The Team That Forever Changed Baseball and America

Memorable Teams in Baseball History

# The Team That Forever Changed Baseball and America

## The 1947 Brooklyn Dodgers

Edited by **Lyle Spatz**

Published by the **University of Nebraska Press**, Lincoln & London, and the **Society for American Baseball Research**

© 2012 by the Society for American Baseball Research
Foreword © 2012 by the Board of Regents of the University of
Nebraska

Chapter 3 has been adapted from *The Black Stars Who Made
Baseball Whole: The Jackie Robinson Generation in the Major
Leagues, 1947–1959* by Rick Swaine. © 2006 by Rick Swaine. Used
by permission of McFarland & Company, Inc., Box 611, Jefferson NC
28640. www.mcfarlandpub.com.

All photographs are courtesy of the National Baseball Hall of Fame
Library, Cooperstown, New York, unless otherwise indicated.

Player statistics courtesy of Baseball-Reference.com.

Library of Congress Cataloging-in-Publication Data

The team that forever changed baseball and America: the 1947
Brooklyn Dodgers / edited by Lyle Spatz.
        p. cm. — (Memorable teams in baseball history)
Includes bibliographical references.
ISBN 978-0-8032-3992-0 (pbk.: alk. paper)
1. Brooklyn Dodgers (Baseball team)—History.  I. Spatz, Lyle, 1937–
GV875.B7T36 2012
796.357'640974723—dc23
2011036311

Set in Sabon.

# Table of Contents

# Foreword

*Mark Langill*

During the last few years of his life, former catcher and longtime baseball executive Bobby Bragan called the offices of Dodger Stadium on the opening of the baseball season with the same question, his voice mixed with pride and apprehension. "How many guys are left from the 1947 team?"

Bragan was referring to his teammates on the 1947 Brooklyn Dodgers. Most sports teams become famous if they perform well in the playoffs at the end of the season, always invited to reunions if the group wins a championship. Although they were crowned National League champions in September, the 1947 squad became forever linked to our national history on April 15, Opening Day, when Jackie Robinson made his debut at Ebbets Field as the first African American player of the twentieth century to appear in the Major Leagues.

In previous years the Dodgers usually found their biggest challenges in the opposing dugout, whether battling their crosstown rival the New York Giants or a St. Louis Cardinals franchise dominating the 1940s with pennants in 1942, 1943, 1944, and 1946. A decade earlier, the biggest hurdle was the team's balance sheet, with the Brooklyn Trust Company serving as the club's chief creditor and fearing bankruptcy during the Great Depression.

But the presence of Robinson in 1947 forced players and coaches to look within themselves and their respective communities back home as their sport became integrated. It also meant learning about Robinson as a teammate and ballplayer through his play on the field.

At age twenty-eight Robinson wasn't a typical rookie, because of life experiences such as being a student-athlete at UCLA, playing professional football, facing racism in the military, and resuming his baseball career in the Negro Leagues. As a second lieutenant in World War II, he was acquitted during a court-martial trial that stemmed from his refusal to move to the back of a military bus when so ordered by the driver, even though the army had commissioned its own unsegregated bus line. And his marriage to UCLA nursing student Rachel Isum before leaving for Triple-A Montreal in 1946 gave Robinson a partner and a solid foundation for the historic rookie season and the final twenty-seven years of his life.

With Brooklyn in 1947, Robinson wasn't there to make friends as a first-year player. His only desire was for the other Dodgers players to respect him as a man while proving blacks and whites could play together on a ball field.

Broadcaster Red Barber admitted his initial uncertainty when tipped off the previous winter to the Robinson plans by Dodgers team president Branch Rickey. The 154 games of the regular season meant Robinson's drama could slowly play out on a national stage and soak into the nation's consciousness as the Dodgers visited the various National League cities.

And one season wouldn't end the problems. Robinson received death threats prior to a 1949 exhibition game in Atlanta, and Robinson's teammates were advised of a possible sniper. Gene Hermanski, an early supporter of Robinson in 1947, suggested that every Dodger wear uniform No. 42 "so they won't know which one to shoot at." The irony, of course, is every Major League player now wears Robinson's number on the April 15 anniversary date.

Stepping back into a time machine, one can only imagine what would have happened with slight changes to the main characters and circumstances.

What if Dodgers team president Larry Mac-Phail had stayed with Brooklyn after the 1943 season and not accepted a commission with the U.S. Army at age fifty-two, prompting the team to lure Rickey from the St. Louis Cardinals? Both MacPhail and Rickey were Hall of Fame executives and powerful advocates of changing the status quo. Would Rickey have tried to integrate baseball with the Cardinals? MacPhail in Brooklyn?

Although Rickey was a visionary, he couldn't see everything in his crystal ball. For example, Dodgers manager Leo Durocher was suspended for the entire 1947 season by Commissioner Happy Chandler for Durocher's "accumulation of unpleasant incidents . . . detrimental to baseball." But Chandler's decision wasn't announced until a week before the season opener, which gave Durocher enough time to set the tone in spring training by defending Robinson in a clubhouse meeting with his players.

If Durocher had stayed with the Dodgers in 1947, how would he compare to his replacement, Burt Shotton, who at age sixty-two didn't want to wear a uniform and therefore was confined to the dugout during games? How would Durocher have reacted to the Ben Chapman episode in Philadelphia when the Phillies manager unleashed a torrent of verbal abuse and bench jockeying, to the point that Dodgers teammates rallied around Robinson because he couldn't fight back?

How does history change if the peaceful scene of Robinson and Chapman shaking hands and smiling in a pregame photo-op, arranged as a favor to Chapman because of public backlash against his behavior, is replaced by the image of "Leo the Lip" punching Chapman in the mouth?

One Robinson story never publicly chronicled centered on eleven-year-old Eddie Hamlin of Mid-dletown, Connecticut, who had been horribly burned in a gasoline fire on January 1, 1947.

"[Hamlin] had been in the hospital for more than six months," wrote Arthur Mann, Rickey's assistant, in a report to his boss after the 1947 season. "His one fear was of dying before he could see Jackie Robinson. I learned about it from a newspaper man (Dan Parker) and, without Parker's knowledge, detoured Robinson on the way to Boston with the express understanding through my contact at Middletown that there would be no reporters and no photographers.

"Robinson visited Eddie, who suffered many skin grafts, most of them in vain, and dozens of transfusions. His mother was trying to work out a $1,500 hospital bill in the kitchen. Robinson spent an hour with the boy, gave him pictures and an autographed baseball and departed. The Hamlin boy was so overcome that he could not speak. Four weeks later, we received a note from Eddie and a picture of him leaving the hospital on crutches with a wide grin."

One man, of course, does not win a pennant. So this book also pays tribute to Robinson's teammates and coaching staff, along with an analysis of the franchise and the various postseason awards.

Although the 1947 Brooklyn Dodgers fell short of becoming the first World Series champion in franchise history, losing a seven-game classic to the New York Yankees, the consolation prize was priceless.

Looking back at the twentieth century, only one Major League team changed a nation.

MARK LANGILL

# Acknowledgments

This book is the result of the work of many members of the Society for American Baseball Research (SABR). Mark Armour, the chairman of SABR's Bio-Project Committee, and Bill Nowlin, in charge of team projects, first had the idea for books devoted to specific teams. It was Mark and Bill who convinced the SABR Board of Directors and Rob Taylor, our editor at the University of Nebraska Press, of the appeal a book on the 1947 Brooklyn Dodgers would have.

I thank all the contributors, those who wrote player biographies and those who wrote articles, for their patience and cooperation. It was a long and often frustrating process from the germ of an idea to publication.

I offer my grateful appreciation to Len Levin and Maury Bouchard. Len and Maury read every word of the text and made numerous corrections to both language and statistics. Tom Bourke researched the genealogical history of every player and in many cases spoke to their descendants. Stephan Saks of the New York Public Library helped track down some difficult-to-find 1940s New York newspaper stories.

Bobby Bragan, Ralph Branca, Gene Hermanski, Don Lund, Howie Schultz, Ed Stevens, and Johnny Van Cuyk—all members of the 1947 Dodgers—were most generous in sharing their remembrances of their careers, as were the families of many of the players.

Gabriel Schechter, a former research associate at the National Baseball Library and Archive in Cooperstown, provided various authors access to their subject's player files. And Patricia Kelly, of the National Baseball Library and Archive, and Mark Langill, the team historian for the Los Angeles Dodgers, furnished the photographs that appear in the book.

# Introduction

*Lyle Spatz*

Of the several thousand team-seasons in baseball history, only a select few stand out, and only a handful might be said to have national appeal. Foremost among those with such national appeal is the 1947 Brooklyn Dodgers, the first racially integrated Major League team of the twentieth century.

The addition of Jackie Robinson to the 1947 Dodgers changed not only baseball but also the nation. Robinson, however, was just one member of that memorable and iconic club. This was a team that had many great players on its roster, some at the beginning of their careers and some at the end. Along with Robinson, they include Carl Furillo, Gil Hodges, Pee Wee Reese, Pete Reiser, Duke Snider, Eddie Stanky, Arky Vaughan, and Dixie Walker. Also associated with the team was a quartet of baseball's most unforgettable characters: Branch Rickey, Walter O'Malley, Leo Durocher, and Red Barber.

Several memorable subplots marked the Dodgers' 1947 season. Just before Opening Day, Commissioner Happy Chandler suspended manager Durocher for the entire season, whereupon Rickey lured his old friend Burt Shotton out of retirement to replace him. Meanwhile, co-owner Walter O'Malley had already begun his maneuverings to take control of the club from Rickey.

Gifted outfielder Pete Reiser was again sidelined after running into an outfield fence; nevertheless, the Dodgers won the National League pennant over their old rivals, the heavily favored St. Louis Cardinals. Despite the one-game heroics of Cookie Lavagetto and Al Gionfriddo, whose feats have become part of baseball lore, they lost in a dramatic seven-game World Series to the New York Yankees.

But the biggest story of the season was Jackie Robinson. Historians have said that by joining the Dodgers in 1947, Robinson not only integrated baseball, he also set the stage for the Supreme Court's groundbreaking *Brown v. Board of Education* decision in 1954 and all the civil rights legislation that followed.

During spring training, a mini-revolt by some Dodgers players opposed to Robinson's joining the team was quashed by Durocher and Rickey. Robinson slowly overcame the enmity of some of his teammates, and he withstood the vicious assaults on his dignity from other players, managers, and fans to win the Rookie of the Year Award. Along the way, he helped the Dodgers set single-game attendance records in cities around the National League, while also changing the face (literally) of product advertisements.

For all these reasons, the 1947 Brooklyn Dodgers remain one of baseball's most treasured teams.

# Chapter 1. **How the 1947 Team Was Built**

*Lyle Spatz*

The 1947 National League champions.

## Pitchers

HUGH CASEY: Taken in the Rule 5 draft from the Memphis Chicks of the Southern Association on October 4, 1938.

JOE HATTEN: Acquired before the 1940 season from the Crookston Pirates of the Northern League.

KIRBY HIGBE: Acquired from the Philadelphia Phillies on November 11, 1940, in a trade for pitcher Bill Crouch, pitcher Vito Tamulis, Minor League catcher Mickey Livingston, and $100,000.

WILLIE RAMSDELL: Acquired before the 1941 season from the Big Spring Barons of the West Texas–New Mexico League as part of a Minor League working agreement.

HANK BEHRMAN: Signed as an amateur free agent in 1941.

HAL GREGG: Signed as an amateur free agent in 1941.

VIC LOMBARDI: Signed as an amateur free agent in 1941.

RUBE MELTON: Acquired from the Philadelphia Phillies on December 12, 1942, in a trade for pitcher Johnny Allen and $30,000.

REX BARNEY: Signed as an amateur free agent in 1943.

RALPH BRANCA: Signed as an amateur free agent in 1943.

HARRY TAYLOR: Acquired from the St. Paul Saints of the American Association before the 1944 season as part of a Minor League working agreement.

JACK BANTA: Signed as an amateur free agent in 1944.

CLYDE KING: Signed as an amateur free agent in 1944.

ED CHANDLER: Signed as a free agent in 1945.

ERV PALICA: Signed as an amateur free agent in 1945.

JOHNNY VAN CUYK: Signed as a free agent in 1945.

PHIL HAUGSTAD: Signed as an amateur free agent in 1946.

GEORGE DOCKINS: Purchased on waivers from the St. Louis Cardinals on April 19, 1946.

DAN BANKHEAD: Purchased on August 24, 1947, from the Memphis Red Sox of the Negro American League.

## Catchers

BRUCE EDWARDS: Signed as an amateur free agent in 1941.

GIL HODGES: Signed as an amateur free agent in 1943.

BOBBY BRAGAN: Acquired from the Philadelphia Blue Jays on March 24, 1943, in a trade for pitcher Jack Kraus and cash.

## Infielders

COOKIE LAVAGETTO: Acquired, along with pitcher Ralph Birkhofer, from the Pittsburgh Pirates on December 4, 1936, in a trade for pitcher Ed Brandt.

STAN ROJEK: Signed as an amateur free agent in 1939.

PEE WEE REESE: Acquired from the Boston Red Sox on July 18, 1939, in a trade for four players to be named and $35,000.

SPIDER JORGENSEN: Signed as an amateur free agent in 1941.

ED STEVENS: Signed as an amateur free agent in 1941.

HOWIE SCHULTZ: Acquired from the St. Paul Saints of the American Association in August 1943 in a trade for pitcher Rube Melton, infielder Joe Oren-go, Minor League pitcher Ed Spaulding, Minor League infielder Jack Bolling, and $40,000.

TOMMY BROWN: Signed as an amateur free agent in 1944.

EDDIE MIKSIS: Signed as an amateur free agent in 1944.

EDDIE STANKY: Acquired from the Chicago Cubs on June 6, 1944, in a trade for pitcher Bob Chipman.

JACKIE ROBINSON: Signed as a free agent in 1945.

## Outfielders

PETE REISER: Signed as a free agent in 1938.

DIXIE WALKER: Purchased on waivers from the Detroit Tigers on July 24, 1939.

CARL FURILLO: Was a member of the Interstate League's Reading Chicks team, which Brooklyn purchased following the 1940 season.

TOMMY TATUM: Signed as a free agent in 1940.

GENE HERMANSKI: Signed as a free agent in 1941.

MARV RACKLEY: Signed as an amateur free agent in 1941.

ARKY VAUGHAN: Acquired from the Pittsburgh Pirates on December 12, 1941, in a trade for pitcher Luke Hamlin, catcher Babe Phelps, infielder Pete Coscarart, and outfielder Jimmy Wasdell.

DICK WHITMAN: Signed as an amateur free agent in 1942.

DUKE SNIDER: Signed as an amateur free agent in 1943.

DON LUND: Signed as an amateur free agent in 1945.

AL GIONFRIDDO: Acquired, along with $100,000, from the Pittsburgh Pirates on May 3, 1947, in a trade for pitcher Kirby Higbe, pitcher Hank Behrman, pitcher Cal McLish, catcher Dixie Howell, and infielder Gene Mauch.

# Chapter 2. **Spring Training in Havana**

*Irv Goldfarb*

"You could not possibly train a baseball squad in Havana. The distractions are too great. . . . The after-dark program down there would kill a team before it ever had a chance to appear in National League competition." So opined baseball legend John McGraw when asked why he never took his New York Giants to Cuba, though he often vacationed there himself. "There are too many women, there is too much drinking, there is too much gambling, and the climate is much too hot."[1] Despite McGraw's warnings, another brilliant baseball mind was to test that theory, and for a very specific reason.

Mention the Brooklyn Dodgers and the year 1947, and any baseball fan will immediately acknowledge it as a landmark season for both the franchise and Major League Baseball. But besides the obvious reason for the familiarity of the year—the signing of Jackie Robinson and the official integration of the Major Leagues—the '47 season was unique for team president Branch Rickey and his club in other areas as well. The Dodgers became the first team in baseball history to have their manager suspended before the season had even begun. Leo Durocher, a character not unfamiliar with controversy, had become fodder for the New York tabloids during the previous year by indulging in violent altercations with umpires, hitting a fan, and allowing actor George Raft to borrow his apartment and conduct a dice game in his living room. Leo added to the chaos when he wed divorced actress Laraine Day, an event that caused the Brooklyn chapter of the Catholic Youth Organization to withdraw its support of the famed Dodgers Knothole Gang.

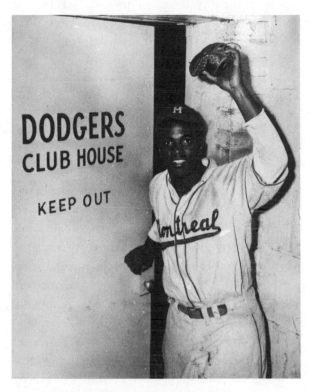

The Dodgers promoted Jackie Robinson from Montreal just before the season began.

Durocher then capped it off when he accused New York Yankees president and co-owner Larry MacPhail of entertaining two alleged gamblers at an exhibition game between the clubs. Pointing to MacPhail's private box, Durocher chided, "If that was my box I'd be barred from baseball."[2] The two gamblers, Connie Immerman and Memphis Engelberg, were actually in the box *behind* the Yankees executive's, but the incident was the proverbial straw, forcing Commissioner Albert "Happy" Chandler to call for two hearings between the parties. On April 9, just before the season began, Chandler suspended Durocher for the season for "conduct detrimental to baseball." Leo and his team were stunned.

The incident that touched off this baseball war was historically important for more than just the fact that it led to the suspension of the Dodgers' manager: the private box in question was located at Gran Stadium in Havana, Cuba, the site chosen by Rickey for his team to train that spring.

The Dodgers were not totally unfamiliar with Cuba, having previously used Havana's La Tropical Stadium as their spring training site for the 1941 and 1942 seasons, before Rickey arrived from St. Louis. Wartime travel restrictions, however, ended that experiment. And as early as 1943, Rickey had shown interest in having heralded Cuban Leaguer Silvio Garcia become the first player to test Major League Baseball's color barrier. According to Cuban baseball authority Edel Casas, Rickey traveled to Cuba and, thinking ahead to possible racial abuse, asked Garcia during the interview, "What would you do if a white American slapped your face?" When Garcia declared, "I kill him," Rickey moved on.[3] (However, a less popular version of the tale claims Rickey sent Walter O'Malley to Havana with a $25,000 letter of credit to sign the shortstop. When O'Malley got there, Garcia was gone, probably having enlisted in the Cuban army.)

When Jackie Robinson trained with the Montreal Royals in Daytona Beach in the spring of 1946, Rickey began to witness some of the racial confrontations he had feared. Trying to avoid as much of this as possible while preparing Robinson for his Major League debut, Rickey cited Cuba's passion for baseball and its easy access from the mainland as two good reasons to hold training camp there in 1947. Another valid reason, no doubt, was the fact that blacks had been playing baseball in Cuba since the turn of the century. A city that had seen the likes of Oscar Charleston, Josh Gibson, and Satchel Paige appeared safe from any social upheaval at the sight of the Dodgers' rookie.

If an under-the-radar arrival in Cuba is what Rickey wanted, that's exactly what he got. The week the team landed, the new Gran Stadium (Gran Estadio de La Habana, to be exact) hosted the climactic three-game series between perpetual rivals Havana and Almendares in what was probably the greatest pennant race in the history of the Cuban League. Almendares needed to sweep the series to take the flag, and they sent former Cardinal Max Lanier (in exile from the Major Leagues as a jumper to the Mexican League) to the mound. Lanier won the first game, 4–2. Almendares won again the next day, 2–1. An overflow crowd of almost 40,000 attended the third game, and watched in a frenzy as Lanier went out on one day's rest and defeated Havana 9–2 to sweep the series and capture the title.

With the local baseball season at an end, it was the Dodgers' turn to take over Gran Stadium. Built only the year before as part of Havana's burgeoning modernization, the ballpark reportedly included a playing field and lighting system of Major League quality. Along with these fine facilities, the players were housed at the best resort in the city, the Hotel Nacional. These opulent quarters boasted beautiful swimming pools and fine restaurants, and the players were quartered with visiting diplomats and international businessmen. The Class Triple-A Royals were housed at the Havana Military Academy, a prep school attended by the wealthy offspring of government employees. The black members of both squads, however, stayed at neither of these locations.

Robinson and the Royals' other black players— Roy Campanella, Don Newcombe, and Roy Partlow—were taken instead to the Hotel Boston in "old" Havana. Jackie was irate. "I thought we left Florida . . . so we could get away from Jim Crow," he complained to the Dodgers' traveling secretary, Harold Parrott. "So what the devil is this business of segregating the Negro players in a colored nation?"[4] Parrott explained to Robinson that the whole thing was Rickey's idea. Though the Hotel Nacional was fully integrated, the Dodgers' head man didn't want to take the chance of any incidents while his team was staying there. "I'll go along with Mr. Rickey's judgment," Jackie finally said. "He's been right so far."

Some have questioned whether Rickey was right in segregating the black players from the rest of the team, believing it was an overreaction. Where the team stayed, however, made no difference to a number of white Dodgers who were nonetheless offended by Robinson's presence. Led by Dixie Walker, the de facto leader of the team, the group attempted to keep Jackie off the club. During a trip to Panama for a three-game series against the Royals, Durocher, still the Dodgers' manager, caught wind of the uprising and exploded.

"I told them what they could do with their petition, and I don't think I got much back talk on it," he said years later. "I told the players that Robinson was going to open the season with us come hell or high water, and if they didn't like it they could leave now and we'd trade them or get rid of them some other way. Nobody moved."[5] (This quotation is likely also in Maury Allen's biography of Robinson.) Rickey confronted his mutinous players in his hotel room and reiterated that anybody who wanted to leave the team would be accommodated. The petition got no further. Though some tension undoubtedly remained into the regular season, there were no more internal flare-ups in Cuba.

While in Havana, the team played "home" series against the Yankees and Boston Braves, along with games against the Royals and a team of Cuban all-stars. In addition to the trip to Panama, they took quick jaunts to play in Caracas, Venezuela, and the Panama Canal Zone, before finally breaking camp during the first week of April and heading home to Brooklyn.

The Havana experiment lasted only a single spring. The club's training camp costs that year were reported as being the highest in the Majors. Surprisingly, the fans in the baseball-hungry country didn't show up in the numbers the Dodgers had expected. Attendance for their series against the Braves was so low that the visiting Boston club lost money on the deal, causing even the St. Louis Browns to cancel their upcoming trip. The prevailing thought may have been that the city, having just experienced the most pressurized pennant race in Cuban League history, had seen enough baseball for a while. But this was disproved later that spring when the All-American Girls Professional Baseball League, featuring the champion Racine Belles, arrived. Fifteen thousand fans showed up for that league's first *practice* game in Havana. In the end, the Dodgers opted not to return in 1948, choosing the less expensive Dominican Republic as their spring training site.

The Dodgers, by then located in Los Angeles, did return to Cuba one more time. When heavy Florida rains threatened a weekend set in 1959 against the Cincinnati Reds, the teams opted to move the series to Gran Stadium. It was the last time the team played there; that same year, Fidel Castro took power in Cuba, and baseball's official dealings with the nation ended. Still, despite John McGraw's warnings, that spring in Havana became a milestone in Dodgers history. The team may have lost a manager but gained a leader, Jackie Robinson, who subsequently changed the fate of their franchise, and baseball, forever.

## Chapter 3. **Jackie Robinson**

*Rick Swaine*

| AGE | G | AB | R | H | 2B | 3B | HR | TB | RBI | BB | SO | BAV | OBP | SLG | SB | GDP | HBP |
|-----|-----|-----|-----|-----|-----|-----|-----|-----|-----|-----|-----|------|------|------|-----|-----|-----|
| 28 | 151 | 590 | 125 | 175 | 31 | 5 | 12 | 252 | 48 | 74 | 36 | .297 | .383 | .427 | 29 | 5 | 9 |

Jackie Robinson is perhaps the most historically significant baseball player ever, ranking with Babe Ruth in terms of his impact on the national pastime. Ruth changed the way baseball was played; Jackie Robinson changed the way Americans thought. When Robinson took the field for the Brooklyn Dodgers on April 15, 1947, more than sixty years of racial segregation in Major League Baseball came to an end. He was the first acknowledged black player to perform in the Major Leagues in the twentieth century and went on to be the first to win a batting title, the first to win the Most Valuable Player Award, and the first to be inducted into the Baseball Hall of Fame. He won Major League Baseball's first official Rookie of the Year Award and was the first baseball player, black or white, to be featured on a U.S. postage stamp.

The raw statistics only scratch the surface in evaluating Jackie Robinson as a ballplayer. Because of institutionalized racism and World War II, he did not play his first big league game until he was twenty-eight years old, and therefore his Major League career spanned only ten seasons. His lifetime batting average was a solid .311, but because of the brevity of his career, his cumulative statistics are relatively unimpressive by Hall of Fame standards.

But in what would be considered his prime years, ages twenty-eight to thirty-four, Robinson hit .319 and averaged more than 110 runs scored per season. He drove in an average of 85 runs, and his average of nearly 15 home runs per season was outstanding for a middle infielder of that era. And he averaged 24 stolen bases a season for a power-laden team that didn't need him to run very often.

Jackie Robinson overcame a most difficult entrance to the Major Leagues to win Rookie of the Year honors.

Colorfully described as a tiger in the field and a lion at bat, the right-handed-hitting Robinson crowded the plate and dared opposing hurlers to dust him off—a challenge they frequently accepted. He was an excellent bunter, good at the sacrifice and always a threat to lay one down for a hit. Not known as a home-run hitter, he displayed line-drive power to all fields, had a good eye for the strike zone, and rarely struck out. For his entire big league career, he drew 740 walks and struck out only 291 times—an extremely impressive ratio.

Second base was Robinson's best position. In a 1987 "Player's Choice" survey, he was voted the greatest second baseman of his era despite having played there regularly for only five seasons. Though not a smooth glove man in the classic sense, he was sure-handed and possessed good range and instincts. He made up for an average arm by standing his ground on double plays and getting rid of the ball quickly. Robinson also displayed his versatility by playing regularly at first base, at third base, and in left field when the needs of the team dictated it.

It was running the bases, however, where Robinson's star shined brightest. He was a dynamo on the base paths—fast, clever, daring, and rough. He was the most dangerous base runner since Ty Cobb, embarrassing and intimidating the opposition into beating themselves with mental and physical errors. Former teammate and big league manager Bobby Bragan, who initially objected to Jackie's presence on the Dodgers, called him the best he ever saw at getting called safe after being caught in rundown situations. He created havoc by taking impossibly long leads, jockeying back and forth, and threatening to steal on every pitch. His mere presence on base was enough to upset the most steely nerved veteran hurlers.

Robinson revived the art of stealing home, successfully making it nineteen times in his career—tied with Frankie Frisch for the most since World War I. At the age of thirty-five in 1954, he became the first National Leaguer to steal his way around the bases in twenty-six years, and a year later he became one of only twelve men to steal home in the World Series.

Throughout his career, Jackie Robinson was a fearless competitor. As Leo Durocher, first his manager and later an archrival, so elegantly phrased it, "You want a guy that comes to play.

But [Robinson] didn't just come to play. He came to beat you. He came to stuff the damn bat right up your ass."[1]

Jack Roosevelt Robinson was born on January 31, 1919, in Cairo, Georgia, a sleepy southern town near the Florida border. Jackie was the youngest of five children, four boys and a girl, born to impoverished sharecroppers Jerry and Mallie Robinson. Jerry Robinson deserted the family six months after Jackie was born. Mallie Robinson, a strong, devoutly religious woman, moved the struggling family across the country by rail to Pasadena, California, in 1920 when Jackie was fourteen months old. She worked as a domestic to support her family; leftovers from the kitchens of families she worked for often constituted their daily diet. With the help of a welfare agency, the Robinson family purchased a home in a predominantly white Pasadena neighborhood, where neighbors immediately petitioned to get rid of the newcomers and even offered to buy them out. When those ploys failed, the family was harassed for several years. The Robinson boys often had to fight to defend themselves, and young Jackie was involved in his share of scrapes with white youths and had some run-ins with authorities.

Jackie's athletic talent became evident at an early age. But he wasn't the only gifted athlete in the family. His older brother Mack became a world-class track star, finishing second in the 200-yard dash to Jesse Owens in the 1936 Olympics. But after Olympic stardom and college, the only job Mack Robinson could find was janitorial work for the City of Pasadena. It was a position he soon lost. As in most of the country at that time, Jim Crow rules prevailed in Pasadena. Black citizens were permitted to use the city's public swimming pool only one day a week. When a judge ordered full access to the pool for black citizens, the city fathers responded by firing black employees, including Mack Robinson.

After starring in baseball, football, basketball,

and track at Muir Technical High School and Pasadena Junior College, Jackie declined many other offers to enroll at the University of California at Los Angeles, near his Pasadena home.

Robinson gained national fame at UCLA in 1940 and 1941. He became the school's first four-letter man and was called the "Jim Thorpe of his race" for his multisport skills.[2] Sharing rushing duties with Kenny Washington, who later became one of the first black men to play in the National Football League, Jackie averaged eleven-plus yards per carry as a junior. *Sports Weekly* called him "the greatest ball carrier on the gridiron today."[3] On the basketball court, Jackie led the Pacific Coast Conference in scoring as a junior and as a senior.

Although he wasn't named to the first, second, or third all-conference teams, one coach called him "the best basketball player in the United States."[4] Already the holder of the national junior college long-jump record, he captured the NCAA long-jump title and probably would have gone to the 1940 Olympics had they not been canceled because of the war in Europe. In addition, he won swimming championships, reached the semifinals of the national Negro tennis tournament, and was the UCLA Bruins' regular shortstop. Baseball was probably Robinson's weakest sport at the university, although he'd been voted the most valuable player in Southern California junior college baseball.

Financial problems at home forced Robinson to drop out of college in his senior year a few credits short of graduation. He took a job as an athletic coach for the National Youth Administration and played semipro football for the Los Angeles Bulldogs. In the fall of 1941, he signed on to play professional football with the Honolulu Bears. Already a gate attraction and a hero in the black community, he got top billing as "the sensational all-American halfback."

Upon returning home from Hawaii shortly after Pearl Harbor, Robinson was drafted into the army in 1942. Stationed at Fort Riley, Kansas, he was originally denied entry into Officer Candidate School despite his college background. Intervention by a fellow soldier, boxing great Joe Louis, who was also stationed at the base, managed to get the decision reversed. Yet Jackie was not allowed to play on the segregated camp baseball team, which infuriated him so much that he refused to play on the football team even when superior officers pressured him to do so. After OCS, Robinson was appointed morale officer for the black troops at Fort Riley and won concessions for them that predictably angered a few higher-ups in command.

Reassigned to Ford Hood, Texas, Jackie continued to be controversial. On July 6, 1944, he defied a white bus driver's orders to move to the back of the bus "where the coloreds belonged." When the base provost marshal and military police supported the driver, Robinson objected vehemently and was subject to court-martial. Facing a dishonorable discharge, Jackie prevailed at the hearing. But the army had had enough of the controversial young black lieutenant and quickly mustered him out with an honorable discharge.

It's ironic that Jackie Robinson's difficulties with white authority in the military led directly to his rise to the top of Branch Rickey's list of candidates to break baseball's color barrier. Rickey, the orchestrator of Organized Baseball's desegregation, was the president, the general manager, and a part-owner of the Brooklyn Dodgers. Rickey's scouts had been surreptitiously scouring the Negro Leagues for Major League talent for some time before tapping Robinson to break the unwritten, and diligently enforced, gentlemen's agreement that banned blacks from participating in Organized Baseball.

Rickey was looking for a black pioneer who—in addition to possessing the requisite talent—was educated, sober, and accustomed to competing with and against white athletes. Robinson met those conditions. He grew up in a racially mixed environment, attended school with white class-mates, and matriculated at UCLA. He'd been an officer in the military. He was well-spoken, personable, and comfortable in front of crowds. He had experienced the glare of the spotlight and reveled in it. Also extremely important to the pious Rickey was the fact that Robinson was a nonsmoker and nondrinker. Nor was he a womanizer; he was planning to marry his college sweetheart, Rachel Annetta Isum. In addition, Jackie was a Methodist, as was Rickey, and he coincidentally shared a birthday with Branch Rickey Jr. Jackie and Rachel were married in Los Angeles on February 10, 1946.

Certainly there were other black ballplayers who possessed the qualifications Rickey sought. Monte Irvin and Larry Doby were two obvious candidates. But when Rickey sent his scouts to search the nation for the best black player, Irvin and Doby were overseas, still in the armed forces. Robinson, though he was far from being considered the best player in Negro baseball, was available due to the early termination of his own military obligation.

After his discharge, Robinson had joined the Kansas City Monarchs of the Negro American League for the 1945 season. The Monarchs, one of the most successful franchises in the Negro Leagues, had been ravaged by the manpower demands of the war, but their roster still included veteran stars Ted "Double Duty" Radcliffe, Hilton Smith, and Satchel Paige. Flashy-fielding veteran Jesse Williams moved over to second base to make room for Jackie at shortstop. Though Robinson hit well over .300 and showed speed and power as a rookie, he disliked the nomadic and often boisterous barnstorming life and was incensed by the Jim Crow laws that the Monarchs often encountered on the road.

On October 23, 1945, it was announced to the world that Robinson had signed a contract to play baseball for the Montreal Royals of the Interna-tional League, the top Minor League team in the Dodgers organization. Robinson had actually signed a few months earlier. In that now-legendary meeting, Rickey extracted a promise that Jackie would hold his sharp tongue and quick fists in exchange for the opportunity to break Organized Baseball's color barrier.

The integration movement in general had picked up steam during World War II as black American soldiers fought and died beside whites. In fact, the decade leading up to Robinson's signing had been marked by significant progress in efforts to gain equal rights for minorities in all facets of life. Yet the moguls running Major League Baseball stubbornly resisted efforts to integrate the sport, refusing to consider black players even as the talent pool was depleted by the war and a one-armed and a one-legged player could be found among the old-timers, teenagers, and 4-Fs gracing big league rosters. But in November 1944, longtime baseball commissioner Kenesaw Mountain Landis, who was generally thought to be against integration, died of a heart attack. Landis's passing was the break Branch Rickey needed to begin implementing his plan to integrate the Dodgers.

When Robinson's signing was announced, the news was heralded in black newspapers and generally received positive reviews in national publications despite objections and attacks from predictable quarters. But Rickey and the Dodgers faced near-unanimous disapproval from the Organized Baseball establishment. After the initial furor died down, a campaign to downplay Robinson's talent and the import of the event began. The *New York Daily News* rated Robinson's chances of making the grade as 1,000 to 1. An editorial in *The Sporting News* deemed Robinson a player of Class C ability and predicted, "The waters of competition in the International League will flood far over his head."[5] Star pitcher Bob Feller of the Cleveland Indians said that Robinson had "football shoulders and couldn't hit an inside pitch to save his neck."[6]

Muscularly built with a thick neck and wide shoulders, Robinson did look more like a half-back than an infielder. He suffered from rickets as a child and walked with a pigeon-toed gait, but on the diamond he moved with amazing quickness. He stood five feet eleven and weighed 190 to 195 pounds in his prime, although he thickened noticeably in the latter stages of his career. In the decades prior to Robinson's entry into Organized Baseball, there were several Major Leaguers whose skin tone caused doubts about their racial background. There could be no doubt about ebony-skinned Jackie Robinson. Columnist John Crosby called him "the blackest black man, as well as one of the handsomest, I ever saw."[7]

Plagued by a sore arm during the Royals' 1946 spring training camp, Jackie performed poorly, generating numerous "I told you so" claims. But when Montreal opened the season on April 18, 1946, against the Jersey City Giants at Roosevelt Stadium in Jersey City, Robinson was playing second base and hitting second in the batting order.

The first twentieth-century appearance by an acknowledged black player in Organized Baseball was a preview of things to come. In front of a packed house, Jackie lashed out four hits and scored four times to lead Montreal to a 14–1 victory. After grounding out in his first at-bat, he blasted a three-run homer over the left-field wall in the third inning. In the fifth inning he bunted for a hit, stole second, and made a daring play to take third on a grounder to the third baseman. From third base he danced far off the bag, darting back and forth and bluffing a steal until the harried pitcher balked him home. Two innings later, he singled sharply to right field and stole second base again before scoring on a triple. In the eighth Jackie again bunted safely. He once again took an extra base, advancing from first to third on an infield single, and again scored by provoking a balk by the Jersey City hurler.

The next day, the headline in the *Pittsburgh Courier* read "Jackie Stole the Show."[8] According to Joe Bostic of New York City's *Amsterdam News*, "He did everything but help the ushers seat the crowd."[9]

Baseball's defense for keeping the game segregated hinged primarily on two points. The first was the contention that there just weren't any black players good enough to merit a shot at the Majors at the time. The second centered on financial concerns—the fear that white fans wouldn't pay to watch Negro players and didn't want to sit in the stands beside black fans. There was also much feigned concern about the financial impact on the established Negro Leagues.

But Jackie Robinson's first year in Organized Baseball emphatically dispelled those tired excuses. He was a sensation on the field, the Royals dominated the International League, and the turnstiles hummed. Thanks to Jackie, the Royals established a new attendance record in Montreal, and his impact on the road was even greater, as attendance at Royals games in other International League cities almost tripled over the previous year. More than a million people came to watch Robinson and the Royals perform that year, an amazing figure for the Minor Leagues at the time.

For the season Robinson led the International League with a .349 batting average and scored 113 runs in 124 games to pace the circuit in that department as well. His forty stolen bases were the second-highest total in the league, and he led the league's second basemen in fielding. Jackie led the Royals to the International League pennant, by a 19½-game margin, and to victory in the Little World Series. After the Series, ecstatic fans wanted to hoist Jackie on their shoulders in celebration, but Jackie had a plane to catch. They chased him for three blocks, prompting a journalist to observe, "It was probably the only day in history that a black man ran from a white mob with love instead of hate on its mind."[10]

In preparation for the 1947 campaign, the Brooklyn Dodgers and their top farm clubs set up spring training camp in Havana, Cuba. Based on his performance at Montreal, it seemed a foregone conclusion that Robinson would get a chance with the parent team, but he was still listed on the Royals' roster when the workouts started. Rickey chose Havana to avoid the racial attitudes of the spring training sites in the South. His plan was to allow the Dodgers' veterans to gradually get used to having Jackie around and to see for themselves what an asset he would be to their pennant prospects. Three other black players, Roy Campanella, Don Newcombe, and Roy Partlow, were also on hand. Rickey scheduled a seven-game exhibition series between the Dodgers and the Royals to showcase Robinson's skills, and Jackie dominated the contests with a .625 batting average.

One problem that Rickey and Robinson had to overcome was that the Dodgers already had Eddie Stanky playing second base. Robinson's Major League debut would come at first base, a strange position for a man who had always been involved in the action in the middle of the diamond.

During training camp, a crisis arose when several players on the team began to circulate a petition against Robinson. The dissenters were reportedly led by outfielder Dixie Walker, who initially dismissed the news of Robinson's signing with the comment, "As long as he isn't with the Dodgers, I'm not worried."[11] Rickey and manager Leo Durocher promptly quashed the mini-rebellion. Shortly thereafter, Durocher, an avid Robinson supporter, received a one-year suspension from the commissioner's office for associating with gamblers and other "unsavory" characters. Rickey deftly took advantage of the cover provided by the resulting clamor to quietly transfer Robinson to the Brooklyn roster.

Contrary to dire predictions, Robinson's first season in the Major Leagues went fairly smoothly as the rookie steadfastly stuck by his promise to Rickey to turn the other cheek. Tension sur-

rounding his first game was defused by a series of preseason exhibition contests against the Yankees in New York, and Jackie's Opening Day debut against the Braves was actually somewhat anticlimactic.

He received death threats when the club visited Cincinnati, but in an oft-told but undocumented story, Dodgers shortstop Pee Wee Reese, a native son of Kentucky, draped an arm over the shoulders of the nervous rookie infielder in a courageous public show of support. Later, a threatened strike by the St. Louis Cardinals was short-circuited by a show of force by league president Ford Frick.

Jackie's worst experience came at the hands of the Philadelphia Phillies. Led by manager Ben Chapman, the Phils baited Robinson so cruelly that he later admitted, "It brought me nearer to cracking up than I had ever been."[12] But the Chapman episode actually served to strengthen support for Robinson and even converted some of his detractors. Stanky, who originally had opposed playing with Robinson, challenged the Phillies to pick on someone who could fight back. Public reaction against Chapman was so severe that he had to ask Robinson to pose for a photo with him to save his job. Jackie graciously complied.

For his rookie campaign, Robinson hit .297, led the league with 29 stolen bases, and finished second in the National League with 125 runs scored. In 151 games he lashed out 175 hits, including 12 home runs. Usually hitting second in the batting order, he walked 74 times and led the league in sacrifice hits. On defense, his 16 errors at first base were the second-highest total in the league, but his fielding was generally considered adequate.

With Robinson the biggest addition to the lineup, the Dodgers captured the National League pennant. In the World Series, Jackie and his teammates lost to the powerful Yankees in a thrilling seven-game classic. The 1947 season was the first in which the full membership of the Baseball Writers' Association of America selected a Rookie of the Year, and Robinson beat out twenty-one-game winner Larry Jansen of the New York Giants for the award. In the NL Most Valuable Player voting, he finished fifth. At season's end, Dixie Walker admitted that "[Robinson] is everything Branch Rickey said he was when he came up from Montreal."[13]

The integration of Major League Baseball proceeded without critical incident. Though Robinson was scorned by some of his teammates, was harassed by enemy bench jockeys, and received a steady diet of fastballs close to his head, he faithfully abided by his promise to Rickey to turn the other cheek. Even when veteran outfielder Enos "Country" Slaughter of the Cardinals appeared to deliberately try to maim him with his spikes in an August 20 game at Ebbets Field, Jackie didn't retaliate.

In fact, baseball's "Great Experiment" was a huge success. Despite the concerns of the owners, integration proved to be a financial windfall for Major League Baseball. Robinson and the Dodgers eclipsed the home attendance record they had set the previous year. They also broke single-game attendance records in every National League ballpark they played in during the 1947 season, with the exception of Cincinnati's Crosley Field, where the attendance record for the first Major League night game held up. Near the end of the season, Jackie was feted by fans with a day in his honor. At year's end, he finished runner-up to crooner Bing Crosby in a national popularity poll.

Before the 1948 season, Eddie Stanky was swapped to the Boston Braves to open up the Dodgers' second-base slot for Robinson. Jackie reported to camp out of shape and got off to a poor start. He was shifted back to first base for thirty games while utilityman Eddie Miksis manned second for the Dodgers. Eventually, Gil Hodges emerged as the club's regular first baseman, and Robinson returned to second. He finished strong at the plate, ending the year with a .296 batting

mark and leading the league's regular second basemen in fielding percentage. Spending more time in the power spots in the batting order, he drove in eighty-five runs, tops on the disappointing third-place squad.

In 1949 Robinson enjoyed the best season of his career, establishing career highs in games played, hits, batting average, slugging, runs batted in, and stolen bases as the Dodgers captured the National League pennant by a single game. He won the batting title with a .342 mark, and his Major League–leading 37 steals were the highest total in the NL in nineteen years. He finished second in the league in runs batted in (124), hits (203), and on-base percentage (.432), and third in slugging average (.528), runs scored (122), doubles (38), and triples (12). His efforts were rewarded with his selection as the National League's Most Valuable Player.

Robinson enjoyed two more superb seasons in 1950 and 1951, batting .328 and .338 and finishing second and third, respectively, in the batting race. Both years, the Dodgers lost the pennant on the last day of the season, although Jackie's heroics kept them in the hunt until the bitter end. In 1951 his spectacular play forced the playoff with the Giants that would be decided by Bobby Thomson's momentous home run. In the final regular-season contest against the Phillies, Robinson prevented the winning run from scoring in the ninth inning with a sensational diving catch, and he blasted a game-winning homer in the fourteenth inning.

The Dodgers returned to the top of the National League standings in 1952 as Robinson hit .308, scored 104 runs, stole 24 bases, and belted 19 homers. During the 1953 season, Jackie Robinson may have had his finest moment. He had worked hard to develop into a fine defensive second baseman. In 1951 he led NL second sackers in fielding and double plays, and he repeated as the double play leader in 1952. But the Dodgers had a young black second baseman in their system, Jim Gilliam, who was ready for the big time.

Jackie graciously agreed to move to another position to make room for the rookie. The thirty-four-year-old veteran played seventy-six games in the outfield and appeared forty-four times at third base, nine times at second, and six times at first base during the 1953 campaign. He even filled in at shortstop in one game, the only time he played his original position as a Major Leaguer. He hit .329, drove in 95 runs, and scored 109 times. Gilliam expertly filled the Dodgers' lead-off spot and was selected the National League Rookie of the Year.

The 1954 campaign was Robinson's last good season. Again shuttling between left field and third base, he batted .311, but age and accumulated injuries were starting to catch up with him. He stole only seven bases and missed thirty games.

In 1955, the year the Brooklyn Dodgers captured their first world championship, Robinson had the worst season statistically of his outstanding career. Sharing third base with light-hitting Don Hoak, he appeared in the field in fewer than one hundred games and batted only .256. In the Dodgers' epic World Series victory, Robinson was at third base for six of the seven contests, and though he hit poorly, he scored five times, including his shocking Game One steal of home.

Jackie rallied to hit .275 in 1956, his final season, while sharing third base with newly acquired Randy Jackson and occasionally filling in at second. Though a mere shadow of his former self, the thirty-seven-year-old veteran was still a force at the plate and on the base paths. In the Dodgers' seven-game World Series loss to the Yankees, Jackie drew five walks, scored five times, and blasted a home run. He struck out in his last professional at-bat, but fittingly he went down fighting. Yankees catcher Yogi Berra had to throw him out at first base after dropping the third strike.

Jackie's last years with the Dodgers had not been harmonious. He disliked both manager Walt Alston and owner Walter O'Malley, whose power play forced Branch Rickey out of the Brooklyn front office in 1950. Though the Dodgers had captured the 1956 pennant, the once dominating nucleus was growing old. Robinson himself was no longer a top performer on the field and had become increasingly outspoken on racial issues both inside and outside of baseball. The Dodgers' brass was hoping he'd step down gracefully, but Jackie refused to announce his retirement. Finally the club forced his hand by swapping him to the New York Giants on December 13, 1956, for journeyman hurler Dick Littlefield and $30,000 in cash.

On January 22, 1957, Robinson's retirement from baseball was announced in an exclusive article in *Look* magazine, in which he took a few parting shots at the remaining segregated teams in the Majors. Jackie had actually decided to retire before he was dealt to the Giants, but couldn't say anything earlier because of his deal with *Look*. The Giants reportedly offered him $60,000 to stay, and the prospect of playing alongside Willie Mays definitely had some appeal. But when Brooklyn general manager Buzzy Bavasi publicly implied that Robinson was just trying to use the magazine article to get a better contract, he decided to prove the Dodgers wrong and declined the Giants' offer.

Though Robinson's career as a Major League baseball player was over, he wasn't about to retire from the spotlight. He joined the Chock full o'Nuts coffee company as a vice president and served as the chairman of the board of Freedom National Bank, founded to provide loans and banking services for minority members, who were largely being ignored by establishment banks. He authored several autobiographical works, wrote a weekly newspaper column, and hosted a radio show. Earlier, he had even tried his hand at acting, starring in the 1950 movie *The Jackie Robinson Story*.

Robinson remained an unofficial spokesman for African Americans and a relentless crusader for civil rights. He became embroiled in politics. Though a strong supporter of Martin Luther King and the NAACP, he endorsed Richard Nixon over John F. Kennedy for president in 1960 because he felt Kennedy had not made it "his business to know colored people." Reportedly, it was an action that he later came to regret.

In 1962 Robinson was elected to the National Baseball Hall of Fame. He was inducted along with former Cleveland pitching great Bob Feller, who had once predicted that Jackie's "football shoulders" would keep him from hitting big league pitching.

A few years after his retirement from baseball, Robinson acknowledged that he suffered from diabetes. His health declined under the ravages of the disease, and at the age of fifty-three he suffered a fatal heart attack at his home in Stamford, Connecticut. He died on October 24, 1972, only months after his No. 42 was officially retired by the Dodgers.

Although he always denied it, there's evidence that Robinson may have been the first insulin-dependent diabetic to play Major League baseball, despite his claim that it hadn't been diagnosed while he was an active player. But former tennis great Bill Talbert, a close friend of Robinson's and the first famous athlete known to perform with diabetes, believed that Jackie became insulin-dependent in midcareer.

"I think Jackie felt it was a weakness. With all the publicity about blacks in baseball, he didn't want another thing to talk about," Talbert said after Robinson's death.[14]

More than two thousand people packed Riverside Church on Manhattan's Upper West Side to hear the young Rev. Jesse Jackson deliver Jackie Robinson's eulogy. Tens of thousands lined the streets of Harlem and Bedford-Stuyvesant to watch the passage of his mile-long funeral procession. Robinson is buried in Cyprus Hill Cemetery in Brooklyn, along with his mother-in-law, Zellee Isum, and his son Jack Roosevelt Jr. He was sur-

vived by his wife, Rachel, his son David, and his daughter, Sharon.

Shortly after his death, Robinson's ordeals and accomplishments were the subject of a Broadway musical, *The First*. In 1987, on the fortieth anniversary of his breaking of the color barrier, the Rookie of the Year Award was redesignated the Jackie Robinson Award in honor of its first recipient. On the fiftieth anniversary of his debut, his No. 42 was permanently retired by all Major League teams, although current Major Leaguers already wearing the number were allowed to keep it for the remainder of their careers.

Among the adjectives often used to describe Robinson's personal makeup are *fearless*, *courageous*, *dynamic*, *defiant*, and *proud*. But probably the most frequently used descriptor is *aggressive*. It's a word that defines his public life as a tireless campaigner against discrimination as well as his history-making athletic career.

Jackie, who was not known for self-deprecation, made the greatest understatement of his life in 1945 at the announcement of his signing. "Maybe I'm doing something for my race," he ventured.[15]

Former teammate Joe Black, speaking for generations of black ballplayers, later said, "When I look at my house, I say 'Thank God for Jackie Robinson.'"[16]

# Chapter 4. Branch Rickey

*Andy McCue*

Branch Rickey was baseball's greatest innovator.

Branch Rickey was "a man of strange complexities, not to mention downright contradictions," wrote the *New York Times*'s John Drebinger. The great decision to break baseball's policy of excluding blacks, for which he is justly praised, has, in recent decades, tended to overwhelm the highly negative image he had earned before that decision. He went from "El Cheapo" to moral beacon in just a few years, and richly deserved each characterization.

He was deeply religious, sowing biblical quotations and religious axioms much as Johnny Appleseed sowed apple seeds.

He was a tightwad. "Rickey believes in econo-my in everything except his own salary," wrote the *New York Daily Mirror*'s Dan Parker. *Daily News* columnist Jimmy Powers tagged him El Cheapo after Rickey dumped a number of the Dodgers' older, and better-known, players soon after taking over.

He was politically and socially conservative. He preached on the temperance circuit as a young man and, as an older man, would regularly attack Communism, Communists, and liberal politicians.

He preached courage and honesty, yet he was devious. Bob Broeg of the *St. Louis Post-Dispatch* dubbed him Branch Richelieu. When a decision by Commissioner Kenesaw Landis deprived Rickey of a promising player, he could actively work to subvert the decision through fake transfers. Rickey could "think up many a little scheme that, while not dishonest, still will not leave Rickey & Co. holding the sack on the snipe hunt," wrote Bill Corum in the *New York Journal-American*.

He could bring Jackie Robinson to the Majors, and tell stories of being deeply moved when an African American player he coached in college sought to rub off his skin color to escape the prejudices of white America, but he could also relate dialect jokes. He made anti-Catholic remarks at the dinner table and characterized a potential Dodgers purchaser as being "of Jewish extraction and characteristics."

He was articulate, if inclined to overblown rhetoric and dramatic vocabulary. "Rickey's natural element is the pulpit," wrote Red Smith. "He talks with such pontifical oratory that he could and would make a reading of batting averages sound as impressive and as stirring as Lincoln's Gettysburg Address," said the *New York Times*'s Arthur Daley. Players who stumbled out of salary-negotiating sessions were amazed at the verbal rings that had been run around them, and at the salaries they had accepted.

At home, he acknowledged he had been going on too long when his five daughters all wound up with fingers next to their noses, the family code that somebody was talking too much. Jane Moulton Rickey, whom he met when she was twelve, proposed to a hundred times, and married at twenty-four, could note, "Mr. Rickey is not, and never has been, one of the ten best-groomed men in America." And he was absent-minded, often tossing lighted matches into trash cans filled with paper.

He was fearsomely intelligent, well read, and thoughtful.

Wesley Branch Rickey was born on December 20, 1881, in Scioto County, located on the Ohio River in south-central Ohio, to the modest farming family of Jacob Franklin "Frank" Rickey and Emily Brown Rickey. Branch had an older brother, Orla, born in 1875, and a younger brother, Frank, born in 1888. As Branch's first name would indicate—John Wesley was the founder of Methodism—it was a pious, Methodist household. Rickey finished grade school in Lucasville, Ohio, but then farm labor called. With help from a sympathetic retired educator, he read as widely as the resources of Scioto County allowed in the 1890s. He educated himself enough to become the teacher at the local grade school, saving money for college. Eventually, he went off to Ohio Wesleyan University. For the next decade, Rickey's life was a welter of sporadic academics, sports, and, eventually, coaching.

He played baseball and football at Ohio Wesleyan and, realizing he could make money to pay for his studies, entered baseball's semipro summer circuit in 1902 and began to coach the university team the next spring. That summer, he moved to the Minor Leagues, playing in Terre Haute, Indiana; LeMars, Iowa; and Dallas, Texas. In 1904, after graduation, Rickey returned to Dallas, and he was purchased by the Cincinnati Reds near the end of the season.

He spent parts of the next three seasons in the Majors, earning a reputation as a marginal catcher, a poor hitter, and an odd duck for refusing to play baseball on Sundays. In Cincinnati his refusal to play on Sundays infuriated manager Joe Kelley, who released him back to Dallas before he appeared in a league game. For the winter, Rickey moved to Allegheny College in Meadville, Pennsylvania, where he served as football and baseball coach.

That winter, the White Sox purchased Rickey's contract, but they sent him to the St. Louis Browns after deciding they could not afford a catcher who took Sundays off and would not report until his college coaching duties were done. He made his Major League debut on June 16, 1905. That one appearance was it for the year, as his mother became ill and Rickey went back to Lucasville. After she recovered, he went back to Dallas before heading to Allegheny for another year of coaching. There, he became disillusioned with the semiprofessional character of college football and left before the baseball season began.

By the time the 1906 season began, Rickey was back with the Browns. He had his best year that summer, playing in sixty-five games and hitting .284. The left-handed-hitting Rickey had his first Major League safety, a single, on April 23 off Detroit southpaw Ed Killian at Sportsman's Park. The offensive highlight of his career came on August 6 against the New York Yankees. Rickey hit a two-run homer in the bottom of the second inning to chase Jack Chesbro and extend the Browns' lead to 5–0. He then hit a "fluke" inside-the-park home run off reliever Walter Clarkson in the sixth, to make the score 6–2. But by the end of the summer, his arm was hurting. He returned to Ohio Wesleyan to coach and complete the courses he needed to enter law school. In late winter the shoulder pain returned.

During the off-season Rickey had been sold to the Yankees. Despite a spring training visit to Hot Springs, Arkansas, his arm did not improve. Rickey played sporadically, and the league noticed his inability to throw. On June 28, 1907, the Washington Senators stole thirteen consecutive bases against him, and Rickey had stopped bothering to throw by the end of the game. It's a record that stands a century later. Offensively, his average fell to .182 in fifty-two games. He would make a cameo two-game appearance for the Browns in 1914, but otherwise his playing career was finished. In all, he played in 120 games over four seasons and had a .239 lifetime batting average.

After marrying Jane in Lucasville in June 1906, he turned to a laundry list of jobs. He was Ohio Wesleyan's athletic director, while also coaching football, basketball, and baseball at the college. He was secretary of the YMCA in Delaware,

Ohio, and he taught beginning law classes even while taking other law classes as a student. As 1908 rolled in, Rickey threw himself into William Howard Taft's campaign for the presidency and the work of the Anti-Saloon League. By the end of 1908, perhaps run down from his schedule, Rickey was diagnosed with tuberculosis, the biggest medical killer of the time.

He spent much of 1909 in a sanatorium in upstate New York, leaving only to begin his first semester at the University of Michigan law school in the fall. By early 1910 his health had improved enough for him to supplement his savings by coaching the university's baseball team.

In 1911, nearing age thirty, Branch Rickey graduated from law school and chose Boise, Idaho, as the site of his law office. He was, by his own accounts, a miserable failure, gaining only one client, who did not even want a lawyer. But the impressions he had made as a baseball player and coach came to his rescue. Even while in Boise, he had spent his summer scouting for Robert Hedges, owner of the St. Louis Browns, who had been impressed with Rickey's intelligence and articulate presentations when he was a player. After his second unsuccessful winter in Boise, Rickey was only too happy to respond to Hedges's request for a meeting in Salt Lake City to discuss a full-time job with the Browns. He borrowed the train fare from Hedges and began a half century of life in professional baseball.

Rickey's initial role was somewhere between scout and general manager. With the help of full-time scout Charley Barrett, Rickey evaluated and tracked players from the Midwest and South. In the winter of 1912, he produced a list of players the Browns could draft from Minor League teams, and 30 of the 105 players chosen that winter were taken by the Browns. By mid-1913 Rickey was the field manager of the Browns. He began teaching his players with a blend of lectures, heart-to-heart talks, and drills. He also began his lifelong fascination with statistical analysis, hiring a young man to sit behind home plate and keep track of how many bases each player made for himself and advanced his teammates. The team improved in 1914, but slid back in 1915 amid accusations that Rickey was too intellectual in dealing with his players.

That winter, Hedges sold the Browns to Phil Ball after granting Rickey a long-term contract. Ball, however, was contemptuous of Rickey's religious views and his approach to the game. He brought in Fielder Jones as field manager while Rickey chafed in his former role of finding players for the Browns. By the spring of 1917, a new ownership group for the National League's St. Louis team persuaded Ball to let Rickey out of his contract to become the Cardinals' president.

Although he was still in St. Louis with his growing family, running the Cardinals was not a dream job. The new ownership was undercapitalized. The team had finished in the top half of the league once in the previous quarter century. Rickey and Cardinals manager Miller Huggins clashed over Rickey's "theoretical" approach to the game. The 1917 Cardinals struggled to their best record since 1891, but it was good only for third place. After the season, Huggins was lured away by the New York Yankees, and Rickey hired Jack Hendricks to take his place.

In August 1918 Rickey joined the Army Chemical Corps, then a new field with cachet. He was commissioned a major and joined a unit with Captains Ty Cobb and Christy Mathewson. In the weeks leading to the November 11 armistice, Rickey's unit supported a number of American attacks on the Germans. He was back in the United States on December 23 and in Lucasville with the family for Christmas.

The Cardinals team he returned to was in serious financial trouble. Rickey borrowed Jane's family heirloom rugs to make his barren office look respectable, and he made himself manager to save

a salary. But he was building the foundation that would make the Cardinals a dominant team for the next three decades.

Rickey's record as manager of the Cardinals was mediocre. For his first three years, he increased the win totals each year, and the Cardinals reached third place by 1921. But in 1922 the team slipped to fourth, then fifth, then sixth, before he was replaced early in 1925. Angry and humiliated, he contemplated quitting, but eventually decided to remain as general manager. For those who questioned Rickey's ability to lead and motivate players, they had their prejudices confirmed when Rogers Hornsby took the Cardinals to the 1926 pennant.

While the critics savaged Rickey as a manager, no one doubted his abilities in the front office. It was only when Rickey was kicked upstairs from the Cardinals' dugout that he found his true role. "Rickey practically created the office of business manager as it is understood today," wrote the *New York Times*'s John Drebinger in 1943.

Rickey's first great innovation was the farm system. "When the Cardinals were fighting for their life in the National League, I found that we were at a disadvantage in obtaining players of merit from the minors," Rickey said. "Other clubs could outbid. They had money. They had superior scouting machinery. In short, we had to take what was left or nothing at all. . . . Thus it was that we took over the Houston Club for a Class A proving ground in 1924. . . . Still, I do not feel that the farming system we have established is the result of any inventive genius—it is the result of stark necessity. We did it to meet a question of supply and demand of young ballplayers," he told *The Sporting News*'s Dick Farrington.

The Cardinals eventually created a chain of Minor League teams so they could sign players cheaply, winnow the good from the great, win pennants, and make money. Rickey would sell the good to others and keep the great for the Cardinals.

Rickey proved a cold-blooded judge of talent, and a man with the knack for nurturing what talent he had. He was not the sentimentalist to hang on to an aging player who had contributed greatly to the team's past success. It is better to trade a man a year too early than a year too late, he preached. He created the concept of the "anesthetic ballplayer," the one who is good enough to be a Major Leaguer, but not good enough to help win a pennant or a World Series. Trading the anesthetics and the fading stars filled holes the farm system could not. And in the Minors, Rickey was an innovator not just in creating but in teaching.

He came up with sandpits to teach players to slide; a set of strings to define the strike zone and help pitchers with their control; the batting tee to help hitters hone their swings; and chalk talks. After World War II, when Rickey was with the Dodgers, he expanded on the statistical analysis he had first tried with the Browns. He hired Allan Roth, who charted where Dodgers batters' hits fell.

Rickey was observant in a way that amazed even other baseball men. There was the story of one pitch—a foul ball—while Rickey was sitting behind the plate one day. After the pitch he turned to an aide and dictated the following notes: The center fielder had failed to get a jump on the ball, the pitcher had an unbalanced motion and would not be able to field his position, and the catcher had blinked as the batter swung, causing him to miss the foul tip.

Rickey's player-evaluation skills built the Cardinals' machine that dominated the National League, winning nine pennants and six World Series between 1926 and 1946. This machine, built on the ownership of Minor League clubs, did not run smoothly. Baseball commissioner Kenesaw Landis did not like to see Minor League teams run simply as talent suppliers for the Major Leagues. He wanted them to act as independent businesses. He wanted players to have the fullest freedom to exploit their talent and not get stuck in the Minor League systems of talent-rich organizations. Rickey, whose plan had been followed by the other Major League teams, argued that Major League ownership had allowed the Minor Leagues to survive the Depression of the 1930s.

In 1938, in what became known as the Cedar Rapids decision, Landis freed at least seventy-four Cardinals farmhands. Landis found that the Cardinals had relationships with more than one team in some leagues, meaning it could affect pennant races by moving players between these teams. He offered no evidence that they had done so. The one released player of unusual talent was Pete Reiser, and Rickey set out to subvert Landis's decision by making sure his protégé, Larry MacPhail of the Brooklyn Dodgers, picked up Reiser with a promise to return him to the Cardinals once the hullaballoo calmed down. Reiser, however, performed so well in spring training that press and public pressure to keep the young outfielder led MacPhail to renege on his promise.

In public, Rickey's reputation as a shrewd executive and motivational speaker grew. He was asked to speak often, and he was never afraid to tie his conservative religious and political beliefs with his baseball success. He befriended political figures, usually conservative Republicans. He was approached to run for governor of Missouri. He was described as one of Republican presidential candidate Thomas Dewey's closest friends and supporters and touted as his successor as New York governor if Dewey was elected president.

By late 1942 Rickey's relationship with Cardinals owner Sam Breadon had become strained. The two were fighting over Rickey's bonus payments and Breadon's dismissal of Rickey protégés in the farm system. Rickey reportedly was upset at Breadon's refusal to back him over the Cedar Rapids decision and with Breadon's paying a large bonus to himself while cutting Rickey's budget for salaries. Rickey was considering a top executive post with a large insurance company.

In 1937, when Brooklyn Dodgers board member James Mulvey had first approached him, Rickey had not been prepared to leave a comfortable life in St. Louis. By late 1942 he was. The wooing was relatively quick. The *New York Times* first reported Brooklyn-Rickey talks on October 4, 1942. The move was announced on October 29, a day when Rickey was introduced as the new general manager at a lunch at the Brooklyn Club. At that lunch Rickey also was introduced to Walter O'Malley, a thirty-nine-year-old lawyer who shared the Brooklyn Trust table with him.

In Brooklyn, Rickey saw a different team than the press and the fans did. They saw the 1941 pennant winner and a 1942 team that had finished second. Rickey saw a team that was old, with a roster about to be ravaged by the needs of military service. It was the disposal of aging stars that earned him the nickname "El Cheapo." It was his response to World War II that would build the foundation of the Boys of Summer.

With the draft in place, most teams cut back on signing players, bowing to the uncertainties of wartime. In response, the number of Minor League teams shrank from forty-one in 1941 to ten in 1944. But Rickey, reasoning that the war had to end someday, signed talent in buckets, seeking to repeat his success in building the Cardinals' Minor League system. Players like Gil Hodges would make token appearances in the Major Leagues before disappearing into boot camp, then emerge after the war to stock baseball's richest farm system. Rickey earned another nickname, "The Mahatma," after sportswriter Tom Meany read a portrait of Indian political leader Mohandas "Mahatma" Gandhi that described Gandhi as a combination of "your father and Tammany Hall."

In the years immediately after the war, Rickey blended prewar players like Dixie Walker, Hugh Casey, and Pee Wee Reese with the results of his player-development program. That program had led to another Rickey innovation—the spring training complex. With more than seven hundred players under contract, the Dodgers needed a large facility if they wanted to ensure uniform training and easy analysis of their prospects. In 1947 Rickey struck a deal with the town of Vero Beach, Florida, for the use of the former U.S. Navy pilot training base on the west edge of town. Using a complex system of colors and numbers, the Minor Leaguers were sorted, trained, analyzed, graded, and eventually assigned to their Minor League teams, all according to the Rickey methods.

Except for the Vero Beach facility, which would become a model for other teams, the methods were those Rickey had developed with the Cardinals. But in Brooklyn he took another step, one that would raise him from talented baseball executive to sainted agent of progress.

Rickey's decision to seek black baseball talent came fairly soon after he joined the Dodgers. His pursuit of black players was a typical combination of motives and methods. It was a product of his religious beliefs; of his desire to win and draw fans; and of his ability to see baseball in the context of American society. It was conducted not by looking for just the best baseball talent, but for the best combination of on-field talent, maturity, and intelligence. For his African American torchbearer, he chose a college-educated man who would be twenty-seven before he played even one game in the white Minor Leagues. He chose Jackie Robinson in part because he was from California, in whose milder racial climate he had played most of his life on integrated athletic teams. Rickey encouraged him to marry his fiancée, a move he felt always helped a ballplayer's career. Robinson went on to justify Rickey's gamble in every way and cement a lifelong relationship between the two men.

But his relationships with his partners were not so strong. By 1950 Rickey knew his lucrative contract would not be renewed, and he began the steps that would put Walter O'Malley in control of the

Dodgers and himself at the general manager's desk in Pittsburgh.

In Pittsburgh, Rickey set out to build the kind of dominant organization he had constructed in St. Louis and Brooklyn. Rickey's one original move in Pittsburgh came too late to save him. In 1955 he sent Howie Haak, his best scout, to begin scouring the Caribbean for talent. This move would bear immense fruit for the Pirates in the 1960s, but by then Rickey was gone.

After the 1955 season, Rickey stepped down as general manager, saying he would spend the rest of his ten-year contract as a senior consultant to the team. But it was clear that consulting was a cover for being at loose ends, a situation that did not change until late in 1958, when Rickey began talking with a New York lawyer named William Shea. In the wake of the Dodgers' and Giants' departures for the West Coast, New York City mayor Robert Wagner Jr. had asked Shea to head an effort to bring National League baseball back to New York. Shea turned for advice to George V. McLaughlin, a New York banker and civic luminary who had brought O'Malley to the Dodgers in 1940. McLaughlin suggested that Shea talk to Rickey. Rickey, who had apparently been mulling the idea for a while, suggested a third league.

For the next two years, Rickey headed the Continental League. He wooed ownership groups, promised his league would find players even while honoring Major League Baseball's reserve clause, and worked through Congress to bring pressure to limit the Major Leagues' control of their players. The league collapsed in late 1960, when both the National and American leagues committed to expansion.

For two years he puttered, but then he jumped at a chance to return to the Cardinals as a "senior consultant." It was an awkward relationship. General manager Bing Devine felt threatened by owner Gussie Busch's hiring of Rickey. Rickey's opposition to a trade that brought shortstop Dick Groat

to the Cardinals worsened the situation. And when a strongly worded memo urging Stan Musial's forced retirement leaked to the press, Rickey's status became fragile. He was not helped when Busch decided to fire Devine in mid-1964, a move that was interpreted as interference by Rickey. The move embarrassed Busch, as the Cardinals rallied to win the pennant with a team Devine had assembled. After the World Series, won by the Cardinals, Busch fired Rickey as well.

In 1965 Rickey finished his work on *The American Diamond: A Documentary of the Game of Baseball*, the closest thing to an autobiography Rickey would do. It contained portraits of a group Rickey called the sports immortals, as well as reflections from his years in the game.

He died on December 9, 1965, and was buried in Rushtown, Ohio, just across the Scioto River from Lucasville. Jane Rickey died on October 16, 1971, and was buried next to him.

## Chapter 5. **Leo Durocher**

*Jeffrey Marlett*

From his birth in 1905 in West Springfield, Massachusetts, to his death in 1991 in Palm Springs, California, Leo Durocher witnessed a great deal of social, political, and international change, some of which he helped bring about. Durocher played an important supporting role in the integration of Major League Baseball. His frank assessment of African American baseball talent remains a simple, if coarse, endorsement of the American belief in meritocracy. He stood in the third-base coach's box for one of baseball's most memorable home runs, Bobby Thomson's 1951 "Shot Heard 'Round the World" off Ralph Branca. He led the New York Giants to a surprising World Series victory in 1954.

More than a decade later, he piloted the Chicago Cubs through six and a half frustrating seasons, always falling short of the postseason. Along the way Durocher kept company with movie stars, entertainers, and an entire retinue of shady underworld characters. He had legal difficulties, four divorces, and fights with fans, jilted women, and angered husbands, fathers, and boyfriends. Through it all he maintained the utmost confidence in his own ability to come out ahead. Then as now, many have seen Durocher's competitiveness as an excuse for playing dirty.

Durocher found success in both playing and managing, winning World Series titles while playing shortstop for the 1928 Yankees and 1934 Cardinals and then as the manager of the 1954 Giants. He won National League pennants but no world championships with the 1941 Brooklyn Dodgers and the 1951 Giants. Finally, the famous phrase "Nice guys finish last," attributed to him,

Leo Durocher's one-year suspension stunned the baseball world.

has achieved recognition throughout American culture.

Leo Ernest Durocher was born on July 27, 1905, to George and Clarinda (Provost) Durocher in West Springfield, Massachusetts. He was the youngest of four sons, but at five feet ten grew to be the tallest. His French Canadian parents often spoke French at home. Like his older brothers, Leo served Mass at the local Quebecois parish, St. Louis.

He also became quite adept at playing pool and soon frequented the local pool halls to hustle money. His athletic abilities also became evident. While playing several sports, Leo became a local baseball prodigy. Company teams offered him increasingly lucrative and easy jobs if he would play for them and not for competing companies.

Discovered by a Yankees scout, he broke into professional baseball in 1925 with Hartford of the Eastern League, earning a call-up to the Yankees that season. He got into two games and had one at-bat. Durocher spent the next two seasons in the Minor Leagues, at Atlanta of the Southern Association (1926) and St. Paul of the American Association (1927). He came back to the Yankees in 1928 and never completely left the Major Leagues until his retirement in 1973.

Durocher's time with the Yankees was volcanic. Protected by manager Miller Huggins, he quickly made enemies with his incessant yapping, extravagant living, and antagonizing of Yankees stars like Babe Ruth and Lou Gehrig. Ruth nicknamed Durocher the "All-American Out" for his diminutive batting average. Ruth also accused him of stealing his watch, a charge Durocher denied vehemently.

Durocher lost his protective mantle when Huggins died in 1929, and he was waived to the Cincinnati Reds before the 1930 season. In Cincinnati he found his gambling appetite even more easily indulged than in New York. He married Ruby Hartley in 1930 and fathered a child. The marriage quickly fell apart, and the couple divorced in 1934. Durocher omitted this first marriage—and his only biological child—in his 1975 autobiography. Midway through the 1933 season, mired in debt and a dissolving marriage, Durocher was traded to the St. Louis Cardinals. He became captain of the famous Gashouse Gang, the 1934 Cardinals team that fought with one another as much as with the opposition and won the World Series against Detroit in seven games.

On September 27 Durocher took time to remarry, this time to Grace Dozier, a prominent St. Louis businesswoman and fashion designer who paid off Leo's substantial debts. After the 1937 season, friction between Leo and the Cardinals' player-manager, Frankie Frisch, led to a trade to the Brooklyn Dodgers. There Durocher reunited with Larry MacPhail, who had traded him from Cincinnati to Branch Rickey's Cardinals. After the 1938 season, Durocher became the Dodgers' player-manager.

Leo received his nicknames "The Lip" or "Lippy" during his first full year in the Majors, 1928. The roots for these names, and the behavior that spawned them, reached back to his boyhood days in West Springfield. Durocher dutifully idolized Walter "Rabbit" Maranville, the Boston Braves' diminutive shortstop who hailed from nearby Springfield. Maranville, only five feet five and weighing 155 pounds, recognized that smaller players needed a mental edge to compensate for their lack of size.

Maranville came to know of the neighborhood's emerging star. He once told the young Leo, "Never back up," because "the first backward step a little man takes is the one that's going to kill him."[1] Maranville meant this advice to apply to fielding the ball, but one might wonder if Leo took Maranville a bit too literally. George Durocher and his other sons exhibited the rock-ribbed but nonetheless quiet stoicism French Canadian immigrants were known for in the Northeast. Maranville's words could also be understood as "Don't back down from a fight," advice Leo often took to heart.

The tutorials in baseball's mental game continued as Leo progressed through the Minor Leagues. Miller Huggins completed Leo's apprenticeship when he reached New York. During the 1928 season with the Yankees, Durocher became a full-blown, loudmouth bench jockey. The verbal assaults continued through his managing years.

Boyhood friends who visited Durocher for games would note that almost every one of Leo's sentences included several obscenities. Branch Rickey once remarked that when Durocher was pushed into a corner, "He's still that kid from West Springfield with a pool cue butt in his hand."

From the earliest days of his playing career to the end of his managing days, Durocher loved to yap. Miller Huggins had encouraged the 160-pound youngster to compensate for his weak bat with hustle. Huggins, Leo said, "kept telling me I'd stick around for a long time if I kept my cockiness and my scrappiness and that fierce desire to do anything to win."[2] Durocher willingly obliged his mentor. First as a player, then as a manager, he never shied away from verbal combat. As of 2010, Durocher ranked third all-time for the most times ejected from a Major League game as a player or a manager. Strictly as a manager, Durocher ranks fourth.

As a player, Durocher also distinguished himself with his fielding. Throughout his managerial career, he often reverted to his boyhood games, playing pepper with players several decades younger than himself. Even when he managed the Cubs in his sixties, Durocher surprised two of his stars, Ernie Banks and Ron Santo, with his ability to keep up with the younger players.

Durocher was certainly not a threat with the bat. He was a career .247 hitter, with just 24 home runs. His highest batting average came in 1936, when he hit .286 for the Cardinals. Overall, though, he performed better the preceding year, hitting .265 in 143 games. That season (1935) included career highs in home runs (8), slugging percentage (.376), and RBIs (78).

Durocher's already limited productivity tailed off significantly in the 1940s. In 1940 he played in little more than half the games (62) he had the year before and came to bat only 175 times. In 1939 Durocher came in eighth in the MVP voting, and he was second among shortstops. In 1941, 1943,

and 1945, his last three years playing, he appeared in only 26 games total, batting just 67 times. (He managed, but did not play for, the Dodgers in 1942 and 1944.)

In 1941 Brooklyn won its first pennant since 1920 but lost the World Series to the Yankees, four games to one. The next year, the Dodgers won 104 games but lost the pennant to the Cardinals. Brooklyn finished third in 1943, the same year Durocher and Grace Dozier divorced.

With the players who had been in the military returning in 1946, Leo shifted over to managing full time. It was in that season that he purportedly made his well-known statement "Nice guys finish last." Aimed at the last-place Giants and their manager, Mel Ott, the phrase quickly took on a life of its own, appearing in all sorts of publications, popular and scholarly, ever since.

The groundbreaking 1947 season was noticeable for Durocher's absence. He had been present during spring training in Havana, Cuba, playing along with Branch Rickey's orchestration of Jackie Robinson's promotion to Brooklyn. Throughout the winter Rickey had planted stories that Durocher was "pressuring" him to add Robinson to the Dodgers' roster. However, just when Rickey was ready to announce that Robinson would in fact start on Opening Day, Durocher's past threw Rickey and the Dodgers an exploding curve ball.

On the very day Robinson was to be introduced, Commissioner Albert B. "Happy" Chandler suspended Durocher from baseball for a year. Chandler claimed that Durocher had once again associated with known gamblers. Prior to a 1947 spring training game in Havana, Durocher noticed two such men sitting with Yankees owner Larry MacPhail. Rickey and Durocher complained to Chandler about double standards. MacPhail responded by decrying the charges as slanderous. Chandler fined both owners and suspended Durocher, a move that astonished Rickey, Durocher, and Brooklyn's fans.

This latest fiasco concerning Durocher only added to Rickey's headaches. In January, Leo had made headlines again—this time for his marriage to actress Laraine Day, whom he had met in 1945. The Utah-born Day was already married to Ray Hendricks, but in January 1947, Day divorced Hendricks in Mexico, then married Durocher the next day in El Paso, Texas. Back in California, Durocher and Day, who still had a year to wait before her California divorce from Hendricks was final, had to plead before a judge so she could avoid conviction for bigamy.

Compounding the scandal's impact was a boycott of the Dodgers by the local chapter of the Catholic Youth Organization (CYO). The director of the Brooklyn CYO, Rev. Vincent Powell, removed CYO support for the "Knothole Gang" and published a letter in the newspapers on March 1, 1947, charging that Durocher was "undermining the moral training of Brooklyn's Roman Catholic youth." The CYO contributed both youths and money to the Brooklyn Knothole Gang, the team's adolescent fan base. Supported by U.S. Supreme Court Justice Frank Murphy, the Brooklyn Diocese had presented Rickey with an ultimatum: fire Durocher for his moral turpitude or face a boycott.

Durocher's suspension solved the boycott issue; nevertheless, with the beginning of the 1947 season a week away, Rickey had no manager for his new team. Eventually he named Burt Shotton as interim manager. Shotton promptly led the team to the National League pennant.

Before he left, Durocher did manage to contribute significantly to the Dodgers' 1947 season. In Havana the Dodgers learned of Rickey's plan to integrate the team with Robinson. Some players circulated a petition protesting Rickey's move. As soon as he heard of it, Durocher called a team meeting—at midnight. Surrounded by sleepy and cross players, Durocher flatly told them to "wipe [their] ass" with the petition. Finally, Leo concluded, many black players shared his own fierce desire

to win. They were hungry, and unless the Dodgers and the other white players themselves played harder, they would find themselves replaced. Leo cared about winning, and if that meant starting black players, he had no problem doing so. He went public with his support for Robinson: "I don't care if he is yellow or black or has stripes like a fucking zebra. I'm his manager and I say he plays."

Underneath his coarse language, Leo believed in meritocracy. Those who are most able are the ones who start, regardless of appearance or background. This managerial approach led him to start three African Americans in the 1951 World Series (Monte Irvin, Willie Mays, and Hank Thompson). Hank Thompson recalled Durocher's introduction when Hank arrived at the Giants' spring training camp: "I'm only going to say one thing about color: You can be green or be pink on this team. If you can play baseball and help this team you're welcome to play." Thompson concluded, "And it was true."[3]

Throughout the 1947 season, Rickey assured Durocher that he would get his manager's job back. Shotton's performance—winning the pennant and pushing the Yankees to seven games in the World Series—made Rickey reconsider his promise, but in the end he kept it. When Leo arrived at spring training in 1948, he did seem changed. Reporters, players, and even Rickey himself noticed that the marriage (and perhaps the suspension) had mellowed him. The old Leo resurfaced briefly when Jackie Robinson reported to camp. Over the winter Robinson had gained significant weight. Durocher reverted to his older hectoring self, badgering Robinson incessantly. Robinson lost the weight and regained his playing form.

Rickey, though, remained unsatisfied. Wishing perhaps for a managerial change himself, Rickey often mused aloud that the team needed shaking up. The season's start bore out Rickey's worries as the Dodgers stumbled to a 35-37 record. When

Horace Stoneham, owner of the crosstown archrival Giants inquired about Burt Shotton's availability as a replacement for Mel Ott, Rickey had his chance. With Durocher away in Montreal on a scouting trip, Rickey and Stoneham met. While Rickey did not offer Durocher's services, he also did not refuse when Stoneham asked for Durocher instead of Shotton.

Thus, the Dodgers' irascible manager switched in midseason to manage their hated rivals. Fans of both teams were stunned, as was Leo, who did not learn of the managerial trade until he returned. The night the deal was completed, Stoneham visited Laraine Day at the couple's Manhattan apartment. When she learned the news, she switched off the radio broadcast of that night's Dodgers game, saying, "Then why am I listening to this?"

Many of Ott's players were slow-footed veterans, and Durocher's aggressive, gambling style did not sit well. He did manage the team to a .519 record (41-38) for the rest of the season. That was only good enough for fifth place in the National League. The next season, 1949, was Durocher's worst with the Giants; the team finished fifth again, but this time with a 74-83 record. From 1950 through 1955, though, the Giants and Durocher enjoyed five winning seasons, never finishing lower than third. During that span the Giants won two NL pennants and the 1954 World Series. In 1951 they made up a thirteen-game deficit in August against the Dodgers and forced a three-game playoff for the pennant.

The Giants won the third game 5–4 on Bobby Thomson's famed home run. According to author Joshua Prager, Leo did more than just watch; his rudimentary telescope-and-bell system rigged in the Polo Grounds offices 483 feet away from home plate had tipped Durocher, Thomson, and the Giants that Branca was about to throw a fastball. The Giants then lost a hard-fought World Series to the Yankees, four games to two. In 1954 the Giants swept the heavily favored Cleveland Indians in four games. The next year they finished third, a distant eighteen and a half games behind the Dodgers. After that 1955 season, Stoneham replaced Durocher with Bill Rigney.

Durocher's stint with the Giants ranked second only to his time with the Dodgers. He managed the Giants for almost seven and a half seasons and finished with a .549 winning percentage (637-523). He managed the Dodgers for eight and a half seasons and finished only slightly better (738-565).

After the Giants replaced him, Durocher pursued his long-desired goal of shifting careers to show business. However, despite his several celebrity friends, most endeavors quickly fell through. His attempt to host a variety show on NBC flopped. Durocher appeared on several television shows, but he made more money doing baseball broadcasts on radio and television. Day divorced him in 1960. Durocher served as a coach for the Los Angeles Dodgers from 1961 to 1964. True to form, he often criticized manager Walter Alston for indecisiveness and tentative leadership.

In 1966 the Chicago Cubs named the sixty-year-old Durocher manager. That season, he suffered through his worst year as a manager, going 59-103. But much like his stint with the Giants, Durocher then led his team through several winning seasons. From 1967 to 1971, the Cubs enjoyed five straight winning seasons.

The club stood at 46-44 when owner Phil Wrigley fired Durocher midway through the 1972 season. Durocher's time with the Cubs is remembered mostly for what did not happen. For several years the talent-laden club finished below expectations. The 1969 season was the best example. The Cubs led the National League East division for more than one hundred days and were nine and a half games ahead of the New York Mets in August. However, the team faltered badly.

As the season wore on, he misused his pitchers, and his tendency to berate players often backfired. Once again, Durocher's hard-driving style had begun to wear thin. During two weeks in September, the Cubs fell from five games ahead of the Mets to four and a half games behind them, eventually finishing eight games back.

The Cubs finished second again in 1970, albeit without the spectacular meltdown. In 1971 they wound up third. That year the locker room finally boiled over with fights between Durocher and the players. Unlike in previous stints with the Dodgers and Giants, Leo never related well to the Cubs' African American players.

One of his most common managerial tactics was to belittle and enrage players so they would play better. He had picked up this technique from Miller Huggins, and it worked quite well with stars like Jackie Robinson and Sal Maglie. With the Cubs it backfired. Pitcher Ken Holtzman took offense at Durocher's repeated use of anti-Semitic remarks. In the years after Curt Flood's legal challenge to the reserve clause, Durocher's well-known hostility to union organizing appeared shockingly retrograde. Halfway through the 1972 season, owner Phil Wrigley had had enough and replaced Durocher with Whitey Lockman.

Leo did not remain idle for long. The Houston Astros made him skipper for the last thirty-one games of 1972. As before, he wrangled with the team's established stars, in this case pitcher Larry Dierker. Durocher managed the entire 1973 season, going 82-80, before retiring for good.

Leo moved back to California and waited for the Hall of Fame recognition he felt he was due. He and his fourth wife, Lynne Walker Goldbatt, divorced in 1981, but the couple had already separated years earlier. Durocher had married the Chicago socialite in 1969.

As the years went by, Leo rediscovered his Catholic faith. He served faithfully as an usher at the Saturday evening Mass at his local parish. He also became increasingly bitter over his perceived slight by the Hall of Fame. He died on October 7, 1991, and was buried in Hollywood Hills Cemetery in Los Angeles. The Hall of Fame recognition finally came in 1994. On Induction Day, Laraine Day accepted the award.

Durocher's posthumous election to the Baseball Hall of Fame rested exclusively on his managerial career. In twenty-four seasons, Durocher amassed 2,008 victories and 1,709 losses, a .540 winning percentage. However, Durocher's effectiveness as a manager exceeded the raw numbers. Throughout his managerial career, he displayed a tough, scrappy, take-no-prisoners approach to the game. Only at the end of his managerial career did Durocher encounter significant player resistance to his style. When he retired, he seemed a relic from an earlier baseball age.

## Chapter 6. **Kirby Higbe**

*Ralph Berger*

| AGE | W | L | PCT. | ERA | G | GS | GF | CG | SHO | SV | IP | H | BB | SO | HBP | WP |
|-----|---|---|------|-----|---|----|----|----|-----|----|----|---|----|----|-----|-----|
| 32 | 2 | 0 | 1.000 | 5.17 | 4 | 3 | 0 | 0 | 0 | 0 | 15.2 | 18 | 12 | 10 | 1 | 1 |

Kirby Higbe, a good old boy from South Carolina, was a hell-raiser all his life. He was a hard thrower who developed his fastball in childhood by tossing rocks and later saw it compared to Bob Feller's. Higbe had a taste for alcohol and a lust for living that landed him in trouble a few times, but he was honest about himself, admitting he had made mistakes that he regretted.

Although a southerner by birth, Higbe had some northern roots. His paternal grandfather, Wellington William Higbe, was born in Akron County, Ohio, in 1849 and served in the infantry for the Union Army after the Civil War. By 1870 Private Higbe was stationed in Warrenton, Georgia, and then later married Mary Elizabeth Baugh of South Carolina; the two settled in Richland County and raised a family there. Wellington Higbe later became chief of police in Columbia, South Carolina.

Walter Kirby Higbe was born in Columbia on April 8, 1915. His father, Lloyd Wellington Higbe, was a glass blower and later a bottle salesman for Lauren's Glass Works. Kirby adored his mother, Cynthia (Kirby) Higbe, a gentle, understanding, churchgoing woman, and regretted the trouble he caused her.

Kirby had an older brother, Lloyd, and a younger brother, Harold. In 1918, when the flu epidemic hit the nation, the family moved to Jacksonville, Florida, trying to escape the outbreak, but Harold contracted the disease and died. The family returned to Columbia to bury Harold. Subsequently, Lloyd and Cynthia had two more children—a daughter, Cynthia, and a son, Frazier.

The Great Depression hit the Higbe family hard. Kirby quit school after the seventh grade

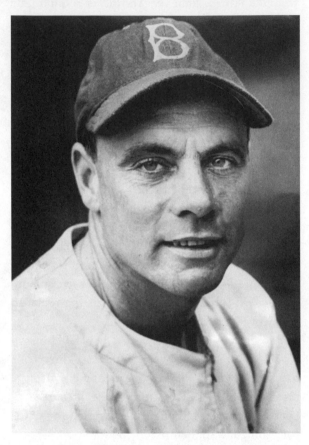

Kirby Higbe's opposition to Jackie Robinson led to his being traded to Pittsburgh in May.

and took a job as a messenger boy for the Southern Railroad for $50 a month. He later regretted the decision to quit school but felt obligated at the time to help the family.

In 1931 Higbe left the railroad to take a job at Claussen's Bakery and pitch on its baseball team. Later he pitched for an American Legion team. Higbe was a hard thrower who knew nothing of the mechanics of pitching.

Scouts from the Pirates took notice of his fast-ball and signed Kirby to pitch for Tulsa (Oklahoma) in the Western League in 1932. But he hit so many batters in batting practice that when the team broke camp, Higbe was left behind with a catcher to work on his control. Only seventeen, he got homesick and returned to Columbia, where he pitched for a semipro team.

Higbe pitched briefly at the Class A level in each of the next two seasons. He went 1-4 in eight games for the Wichita/Muskogee Oilers of the Western League in 1933, and 0-2 in six games for the Southern Association's Atlanta Crackers in 1934. Higbe was with the Portsmouth (Virginia) Truckers in the Class B Piedmont League, a Chicago Cubs affiliate, in 1935. In his first full season as a professional, he had ten victories (10-13) and 206 innings pitched. Higbe won eleven games and lost twelve while splitting the 1936 season between Portsmouth and the Columbia Senators of the South Atlantic League.

In 1937 the twenty-one-year-old Higbe went to spring training with the Cubs. Manager Charlie Grimm told him he had Major League stuff but needed seasoning. Grimm sent Kirby to the Moline (Illinois) Plow Boys in the Class B Three-I League but promised to bring him back at the end of the season if he had a good year.

Kirby had a great year, going 21-5 and leading the league in wins, winning percentage, innings pitched, strikeouts, and walks. Higbe gave credit for his success to his new bride, nineteen-year-old Columbia native Anne Ellerbe, whom he married on May 27, 1937.

The Cubs did call him back, and Kirby got to pitch his first Major League game, against the St. Louis Cardinals at Wrigley Field on October 3, the last day of the regular season. He pitched the final five innings of Chicago's 6–4 win, earning his first Major League victory. In 1938 Higbe headed to Catalina Island, where the Cubs trained, but got homesick and went only as far as Knoxville, Tennessee. He called the Cubs and asked them if he could play at Birmingham and when they needed him he would come. The Cubs agreed, and Kirby played for the Birmingham (Alabama) Barons of the Class A Southern Association until September, winning fifteen games before the Cubs recalled him.

The Cubs were five games behind the league-leading Pirates when Higbe made his first Major League start on September 8, 1938, at Sportsman's Park in St. Louis. Chicago took the early lead but Kirby couldn't hold it, giving up four runs over six innings. Higbe started again in the first game of a doubleheader in Philadelphia on September 23, lasting only four innings. He had pitched ten innings for the Cubs in two starts, allowing sixteen base runners and six runs, but years later he remembered feeling good about things. His homesickness was a thing of the past, and he felt he was in the big leagues to stay.

In 1939 Higbe pitched well early, mostly in relief, winning two games and losing one with a 3.18 ERA. On May 29 the Cubs traded him, along with pitcher Cowboy Harrell and outfielder Joe Marty to the Phillies for pitcher Claude Passeau. Kirby went from the reigning National League champs to a perennial cellar dweller. Regardless of how well he pitched for the Phillies, it was hard to come up with wins. He was 10-14 for his new club, with a 4.85 ERA. His combined 123 walks for the two franchises led all NL pitchers.

In 1940 the Phillies were last again. Higbe, 14-19, again led the league in walks, but now also led in strikeouts. He was selected to the All-Star team but did not play. While it may have been painful to play for a losing team, the regular work helped Kirby a great deal, work he likely would not have had on a pennant contender.

On November 11, 1940, Philadelphia traded Higbe to the Dodgers—who no doubt were influenced by his five 1940 victories over the Giants—for three players and, at that time, a whopping $100,000. Dodgers general manager Larry MacPhail said Higbe possessed the best curve ball in baseball and was sure to be a twenty-game winner for Brooklyn. The deliriously happy Higbe also got a salary increase to $10,000 a year.

The five-foot-eleven, 190-pound right-hander had his best year in 1941, winning a league-leading twenty-two games and losing nine. Higbe established career highs in many pitching categories, including forty-eight appearances, thirty-nine starts (also leading the league in both categories), and 298 innings pitched. His performance was good enough for seventh place in the MVP voting.

Not surprisingly, Higbe loved playing in Brooklyn. The fans were great and he was with a top team. He acquired the name "Laughing Boy" from Dick Young of the *New York Daily News*, who noted that he had a grin as wide as that of comedian Joe E. Brown.

The Dodgers won the pennant, their first since 1920, and Higbe was their starting pitcher in Game Four of the World Series against the Yankees. He was behind, 3–0, when he left with two outs in the top of the fourth. The Dodgers rallied to take a 4–3 lead going into the top of the ninth. The stage was set for Mickey Owen's infamous error allowing Tommy Henrich to reach first base and set up the Yankees' miracle comeback. The Yankees closed out the Series the next day. It was Kirby Higbe's only World Series appearance.

Higbe won sixteen and lost eleven in 1942 as the Dodgers won 104 games, only to finish two games behind the Cardinals. He was plagued by arm trouble after the season, and in 1943 he had a mediocre 6-10 record in the middle of July. His arm came around, however, and he won seven consecutive decisons, finishing a respectable 13-10.

On October 16, 1943, Higbe was drafted into the army at Fort Jackson, near his home in Columbia, South Carolina. He was assigned to the military police, which meant, essentially, standing guard, but he was primarily there to play baseball. That did not last, however, and Higbe was sent to Camp Livingston, Louisiana. There he underwent basic training and became a rifleman. He

still managed to play some ball and was selected to play in the National Baseball Congress Semi-Pro tournament in 1944. He participated while on furlough and made the All-Star team.

In 1945 Kirby found himself in Germany. He was frightened as he went into combat at Cologne; seeing dead bodies shook him badly. His unit fought all the way to Berndorff, Austria. Shipped home after the war in Europe ended, Higbe and his fellow soldiers took more training and sailed for the Philippines. When they arrived there, they learned the Japanese had surrendered. While in the Philipines, Higbe managed the Manila Dodgers, and when he wasn't playing baseball, he was selling beer to the locals.

Kirby was late getting to spring training in 1946 because he wasn't discharged until late March, but he had a successful season, winning seventeen and losing eight with a career low ERA of 3.03. The Dodgers tied the St. Louis Cardinals for first place, but lost the pennant in Major League Baseball's first-ever playoff series, two games to none. Higbe relieved starter Ralph Branca in the first game and was the fourth of six pitchers Brooklyn used in the second contest. Kirby pitched in the 1946 All-Star Game in Fenway Park, a game won by the American League 12–0. While he did not get the loss, he yielded four runs on five hits in one and one-third innings, including the first of Ted Williams's two home runs.

Baseball's color line was broken in 1947 when Jackie Robinson was brought up from Montreal to Brooklyn. When Branch Rickey announced that Robinson was to play for the Dodgers, Higbe was one of a group of Brooklyn players who protested Rickey's decision. Subsequently, Kirby was traded to the Pittsburgh Pirates on May 3, 1947, along with pitchers Hank Behrman and Cal McLish, catcher Dixie Howell, and infielder Gene Mauch in exchange for Al Gionfriddo and $100,000. After going 2-0 with a 5.17 ERA for the pennant-winning Dodgers, he was 11-17 with a 3.72 ERA for

Pittsburgh. He walked 122 batters, leading the league for the fourth and last time in that category.

Higbe went 8-7 for the Pirates in 1948, pitching mostly out of the bullpen. He had a terrible start to the '49 season, giving up twenty-three earned runs in fifteen and one-third innings. On June 6, Pittsburgh traded him to the Giants for pitcher Ray Poat and infielder Bobby Rhawn. Pitching mostly in relief for the Giants, he was 2-2 for the season, and according to Tommy Henrich's book, *The Way To Better Baseball*, he was now almost exclusively a knuckleballer. Overall, he appeared in forty-four games for both clubs but pitched just ninety-five and two-thirds innings, his lightest workload since 1938.

Higbe, now thirty-four years old, made his last Major League appearance on July 7, 1950, at Braves Field in Boston, pitching two scoreless innings in relief. On July 12 the Giants sent him to the Minneapolis Millers, their Class Triple-A affiliate in the American Association. Higbe finished his big league career with 118 wins, 101 losses, a 3.69 ERA, and 24 saves. He was, however, very good during his five seasons with the Dodgers, going 70-38 with a 3.29 ERA.

Higbe won five games and lost eight for the first-place Millers in 1950. He also appeared in four games for the Pacific Coast League's Seattle Rainiers, dropping two decisions. He did better in 1951, winning seventeen games for Class A Montgomery and Class Double-A Atlanta. He spent the entire 1952 season with Montgomery in the South Atlantic League, going 13-14 with a 2.79 ERA. Sliding down the Minor League ladder, Kirby pitched in the Tarheel and Tri-State leagues in 1953, winning eighteen games despite arm trouble. He pitched his last game with a semipro team and called it quits. In recognition of his twenty years of professional baseball, Higbe was inducted into the South Carolina Athletic Hall of Fame.

Higbe was now just an ordinary workingman. He landed a job with the post office in Columbia. Kirby began seeing another woman, Betsy Ains,

whom he married in 1960 when their divorces were final. They had two sons, David Parks Higbe, born in 1961, and Hugh Whitlow Higbe, born in 1963, named after Higbe's two best friends in baseball—Hugh Casey and Whitlow Wyatt.

Kirby resigned from the post office and signed on with a chemical company, but that job evaporated in nine months, putting him out of work. Bills were piling up with no money coming in. A desperate Higbe wrote several bad checks and was ordered to pay them off. When he could not, he was sentenced to sixty days in the Richland County Jail.

A sympathetic guard got Higbe a job in the jail as a trustee, cleaning the cells, and Higbe had his own room in the jail. Not only did he get out after forty days but he also got a job as a guard at the jail. He stayed there for two years, then quit, thinking he was about to get a better job with the South Carolina Tax Commission. That did not happen, and Kirby was out of work for six months.

Finally, he got a job at the state penitentiary as a guard. But Higbe could not keep out of trouble. To make extra money, he began smuggling sleeping pills into the prison for the inmates. He was eventually caught and pleaded guilty. The judge was lenient and gave Higbe a three-year suspended sentence and three years' probation. Kirby got some relief when he started receiving $209.93 a month under the Major Leagues' pension plan.

Higbe wished he had finished high school and taken advantage of the GI Bill to go to college. But he never regretted being a big league ballplayer. He loved every minute of being in the Majors. Also, he gave back to baseball and to young players by coaching American Legion teams in his hometown. Higbe died of emphysema on May 6, 1985, in Columbia, South Carolina, and is buried in that city's Elmwood cemetery. He was seventy years old. He was survived by his sons, Hugh and William.

# Chapter 7. **Bobby Bragan**

*David L. Fleitz and Maurice Bouchard*

| AGE | G | AB | R | H | 2B | 3B | HR | TB | RBI | BB | SO | BAV | OBP | SLG | SB | GDP | HBP |
|-----|---|----|---|---|----|----|----|----|-----|----|----|-----|-----|-----|----|-----|-----|
| 29 | 25 | 36 | 3 | 7 | 2 | 0 | 0 | 9 | 3 | 7 | 3 | .194 | .326 | .250 | 1 | 0 | 0 |

Bobby Bragan was a backup catcher whose pinch-hit double in Game Six of the 1947 World Series was his final moment of glory as a Major League player. However, Bragan left an enviable legacy as a manager and executive at the Major and Minor League levels. He managed three Major League clubs, developed the farm system of the nascent Houston Colt .45s, was president of the Texas League, served as president of the National Association of Professional Baseball Leagues (the umbrella organization for all Minor Leagues), and then built a new career in public relations for the Texas Rangers. His self-avowed greatest achievement, though, is the more than four hundred scholarships awarded through the Bobby Bragan Youth Foundation.

Robert Randall Bragan was born Robert Randall Downs on October 30, 1917, in Birmingham, Alabama, the second son of Walter Lee and Corinne (Roberts) Downs. After Walter died in 1921, Corinne met and married George Washington Bragan Jr., a widower with two young children. George adopted Corinne's two sons, Walter Lee Jr. and Robert, who never considered anyone other than George to be their father.[1] From the tragedy each endured, George and Corinne created a loving, close-knit family that eventually grew to seven sons and two daughters.

The Bragan boys, who worked after school, nonetheless found time to play baseball. Four of them eventually signed professional contracts. Robert, a shortstop, was the best of the lot. After graduating from Phillips High School, he accepted a baseball scholarship to Birmingham's Howard College (now Samford University), but he left after

Bobby Bragan was opposed to playing with Jackie Robinson initially but later changed his mind.

one semester when he was offered $65 a month to play for the Panama City (Florida) Pelicans in the Class D Alabama-Florida League.

Bobby, five feet eleven and weighing 175 pounds, spent the 1937 season with Panama City, where he hit .285 with 56 runs batted in. Before the start of the next season, the Pelicans sold his contract to the Pensacola (Florida) Pilots of the Class B Southeastern League for $500. A strong-armed, good-fielding shortstop, he batted .298 for Pensacola in 1938. The next season, Bragan hit .311 with 29 doubles, 10 triples, and 12 home runs. The Philadelphia Phillies, who had a working agreement with the Pilots, took notice.

The Phillies bought Bragan's contract in early 1940 and invited him to spring training. Bobby performed well during the exhibition season, and manager Doc Prothro gave him the starting job with a $2,500 salary. In his memoir Bobby wrote, "I was lucky in that I was in the right organization at the right time trying to win a job at the right position."[2]

Bragan, a right-handed batter, was used sparingly to start the season, getting in only as an occasional defensive replacement. But with regular shortstop George Scharein struggling at the plate, Bragan got the start in Pittsburgh on April 30. He played errorless ball and had his first Major League hit, a single off Pirates reliever Ken Heintzleman that scored two runs. From May 9 through the rest of the season, he was the Phillies' regular shortstop.

Overall, Bragan batted .222 in 132 games with 7 home runs and 44 runs batted in for the last-place Phillies. Defensively, he had a .936 fielding percentage, the lowest among the National League's regular shortstops. He was an adequate Major League shortstop at best, with a good throwing arm but poor speed.

During the off-season, life changed for the twenty-three-year-old Bragan. He had been courting Frances Best, known to all as Gwenn, who was still a high school senior. The relationship got serious and the couple married in a secret ceremony on March 2, 1941. The marriage lasted until Gwenn's death in 1983.

Bragan played all 154 games at shortstop for the Phillies in 1941. He raised his batting average to .251 with sixty-nine runs batted in, but he struggled against curve ball pitchers. Opponents exploited his weakness against the breaking ball and Bragan slumped the following season, hitting just .218 in 109 games. Bobby recognized that he did not have the talent required to succeed in the Majors as an infielder, so he volunteered to catch. He caught a full Major League game for the first time on July 30, 1942, and filled in as a part-time shortstop and catcher for the remainder of the season.

On March 24, 1943, the Phillies sent Bragan to the Brooklyn Dodgers for Minor League pitcher Jack Kraus and an undisclosed amount of cash. While the trade barely registered in the sports pages of the day, it was a seismic event in the life of Bobby Bragan. At Brooklyn's spring training camp in Bear Mountain, New York, Bragan met the Dodgers' new president and general manager, Branch Rickey. Bragan later said that no one had a greater impact on his life than Branch Rickey.

With rosters unsettled during the war years, Dodgers manager Leo Durocher used Bragan as both an infielder and a catcher in 1943 and 1944. It was during this time that Bragan decided he wanted to be a manager. "My reasoning was simple," he explained years later in his memoir. "Even in war ball, so to speak, I couldn't stay in a major-league starting lineup. Playing at my best, I still was skilled enough only to be a reserve. And when the war was over and the best players got back, marginal players would quickly be cut. My luck was to be playing for Leo, so I could watch the best and learn from him."[3]

Though married with two children (son Robert Jr. was born in 1942 and daughter Gwenn was born the next year), Bragan was called into military service on April 19, 1945, but was not sent overseas. He was discharged in late January 1947 and immediately traveled to Havana, Cuba, where the Dodgers were conducting spring training. Bragan, twenty-nine, had missed two full Major League seasons.

In Havana, Bragan discovered that he would be a teammate of Jackie Robinson, the first African American Major League player of the twentieth century. Bragan was one of several Dodgers who objected to the presence of Robinson on the Brooklyn club. As Bragan recalled years later, Branch Rickey called all five recalcitrant players into his office, one at a time, and stated that if Robinson was talented enough to make the team, then he would open the season with the Dodgers. "If it's all the same to you, Mr. Rickey," replied Bragan, "I'd prefer to be traded to another team." Rickey then asked if Bragan would play differently if Robinson was his teammate, to which Bragan answered in the negative. "No, sir," he said, "I'd still play my best."[4] This answer seemed to satisfy Rickey, and when the 1947 season began, both Bragan and Robinson were Dodgers.

As the season wore on, Bragan's attitude changed. He grew to respect Robinson, not only for his playing ability but also for his courage and dignity in the face of relentless abuse from opposing managers, players, and fans. Bragan dropped his trade request, and by the spring of 1948, he and Robinson had formed a friendship that lasted until Robinson's death in 1972.

Bragan spent the 1947 season as a bullpen catcher and late-inning defensive replacement. He appeared in only twenty-five games, batting .194. In his only appearance in the World Series against the Yankees, he had a pinch-hit double in the sixth inning of Game Six.

Bobby opened the 1948 season with the Dodgers, but in June he was offered a job managing the Fort Worth Cats, Brooklyn's Class Double-A farm club in the Texas League. Bragan was thrilled with the offer and accepted immediately. Overall, he had played in nearly 600 big league games, including 415 at shortstop and 140 as a catcher. His lifetime batting average was .240 with fifteen home runs.[5]

As a player-manager, Bragan caught sixty-seven games and hit .274 for the first-place Cats, who went on to win the postseason playoffs and the Texas League championship. They then faced the Birmingham Barons in the Dixie Series, capturing that title as well. In 1949 Fort Worth easily finished first in the regular season but lost in the league finals.

Bragan managed the Cats for three more seasons, finishing second, fourth, and second. He continued to write his own name on the lineup card most days, playing in 309 games from 1950 through 1952. Bragan maintained that as the catcher he was uniquely positioned to manage the game, especially the pitchers.

In 1953 Rickey, then the general manager of the Pittsburgh Pirates, tapped Bobby to manage the Hollywood Stars of the Pacific Coast League—a club that had won the PCL pennant in 1952. Bragan played in ninety-eight games in 1953 while leading the Stars to their second consecutive pennant. After the season, *The Sporting News* named him its Minor League Manager of the Year, noting the players were "inspired by Bragan's fighting leadership."[6] After Hollywood finished second in 1954 and third in 1955, Rickey hired Bragan to manage the Pirates for 1956.

The Pirates were loaded with talent, most of it still raw, and Bragan was determined to mold it in the "Rickey-Durocher" image. Mostly, it didn't work. Future Hall of Famers Bill Mazeroski and Roberto Clemente were at least two seasons away from All-Star status. Shortstop Dick Groat especially did not thrive under Bragan's caustic comments and frequent fines; the future National League MVP considered quitting baseball more than once during Bragan's tenure as skipper. Pittsburgh finished seventh in 1956 and was on its way to another seventh-place finish in 1957, when GM Joe Brown fired Bragan in August. Bragan later admitted that he had tried too hard, was too much of a taskmaster and perfectionist, and was not the right manager for the Pirates of the late 1950s.

Hank Greenberg, general manager of the Cleveland Indians, hired Bragan to lead the Indians in 1958, but two weeks after the hiring, Greenberg was fired and replaced by Frank Lane. Bragan was dismissed after only three months. He later recalled that Lane broke the news by saying, "I don't know how we'll get along without you, Bobby, but starting tomorrow we're going to try."[7]

For the 1959 season, the forty-one-year-old Bragan returned to the Dodgers organization as manager of the PCL Spokane Indians. Ever the teacher, Bragan had a particularly beneficial effect on twenty-six-year-old Maury Wills, who was about to start his ninth year in the Minor Leagues. Bobby turned him into a switch-hitter and encouraged him to use his speed to steal bases. By 1962 Wills was the National League's Most Valuable Player.

In 1960 Bragan joined the Los Angeles Dodgers as the third-base coach under Walter Alston. After the season, Gabe Paul, the general manager of the expansion franchise in Houston, offered Bobby the farm director position. Bragan's dream was to someday manage the Dodgers, but the gravitational pull from Texas, where he and Gwenn still lived, was too great, and Bobby accepted Paul's offer.

Bragan enjoyed the challenge of building a farm system and scouting for talent in 1961, but by 1962, after a disagreement with the owner, Gabe Paul quit and was replaced by Paul Richards. Bragan spent a miserable 1962 as Houston's bullpen coach. The move to Houston, he later claimed, was the biggest mistake of his baseball life.

When Milwaukee offered Bragan $35,000 to manage in 1963, he wasted little time accepting. The Braves were fresh off a fifth-place finish in 1962, but Bragan's style did not wear well in Milwaukee, and the club slipped to sixth place in 1963 before finishing fifth again in 1964. As lame ducks in Milwaukee in 1965, the Braves team endured a very angry fan base and critical press corps. The Braves won eighty-six games despite a season full of problems. Bragan considered it his finest managerial effort. It was Bragan who persuaded twenty-six-year-old Phil Niekro to go back to the Minors in 1966 to develop his knuckleball.

The Braves, in their first season in Atlanta, led the league in runs scored, but their pitching was weak, and Bragan was fired in August. Beginning in 1969, Bragan served seven seasons as president of the Texas League, a post that allowed him to continue living in his adopted hometown of Fort Worth.

Ever the innovator, Bragan brought the designated hitter to his league in the early 1970s, and then as a member of the Baseball Rules Committee was instrumental in instituting the DH in the American League in 1973. He also called for interleague play, synthetic grass at all stadiums, and more domes. A three-year stint as president of the National Association of Professional Baseball Leagues followed, after which Bragan, at the age of sixty-one, became an assistant to Baseball Commissioner Bowie Kuhn.

Four years later, Bragan took a post in public relations for the Texas Rangers. He worked in that capacity until he was well past his eightieth birthday, giving speeches and making public appearances on behalf of the team. Bragan was inducted into the Alabama Sports Hall of Fame in 1980, the Texas Baseball Hall of Fame in 1981, and the Texas Sports Hall of Fame in 2005. Also, in 2005, at the age of eighty-seven, Bragan managed his former team, the Fort Worth Cats, for one day, surpassing Connie Mack as the oldest manager in the history of professional baseball. As late as 2009, Bragan was listed as a special assistant for community relations in the Texas Rangers front office.

Bobby and Gwenn had been married for forty-two years when she died in 1983. On March 27, 1985, Bobby married Roberta L. Beckman; the happy marriage lasted until Roberta died in 1993. Bragan continued in his role as chairman and CEO of the Bobby Bragan Youth Foundation, going to the office at least three days a week.

Bobby Bragan died in Fort Worth, Texas, at age ninety-two on January 21, 2010. He is buried in Fort Worth's Greenwood Memorial Park.

# Chapter 8. **Dixie Walker**

*Lyle Spatz*

| AGE | G | AB | R | H | 2B | 3B | HR | TB | RBI | BB | SO | BAV | OBP | SLG | SB | GDP | HBP |
|-----|-----|-----|-----|-----|-----|-----|-----|-----|-----|-----|-----|-----|-----|-----|-----|-----|-----|
| 36 | 148 | 529 | 77 | 162 | 31 | 3 | 9 | 226 | 94 | 97 | 26 | .306 | .415 | .427 | 6 | 9 | 1 |

During Dixie Walker's playing days, he won a batting championship and a runs-batted-in title, and he played in two World Series and four All-Star Games. Yet modern-day fans remember him mostly for the charge that he was the player most responsible for trying to keep Jackie Robinson from joining the Brooklyn Dodgers.

Dating from his Major League debut as a twenty-year-old in 1931, Walker's abilities were so apparent as to make many in the media call him the eventual successor to Babe Ruth in the Yankees outfield. A series of recurring injuries throughout Walker's eight-year American League career prevented that from ever happening. In May 1936 the Yanks sold him to the Chicago White Sox to clear a roster spot for the man who truly would be the Babe's successor—Joe DiMaggio.

Overall, the left-handed-hitting Walker batted .306 and accumulated 2,064 hits during his eighteen-year big league career. Tall and lean, at six feet one and 180 pounds, he was a solid hitter, a fine defensive player with an excellent throwing arm, and, in his early days, among the fastest players in the game.

Of Scotch Irish descent, Fred Walker was born in a log cabin in Villa Rica, Georgia, on September 24, 1910. Villa Rica was a small railroad and factory town about thirty-five miles west of Atlanta. He was the first child born to Ewart and Flossie (Vaughn) Walker. Ewart, also known as Dixie, was in his second season as a right-handed pitcher for the Washington Senators when Fred was born. In four seasons with Washington, the original Dixie Walker won twenty-five games and lost thirty-one. After his Major League career ended,

Dixie Walker, the team's clubhouse leader, made the best of his self-created awkward situation with Jackie Robinson.

he returned to the Minor Leagues, where he had a long career as a manager. Ewart's younger brother, Ernie, also reached the Major Leagues, as an outfielder for the St. Louis Browns from 1913 to 1915.

Young Fred left school at the age of fifteen to take a job with the Tennessee Coal and Iron Company, a Birmingham steel mill, working at the open hearth. It was hot, backbreaking work, and Walker never forgot it.

As the son and nephew of Major Leaguers, Fred,

36

like his younger brother Harry, also a future National League batting champion, spent his whole life in baseball. He began his professional career in 1928 as an outfielder/third baseman, splitting the season among Greensboro (North Carolina) of the Piedmont League, Albany (Georgia) of the Southeastern League, and Gulfport (Mississippi) of the Cotton States League. In 1929 Walker was back in the Class D Cotton States League, where he batted .318 for the Vicksburg (Mississippi) Hill Billies. That earned him a promotion to the Class B Greenville (South Carolina) Spinners of the South Atlantic Association in 1930. Walker was batting a sensational .401 at midseason, when the New York Yankees purchased his contract and assigned him to Jersey City of the International League. He continued his steady hitting, compiling a .335 mark in eighty-three games with the Skeeters. Showing power and speed, he had a combined 104 RBIS and 32 stolen bases for the season.

In 1931 the Yankees invited the twenty-year-old Walker to spring training in St. Petersburg, Florida, where he impressed everyone with his batting, fielding, and throwing. He started the year with the Toledo Mud Hens of the American Association; however, two weeks into the season, Yankees manager Joe McCarthy found himself short of outfielders due to injuries, and he recalled Walker.

Dixie made his Major League debut at Washington on April 28, 1931, in a fourteen-inning game called because of darkness. Walker had three hits in seven at bats, including his first big league hit, a single off Sam Jones. Shortly thereafter, sidelined outfielders Babe Ruth, Sammy Byrd, and Myril Hoag returned, and Walker went back to Toledo.

When the Mud Hens hit a financial crisis in midsummer, they asked the Yankees for salary relief for Walker and shortstop prospect Bill Werber. The Yanks responded on July 8, sending Walker back to Jersey City. He spent the rest of the 1931 season in the International League. Playing for Jersey City and Toronto, he batted a combined .352, third best in the league.

In 1932 Walker went to spring training with the International League's Newark Bears, a club that Yankees owner Jacob Ruppert had purchased the previous November. He spent the entire season with the Bears, batting .350 with 105 RBIS, and was voted to the International League All-Star team.

Ruth, Earle Combs, and Ben Chapman would be the Yankees' starting outfield in 1933, with Sammy Byrd slated for one of the two reserve slots. McCarthy chose Walker for the other. A feature story in *The Sporting News* on May 4, 1933, said the Yanks thought Walker could be next in line for a full-time spot in the outfield, maybe as the eventual replacement for Ruth. In June, when the thirty-four-year-old Combs slumped at bat, Walker replaced him in center field. Playing in ninety-eight games as a rookie, he batted .274 with fifteen home runs, the most home runs he would ever hit in the big leagues. *The Sporting News* selected him as the right fielder on its unofficial American League rookie team for 1933.

Walker was also involved in two of the more memorable moments of that season, four days apart in late-April games against the Washington Senators. In a game at Griffith Stadium on April 25, Chapman slid very hard into Senators second baseman Buddy Myer, knocking him over. When Myer retaliated by kicking Chapman, a full-scale battle broke out between the two teams. After the umpires ejected Chapman and Myer, Washington pitcher Earl Whitehill cursed at Chapman as he left the field, and Chapman responded by punching Whitehill in the face, setting off an even rowdier battle. Walker, Chapman's friend as well as his neighbor in Birmingham and his Yankee roommate, came rushing out of the dugout to help. A large group of angry Washington fans surrounded Walker, who was finally rescued by teammates

Tony Lazzeri, Lefty Gomez, and Bill Dickey. Walker was ejected and several fans arrested before order was finally restored.

Four days later, the Yanks were trailing the Senators, 6–3, in the bottom of the ninth. Lou Gehrig was on second base and Walker on first with no outs when Tony Lazzeri hit a drive into right-center field. Right fielder Goose Goslin got to the ball quickly and relayed it to shortstop Joe Cronin, who threw it to catcher Luke Sewell. With ball in hand, Sewell first tagged the slow-footed Gehrig and then tagged Walker, who was only steps behind Gehrig, to complete the unusual double play.

Walker hit his first big league home run at Boston's Fenway Park off Johnny Welch on June 11, 1933. By late June the rookie had gradually begun to take over the center-field job from Combs. But after tearing tendons in his right shoulder in a game on September 19, he sat out the rest of the season, except for a brief appearance on the last day.

At spring training in 1934, almost everyone connected to baseball was again predicting stardom for Walker. However, he developed a sore arm in the spring and did little more than pinch-hit and pinch-run all season. In mid-August the Yanks took Dixie off the roster and put him on the voluntarily retired list.

By March of 1935, Walker was throwing from the outfield with apparent ease. But during an exhibition game at West Point in April, he dislocated his right (throwing) shoulder while sliding into second. The injury put him out indefinitely, and it would take several years before he regained full throwing ability. He played a few games in late May and early June, before the Yankees sent him back to Newark. Dixie played in eighty-nine games for the Bears, batting .293, with seventeen home runs. In what should have been two prime seasons with the Yankees (1934–35), Walker had appeared in just twenty-five games for them.

On May 1, 1936, the Yankees sold Walker to the Chicago White Sox for a reported $20,000. The next day, before the White Sox left New York, Walker pushed up his wedding plans and married native New Yorker Estelle Shea, a young woman who worked at the prestigious Music Corporation of America talent agency.

Although he had to leave the pennant-contending Yankees for the White Sox, Walker was glad to have a chance to play every day. He started poorly for Chicago, with only one hit in his first few games before collecting five in a 19–6 shellacking of the St. Louis Browns on May 11. But on May 23, Walker again dislocated his right shoulder. A collision with Browns first baseman Jim Bottomley sidelined him for three months. In all, he played just twenty-six games for Chicago, which along with the six he played for the Yankees added up to his third consecutive injury-shortened season.

That winter Walker had surgery on the shoulder that involved the refastening of tendons. After resting the arm all winter, Dixie was in right field and batting third on Opening Day against the Browns. Free from any major injury for the first time as a big leaguer, Walker played in all 154 games in 1937 for the White Sox. He batted .302 with 95 runs batted in, and his 16 triples tied him for the American League lead.

Nevertheless, on December 2, 1937, Chicago traded Walker, along with pitcher Vern Kennedy and infielder Tony Piet, to the Detroit Tigers for outfielder Gerald "Gee" Walker (no relation), third baseman Marv Owen, and Minor League catcher Mike Tresh. The deal was extremely unpopular in Detroit, where fans reacted angrily to the trading away of Gee Walker, one of the best-liked players ever to wear a Tigers uniform.

As the replacement for the very popular Gee Walker, Dixie had a difficult time in Detroit. Although he batted .308 in 1938 and was playing a sensational left field, the hometown fans continued to boo him. In late July 1939, Walker, who had tied the American League record by scoring five runs in a game on April 30, was batting .305. But torn knee ligaments had limited his playing time, leading the Tigers to put him on waivers. Despite his many injuries, Walker had compiled a .295 batting average during his eight years in the American League.

On July 24, 1939, Brooklyn's Larry MacPhail purchased Walker's contract from the Tigers. Thus began the transformation of Dixie Walker from one of the most *un*popular players ever to wear a Detroit uniform, to perhaps the most popular one ever to wear a Brooklyn uniform. The Dodgers had not won a pennant since 1920, but under their new president, MacPhail, and first-year manager Leo Durocher, the team was very much on the upswing.

Dixie made his first start for Brooklyn on July 27, 1939, after striking out as a pinch hitter two days earlier. Over the remainder of the 1939 season, he batted .280, while establishing himself as the team's center fielder. The addition of rookies Pee Wee Reese and Pete Reiser and a trade for Joe Medwick helped the Dodgers climb to second place in 1940. Walker led the club in batting (.308) and doubles (37), while finishing sixth in the voting for the National League's Most Valuable Player. He was also quickly becoming a favorite of the Brooklyn fans. A .435 batting average against the hated New York Giants in 1940 helped fuel his popularity, eventually earning him the title of "The People's Choice." However, the year was not without heartbreak for Dixie and for Estelle. On May 23, their four-month-old daughter, Mary Ann, died of pneumonia.

Before the start of spring training in 1941, the Dodgers signed former Pittsburgh Pirates great Paul Waner. The future Hall of Famer played well in spring training, leading Durocher to announce that the thirty-eight-year-old Waner, not Walker, would be his Opening Day right fielder. Five thousand outraged Brooklyn fans signed a petition supporting Walker, but Durocher, backed by

MacPhail, refused to yield. However, when Waner got off to an atrocious start, the Dodgers released him and reinstalled Walker in right, where, with occasional exceptions, he would remain a fixture for the next seven years.

A trade for second baseman Billy Herman on May 6 fortified an already strong Dodgers infield that had Dolph Camilli at first base, Pee Wee Reese at shortstop, and Harry Lavagetto at third. Mickey Owen caught a pitching staff that included Whit Wyatt, Hugh Casey, and newly obtained Kirby Higbe. The blossoming of Reese and Reiser, combined with the excellent group of veterans acquired by MacPhail and Durocher, turned the Dodgers into winners. They captured their first pennant in twenty-one years, finishing two and a half games ahead of the St. Louis Cardinals. In an all–New York City World Series, they lost to the Yankees in five games. Walker was tenth in the MVP voting, earning his place on the list with a .311 batting average, eighth best in the league, along with placing in the top ten in numerous other offensive categories.

When the Dodgers opened a ten-game lead on St. Louis in early August 1942, they appeared on their way to a repeat pennant and another shot at the Yankees. But the Cardinals mounted one of the great comebacks ever, to edge Brooklyn by two games. MacPhail had warned the club that they were losing ground and predicted that St. Louis would pass them, a prediction that several players, primarily Walker, had ridiculed. An ankle injury in late April and a leg injury in June, the latter suffered in an on-field brawl with the Cardinals, limited Walker to 118 games in 1942. He batted .290—his only sub-.300 season as a Dodger, and the only one in which he failed to get any MVP votes.

By 1943 all of baseball was losing players to the war; the Dodgers, minus Reese, Reiser, and Casey, dropped to third place. Walker bounced back from a subpar 1942 with a solid season, finishing in the top ten in batting, runs, hits, and doubles, and appeared in his first All-Star Game.

The year was not without controversy in Brooklyn. Few years were. On July 10 the Dodgers almost to a man refused to take the field for a game against the visiting Pittsburgh Pirates. Arky Vaughan had organized the boycott to protest manager Durocher's three-game suspension of pitcher Bobo Newsom for insubordination. At the last minute, GM Branch Rickey persuaded Vaughan and the others to play. Durocher was particularly upset with Walker for siding with Vaughan and threatened to trade him.

Although baseball injuries to his knee and shoulder exempted him from military service, Dixie did a lot to help the war effort in other ways. During the off-season, he worked for the Sperry Gyroscope Company on Long Island and also served as their athletic director. In December, Walker was part of a USO tour group of players who visited American servicemen in Alaska and the Aleutian Islands.

As with all the other big league teams, the Dodgers' 1944 roster was composed mostly of aging veterans, fuzzy-cheeked kids, and 4-Fs. In all, it was a disastrous season for Brooklyn, the worst in Durocher's tenure with the club. The Dodgers finished in seventh place, forty-two games behind the Cardinals, who captured their third consecutive pennant.

Meanwhile, Walker, at the age of thirty-three, had the best season of his career, winning the National League batting championship with a .357 average. In addition, he drove in ninety-one runs, finished in the top five in hits, doubles, on-base percentage, slugging percentage, and total bases, and was the starting right fielder in the All-Star Game. Walker, the father of three, also received a notable off-the-field honor: the National Father's Day Committee voted him the "Sports Father of the Year."

Walker's outstanding season earned him a close third-place finish in balloting for the Most Valuable Player Award. *The Sporting News* placed him on its Major League All-Star team, and the New York chapter of the Baseball Writers' Association of America honored him with the prestigious Sid Mercer Award as the Player of the Year.

In November 1944 Walker again joined a group of players and umpires that visited various theaters of operation as part of a USO-sponsored program to entertain the troops. With even more players lost to the military, talent for the 1945 season was at an all-time low. Walker did not repeat as batting champion—he hit an even .300—but he did win the runs-batted-in title with 124.

The end of the war made the competition for roster spots in 1946 more competitive than ever. Walker ultimately kept his job and joined rookie Carl Furillo and the returning Pete Reiser as outfield starters. In his first at bat of the spring, Dixie hit a bases-loaded triple against the Montreal Royals at Daytona Beach. The game was among the most significant in spring training history, with ramifications that affected not only baseball but also the course of American history.

Playing second base for Montreal, Brooklyn's top farm team, was Jackie Robinson, a black man signed by Rickey during the off-season. The game marked the first appearance of an integrated team in Organized Baseball in the twentieth century. The teams played several times, without incident. "As long as he's not on the Dodgers, I'm not worried," said Walker. Robinson remained with the Royals in 1946, where he won the International League batting championship.

After a season-long battle with a surprising Dodgers team, the Cardinals captured the pennant in the first postseason playoff in Major League history. Walker, Brooklyn's best player, had another outstanding season. His .319 batting average was third best in the National League, and his 116 runs batted in were second best. Though now an "old man" by baseball standards, the thirty-five-year-old Walker had 9 triples and a career-high 14 stolen bases. He was the starting right fielder for the NL in the All-Star Game, and he finished second to Stan Musial in the vote for the league's MVP.

Although Dixie Walker was a gentle man off the field, he was a fiery competitor on it. That trait had led to his involvement in the 1933 battle with the Washington Senators. In 1946 it landed him in a pair of melees with the Chicago Cubs, centering on another southern teammate, Eddie Stanky, and Cubs shortstop Lennie Merullo.

A fight broke out between the two in the tenth inning of a game at Ebbets Field on May 22 when Merullo slid into second baseman Stanky with his spikes high. The two men then started punching each other, precipitating a brawl between the two teams. The next day policemen, anticipating more trouble, sat along the dugouts of both clubs. Yet despite their vigilance, a pregame fight broke out between Walker and Merullo in the batting cage. The fight cost Walker, Merullo, Pee Wee Reese, and Cubs first baseman Phil Cavarretta, who punched Leo Durocher, $650. Additionally, Walker, Merullo, and Cubs coach Red Smith all received brief suspensions.

When the Major League Players Association was set up in 1946, Walker was chosen the Brooklyn representative, as well as the overall National League representative. New York Yankees pitcher Johnny Murphy was chosen as the American League representative. Their primary goal was the institution of a pension plan for Major League players. That goal was achieved early in 1947. Commissioner Happy Chandler announced a plan under which players with five years' experience would receive $50 a month at age fifty, and $10 a month more for each of the next five years.

By the end of the 1946 season, Walker was, in the words of Dodgers broadcaster Red Barber, the most popular player in Brooklyn history. That would begin to change the following spring. On April 10, 1947, during an exhibition game against the Montreal Royals at Ebbets Field, the Dodgers announced that they had purchased the contract of Jackie Robinson and that "he will report immediately." No one knew what effect the addition of the first black man to play in the Major Leagues in the twentieth century would have on the Dodgers. To complicate the situation further, the announcement came one day after Commissioner Happy Chandler had suspended manager Leo Durocher for the season.

On Opening Day at Ebbets Field, interim manager Clyde Sukeforth's lineup card had Robinson at first base and Walker in right field. Robinson and Walker were in those same positions when Burt Shotton took over as manager a few days later, and, despite rumors that Walker would be traded, they remained there for the rest of the season.

The relationship between Dixie Walker and Jackie Robinson is, of course, one that transcends the playing field and is more a reflection of race relations in America, especially as they were in 1947. Although Walker was a lifelong southerner, he did not "hate" Robinson; however, there is no doubt that he did not want Robinson, or any other black man, as a teammate. Announcer Red Barber, himself a southerner, has written of the problem he had in merely *broadcasting* a game in which Robinson took part.

Walker, who had a hardware store in Birmingham, feared his playing with a black man would hurt his business. Yet despite his distaste for integration, Walker never went out of his way to be unpleasant to Robinson, who later described him as a man of innate fairness.

Robinson had a most difficult season, enduring racial insults from players and fans. Perhaps the worst insults came from Philadelphia Phillies manager Ben Chapman, Walker's good friend. With incredible courage and self-restraint, Robinson not only showed he "belonged," he was also honored with the Major Leagues' Rookie of the

Year Award. The baseball "odd couple" of Robinson and Walker, who batted .306 and had a team-leading ninety-four runs batted in, helped lead the Dodgers to a pennant. After the season, Walker paid tribute to his teammate. He said only Bruce Edwards had done more to put the Dodgers on top. He agreed that Robinson was very much the excellent ballplayer Branch Rickey had claimed he would be.

Walker and Robinson had made the best of a very awkward situation. Robinson would go out of his way to avoid putting Walker in a situation that might be perceived in Alabama as an acceptance of integration, while later acknowledging how grateful he was for a batting tip Walker gave him when he was struggling at the plate.

Walker had grown up believing blacks did not have what it takes to play at the Major League level. Robinson's athletic ability and the mental and emotional strength he exhibited in withstanding all that was thrown at him convinced Walker otherwise. "A person learns, and you begin to change with the times," Dixie would later say. The two never became friends, but Walker continued to praise Robinson's abilities and character for as long as he lived.

Performing under difficult personal circumstances, Walker had continued to produce and had done nothing to disrupt the team's drive to the pennant. In the MVP voting for that year, he received one first-place vote, but, strangely, the other twenty-three writers left him off the ballot.

The 1947 World Series was one of the most thrilling ever, but the result was another loss to the Yankees, this one in seven games. Walker's groundout to the second baseman leading off the ninth inning of Game Seven turned out to be his last at bat in a Brooklyn uniform.

During spring training Walker had been among a group of Dodgers players who had asked management not to add Robinson to the team. When that failed, he took what he believed to be the best

way out of his integration dilemma. He wrote a letter to Branch Rickey in which he asked Rickey to trade him as the best solution for all concerned. Rickey tried, somewhat reluctantly, not wanting to lose his most productive hitter. Following the season, Rickey offered Walker a chance to stay in the organization as the manager of the American Association's St. Paul Saints at a salary of $15,000. Or, Rickey said, he could send him to Pittsburgh, where Walker could make more money.

Walker wanted to manage eventually, but not yet; nor did he want his salary reduced to $15,000. So Rickey sold him to Pittsburgh for one dollar, with the proviso that the Pirates add the $10,000 waiver price to Dixie's 1948 contract. Rickey chose not to make this public, instead announcing that Walker was part of the big trade that brought Preacher Roe and Billy Cox to Brooklyn.

With Pittsburgh in 1948, Walker topped the .300 mark for the tenth time in twelve seasons, helping the Pirates climb from last place to fourth. Meanwhile, the Brooklyn fans showed they had not forgotten him. On the Pirates' first visit to Ebbets Field, they staged a Dixie Walker Day that included, among other gifts, a new car for their longtime favorite.

By 1949 Walker's playing career had reached its end. He played in just eighty-eight contests—though he led the National League with thirteen pinch hits. He hit his only home run, the final one of his career, on July 20 off Ralph Branca as a pinch hitter. Appropriately, it came at Ebbets Field, sailing over the right-field wall and landing on Bedford Avenue.

The Pirates released Walker after the season, and he began immediately looking for a managerial job, at either the Major League or high Minor League level. On December 5, 1949, he signed to replace Cliff Dapper as manager of the Atlanta Crackers of the Southern Association. In his first season, 1950, Walker led the Crackers to the regular-season pennant. Dixie returned to Atlanta in

1951, where his team finished sixth before rising to second in 1952.

The St. Louis Cardinals added Walker to their coaching staff in 1953, but in late July they asked him to take over the Houston team in the Texas League. Walker stayed with Houston through 1954, but then spent the next five years managing in the International League. In 1955 and 1956 he led the Rochester Red Wings, and from 1957 through 1959, the Toronto Maple Leafs.

The Braves, now in Milwaukee, employed Walker as a scout from 1960 to 1962. Bobby Bragan, his onetime Dodgers teammate, took over as the Braves' manager in 1963 and added Walker to his coaching staff, primarily as a hitting instructor. After the Braves moved to Atlanta in 1966, they put Dixie in charge of their scouting in the Southeast.

When Los Angeles Dodgers batting coach Duke Snider left in 1968, the Dodgers replaced him with Walker. At training camp in 1969, Walter Alston praised Walker for his work with the team's younger players. The Dodgers kept Walker with the club all season as batting coach, a move highly praised by the players. Over the years, Walker helped improve the batting of countless Dodgers. Among the Los Angeles players who praised him for his help with their batting were African American stars Dusty Baker, Jim Wynn, and Maury Wills.

Walker's rehabilitation, at least in the Dodgers' family, was complete. At spring training in 1971, Walter O'Malley presented him with a silver bat worth $2,500, emblematic of his 1944 batting championship. O'Malley also included Dixie in his personal all-time Dodgers outfield, along with Duke Snider and Carl Furillo.

After the 1974 season, the sixty-four-year-old Walker stepped down as the Dodgers' hitting coach, saying he now preferred to work with the team's Minor Leaguers. He retired from baseball after the 1976 season and returned to Birmingham.

Dixie Walker died of colon cancer on May 17, 1982, at St. Vincent's Hospital in Birmingham and is buried in that city's Elmwood Cemetery. He was survived by Estelle, who lived for another twenty years, daughters Mary Ann and Susan, and son Stephen. Two of his sons predeceased him. Fred Jr. died in a scuba diving accident in 1971, and Sean of an accidental gunshot wound in 1975.

# Chapter 9. **Carl Furillo**

*John T. Saccoman*

| AGE | G | AB | R | H | 2B | 3B | HR | TB | RBI | BB | SO | BAV | OBP | SLG | SB | GDP | HBP |
|---|---|---|---|---|---|---|---|---|---|---|---|---|---|---|---|---|---|
| 25 | 124 | 437 | 61 | 129 | 24 | 7 | 8 | 191 | 88 | 34 | 24 | .295 | .347 | .437 | 7 | 17 | 1 |

People who saw Carl Furillo play talk most often about his throwing arm. He was given nicknames because of it, including "The Reading Rifle" and "The Arm." On August 27, 1951, Pirates pitcher Mel Queen learned about Furillo's arm the hard way—thrown out at first base after hitting an apparent single to right. It was one of Furillo's twenty-four assists that season. In his career he threw out seven men who rounded first too widely, throwing behind them. Another of Carl's nicknames was "Skoonj," short for one of his favorite foods—the Italian seafood dish scungilli, the edible part of an aquatic snail.

Furillo, who batted and threw right-handed, was a .299 career hitter and a batting-title winner in 1953. Nevertheless, people wanted to talk about the way he played the right-field wall at Ebbets Field. The wall was nineteen feet high, with a nineteen-foot screen on top (which was in play), and the scoreboard with a Bulova clock atop it sat in right center. The wall was concrete and concave, with a vertical top half and an angled bottom half. According to Philip J. Lowry in *Green Cathedrals*, there were nearly three hundred angles a ball could take after hitting different parts of the wall.

Furillo described how he played the wall. "Will it hit above the cement and hit the screen? Then you run like hell toward the wall, because it's gonna drop dead. Will it hit the cement? Then you gotta run like hell to the infield, because it's gonna come shooting out. I can't even tell you if it's gonna hit the scoreboard. The angles were crazy."[1]

Carl Anthony Furillo was born on March 8, 1922, in the same town in which he died—Stony Creek Mills, Pennsylvania, a suburb of Reading.

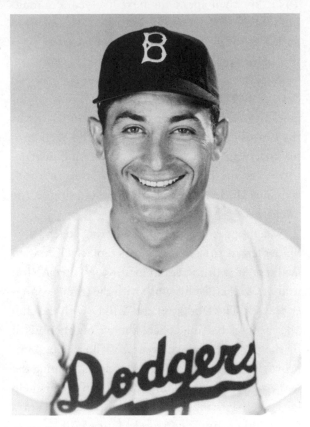

Carl Furillo had been in Leo Durocher's doghouse and benefited from Leo's suspension.

The son of Italian immigrant parents, Michael and Filomena Furillo, he dropped out of school after completing the eighth grade. His was a close-knit family, and Carl worked at various jobs, including picking apples and work in a woolen mill. However, he always played ball. After the death of his mother, when he was eighteen, he was able to leave the family to pursue baseball professionally.

Furillo spent most of the 1940 season with the unaffiliated Pocomoke City (Maryland) Chicks of

44

the Class D Eastern Shore League, batting .319 and slugging .523 in seventy-one games. His salary was $80 a month. Furillo was a center fielder, but he also pitched in eight games, compiling a 2-3 record. That season, he also played eight games for the unaffiliated Reading team of the Class B Interstate League. After the 1940 season, the Dodgers purchased the Reading club, including its twenty players and two sets of uniforms.

Furillo batted .313 for the Reading Brooks in 1941, slugging .490 in 125 games. In the outfield he had twenty-five assists. His pitching days were over. "He could certainly throw," said his manager Fresco Thompson, "but who knew where? He broke four ribs and two wrists [on batters] before we decided as an act of public safety to make him spend all his time in the outfield."[2]

Carl moved up to Montreal of the International League in 1942 and batted .281. He was the second-youngest player on the team, and the most prominent future Major Leaguer on the Clyde Sukeforth–managed squad.

The army called, and Furillo missed the next three seasons. He served in combat in the Pacific Theater, received three battle stars, and was wounded. Peter Golenbock says in his book *Bums* that Furillo turned down a Purple Heart medal for his wounds, saying he hadn't been sufficiently valiant.

On January 22, 1946, Furillo reported to Sanford, Florida, for "advanced training" designed for returning servicemen. According to Carl, he was offered a contract of $3,750 to play with the Dodgers, and when he balked, manager Leo Durocher told him, "Take it or leave it."[3] Salary was one of several areas where the rookie and the manager had conflicts.

Additionally, Furillo had to deal with rumors, embraced by Durocher, that he was a heavy drinker. Furillo steadfastly denied the accusation and was incensed that Durocher branded his denial a lie. Carl decided there was no hope of their having a good relationship. He said, "[Durocher] knew

his onions. . . . He knew his baseball, and that's about all. . . . He didn't know how to handle young players."[4]

In spite of the animosity, however, and in spite of a lackluster spring, Furillo displaced Brooklyn's prewar center fielder Pete Reiser. At the end of spring training, Durocher said, "Furillo is all right now. I'm sure he'll prove his ability."[5]

On Opening Day 1946, Furillo was the starting center fielder, batting sixth. He went 2 for 4 in the Dodgers' 5–3 loss to the Boston Braves. Brooklyn finished the season in a tie for first place with the St. Louis Cardinals. Furillo played 103 games in center field and 117 games overall, batting .284.

In the best-of-three playoff at the end of the season, the Dodgers were swept in two games. Furillo went 1 for 8 with a run scored and an RBI. It was the first of nine seasons in his fifteen-year big league career that Carl's team finished in first place or tied for first place.

With Jackie Robinson joining the club for the 1947 season, the Dodgers and their Montreal affiliate held spring training in Cuba, the Dominican Republic, and Panama. At the stop in Panama, Durocher, soon to be suspended for his connections to gamblers, got wind of a possible petition protesting the inevitable inclusion of Robinson on the Dodgers' roster. He quashed it immediately, and that was the end of the matter. Dodgers general manager Branch Rickey then met individually with each of the alleged participants. Furillo, the only northerner in the group, apologized, "saying he'd made a mistake," according to author Jonathan Eig in *Opening Day*.[6]

Peter Golenbock in *Bums* has a different version. He wrote that, while training in Havana, a teammate asked Furillo what he would do if Robinson came after his job. Carl said, "I'd cut his legs off." Golenbock wrote that Furillo added, "You couldn't retract it. But I got along good with Jackie. And I told Jackie about it. I said, 'I'm sorry, but I didn't mean it the way they put it.' Jackie said, 'Don't worry about it.'"[7]

Given to the occasional intemperate remark, Furillo was variously described as "hot-headed," "carrying chips on both shoulders," and having "a particularly low boiling point." However, he was also someone who had a lifelong reputation as a straight shooter; he might have made the same statement if the name "Hodges" were substituted for "Robinson."

On April 15, 1947, Robinson's debut, Carl did not start, but he played right field in the late innings. Arthur Daley of the *New York Times* wrote, "Carl Furillo remained forgotten on the bench. The rookie sensation of a year ago had been in Durocher's well-occupied doghouse all during spring training and it looks as though Leo the Lip neglected to leave the key behind."[8] Furillo claimed that Durocher was on him because he bailed out on curve balls from right-handed pitchers. Furillo also complained about being platooned, which Durocher took as a challenge to his authority.

Still, by June 23 Furillo was fifth in the National League with a .325 batting average, though he had only 123 at bats. Later that season, a group of Dodgers fans collected the funds to buy a new Buick, which was presented to Carl before a game on August 14, with middleweight boxing champion Rocky Graziano among those doing the honors. At Furillo's request the excess money collected to purchase the car was donated to the Damon Runyon Memorial Cancer Fund. After his base hit drove in the only run in a 1–0 Dodgers victory, he called it "the happiest day of my life."[9]

The Dodgers won the National League pennant in 1947. Furillo played 93 of his 121 outfield games in center field, batting .295 with eighty-eight runs batted in. In the World Series, the Dodgers lost to the Yankees in seven games. Carl played in all the games but the second, leading Dodger regulars with a .353 batting average.

In 1948 Furillo was injured in midseason and played in only 108 games. He finished with a .297 batting average and, despite playing only two-thirds of the season, had thirteen assists. On July 6 Carl married the former Fern Reichart, from Reading. The Dodgers had swept the Phillies in a doubleheader in Philadelphia on July 5 and had a night game on the sixth, from which Carl was excused.

On July 20, two weeks after the wedding, Furillo suffered a broken nose and deviated septum when a batted ball hit him during fielding practice. Furillo had surgery to remove a bone chip but required a second surgery a week later to rebreak and reset the nose. He missed about three weeks, and after coming back, he did not play in every game.

The 1948 Dodgers were a team in transition, finishing in third place. Leo Durocher resigned midway through the season (signing to manage the archrival Giants), and Burt Shotton came out of retirement to retake the helm. Additionally, the Brooklyn team was the youngest in the league.

In 1949 Brooklyn returned to the World Series, again facing the Yankees. With Duke Snider now the regular center fielder, Furillo played all of his 142 games in right field and equaled his 1948 total of 13 assists. He had his best year at the plate, to that point, batting .322 (fourth in the National League) with 18 home runs and 106 RBIs. In the September 22 game against the first-place Cardinals, Furillo had one of the finest offensive performances of his career. The Dodgers won 19–6, and Carl went 5 for 6, with 3 consecutive doubles, and drove in 7 runs.

Furillo sported a .431 average over the final forty-six games. In the last game of the season, in which the Dodgers clinched the pennant with a ten-inning 9–7 victory at Philadelphia, he went 4 for 6, scoring two runs. Carl finished sixth in the National League MVP voting, behind teammates Robinson (the winner) and Pee Wee Reese (fifth).

The 1949 World Series ended with the Yankees winning in five games. Furillo, hobbled by a groin injury suffered on a muddy field in Boston, started only Game One and Game Three, with one hit in eight at bats.

In 1950 the Dodgers finished second, two games behind the pennant-winning Philadelphia Phillies. Furillo racked up 189 hits, good for third in the National League, and he matched his 1949 totals of 18 home runs and 106 RBIs. Defensively, he recorded 18 assists.

On June 28 of that season, Furillo was beaned just above the ear in a game against the Giants at Ebbets Field. He had belted a two-run homer in the fourth inning, and in the eighth, he could not evade a high inside pitch from the Giants' Sheldon Jones. He was carried off on a stretcher, with players from both the Giants and the Dodgers at his side. Despite the circumstance of the earlier home run, the *New York Times* account of the beaning took great pains to state that it was accidental. Doctors ruled out a concussion. Carl was batting .325 at the time of the beaning, and he finished the year at .305.

Furillo's version of the incident is darker. Interviewed by Roger Kahn for *Boys of Summer*, he said that Giants manager Durocher told him before the game, "We had you skipping rope with the left hander last night. Tonight . . . you'll be ducking."[10] He said Herman Franks, a Giants coach, warned him, "Tonight we get you, Dago."[11] The next day, Furillo said, Jones visited him in the hospital to apologize, and he indicated that he was under orders from Durocher. (Kahn's book mistakenly has the incident occurring in 1949.)

In April 1951 at the Polo Grounds, Furillo got a measure of revenge with a game-winning home run in the tenth inning against Giants pitcher Sal Maglie. Furillo was used as the lead-off batter by manager Chuck Dressen ninety-one times in 1951. His numbers that season (.295, 16 home runs, 91 RBIs) were typical for Furillo, but he was not a prototypical lead-off man. He drew only 43 walks, equaling his career-high to date. Leading off for the highest-scoring offense in the Majors, he led

the league with 724 plate appearances. He chipped in a career-high 24 outfield assists.

Furillo was hitless in fourteen at bats in the Dodgers-Giants playoff at the end of 1951. Giants players accused Carl and other Dodgers of yelling tauntingly through the clubhouse wall after the first game, insulting Durocher and the Giants. Monte Irvin said that Robinson and Furillo could clearly be heard.

Furillo suffered his worst season to date in 1952. After years of threatening to hold out, he actually signed a blank contract for the season, receiving a salary in the $20,000 range. Manager Dressen removed him from the lead-off spot, and he often batted eighth. Furillo's batting average hovered around .230 for most of the year, and he finished at .247. While his fielding percentage of .988 was the best of his career, his twelve assists, impressive enough for most outfielders, were his fewest in five years. Nevertheless, Furillo was named to the National League All-Star team for the first time.

His slump extended into the '52 World Series. The Dodgers once again met the Yankees, and they lost in seven games. Furillo played in all seven games, batting .174.

In January 1953 Carl underwent eye surgery to remove cataracts. He responded with the highest batting average of his career, a batting title, a second trip to the All-Star Game, and a ninth-place finish in the MVP voting. The Dodgers won the pennant by thirteen games, but lost the World Series to the Yankees in six games.

Furillo renewed his ongoing feud with Leo Durocher that season. On September 6, after going 4 for 4 in the previous game, Carl was hit on the right wrist by a Ruben Gomez pitch in the second inning. Enraged, Furillo attempted to get at Gomez, but Giants catcher Wes Westrum, Dodgers manager Dressen, and two umpires intervened. While on first base, Furillo looked toward the Giants' dugout. When the count on batter Billy Cox went to 2-2, Furillo called time, charged the Giants' bench, and was met by Durocher. The two grappled. Durocher's hat fell off, and Furillo had him in a headlock. Roger Kahn's book *The Era* says that Durocher's bald head "turned pink, then red, then purple."[12]

Finally, Monte Irvin and Giants pitcher Jim Hearn managed to separate the two combatants, but not before someone stepped on Furillo's left hand. He sustained a fractured metacarpal bone. Both Furillo and Durocher were ejected, and Furillo had to dodge debris thrown by Giants fans as he walked up the steps to the Dodgers' clubhouse that abutted the left-center-field bleachers.

Gerald Eskenazi's biography of Durocher, *The Lip*, says Durocher taunted Furillo as a "crybaby" after he was hit. Furillo told reporters that Durocher was motioning to him with his index finger, as if to beckon him, and "mumbling something . . . though I did not hear what he was saying." For his part, Durocher said, "I never called him, never motioned for him. The first thing I saw is Furillo pointing and then charging, so I came out to meet him."[13]

Furillo said in the clubhouse after the game, "I'll get him the next time I see him. The next time we come face to face . . . I'll let him have it." For his part, the five-foot-ten Durocher, whose playing weight was 160 pounds, had a response for the six-foot, 190-pound Furillo: "I'll be there."[14]

National League president Warren Giles called Furillo into his office because of his threat, but he ordered no suspensions. Furillo did not return to action until the World Series with the Yankees, his league-leading batting average frozen at .344. The Dodgers lost the Series, despite having a team that won 105 regular-season games. Furillo was 8 for 24, playing in all six games and hitting a home run that temporarily tied the score in the ninth inning of the sixth and final game.

Coming off his superb season, in which he made that All-Star team for the second year in a row, and in which he finished ninth in the MVP balloting, Furillo was rewarded with a contract of around $28,000 for 1954. His batting average reverted to his career norm, .294, and he hit 19 home runs and drove in 96 runs for the second-place Dodgers, now under the direction of Walter Alston.

Furillo's pay was cut slightly for the 1955 season. If he was upset about it, he had the consolation that "next year" had finally arrived, and he received a World Series share of $9,768. Furillo had his best power numbers, clouting a career-high twenty-six home runs and slugging .520, his second best. He batted .314 and recorded double-digit assists for the eighth consecutive season.

The Dodgers met the Yankees for their fifth Subway Series in nine years. Furillo hit .296 for the Series and played a flawless right field. In a rare show of emotion, Furillo years later recalled the feeling of winning that Series: "Oh God, that was the thrill of all thrills. . . . I never in my life seen a town go so wild. . . . We accomplished something. . . . You did it for yourself, too, but you did it for the people."[15]

The Dodgers repeated as National League champs in 1956. Furillo contributed 21 home runs and a .289 batting average to the cause, as well as 10 assists. He batted .240 in the World Series, as the Dodgers fell to the Bronx Bombers in seven games.

Furillo did not join other Dodgers players for a goodwill tour of Japan after the Series. In December he had surgery for acute appendicitis and played in only 119 games in 1957, his fewest since 1948. August 28, 1957, was Carl Furillo Night at Ebbets Field. He received a $6,000 automobile, a Shetland pony for sons Carl Jr. and Jon, and an inscribed silver tray from his teammates. He also received telegrams from President Dwight D. Eisenhower and the governors of New York and Pennsylvania. Furillo said, "The fans, ya loved 'em. They'd say, 'Please Carl, win tomorrow. My husband gets mad, he won't eat."[16]

The club moved to Los Angeles for the 1958 season. For their first four years in LA, the Dodgers played in the Los Angeles Memorial Coliseum. The left-field wall was a mere 250 feet from home plate, but a high screen was atop the wall so that short fly balls would not be turned into home runs. Furillo played in 122 games in '58, stroking 18 home runs and batting .290, with 83 runs batted in. Playing in a cavernous right field, he had only 5 assists.

The Dodgers placed seventh in 1958, posting seventy-one victories, their lowest total since 1944. Arthur Daley, still keeping tabs on the club, wrote of Furillo in August: "The only old-timer who is still operating under a full head of steam is Carl Furillo. When he found some of the younger players making jokes after a particularly galling defeat, he let fly with expletives that blistered their ears."

Furillo's 18th and last home run in 1958 was the 192nd and last of his career. He played in only fifty games in 1958 and eight in 1959. Nagging injuries were taking their toll on his thirty-seven-year-old body: leg cramps, a cracked rib suffered in a May exhibition game, spinal disc issues, and a calf injury suffered while legging out a hit.

After the last scheduled games of the 1959 season, the Milwaukee Braves were tied with Los Angeles for the league lead, and so the Dodgers were involved in a playoff for the third time in fourteen years. They swept the best-of-three series in two games. Furillo didn't start either game, but in Game Two his infield single drove in the pennant-clinching run in the bottom of the twelfth inning.

At thirty-seven, Furillo was the oldest Dodger on the World Series roster as Los Angeles beat the Chicago White Sox in six games. He made four pinch-hitting appearances, and his bad-hop pinch single in the seventh inning of Game Three broke a scoreless tie and provided the margin of victory in the 3–2 win.

Persistent pains in his legs caused the Dodgers to place Furillo on the inactive list on May 12, 1960. On May 17 they gave him his unconditional release. If Furillo had finished the season, he would have received a monthly pension of $285 starting at the age of fifty, instead of the $255 he would now receive. He also was slated to receive $33,000

for the season, but he had been paid only $12,000 of it at the time of his release. He sued the Dodgers on the grounds that he was released while injured.

In August the Dodgers announced that Furillo had been hired to be an instructor at the Dodgertown Summer Camp in Vero Beach. However, Carl continued the suit. It was settled in May 1961, with Furillo being awarded the $21,000 remaining from his 1960 salary. Despite repeated entreaties to every Major League club, Furillo received no job offers as either a coach or a scout.

He moved the family back east, first to Reading, and in 1963 into a split-level home in Flushing, Queens. He bought a half interest in a delicatessen, which was renamed Furillo and Totto's, and worked long hours at that business for seven years. Then he moved the family back to the Reading area and took a construction job, among other things installing doors on Otis elevators at the World Trade Center. This was hard work, out in the elements, but he planned to do it only until he turned fifty, when his baseball pension would kick in. He spent weekends with the family in Reading and spent weekdays on the job.

After the construction job was over, Furillo took a job as a security guard near his home, four nights a week as a night watchman. He later was diagnosed with chronic leukemia and died in his sleep of heart failure on January 21, 1989, forty-six days short of his sixty-seventh birthday. He was survived by Fern, his two sisters, his two sons, and five grandchildren. Former teammates Sandy Koufax, Joe Black, Johnny Podres, Clem Labine, Billy Loes, Cal Abrams, Carl Erskine, and Peter O'Malley, the Dodgers' owner, attended his funeral at Forest Hills Memorial Park in Reiffton, Pennsylvania.

Erskine recalled, "I remember how tough he was, how strong he was, how consistent he was as a player. When he hit a single, it was a bullet. When he hit a homer, it was a rocket. And his arm portrayed his strength."[17]

Even in the end, it all came back to "The Arm."

# Chapter 10. **The Suspension of Leo Durocher**

*Jeffrey Marlett*

Pee Wee Reese and Hugh Casey (*standing*), Pete Reiser (*shaking hands*), Gene Hermanski, and Dixie Walker say good-bye to Leo Durocher following his suspension.

Leo Durocher made the cover of *Time* magazine just once: the April 14, 1947, issue. Published the day before Jackie Robinson broke into the Major Leagues with the Brooklyn Dodgers, the *Time* article did not cast the Dodgers' manager in a kind light. The words "I don't want any nice guys on my ball club" ran beneath Leo's portrait. The background picture depicted Leo giving an umpire an earful of abuse, standard operating procedure for the manager nicknamed "The Lip."

Just five days earlier, Durocher had been suspended from baseball for a year. Commissioner Albert "Happy" Chandler cited Durocher's string of moral shortcomings: gambling debts, associations with known gamblers and nightlife figures,

and a scandalous marriage with charges of adultery, bigamy, and contempt of court. Dodgers owner and general manager Branch Rickey often said Leo possessed "the fertile ability to turn a bad situation into something infinitely worse," but Leo seemed finally to have hit rock bottom.[1] Outside of Brooklyn, many baseball fans and observers gloated. Dodgers fans were devastated. Durocher's suspension was shaping up as baseball's "story of the year" before the season had even started.[2]

Then Robinson took the field in Brooklyn. Led by Burt Shotton, a sort of anti-Durocher, the Dodgers won the pennant. They pushed the Yankees to a seventh game before losing the World Series. Leo and his troubles had quickly receded into memories of spring training. The 1947 season could have provided an opportunity for Durocher to shine along with Brooklyn's new star. Instead, the *Time* cover would be the highlight of Durocher's 1947 season. His unerring ability to find trouble and draw attention removed him from a landmark season in baseball history.

When he broke into the American League, Leo Durocher gained notoriety for his brash actions as well as his quick glove. In 1928, at the age of twenty-two, he was playing shortstop for the New York Yankees, yet he was garnering more attention from his sartorial and off-field choices. Before that first season was a month old, Yankees manager Miller Huggins had to reprimand the young Durocher for brashly overdressing. Leo might have made rookie money, but he spent profligately, routinely overdrawing his bank account. Leo acquired his nicknames "The Lip" and "The All-American Out" from Babe Ruth himself. Before the 1928 season concluded, Ruth had also accused Durocher of stealing his watch.[3]

Durocher's financial troubles followed him after his trade to Cincinnati in 1930. Gambling opportunities beckoned from Kentucky, just across the Ohio River. When traded to St. Louis during the 1933 season, he needed the Cardinals' general manager, Branch Rickey, to cover his outstanding debts. During the 1934 season, Durocher married a wealthy local businesswoman, Grace Dozier, with Rickey's permission and blessing. Eventually, though, Leo reverted to his old habits. Things didn't change much when he was traded to Brooklyn before the 1938 season. His spending and gambling continued apace, but nobody could deny his will to win. After a year, team president Larry MacPhail appointed him manager for the 1939 season.

Dodgers broadcaster Red Barber once wrote about the 1947 season, "Try to untangle Durocher from either Rickey or MacPhail and it's no

story."[4] Barber had a point. Durocher's 1947 season-long suspension resulted partially from the ongoing feud between the two baseball executives. Both had handled Durocher as a player; in fact, Rickey and MacPhail together had orchestrated Durocher's trade to Brooklyn. When MacPhail entered the army after the 1942 season, Rickey took over as Brooklyn's team president. That meant he had Durocher on his hands again, now as a player-manager. Durocher had led the Dodgers to the 1941 pennant, two second-place finishes (1940, 1942), and a third-place finish in his inaugural season. After Rickey took over, the Dodgers stumbled, finishing third twice and even falling as far as seventh in 1944. By 1946 Leo had led the Dodgers back to second place, narrowly losing the pennant again to the Cardinals.[5]

Rickey biographer Lee Lowenfish writes that even as the 1946 season ended, Rickey recognized that his manager still swam in dangerous waters. Durocher's friendship with actor and avid gambler George Raft seemed particularly worrisome.[6] During his climb to Hollywood fame, Raft had befriended several baseball stars. With Durocher, though, Raft had found a true buddy—a quick-witted, gambling, nightlife-loving buddy. Raft and Durocher stayed at each other's apartment when visiting the other's home city. Raft once said, "We used each other's suits, ties, shirts, cars, girls."[7] In 1944, with Durocher away at spring training in nearby Bear Mountain, New York, Raft hosted a gambling night at Leo's apartment during which a wealthy patron lost several thousand dollars in a rigged craps game. By 1946 rumors had surfaced connecting Durocher and Raft with New York mobsters Joe Adonis and Bugsy Siegel. The Brooklyn district attorney's office had tapped Durocher's telephone, and the manager's name had surfaced amid a check-cashing scandal at the Mergenthaler Linotype Company in Baltimore.[8]

Westbrook Pegler, a syndicated columnist for the *New York Journal-American*, had seen enough. In October 1946 he began a series of articles decrying Raft and Durocher as threats to society. In a phone conversation with Rickey, Pegler proclaimed Durocher a "moral delinquent" who would eventually "drag Rickey and baseball down to his own level of shame and shameful companions."[9] As Lowenfish writes, "Rickey could not effectively say to Leo Durocher, 'You *must* cut all ties to George Raft.' Somebody else would have to do it."[10] In November, Rickey sent Arthur Mann, his new assistant, to Chicago to arrange a meeting between the commissioner and Durocher. Mann told Chandler of Rickey's wish: "Any reasonable method for telling Durocher emphatically that he must sever connections of all kinds with people regarded as undesirable by baseball—gangsters, known gamblers, companions of known gamblers, and racketeers. Regardless of names or identity, anybody whose reputation could hurt Leo or baseball."[11]

Chandler finally tracked Durocher down at an NBC studio where Durocher was rehearsing for a spot on the Jack Benny radio show. Chandler insisted that Durocher meet him on November 22 at the Claremont Country Club in Berkeley, California. Mann returned to Brooklyn, presuming his confidential business concluded.[12]

At the appointed time, Chandler and Durocher strolled across the greens. The commissioner produced a list of those whom Leo should avoid at all costs. Arthur Mann writes, "Raft, Adonis, Siegel, Engelberg, etc.—a special coterie of men to avoid; and Leo readily agreed, even though it meant cutting off some apparently harmless associations of nodding acquaintance. Chandler was firm, but not threatening. He told Leo that the time had come to choose between undesirables and baseball, to halt wagging tongues; that there would be no trouble if he, Durocher, created none."[13]

Leo acknowledged that the break would be difficult, but worth it. Chandler seemed satisfied. However, at just this moment, Leo sprang something new on the commissioner. He told Chandler about his love affair with the actress Laraine Day. They would be married just as soon as her divorce was final. Leo neglected to tell the commissioner that when he first met Laraine in 1942, he also was married. (His divorce from Grace Dozier went through in 1943.)[14]

Chandler hoped the furor could be contained, but in January 1947 Day and Durocher's marriage hit the headlines. Day had filed for divorce from her husband, Ray Hendricks, a bandleader and manager of the Santa Monica airport. Hendricks accused Durocher of stealing Day's affections. The press loved it. A divorce settlement soon was reached, but the California divorce decreed a year's wait before Day could remarry. However, Day darted across the border to Juarez, Mexico, to obtain a "quickie divorce." She then returned to El Paso, Texas, and married Durocher the same day, January 21, 1947.

As Arthur Mann wrote, "Could Chandler understand and appreciate that, more often than not, Durocher would parlay a simple situation into a complex problem through abysmal thoughtlessness?"[15] Meanwhile, Chandler found himself facing unwanted and unpleasant comparisons to his predecessor, Kenesaw Landis. Chandler's unwillingness to tackle Durocher preemptively stood in contrast to Landis's swift and stern punishments for those he discovered gambling on baseball.

With Day and Durocher's marriage, the simmering scandal threatened to boil over. Judge George Dockweiler, who had granted Day's interlocutory divorce decree, now considered charging her with adultery. In the eyes of the California court, Day remained married to Hendricks. With her actions in Texas, she now had two husbands. Durocher realized that Dockweiler had capitalized on their celebrity status to make his point. Dockweiler admitted he would not have pressed another, less recognized couple so hard. "That judge," Leo proclaimed to the press, "is nothing more than a pious, Bible-reading hypocrite."[16] Eventually Dockweiler was removed from the case, and Day and Durocher remarried in California in 1948.[17]

At the time, though, the scandal surged ahead. Leo's marital fanfare drew the attention of U.S. Supreme Court Justice Frank Murphy. A former governor of Michigan, mayor of Detroit, and lifelong bachelor, Murphy devoutly practiced his Roman Catholic faith. He gladly wore the mantle of the top court's morality crusader. Murphy urged Commissioner Chandler to take swift and permanent action, reminiscent of Landis's tenure, against the unrepentant Durocher.

Just after the 1946 season, the Roman Catholic Diocese of Brooklyn had threatened Rickey that the Brooklyn Catholic Youth Organization (CYO) would boycott Dodgers games. CYO members constituted the largest block of the Dodgers' Knothole Gang, a youth outreach endeavor Rickey had begun in Brooklyn as he had in St. Louis. Church groups were solicited to make attending baseball games part of their moral and social recreation programs. A CYO boycott of Dodgers games would greatly reduce attendance at Ebbets Field. As national president of the CYO, Justice Murphy went even further, threatening Chandler with a nationwide CYO ban on baseball. On March 1, 1947, the Brooklyn CYO made good on its threat and withdrew from the Dodgers' Knothole Gang.[18]

Meanwhile, the Dodgers prepared for spring training in Havana, Cuba. Durocher tried being on his best behavior, but found it tough going when he kept meeting old friends like Memphis Engelberg and Connie Immerman. Durocher and Immerman knew each other from the 1920s, when the young Yankees shortstop frequented the Cotton Club. Now Immerman was managing a new casino in Havana. Engelberg, a well-known New York–area horse handicapper, was a good friend of both Durocher and Charlie Dressen, who was now coaching with the Yankees.[19]

Writing thirty-five years later, Red Barber pointed out an important but often ignored precedent to Chandler's decision. On April 3, 1947, Bert Bell, commissioner of the National Football League, made public his belated decision to suspend indefinitely two New York Giants football players, Merle Hapes and Frank Filchock. Gamblers had offered the two players bribes to throw the 1946 NFL championship game. Hapes and Filchock took a week to notify team officials. News of the attempted bribery made headlines on December 5, the morning of the game (which the Giants lost to the Chicago Bears, 24–14). Even though the two players' culpability lay in their delayed response to the bribes, Bell took a few months to respond. His decision to suspend Hapes and Filchock indefinitely was the harshest punishment for professional athletes since Landis's suspension of the eight Black Sox players in 1921. New York's sportswriters reacted positively to Bell's strong (if not necessarily swift) decision. Barber thus mused: "Did Chandler note the widespread approval that Bell received, or had Chandler made up his mind on his decision before April 3? Was Bell's decision, and its timing, the final nail in the lid of Durocher's coffin?"[20]

These forces—the nation's ongoing concern about gambling in baseball and other sports, Chandler's ascension to baseball commissioner, Rickey's simmering feud with MacPhail, and Leo's spotty record on non-baseball activities—provided the material causes for his suspension. As will be seen shortly, the efficient cause—the actual act that resulted in suspension—came in early April. The formal cause, though, remained Leo's highly visible and public refusal to play according to "the rules" set down by baseball's watchdogs. Historian Jules Tygiel has dismissed another commonly assumed formal cause: Chandler and MacPhail's opposition to Rickey's plan to integrate the Dodgers.[21]

Rickey had been planning to integrate the team since 1945 and had carefully chosen army veteran and Negro Leagues player Jackie Robinson for the task. Leo actually played a small but pivotal role in assuring Robinson's Major League debut. While training in Havana, the Dodgers traveled to Panama for a weekend series against some Caribbean All-Stars. Durocher learned that several Dodgers players had created a petition in opposition to Robinson. Durocher called a team meeting at midnight. The coaches assembled the team in an empty dining-hall kitchen. Still in his night robe, Leo told the players they could "wipe [their] ass" with the petition. Rickey, he assured them, would trade anybody unwilling to play with Robinson. For his part, Leo declared,

> I'm the manager of this ballclub, and I'm interested in one thing: winning. . . . This fellow is a real great ballplayer. He's going to win pennants for us. He's going to put money in your pockets and money in mine. And here's something else to think about when you put your head back on the pillow. From everything I hear, he's only the first. *Only the first, boys!* There's many more coming right behind him and they have the talent and they're gonna come to play. . . . Unless you fellows look out and wake up, they're going to run you right out of the ballpark.

Roger Kahn adds that Leo concluded, "Fuck your petition. The meeting is over. Go back to bed."[22] The short speech captured Durocher's meritocratic worldview. Winning, especially financially lucrative winning, erased all surface differences.

That, Kahn has written, might have been Leo's finest hour. Had he not been suspended for the entire 1947 season, Robinson would have enjoyed the support of Leo's (in)famous commitment to winning.[23] Leo's willingness to engage umpires, opposing players and managers, and fans themselves would have buffered Robinson from at least some of the abuse he encountered.

The events leading to Leo's suspension soon followed. In March 1947 the Yankees came to Havana for an exhibition series against the Dodgers. This meant Durocher's good friend and former assistant, Charlie Dressen, now sat in the opposing dugout as a Yankees coach. The two friends had been teammates for two seasons on the Cincinnati Reds (1930 and 1931). Off the field, they both enjoyed card games and receiving horse-betting tips, especially from Memphis Engelberg.

Dressen's defection to the Yankees had upset Durocher, and Leo, characteristically, struck back. The *Brooklyn Daily Eagle* regularly ran a column titled "Durocher Speaks" so the Dodgers' manager could weigh in on various issues. Harold Parrott, a former sportswriter now working for the Dodgers, actually ghostwrote the pieces. The March 3 column claimed that because Yankees owner Larry MacPhail had failed to sign Durocher as the new Yankees manager, he now sought revenge by signing Dressen. With unreflective irony, Durocher accused MacPhail of unsportsmanlike conduct. Reverting to his Dodgers past when he routinely fired and rehired Durocher, MacPhail erupted, demanding that Commissioner Chandler punish the Dodgers' manager.

Then Leo made things even worse. On March 9, in another game with the Yankees at Havana's new Estadio del Cerro, Durocher noticed Engelberg and Immerman sitting directly behind the Yankees dugout. MacPhail had given them the choice seats and sat himself just a few feet away. Durocher immediately complained, "If I did that, I'd get kicked out of baseball." Rickey too had noticed the same two characters in MacPhail's box seats in the previous day's game. Dick Young of the *New York Daily News* quoted Durocher complaining that MacPhail associated with the very same gamblers Leo had to avoid. In other words, Durocher viewed this situation as analogous to his confrontation with Judge Dockweiler: while Durocher must atone for every infraction, others were allowed to commit the same sins without fear of retribution.[24]

On March 16 MacPhail filed a protest charging Durocher and Rickey with slander. He also named Engelberg and Immerman as Durocher's friends, implying that the manager still associated with gamblers. Chandler now had no choice. Durocher and Rickey had questioned the commissioner's leadership as well as MacPhail's off-field associations. Chandler called a meeting for March 24 with Durocher and MacPhail. After MacPhail finished reviewing the charges, Durocher apologized, claiming, "It's all baseball jargon. I didn't mean anything derogatory in that article about you. . . . I needled you, but it was purely baseball and nothing personal." Durocher effectively admitted that he and Parrott had directed the column at Chandler's decisions, not MacPhail himself or his friends (who, of course, were also Durocher's!). Momentarily outgunned on the ball field, Leo had sought an advantage on his former boss. As he had done several times as the Dodgers' owner, MacPhail tearfully embraced Durocher and claimed the incident finished. "You've always been a great guy with me and always will be a great guy. Forget it. It's over," MacPhail declared.[25]

It turned out MacPhail was wrong. At the same meeting, Durocher had reminded Chandler that the commissioner himself had named Engelberg and Immerman among those to be avoided. Chandler responded by querying Leo about gambling in the Dodgers' locker room. After Leo answered, Chandler then asked MacPhail if he had offered Leo the Yankees' manager job. MacPhail stalled. Arthur Mann noted that Chandler did not ask Leo the same question. Chandler likewise did not rule on MacPhail's charges. At a March 30 meeting, held with Rickey present, it became clear that Yankees management could have handed Immerman and Engelberg the tickets.

Rickey and co-owner Walter O'Malley considered the matter closed. However, they then received an ominous sign. Chandler dismissed MacPhail and then casually asked Rickey and O'Malley, "How much would it hurt you folks to have your fellow out of baseball?"[26]

Presuming order restored, the Dodgers returned to Brooklyn. Rickey set about finalizing the plans for Robinson to start on Opening Day at Ebbets Field. On April 9, while Durocher met with Rickey to discuss starting Robinson in an exhibition game that afternoon at Ebbets Field, Chandler telephoned with his decision. Both teams were fined $2,000 each for detrimental conduct. Harold Parrott was fined $500 and ordered to stop publication of "Durocher Speaks." Dressen was suspended for thirty days for signing with the Yankees while still under contract with the Dodgers. Durocher was suspended from baseball for one year.[27]

Rickey exploded, repeatedly yelling, "You son of a bitch!" Durocher and Arthur Mann both knew something was wrong when the normally abstemious Rickey used such profanity. Leo, uncharacteristically, responded with only an indignant "For what?" Later, Leo said, "To this day, if you ask me *why* I was suspended, I could not tell you. Neither could any sportswriter who followed the case."[28]

The suspension made news nationwide. Dodgers fans regarded the decision as cowardice prompted by Chandler's acquiescence to MacPhail, who, according to Brooklyn fans, had instigated the affair. Arthur Daley wrote in the *New York Times*, "The Lip is in a comparable position to the chap hauled into traffic court for driving through a red light and then being sentenced to the electric chair."[29] Nationally, though, Leo's suspension appeared as proof that repeat offenders could not always expect to escape punishment. The Catholic press took special glee in noting that Leo finally had his comeuppance.[30]

Durocher glumly accepted his fate, moving into a secluded house in the Santa Monica hills with Laraine Day. He occupied himself with yard work, the Hollywood night life, and following the Dodgers via Red Barber's broadcasts. Rickey promised

Leo his full year's salary and then named Burt Shotton as interim manager.[31]

With Durocher gone, Robinson was left to face alone the racist opposition of men like Philadelphia Phillies manager Ben Chapman. Robinson's teammates, led by Pee Wee Reese, embraced Robinson and provided instead a quieter, perhaps more stable, support than Durocher's combat-ready mentality could have done. It cannot be assumed that Robinson would have suffered less if Leo had not been suspended for that year. Durocher and Robinson had their own conflicts in the 1948 season before Leo left to manage the archrival Giants.

In his memoirs Chandler solely blamed Durocher. He had "run a thousand red lights," Chandler said in reference to Daley's remark.[32] Later on, Dodgers chroniclers such as Peter Golenbock and Roger Kahn would suggest that at least partial blame could be pinned on Walter O'Malley. The future Dodgers owner repeatedly failed to defend Durocher successfully before Chandler and Brooklyn's Catholic leaders.[33] Durocher and others blamed Branch Rickey. Day repeatedly told Durocher, "That man is not your friend." Rickey, according to Day, put up a pious front while watching to take any advantage.[34] The Day-Durocher-suspension saga still receives attention from baseball aficionados. Day's death in November 2007 rekindled interest, six months after Major League Baseball and the entire nation recognized the sixtieth anniversary of Robinson's Opening Day start with the Dodgers.[35]

The 1947 season concluded with the Yankees beating the Dodgers in a tight seven-game World Series. After the final out, MacPhail sought out Rickey, who politely shook hands while whispering a rebuke. MacPhail then went on a drunken rampage that involved fistfights and firing George Weiss, the Yankees' farm director.[36] When Chandler had asked Rickey and O'Malley how much it would hurt to lose Durocher, Rickey replied that Durocher "has more character than the fellow you just sent out of the room," referring to MacPhail, whom he had come to dislike intensely.[37]

Durocher certainly committed his fair share of what might be called "surface crimes." He gambled and allowed gamblers access to his players, and his personal life ran antithetical to the very traditional values baseball was supposed to represent and defend. When confronted with a deeper crime like the racism displayed by some Dodgers players during spring training, Durocher revealed his pragmatic, yet moral, side.[38] What and whom Leo defended that night in Panama became the lasting story of the 1947 season, not his suspension which began the season.

# Chapter 11. **Branch Rickey and the Mainstream Press**

*Joe Marren*

Wesley Branch Rickey—even the name is wonderfully quirky and unique. And the man himself lived up to the matchlessness of his name. He was another Lincoln; he was Simon Legree; he was a saint, and he was a grievous, unrepentant sinner; he was one of baseball's best executives and innovators, or he was one of the worst of them to his bosses in St. Louis, Brooklyn, and Pittsburgh. As Ed Fitzgerald wrote in a November 1947 profile of Rickey in *Sport* magazine, "Rickey is about as uncomplicated as a Rube Goldberg contraption for feeding yourself in bed."

Rickey was "The Mahatma" or "El Cheapo," depending on who was writing about him. After signing Jackie Robinson in 1945, and then after promoting him to the Dodgers in '47, Rickey was both praised and damned at the same time; there was no in-between. Shortly after his death on December 9, 1965, he was lionized and beatified. A few years later, the revisionists looked at his feet of clay and questioned his integrity. Now the neo-revisionists are reexamining Rickey and his legacy. Since Rickey is already long buried, they will praise him and resurrect the good about him that was interred with his bones.

But which Rickey was onstage in Brooklyn in 1947? The answer is easy: all of them. And it is the press that will guide the tour of that season.

The first stop is a January meeting in the Waldorf-Astoria Hotel in New York City. Rickey told the assembled Major League owners that he intended to promote Jackie Robinson that spring. The owners were shocked and voted 15–1 against the move, thereby putting Rickey and Commissioner Happy Chandler on notice. There was noth-

Ambivalent press coverage dogged Branch Rickey and his teams throughout his long career in baseball.

ing the owners could do to prevent Rickey from doing what he felt was best for his club, but it did take steel nerves on Rickey's part to continue with his plan. What may have worried the other owners was a 1946 report by Yankees boss Larry MacPhail that said owners should brace themselves for poor black fans driving away prosperous white fans.

A second stop takes place on the wintry night

of Tuesday, February 5, at the Carlton YMCA in Brooklyn, where Dodgers executive secretary Herbert T. Miller had gathered together thirty "distinguished Brooklyn Negroes" to meet Rickey, according to an article in an October 1951 issue of *Sport* magazine. They probably expected to hear that Jackie Robinson would be promoted to the parent Dodgers after a successful 1946 season with the club's top farm team in Montreal. After all, Robinson had successfully made the switch from shortstop to second base, batted .349, stolen forty bases, and helped the Royals win the Little World Series. But it was a vintage Rickey performance, because the crowd didn't get what it expected.

He bluntly told his guests that the biggest threat to Robinson's success, if he was promoted, would be that "the Negro people themselves will ruin it. . . . We don't want what can be another great milestone in the progress of American race relations turned into a national comedy and an ultimate tragedy. If any individual group or segment of Negro society uses the advancement of Jackie Robinson in baseball as a social 'ism' or schism, I will curse the day I ever signed him to a contract, and I will personally see that baseball is never so abused and misrepresented again."

Yet for some reason the audience of community leaders and other respectable middle-class citizens bought Rickey's idea. They knew that society would be watching and judging. So they hastily started a campaign based on the phrase "Don't Spoil Jackie's Chances" and urged restraint and moderation among Robinson's fans.

Why did they buy it when millions identified with Robinson? In him they saw their own chances at gaining that promised equality too long denied. Perhaps they realized that this first step was a cautious one, fraught with danger both personal for Robinson and monumental for America. Or perhaps they were simply mesmerized by Rickey's blunt assessment of the nation's psyche. As Fitzgerald wrote in that November 1947 is-

sue of *Sport*, "Branch Rickey is a man who possesses tremendous magnetism. Measured in terms of candlepower, his personality lights up a whole room. There's an intensity about him that thrusts itself upon your imagination and kindles a fire of interest in you. When he speaks, you find yourself leaning forward to catch every word. There's something about the way he talks, easily but deliberately, that makes you certain the things he's saying are of deathless importance. Whatever that elusive quality is that enables one man to dominate a group of his fellows, Rickey has it."

Not all the ballplayers who played for Rickey, or the sportswriters who covered those players and those teams, would completely agree with Fitzgerald's assessment. (Enos Slaughter supposedly once said that Rickey had to open the vault to get a nickel change.) But it is a measure of the man that he could indeed make people talk about him, curse him, and debate his tactics during his life and decades after it ended.

What Rickey didn't tell his audience that wintry night in Brooklyn was that he had a plan. The first step was to move spring training away from segregated Florida to sites and games in more tolerant Cuba and Panama. Along the way, Rickey thought, Robinson's outstanding play in camp and in exhibition games would naturally lead to the Dodgers' players clamoring for him to be promoted. (Robinson had a .625 batting average and also stole seven bases that spring.)

But there were two immediate obstacles (not counting what would happen if Robinson didn't perform up to expectations): Rickey wanted Robinson to switch to first base because the Dodgers were weak there, and some players threatened to organize a petition against Robinson's expected promotion.

The plans also called for manager Leo Durocher to demand that Robinson be called up for the good of the team. That part of Rickey's plan failed miserably, since Commissioner Chandler suspended Durocher for the season on April 9 for a host of indiscretions. The suspension had a polarizing effect on baseball. As Chandler put it, "A good many New York sports writers, no fans of mine anyhow, jumped to the defense of their fallen hero. . . . *Time* magazine made an accurate summation of that situation saying: 'Commissioner Chandler had done the seemingly impossible; he has made Leo Durocher a sympathetic figure.'" Chandler wrote in his autobiography that "I'll have to confess, I didn't think anybody could do that."[1] Another point of view was summed up by *Washington Post* sportswriter Shirley Povich: "Maybe the punishment was in excess of the crime, but who can shed a tear for Durocher?"[2]

Durocher was first replaced by Dodgers scout, coach, and one-time Minor League manager Clyde Sukeforth. But Sukeforth was just a stopgap as Rickey searched for someone to guide the Dodgers for the season.

The names of former Yankees manager Joe McCarthy and former Giants player-manager Bill Terry were mentioned before Rickey decided to offer the job to old friend Burt Shotton, who had retired from his coaching job with the Cleveland Indians a few years previously. The sixty-two-year-old Shotton's last full season as a big league manager was with the seventh-place Philadelphia Phillies in 1933. Rather than wear a uniform again, Shotton said he would manage in his street clothes, which meant he could not go on the field. That was a crucial decision, since it essentially meant that Robinson would not have someone as fiery as Leo Durocher arguing with the umpires for him.

Just a day after Chandler's bombshell, Rickey stealthily slipped in one of his own. During the top of the sixth inning of an afternoon exhibition game on April 10 in Ebbets Field—against Montreal—he announced, "The Brooklyn Dodgers today purchased the contract of Jackie Roosevelt Robinson from the Montreal Royals. He will report immediately."[3]

Robinson had to endure a storm of protest about his promotion to the parent club. And some of the hostility came from fellow Dodgers. A spring training survey in *The Sporting News* said the team was "mainly antagonistic" toward calling up Robinson.[4] It was Rickey who headed off the nascent rebellion from within the ranks. While it may have been naive on his part to believe the team would clamor for Robinson's promotion in order to bring them a share of any potential World Series wealth, Rickey nevertheless realistically told the rebels they could play with Robinson or be traded.

Two of the more disgruntled players were reserve catcher Bobby Bragan and popular outfielder Fred "Dixie" Walker. During a heated meeting with Rickey in spring training, Bragan said he wanted to be traded. Walker also asked to be traded in a letter to Rickey on March 26. Walker's wish almost came true; a deal with Pittsburgh was agreed to in principle before Rickey vetoed it. With both stars and reserve players discontented, Rickey had to act decisively. Lester Rodney, the sports editor of the Communist Party's *Daily Worker*, credited Rickey with standing up to the pressure from the players: "Kirby Higbe was traded immediately. . . . And when Carl Furillo said . . . 'I ain't gonna play with no niggers!' Rickey snapped back, 'You don't want to play with no niggers? Then you can go back to Pennsylvania and pound railroad ties for $15 a week. You'll never set foot on a big-league baseball field again.' Carl played. They all played."[5] A postscript must be noted here: by the end of the 1947 season, Furillo, Bragan, and Walker had come to admire Robinson.

It was that sort of hyper-attention from the press that Rickey was continually adapting to in Brooklyn. Ambivalent press coverage dogged Rickey and his teams throughout his long career in baseball. In 1947 coverage started out positively with a May editorial in *Crisis* magazine that gave Rickey all the credit for "shrewdly picking" Robinson in 1945 and then wisely delaying the announcement of his promotion to the big leagues until just five days before the season opened. Then, just as Rickey had asked in his February 5 speech at the Brooklyn YMCA, the magazine also asked "Negro newspapers" to provide balanced coverage and not dwell solely on Robinson. Just as Rickey asked in that speech, the editorial concluded by urging all Americans to respect Rickey's "judgment and courage" and Robinson's "skill and courage."

In its September 22 issue, *Time* magazine ran a story about Robinson's winning the Rookie of the Year Award from *The Sporting News*. The article did more than praise Robinson; it also labeled Rickey "the smartest man in baseball." The cover story gave credit to Robinson for enduring "the toughest first season any ballplayer has ever faced." But it also praised Rickey for hiring *Pittsburgh Courier* sportswriter Wendell Smith to travel with the team as a companion for Robinson, and for setting up "how-to-handle-Robinson" committees of prominent African Americans in National League cities.

Rickey wrote that he "picked" Robinson both for his play on the field and for his strength and character off the field. He asked Robinson not to retaliate when jeered. Yet the support committees would seem to have been ineffective, for between the positive *Crisis* editorial near the start of the 1947 season and the laudatory article in *Time* near the end of that season came the slings and arrows of less complimentary screeds. (Supposedly the character of Judge Goodwill Banner in Bernard Malamud's novel *The Natural* was partly based on Rickey's habit of talking over people's heads and being too theoretical.)

And Jimmy Powers of the *New York Daily News* did a lot of slinging, branding Rickey "El Cheapo" around 1945. It got so bad that in 1946 Rickey considered suing Powers. Fitzgerald's article in the November 1947 issue of *Sport* assessed the situation: "Powers misses no opportunity to sink another shaft into Rickey. It can hardly be denied that the Dodgers' chief executive is an inviting target. Sometimes it seems he delights in furnishing critics like Powers with more ammunition. Nothing Rickey does convinces Powers, who, of course, doesn't want to be convinced. He has more fun, and keeps his readers more excited that way."

Rickey didn't try to mislead the press, said his friends and allies both in the press and in the Dodgers' office; he just had a tendency to over-answer, and not everyone could follow his logic. And yet there were probably times, his biographers wrote, when Rickey probably "preferred not to be understood."[6] Baloney, wrote *New York Daily News* writer Dick Young in a January 1953 issue of *Baseball Digest*:

Branch Rickey, though he reflects an aloofness in his relations with the press, is profoundly aware of the newspaper criticism directed against him. And yet much of the adverse comment written about Rickey results from his condescending approach to the press. Writers not so much resent his evasiveness, but rather his insufferable belief that he is getting away with it. Rickey, while talking to newsmen, creates the impression in his audience that he is thinking: "I can wrap these lame-brains around my little finger with my rhetoric."

Few men have the nimble brain of Branch Rickey, including the newsmen whom he tries to deceive, but baseball writers are proud of the trust which is often placed in them. Rickey, inordinately suspicious, fails to project this feeling of trust. He substitutes arrogance and scorn, and as a result receives the "bad press" he cannot understand.

One of the reasons he got some bad press was his seeming contradictions and chutzpah in claiming the Robinson story as his own. For example, Commissioner Chandler felt slighted in having his role in Robinson's breakthrough ignored, and he blamed Rickey:

During our hours together out in the cabin I kept getting the impression that Rickey felt he was God Almighty, and that he was somehow the Savior of the black people. He tried his best—and this I know—he and his whole outfit moved in to give him the full credit for breaking the baseball color line. They wanted to keep everybody else, including me, out of it. But of course he couldn't have done it without my approval. When he came down to Versailles [Kentucky], he had two chances: slim and none. But I did it for him, made it possible. I never could understand why he always cut me out of it, every time he mentioned the Jackie Robinson decision. I was surprised, and I suppose somewhat hurt by his attitude.[7]

Also feeling slighted was the *Daily Worker*, which had been actively campaigning since the mid-1930s to integrate baseball. Historian Jules Tygiel once credited the Communist press and the African American press for continually pushing the idea that baseball should be integrated. *Daily Worker* sports editor Lester Rodney said, "Of course, it always rankled me that [Rickey] never acknowledged the role of the *Daily Worker* in all this. But he was a big anti-Communist and he hated the idea of us getting credit for anything—especially for breaking the color line. He didn't want anyone to think that he had succumbed to pressure from the Reds."[8]

That may or may not settle the "how" of the decision, but it certainly doesn't settle the "why"—and there again, Rickey offered conflicting reasons. He once told *Look* magazine sports editor Tim Cohane, in a piece published in the magazine on March 19, 1946, "I cannot face my God much longer knowing that His black creatures are held separate and distinct from His white creatures in the game that has given me all my own."

That quote, as well as the story that Rickey was a crusader for equal rights after witnessing Charley Thomas (an African American catcher on Rick-ey's Ohio Wesleyan team) cry in his South Bend, Indiana, hotel room in 1903 because of discrimination, is an example of what former *Daily Worker* sportswriter Bill Mardo calls the bubba meise school of history. ("Bubba meise" is a Yiddish expression that loosely translates as something akin to myth.)

In other talks with reporters, Rickey said that signing and then promoting Robinson was based solely on winning a pennant for the Dodgers. An article by John Chamberlain in an April 1948 issue of *Harper's* magazine quoted Rickey (who got right to the point of the matter, which seemed to surprise the writer, who expected Rickey to be evasive) as saying that Robinson was not promoted "to solve a sociological problem." Instead, Rickey answered succinctly: "I brought him up for one reason: to win the pennant. I'd play an elephant with pink horns if he could win the pennant."

The 1947 season was a trying one for the Dodgers. It was a season in which some people made fundamental personal changes in their beliefs that also indirectly helped shape a country. And Branch Rickey led them the whole way. At the end of it all, after losing a heartbreaking World Series to the New York Yankees, four games to three, Rickey encountered Yankees boss Larry MacPhail outside the clubhouse. The two had once been close. But MacPhail's role in Rickey's problems with the owners and Durocher's suspension was a sore spot. Worst of all, MacPhail's name kept popping up at odd times.

As Rickey biographer Lee Lowenfish wrote, "The last straw may have been the recent comment by the combustible Yankees president that Leo Durocher would never have been suspended if Branch Rickey didn't really want it to happen. In front of a swarm of photographers MacPhail offered a handshake to his defeated rival, but Rickey whispered, 'I am taking your hand only because people are watching us, but never speak to me again, never.'"[9]

# Chapter 12. Timeline, April 15–April 30

*Lyle Spatz*

Tuesday, April 15, vs. Boston—Coach Clyde Sukeforth filled in for suspended manager Leo Durocher on Opening Day at Ebbets Field. Spider Jorgensen, at third, and Jackie Robinson, at first, made their Major League debuts. Robinson became the first African American to play in the Major Leagues in the twentieth century. He went 0 for 3. Also making his big league debut was Marv Rackley, as a pinch runner for catcher Bruce Edwards. Pete Reiser's seventh-inning double drove in the winning run in the Dodgers' 5–3 victory over the Boston Braves. Hal Gregg, in relief of Joe Hatten, was the winner. 1-0, First (T), 1 game ahead.

Wednesday, April 16, vs. Boston—Rained out. 1-0, First (T), ½ game ahead.

Thursday, April 17, vs. Boston—Spider Jorgensen drove in six runs in a 12–6 win over Boston. Kirby Higbe, with relief help from Harry Taylor and Hugh Casey, got the win. Jackie Robinson got his first hit, as did twenty-year-old Duke Snider, playing in his first big league game. 2-0, First (T), ½ game ahead.

Friday, April 18, at New York—The Giants hit six home runs in a 10–4 win at the Polo Grounds, spoiling Dodgers manager Burt Shotton's debut. Winning pitcher Dave Koslo yielded Jackie Robinson's first Major League home run. Vic Lombardi suffered his first loss against the Giants after nine consecutive wins. Brooklyn's Ed Chandler made his Major League debut, pitching three innings in relief. 2-1, Second, 1 game behind.

Saturday, April 19, at New York—Jackie Robinson had three hits, but Ralph Branca lost to the Giants, 4–3. 2-2, Third, 2 games behind.

Sunday, April 20, at Boston—Snowed out. 2-2, Third, 2 games behind.

Monday, April 21, at Boston—Snowed out. 2-2, Third (T), 2 games behind.

Tuesday, April 22, vs. Philadelphia—Hal Gregg pitched a one-hitter in shutting out the Phillies, 1–0. The only hit he allowed was a first-inning double by Del Ennis. Gene Hermanski's eighth-inning single scored Jackie Robinson, who had singled and stolen second. 3-2, Second, 1½ games behind.

Wednesday, April 23, vs. Philadelphia—Joe Hatten pitched a complete game to lead the Dodgers over the Phillies, 5–2. Eddie Stanky, Pete Reiser, and Carl Furillo each had two hits. 4-2, Second, 1½ games behind.

Thursday, April 24, vs. Philadelphia—Ralph Branca and Hugh Casey combined to shut out the Phillies, 2–0, giving Brooklyn a sweep of the three-game series. Dixie Walker's first-inning single off Tommy Hughes drove in the only runs of the game. 5-2, Second, ½ game behind.

Friday, April 25, vs. New York—Rained out. 5-2, Second, ½ game behind.

Saturday, April 26, vs. New York—The Dodgers moved into first place with a 7–3 win over the

Giants. Dixie Walker's four consecutive singles, and a two-run homer by Gene Hermanski off Bill Voiselle, led the offense. Vic Lombardi, in relief of Kirby Higbe, got the win. 6-2, First, ½ game ahead.

Sunday, April 27, vs. New York—Eddie Stanky's ninth-inning sacrifice squeeze scored Marv Rackley, giving the Dodgers a 9–8 win. Hugh Casey, Brooklyn's fifth pitcher, was the winner. 7-2, First, 1 game ahead.

Monday, April 28—Not scheduled. 7-2, First, 1 game ahead.

Tuesday, April 29, vs. Chicago—A bases-loaded double by Dixie Walker and a two-run home run by Carl Furillo highlighted a 10–6 defeat of the second-place Cubs. Joe Hatten, with relief help from Hugh Casey, was the winner. It was Brooklyn's sixth consecutive win and their eighth without a loss at Ebbets Field. 8-2, First, 2 games ahead.

Wednesday, April 30, vs. Chicago—Chicago's Bill Nicholson hit a ninth-inning two-run blast over the right-field screen to give the Cubs a 3–1 victory. Doyle Lade ended Brooklyn's six-game winning streak, outdueling Ralph Branca. The loss was the Dodgers' first at home after eight wins. 8-3, First, 1 game ahead.

# Chapter 13. Ebbets Field, 1947

*Bob McGee*

Ebbets Field: The greatest ball park ever. (Courtesy of the Los Angeles Dodgers)

In the spring of 1947, Ebbets Field was entering its thirty-fifth season, and in that year more fans would pass through the fabled ball yard's portals than in any other.

The old ballpark was "the fun house of baseball," as artist Andy Jurinko has said, with its cozy stands bringing fans near enough to the action to make matters up close and personal, whether for players, umpires, or the person sitting next to you.

It was close enough to hear the players' chatter, close enough, if you were sitting in line with the first base bag, to see the whites of the first baseman's eyes. It was close enough for those who were

on the field to see and hear you. And to be seen and heard in Brooklyn, at Ebbets Field, was not to be forgotten.

It was a palette of color, from the ads on the outfield walls from the right-field corner to the left, whether for Coca-Cola, Botany Ties, Burma-Shave, Gem Blades, or a host of others, save for a hitter's blackened background in straightaway center.

There was the scoreboard that jutted out from the right-center-field wall, along the right-field wall that separated Bedford Avenue's sidewalk from the field; it was the only wall in the ballpark that did

64

not have a double-decked stand behind it. The scoreboard, at each side, angled back to the wall, which was nineteen feet high, topped by a nineteen-foot screen. The top nine and a half feet of that wall was straight; the bottom nine and a half feet was angled back toward the infield, wreaking unpredictable havoc with caroming fly balls.

The angled wall ran over from the right-field corner to a double-door exit gate in deepest right-center field that President Roosevelt's limousine had driven through merely two and a half years before. There was enough of a crack under those doors for children—hell, not just children but adults, too—to lie flat on their stomachs to watch a game. Occasionally, a street cop would come along and tap their heels with a billy club—time to move.

Atop the scoreboard was a Bulova clock. In May of 1946, the 30th to be exact, Bama Rowell of the Braves had stopped that clock in the second inning of a doubleheader's nightcap, at precisely 4:25 in the afternoon. The ball stayed inside the clock for a double, the inspiration, of course, for a similar incident in the movie version of Bernard Malamud's book *The Natural*.

Below the clock, atop the scoreboard, there was a sign—not yet the Schaefer sign with the illuminating "h" and "e" for hit and error, which would come a year later; this sign invited you to "Shave Electrically." And of course, there was the sign below the scoreboard, the Abe Stark sign, the sign that beckoned all to "Hit Sign, Win Suit." Ten years earlier, traded to the Dodgers in late career, the right-handed, right-field slice hitter Woody English had done so, and more than once.

But did you get a suit, Woody?

"The ball had to hit the sign on a fly, and the official scorer had to verify it," English remembered. "By the end of the season I had hit the sign three times, so I went down to pick up my suits. A tailor was there—it wasn't Abe Stark—and he went over to the counter and looked it up and sure enough,

he saw that I had three coming. He said, 'Right this way Woody' and brought me over to this rack. He showed me these three pretty cheap lookin' things . . . and I said, 'Listen, just give me . . . one . . . good . . . suit.'

"He chuckled and said, 'All right, Woody, c'mon back here.' He took me to the back, where the good suits were. And that's what I got; one good suit."

The walls were not padded. Pete Reiser had a nasty habit of running into them. It did not stop him. Another year would go by before that changed, and by that time the prodigious promise of Pistol Pete would be largely spent, a product of the pounding.

It was 343 feet down the left-field line; 297 down the right. Some 850 box seats had been added over the winter, bringing in the fences slightly; although the deepest recesses of right-center field were 407 feet, straightaway center field was only 386 feet, down 14 feet from the year before.

Up in the bleachers, there were the leather lungs of Hilda Chester, who, warned by her doctors about the fragility of her heart, was given a school bell that she flagged relentlessly, while not abating the yelling at all. One time, when umpire Beans Reardon asked her why she yelled at the men in blue all the time, she replied, "Open your other eye, joik, you've got noive like a toothache."

In the box seats, there was Jack Pierce, who would buy an extra seat for his helium tank; he'd spend time blowing up balloons, yelling "Cooooooooo-kie!" serenading the man whose last name was Lavagetto.

In section 8, there was Shorty Laurice and the Sym-Phony Band, an ever-changing crew of musicians that included JoJo Delio, Lou Soriano, Patty George, Jerry Martin, Joe Zollo, and Zollo's son Frank, the stalwarts. They routinely razzed the umpires with "Three Blind Mice." No adequate adjustment was made when a fourth member was added to the crews.

When opposing hitters struck out, they were accompanied on their solemn walk to the dugout with "The Worms Crawl In, the Worms Crawl Out," cymbals and chords blaring when the player took his seat on the bench. Catcher Walker Cooper once tried to outsmart them. He didn't sit for several innings. When he finally did, they got him, drum and cymbals matching the posterior's point of impact on the pine.

Public address announcer Tex Rickard would routinely intone that fans sitting along the rail in left field should please remove their clothes. Fans sitting along the third base line back toward that left-field corner had good reason for removing their clothes from that special perch: for the last fifteen or so feet up to the wall, the foul line was painted right on the fence rail. If you were leaning against the rail, you were in fair territory.

Gladys Gooding, who for years played the organ at RKO and Loew's Theaters before coming to Ebbets Field, was the answer to a trivia question about being the only person who ever played for the Dodgers, the Rangers, and the Knicks.

Yet it's the ethereal things that are hardest to pin down. The Ebbets Field smell has been alternately characterized as oily, inky, beery, a combination scent of hot dogs, mustard, peanuts, a smell of the grass intermingled, picked up even when walking through the Rotunda's turnstiles down in the caverns, panoplied by the wafting aromas of the Bond Bread Bakery a few blocks away. Sweet.

The most enduring image: the ballpark façade.

At the junction of Sullivan Place and McKeever Place, in spring 1947, EBBETS FIELD, writ large in the setback, just below the ballpark's crown, a flag rising precisely in the middle above, testified silently to the beauty of an immortal piece of Americana, and with it, the promise of what the American summer would bring.

And that façade itself, beauty incarnate: fourteen rows of small pane, Federal-style windows, separated by brick pilasters, running from the sidewalk or just above the main gate's galvanized iron marquee above the entryway almost to the top of the wall, with gargoyles marking the spring line for the crowning, semicircular windows above each row, where an ornamental circle of brick-belt coursing surrounded the windows, bas-relief medallions of baseballs populating the space in between each of them, a perfect tableau before entering the eighty-foot-diameter Rotunda, with ball-and-bat chandelier dangling unobtrusively from the twenty-eight-foot-high elliptical ceiling. If the chandelier seemed high, it was only because the ballpark's roof itself was only eighty feet off the ground.

Crowded, teeming, the Rotunda was all that symbolized what was wrong and right about the intimacy and design of Ebbets Field, inasmuch as the ticket sellers' lines cascaded from interior ticket windows to the room's center, while those holding tickets pushed their way through. But never mind! This was Ebbets Field, where the smell of the grass was already in your nostrils; this was the place where, on Opening Day 1947, a teenager standing and waiting to buy tickets in the morning at the advance sale window heard a commotion, and turned around to see a squad of policemen surrounding a black man who was a head taller than each of them.

This was the moment, the very moment, Jackie Robinson stepped across the threshold of the nineteenth and twentieth centuries and prepared to take it to the world, which, as everyone from Brooklyn who ever crossed a bridge understood, is what life is all about.

# Chapter 14. **Jackie Robinson's First Game**

*Lyle Spatz*

Third baseman Spider Jorgensen, second baseman Eddie Stanky, shortstop Pee Wee Reese, and first baseman Jackie Robinson composed the Brooklyn infield on Opening Day 1947.

Jackie Robinson's Major League debut was more than just the first step in righting a historical wrong. It was a crucial event in the history of the American civil rights movement, the importance of which went far beyond the insular world of baseball.

The Dodgers signed Robinson to a Major League contract just five days before the start of the 1947 season. Baseball people, especially those in Brooklyn, were still digesting the previous day's news of manager Leo Durocher's one-year suspension (for conduct detrimental to baseball), when the story broke of Robinson's promotion from the Montreal Royals. He would be the first black American to play in the Major Leagues since

catcher Fleetwood Walker played for the Toledo Blue Stockings of the American Association back in 1884.

Robinson had played second base for the International League's Montreal Royals in 1946, but on orders from the Dodgers he had been working out at first all spring. He played first base in Brooklyn's final three exhibition games against the Yankees, and again two days later when the Dodgers opened the season at Ebbets Field against the Boston Braves. Rumors of a sellout may have discouraged some fans from attending, but whatever the reason, a crowd of only 26,623 saw Robinson's debut.

Jack made the game's first put-out, receiving

the throw from fellow rookie Spider Jorgensen on Dick Culler's ground ball to third base. Interim manager Clyde Sukeforth had Robinson batting second, so after Eddie Stanky grounded out, Jack stepped in against Johnny Sain for his first Major League at bat. Sain, the National League's winningest right-hander in 1946, retired him easily on a bouncer to third baseman Bob Elliott. After flying out to left fielder Danny Litwhiler in the third inning, Robinson appeared to have gotten his first big league hit in the fifth. But shortstop Culler made an outstanding play on his ground ball and turned it into a well-executed 6-4-3 double play.

When he next batted, in the seventh, Brooklyn was trailing 3–2. Stanky was on first, having opened the inning by drawing Sain's fifth walk of the afternoon. It was an obvious bunt situation and Robinson laid down a beauty, pushing the ball deftly up the right side. Boston's rookie first baseman, Earl Torgeson, fielded it, but with Robinson speeding down the line, he was forced to hurry his throw. The ball hit Jack and caromed away, allowing him to take second and Stanky to reach third. Pete Reiser's double scored both runners and finished Sain. Reiser later scored on Gene Hermanski's fly ball off reliever Mort Cooper as the Dodgers won 5–3. Hal Gregg, in relief of starter Joe Hatten, got the win, and Hugh Casey got the first of his league-leading eighteen saves. Of course nobody had ever heard of "saves" in 1947, and Casey would die never knowing that he had twice been the National League leader.

When the Dodgers took the field in the ninth inning, Robinson remained on the bench as veteran Howie Schultz took over at first base. Sukeforth had inserted Schultz as a defensive measure, but the Dodgers soon realized that Robinson needed no help. Schultz played in only one more game before Brooklyn sold him to the Philadelphia Phillies. Ed Stevens, the team's other first baseman, played in just five games before he was sent back to the Minors.

The popular Pete Reiser, coming back from yet another injury, clearly had been the star of the game, and it was he, not Robinson, who was the focus of the story in the next day's *New York Times*. Roscoe McGowen's game account mentioned Robinson only in relation to his play, leaving columnist Arthur Daley to take note of his debut, which he called uneventful. In retrospect, it would be easy, and fashionable, to attribute the writers' casual treatment of this history-making game to racism. However, I prefer to think they handled it in this way because it took place at a time when baseball reporters believed that's what they were: baseball reporters, men who felt their sole duty was to report what took place on the field. Red Barber and Connie Desmond, the Dodgers' radio broadcasters, did the same. The mind boggles to think how the media would cover such an event today.

# Chapter 15. Clyde Sukeforth

*James L. Ray*

Clyde Sukeforth was a backup catcher who played parts of ten seasons in the Major Leagues for the Cincinnati Reds and Brooklyn Dodgers. Over those ten seasons, Sukeforth hit .264 with only 2 home runs and had 96 runs batted in. Although his accomplishments as a player were minimal, Sukeforth's subsequent years as a Minor League scout and big league coach led him to play key roles in three momentous baseball events: the discovery of Jackie Robinson, the signing of Roberto Clemente, and the decision to send in Ralph Branca to pitch to Bobby Thomson, a decision that led to Thomson's 1951 "Shot Heard 'Round the World."

Clyde Leroy Sukeforth was born on November 30, 1901, in Washington, Maine, a tiny rural town. His father was Pearle Leroy Sukeforth, who as a young man was a cooper but who later became a dairy farmer. Clyde's mother was Sarah M. Grinnell, known as Sadie. Pearle and Sarah were married in May 1899 and had their first child, a daughter named Hazel, in November 1899.

The Sukeforths received out-of-town news only from the *Boston Post*, which was delivered by stagecoach every evening to the local library. From the time he was a young boy, Clyde journeyed to that library to read about his favorite baseball players. Most of those players were members of the Boston Red Sox, who just happened to be the best team in baseball during Clyde's adolescent years.

But Sukeforth did not just read about the game; he played it whenever he got the chance in the brief summers of southern Maine. "Every kid played baseball in my day. That's all there really was to do. There was no organization to it, but we played

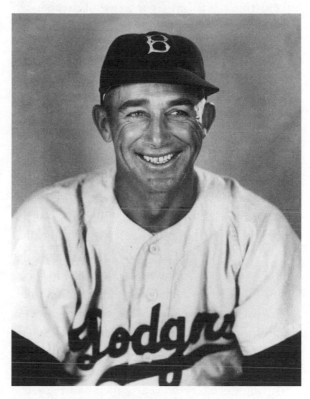

Clyde Sukeforth managed the Dodgers to victories in the first two games of the season.

seven days a week. And every kid had a ball and a glove," Sukeforth said in a 1991 interview.

In 1916 Sukeforth enrolled in the Coburn Classical Institute, a college preparatory high school in nearby Waterville. By the end of World War I, Maine had become one of the leading paper-manufacturing states in the nation. Massive sawmills, pulp mills, and paper plants popped up around the state, creating jobs and giving rise to a number of company-sponsored baseball teams. After graduating from high school, Sukeforth played two seasons for the Great Northern Paper Company in Millinocket, Maine. He later recalled, "They recruited all of the better players around, [and] they paid us more than the good ballplayers were getting in the minor leagues."[1]

After playing two years for Great Northern, Sukeforth enrolled at Georgetown University in Washington DC in the fall of 1923. During his two years at Georgetown, Clyde starred on the school's baseball team as a catcher and left fielder. He also continued to follow the Major Leagues, keeping a close watch on the local Washington Senators. In 1924 Sukeforth watched from the stands as Washington's Walter Johnson pitched against the New York Giants in the World Series.

In 1926 Sukeforth went to spring training with the Cincinnati Reds. He showed well but was sent down to play for the Nashua Millionaires of the Class B New England League. The Reds recalled him in late May, and he made his big league debut on May 31, when he struck out as a pinch hitter for Eppa Rixey. That was the extent of Sukeforth's stay with the Reds. After appearing in four games for the Minneapolis Millers of the American Association, he spent the rest of 1926 with the Manchester Blue Sox of the New England League.

During the next two years, 1927 and 1928, the left-handed-hitting Sukeforth served as the backup to the Reds' longtime starting catcher, Bubbles Hargrave. During those two seasons, he played in seventy-one games, batting .162 with five RBIs. Sukeforth had his first Major League hit on May 21, 1927, a double off Philadelphia's Alex Ferguson.

In 1929 Sukeforth had the best season of his career. Playing for a Reds team that finished in seventh place, he batted .354 with thirty-three RBIs in eighty-four games. In 1930 he played in ninety-four games and batted .284. Although the five-foot-ten Sukeforth weighed only 155 pounds, he caught 106 games in 1931, with a .256 batting average. He also committed thirteen errors, the most by a National League catcher that season.

On November 16, 1931, Sukeforth was accidentally shot in the eye while rabbit hunting. At first, doctors thought he would never be able to play ball again, and even feared he might lose the eye. But his eye improved quickly enough that he was released from the hospital on December 2. Sukeforth's only complaint about the injury, revealed in interviews years after the fact, was that he "couldn't read too well without squinting."[2]

On March 14, 1932, the Reds traded Sukeforth, second baseman Tony Cuccinello, and third baseman Joe Stripp to the Brooklyn Dodgers for three players, including future Hall of Fame catcher Ernie Lombardi. Sukeforth played in 106 games as a backup catcher for the Dodgers over the next three years. After the 1934 season, the Dodgers optioned him to the Toledo Mud Hens, but he decided he did not want to play in the American Association for the money offered. While mulling his future, Clyde played semipro ball in Maine during the summer of 1935. He was, however, still under contract with the Dodgers, who decided he might work out well as a manager of one of their lower-level Minor League clubs.

So in 1936 Sukeforth managed the Leaksville-Draper-Spray Triplets of the Class D Bi-State League to a third-place finish. He also caught in fifty-one games and hit .365 with seven home runs.

In 1937 Sukeforth managed the Clinton (Iowa) Owls of the Class B Three-I League to a first-place finish. He spent the next two seasons with Elmira in the Class A Eastern League. In 1938 Elmira won the league championship in the postseason playoffs. He also continued to play, appearing in twelve games in 1938 and thirty-one games in 1939. Sukeforth's success led to a promotion to manage the Dodgers' top farm team, the Montreal Royals in the International League.

After Clyde spent three years with Montreal,

Brooklyn's new general manager, Branch Rickey, hired him to serve on the Dodgers' coaching staff in 1943. In 1945, at the age of forty-three, he played in eighteen games for the Dodgers to fill a void created by the player shortages of World War II. He played surprisingly well, hitting .294 in fifty-one at bats.

Sukeforth's main job that season, however, was as a scout for Rickey. His most important target was a twenty-six-year-old African American player named Jack Roosevelt Robinson. "Mr. Rickey had sent me to Chicago to see Robinson play. Mr. Rickey wanted me to check Robinson's arm."[3] However, Robinson had suffered an arm injury and was out of the lineup. Sukeforth introduced himself to Robinson and told him Rickey wanted to meet with him in New York. Robinson agreed to make the trip.

When they arrived in New York, Sukeforth took Robinson to the Dodgers' offices in Brooklyn, where he met with Rickey. Sukeforth stayed in the room for the conference between the two men. It was August 28, 1945. Rickey told Jackie that the plan was to have him play for Montreal in 1946. Then, if everything worked according to schedule, he would bring Robinson to Brooklyn.

The 1946 season was a busy one for Sukeforth. He served on manager Leo Durocher's coaching staff, performed special scouting assignments for Rickey, and, perhaps most important, helped create the new Nashua Dodgers of the Class B New England League. In that role Sukeforth was instrumental in forging ties with the New Hampshire community, and he eased the racial integration of the league by adding Roy Campanella and Don Newcombe to the roster.

Prior to the start of the 1947 season, Durocher was suspended for the entire year by Commissioner Happy Chandler for consorting with gamblers. Rickey asked Sukeforth to take over as manager, but Sukeforth did not want the job. He did, however, fill in for the first two games of the season, the first of which featured the debut of Robinson. "I didn't tell Jack anything special [before the game]," he recalled. "Jack had enough to think about."[4]

On April 18, before the game against the New York Giants at the Polo Grounds, the Dodgers announced that Burt Shotton, a longtime Rickey favorite, had been hired as manager. After two games as the manager, Sukeforth was again a coach.

Four and a half years later, Sukeforth played a key role in another memorable moment in baseball history. On October 3, 1951, the Dodgers and the New York Giants played the final game of a three-game playoff to determine who would meet the Yankees in the World Series. At the time, Sukeforth was the Dodgers' bullpen coach.

"I was the bullpen coach catching the two relief pitchers who were warming up for the Dodgers at the time. Don Newcombe had been throwing pretty good for the Dodgers during the game. He had pretty good control of the game until that ninth inning [when he began to tire]. So I began catching Carl Erskine and Ralph Branca in the bullpen. I didn't think that Erskine was throwing as good as Branca was that day. Then came the call from the manager (Charlie Dressen). He wanted to know who was throwing the best for us."[5] Sukeforth picked Branca, who then yielded Thomson's pennant-winning home run.

Two months later, on December 2, Sukeforth married thirty-five-year-old Grethel Winchenbach of Waldoboro, Maine, a widow who was fifteen years younger than Clyde. They would remain married until Grethel died in 1999. Grethel was Clyde's second wife. On December 8, 1933, he had married Helen F. Miller of Cincinnati. She died in 1938, about two weeks after the couple's only child—their daughter, Helen—was born.

Although Sukeforth stayed on with Brooklyn for the 1952 season as a coach, the Dodgers fired him when the season ended. Many blamed the Branca choice for his sacking by the Brooklyn brass. Sukeforth moved on to the Pittsburgh Pirates, where Rickey was now the executive vice president and general manager. There, as a coach and an occasional scout, he played a role in the drafting of Roberto Clemente from the Brooklyn organization in the 1954 Rule 5 draft. Sukeforth recalled the discussion that Pirates executives had before the draft.

"[Branch Rickey asked me,] 'Clyde, do you have a candidate?' I said, 'Yes sir, Clemente. Any of you fellas seen Clemente? I saw his arm. I sure did, some question in my mind whether it's better than Furillo's, but I'll guarantee you it's as good, and Furillo had the best arm in the league!'"[6]

Sukeforth retired as a coach at the end of the 1957 season, but he remained in the Pirates organization as a scout and occasional Minor League manager through 1962. He spent the final years of his baseball career as a coach and a scout for the Braves, first in Milwaukee and then in Atlanta.

Sukeforth remained close with many of the players he managed and coached, including Jackie Robinson. Not long before Jackie died in 1972, Clyde saw him for the last time. "I knew Jack wasn't feeling well," he recalled, "so when I heard he was being honored by the Virgin Islands at Mama Leone's restaurant, I figured I'm not going to have many opportunities to see this fellow again. I didn't expect to have to say anything, I just wanted to see Jack, but they asked me to speak.

"I told them I didn't think my part in Jack's career was that important. My relationship with Jack was the same as it would have been with any ballplayer, black or white. He sent me a letter a few days later saying he appreciated my modesty, but he thought I was a little more helpful than that. That was kind of him."[7]

Sukeforth died at age ninety-nine in Waldoboro, Maine, on September 3, 2000. At his request, no services were held. He is buried in Wal-

doboro, and rather miraculously, a fresh baseball can be found on his gravesite at all times.

Among those who remembered Sukeforth fondly was Rachel Robinson, Jackie's widow. After his passing, Mrs. Robinson recalled in an interview, "I stayed in touch with Mr. Sukeforth through the years. He was very kind to both of us. He was probably one of the most influential people in my husband's life, especially getting to the big leagues. Mr. Sukeforth cared about Jackie and our entire family. He never forgot us, nor did we ever forget him."[8]

## Chapter 16. **Burt Shotton**

*Rob Edelman*

Unlike Leo Durocher, the man he replaced as the Brooklyn Dodgers' manager for the 1947 season, Burt Shotton was no gruff, umpire-baiting field general. He was instead a calm, serious baseball lifer who, like the more illustrious Connie Mack, wore his street clothes in the dugout during his tenure in Brooklyn. His quiet demeanor did not win him headlines or make him one of the game's beloved characters. In 1931, when he was managing the Philadelphia Phillies, New York sports columnist John Kieran described him as "one of those strong silent men."[1]

Even though he led the Dodgers to National League pennants in 1947 and 1949, the bespectacled, teetotaling Shotton never earned the respect of the Brooklyn fans for his managerial acumen. Perhaps this would have been different had his team topped the hated New York Yankees at least once in those Fall Classics. Or perhaps his strong and silent persona contributed to his diminished status. Arthur Daley, another observer of the New York sports scene, commented several weeks after Shotton's passing, "Successful as he was, [his] quiet and unspectacular direction left him one of the least-known of all Brooklyn managers."[2] But to his credit, Shotton won more pennants than many other big league skippers, and he guided the Dodgers during one of their most momentous and controversial seasons: 1947, the year Jackie Robinson broke the Major League color line.

Burton Edwin Shotton was born on October 18, 1884, in the township of Brownhelm, Ohio, twenty-eight miles west of Cleveland. He was the second of four children born to John Matthew Shotton and Mary Alice (Bacon) Shotton. He had

Burt Shotton came out of retirement to lead the Dodgers to the pennant.

an older sister, Cora, and two younger brothers, John and Frank. Despite his below-par eyesight, he delighted in playing baseball. Shotton was a left-handed-hitting, right-handed-throwing center fielder, and he possessed blinding speed. He earned the nickname "Barney," reportedly after Barney Oldfield, the celebrated late nineteenth-century/early twentieth-century bicycle/auto racer. As Shotton aged, he became known as Old Barney.

Shotton began his professional career in 1908, batting .244 in twenty-two games for Erie in the Ohio-Pennsylvania League. He reached the Majors the following season, when he made it into seventeen games with the St. Louis Browns. In his first Major League at bat, on September 13, 1909, in Detroit, Shotton singled off George Mullin. He had his first Major League home run, an inside-the-parker, on June 22, 1912, at Comiskey Park off Joe Benz. In 1913 he had twenty-nine outfield assists, second to Tris Speaker, who had thirty.

Shotton remained with the Browns through 1917, when he and shortstop Doc Lavan were dealt to the Washington Senators for pitcher Bert Gallia and $15,000. After spending the 1918 season with the Nats, Shotton was claimed on waivers by the St. Louis Cardinals. He appeared in one game with the Cardinals in 1923, his final big league campaign. During the course of his fourteen seasons in the Majors, the five-foot-eleven 175-pounder played in 1,387 games and had 1,338 hits. His career batting average was .271, and he hit just 9 home runs. As a left-handed batter, he was at his best in the leadoff spot, where he could utilize his speed; during his career, he totaled 293 stolen bases. In 1913 and 1916, he led the American League in walks.

In 1913 Shotton met and befriended the man who would have the most impact on his career. That season Branch Rickey had taken over as manager of the Browns for their final twelve games. From the outset, Rickey respected his fellow Ohioan's soft-spoken personality, grasp of the game's fundamentals, and talent for imparting them to younger players. Rickey had vowed to his mother, a deeply pious woman, that he would avoid ballparks on Sundays. He sensed that he could trust Shotton and, in 1914–15, Burt became the Browns' "Sunday manager." In 1919, after Rickey was hired by the Cardinals as vice president, general manager, and field manager, he acquired Shotton from Washington on waivers.

After retiring as a player, Shotton spent the next two decades in professional baseball. For a good portion of this time, he remained connected to Rickey. He was a Cardinals coach from 1923 through 1925. When Rickey felt overwhelmed by the responsibilities of managing the team on the field and running its front office, he briefly considered hiring Shotton as his on-field replacement.

During the decade, Rickey began investing in Minor League teams, using them to develop players for the parent club. The Cardinals thus became part-owners of the International League Syracuse (New York) Stars, and Rickey named Shotton manager for the 1926 campaign. During his second season, as the Stars won 102 games and finished in second place, Shotton further enhanced his reputation for mentoring younger players. His solid effort at Syracuse led to his becoming manager of the lowly Philadelphia Phillies in 1928. He held the spot for six seasons, but all were undistinguished.

During his debut campaign, Shotton could do little to improve the team's prospects. In a baseball season preview piece, the *New York Times*'s James R. Harrison reported, "By a unanimous vote the Baker misfits have again been consigned to their old berth in the cellar," adding that "the Phillies look as hopeless as ever."[3]

Despite the "amazing amount of fortitude" he brought to the job, Shotton led the Phils to a last-place finish with an abysmal 43-109 record.[4] In 1932, Shotton's best season in Philadelphia, the team ended at 78-76.

During the off-season, when he was away from baseball and inquiring sportswriters, Shotton savored hunting and fishing and what for him was a new pastime: target shooting. In 1929 the novice shooter won top honors in the feature event at the Midwinter Handicap target tournament at Pinehurst, North Carolina.

Despite Shotton's belief that the Phillies would be in the mix for the National League pennant in

ROB EDELMAN

1933, the team finished in seventh place. In December, Shotton was let go by Phillies president Gerry Nugent, and he resurfaced in Cincinnati as a coach under new manager Bob O'Farrell.

Rickey reentered Shotton's professional life in June 1935, hiring him to take over for Eddie Dyer as skipper of the International League Rochester (New York) Red Wings, a Cardinals affiliate. The following season Shotton began managing another Cardinals Minor League team, the Columbus (Ohio) Red Birds of the American Association. In 1937 he led Columbus to the league championship, losing the Junior World Series to the Newark Bears. The Red Birds won the title again four years later. This time, they were the Junior World Series champs, defeating the Montreal Royals, and *The Sporting News* named Shotton Minor League Manager of the Year. During his time with Columbus, Shotton managed such future Cardinals stars as Enos Slaughter, Max Lanier, Mort Cooper, Mickey Owen, Harry Brecheen, Murry Dickson, and Harry Walker.

Shotton remained with the Red Birds through the 1941 season. That December he returned to the Majors as third base coach with the Cleveland Indians, working under player-manager Lou Boudreau. After the 1942 campaign, Rickey became president of the Brooklyn Dodgers and Shotton was rumored to be in line to replace the Dodgers' skipper, Leo Durocher. However, Leo remained the team's manager. Shotton, meanwhile, stayed in Cleveland through the World War II years, leaving the club after the 1945 campaign.

The following year Shotton reunited with Rickey yet again, hiring on with the Dodgers as a scout. Now sixty-two years old, the silver-haired baseball veteran began the 1947 season as supervisor of the team's Minor League training camp in Pensacola, Florida. He considered himself to be in semiretirement and assumed that his on-field baseball career was over.

Meanwhile, Durocher remained the Dodgers'

skipper until April 9, 1947, when baseball commissioner A. B. "Happy" Chandler meted out a one-year suspension to him "as a result of the accumulation of unpleasant incidents, in which he [Durocher] had been involved, which the commissioner construes as detrimental to baseball."[5] In Durocher's absence, Clyde Sukeforth, one of his coaches, took over the team for two games. But Sukeforth preferred life in the coaching box to the daily stresses that came with managing. As a more permanent replacement, Rickey initially tried to hire Joe McCarthy, the longtime New York Yankees skipper, who had quit the team midway through the previous season. After McCarthy turned him down, Rickey called on Shotton.

On April 17 Rickey shot off a telegram to Shotton at his home in Bartow, Florida. "Be in Brooklyn tomorrow morning," he instructed. "See nobody. Say nothing."[6] Shotton complied, arriving at the Dodgers' headquarters on Montague Street the next morning. Rickey apprised him of the situation and offered him the post as Durocher's replacement.

Shotton accepted the offer, and the appointment became official at noon on April 18. The announcement was brief and succinct: "Burton Edwin Shotton has accepted the management of the Brooklyn Dodgers and will take charge of the team today."[7] By 1:30 p.m., the new skipper, garbed in topcoat and gray fedora, was ensconced in the visiting team's dugout at the Polo Grounds. The *New York Times*'s John Drebinger observed that Shotton "appeared on the scene like something whisked out of a magician's closet by Prof. Branch Rickey."[8] When asked to comment on the day's events, Shotton could only utter, "It was a complete surprise to me."[9]

The Dodgers' new skipper did not sign a contract and had no idea of his salary. "I'm just here," he added. "I haven't had a contract in all the years I've held jobs with Mr. Rickey as a player, manager, or coach, so I didn't think it necessary to bother about one now."[10] He observed that he would not be dressing in a team uniform. "That's part of the deal," he noted. "I took it off for the last time several years ago. Anyway, with the bunch of coaches we have on this club, why should I?"[11] While in the dugout, Shotton wore his street clothes, along with his gold-rimmed spectacles. On some occasions, he added a team cap and warm-up jacket or windbreaker with "Dodgers" emblazoned on its front. On warmer, sunnier days, he was decked out in slacks, a sports shirt, and a wide-brimmed hat.

When he came to Brooklyn, Shotton was completely unfamiliar with the team. "As soon as I think I know something about the club and can help, I'll start to work," he explained. "Until then, I'll just watch."[12]

Unlike in Philadelphia, Shotton was armed with a talented ball team. While the Dodgers finished the 1947 campaign with a 94-60 record and the National League flag, Shotton's impact on the team extended beyond won-lost records. Under Durocher, celebrities from George Raft to Danny Kaye to New York City mayor William O'Dwyer were a regular presence in the Ebbets Field clubhouse. Now, the atmosphere in the team's locker room and manager's office was more subdued.

Additionally, Shotton exhibited an even-handed confidence in his team, especially in his younger players. Early in the season, during the Dodgers' first western trip, rookie hurler Harry Taylor had a rough outing against Cincinnati. The Dodgers' hierarchy wanted to dispatch the pitcher to the Minors, but Shotton was convinced that Taylor had it in him to be a successful big leaguer. He expressed this view to the front office and repeated it to Taylor. The youngster responded with a slew of solid outings before pulling a tendon in his arm in August. He finished the season with a 10-5 record and a nifty 3.11 ERA.

But most significantly, Shotton had the distinction of being Jackie Robinson's first full-time Major League skipper. Robinson's reception among his teammates and opponents has been well documented. Perhaps it would have been more tumultuous had he had a firecracker for a manager. Even though Shotton was the Dodgers' skipper out of necessity rather than choice, his even temperament allowed Robinson an easier fit in the clubhouse and helped the entire team meld into a pennant winner.

On September 22 the idle Dodgers clinched the National League flag when the second-place Cardinals lost to the Chicago Cubs. "It's been a long pull, but a pleasant one," Shotton observed. "I'll congratulate the boys when they report at Ebbets Field tomorrow for the game with the Giants."[13] At sixty-two years and eleven months, he was the oldest manager ever to make his World Series debut.

After the New York Yankees defeated the Dodgers in the Series, four games to three, Shotton admitted that the better team won. But he also predicted that the Dodgers "will beat the Yankees during the next ten years a whale of a lot more times than they will beat us."[14] However, the question of the moment was whether Shotton would lead the Dodgers to those victories.

Throughout the 1947 season, Durocher told the media that he definitely would return as Dodgers skipper once his ban was lifted. Shotton usually responded to such declarations with a polite "No comment." When the Dodgers won the pennant, Rickey told the press that he was "pleased with manager Burt Shotton."[15] Yet Durocher was present for all seven World Series games. Immediately after the Series, fans and sportswriters began speculating as to who would manage the club in 1948.

Rickey began the off-season by conferring with Shotton and his coaches on the club's weaknesses and strengths. Rickey met with Durocher and his wife, actress Laraine Day, for three-plus hours on the evening before they returned to California, and the ex-skipper fully expected reinstatement.

By early December, after being assured by Chandler that the commissioner's office would

ROB EDELMAN

not oppose the move, Rickey decided to reinstate Durocher. The announcement came on December 6. "I'm right where I was before," Shotton, ever the loyal soldier, told reporters. "I'm going back to Bartow as soon as I can leave here. I didn't expect to manage last season, nor did I expect to manage the Dodgers next year."[16]

Shotton remained with the club as a supervisor of Minor League managers. He said Rickey had been considering him for this position for several years. "I didn't want to take it if I had to travel all over the system looking at different minor-league managers," he noted, "but when Rick said: 'How about going back to Bartow, being your own boss and going where and when you please,' why, I said okay."[17]

For the upcoming season, Durocher reportedly was willing to step aside as manager of the 1948 National League All-Star team in favor of Shotton. But NL president Ford Frick announced that according to Major League rules, an All-Star Game manager must be under Major League contract. Only Durocher, the reinstated skipper, could lead the squad.

In January 1948 the New York chapter of the Baseball Writers' Association held a private party in Shotton's honor. That month, he declared, "Never again will I manage a ball club."[18] With the arrival of April and the start of the baseball season, Durocher was in the Brooklyn dugout and Shotton was back at the Dodgers' training camp in Vero Beach, Florida, evaluating Minor Leaguers in the morning and spending the afternoon bass fishing. But this routine was fated to be upended yet again. On July 16, in a move that stunned the baseball world, Durocher abruptly left the Dodgers and signed to manage the New York Giants, who had fired their skipper, Mel Ott. Reportedly, Horace Stoneham, the Giants' principal owner, wanted to sign Shotton. However, when Rickey offered him a choice between Shotton and Durocher, he selected Durocher.

Once again it was Shotton to the rescue in Brooklyn as Rickey called on him to take over the Dodgers. The mood of the moment in Brooklyn was summed up by one anonymous fan, who observed, "That Branch Rickey sure is a smart guy. He gets rid of a manager who is liked by only half the people and hires a new one that everyone likes for a lot less money."[19]

Shotton joined the Dodgers in Cincinnati and immediately got down to the business of running the team. The 48-33 record he compiled was more than respectable; however, the team ended the campaign in third place, trailing Boston and St. Louis. At the close of the season—and despite rumors that just-deposed New Yankees manager Bucky Harris would be signed to lead the Dodgers—Rickey announced that Shotton would stay on as manager in 1949.

For the first time, Shotton began the new season as the Dodgers' skipper. From the outset, he confidently predicted that the team would return to the World Series. And so it did, as he led the Dodgers to a 97-57 record and a first-place finish. Despite his even temperament, Shotton was capable of spewing venom when he deemed it necessary. In mid-May the Dodgers dropped three straight games to the Boston Braves, and Shotton, according to Associated Press writer Joe Reichler, "ripped into his players with a tongue-lashing the likes of which they had not heard since the departure of Leo Durocher."[20]

The Dodgers again faced the Yankees in the Fall Classic, and again they were beaten, this time by four games to one. Rickey defended Shotton, whose decision making—and, in particular, his handling of the pitching staff during the Series—was questioned by fans. "The manager did not lose this series," he observed. "Both [New York skipper] Casey Stengel and Shotton played sound baseball. I have no criticism to make of the way Shotton handled our men and I daresay the players hold the same opinion."[21]

So Shotton remained on board as the Dodgers' skipper. Upon signing for the 1950 season, he declared, "We have a great club. It will win the pennant again and I think that it also can win the World Series."[22] What Shotton did not count on was the full emergence of the Whiz Kids of Philadelphia. His former team won the pennant on the first day of October, when Dick Sisler smacked a dramatic home run off Don Newcombe in the tenth inning for a 4–1 victory. At 89-65, the Dodgers finished in second place, two games behind the Phillies.

Before the year's All-Star Game, Shotton found himself at the center of a minor brouhaha. As skipper of the league champions, he was set to manage the National League All-Stars. His starting outfielders were Enos Slaughter, Ralph Kiner, and Hank Sauer, none of whom was a center fielder. Shotton might have started Slaughter in center, because he possessed the speed to play the position, but he decided to bench Sauer and replace him with Duke Snider. Of course, Snider was Shotton's player, but Sauer was a Chicago Cub, and the game was to be played in Chicago's Comiskey Park. Windy City fans were livid. When Shotton was introduced as the NL skipper, he reportedly was booed for five minutes. In the meantime, Happy Chandler ordered Shotton to play Sauer. He had no choice but to comply, and he started Sauer in right field. In the end, the NL emerged victorious with a fourteen-inning 4–3 victory.

This controversy, and the Dodgers' second-place finish, did not necessarily doom Shotton's future in Brooklyn. What did was the event that occurred on October 16, 1950. On that date the Dodgers failed to renew Rickey's contract. He was replaced as team president by Walter O'Malley. The following month, Rickey sold his 25 percent interest in the team and signed a five-year contract as general manager and executive vice president of the Pittsburgh Pirates.

While Shotton was Rickey's man, he still hoped to remain with the Dodgers. But O'Malley surely was not pleased when Rickey joined Shotton on a hunting trip in Virginia. This action indicated that the skipper had remained in Rickey's corner—and so he would not be the right man to manage in Brooklyn in 1951. On November 28 Shotton was replaced by Charlie Dressen.

Shotton deeply resented his unceremonious firing. "The deal I got this time made me a little sour," he declared the week after Dressen was hired.[23] Yet he remained a Dodgers loyalist, and he was stunned and disappointed when the team lost the 1951 pennant to the Giants on Bobby Thomson's "Shot Heard 'Round the World."

Not surprisingly, Shotton was rumored to be joining Rickey in Pittsburgh. "I would like to get back into baseball," he said in an October 1951 interview, "but no one has anything where I could fit in."[24] No offers were forthcoming, and the sixty-six-year-old became a full-time retiree.

Shotton remained in Florida for the final decade of his life. He held one last baseball job. In 1960 Rickey hired him as a consultant for the Continental League, his planned third Major League, and as the supervisor of managers in the Class D Western Carolina League, which would supply the new league with ballplayers.

Shotton died of a heart attack on July 30, 1962, while at his Lake Wales home. He was survived by his wife, the former Mary Louise Daly, whom he had married in 1909, and two sons, Burt Shotton Jr. and Dr. James Shotton, a veterinarian.

History has not been sympathetic toward Shotton. However, according to accounts written during his managerial stints, he was a players' advocate. After the 1947 season, Shotton was casually referred to in *Time* magazine as "well-liked."[25] The following year, upon rejoining the team after Leo Durocher's departure, he was vocally supported by a number of Dodgers. "I love playing for Shotton," said Jackie Robinson. "When Shotton wants to bawl out a player he takes him aside and

ROB EDELMAN

does it in private. That gives you a sort of lift."[26] While acknowledging that he was a Durocher fan, Pee Wee Reese observed, "I think Shotton has a great way with young ballplayers, maybe does better with some of them than Leo did. Burt is a good manager, no mistake about that."[27]

Decades later, Carl Furillo, while being interviewed by Peter Golenbock, referred to Shotton as "a prince."[28] Don Newcombe called him "a damn nice man."[29] Carl Erskine, while noting that Shotton was "from the old school," labeled him "an outstanding man" and "a class individual."[30] Ralph Branca, however, expressed a different point of view, telling Golenbock that Shotton "just wasn't competent enough to be a big league manager, except he was a friend of Rickey's."[31]

According to Branca, the Dodgers won in spite of their manager. Rex Barney added, "I was anti-Shotton. I thought the game got by him, and I didn't like the cute things he did, like not wearing a uniform on the bench." He also described Shotton as "cold and indifferent."[32]

This dichotomy also existed with relation to Shotton's handling of the race issue. On May 25, 1947, in what was described as his breakthrough game, Jackie Robinson spearheaded a 5–3 victory over the Phillies. Afterward, Shotton declared, "[Jackie] has finally become relaxed and is playing the kind of ball that earned him his major-league chance." After dissecting Robinson's early-season problems, he concluded, in a remark that indicated he was well aware of Jackie's anxiety, "Guess he had too much on his mind."[33] Red Barber further observed that the manager was a calming influence in the Dodgers' clubhouse throughout the 1947 season. Roger Kahn, on the other hand, believed that Shotton "simply ignored the terrible racial tension tormenting Jackie Robinson."[34]

In November 1947, *Time* magazine readers offered suggestions for its Man of the Year. They included President Harry Truman, Secretary of State George C. Marshall, General Douglas MacArthur, Senator Robert A. Taft, Senator Arthur H. Vandenberg, Arturo Toscanini, Yehudi Menuhin—and Burton Edwin Shotton. W. R. Puffer of El Segundo, California, proclaimed that by "demonstrating that the vulgar crudities . . . are not, essentially, an integral part of a winning baseball team, Mr. Shotton has given a renewed respect, a freshened impulse, to our National Pastime."[35] Yet Shotton's lack of flair did not endear him to those local sportswriters who preferred covering the more flamboyant—and more quotable—Durocher. One of them, the *Daily News*'s Dick Young, sarcastically referred to Shotton in print as KOBS (or Kindly Old Burt Shotton).[36]

This point of view was emphasized in Shotton's *New York Times* obituary. Its unnamed author wrote that Shotton was "the kind of manager whose gentle and at times austere touch confused many. Perhaps his attitude was too kindly for hardened major-league baseball players. He led the Dodgers to National League pennants in 1947 and 1949, but the fans in Brooklyn did not accord him the tributes he deserved."[37]

The writer continued, "Mr. Shotton was never particularly popular with players, fans, or writers covering the game. But he had a kindness that few understood."[38]

# Chapter 17. **Ray Blades**

*Russell Wolinsky*

On April 9, 1947, the *New York Post*'s back-page headline screamed, "DUROCHER SUSPENDED FOR SEASON: BLADES LIKELY TO TAKE OVER JOB."[1] That Ray Blades, recently hired to replace Charlie Dressen as Durocher's first lieutenant, would succeed the recently suspended Brooklyn manager seemed a reasonable supposition. After all, he had assumed the managerial reins when Durocher left the club's spring training site for a few days in mid-March. A week later, Branch Rickey chose his old friend Burt Shotton as Durocher's successor.

Blades too had a relationship with Rickey, one that dated back to 1919, when the Rickey-managed St. Louis Cardinals traveled to Mount Vernon, Illinois, for an exhibition game against the local semipro Carbuilders. Blades, a Mount Vernon native, was at second base for the home team. Francis Raymond Blades had been born there on August 6, 1896, one of eight children of Francis Marion and Mary Magdalene Blades.

The Cardinals, with Rogers Hornsby in the lineup, were beaten by the scrappy locals 2–1. Impressed by the Carbuilders' high-quality play and hustle, Rickey immediately signed three of their players, including Blades, who was twenty-three years old and a veteran of the World War.

The switch-hitting Blades made his professional debut with Memphis of the Southern Association in 1920, and then he moved to Houston of the Texas League the following year. He remained with the Buffaloes for two seasons, where at the urging of Rickey he abandoned switch hitting and became a right-handed batter exclusively.

Blades was batting a league-leading .330 with

Ray Blades was expected by some in the media to replace the suspended Leo Durocher as Brooklyn's manager, but he remained the team's third base coach.

Houston when the Cardinals called him up on August 18, 1922. He made his Major League debut the following afternoon at Sportsman's Park, playing left field and batting sixth. He stroked a single in four at bats in an 8–7 Cardinals loss to Philadelphia. Playing thirty-seven games in his rookie season, the five-foot-seven, 163-pound Blades batted an even .300.

Primarily a second baseman, Ray had committed 142 errors in three Minor League campaigns. His uneven fielding at second base and the presence of Rogers Hornsby at the keystone position for St. Louis necessitated a switch.

Either Rickey or Cardinals coach Burt Shotton suggested to Ray that his best chance to remain with the Cardinals was either at third base or in the outfield. Blades tried the hot corner first: "[Shotton] hit ten balls to me. I missed nine of them, picked up the tenth, and threw it into the stands."[2] After that final muff at third, the Cardinals decided that Blades was best suited for the outfield.[3]

The tragic death of twenty-seven-year-old Cardinals left fielder Austin McHenry in November 1922 created a void at the position for Blades to fill. "No one ever worked longer or harder to stick in the majors [and master outfield play]," wrote Chicago sportswriter Edgar Munzel. "Finally he earned the accolade as one of the finest defensive gardeners in the NL."[4] His fielding in left improved to the point where Hornsby would opine in a syndicated column, "I always figured Ray Blades and Ross Youngs . . . as two of the greatest outfielders in the game."[5]

Blades, who had a career on-base percentage of .395, never changed his hitting philosophy: "Just deaden the ball a little." After a terrific 1925 season, he was recognized as one of the best lead-off batters in the game. Appearing in 122 games, he batted .342, with a .423 on-base percentage and a .535 slugging average. During one stretch, he reached base in fifty-four consecutive games. Blades marked another milestone in 1925: in October, he married Ruth Bennett.

On August 17, 1926, a gray, drizzly afternoon in St. Louis, Blades raced toward the left-field wall in an attempt to snare a drive hit by Brooklyn's Gus Felix. He climbed a recently erected chicken-wire fence strung along the outfield wall and got a spike caught in the mesh fence. Ray had to be helped off the field, suffering what was originally reported as a badly bruised kneecap.

His leg set in a plaster cast, Blades returned home to Illinois. Aside from a pinch-hitting appearance on August 27, he was unable to play again in 1926. That December, Blades had surgery on the knee for a series of badly torn ligaments. The operation was a success, though Blades walked with a slight limp for the remainder of his life.

Ray returned to action in May 1927, but he was never the same player. The surgery had robbed him of much of his speed. Whatever power he had at the plate was gone as well. After a 1928 season in which he had a mere eighty-five at bats and hit a career-low .235, Blades spent 1929 back in the Minors playing for St. Louis farm clubs in Rochester and Houston.

The Cardinals signed him as a player-coach for the 1930 season, but there was really nowhere for him to coach; manager Gabby Street was at third and Buzzy Wares was at first. He batted only 101 times during the season, compiling a surprising .396 average. An errant pitch by teammate Wild Bill Hallahan during spring training had shattered the bone in his left foot, necessitating more surgery that December.

By 1932 Blades knew his days as a big league player were over. On May 8 there was another collision with the wall at Sportsman's Park, this time in right field. He played eighty games for St. Louis, more than in any season since 1926, but hit just .229. In 1933 Blades, now thirty-six, took over as manager of the Columbus Red Birds, the Cardinals' affiliate in the American Association. As a player-manager, he led the club to Junior World Series championships in 1933 and 1934.

By 1934 the American Association had suspended Blades three times and fined him even more often, usually for infractions concerning abusive language to umpires. He was suspended again in 1935, this time for encouraging his players to stall in a game against Minneapolis.

After Columbus, Blades managed Rochester in the International League for three years with mixed results. He led the Red Wings to a second-place finish in 1936, a disappointing sixth-place finish in 1937, and a third-place finish in 1938. Then, on November 6, 1938, the Cardinals named Blades to succeed manager Frankie Frisch.

Blades immediately began shaping an unsettled club in his own image. If the rookie pilot had one advantage taking over the St. Louis managerial reins, it was that at either Columbus or Rochester he had led sixteen members of the current big league squad.

Blades's pitching philosophy, in an era in which pitchers were expected to complete, or nearly complete, their starts, became the most controversial aspect of his managerial style. "My idea is never to save anybody for tomorrow. . . . Let's win today's game today. . . . Save a man for tomorrow and you may lose two games. I'll relieve with anyone who can relieve. . . . There won't be any regular rotation necessarily. . . . In a short series I believe in trying to beat the other club's best pitcher with my best pitcher. And with all my pitchers if necessary."[6] St. Louis's forty-five complete games were the lowest in the Major Leagues in 1939.

The Cardinals won ninety-two games and finished just two games behind Cincinnati. Blades summed up the season philosophically: "We gave 'em a good fight, didn't we?"[7] On November 14 Breadon rewarded him with another one-year pact.

In 1940 Johnny Mize, Joe Medwick, shortstop Jimmy Brown and his replacement, Marty Marion, and center fielder Terry Moore all suffered injuries. The pitching collapsed and Blades panicked. Going into June, neither Curt Davis nor Mort Cooper had won a single game. The manager began yanking hurlers with abandon: he used eighty-six pitchers in the first thirty games with only six going the distance. St. Louis finished in sixth place, thirteen and a half games behind Cincinnati.

With the drop in the standings came an expected decrease at the gate. A paid crowd of 7,661 for the June 2 doubleheader against Philadelphia "was one of the smallest Sunday doubleheader crowds in years."[8] Sam Breadon took note. The hammer fell on June 7. Breadon made the change without even consulting Rickey, replacing Blades with Billy Southworth, who had succeeded Blades as the manager at Rochester.

Ray returned home to McLeansboro, Illinois, where he had his first summer vacation in twenty years. Wishing to remain in baseball, he returned to the Southern Association, where his professional baseball career had begun in 1920. In December he accepted a position as skipper of the league's New Orleans club, a Dodgers affiliate.

Blades led the Pelicans to a surprising third-place finish in 1941 and then spent 1942 as a coach with the Cincinnati Reds. He resigned after the season and returned to New Orleans, where in 1943 the Pelicans finished first in the season's second half. After three controversial seasons managing the American Association's St. Paul Saints, which culminated in his abrupt resignation during the 1946 playoffs, the Dodgers chose him to replace the departed Dressen.

Blades was "given credit for much of the smart playing by the Dodgers" in 1947, wrote *The Sporting News*.[9] His baseball experience and acumen added new dimensions to a Brooklyn club devoid of its spiritual leader, Durocher. Regardless of his baseball "smarts," Blades's coaching was sometimes criticized while he was with Brooklyn. "Ray Blades unaccountably sent Carl Furillo home [on a ground ball to Yankees shortstop Phil Rizzuto] where he was a dead pigeon all the way," wrote Arthur Daley in his game account of 1947 World Series Game Seven, which Brooklyn lost. "[A] sepulchral voice in the press box asked, 'Is Charlie Dressen still coaching at third?' It was the nastiest crack of the series."[10]

In August 1948 Blades traded coaching assignments with Jake Pitler; Ray switched to the first base box while Pitler moved to third. In October, Rickey took him off the playing field altogether and named him troubleshooter for the Dodgers' Minor League system.

Ray remained with Brooklyn, chiefly as a scout, for two more seasons. In November 1950 Marty Marion was named to manage the Cardinals. One of Marion's first personnel decisions was to hire the fifty-four-year-old Blades, his first Major League manager, as "supervisor" and third base coach.

Blades was released from the St. Louis organization for the final time in October 1951, for what owner Fred Saigh described as "economic reasons." Ray was believed to have been the highest paid of the four Cardinals coaches, a number the owner believed was too many.

Another round of knee surgery kept Ray out of baseball entirely in 1952, but an old baseball acquaintance was there to bring him back. Wid Matthews, who had worked with Blades in New Orleans in 1943, was now personnel director of the Chicago Cubs. Matthews hired Blades to serve as a "coach-scout . . . a sort of personal handyman." (The "coach-scout" contract would be voided by the commissioner's office—scouts did not receive pension benefits—and eventually was changed to call for coach's duties alone.)

He performed both duties for Chicago, regardless of the wording of his contract, and became the first-ever advance scout for the franchise.[11] Ray was among the Chicago brain trust to scout, and highly rate, future Hall of Fame shortstop Ernie Banks. On October 11, 1956, Ray Blades retired from professional baseball at the age of sixty.

*Washington Post* columnist Shirley Povich caught up with Blades at the Laurel Park racetrack in Maryland in 1962. Ray was "chauffeuring" the spread-eagle starting gate. "All I do is steer," the sixty-five-year-old baseball retiree said of his new career.

Blades remained a visible member of the St. Louis Cardinals family. He was on hand on the weekend of August 5–6, 1961, for the thirtieth anniversary of the 1931 champions. In March 1976, the 1926 world champion team was given a golden-anniversary salute by St. Louis writers. Blades, who neither smoked nor drank, and catcher Bob O'Farrell, both seventy-nine years old, were the oldest of the ten surviving team members. Two years later, his high-school baseball uniform was retired. "The greatest baseball man to ever play at McLeansboro High School," read a plaque in front of Blades's glass-encased jersey.

Ruth Bennett Blades, Ray's wife, died on January 30, 1968, in Mount Vernon. They had no children. In 1970 Ray married Ruth Daley Wright. He died on May 18, 1979, at Abraham Lincoln Hospital in Lincoln, Illinois. He was eighty-three years old. In addition to his wife, he was survived by a stepdaughter.

# Chapter 18. **Spider Jorgensen**

*William H. Johnson*

| AGE | G | AB | R | H | 2B | 3B | HR | TB | RBI | BB | SO | BAV | OBP | SLG | SB | GDP | HBP |
|-----|-----|-----|-----|-----|-----|-----|-----|-----|-----|-----|-----|-----|-----|-----|-----|-----|-----|
| 27 | 129 | 441 | 57 | 121 | 29 | 8 | 5 | 181 | 67 | 58 | 45 | .274 | .360 | .410 | 4 | 5 | 1 |

On April 15, 1947, in Brooklyn, New York, an African American player took the field in a Major League baseball game for the first time in the modern baseball era. In descriptions of Jackie Robinson's arrival, there is rarely mention of another rookie who debuted for the Brooklyn Dodgers that afternoon, a third baseman who batted seventh and wore No. 21, Spider Jorgensen.

John Donald Jorgensen was born on November 3, 1919, in Folsom, California, near Sacramento. He was the seventh child (along with two sisters and four brothers) of Walter and Winifred (Carney) Jorgensen. Walter, the son of a Danish-born father and Irish American mother, was a California-born dredge operator in the Sacramento River delta. Winifred, also born in California, was the daughter of Irish immigrants. There is little documentation regarding Jorgensen's early life or scholastic athletic career. At Folsom High School, from which he graduated in 1936, John acquired the nickname "Spider." In the June 1998 issue of *Baseball Digest*, sportswriter Phil Elderkin wrote that the nickname came from a pair of black shorts with an orange stripe down the side that Jorgensen wore playing basketball. "The weekend before, a teacher had been cleaning out a woodshed and had to kill a black widow spider," Jorgensen related. "When he saw me, he told everyone I reminded him of the spider."

A proposed scholarship to study business at the University of Santa Clara fell through; consequently, Jorgensen spent two years at various jobs in Sacramento and playing baseball in the semipro Sacramento Winter League. In 1939, and again in 1941, he played baseball at Sacramento City Col-

Spider Jorgensen's only Major League season as a regular was 1947.

lege. A second baseman when he entered college, he was moved to third base when the team's regular third baseman was injured.

In 1940 Jorgensen participated in a Dodgers tryout camp run by scout Tom Downey in San Mateo, California. He performed well enough that, in 1941, after he had finished at Sacramento City College, scouts Downey and Bill Svilich persuaded him to sign a contract with Brooklyn. The twenty-one-year-old left-handed-hitting infielder was assigned to the Dodgers' Santa Barbara team in the Class C California League. There, in his first pro season, Jorgensen appeared in 140 games and batted .332 with 9 home runs and 43 doubles. Although he also made 48 errors at third base, he still was named the league's Most Valuable Player, as Santa Barbara won the league championship.

The Japanese attack on Pearl Harbor put Jorgensen's career on a four-year hold. On February 17, 1942, he enlisted in the U.S. Army. He was assigned to the Army Air Corps, and during the war reached the rank of technical sergeant while serving at duty stations in Idaho, Arizona, and Texas. In Texas he met Lenore Jones and married her in October 1946. In addition to Lenore's two children from a previous marriage, the couple had a daughter, Jonel. Spider and Lenore remained married until her passing in 1995.

Jorgensen was discharged in 1945, and in 1946 he reported to the Class Triple-A Montreal Royals, the Dodgers' affiliate in the International League. At Montreal, Spider became part of an infield that included Jackie Robinson at second and future Dodgers general manager Al Campanis at shortstop. Jorgensen hit .293 in 117 games with the Royals.

After spring training in Cuba in 1947, Jorgensen assumed he was heading back to Montreal. But injuries to veteran infielders Cookie Lavagetto and Arky Vaughan forced the Dodgers to keep him. Jorgensen told writer Phil Elderkin, "I came into Ebbets Field on Opening Day, scared to death. I didn't think I was going to play. I didn't have any equipment with me. My glove, bats, everything else went to Syracuse because the Montreal club opened up there. Then Jackie comes over and says 'Here, use my second base glove.' He was going to play first base. So I used his glove and borrowed a pair of spikes and I'm in the lineup. So I really didn't have time to get nervous."

Spider logged a walk and an RBI in three at bats

that day. Two days later, on April 17, he had what proved to be one of his best days in the Majors, driving in six runs on a home run and two doubles. In the twenty-seven-year-old rookie's only Major League season as a regular, he played 128 games at third base and hit .274, with twenty-nine doubles and eight triples. Dan Daniel, writing in the August 13 edition of *The Sporting News*, called him the "best of the hot corner rookies." Jorgensen played in all seven games in the World Series loss to the Yankees that fall, getting four hits with three runs batted in.

During the winter the five-foot-nine, 155-pound Jorgensen bruised his arm—due to the recoil from a hunting rifle—and then damaged it permanently by throwing too aggressively in spring training. In April, manager Leo Durocher told *The Sporting News* not to be surprised if Jorgensen was his starting third baseman again in 1948. But, most likely due to the sore arm, Jorgensen started the season as a reserve and was replaced at third base by the newly acquired Billy Cox.

Jorgensen was left in St. Louis on June 6 after a series with the Cardinals for further testing of his arm and shoulder. He did not get into any more games, and within two weeks the Dodgers sent him to their American Association farm team in St. Paul. It was the beginning of the end of Jorgensen's Major League career. While he had hit .300 in 31 Dodgers games in 1948, he appeared in only 107 Major League games after that season.

Spider was a Dodgers reserve in 1949, and he played in his second World Series that fall, hitting just .182 (2 for 11) with two doubles. On May 17, 1950, after appearing in only two games, the Dodgers sold Jorgensen to the New York Giants for what *The Sporting News* described as likely well over the $10,000 waiver price. The thirty-year-old infielder played in twenty-four games for the Giants with 5 hits in 37 at bats. He also played in sixty-four games for the Class Triple-A Minneapolis Millers, batting .330 in 215 at bats.

Spider played his final game in the Majors on June 30, 1951, flying out as a pinch hitter. The next day the Giants traded Jorgensen, hitting just .235, and pitcher Red Hardy to the Oakland Oaks of the Pacific Coast League for outfielder Earl Rapp.

Between 1951 and 1955, Jorgensen played third base, shortstop, and the outfield for the Oaks under managers Mel Ott, Augie Galan, Charlie Dressen, and Lefty O'Doul. In 1956 the Vancouver Mounties replaced Oakland in the league, and in 1957 the Mounties became a Baltimore Orioles farm club. Spider continued to parlay his reliable defense and sufficient offensive skill into three more years of professional baseball. His regular playing career ended after the 1958 season, but the forty-year-old returned to the Dodgers' family the next year as a spring training mentor, and then coached for the Mounties during the season.

His skill in dealing with younger players garnered positive attention, so in 1960 Spider was named player-manager (although he played in just four games) of the Dodgers' Great Falls (Montana) Electrics in the Class C Pioneer League. The next season Jorgensen dropped a level to manage the Artesia (New Mexico) Dodgers of the Class D Sophomore League. That league was a purely instructional entity and Jorgensen remained at that level in 1962, shifting within the organization to the St. Petersburg Saints of the Florida State League.

After the 1962 season with St. Petersburg, Jorgensen left professional baseball and returned to his home in Sacramento. However, he could not stay away from the sport. Although unpaid, he put his knowledge and experience to work coaching amateur baseball, serving as head coach of the Fair Oaks American Legion team, a squad that won the Legion North Division championship in 1967. Jorgensen may have had more raw talent on that Legion team than on any of the three Minor League teams he had managed, as the squad was led by future Major League star Dusty Baker. In a 2010 book, *How to Be Like Jackie Robinson*, Baker, by then the manager of the Cincinnati Reds, was quoted as saying, "In all the time he coached us, I never knew Spider played for the Dodgers. I knew he was a terrific coach, but he never once mentioned he was a former player."

In 1969 Jorgensen returned to professional baseball as a scout and spring training instructor for the Kansas City Royals. As a scout, he was directly responsible for signing future Major Leaguers Greg Minton, Doug Bird, and John Wathan. He also had a stint of sixty-nine games managing the Royals' Winnepeg Goldeyes in the short-season Northern League.

After Kansas City, Jorgensen scouted for the Philadelphia Phillies for a few years, and found pitcher Bob Walk, among others. As a scout for the Chicago Cubs, he persuaded the team to draft Mark Grace, who proved to be one of the finest hitters of the 1990s.

Years later, in an obituary written by Jim Gazzolo, others commented on Spider's scouting ability and on his character. "I don't think there is a person in the world who didn't love him," Ontario High baseball coach Bob Beck told Gazzolo. "To my knowledge, he didn't have an enemy in the world. He had an unassuming manner about himself. He was just very friendly, accommodating, but he didn't miss a trick. He always knew what was going on."

In 1996 Jorgensen was a member of the first group of inductees into the Sacramento City College Athletic Hall of Fame. A baseball man to the end, Jorgensen was still scouting locally for the Cubs when he died on November 6, 2003, at San Antonio Hospital in Rancho Cucamonga, California, three days after his eighty-fourth birthday. He is inurned at Lakeside Memorial Lawn Cemetery in Folsom, California.

# Chapter 19. **Hal Gregg**

*James L. Ray*

| AGE | W | L | PCT. | ERA | G | GS | GF | CG | SHO | SV | IP | H | BB | SO | HBP | WP |
|-----|---|---|------|-----|---|----|----|----|-----|----|-----|-----|----|----|-----|----|
| 25 | 4 | 5 | .444 | 5.87 | 37 | 16 | 5 | 2 | 1 | 1 | 104.1 | 115 | 55 | 59 | 4 | 1 |

We often read or hear about pitchers developing arm strength and accuracy in their youth by throwing rocks at a target. Hal Gregg's missile of choice was citrus—specifically, an orange. Born in Anaheim, California, on July 21, 1921, Harold Dana Gregg grew up on an orange farm. His parents, Calvin and Margaret (Smylmo) Gregg, were orange farmers, and they had a large grove right behind the family house.

Young Hal had no interest in baseball; he wanted to be like his father. At a very young age, he began working on the farm: planting, picking, watering, and doing every chore his father assigned him. Hal competed with the other workers during breaks to see who could "pick" an orange off a branch by firing another orange at it.

Although he didn't play baseball in his youth or adolescence, he developed a feeling for the game by watching his older brother. James Gregg was a standout baseball player in high school and eventually played some semipro ball. Hal had another brother, Malcolm, born in 1914, two years after James.

One day James noticed that his little brother could throw as hard and as far as he could. Accordingly, he encouraged Hal to try baseball, but the younger Gregg wanted no part of the game. He wanted to go to work. It was the heart of the Great Depression. Money was tight. Jobs were scarce. So when he was offered a job at a local feed mill loading 160-pound sacks of grain onto trucks, Hal jumped at the opportunity. The decision would affect him for the rest of his life.

Teenagers rarely got such chances to work at what was then considered a good job, but even as

Hal Gregg was the Dodgers' winning pitcher in the historic 1947 opener.

a fifteen-year-old Hal was already very big and very strong. (He eventually grew to a height of 6 feet 3½ and a weight of 195 pounds.) He used that brawn to load the trucks with those heavy sacks. It was brutally hard work. After a couple of years, the repeated stress of lifting more than thirty tons of grain every day—about 375 sacks—

87

took its toll on young Hal's back. He tried to work through the pain, but eventually strained his back to the point where he had to give up his career as a sack-thrower.

Although Hal was already eighteen years old and had never competed in a real baseball game, James encouraged him to sign up for the Dodgers' baseball school in Long Beach, California. Feeling he had nothing to lose, and knowing he could throw harder than anyone he had ever met, Hal signed up.

While at the school, he impressed Dodgers scout Ted McGrew, who later boasted that he had made up his mind to give Gregg a Minor League chance after seeing the youngster throw only two fastballs. Gregg did not begin his Minor League career until the next spring (1941), when he debuted as a relief pitcher for the Santa Barbara Saints of the Class C California League.

Gregg made only four appearances for the Saints before the Dodgers assigned him to the Olean (New York) Oilers of the Class D PONY League. He was an unimpressive 1-5 for Olean with an earned run average of 4.59. Moreover, the repetition of the pitching movement had again worn down his fragile back. In midseason Gregg threw a hard fastball and heard something crack. He later found out that he had dislodged a vertebra. The team sent him to the Johns Hopkins University Hospital in Baltimore, where surgeons removed a bone from one of Hal's ribs and used it as a replacement vertebra for the one he had ruined. The surgery gave Gregg little relief; nevertheless, he forged ahead with his pitching career.

In 1942, the first wartime season, Hal was back playing for Santa Barbara. He was 4-6 with a 3.66 ERA when the league folded at the end of June because too many players had been drafted. Gregg had tried to enlist the day after Pearl Harbor, but his draft board classified him as 4-F because of his back.

In the fall Gregg headed to the hospital again, where he underwent more surgery, this time to fuse his spine. The surgery was successful, and the vertebra problem that had haunted him for so long seemed healed. Pain-free for the first time in years, Gregg pitched for the International League's Montreal Royals in 1943. In twenty-three games for the Dodgers' top affiliate, he had a mediocre 11-11 record, but his ERA was just 3.17 and he was becoming known for his blazing fastball. His pitching caught the attention of Dodgers manager Leo Durocher and general manager Branch Rickey. Brooklyn had lost several key veterans to the service and was now struggling to win games and, more important, to fill the seats.

In mid-August, Durocher decided it was time for a youth movement. He stormed into Rickey's office and demanded the team call up some young players from the Minors. The next day Rickey summoned Gregg and teammate Rex Barney, another young hard-thrower, from Montreal. When Rickey met the two pitchers upon their arrival in Brooklyn, he told them to relax and get acclimated, predicting that Durocher wouldn't want to start either pitcher for a week or so. He was wrong. That afternoon Durocher started both youngsters in a doubleheader against the Chicago Cubs.

Gregg pitched the opener and allowed three runs in the first inning. He held the Cubs scoreless in the second, but in the third inning Dom Dallessandro hit a line drive that smacked Gregg's right ankle, dropping him to the ground. He remained on the field, unable to rise, for several minutes. He was eventually helped off the field, but he was done for the day. Gregg's pitching line for his first big league game was 2⅓ innings pitched, 6 walks, 4 hits, 6 runs, and 2 wild pitches. To complete his miserable debut, he was hit by a Claude Passeau pitch in his first Major League plate appearance. The rest of the 1943 season wasn't much better for Gregg. In five appearances overall, four of them starts, he was 0-3 with a 9.64 ERA. Gregg's biggest problem was a lack of control. He walked twenty-one in 18⅔ innings.

Despite his dismal performance in his first few Major League appearances, Gregg showed enough promise at spring training in 1944 to make the Dodgers' war-depleted roster. He pitched well initially, but once again injured his back during the summer. Fortunately, the doctors were able to fashion a back brace that held his strained spine in place.

Limited by these physical ailments, Gregg again struggled with his control in '44 and led the National League in walks (137 in 197⅔ innings), wild pitches (10), and hit batsmen (9). He won only nine games and lost sixteen. His ERA was an uninspiring 5.46. It was far from stellar, but in those times of manpower shortages, it was enough to keep Gregg in the big leagues if he could stay healthy.

In the winter of 1944–45, Gregg pitched semi-pro ball in California in an effort to rehabilitate his back. When he returned to spring training in 1945, he appeared to be a different man, telling Durocher and Rickey that he no longer had the back pain that had limited his performance in prior years. But Durocher soon noticed that Gregg was using a cramped, shot-put-type delivery—probably out of fear of more injury—which greatly slowed down his fastball. He asked Gregg to loosen up and put everything he had into each pitch.

Gregg made his 1945 debut against the Philadelphia Phillies on April 19, allowing only two hits and just one earned run for a complete-game victory. With his overpowering fastball, he struck out seven Phillies. But he also struggled with control of his curve ball and walked six batters. It could have been worse but for Gregg's catcher that day. Clyde Sukeforth, who had come out of retirement at the age of forty-three to play a few games behind the plate, deftly handled Gregg's erratic pitches.

Sukeforth's handling of Gregg led Durocher to assign the older man to be the wild man's personal catcher. The two soon became a strong battery.

Gregg's wildness was diminishing with experience and Sukeforth's coaching, and with greater control came more confidence, and more wins. By midseason the twenty-three-year old had become one of the best pitchers in the National League. He did not get the chance, however, to pitch in an All-Star Game.

Because of the war effort, the owners agreed to cancel the Midsummer Classic, and as a result, Major League Baseball did not name All-Stars for the 1945 season. A group of baseball writers from the Associated Press picked their own standouts based on nominations from the league's managers. Hal Gregg was the consensus best starting pitcher in the National League.

From late July to early August, Gregg went on a five-game winning streak. On August 3 he held the Boston Braves hitless for seven innings, facing the minimum twenty-one batters. Although he lost the no-hitter in the eighth, he won the game, 3–1, allowing only an unearned run. Gregg followed with another strong performance on August 8, a complete-game 1–0 shutout of the Cincinnati Reds. It was his first career complete game, and the win improved his record to 15-6. Everyone in baseball—players, managers, writers—was taking notice. Hal Gregg had special talent. He had a bright future.

But Gregg slumped badly in the final two months of the season. He was 1-7 before finishing the season with two dominating wins against the last-place Phillies. Gregg had a final record of 18-13, and his 3.47 ERA was two runs lower than his 1944 mark. He was still struggling with his control, leading the league with 120 walks and finishing second in wild pitches and hit batsmen.

After a strong start in 1946, Gregg pulled a muscle in his throwing arm on May 15, and the injury kept him out for six weeks. When he did pitch, Gregg was still a force, winning six games while losing four and posting a career-best 2.99 ERA against the strengthened postwar rosters.

On May 2, 1946, Gregg married Alice Wyatt, a twenty-one-year-old fashion model from Forest Hills, New York. The two were married at St. Paul's Episcopal Church in Mount Vernon, New York. The couple had three sons, Harold Jr., Gregory, and James. They remained married until Hal's death forty-five years later.

By holding the Braves scoreless for the final two and one-third innings, Gregg was the winning pitcher on April 15, 1947, the game in which Jackie Robinson made his historic debut. Gregg's performance encouraged manager Burt Shotton to start him against the Phillies a week later. Gregg did not disappoint. He pitched a complete-game shutout in a 1–0 win, at one time retiring twenty consecutive batters. Gregg told reporters after the game that he never felt so confident in his whole life, but the rest of the season did not go as well as those early outings. Gregg made fifteen more starts, but by the end of the season, he was working almost solely out of the bullpen. Although he was just 4-5 with a 5.87 ERA, Gregg pitched well in relief down the stretch, and in doing so gained the confidence of his manager. When asked about Gregg's late-season surge, Shotton said that Gregg could be the ace of the staff.

The 1947 World Series pitted the Dodgers against the New York Yankees. Gregg made his first Series appearance in the fifth inning of Game Two, allowing an inherited runner to score and surrendering another run in two innings of work.

In Game Four, Gregg relieved rookie starter Harry Taylor, who faced only four batters and left with his team down 1–0 and the bases loaded with nobody out. Gregg disposed of the threat and surrendered just one run over the next six innings. His performance held the Yankees at bay and helped set the stage for Cookie Lavagetto's two-out, ninth-inning double that spoiled Floyd Bevens's potential no-hitter and won the game for Brooklyn.

Gregg's outstanding performance in Game

Four prompted Shotton to name him his Game Seven starter. It was a surprise move for a pitcher who had been working almost exclusively out of the bullpen since midseason. But Gregg was not up to the task. His line for the game was 3⅔ innings pitched, 3 hits, 3 earned runs, 4 walks, and 3 strikeouts. The Yankees went on to win the game, with Gregg taking the loss.

On December 8, 1947, the Dodgers traded Gregg and pitcher Vic Lombardi to the Pittsburgh Pirates for third baseman Billy Cox, utility infielder Gene Mauch, and pitcher Preacher Roe. In a separate deal that day, the Dodgers sold Dixie Walker to the Pirates for the $10,000 waiver price.

Gregg's time in Pittsburgh was marred by arm injuries and declining performance. After a disappointing 2-4 season in 1948, he shuttled back and forth between the Pirates and the Minor Leagues in 1949 and 1950. Disgusted and distraught, Gregg quit baseball after the 1950 season. His arm hurt, his bad back was now a chronic problem, and he had been on a steady decline for three years. He moved back home to Anaheim and began working full time at his orange-growing business.

Yet when the Pirates asked if he wanted a tryout at spring training in 1952, Gregg accepted the offer. He was the final man cut from the Major League roster. Once again, he retired. That is, until later that spring when Mel Ott, the manager of the Oakland Oaks of the Pacific Coast League, paid Gregg a visit and persuaded him to give the game one more chance. A few days later, Gregg signed to pitch for Oakland. By the middle of June, he was 11-3. On June 13, 1952, the Durocher-managed New York Giants purchased Gregg's contract from the Oaks for $35,000.

On June 17, 1952, in his first big league game in more than two years, Gregg pitched admirably for six innings, holding the Pirates to one run on five hits. Things went awry in the seventh when he yielded a bases-loaded home run to Gus Bell and ended up the losing pitcher. In all, he appeared in sixteen games for the Giants, including his final one on August 17 against the Braves at the Polo Grounds. He returned in 1953 for one game with Oakland before retiring from baseball.

Hal went home to Anaheim, where he and Alice raised their three children and ran the orange business, as he had intended from his childhood days. On May 13, 1991, Hal Gregg died at the age of sixty-nine at his home in Bishop, California, where he had lived for the prior decade. Gregg, who was cremated, was survived by his wife and their three sons. His obituary in the local paper noted that few people in town even knew that he had been a Major League baseball player.

## Chapter 20. Timeline, May 1–May 20

*Lyle Spatz*

Thursday, May 1, vs. Chicago—The Dodgers took advantage of ten walks to top the Cubs, 5–2. Eddie Stanky had three hits, and Jackie Robinson ended a 0-for-20 slump with a first-inning double off Bob Chipman. Kirby Higbe was the winner, aided by three and one-third innings of strong relief by Ed Chandler. 9-3, First, 1½ games ahead.

Friday, May 2, vs. Cincinnati—Rained out. 9-3, First, 1½ games ahead.

Saturday, May 3, vs. Cincinnati—Rained out. The Dodgers traded pitchers Kirby Higbe, Hank Behrman, and Cal McLish, infielder Gene Mauch, and catcher Dixie Howell to the Pittsburgh Pirates for outfielder Al Gionfriddo and a reported $100,000. Higbe had allegedly been one of the most vocal Dodgers in his opposition to playing with Jackie Robinson. 9-3, First, 1½ games ahead.

Sunday, May 4, vs. Pittsburgh—Rained out. 9-3, First, 1½ games ahead.

Monday, May 5, vs. Pittsburgh—Rained out. 9-3, First, 1½ games ahead.

Tuesday, May 6, vs. St. Louis—Following four straight rainouts, which wiped out a two-game series with the Reds and Pirates, the Dodgers returned to action. They defeated the Cardinals 7–6 in the first meeting between the two teams since the 1946 playoff. Hugh Casey entered the game in the seventh inning with the score tied at 6–6 and pitched three scoreless innings to earn the win. Carl Furillo's bases-loaded triple in the sixth in-ning tied the score, and Pee Wee Reese's seventh-inning home run was the game winner. 10-3, First, 2 games ahead.

Wednesday, May 7, vs. St. Louis—After three straight losses, Cardinals ace Howie Pollet won his first game of the season. Despite yielding nine hits and eight walks, he edged the Dodgers 2–1. Pollet's teammates backed him with four double plays, and Terry Moore's two-run homer off Vic Lombardi in the seventh was the difference. 10-4, First, 1 game ahead.

Thursday, May 8, vs. St. Louis—World Series hero Harry Brecheen held Brooklyn scoreless for eight innings in the first night game of the season at Ebbets Field. The Dodgers finally pushed across a run in the ninth, but fell to St. Louis, 5–1. Starter Ralph Branca was ineffective, suffering his third defeat of the season. Owner Branch Rickey re-fused to comment on a rumor that Dixie Walker, the alleged ringleader in the opposition to Jackie Robinson, would be sold to Cincinnati. The team did make one move, sending pitcher Paul Minner to Mobile of the Southern Association. Nation-al League president Ford Frick announced that a threatened strike by the Cardinals against Robin-son had been averted. 10-5, First, .020 percentage points ahead.

Friday, May 9, at Philadelphia—The Phillies topped the Dodgers 6–5 in eleven innings, deal-ing Brooklyn its third consecutive loss and knock-ing them out of first place. The Dodgers tied the score with four runs in the eighth inning, but in the last of the eleventh, Emil Verban's single off Hugh Casey drove in Andy Seminick with the winning run. Before the game, Phillies manager Ben Chapman obliged reporters by shaking hands with Jackie Robinson. Nevertheless, Chapman, perhaps the most virulent racist in the league, continued his verbal assaults once the game began. Meanwhile, the Dodgers, seemingly satisfied that Robinson was up to being their full-time first baseman, sold Howie Schultz to the Phillies. Schultz had shared the position with Ed Stevens in 1946. 10-6, Third, 1 game behind.

Saturday, May 10, at Philadelphia—Pete Reiser hit a home run in Brooklyn's 4–2 win. Joe Hatten won his third straight decision, while the Phillies' Tommy Hughes fell to 0-5. 11-6, First, .015 percentage points ahead.

Sunday, May 11, at Philadelphia (2)—The Dodgers lost both ends of a doubleheader, 7–3 and 5–4, before a Shibe Park record crowd of 40,952. Dutch Leonard, in the first game, and Schoolboy Rowe, in the second, each earned his fifth win of the season. Leonard bested Vic Lombardi, and Rowe, with four innings of relief from Ken Heintzelman, defeated rookie Ed Chandler in the nightcap. Gene Hermanski's two home runs off Leonard accounted for all of Brooklyn's runs in the opener. 11-8, Third, 2 games behind.

Monday, May 12, vs. Boston—Leading 2–1, the Dodgers exploded for four fifth-inning runs against Mort Cooper on the way to an 8–3 victory. Ralph Branca went the distance. Rookie first baseman Earl Torgeson knocked in all the Braves' runs off Branca with a double and a home run. Jackie Robinson had two stolen bases and was leading the National League with twenty runs scored. 12-8, Second, 1½ games behind.

Tuesday, May 13, at Cincinnati—The Dodgers began their first western trip with a 7–5 loss under the lights at Crosley Field. Harry Taylor lasted just two innings in his first start of the season. Taylor, Rube Melton, Clyde King, Hal Gregg, Ed Chandler, and Rex Barney, who struck out the side in the two innings he pitched, combined to walk eight batters. The Reds were also helped by three Brooklyn errors. After again denying he would sell or trade Dixie Walker, Branch Rickey sold little-used outfielder Tommy Tatum to the Reds. Tatum started in center field for Cincinnati and contributed a two-run single. Brooklyn had thirteen hits, including three by Bruce Edwards. 12-9, Third, 1½ games behind.

Wednesday, May 14, at Cincinnati—Tommy Tatum, sold by the Dodgers to Cincinnati a day earlier, hit his first Major League home run in the first inning. It came off Joe Hatten and was all Ewell Blackwell needed in handing Brooklyn its first shutout of the season, 2–0. Pete Reiser had a first-inning single that ran his consecutive on-base streak to nine (six hits and three walks). Jackie Robinson had two hits, extending his consecutive-game hit streak to eleven. 12-10, Third, 2 games behind.

Thursday, May 15, at Pittsburgh—Ralph Kiner slugged two home runs and Billy Cox had a homer and a triple in the Pirates 7–3 victory at Forbes Field. Ed Bahr pitched eight and one-third innings for the win. Kiner's first home run, off loser Vic Lombardi, came on a 3-0 pitch with two men aboard. Eddie Stanky had three hits and Jackie Robinson two for the Dodgers, who fell to fifth place. 12-11, Fifth, 2 games behind.

Friday, May 16, at Pittsburgh—Ralph Branca captured his third win of the season, 3–1, aided by two and one-third innings of relief by Hugh Casey. Pittsburgh's Kirby Higbe allowed only four hits in eight innings against his former teammates, but one was a two-run homer by Pee Wee Reese. 13-11, Fourth, 1 game behind.

Saturday, May 17, at Pittsburgh—Thirty-nine-year-old lefthander Fritz Ostermueller allowed twelve hits, all singles, but shut out the Dodgers, 4–0. Rube Melton, making his first start of the season, gave up a two-run homer to Hank Greenberg in the first inning. Jackie Robinson's two hits stretched his hitting streak to fourteen games. Robinson received encouragement from Greenberg, who told him to "stick in there. You're doing fine." 13-12, Fifth, 1½ games behind.

Sunday, May 18, at Chicago—Jackie Robinson's presence in the Dodgers' lineup continued to generate attendance records. More than 46,000 saw Robinson's first game at Wrigley Field, a 4–2 Brooklyn win, and the end of Robinson's fourteen-game hitting streak. Cubs left-hander Johnny Schmitz had nine strikeouts and a 2–0 lead after six innings, but the Dodgers struck for four runs in the seventh. Pete Reiser's double with the bases loaded was the key blow. Starter Joe Hatten pitched six innings and was the winner. Hugh Casey tossed three scoreless innings in his twelfth relief appearance of the season. 14-12, Third (T), 1 game behind.

Monday, May 19, at Chicago—In a game interrupted by rain for more than an hour, the Dodgers battled back from a 7–3 deficit, but left the tying run on base in two separate innings and lost, 8–7. The Cubs ended a five-game losing streak, while the Dodgers suffered their tenth loss in fourteen games and dropped back to fifth place. Hal Gregg, the first of five Brooklyn pitchers, was the loser. 14-13, Fifth, 1½ games behind.

Tuesday, May 20, at St. Louis—Rained out. 14-13, Fifth, 1½ games behind.

# Chapter 21. **Hank Behrman**

*Rob Edelman*

| AGE | W | L | PCT. | ERA | G | GS | GF | CG | SHO | SV | IP | H | BB | SO | HBP | WP |
|-----|---|---|------|-----|---|----|----|----|-----|----|------|----|----|----|-----|----|
| 26 | 5 | 3 | .625 | 5.48 | 40 | 6 | 16 | 0 | 0 | 8 | 92.0 | 97 | 48 | 33 | 0 | 3 |

Hank Behrman was a minor contributor to the golden age of baseball in Brooklyn. His career was all promise and little delivery. Yet the five-foot-eleven, 174-pound right-hander did have one sterling season for the Dodgers. In 1946, his rookie campaign, he appeared in forty-seven games and posted an 11-5 record with a sparkling 2.93 ERA. A year later his cumulative ERA for the Dodgers and Pittsburgh Pirates jumped to 6.25, and by 1950 he was out of the Majors for good, at the age of twenty-nine.

Henry Bernard Behrman was born in Brooklyn on June 27, 1921. By the time he reached high school, his family had moved to Maspeth, in the borough of Queens. The Dodgers signed Behrman after he attended a tryout at Ebbets Field in 1940. The youngster spent the 1941 campaign playing for the Valdosta Trojans in the Class D Georgia-Florida League. His 18-10 record and 3.11 ERA earned him a promotion to the Durham (North Carolina) Bulls in the Class B Piedmont League for 1942. On July 25 he tossed a no-hitter for the Bulls at Asheville, and completed the season with a 14-11 record and a 2.92 ERA.

At the close of the 1942 campaign, Behrman entered the army. After basic training, he was assigned to the 326th Glider Infantry Regiment. He spent the bulk of his time in the service at the Alliance Army Air Base in Nebraska, where he pitched for the base team. In February 1945, the 326th arrived in France. With the end of the war in Europe in May, Behrman was selected to play for the Thirteenth Airborne Division Black Cats, who compiled a 33-4 record. The 326th returned to

Hank Behrman was traded to Pittsburgh in May and returned to the Dodgers in June.

the United States in August and, on January 30, 1946, Behrman was mustered out of the military. The Dodgers assigned him to the Montreal Royals, their top farm club.

Despite his status as a raw rookie, Behrman proclaimed that he would rather quit baseball than spend the 1946 season in the Minors. During spring training, the twenty-four-year-old hurler impressed the Dodgers' brass with his rubber arm and his money pitch, a lively fastball that zoomed upward or sank as it neared home plate. On April

2 Behrman started for Montreal against the Dodgers and held them to six hits and no runs in seven innings.

"He has what it takes to win," observed Branch Rickey Jr., head of the Dodgers' Minor League operation.[1] "He's the sleeper of this camp." Fresco Thompson, the team's new assistant farm director, noted, "He pitched a couple of innings the other day, right after having been laid up with the flu, and he made me sit up and take notice. He has something more than a chance of making the grade in a hurry."[2]

The day before the start of the 1946 season, Behrman was reassigned to the parent club—and quickly proved himself a stellar addition to the Dodgers' mound staff. He began the campaign in the starting rotation and impressed in his Major League debut, turning back the Braves in Boston on April 17. After a shaky two innings, in which he allowed four hits and two runs, Behrman settled down and gave up just five more safeties in the final seven frames.

Behrman eventually was relegated to the bullpen, where manager Leo Durocher felt he was most needed. On June 24 he relieved Kirby Higbe in the second inning of a game against Cincinnati and whiffed seven of the first eleven hitters he faced. Three days later he took over for Joe Hatten against Boston with two outs and the bases loaded in the fifth inning. In what *New York Times* sportswriter Roscoe McGowen described as an "almost flawless pitching performance," Behrman got out of the inning and pitched four more frames, allowing just one Brave to reach base.[3]

In 1947 Behrman reported to spring training underweight and promptly hurt his arm. On May 14 he married Ellen Leffert, a Long Island native; they eventually became the parents of five offspring. Yet that same year, a further distraction for the hurler came when he was hit with a paternity suit. His preference for the nightlife over keeping fit was being recognized within the Dodgers' inner circle.

Behrman appeared in forty games for the 1947 Dodgers, posting a 5-3 record—but with a 5.48 ERA. Then again, he did not spend the entire campaign with the team. On May 3, he, pitchers Kirby Higbe and Cal McLish, catcher Dixie Howell, and infielder Gene Mauch were traded to Pittsburgh for outfielder Al Gionfriddo and a sum that was reported to be between $100,000 and $200,000. Behrman's performance in Pittsburgh was lackluster. He got into just ten contests, losing two with no victories. His ERA was an abysmal 9.12. However, his trade to the Bucs was conditional. If the Pirates wished, they could return Behrman to Brooklyn without explanation. And so on June 14, six weeks after being dispatched to Pittsburgh, Behrman was sold back to Brooklyn for $25,000. (Some accounts list the sum at $50,000.)

Upon his return to the Dodgers, sportswriter Herbert Goren observed that "it seemed as if some of the zing was off his fastball."[4] Behrman was inconsistent for the rest of the season, with his outing in Pittsburgh on September 17 being one of the high points. In the eighth inning, he replaced Hal Gregg, and the 33,916 fans who had packed into Forbes Field greeted him with boos. Behrman promptly quieted the crowd by striking out two future Hall of Famers, Ralph Kiner and Hank Greenberg. Then he set the Bucs down in order in the ninth inning, preserving Brooklyn's 4–2 victory. Behrman appeared in five games during the 1947 World Series, all in relief, giving up nine hits in six and one-third innings.

In February 1948 the Dodgers assigned Behrman to Montreal. His reputation as an irresponsible young man who was not reaching his potential as a frontline hurler now was firmly in place among the Dodgers' higher-ups—and his demotion to the Royals reportedly was a disciplinary measure. On March 3 Behrman disclosed that Dodgers boss Branch Rickey had given him the okay to try to make a deal for himself with another team. He had been unable to do so. But he promised that his foray to the Minors would be temporary. "Maybe," he mused, "this is just what I needed. I know I've made some mistakes. I'll work my head and arm off for Montreal and then next spring maybe they'll give me another chance. I know I've got the stuff to win for them."[5]

Buzzy Bavasi, the Montreal general manager, reported that Behrman stayed in shape and was well-behaved. "He's the first guy to check in every night," Bavasi said.[6] Behrman compiled a snazzy 6-2 record that earned him a return to the Dodgers. Curiously, he initially balked at the move. "I am very happy where I am and I want no part of the Dodgers," he claimed, but then he relented after conferring with Bavasi.[7]

Still, the Dodgers' brass was not pleased. Behrman was optioned back to Montreal for what were described in the press as "personal reasons." After winning two more games for the Royals and compiling an overall ERA of 2.55—that at season's end was second best in the International League—he was summoned back to Brooklyn. Behrman was described by Roscoe McGowen as "the returned prodigal."[8]

Behrman got into thirty-four games for the 1948 Dodgers; his record was 5-4, and his ERA was 4.05. On August 25 he was a key participant in a controversial play. In a game against Pittsburgh, Carl Erskine relieved Hugh Casey in the ninth inning with two outs and runners on first and third. With the count on Eddie Bockman at three balls and one strike, manager Burt Shotton replaced Erskine with Behrman. On Behrman's first pitch, Bockman grounded to Pee Wee Reese for a force play at second, ending the game with the Dodgers in front, 11–9.

However, according to Major League rules, a reliever who enters a game must complete pitching to at least one batter before being replaced. The Pirates disputed Erskine's quick exit. Their protest

was allowed by National League president Ford Frick; Bockman's at bat was erased and the contest was scheduled for completion on September 21. In the replay, Erskine walked Bockman to load the bases. Behrman then entered the game. His first three pitches to Stan Rojek were balls. His next two were called strikes. Then Rojek hit a bounder that caromed off the glove of third sacker Tommy Brown, and the tying and winning runs scored.

In January 1949 Branch Rickey hired Behrman to work at Ebbets Field as an assistant groundskeeper. Rickey did so to keep tabs on the errant hurler. For eight hours a day, at ninety cents an hour, Behrman toiled to prepare the Ebbets Field turf for the coming season, trading his baseball uniform and glove for work clothes and a rake, pick, and shovel.

"I've worked in the yard at home, but this is a big yard," he told the *Brooklyn Daily Eagle* in February. "I like the work even if it does get me up at six o'clock in the morning. There won't be any alibi for Pee Wee Reese fumbling a ground ball behind me when I get through smoothing out this infield."[9]

Behrman was eagerly anticipating the coming campaign. "I hope Mr. Rickey will let me start this year," he declared. "I could win fifteen for the Dodgers. Twelve if he keeps me on relief. I didn't have such a lousy record last season, either. But I would have to go out for a pinch-hitter and the next guy to come in would blow the ball game wide open."[10]

Rickey optimistically observed, "This may be the making of that boy. He told me he never had worked for wages in his life."[11] The general manager surely must have been smiling when Behrman noted, "I like [the groundskeeper position]. But, boy, am I tired when I get home at night! I eat my dinner and go right to bed at 7:30."[12] Rickey's mood quickly changed when, after two weeks on the job, Behrman abruptly left Brooklyn and headed to Vero Beach before he was scheduled to report for spring training. Rickey soured even further when the pitcher made public his claim that the team refused to pay him the $75 he had spent while awaiting the opening of camp. After driving from New York to Florida, Behrman was rebuffed when he tried to enter Dodgertown—even though Pee Wee Reese, Ralph Branca, and several newspapermen already were living on the grounds. Behrman was forced to move into a Vero Beach inn.

Even though he had signed his contract for the 1949 campaign, an irate Behrman promised to not officially report to spring training. He now claimed that laboring with the Ebbets Field grounds crew had affected his health, resulting in his "coughing every day." He said that "working under those damp stands in Ebbets Field was no good for me. Since I've been down here, my coughing has stopped almost completely."[13]

Before the close of spring training, Rickey sold Behrman to the New York Giants for a reported $25,000. He pitched in forty-three games, including four starts, and compiled a 3-3 record with a 4.92 ERA. Behrman returned to the Giants in 1950 and suffered through a difficult spring training. He was sidelined by a badly bruised left knee and a series of nosebleeds, and he had a cyst removed from the left side of his face. Despite these maladies, he was pitching in exhibition games by mid-March. As the spring workouts neared their close, however, Behrman was released outright to the Pacific Coast League Oakland Oaks.

Behrman had seen his last days as a big leaguer. During his career he primarily worked in relief, starting only 27 of the 174 Major League games in which he appeared, and compiling a 24-17 record and 4.40 ERA. As *Brooklyn Daily Eagle* writer Tommy Holmes noted a couple of years after the hurler's departure from the big leagues, "Behrman had the arm. He could knock the bat out of your hands with his fast ball and catch you looking at his curve."[14]

But his time in the Majors is most notable for what he did off the field rather than on—and for his well-earned reputation for disobeying the rules. While on the road, he often ignored curfews; it was no different when the Dodgers were at home. "Hank lived at St. Albans, on Long Island, and rarely made it to Ebbets Field on time," reported Loren McMullen in the October 1951 issue of *Baseball Digest*. "But he never was caught without an excuse. Either the train broke down, or his mother suffered an appendicitis attack, his brother was chased by gunmen, or a tornado struck his community."[15]

After finishing in the Majors, Behrman hung around professional baseball for a few more seasons. In 1950 he compiled a snazzy 17-8 record in Oakland, with a more than respectable 4.25 ERA. It was Behrman's last top-flight campaign. He spent the next season playing for the Class Double-A Oklahoma City Indians in the Texas League and the Class Triple-A San Francisco Seals and Oakland Oaks of the PCL. In 1952 Behrman was hurling for the Class Triple-A American Association Toledo Mud Hens and Charleston Senators. He was back with the Senators in 1953, but went 6-16 with a 4.87 ERA, and was plagued by arm trouble. Charleston released him the following spring, and his baseball career was over.

Behrman returned to New York, found employment as a truck driver for a food concessionaire, and faded into obscurity. In late 1986 he underwent a triple heart bypass, and he passed away the following January 20. The causes of death were complications from the operation and the onset of pneumonia. He was sixty-five years old and was survived by his wife and five children. Behrman is buried in Calverton National Cemetery on Long Island.

# Chapter 22. **Rube Melton**

*Jack V. Morris*

| AGE | W | L | PCT. | ERA | G | GS | GF | CG | SHO | SV | IP | H | BB | SO | HBP | WP |
|---|---|---|---|---|---|---|---|---|---|---|---|---|---|---|---|---|
| 30 | 0 | 1 | .000 | 13.50 | 4 | 1 | 0 | 0 | 0 | 0 | 4.2 | 7 | 7 | 1 | 0 | 0 |

There was no digging in at home plate when Rube Melton was on the mound. Standing six feet five and weighing 205 pounds, Melton was blessed with a right arm capable of throwing a baseball with speed that few possessed. *Brooklyn Daily Eagle* columnist Tommy Holmes wrote that Melton was "very fast and uncommonly wild."[1] In 1942, the only season in which he pitched more than two hundred innings in the Major Leagues, he led the National League in both walks and wild pitches. He had incredible potential, though, which was why general managers put up with his wildness over six Major League seasons.

He was born Reuben Frank Melton, and for most of his first twenty years he was simply Frank Melton. But his antics off the field, and sometimes on, caused sportswriters and teammates to nickname him "Rube," a name he hated.

While in the Minors, he once disappeared between innings of a game he was pitching. When he finally ran out to the mound, after delaying the game, he explained that he had been talking to a friend in the parking lot.[2] Another time during his tenure in the Minors, he lit a pile of rags on fire in his hotel room to keep the mosquitoes away. His roommate put out the fire, much to Melton's chagrin.[3]

While newspapers laughed at Melton's eccentricities, he was more than just a country bumpkin. He was always angling for a better salary, becoming famous for his lengthy spring training holdouts; he possessed such great raw talent that scouts and general managers fought (and paid highly) for his services.

Born on February 17, 1917, in Cramerton, North

Rube Melton's outing on June 3 was his last Major League game.

Carolina, Melton was the sixth of ten children born to Reuben Judson Melton and Minnie Dulcenia (Haynes) Melton. When Melton's father found work at a cotton mill near Gastonia, North Carolina, he moved his family to Victory-Winget, a company town named for two cotton mills whose employees lived there.

Baseball was a big part of a mill company town's existence. Young Frank showed great promise on the diamond. By the time he turned sixteen, the lanky Melton was turning heads with his fastball.

In 1933 he was on the mound for the local American Legion Junior baseball team, Gastonia Post 23, a state and national power in Legion baseball.[4]

Melton also played football and basketball for Gastonia High School. But with his flaming fastball, baseball was his game. By 1934, at seventeen and with a year to go in high school, Melton was too old for American Legion ball, so he latched onto a mill team in the local industrial league.[5]

In early 1935 Melton signed a professional contract with the Southern Association's Chattanooga Lookouts, a Washington Senators affiliate.[6] But he spent June and July pitching in the Western Carolina League and the Tobacco State League. With the summer winding down, Melton enrolled at Wake Forest College.[7] He stayed for a semester, even playing on the freshman football team, before leaving the school to attend Campbell Junior College, now known as Campbell University, for the spring semester.

At Campbell, Melton gained the notice of St. Louis Cardinals scout Frank Rickey, the younger brother of Branch Rickey, the Cardinals' business manager. Frank Rickey signed Melton and sent him to the Asheville Tourists of the Class B Piedmont League. Before playing a game, though, Melton was sent down to the Class D Pennsylvania State League's Greensburg Red Wings.[8] The nineteen-year-old Melton dominated the Class D opposition, going 13-4 and leading Greensburg into the playoffs. He was named the league's best right-handed pitcher.[9]

In 1937 Melton went to spring training with the Columbus (Ohio) Red Birds, the Cardinals' team in the American Association. *The Sporting News* called him a "reliable first-string pitcher," but the deep Cardinals farm system prevented him from making the Columbus team.[10]

Melton was returned to Asheville, but after just one exhibition game, he was sent to the Albany (Georgia) Travelers in the Class D Georgia-Florida League. Before leaving Asheville, Rube married

Hazel Bunting on April 3, 1937. In his first start at Albany, Melton set a league record by striking out fifteen Thomasville Orioles. He soon faltered, though, posting a 6-11 record and a 4.01 ERA.

At the end of the 1937 season, Melton made a bold move. For the last two years, he had been paid $75 a month to play ball. With a new wife and a child on the way, he decided a change was necessary. So in 1938 he jumped to Valdese of the outlaw Carolina League, where he was paid $75 a week.[11]

But on August 5, Valdese quit the league.[12] Organized Baseball had blacklisted all of the Carolina League players, so Melton found his way instead to several top-notch semipro teams. He pitched for whoever paid him the most money. Late in the 1939 season he was with the Bona-Allen Shoemakers of Buford, Georgia. Bona-Allen was the defending champion of the prestigious National Baseball Congress semipro World Series.

Scouts flocked to the tournament in Wichita, Kansas, and were wowed by Melton's pitching. However, the Cardinals still owned his rights. Frank Rickey offered Melton $400 a month to play with Columbus.[13] Melton accepted, and on February 14, 1940, he was reinstated to Organized Baseball.[14]

Melton went to spring training with the Cardinals, but back problems kept him from competing for a spot on the big league club, and he was sent to Columbus.[15] The Red Birds used him as both a starter and reliever. By July he had relieved in sixteen games with eleven saves.[16] Later in the season they used him primarily as a starter. On August 22 manager Burt Shotton started him in both ends of a doubleheader against the Minneapolis Millers.

Unbeknown to Branch Rickey and the Cardinals organization, Melton was eligible for the Rule 5 draft. The Major Leagues had decided that his two years out of Organized Baseball had counted toward his eligibility for the draft. The Philadelphia Phillies, with the worst record in the Majors in 1939, had the first pick. They selected Melton, then immediately sold him to Brooklyn for $15,000.[17]

Commissioner Kenesaw Landis was suspicious of the deal and never signed the paperwork. At the winter meetings, Landis's secretary, Leslie O'Connor, accused Phillies owner Gerry Nugent and the Dodgers' Larry MacPhail of collusion. Shortly after the meeting, Landis nullified the sale.[18]

Landis, knowing the Phillies' precarious financial position, said Melton could still be traded, but not to the Dodgers; he barred them from trading Melton to Brooklyn for at least three years. When Melton flew to Philadelphia to negotiate his contract, he had a surprise for Nugent. He had suffered a bruised knee in a car accident.[19]

At spring training with the Phillies in 1941, manager Doc Prothro taught Melton how to throw a change-up. In early March, Prothro declared him his number one pitcher. Rube started against Boston in the third game of the season and failed to last through the third inning. The "number one pitcher" started only four more games. Most of his work came in relief. When he did pitch, he hardly lived up to his billing.

Melton was unhappy about his role on the team and his poor performance. By July 16 he had had enough. After getting pounded by Chicago that afternoon, he went home. Nobody knew about it until the next day when he failed to show up for the game with the Cubs. Prothro was livid. Rumors cropped up that he and Melton had had a fight, but Prothro denied it.

Melton wrote owner Nugent soon after and told him his young son was ill.[20] Yet in the same interview, he told reporters, "I was worried and everything had been going badly for me. So I just went home."[21] He returned to the team on July 24 and was fined a week's pay.[22] His poor pitching continued to the end of the season. He finished with a 1-5 record and a 4.73 ERA in twenty-five games.

What the Phillies did not know, however, was that Melton had torn a muscle in his arm.[23] It was the first of many arm injuries that would ultimately force him from the Major Leagues.

On his way to spring training in 1942, Melton was arrested in Hialeah, Florida, on charges of disorderly conduct and annoying women. Nugent, clearly fed up with his flighty pitcher, let him sit in jail overnight before paying his $300 fine.[24]

Despite that inauspicious start, 1942 turned out to be, in many ways, Melton's best season in the Major Leagues. Playing on an atrocious Phillies team (42-109), he started a career-high twenty-nine games and pitched 209⅓ innings. His record was 9-20, but his ERA was a full run lower than 1941 at 3.70.

On December 12, 1942, the Phillies traded Melton to the Dodgers for pitcher Johnny Allen and $30,000. Though the Dodgers were barred from trading for Melton under Judge Landis's earlier ruling, Landis allowed the deal because of Nugent's mounting debts.[25]

Branch Rickey, Brooklyn's new president, was ecstatic. "Melton can throw a ball as hard as any man living," he told *The Sporting News*.[26] Rickey, whose pitching staff had been hit hard by the wartime draft, was also happy that because Melton had a wife and two children, he was deferred from military service.

Melton too was happy with the trade; still, he sent his initial contract back to Rickey unsigned. By March, Melton was listed as an official holdout.[27] Rickey and Melton finally agreed to terms on March 19. Melton won a raise of $3,500 from his 1942 Phillies salary of $5,000.[28]

Rube got his first win as a Dodger in his third start, defeating the defending World Series champion St. Louis Cardinals, 1–0, and driving in the only run of the game. Four days later, he beat them again. Unfortunately for Rube, that was the highlight of his 1943 season. By mid-August the Dodgers had seen enough, and they sent him to their

St. Paul team in the American Association. At the time Melton had a record of 5-7. Rickey told the press, "I think the same of Melton as I did in the spring. He's a good pitcher and will be back with us next spring."[29]

Actually, Melton made it back with the Dodgers by September 17, after St. Paul's season had ended. However, he was used only in relief as the Dodgers limped to a third-place finish.

When Melton received his 1944 contract, which called for a pay cut of $1,500, he again returned it unsigned. For the second straight year, he was holding out. But in late March, many of the men previously considered unfit for duty were reclassified. Melton was now 1-A and subject to the draft. Rickey suspended salary talks and instructed Melton to stay home rather than report to spring training.[30]

Instead of heeding Rickey's instructions, Melton hurried to the Dodgers' training camp in Bear Mountain, twenty pounds overweight.[31] In May it was reported that the navy had accepted Rube for active service and he would be notified when he was needed.[32] But Melton was never called to duty that spring, and by June the *New York World Telegram* called him the "new ace of the Dodger staff."[33] Melton ended the season with a 9-13 record and a 3.46 ERA for the seventh-place finishers. More impressively, in 187 innings pitched, he gave up only one home run.

Melton was drafted into the army and was inducted on December 7, 1944, and sent to Fort Bragg, North Carolina. He was transferred to Camp McClellan in Anniston, Alabama, where he played basketball on the camp team.[34] Later in the year he was shipped to the Pacific. While the war was over by the start of the 1946 season, Melton's service was not. He was still in the army during spring training and was not discharged until May 22. The Dodgers used Melton mostly in relief in 1946. Though he pitched in only twenty-four games, he recorded an ERA of 1.99 while go-

ing 6-3, his only winning season in the Major Leagues.

In 1947 Melton reported to Havana for the opening day of spring training—the first time he had done so since 1942—suffering from more than the usual arm soreness. From Havana, the Dodgers sent him to Fort Clayton in Panama. A military doctor X-rayed Melton's arm and discovered that he had bone chips floating in his elbow.[35] Rube flew to Baltimore, where he had surgery at Johns Hopkins Hospital.[36]

Meanwhile, the Dodgers opened the season with a desperate need for pitching, so they rushed Melton back to the team. They soon discovered the surgery had robbed him of his fastball. On June 3, 1947, Melton pitched his last game as a Major Leaguer. The Dodgers, in need of live arms, sent him outright to their Montreal Royals farm team.[37] Melton had hoped to be sent somewhere in the South where the weather was warmer. He appeared in only eight games for the Royals. After the season, the Dodgers released him.

The rest of Melton's baseball career was marked by brief appearances in the Minors over the next four years. He retired from baseball after the 1951 season and settled in Greenville, South Carolina, where he became a sand and gravel contractor, calling his company the Rube Melton Sand Company.

On September 11, 1971, Melton and his wife, Hazel, were killed in a two-car accident near Greer, South Carolina. The driver of the other automobile was also killed. Melton was fifty-four years old. He is buried in Woodlawn Memorial Park in Greenville.

# Chapter 23. Jackie Robinson and the Jews

*Rabbi Rebecca T. Alpert*

The subject of Jews and baseball is one that often inspires nostalgia, not thoughts about Jewish values. But for me, thinking about Jews and their role in "America's game" is primarily about the Jewish passion for social justice. The connection begins with one of my favorite quotations, from the Hebrew Bible in the book of Jeremiah. The prophet relays what he hears as God's words to Israel: "I will remember you because of the *hesed* [loving kindness] of your youth" (2:2). The quotation inspires a memory from my youth—a moment in time when American Jews acted with *hesed*. When we thought not only about what was good for the Jews, when we felt emboldened to hope for a better world for everyone, and when we actually played a role in trying to make that world a reality.

In 1947, Israel (the nation-state) was still one year from its founding. The Holocaust was too painful even to contemplate. And Hank Greenberg was playing his final year in the Major Leagues, at first base for the Pittsburgh Pirates. Greenberg was the most successful Jewish sports figure in the mid-twentieth century in the national pastime. He hit more home runs in one season than anyone but Babe Ruth. (Some say it was anti-Semitism that kept him from passing the Babe, but baseball historians argue that's unlikely.)[1] Greenberg played in many All-Star Games and in several World Series, served his country in World War II—one of the first ballplayers to enlist—and ended up as one of only two Jewish players (the other, Sandy Koufax) in the Hall of Fame. But more important, Hank refused to play on Yom Kippur (of course he did play on Rosh Hashanah, but that's another story). He

inspired a poem, a banner headline in the Detroit press, and the love of Jews everywhere.[2]

But my interest in Hank Greenberg is not because of what he meant to the Jews, but because of what he meant to Jackie Robinson, and what that connection meant to Jews who are passionately committed to social justice. The 1947 season wasn't only Greenberg's last year as a Major League player; it was also Robinson's first. And while it wasn't easy for Greenberg to endure the anti-Semitism in the Majors, it didn't compare to the abuse Jackie Robinson experienced when he became the first African American to play in Organized Baseball in the twentieth century, after blacks were barred from the sport not by law, but by a "gentleman's agreement" among the owners.

Robinson and Greenberg met one afternoon when Jackie reached first and Hank was the first baseman. In that encounter at first base, Robinson reported that Greenberg treated him with respect and said words of support to him. And in the Jewish press (and the *New York Times*), that was news.[3] That moment became a legend in Jewish baseball history, preserved in every account about Greenberg (and Robinson) that Jews write.

That moment is important to me because it reminds me that in those days Jews saw it as part of our role as Americans to support unpopular causes in the name of justice. We could be the ones who would set an example by welcoming Robinson into an America that was learning to denounce bigotry. We pride ourselves on our role in the civil rights movement, on the fact that Rabbi Abraham Joshua Heschel marched with Martin Luther King. That moment reminds me that Jews should also take pride in the fact that our passion for civil rights started much earlier (some suggest as far back as the beginning of the century) and had one of its greatest moments when we stood up for Jackie Robinson.

I grew up in Brooklyn in the Robinson era, listening to the stories my parents told me about the importance of being a Brooklyn Dodgers fan because they had the courage to break the color line. And I certainly was not alone. Fiction and memoir writers have immortalized the moment when Robinson came up to bat to the Jewish cries of "Yankel, Yankel" (the Yiddish name for Jack) from avid supporters.[4] In the Ken Burns documentary *Baseball*, the segment about Robinson ends with a quote from the family of Eric Foner describing their experience on Passover that year. When the youngest asked the question at the seder, "Why is this night different from all other nights?" the family replied, "Because tonight for the first time in this century, a black man played on a white team."[5]

Jews were also actors in the process that brought the event about. Though much credit is given to Dodgers owner Branch Rickey, and of course to Robinson himself, the real campaign to integrate baseball had been going on for almost two decades. It was led by the African American press, with a vigorous supporting role played by the radical Jews who were sportswriters at the Communist *Daily Worker*. And we also note the courage of Isadore Muchnick, the Boston city councilman from a liberal Jewish district who used the power of his office to put pressure on the Boston teams to give Robinson a tryout, knowing his district would stand by him, defending his actions based on the teaching of the prophets.[6]

Robinson himself acknowledged and appreciated the support he received from the Jewish community, and like many blacks of his era, he saw in the Jews the model for the black community to achieve success in this country. Robinson defended the Jews even when the black-Jewish alliance began to rupture in the late 1960s, up until his death in 1973.[7]

Is this only a happy story? Of course, the fact that Robinson had to defend us means that the Jewish-black alliance had already begun to come apart by the 1970s. And of course there were Jews who didn't want Jackie Robinson and his family to live in their neighborhoods in Brooklyn in the 1940s, and others who didn't want him to join their country clubs in Connecticut in the 1960s. And there were certainly those who fought for Robinson because they believed that the advancement of African Americans would also be good for the Jews. But I'd like to remember the part of our Jewish heritage that encourages Jews to remember the *hesed* of our youth; to stick our necks out, support causes that may not be popular, that may not even be in our own self-interest. It's part of who we are as Jews and what Jeremiah wants us to remember.

RABBI REBECCA T. ALPERT

## Chapter 24. **Timeline, May 21–June 15**

*Lyle Spatz*

Wednesday, May 21, at St. Louis—Cookie Lavagetto's single in the tenth inning drove in Pete Reiser with the winning run in Brooklyn's 4–3 win over the Cardinals. Hugh Casey won in relief of starter Joe Hatten, while loser Harry Brecheen went the distance for St. Louis. 15-13, Fifth, 1½ games behind.

Thursday, May 22—Not scheduled. 15-13, Fourth, 1½ games behind.

Friday, May 23, vs. Philadelphia—After trailing 4–0, Brooklyn rallied to win, 5–4. After starter Dutch Leonard left in the seventh inning with the bases loaded, walks issued by Ken Heintzelman and Tommy Hughes accounted for the tying and winning runs. Starter Ralph Branca allowed all of Philadelphia's runs. Rex Barney won his first game of the season, with the help of two innings of scoreless relief by Hugh Casey. 16-13, Third, 1 game behind.

Saturday, May 24, vs. Philadelphia—Carl Furillo's first-inning pinch-hit home run gave Brooklyn a 3–0 lead, but the Phillies came back to win, 4–3 in ten innings. Reliever Hugh Casey was the loser. Later that night, Casey struck and killed a blind pedestrian while driving home. 16-14, Fourth, 1 game behind.

Sunday, May 25, vs. Philadelphia—Joe Hatten gave the Dodgers only their sixth complete game of the season in downing the Phillies, 5–3. Jackie Robinson had three hits, including his second home run. 17-14, Third, 1 game behind.

Monday, May 26—Not scheduled. 17-14, Third, 1 game behind.

Tuesday, May 27, at New York—Playing before a crowd of more than 51,000, Pee Wee Reese hit a three-run homer, Dixie Walker had three hits, and Ralph Branca went the distance as the Dodgers easily defeated the first-place Giants, 7–3. 18-14, Third, ½ game behind.

Wednesday, May 28, at New York—By pounding the Giants 14–2, the Dodgers moved into first place. Harry Taylor gave manager Burt Shotton Brooklyn's third consecutive complete game, while earning his first Major League victory. Rookie third baseman Spider Jorgensen returned to the lineup after missing almost three weeks with a sore knee. Eddie Stanky's ejection was Brooklyn's first of the season. Eddie Miksis, who replaced Stanky at second base, and catcher Bruce Edwards each had three hits. Miksis, Edwards, and Dixie Walker hit home runs, and Edwards drove in six runs. 19-14, First, ½ game ahead.

Thursday, May 29, at New York—Rookie sensation Clint Hartung raised his record to 4-0, pitching the Giants to a 5–4 victory and moving them past Brooklyn into first place. Ken Trinkle pitched the ninth for New York after Gene Hermanski opened the inning with a home run. Joe Hatten was the starter and loser for Brooklyn. 19-15, Second (T), .004 percentage points behind.

Friday, May 30, at Boston (2)—Warren Spahn won game one of the Memorial Day doubleheader,

6–3. It was the left-hander's eighth consecutive win. Rex Barney, making his first start of the season, was the loser, although most of the damage was done after Hugh Casey relieved Barney. In the second game, Charles "Red" Barrett allowed the Dodgers just five singles, shutting them out, 3–0. Vic Lombardi pitched well but suffered his fifth loss. Brooklyn fell two games behind the Giants, who swept a doubleheader from Philadelphia. 19-17, Fourth, 2 games behind.

Saturday, May 31, at Boston—The largest non-Sunday crowd at Braves Field since 1933 saw Ralph Branca earn his fourth straight win, a 5–0 shutout that got the Dodgers back on track after three consecutive defeats. Pete Reiser's home run with a man on was the big blow in Brooklyn's four-run third inning. Braves pitcher Mort Cooper hit Jackie Robinson in the seventh inning. It was the second time Robinson had been hit by Cooper and the sixth time he had been hit this season. 20-17, Third (T), 2 games behind.

Sunday, June 1, vs. St. Louis—The so-far disappointing Cardinals were in last place when they made their second visit to Ebbets Field. Harry Taylor kept them there with a five-hit, complete-game 6–1 win over Harry Brecheen. Dixie Walker broke his 2-for-15 slump with three hits and three runs batted in. Carl Furillo also had three hits. 21-17, Fourth, 1½ games behind.

Monday, June 2, vs. St. Louis—Howie Pollet's two-out single in the tenth inning drove in the winning run in the Cardinals' 5–4 victory. Pollet pitched the entire game, while Ralph Branca, the fourth of five pitchers used by Burt Shotton, was the loser. 21-18, Fourth, 1½ games behind.

Tuesday, June 3, vs. Pittsburgh (2)—After being swept in their previous two doubleheaders, the Dodgers managed their first sweep of the season. They turned back the Pirates, 11–6 and 8–7, in Pittsburgh's 1947 debut at Ebbets Field. Rex Barney, who started the first game and relieved in the second, was credited with the win in each. Kirby Higbe, in his return to Brooklyn, and Preacher Roe were the starters and losers for the Pirates. Eddie Stanky led the Brooklyn attack in the opener with a single, two doubles, and a triple, and three runs batted in. The Dodgers staked Hal Gregg to a 6–0 lead in the nightcap, but he struggled through four innings and the official scorer awarded the win to Barney. 23-18, Third, 1 game behind.

Wednesday, June 4, vs. Pittsburgh—Two days after losing to St. Louis in relief, Ralph Branca went the distance in defeating Pittsburgh, 9–4. Hank Greenberg and Ralph Kiner hit solo home runs for the Pirates, and Bruce Edwards had a two-run blast for the Dodgers. But the big blow of the game was Pee Wee Reese's second-inning grand slam off starter Elmer Singleton. Despite the win, it was a somber day for the Dodgers. While chasing Culley Rikard's long drive in the sixth inning, Pete Reiser crashed into the center-field wall and had to be removed from the field on a stretcher. 24-18, Third, .004 percentage points behind.

Thursday, June 5, vs. Pittsburgh—Brooklyn moved into first place behind Harry Taylor's two-hit 3–0 shutout. Wally Westlake, with a single and a triple, had the Pirates' only hits against Taylor, who pitched his third consecutive complete game. Jackie Robinson had three hits, including a home run. Bruce Edwards also had three hits. Doctors at Swedish hospital reported that Pete Reiser had suffered a brain concussion, but should be back in the lineup in two weeks. 25-18, First, ½ game ahead.

Friday, June 6, vs. Chicago—A four-run second inning sparked the Dodgers to a 6–2 win. Joe Hatten went the distance despite allowing nine hits. Eddie Stanky had three hits, and Jackie Robinson and Spider Jorgensen had two. Jorgensen's double was Brooklyn's only extra-base hit. 26-18, First, ½ game ahead.

Saturday, June 7, vs. Chicago—Rained out. 26-18, First, ½ game ahead.

Sunday, June 8, vs. Chicago—Rained out. 26-18, First, ½ game ahead.

Monday, June 9, vs. Cincinnati—The Reds ended Brooklyn's five-game win streak and knocked the Dodgers out of first place with a 9-6 win. Four Dodgers pitchers followed starter Harry Taylor, who lasted just one and one-third innings. Vic Lombardi was the loser, though it was Hugh Casey who allowed Cincinnati's big blow: Benny Zientara's three-run homer in the eighth. Brooklyn had thirteen hits off three Reds pitchers, including Pee Wee Reese's sixth home run. 26-19, Second, ½ game behind.

Tuesday, June 10, vs. Cincinnati (2)—Cincinnati's Ewell Blackwell outpitched Ralph Branca in the first game of the doubleheader, 3–1. But Brooklyn rallied to win the second game, 6–5, with Branca getting the win with two innings of scoreless relief. Blackwell, who had shut out the Dodgers on May 14, held them scoreless until Marv Rackley singled home Gene Hermanski with two outs in the ninth. Brooklyn jumped on Johnny Vander Meer for a 4–0 lead in the nightcap. Rex Barney held the lead until the Reds scored five runs against him and Hal Gregg in the sixth and seventh. In the home eighth, a solo home run by Jackie Robinson and a run-scoring double by Bruce Edwards provided the Dodgers with the tying and winning runs. Tommy Brown had his first extra-base hit, a double, and first run batted in of the season. 27-20, Second (T), 1 game behind.

Wednesday, June 11, vs. Cincinnati—Jackie Robinson had two singles, a double, and a triple, but Brooklyn lost again to the Reds, 5–4. Cincinnati won with a four-run sixth against starter Joe Hatten. Pinch-hitter Ray Mueller's bases-loaded double was the key blow. Brooklyn remained one game behind the first-place Giants. 27-21, Second, 1 game behind.

Thursday, June 12—Not scheduled. 27-21, Second (T), 1 game behind.

Friday, June 13, at St. Louis—The Dodgers opened their second western swing with a 3–0 loss at Sportsman's Park in St. Louis. George Munger allowed the Dodgers just three hits, singles by Eddie Stanky and Gene Hermanski, and a double by opposing starter Harry Taylor. Ron Northey, with a single, double, and home run, was the hitting star for the seventh-place Cardinals. Bruce Edwards injured his hand during the game, and rookie Gil Hodges would do most of the catching for the next two weeks. Pitcher Hank Behrman, who had gone to Pittsburgh in the Kirby Higbe trade, was returned to Brooklyn. 27-22, Fourth, 1½ games behind.

Saturday, June 14, at St. Louis (2)—St. Louis won both ends of a day-night doubleheader behind complete-game performances by left-handers Al Brazle and Harry Brecheen. The Cardinals had twelve hits in winning the afternoon game, 5–3, including three each by Red Schoendienst and Whitey Kurowski. Meanwhile, the Dodgers committed three errors behind loser Ralph Branca. Schoendienst also had three of St. Louis's fourteen hits in the 12-2 night-game romp. The Cardinals got home runs from Stan Musial, Ron Northey, and Joe Garagiola. Rex Barney, the starter and loser, was followed by Ed Chandler and Hank Behrman, newly returned from Pittsburgh. 27-24, Fourth, 2½ games behind.

Sunday, June 15, at St. Louis—Howie Pollet's 11–3 win gave the Cardinals a sweep of the four-game series and dealt the Dodgers their fifth straight loss. For Pollet, who was 1-7 against the rest of the league, it was his third win of the season without a loss against Brooklyn. The Cardinals battered Joe Hatten and Hal Gregg and had a 10–0 lead before the Dodgers scored their three runs in the eighth inning. Brooklyn dropped to three games behind Boston, the new leader. 27-25, Fourth, 3 games behind.

# Chapter 25. Gene Hermanski

*Leonard Levin and Robert H. Schaefer*

| AGE | G | AB | R | H | 2B | 3B | HR | TB | RBI | BB | SO | BAV | OBP | SLG | SB | GDP | HBP |
|---|---|---|---|---|---|---|---|---|---|---|---|---|---|---|---|---|---|
| 27 | 79 | 189 | 36 | 52 | 7 | 1 | 7 | 82 | 39 | 28 | 7 | .275 | .377 | .434 | 5 | 3 | 3 |

The opportunity for Gene Hermanski to become a member of the Brooklyn Dodgers arose when one of the Class D teams he played for in 1940 folded after the season. When that happened, Hermanski became a free agent. Signed by the Dodgers, he eventually made his way to the big leagues, where he became a reliable backup outfielder on the 1947 pennant-winning Dodgers, and carved out a career playing mostly a utility role for nine seasons.

Eugene Victor Hermanski was born in Pittsfield, Massachusetts, on May 11, 1920, to Stephen and Pauline (Oboyski) Hermanski (the family name was also spelled Horomanski and Horomenski). Stephen, seeking new opportunities, moved his family to Newark, New Jersey, in 1924 shortly after their second son, Roman, was born.[1]

Baseball became an important part of Gene's life at an early age. He played for Newark's East Side High School, winners of the state championship, and also played in the semipro Essex County League.[2] After he graduated, Hermanski signed with the Philadelphia Athletics, and in 1939 he played for Kinston (North Carolina) in the Class D Coastal Plain League and Federalsburg (Maryland) in the Class D Eastern Shore League. Gene, a left-handed-hitting, right-handed-throwing outfielder, hit a combined .244 in seventy-six games in his first season of professional baseball.

In 1940 he again played at Kinston and Federalsburg but ended the season with the Pocomoke City (Maryland) Chicks of the Eastern Shore League. Though the Chicks were an Athletics affiliate, Hermanski teamed there with a future Dodgers teammate, All-Star outfielder Carl Furillo. At

Gene Hermanski started all seven games of the World Series against the Yankees.

Federalsburg and Pocomoke City, Hermanski hit a combined .309 with eleven home runs.

Pocomoke City, which finished last in the eight-team circuit, disbanded at the end of the 1940 season, making the twenty-year-old Hermanski a free agent. Gene then notified the Dodgers he was available; they signed him and sent him to the Montreal Royals, their Class Triple-A affiliate in the

International League. Hermanski never played with Montreal, though, because the Royals promptly optioned him to the Olean (New York) Oilers in the Class D PONY League, a team managed by future Dodgers coach Jake Pitler. Gene was a man among boys in the early going. Through mid-June he was leading the league in home runs and hits and was third in batting at .381.[3] In 105 games at Olean, Hermanski hit .341 (third in the league) with 22 doubles, 7 triples, 8 home runs, and a league-leading 142 hits.[4]

Montreal recalled Hermanski after the PONY League season ended, but he did not see any action with the Royals.[5] Due to his outstanding 1941 season, he was expected to have a shot at playing in the International League the next year. World events intervened, as they did for so many young men in the early 1940s. In 1942, with the United States at war, Hermanski joined the Coast Guard. While stationed in Salem, Massachusetts, he played against the Red Sox and the Braves in exhibition games, with some success.[6] On August 8, 1943, he was given leave from the Coast Guard to enlist in the navy's aviation training program. With two months' leave before reporting to his new assignment, Hermanski used the time to play baseball. The Dodgers sent him to the Durham (North Carolina) Bulls, their affiliate in the Class B Piedmont League. In ten games at Durham, Hermanski had a .410 batting average and a .667 slugging percentage.

With their roster depleted by the draft, the Dodgers brought the five-foot-eleven, 180-pound Hermanski to Brooklyn. He made his Major League debut on August 14, 1943, in the first game of a doubleheader against the Reds at Ebbets Field. Gene batted third, played left field, and went hitless in four at bats. He started the nightcap in left field as well and had his first big league hit, a single, off Reds starter Bucky Walters. Gene also had another single in the game and started a double play from the outfield.[7]

In the next day's doubleheader against the Cardinals, Hermanski became a local hero, at least for a day. Gene played right field in the opener and went 2 for 3, with a double and two runs batted in. The Dodgers lost, but they won the nightcap when Gene drove in the game-winning run. St. Louis had taken a one-run lead in the top of the tenth inning, but the Dodgers came right back in the bottom of the frame. With one out, the score tied, and the bases filled, Hermanski, who was 0 for 2 in the game, strode to the plate to face Ernie White. After throwing two wide ones, White was replaced by right-hander Howie Krist.

Gene fouled off the first two Krist offerings, then took ball three. With the crowd going wild, Krist threw ball four to force in the winning run. Hermanski, so caught up in the excitement, headed for the dugout without touching first base. Cooler heads intervened and Hermanski made it safely to first, and the game was over.[8] On August 20 Gene hit a triple in the bottom of the eighth against the Cubs and then stole home as the Dodgers won, 6–3.[9] During his leave he appeared in eighteen games with the Dodgers, with a .300 batting average and twelve runs batted in.

After six months in Naval Aviation, Hermanski failed to make the grade. In 1944 he was returned to the Coast Guard where he managed and played the outfield for the Floyd Bennett Field (Brooklyn) Fliers. Additionally, he was playing nights and weekends for the semipro Brooklyn Bushwicks under the name Gene Walsh. The Bushwicks, who played their home games at Dexter Park in Queens, paid "Walsh" $50 per game, considerably more than the $77 per month he was getting from the Coast Guard.[10]

At war's end Hermanski reported to the Dodgers' spring training camp much further along in his baseball development than many of his contemporaries. Consequently, he started the 1946 season with Brooklyn. The 1946 Dodgers, managed by Leo Durocher, had a starting outfield of Dixie

Walker, Carl Furillo, and Pete Reiser, with Augie Galan and Dick Whitman in reserve. Hermanski appeared in just thirty-four games in the field. He produced a woeful .938 fielding percentage with no assists. Overall, he got into sixty-four games in his rookie season, batting .200 (22 for 110).

Hermanski was Brooklyn's starting left fielder on April 15, 1947, the day Jackie Robinson broke the color barrier. He had a single and a sacrifice fly and helped to deliver the first Dodgers run with a rolling takeout of Braves second baseman Connie Ryan, thereby avoiding an inning-ending double play.[11] The Dodgers prevailed, 5–3, in the historic contest. Gene got into seventy-five games in 1947; he batted .275 and displayed some power.

His first Major League home run came on April 26 before a sellout crowd at Ebbets Field. In the sixth inning, with Dixie Walker on base, Hermanski laced the first pitch from Giants starter Bill Voiselle into Bedford Avenue. The two-run blast gave the Dodgers a lead they never relinquished as they went on to win, 7–3, and take over first place.[12] Hermanski finished Brooklyn's pennant-winning campaign with 7 doubles, 1 triple, 7 home runs, and 39 RBIs. Playing mostly left field, he had 5 assists and made just 2 errors in 112 chances.

Hermanski started all seven games of the World Series against the Yankees, going 3 for 19 in the losing cause. His lasting memory of the 1947 Series is that "I hit the ball very hard, but each time it was right at one of those Yanks."

In 1948 Hermanski became the Dodgers' full-time right fielder and responded with his best season to date. He played in a career-high 133 games, set career marks for hits (116), walks (64), doubles (22), triples (7), home runs (15), runs (63), stolen bases (15), and RBIs (60), and achieved his third-highest batting average (.290). His 15 home runs led the club.

The highlight of Gene's '48 season came on August 5 when he hit three home runs in a nine-inning game at Ebbets Field. His blasts came off

Chicago Cubs pitchers Ralph Hamner in the first and third innings and Jess Dobernic in the eighth. The three home runs accounted for five of the Dodgers' six runs as they defeated the Cubs, 6–4.[13]

Defensively, Hermanski had thirteen assists, tying with teammate Carl Furillo for fifth highest among National League outfielders. However, his .971 fielding percentage was the second lowest in the National League among everyday outfielders.

Ten different players played the outfield for Brooklyn in 1949, with Duke Snider and Carl Furillo as the only two regulars. Hermanski played seventy-seven games in the field, the most among the other eight outfielders. He displayed all his talents on April 26. He hit a home run off Braves starter Johnny Sain in the bottom of the first to knot the score at 1–1. Then in the third, with two aboard and no one out, he made a shoestring catch of a drive that base runners Sain and Eddie Stanky thought he could not reach. He then fired the ball to Robinson at second, who in turn relayed it to first baseman Gil Hodges for the 7-4-3 triple play.[14]

Hermanski hit his two career grand slams in 1949. The first came on July 2 at the Polo Grounds off the Giants' Andy Hansen, and the second on July 28 off Chicago's Bob Rush at Wrigley Field. Gene played in eighty-seven games in '49 and had a career-high .299 batting average. He had 47 walks to go with his 67 hits to yield an impressive .431 on-base percentage. Hermanski perennially had an on-base percentage at least 100 points higher than his batting average.

Once more the Dodgers won the pennant and once more they lost to the Yankees in the World Series. Hermanski appeared in four of the five games, hitting .308 (4 for 13) with 1 triple and 2 runs batted in. After initially balking at his 1950 salary offer, he signed for $12,000, reportedly a "slight raise."[15] Hermanski played in ninety-four games that year and produced almost identical statistics as in the previous two seasons: a .298 batting average, 7 home runs, and 34 runs batted in.

Playing primarily against right-handed pitchers, he had developed into a consistent hitter.

On June 15, 1951, the Dodgers included Hermanski in an eight-player deal with the Cubs. Gene, catcher Bruce Edwards, pitcher Joe Hatten, and infielder Eddie Miksis went to Chicago for catcher Rube Walker, pitcher Johnny Schmitz, infielder Wayne Terwilliger, and outfielder Andy Pafko, the player most coveted by Brooklyn.

Hermanski batted .280 in seventy-five games for the eighth-place Cubs, playing mostly in right field. He was back with the Cubs in 1952, but he batted just .255 with 4 home runs and 34 RBIS, a marked decline from his best days in Brooklyn. Early in the 1953 season, after he had hit only .150 in eighteen games, the Cubs traded Hermanski to the Pittsburgh Pirates as part of a major deal that brought slugger Ralph Kiner to the Cubs. Hermanski batted a meager .177 in forty-one games for the Pirates, giving him an overall season average of .167.

Pittsburgh released Hermanski in mid-April 1954. He left the Majors with a respectable .272 batting average, a .372 on-base percentage, and 259 RBIS in 739 games. Now free to make his own deal, he signed with Oakland of the Pacific Coast League, where he was reunited with former Dodgers coach and manager Charlie Dressen. Gene got off to a great start with the Oaks and was hitting .348 at the end of April.[16] He appeared in 104 of Oakland's 167 games in 1954, hitting .270 with 11 home runs.

In January 1955 Oakland sold Gene's contract to Beaumont of the Texas League.[17] Hermanski, now thirty-four, went to spring training with the Exporters but did not play in a regular season game with them.[18] By June he was a salesman for the Parker-Danner Company of East Providence, Rhode Island, a supplier of heavy construction equipment.[19] He and his wife, Phyllis, settled in Barrington, Rhode Island, and eventually moved to nearby North Attleboro, Massachusetts.[20]

In the 1970s, Gene, residing in North Plainfield, New Jersey, was a salesman for the Mid-West Emery Truck Company of Jersey City.[21] Phyllis died on December 31, 1987. Their daughter, Lynda, born in 1950, died in 1985.

Hermanski was ninety years old when he died in Homosassa Springs, Florida, on August 9, 2010. He was survived by his second wife, Carol, whom he married in 1973.

LEONARD LEVIN AND ROBERT H. SCHAEFER

# Chapter 26. **Hugh Casey**

*Russell Wolinsky*

| AGE | W | L | PCT. | ERA | G | GS | GF | CG | SHO | SV | IP | H | BB | SO | HBP | WP |
|---|---|---|---|---|---|---|---|---|---|---|---|---|---|---|---|---|
| 33 | 10 | 4 | .714 | 3.99 | 46 | 0 | 37 | 0 | 0 | 18 | 76.2 | 75 | 29 | 40 | 2 | 0 |

On Monday evening, September 22, 1947, the "sizzling steaks [were] on the house . . . [and] free gravy down the shirt front" was de rigueur at 600 Flatbush Avenue.[1] Pitcher Hugh Casey, proprietor of Hugh Casey's Steak and Chop House, was optimistically throwing a victory dinner party for his Dodgers teammates. Brooklyn's beloved "Bums" stood poised to clinch their second National League pennant of the decade, and the right-handed relief ace, "a genial, happy host," was delighted to treat.[2]

Some apprehension remained. Brooklyn had lost three consecutive games, allowing three chances to nail down the National League championship slip through their fingers. The Dodgers were idle this Monday. The St. Louis Cardinals, their closest competitors, were playing a double-header at home against the Chicago Cubs. At Casey's joint, a group of Dodgers players and their wives huddled in a booth and anxiously awaited results of the nightcap from St. Louis.

Finally, close to midnight, the tavern's manager happily announced the final score from St. Louis: Cubs 6, Cardinals 3. All hell broke loose, not only at Casey's but on the streets of Flatbush as well. An impromptu party broke out on Flatbush Avenue. Led by an unnamed accordion player, Dodgers players and their wives formed a conga line that joyously marched down Brooklyn's major thoroughfare. The inn's proprietor, Hugh Casey, quietly beamed and joined in the merriment.

Hugh Thomas Casey was born in Atlanta, Georgia, on October 14, 1913. He was the youngest of seven children (five boys, two girls) born to James Oliver Casey, a Fulton County police cap-

Hugh Casey was 10-4 in 1947, his last big season.

tain, and Elizabeth Casey. Young Hugh had already gained some notoriety as a hard-throwing teenage pitcher when he first encountered Wilbert Robinson, the legendary former Brooklyn manager. The two met in the early 1930s at Dover Hall, a former plantation just outside Brunswick, Georgia, that served as a hunting and drinking retreat for vacationing northerners like Robinson. Robby immediately took a liking to the big Georgian—more at first for his hunting prowess than his ability on a baseball diamond—and hired Hugh as a sort of aide de camp.

Casey's baseball talents soon became obvious to the ex-catcher when he noticed the oversized teen tossing rocks at empty whiskey bottles precariously balanced on fences. Robinson noted the pitcher's superior velocity and pinpoint control; he threw hard and never seemed to miss hitting a bottle. Knowing a big league prospect when he saw one, Robby took Hugh under his wing, encouraging and coaching him.

The Detroit Tigers signed Casey after he graduated from high school in 1931. In May 1932, after a brief stay in the Detroit system in which he never appeared in a game, the Tigers dropped him. By 1934 Casey was pitching with his local team, the Southern Association's Atlanta Crackers. It was his second go-around with the Crackers; he had unsuccessfully debuted with them as an eighteen-year-old two seasons earlier. In 1933 Casey logged a 19-9 mark for the Charlotte Hornets of the Class B Piedmont League, and he returned to his hometown with renewed confidence.

In 1934 the Crackers' new president was Casey's old mentor, Wilbert Robinson. Cincinnati Reds general manager Larry MacPhail was in Atlanta on a scouting trip, and Robinson suggested to MacPhail that he sign Casey. MacPhail passed on Casey, but shortly thereafter the Chicago Cubs drafted him.

Casey spent the entire 1935 season with Chicago but saw little action. "Sometimes I think [manager] Charlie Grimm never knew I was with the club. . . . I knew every blade of grass in every bullpen throughout the league," Casey recalled.[3] In his Major League debut, on April 29, he pitched two and two-thirds scoreless innings in a wild 12–11 victory over Pittsburgh at Wrigley Field. The official scorer ruled Casey the winning pitcher, but National League president Ford Frick later overruled that decision. The hard-throwing right-hander ended his rookie campaign having thrown only twenty-five and two-thirds innings in thirteen games, with a 0-0 record and a 3.86 earned run average. He was not included on the Cubs' World Series roster, though he received a full share of World Series money.

Grimm sent Casey to the Los Angeles Angels of the Pacific Coast League the following March. Hugh hurt his arm while with the Angels and lost a great deal of velocity on his fastball. Forced to adapt, he quickly developed what he called a "splitter" to complement his excellent curve ball; skeptics later claimed that Casey's new pitch could be more accurately described by simply eliminating the "l."

Toiling as a starter, Casey spent the next three seasons in the Minors perfecting his craft and reinventing himself on the mound. In 1937, with Birmingham, he led the Southern Association with a 2.56 ERA. Ignoring concerns about Casey's weight—he was six feet one but weighed well over 200 pounds—Brooklyn drafted him off the Memphis Chicks roster following the 1938 season.[4]

"He knows how to pitch," determined new Dodgers skipper Leo Durocher after observing Casey in spring training in 1939.[5] In his first starting assignment, on May 30, Casey drew as his opponent New York Giants ace Carl Hubbell. Before a crowd of nearly 59,000 at the Polo Grounds, Casey outpitched the future Hall of Famer, 3–1.

He finished the 1939 campaign 15-10 for a third-place Dodgers team, working mostly as a starter. At the time, Casey's pitching repertoire consisted of a "sneaky fast" hard one, a pitch quicker than it appeared when juxtaposed with his superior curve, and his "splitter." "He has a head on him—and he has heart," said Durocher. "You won't see him flinch in the jam."[6]

On July 19, 1940, at Wrigley Field, with the Cubs enjoying a big lead, Casey entered the game in the eighth inning and plunked Cubs pitcher Claude Passeau between the shoulder blades. The enraged Passeau immediately hurled his bat toward the pitcher's mound. Casey started toward the plate, but Brooklyn's Joe Gallagher got there first and began pummeling Passeau. A full-scale brawl ensued, requiring the police to intervene. This was far from the last time that Casey—who more than once admitted, "I'm a mean man on the mound"—would hurl a pitch in anger.[7]

Less than a year later, on May 19, 1941, Passeau got his revenge by connecting on a Casey fastball for a second-inning grand slam. Casey, who was the starting pitcher that afternoon, later claimed that the incident marked the start of his career as a reliever. After Passeau's home run, manager Durocher stormed out to the mound to make a pitching change, screaming at his shell-shocked hurler, "You're in the bullpen for the rest of your life."[8]

Casey remained in the rotation until mid-July, but Durocher finally made the switch, and Casey finally found his true niche. In nineteen relief appearances between July 29 and the conclusion of the '41 campaign, Casey posted a 2.23 ERA as the Dodgers stormed to their first pennant since 1920. Averaging two-plus innings pitched per outing, the moon-faced reliever took the hill in six of the Dodgers' ten contests between August 16 and 23. He finished the final ten games in which he appeared that September. "We couldn't have won without Hugh Casey's great relief pitching," said Durocher at the end of the season.[9]

Brooklyn clinched the National League flag on September 25 at Braves Field in Boston. The Dodgers were to face the mighty New York Yankees in the two teams' inaugural Fall Classic meeting. Casey strutted around Yankee Stadium before Game One and announced that he was more than ready for "them damn Yankees." (Casey was never shy about his southern roots.) "Ah promise to protect that advantage with mah life's blood," he exclaimed. "Which is the blood of the old South and the Confederacy, suh!"[10] In the Series opener he made good on his boast, relieving in the sixth inning with two on base and retiring Phil Rizzu-

to and Red Ruffing on fly balls before he was lifted for a pinch hitter in the top of the seventh.

After the Dodgers won Game Two to tie the Series, the scene shifted to Ebbets Field, and Casey's fortunes turned for the worse. Durocher called on him in the eighth inning of a scoreless Game Three after starter Fred Fitzsimmons had been struck on the left knee by a drive off the bat of his mound opponent, Marius Russo. Hugh allowed a pair of Yankees tallies on four consecutive singles, including one by Tommy Henrich in which Casey was slow in covering first base. The final score was 2–1 Yankees.

Game Four was played on October 5, an unseasonably warm Sunday in Brooklyn. Called on to relieve Johnny Allen with two out in the fifth, Brooklyn trailing 3–2, and the bases loaded, Casey got Joe Gordon on a fly to left to end the threat. The Dodgers took a 4–3 lead in the bottom of the inning on Pete Reiser's two-run homer. Hugh doggedly guarded that slim edge until there were two out in the ninth.

Then, with Henrich again at the plate, Casey's 3-2 curve—or was it a spitter?—broke sharply down and away from the mitt of Brooklyn catcher Mickey Owen and toward the backstop. Henrich, equally fooled by the pitch, flailed futilely at it, quickly glanced back, and then hustled to first. He arrived there safely before the frustrated Owen could recover. The Yankees then reached Casey for a single, two doubles, and two walks before he finally got the third out.

The Dodgers failed to score in the bottom of the ninth, and Casey was a loser for the second consecutive day. New York's 7–4 victory gave them a commanding 3–1 lead. When they clinched the title the following afternoon, it seemed almost anticlimactic to Brooklyn fans.

Owen, who was charged with an error on the play, was practically in tears after the Game Four loss. "Sure, it was my fault," he moaned. His batterymate was more philosophical about it, at least to the press. "I guess I've lost 'em just about every way now."[11] For the rest of his life, Casey maintained that the pitch was a curve and not a spitter.

After an off-season that included harrowing memories of the pitch that got away, questions about his military status, a threat by the pitcher to retire from baseball and instead pump gas in Atlanta (a weak ploy for more money), a separation from his wife, Kathleen (Thomas) Casey, whom he had married in 1937, and an intense dieting regimen, it was Ernest Hemingway, and not fate, that nearly knocked Casey out.

With the Dodgers training in Havana, Cuba, in 1942, the author—who spent a lot of time there and was a big baseball fan—invited a group of Dodgers to accompany him for an evening of eating, drinking, and merriment. After several rounds of drinks, Hemingway sized up Casey and challenged him to a few rounds of boxing. Casey demurred at first, but after Hemingway sucker-punched him, Casey donned a pair of gloves and began to batter his host.

Tables, chairs, trays, and glasses went flying as the two inebriated men exchanged blows. At one point, Hemingway's wife, journalist Martha Gellhorn, awakened by the commotion, came down from her bedroom to see what the ruckus was all about. Ernest assured her it was nothing serious. Finally, tired of being knocked down so often, the author administered a shot to Casey's groin and then surrendered.

Both Casey and the Dodgers began the 1942 campaign on fire. Going into a July 18 doubleheader at St. Louis, Brooklyn led the second-place Cardinals by eight games. Casey was sporting a tidy 1.80 ERA after seventy-five innings pitched, spread over twenty-nine appearances. In addition, he was doing his share for the war effort by visiting shipyard workers around the borough and lending a hand to the War Bond drive. Big Hugh was photographed often at one of those shipyards, the ever-present cigar wedged firmly in his mouth.

In the July 18 opener, Casey was nursing a 4–3 lead with two out in the sixth inning when a Stan Musial line drive fractured the pinky finger of his pitching hand.[12] Casey tried to make the play but threw wildly to first, allowing both base runners to score in what eventually became a 7–4 Brooklyn defeat. Once removed from the contest, Casey sat in front of his locker and downed an entire pint of whiskey.[13] His broken finger kept him out of action until August 6.

The Cardinals, nine games behind the Dodgers as play started on August 11, won thirty of their next thirty-six games and vaulted into first place on September 13. Despite Brooklyn's 10-2 streak to end the season, the Cardinals went 11-1, and the Dodgers fell two games short of repeating as National League champions. Casey contributed a 1.64 ERA in six games during that twelve-game span. The disappointment lingered with Casey for years, as military duty prevented him from seeing big league action again until 1946.

Casey reported for active duty with the U.S. Navy in January 1943 and spent the next three years in the military, rising to the rank of chief petty officer. Most of his time in the service, however, was spent playing ball. Released from active duty in December 1945, Casey reported to the Dodgers' training camp in Daytona Beach, Florida, in the spring of 1946. Despite a rocky start and finish, he enjoyed another stellar season in the Dodgers' bullpen, with an 11-5 record and a 1.99 ERA.

On the final day of the season, the Dodgers and the Cardinals were tied for first place. With Brooklyn trailing the Boston Braves 1–0 at Ebbets Field, Casey was called in to hold Boston in the ninth inning. But he allowed a walk and two hits before Durocher removed him. The Dodgers eventually lost, 4–0, but St. Louis lost also, necessitating a tiebreaking playoff for the first time in Major League history. With Brooklyn quickly dropping two straight to the Cardinals—holding a lead only in the first inning of Game Two—the relief ace's talents were not required.

The Dodgers and Casey bounced back to win the pennant in 1947. Once again the Yankees provided the competition in the World Series, and once again Brooklyn came up short. En route to the pennant, some cracks were beginning to appear in the façade of thirty-three-year-old Hugh Casey.

Despite eighteen saves in 1947—a figure that would have led the National League had saves been an official statistic—Casey had to shut down for the regular season in mid-September because of a lame shoulder and a kink in his right elbow. He had become mostly a spectator, albeit an enthusiastic one, when he threw his pennant-clinching bash at his bistro.

Casey's ERA ballooned to 3.99, double what it was in 1946. This was also the first season he served entirely as a reliever, not starting a single game.[14] Late on a May evening in the Park Slope section of Brooklyn, while driving to his Flatbush tavern, Casey struck and killed a blind man. There were no criminal charges pressed against him, nor was he arrested. Questions remained, however, as to the state of his sobriety at the time of the accident.

In many ways the 1947 World Series was a showcase for the teams' ace relievers: Casey and New York's Joe Page. Casey established a World Series record by appearing in six games, five consecutively.[15] He was credited with two wins and a save, allowing only one run and five hits in ten and one-third innings. Page, whose numbers were not as good as Casey's, received the greater accolades primarily for his five relief innings of no-run, one-hit pitching in the decisive Game Seven, won by the Yankees, 5–2.

If there was a moment of redemption for Casey in the '47 Series, it came on a single pitch in the ninth inning of Game Four. With the bases loaded and one out, he induced his old nemesis, Tommy Henrich, to bounce into a 1-2-3 double play. Cookie Lavagetto's pinch-hit, two-run, game-winning double in the bottom of the ninth denied New York's Bill Bevens both a victory and the first World Series no-hitter. To Casey, Brooklyn's dramatic 3–2 win made up for every game the Dodgers ever lost to the Yankees.

By 1948 everything was beginning to go wrong for Hugh Casey. He reported to the Dodgers' spring training camp in the Dominican Republic grossly overweight, and later was sidelined by what was described as "a mysterious ailment."[16] On Opening Day, at the Polo Grounds, Casey was barely able to hang on to a 7–3 Brooklyn lead, allowing three runs to score before finally getting the final out with the tying run on third base.

On May 20, during a loss to St. Louis, Casey beaned Cardinals catcher Del Rice. "The ball wasn't more than an inch or so inside," Casey muttered in his defense. But Cardinals manager Eddie Dyer "half-drawled" to Hugh, "You're a better pitcher than that."[17]

Then, four days later, Casey slipped and fell down a flight of stairs coming from his apartment, directly above his bar. Suffering "torn tendons and ligaments" after landing heavily on his right side, he did not pitch for more than two months.

Casey's heavy drinking was becoming more and more obvious. Dodgers broadcaster Red Barber noted that, according to other Dodgers, Hugh's bedtime routine included cigars, comic books, and a bottle of whiskey. He would lie in bed smoking the stogie, reading the comic books, and drinking his liquor straight until either "the bottle or he was finished."[18]

After his injury, Casey made three successful "rehab" appearances for the semipro Bushwicks in early July before making his first appearance with the Dodgers. Pitching before a crowd of 65,000 at Cleveland's Municipal Stadium on July 14, he tossed four and two-thirds effective innings in an exhibition game against the Indians. After pitching only thirty-six innings and posting an ERA of 8.00 in 1948, the Dodgers released him on September 29.

In October, Casey, now thirty-five, signed with the Pittsburgh Pirates. Used sparingly, he appeared in only thirty-three games in 1949, often in a mop-up role. In two consecutive games against Brooklyn—June 25 and 26—Casey was battered by his ex-teammates. In the June 26 game, he twice threw pitches close to Jackie Robinson. His second delivery hit Jackie in the right knee. Robinson made several comments to the pitcher as he made his way to first base, but Casey just stared at him without saying a word. After the Pirates released him on August 10, Casey signed with the Yankees. He appeared in only four games and was ineffective in three of them.

Casey returned to his hometown Atlanta Crackers for the 1950 campaign, where he was reunited with former Dodgers teammates Dixie Walker, now the Southern Association club's manager, and Whitlow Wyatt, their pitching coach. He won ten games working as both a starter and a reliever for the pennant-winning Crackers.

But in 1950 Casey's personal problems were beginning to mount. He was sued by a Brooklyn woman, Hilda Weissman, who alleged that Casey was the father of her son, Michael Hammond, born the previous November 2. "I know the girl," Casey explained. "She used to hang around the ball park and the ball players in Brooklyn, and come into my bar and grill once in a while. But that's all."[19]

Weissman, however, described four evenings spent with Casey at Brooklyn's St. George Hotel in January and February 1949. After a trial in December 1950, Casey was ruled the father of the child and ordered to pay $20-a-week child support to Weissman. He said he would appeal the verdict, while his wife, Kathleen, who was by his side through the entire trial, was supportive. "My belief in my husband still stands," she proclaimed after the verdict. "I know he is not guilty of being the father of this child."

Meanwhile, Casey's life continued to unravel.

On January 31, 1951, a tax lien for $6,759.36 was filed against him for unpaid income taxes. Now sole proprietor of Hugh Casey's Steak and Chop House, he feared he would lose the bar. Casey desperately tried hooking on with the Dodgers again for the '51 season, but he could get no further than pitching batting practice at Ebbets Field. He pitched once more at Dexter Park, in April 1951, this time as a member of the Hartford Indians against the Bushwicks. In May, Casey and his wife separated again, though Kathleen claimed it had nothing to do with the paternity suit.

A month later, in June 1951, Casey returned to Atlanta, ostensibly to try to settle his tax problems. He checked into the downtown Atlantan Hotel and allegedly told the bellboy that he was suffering from a leaking heart valve and had only ten days to live.

During the early morning of July 3, 1951, Casey made two phone calls from his hotel room. One was to his good friend Gordon McNabb, an Atlanta real-estate agent. The other was to his wife. In both cases, he announced that he was going to kill himself. With the estranged Mrs. Casey on the line begging him not to do it, Casey placed a 16-gauge shotgun to his head. At about the same time, McNabb and his wife were about thirty feet away from Casey's room, rushing to stop him from acting out his threat. All three heard the single shot fired from the shotgun. According to Kathleen Casey, Hugh's final words were, "I am innocent of those [paternity] charges."[20]

When the news reached Casey's bar, a group of patrons raised their glasses one final time to the man whose round face and ample body looked down on them in a portrait. A toast was proposed to "the guy who was kind to everyone but himself."[21] With Dixie Walker and Whit Wyatt serving as pallbearers, Hugh Casey was buried in the Mount Paran Church of God cemetery in Atlanta, Georgia, on July 4, 1951.

## Chapter 27. **Rex Barney**

*Don Harrison*

| AGE | W | L | PCT. | ERA | G | GS | GF | CG | SHO | SV | IP | H | BB | SO | HBP | WP |
|-----|---|---|------|-----|---|----|----|----|----|----|-----|----|----|----|-----|-----|
| 22 | 5 | 2 | .714 | 4.75 | 28 | 9 | 8 | 0 | 0 | 0 | 77.2 | 66 | 59 | 36 | 2 | 5 |

With the possible exception of Sandy Koufax, no Dodgers pitcher ever threw harder than Rex Barney. Throughout the late 1940s, Barney's fastball was the talk of baseball. In 1947, at the age of twenty-two, he struck out Joe DiMaggio with the bases loaded in a World Series game. On a rainy night at the Polo Grounds in 1948, Barney pitched a no-hitter against the New York Giants and appeared on the verge of realizing his greatness. Alas, it was not to be. "Barney pitched as though the plate was high and outside," Bob Cooke wrote famously in the *New York Herald Tribune*.

Born on December 19, 1924, Rex Edward Barney was the youngest of four children of Eugene Spencer and Marie Barney. It was a typical winter night in Omaha, Nebraska—twenty degrees below zero. "My father could not get the old Model T Ford started, so he called somebody to help him rush my mother to the hospital," Barney wrote in his 1993 autobiography. "She told me I was born in the elevator on the way up to the delivery room."

Rex's father worked on the Union Pacific Railroad for forty-five years and eventually became a general foreman. He left home on Sunday night and rode the rails throughout the week before returning on Friday evening. When Rex was born, his sisters, Beatrice and Bernice, were thirteen and eleven, respectively, and his brother, Ted, was nine.

Barney was a star basketball and baseball player at Creighton Prep, a Catholic school for boys in Omaha. He excelled most on the basketball court, leading the team to a pair of state titles and earning all-state recognition. As a high school pitcher, Barney was an angular six-foot-three, 185-pound right-hander who struck out batters by the bushel.

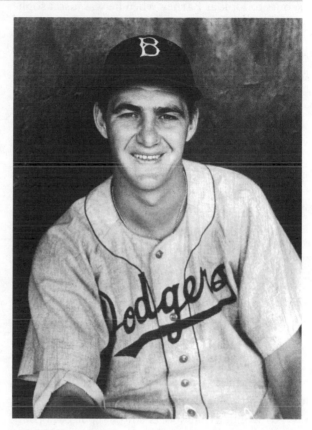

Rex Barney's inability to control his outstanding fastball limited his success.

He was wild, but that is not unusual at that level. Creighton Prep won the state baseball tournament in two of Rex's four years.

Barney credited much of his early success to a man he called "one of Nebraska's greatest high school coaches," Skip Palrang, who coached every sport at Creighton Prep, managed the city's American Legion team, and later became athletic director at Boys Town. Palrang's formidable presence prepared Rex for his years with the volatile Leo

Durocher, first playing for him when he was the Brooklyn manager, and later playing against him when Durocher became the manager of the New York Giants.

The Detroit Tigers, St. Louis Cardinals, New York Yankees, and Brooklyn Dodgers all sent scouts to look at Barney when he was just a sophomore at Creighton Prep. He also began to receive scholarship offers for baseball and basketball from several colleges, most notably Nebraska, Stanford, and Notre Dame.

In the spring of 1943, after Barney's draft board informed him that he soon would be inducted into the army, Rex opted to sign a contract with the Dodgers. The signing bonus was $2,500—but all but $500 of that amount was contingent on Barney's returning from the service and proving he was capable of resuming his baseball career.

Barney enjoyed a meteoric rise through the Dodgers' farm system that spring and summer. He reported to the Class B Piedmont League in Durham, North Carolina, in May and made his debut in relief on June 4 against the Norfolk Tars. His first professional pitch whizzed about five feet above the head of batter Jack Phillips and tore through the chicken-wire screen in front of the field-level press box and conked the local sports editor on the head.

No wonder that sports editor reported, "[Barney's] pitching was of the compass type—he threw in the general direction of the plate." Still, the scribe acknowledged, "The lad has plenty of steam and may develop into a pitcher."

The Dodgers thought so, too. Early on, Durham manager Bruno Betzel took Barney and infielder Gene Mauch aside and told them, "You're the only two guys on this club with a chance to go up." Pitching with a dreadful last-place team, Barney won four games and lost six, but his earned run average was a solid 3.00. He struck out seventy-one batters and walked fifty-one in eighty-one innings.

In late July 1943 both Barney and Mauch were promoted to the Dodgers' top farm club, the Montreal Royals of the International League. Rex appeared in just four games with the Royals and dropped his only decision, but his 2.45 ERA and eighteen strikeouts in twenty-two innings impressed Branch Rickey and the other Dodgers brass. Rex was elevated to Brooklyn for the final five weeks of the season.

As Barney wrote, "The Brooklyn Dodgers, Ebbets Field, and baseball was the greatest triple play God ever executed on this planet. If a player didn't fall in love with Ebbets Field, there had to be something wrong with him. And those fans—their enthusiasm for their beloved Bums was overwhelming. Today they call it chemistry; I prefer to think of it as a love affair. That's what made it such a tragedy when the team left Brooklyn."

The first Major League pitch he threw struck Cubs leadoff hitter Eddie Stanky squarely in the middle of his back. But although he was still nearly four months short of his nineteenth birthday, Rex proved he belonged in the wartime National League, winning two of his four decisions.

Barney entered the army in September 1943 and served at Fort Riley, Kansas, where he played baseball. He and thousands of other apprehensive GIs spent two weeks aboard a troopship, a converted Italian luxury liner, en route from New York to Le Havre, France. Their twelve-ship convoy spent much of the voyage dodging Nazi U-boats; four ships didn't make it.

Assigned to the Fourth and Sixth Armored Divisions of the Third Army, Barney saw action in France and Germany, took German shrapnel in a leg and his back, and was awarded two Purple Hearts and a Bronze Star. His most memorable encounter, though, was with the fiery American general George C. Patton.

Barney was the commander of a lead tank, roaming the advance positions to draw enemy fire from sunup to sundown. On this day, there was a commotion in the rear, and a Jeep flying four stars pulled abreast. "I recognized him immediately," Barney told Dick Young of the *New York Daily News.* "He was my idol. He was sitting behind a 50-caliber machine gun."

They saluted, and Patton said, "Sergeant, where is the front?"

"General," Barney responded, "the front of this tank *is* the front."

"That's too goddamn close for me! Carry on," Patton said, and the Jeep turned around and headed in the opposite direction.

After his discharge Barney rejoined the Dodgers in the spring of 1946. Although the club surprised pundits by challenging the powerful St. Louis Cardinals and tying the Redbirds for the pennant (losing two games to none in the playoff), Rex endured a disappointing year, winning twice and losing five games. Still, the Barney fastball offered considerable promise for 1947.

Just before the start of the '47 season, Dodgers manager Leo Durocher was suspended "for conduct detrimental to baseball" and was replaced by Burt Shotton. Like Durocher, Shotton was perplexed by Barney's inability to cure his wildness. Rex reversed his 1946 record, winning five games and losing two. But his strikeout-to-walk ratio remained a sore point and turned most of his games into nail-biters.

On May 1, 1947, at a Catholic church in Brooklyn, Barney married Beverly Duda, a girl he had known since high school in Omaha. They had two children, Christine and Kevin. The marriage ended in divorce.

For Barney, life on the playing field was far less rewarding, especially late in the season. Nevertheless, Shotton selected Rex to start Game Five of the World Series against the Yankees. For four and two-thirds innings, he allowed just two hits and two runs, but he walked nine batters.

The opening inning epitomized Barney's career. With no outs, the Yankees loaded the bases

on a pair of walks, to George Stirnweiss and Johnny Lindell, sandwiched around Tommy Henrich's double. DiMaggio was due up next. Coach Clyde Sukeforth walked to the mound and told Barney, in words to this effect: "Nothing to worry about. Just strike this bum out and get the next one to hit into a double play."

Well, Barney overpowered the Yankee Clipper with a strikeout, got the second out on George McQuinn's comebacker to the mound, forcing Stirnweiss at the plate, and then fanned third baseman Billy Johnson.

There was more trouble in the third when, with one out, Barney issued consecutive walks to Henrich and Lindell. This time, Rex induced DiMaggio to hit into a 6-4-3 double play.

Pitcher Frank Shea's run-producing single followed a pair of walks in the fourth. With one out in the fifth, Barney tried to throw another fastball past DiMaggio, but this time the Yankee center fielder hit it into the left-field stands. Shotton replaced Rex with two outs in the inning after he gave up his ninth base on balls. Shea won the game, 2–1; Barney took the loss; and the Yankees went on to win the Series in seven games.

Rex seemed to put it together in 1948, winning fifteen games against thirteen losses, including his crowning baseball moment, the no-hitter against the Giants. Rex ranked second in the league in strikeouts, and he tied for second in shutouts with four. His 3.10 ERA ranked fifth in the league. This was his only professional season in which he struck out more batters than he walked, 138 versus 122.

But if '48 was a personal high for Barney, it was a season of transformation and turmoil for the Dodgers. On July 16 the baseball world was astounded to learn that Durocher, back as manager after his yearlong suspension, had resigned from the Dodgers and replaced the fired Mel Ott as the Giants' field leader. Shotton, in turn, returned to Brooklyn to lead the Dodgers.

Barney admitted that he was "devastated" to

see Durocher go. "I cried when he left. I was used to tough managers and I felt that I had begun to turn things around for him and now he was gone."

Rex didn't always see eye to eye with Shotton, but he continued to pitch well. On August 18, he outdueled the Phillies' Robin Roberts with a one-hitter, winning by a 1–0 score in Philadelphia. The Phillies' lone hit was a looping single to center by Ralph "Putsy" Caballero in the seventh inning.

Barney's 2–0 no-hitter against the Giants came on a rainy night at the Polo Grounds. The date was September 9. It had rained throughout the day, but with a sizable advance sale at the gate (36,324), the Giants decided it would be wise to start the game.

The opening inning provided the most angst for Barney. After he walked the leadoff man, Jack "Lucky" Lohrke, on four pitches and retired Whitey Lockman, he fielded Sid Gordon's slow roller and threw wildly in an attempt to get a force out at second base. Then cleanup hitter Johnny Mize walked and the bases were loaded. But Willard Marshall hit the first pitch to second baseman Jackie Robinson, who started a 4-6-3 double play.

The only other Giant to reach base was losing pitcher Monte Kennedy, on Robinson's error in the third inning. Barney retired the last twenty Giants in order, capped by Lockman's foul pop-up to catcher Bruce Edwards for the final out. Remarkably, only 41 of Barney's 116 pitches were wide of the strike zone on this night. Only four Giants went down on strikes.

Durocher, who had been the Dodgers' manager just weeks earlier but was now the Giants' field boss, ran past Barney on his way to the clubhouse. "I'm proud of you, kid," he said to Rex.

Another version of that encounter appears in Peter Golenbock's book *Bums: An Oral History of the Brooklyn Dodgers*. Durocher reportedly told Barney, "You skinny son of a bitch. Why'd you have to do this to me? I'm your greatest fan. Why did you do it to me?"

The plate umpire on this memorable evening,

Babe Pinelli, called Barney "the fastest thing in baseball today. I don't care about Lemon or Feller. I've seen them. This kid is it. And no finer boy in baseball could have pitched it. He has a heart as big as a lion, and a wonderful disposition."

Thirty-two years later, in 1980, the New York Baseball Writers' Association presented the "Casey Stengel You-Could-Look-It-Up" award to Barney at their annual dinner in recognition of the last no-hitter at the storied Polo Grounds. No other Brooklyn pitcher ever no-hit the Giants in their own ballpark.

Unfortunately, Barney had reached his peak at the age of twenty-three. With the notable exception of a second one-hitter, against the Chicago Cubs at Wrigley Field on September 19, Rex was a so-so pitcher with the pennant-winning Dodgers in 1949. He won nine games, dropped eight, and his ERA was a high 4.41.

In the World Series, with the Dodgers trailing the Yankees three games to one, Shotton gave Barney the ball for Game Five. He allowed five runs in two and two-thirds innings and took the loss. The Yankees went on to wrap up Casey Stengel's first world championship as a manager with a 10–6 victory.

The 1950 season ended in disappointment for the Dodgers when they lost the pennant to Philadelphia on the season's final day. Limited to twenty appearances and only one start, Barney won two of three decisions, but his ERA soared to 6.42.

Some observers, and Barney himself, believe that a broken ankle, suffered sliding into second base on the final day of the 1948 season, forced him to alter his pitching style. "In 1949 I won nine ballgames, but from then on, by my own admission, I never had the same motion, never had it again," he told Golenbock. "I never got into the same flow, and in baseball everything is rhythm."

The Dodgers optioned Barney to Fort Worth of the Texas League in 1951, hoping that manager Bobby Bragan, a former Dodgers catcher, could help Rex learn the strike zone. It did not happen. In five appearances with the Class Double-A club, he walked thirty-nine batters in just fourteen innings. In a game against Houston, Barney broke the league record for walks given up by a pitcher in a game by issuing sixteen in seven and two-thirds innings.

In 1952 Rex was assigned to the St. Paul Saints, the Dodgers' farm club in the American Association. His pitching line for the Saints that season read 4 games, 3 innings pitched, 0 victories, 1 loss, 14 walks, 17 earned runs, and a 51.00 ERA. Barney's professional baseball career was over. His Major League won-lost record was 35-31, with a 4.34 ERA. The strikeouts (336) were outnumbered by the walks (410).

At twenty-eight Rex Barney was a has-been. He admitted to contemplating suicide. But then he remembered what Dodgers broadcaster Red Barber had told him a decade earlier: that he had a pleasing radio voice, and he should consider getting into broadcasting when his playing career was over.

Barney did just that. He started a circuitous climb up the radio ladder—some work in his hometown of Omaha; some at a 250-watt station in Vero Beach, Florida; some play-by-play work at WCAW in Charleston, West Virginia; the game-of-the-day for the Mutual Broadcasting System. When the Dodgers and Giants went west in 1958, WOR-TV hired Barney and Al Helfer to bring National League games into New York.

With assistance from Lee MacPhail, the Baltimore Orioles' general manager who had been an office boy during Rex's early Brooklyn days, Barney began a sports talk show in Baltimore in 1965. He became a celebrity in his adopted city.

During the late 1960s he began filling in for Bill Bolling, the public address announcer at Memorial Stadium. When Bolling departed in the spring of 1973, Barney became the Orioles' regular PA man, a job he held during the move to Camden Yards and until his death on August 12, 1997. He is buried in Lorraine Park Cemetery, Woodlawn, Maryland.

His trademark sign-off—"THANK Youuuu"—and cry of "Give that fan a contract!" after a spectator made a nice play in the stands became part of the Baltimore culture. "His voice was almost like a security blanket," said Mike Flanagan, a former Orioles twenty-game winner and television announcer.

Barney's last years were plagued by ill health. He suffered a stroke in 1983 and a heart attack in 1991, one year before he had a leg amputated because of circulation problems associated with diabetes. His second marriage, to a Baltimore schoolteacher named Carole Bennett, also ended in divorce.

"I should have been up there with the greats," he wrote in his autobiography. "I should have gone right up the ladder, but too many rungs were missing."

## Chapter 28. **Tommy Brown**

*C. Paul Rogers III*

| AGE | G | AB | R | H | 2B | 3B | HR | TB | RBI | BB | SO | BAV | OBP | SLG | SB | GDP | HBP |
|---|---|---|---|---|---|---|---|---|---|---|---|---|---|---|---|---|---|
| 19 | 15 | 34 | 3 | 8 | 1 | 0 | 0 | 9 | 2 | 1 | 6 | .235 | .257 | .265 | 0 | 1 | 0 |

Tommy Brown was only nineteen years old and recently discharged from the army when he joined the 1947 Brooklyn Dodgers for spring training in Havana. Playing time would prove difficult to come by for Brown on that Dodgers club with all its players returned from World War II. But the Dodgers could not send him to the Minor Leagues under the rules then in force. Because Brown already had two years on a big league roster, he would have to pass through waivers to be farmed out. The Dodgers were not willing to let Brown go for the waiver price, so he was relegated to end-of-the-bench status.

For the '47 season, the youngster appeared in only fifteen games, including six at third base, three in the outfield, and one at shortstop. The right-handed-hitting Brown even suffered the ignominy of starting a game at third base against a left-handed pitcher but, when the Dodgers knocked the southpaw out of the game in the first inning before he had a chance to bat, being replaced by the left-handed-hitting Spider Jorgensen.

Brown had made quite a splash when he was first called up to the Dodgers on August 3, 1944. With Pee Wee Reese still in the military, the Dodgers had tried Bobby Bragan at shortstop but decided they needed someone more mobile. GM Branch Rickey and manager Leo Durocher remembered Brown from spring training and called him up from the Newport News (Virginia) Dodgers of the Class B Piedmont League. When Brown arrived in the clubhouse, Durocher told him he was playing shortstop that afternoon in a doubleheader against the Cubs. Brown advised Durocher that he had ridden the train all night, but Leo respond-

Tommy Brown, age nineteen, was the third-youngest player in the National League in 1947.

ed that he didn't care. Brown did play the doubleheader, although he was only sixteen years and seven months old. He thus became the youngest position player to appear in a Major League game and the second youngest ever, after Joe Nuxhall, who appeared as a pitcher for the Cincinnati Reds earlier in 1944.

Tommy Brown was a local kid; he was born December 6, 1927, in the Bensonhurst section of

Brooklyn. He never knew his father and was raised primarily by an aunt and uncle. He quit school at a young age to work with his uncle unloading barges on the docks of New York. Brown spent his free time playing baseball on the pavement and cobblestone streets and in the famous Brooklyn Parade Grounds. The Dodgers held open tryouts there in 1943, and a friend who played first base on Tommy's team talked Brown into going with him.

They joined about 2,500 other kids, and Brown arrived without a glove or spikes, items he did not own. After three days the Dodgers told him and a handful of others that they would hear from the team. Brown was only fifteen years old. Over the winter, the club offered him a chance to attend spring training in Bear Mountain, New York. His "bonus" was the 25-cent fee for the ferry.

Brown showed enough promise in spring training to be offered $75 a month to play for the Dodgers' Class D PONY League farm club in Olean, New York. But Jake Pitler, manager of the Class B Newport News team, claimed him, which meant Brown would earn $125 a month. Tommy was barely sixteen when the season opened, but he proceeded to bat .297 in ninety-one games before his call-up by the Dodgers. He also led the league in triples, with eleven, and socked twenty-one doubles. Brooklyn president Branch Rickey called Brown "the second-best prospect in our chain and a veritable Pepper Martin."

When manager Pitler told Brown he was being called up to Brooklyn, he received a surprising response. Tommy told Pitler that he did not want to go but wanted to finish the year with Newport News because he was hitting well and learning so much. But Pitler said, "No, you've got to leave right now."

Brown faced left-hander Bob Chipman of the Cubs in his debut with the Dodgers. In his first at bat he grounded out, but later, in the seventh inning, he slugged a double to left-center. It was in the field, however, that Brown's nervousness was apparent. He let a routine ground ball by Chipman roll through his legs, and in the brief infield practice before each inning in the field, he had the fans behind first base scurrying for cover as he unleashed throws that not even six-foot-six first baseman Howie Schultz could reach. Brown had quickly lived up to his nickname, "Buckshot," which Durocher had given him in spring training because of his scatter arm.

In spite of Brown's shakiness afield and being largely overmatched at the plate, Durocher played him often at shortstop for the rest of the season. Brown finished his rookie campaign with a puny .164 batting average. Still, he managed to make contact most of the time, striking out only seventeen times in 160 plate appearances. In the field, he made sixteen errors, mostly on errant throws.

Brown's boyhood hero was Joe DiMaggio, and early in his career he affected DiMag's widespread stance. At six feet one and 175 pounds, he even physically resembled DiMaggio. Although no one called Brown a future DiMaggio, Tommy was considered a baseball prodigy because of his youth.

Although Reese was still in the navy in 1945, the Dodgers decided to send Brown to the St. Paul Saints of the American Association for some much-needed seasoning. Tommy again performed well, batting a solid .286 in eighty-five games, with ten home runs. That prompted the Dodgers to recall him in mid-July for the stretch run. Brooklyn was in the pennant race and had decided that Eddie Basinski could not cover enough ground to play shortstop every day. For the last two months of the season, Brown became the regular shortstop and did a commendable job, hitting .245 in 196 at bats. He clubbed his first big league home run on August 20 against the Pirates' Preacher Roe in a losing cause.

Tommy was only seventeen years old when he hit that first home run. Five days later, he connected for another circuit blast off Adrian Zabala of the New York Giants. As a result, he is both the youngest and the second-youngest player ever to homer in a Major League game.

Brown remained plagued by inconsistency in the field, both throwing and catching the ball. He once threw a ball to first base that landed in the upper deck. Another time, a ground ball went right through his legs. Tommy, however, continued as if he had caught the ball and made a phantom throw to first baseman Schultz, who stretched as if he were going to catch the throw. The only problem was that they fooled Dodgers left fielder Augie Galan, who didn't see the ball roll by him. The batter circled the bases and Brown was charged with a four-base error.

After the 1945 season, Tommy joined fifteen other Major Leaguers on a barnstorming trip to Manila, Tokyo, and stops in the South Pacific to entertain troops by playing against service teams and holding evening bull sessions about baseball.

Major Leaguers returned from military service in droves in 1946, but Brown, now eighteen, was going against the grain. He was drafted into the army in February after returning from his barnstorming tour. He was discharged in early April 1947 to find Pee Wee Reese holding down shortstop once again and a glut of talent at third base. As a result, Brown played in only fifteen games, mostly in the outfield or as a pinch hitter. He did not appear in the World Series. Manager Burt Shotton was trying to win a pennant and had little time or patience for the development of the raw talent that was Tommy Brown.

Although 1946 and 1947 were pretty much lost years for Brown, he was still only twenty years old and reported to spring training in 1948 with high hopes. Branch Rickey was still enthralled by Brown's potential and was quoted shortly after the '47 season as saying, "Brown is liable to play 154 games for us next year. At what position, we can't be sure. Maybe third base, maybe the outfield, maybe even first base."

Tommy did receive more playing time in 1948, mostly at third base, but found himself in crusty Burt Shotton's doghouse. The sixty-three-year-old Shotton had managed the Dodgers in 1947, following Leo Durocher's one-year suspension. Durocher returned in '48, but when he left in mid-July to take over as manager of the Giants, Shotton returned. Shotton became unhappy with Brown when Tommy bowed out of a game with what Shotton believed was a minor finger injury. For his part, Brown never knew where he stood with Shotton, even though he played thereafter with illness or injury.

In 1948 Tommy became known as the one o'clock batting champion, a reference to his prodigious hitting in batting practice. For the year, Tommy hit 162 batting practice homers in Ebbets Field. He hit only two in fifty-four games and 156 at bats that counted, however. He still had difficulty making solid contact in real competition. Brown batted just .241 for the season. He also had a run-in with his roommate, Carl Furillo. Although the Dodgers hushed up the story, Furillo and Brown got into a fight over an incident in their hotel room. Furillo got much the better of it, and Brown ended up in the hospital.

Although his batting average improved to .303 in 1949, Brown remained a part-time player and pinch hitter, appearing in forty-one games with ninety-five at bats. He made his only World Series appearances in '49, batting twice as a pinch hitter. The next season, 1950, was a virtual repeat of 1949. In forty-eight games and ninety-eight plate appearances, Brown had 27 hits, including 8 home runs, for a .291 average. He also led the National League with 7 pinch hits.

Tommy had his biggest day in the big leagues on September 18, 1950, against the Cubs at Ebbets Field. Batting lead-off, he singled off Paul Minner. He then homered off Minner in the third inning. In the fifth, he again smacked a home run, this time against reliever Monk Dubiel. Dubiel was still pitching in the eighth inning when Brown hit his third home run of the afternoon to cap a 4-for-4 day.

Heading into the 1951 season, Brown was both a seasoned veteran of the big leagues and a perennial prospect. He was still just twenty-three years old but had six years of Major League experience. New manager Charlie Dressen had high hopes for Tommy and intended for him to play left field. Dressen said he wanted to find a position for Brown because "if that kid can play anything like 150 games, it's a cinch that he will hit at least thirty-five home runs. You've got to love that swing he takes at the ball."

But once the season began, Brown again had trouble making solid contact. Finally, on June 8, the Dodgers gave up on Tommy's ever fulfilling his potential and traded him to the Phillies for spare outfielder Dick Whitman and cash. At the time, Brown was hitting just .160 with four hits (and no home runs) in twenty-four at bats. He became a semi-regular with Philadelphia, bouncing between the outfield, second base, and first base. He appeared in seventy-eight games after the trade, hitting only .219, but slugging a promising ten home runs.

Brown was once again lauded as a serious outfield candidate heading into the 1952 season. When camp opened, manager Eddie Sawyer pulled Brown aside and told him that left field was his if he could hit enough to hold it.

Brown could not. He was struggling along with four hits in twenty-nine at bats when the Phillies pulled the plug on June 15, selling him to the Chicago Cubs. Once again, the change of scenery was to Tommy's liking. He parlayed himself into almost an everyday player, hitting .320 for the Cubs in sixty-one games. The Cubs even played Brown at shortstop for thirty-nine games, a position he had not played for seven years.

Brown began 1953 as the frontrunner for the Cubs' shortstop position, but he could not keep up his excellent stick work of 1952. He languished below .200 for most of the year and watched as Roy Smalley and Eddie Miksis shared the shortstop position. Brown was again a part-time player, and though his baseball career was far from over, he had played his last Major League game at the age of twenty-five.

Tommy landed with the Los Angeles Angels of the Pacific Coast League for 1954, holding down third base while batting .263 in 152 games. He began the 1955 season with the Angels, but after twenty-four games he was sold to the Nashville Vols in the Southern Association. There he took over third base and hit a solid .299.

At Nashville in 1956, Brown received some national publicity when, against the Pelicans in New Orleans, he went 4 for 4, 3 for 3, and 3 for 3 in a three-game series. He also had six walks in the series, thus reaching base in sixteen consecutive at bats. When the club returned home to Nashville, Brown walked four straight times, meaning that he had reached base twenty times in a row.

He was voted to the Southern Association All-Star team but, more important, was purchased by the Cincinnati Reds on July 15. However, when he arrived on the train from Nashville, Tommy couldn't lift his right arm above his shoulder. He had apparently landed on the shoulder a couple of weeks earlier when diving for a ball against the Atlanta Crackers. As a result, the Reds quickly sent him back to the Southern Association.

Brown finished the year in Nashville, batting an impressive .316 with 10 home runs and 85 runs batted in. His stellar year earned him an invitation to the 1957 Chicago White Sox spring training in Tampa, Florida. But when the season began, he was back playing third base in Nashville, where he slumped to .256 in 139 games.

He returned to Nashville for the 1958 season, before shifting to the Chattanooga Lookouts in the same league after the Washington Senators organization acquired him. For the year, he hit .266 with eight home runs. He split 1959 between Chattanooga and New Orleans, batting .259. Although he was only thirty-one, Brown was tired of life in the Minor Leagues and retired after that season.

Brown had married a woman from Nashville and so stayed in the area after his playing career, working at the Ford Glass Plant for thirty-five years, before retiring in 1993. He continues to live in retirement in Brentwood, Tennessee.

# Chapter 29. **Harry Taylor**

*Adam J. Ulrey*

| AGE | W | L | PCT. | ERA | G | GS | GF | CG | SHO | SV | IP | H | BB | SO | HBP | WP |
|-----|-----|-----|------|------|-----|-----|-----|-----|-----|-----|-------|-----|-----|-----|-----|-----|
| 28 | 10 | 5 | .667 | 3.11 | 33 | 20 | 2 | 10 | 2 | 1 | 162.0 | 130 | 83 | 58 | 5 | 5 |

Known as "Handsome Harry" for his movie-star good looks, James Harry Taylor was born on May 20, 1919, in East Glenn, Indiana, near Terre Haute in the west-central part of the state. Harry was one of four children born to Cyrus and Lottie (Burk) Taylor. He had two brothers, Paul and Kenneth, and a sister, Betty. In 1938, after graduating from Fayette High School, he signed to play for Tallahassee, a Dodgers affiliate in the Class D Georgia-Florida League, but was released without ever getting into a game.

Nineteen days later, on the advice of scout Chick Mattick, the Chicago White Sox signed Taylor and sent him to the St. Paul Saints of the American Association. Except for a brief stay with Richmond of the Class B Piedmont League in 1939, Harry remained with St. Paul until he enlisted in the army in 1941. Pitching mostly in relief, he won nine games and lost twenty-seven over three years, with an earned run average of 5.30.

During his time in the military, Taylor managed and played for several army teams, pitching three no-hitters. On December 6, 1942, while stationed at Camp Gordon Johnston in Carrabelle, Florida, he married Beulah June "Boots" Collins. Harry's wife was also from Indiana, having been born March 19, 1920, in Tecumseh, Indiana.

When Taylor returned to St. Paul in 1946, the Saints were a Brooklyn Dodgers farm team. His years in the service had been beneficial to his baseball career. Taylor credited his playing baseball in the army with creating a turning point in his career. "Before I went into the army I didn't study the game much," he said. "Because I was the only guy with pro experience on the team, I was made

Harry Taylor was inserted into the starting rotation on May 28 and compiled seven victories and seven complete games in his first ten starts.

manager. Then I came down with an injury and couldn't play so I had to manage the team from the bench. Sitting there and watching, I began to follow the game in all of its phases. I'm sure it had a lot to do with my success after my hitch was over."

Taylor, a six-foot-one, 175-pound right-hander, threw with three different motions: overhand, three-quarters, and side-arm. He liked to make the batter guess what angle the next pitch was coming from. He used either his fastball or his curve as his outpitch, though when in a jam, he preferred to throw the curve ball.

By June 5, 1946, Harry had already won seven games for the Saints and was called the "league's leading chucker" by *The Sporting News*. He was one of six pitchers selected for the eleventh annual American Association All-Star Game. In Louisville, on August 18, he came within a "scratch bingle" of pitching a no-hitter. Overall, he won a league-leading fifteen games against seven losses with an ERA of 3.33 and ninety-one strikeouts. The Dodgers noticed. On September 3 they paid St. Paul $15,000 for Harry's contract. Two weeks later, after the Saints were eliminated from the American Association playoffs, he was called up to Brooklyn.

The Dodgers and the Cardinals were in the midst of a very tight pennant race when Taylor made his Major League debut at Boston on September 22. With two on and one out in the seventh inning, and the Braves up 4–2, Harry struck out the next two batters to end the threat. On September 25 he was one of a then National League–record eight pitchers used in an 11–9 loss to the Phillies. In all, he pitched four and two-thirds innings in four games, with no decisions.

In 1947 Taylor made the team out of spring training, winning a spot in the bullpen. But on May 28, with the Dodgers trailing the Chicago Cubs by a half game, new manager Burt Shotton inserted Taylor into the starting rotation. Harry pitched a complete-game five-hitter to defeat the New York Giants, 14–2. He also had two hits and two runs batted in. Taylor's win and a Cubs loss put Brooklyn into first place. Four days later he pitched another complete game in leading the Dodgers to a 6–1 victory over St. Louis, and he followed with a two-hit shutout against Pittsburgh. By July 4 Taylor had seven victories and seven complete games in ten starts. On July 29 Taylor's three-hit shutout at St. Louis helped the Dodgers stretch their lead to eight games over the New York Giants.

An injury Taylor suffered in a game against the Cardinals on August 18 may have been the reason for his short career. Harry hurt his elbow as he threw a curve to the Cardinals' Whitey Kurowski, and while he got credit for his tenth victory, it would be his last of the season. Taylor did not pitch again for more than five weeks, and when he did come back, he threw just four innings in two relief appearances. He attributed his elbow trouble to an old injury; whether or not that was true, Taylor was never again the same pitcher. He ended the regular season with a record of 10-5 and a 3.11 ERA.

The Dodgers won the pennant, and manager Shotton reluctantly started Taylor against the Yankees in Game Four of the World Series at Ebbets Field. The first four Yankees reached base on two hits, an error, and a bases-loaded walk to Joe DiMaggio. When Dodgers coach Clyde Sukeforth came to the mound to take Taylor out, Harry said stubbornly, "I haven't started to pitch yet, Sukey." Sukeforth replied, "I know, but we haven't any more bases to put those fellows on."

Taylor's inauspicious performance, which would be his only World Series appearance, was overshadowed by the dramatic events at the end of the game. The Dodgers were held hitless by Yankees pitcher Bill Bevens until Harry Lavagetto delivered a game-winning double with two outs in the ninth inning. The Series went seven games before the Yankees triumphed.

Taylor won his first start in 1948, a 5–3 decision over the Giants on April 22. But an emergency appendectomy seven days later kept him from pitching again until he made a two-inning relief appearance on May 26. From there on, he was largely ineffective. By July 19, when he was 1-4 with a 5.16 ERA, the Dodgers sent him back to St. Paul to make room for twenty-one-year-old Carl Erskine. Taylor pitched in nine games for the Saints, logged a 3-4 record with a 3.95 ERA, and returned to the

Dodgers in September. He finished the '48 season with two victories, seven losses, and a 5.36 ERA.

Taylor never again pitched for Brooklyn. He spent the next two seasons with St. Paul, going 11-6 with a 3.89 ERA in 1949 and 13-9 with a 4.02 ERA in 1950. On September 18, 1950, with Taylor out of options, the Dodgers sold him to the Boston Red Sox in a cash deal, variously reported as "considerable" and "not too far from the $100,000 level."

The Red Sox were still in the pennant race, and Taylor wasted no time trying to impress his new manager, Steve O'Neill. He pitched a two-hit shutout against the Philadelphia Athletics on September 25 and a six-hit victory over the Yankees on October 1, the last day of the season. O'Neill liked what he saw and declared that Taylor "will be a big winner for us next year." But when next year came, the magic had disappeared. Taylor's 1951 record was 4-9, and his 5.75 ERA was the worst of his Major League career. He started 8 times in 31 appearances, gave up 100 hits in 81⅓ innings, and walked nearly twice as many (42) as he struck out (22).

In the first week of the 1952 season, Taylor pitched a six-hit victory over the Philadelphia Athletics. On May 4 he pitched one inning in relief against the Cleveland Indians. Soon after, the Red Sox sent him to the Louisville Colonels, where he spent the rest of the season. Back in the American Association, he was 9-10 for the Colonels with a 4.32 ERA in twenty-five games.

Taylor was with the Williston (North Dakota) Oilers of the semipro ManDak League in 1953, where he was 9-2. In 1955 he pitched for the Paris (Illinois) Lakers in the Class D Mississippi–Ohio Valley League, going 7-2 with a 3.82 ERA, and then retired from baseball. In his six Major League seasons, Harry Taylor won nineteen, lost twenty-one, and had a 4.10 ERA.

After leaving baseball, Taylor lived in Shirkieville, Indiana, near his hometown, and did some farming. He later worked for the Bemis Manufacturing Company and Visqueen, a maker of building products. He was a member of the Major League Baseball Players Alumni Association and the West Terre Haute Masonic Lodge.

Taylor's wife, June, had died on February 1, 1984. Harry died on November 5, 2000. He left a son, James, who lives in Florida.

Monday, June 16, at Chicago—Harry Taylor ended the Dodgers' five-game slide with a six-hit 2–1 victory over the Cubs. Both Dodgers runs off loser Doyle Lade—in the second and the fifth—were unearned, the result of errors by first baseman Eddie Waitkus. A bases-loaded walk to Jackie Robinson and a single by Duke Snider drove in the runs. Chicago got its only run in the first inning. 28-25, Fourth, 2½ games behind.

Tuesday, June 17, at Chicago—Rained out. The Dodgers sent outfielder Marv Rackley and pitcher Ed Chandler to the Minors. 28-25, Fourth, 3 games behind.

Wednesday, June 18, at Chicago—Rookie catcher Gil Hodges broke a seventh-inning 3–3 tie with his first Major League home run. It came off veteran Hank Borowy and gave Joe Hatten, who had relieved starter Rex Barney, his seventh win of the season. The Dodgers added a run in the eighth to make the final score 5–3. Hugh Casey pitched two and two-thirds innings of scoreless relief. 29-25, Fourth, 2 games behind.

Thursday, June 19, at Chicago—Brooklyn completed a three-game sweep of the Cubs as Ralph Branca defeated Dodgers nemesis Johnny Schmitz, 5–1. Shut out for five innings, the Dodgers scored two runs in the sixth and three in the seventh. Pee Wee Reese, batting third in Burt Shotton's revised lineup, had a single, double, and triple. 30-25, Third, 1½ games behind.

Friday, June 20—Not scheduled. 30-25, Third (T), 1 game behind.

Saturday, June 21, at Cincinnati—Harry Taylor took a 4–1 lead into the sixth inning, but the Reds scored four runs to go ahead, 5–4. The Dodgers then scored two in the seventh off Harry Gumbert, in relief of Johnny Vander Meer, to win 6–5 and move into second place. Hugh Casey pitched the final three and two-thirds innings for the win. 31-25, Second, 1 game behind.

Sunday, June 22, at Cincinnati (2)—Ewell Blackwell nearly duplicated his teammate Johnny Vander Meer's feat of pitching consecutive no-hitters. After no-hitting Boston in his previous start, Blackwell held Brooklyn hitless for eight innings in the first game of the doubleheader. But Eddie Stanky singled with one out in the ninth, and after Al Gionfriddo made the second out, Jackie Robinson also singled. Blackwell had to settle for a two-hit shutout. Joe Hatten was the loser in the 4–0 defeat. In the second game, the Dodgers built up a 9–2 lead and held on to win, 9–8. Carl Furillo's grand slam and seven runs batted in led the Brooklyn offense. Vic Lombardi, in relief of starter Rex Barney, got the win. Bucky Walters, the first of six Reds pitchers, took the loss. 32-26, Third, 1½ games behind.

Monday, June 23—Not scheduled. 32-26, Second, 1 game behind.

Tuesday, June 24, at Pittsburgh—With the score tied at 2–2 in the fifth inning, Jackie Robinson stole home off Pirates veteran left-hander Fritz Ostermueller. It proved to be the game winner, although the Dodgers later added another run to make the final score 4–2. Pee Wee Reese's homer with a man aboard accounted for Brooklyn's first two runs. Ralph Branca went the distance for his ninth win of the season. 33-26, Second, 1 game behind.

Wednesday, June 25, at Pittsburgh—Two rookies led Brooklyn to a 6–2 win over Kirby Higbe and the Pirates. Harry Taylor pitched a complete game, while Spider Jorgensen drove in five runs. The Dodgers ended this western trip a half game behind the league-leading Braves. 34-26, Second, ½ game behind.

Thursday, June 26, vs. Boston—The Dodgers moved past the Braves into first place with an 8–6 win. A five-run Boston eighth tied the score at 6–6, but Brooklyn scored two in the home half to win. Ralph Branca, Brooklyn's fourth pitcher, got his tenth win, the first on the team to reach double digits. The Dodgers had fourteen hits, including two doubles by catcher Gil Hodges, an Eddie Stanky triple, and a Carl Furillo home run. 35-26, First, ½ game ahead.

Friday, June 27, at Boston—The season's biggest crowd at Braves Fields saw the Dodgers amass fifteen hits off four Boston pitchers to win, 8–5, and raise their lead to one and a half games. Rex Barney faltered in the sixth inning, but Hank Behrman stifled the Braves from there on. Jackie Robinson had three hits, and Carl Furillo and Spider Jorgensen each had two. 36-26, First, 1½ games ahead.

Saturday, June 28, at Boston—Earl Torgeson drove in the winning run with a two-out double in the ninth inning off Hank Behrman. Torgeson had homered earlier off starter Ralph Branca in Boston's 5–4 win that ended Brooklyn's five-game winning streak. Spider Jorgensen and Dixie Walker each had a two-run homer to account for Brooklyn's four runs. Jackie Robinson extended his hitting streak to fourteen games. 36-27, First, ½ game ahead.

Sunday, June 29, at New York (2)—Jackie Robinson had five hits and three stolen bases in the doubleheader split at the Polo Grounds before more than 52,000 fans. With hits in both games, Robinson had hit safely in sixteen consecutive games. Brooklyn won the opener, 4–3, behind Harry Taylor but were trounced in the nightcap, 9–5. It was Robinson's hit and a stolen base that sparked Brooklyn's two-run game-winning rally in the ninth inning of the first game. The Giants won game two with a six-run eighth, which included home runs by Sid Gordon, Johnny Mize, and Willard Marshall. Gordon's came off starter and loser Hal Gregg, while Mize's and Marshall's were off George Dockins, who was making his Dodgers debut. The split dropped Brooklyn into second place, a half game behind the Braves. Catcher Bruce Edwards returned to the lineup after being out for more than two weeks. Veteran Bobby Bragan and rookie Gil Hodges had filled in during his absence. 37-28, Second, ½ game behind.

# Chapter 31. **Ed Chandler**

*James L. Ray*

| AGE | W | L | PCT. | ERA | G | GS | GF | CG | SHO | SV | IP | H | BB | SO | HBP | WP |
|-----|---|---|------|-----|---|----|----|----|-----|----|------|----|----|----|-----|----|
| 30 | 0 | 1 | .000 | 6.37 | 15 | 1 | 4 | 0 | 0 | 1 | 29.2 | 31 | 12 | 8 | 0 | 2 |

World War II interrupted Ed Chandler's dream of pitching in the Major Leagues, but the time he spent in the service proved to be a blessing. It was there, with the guidance of two Major League pitchers, that Chandler truly learned to pitch. The scouts were interested, but it was unlikely they would sign a twenty-nine-year-old prospect. Certainly, there was nothing Chandler could do about his age—or was there?

Edward Oliver Chandler was born in Pinson, Alabama, a small town twenty miles northeast of Birmingham. Although baseball reference works have usually listed Chandler's birth date as February 17, 1922, U.S. census records, army enlistment records, and family members indicate he was actually born on January 31, 1917. Chandler's parents were William M. and Susie Caroline Chandler. The Chandlers had fourteen children; Edward was the seventh of nine sons. Nine boys is the perfect number for a baseball team, allowing the Chandler brothers to field teams in amateur and semipro leagues around the Birmingham area.

By 1941 Eddie, as he was known, was working as a traveling salesman. While on a trip to southern Idaho, he tried out for the Class C affiliate of the St. Louis Cardinals. The tryout was successful, and on August 26 he signed to play for the Pocatello Cardinals of the Pioneer League. The six-foot-two, 190-pound right-hander made only four appearances for the Cardinals. He posted a record of 1-1 and was advised to give up baseball. Undeterred, Chandler attended Idaho Southern University (now Idaho State) and played on the Bengals baseball team. While his overall record for ISU is not known, it is known that in one game in 1944,

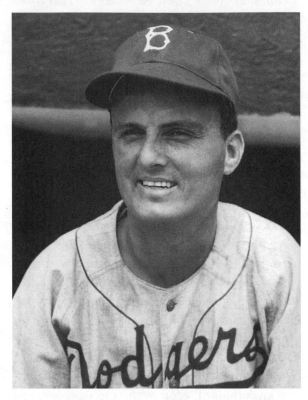

Ed Chandler made the club out of spring training but was returned to the Minors on June 17.

Chandler struck out nineteen batters through nine innings and twenty-three overall when the game was declared a tie after twelve innings.

World War II interrupted many careers, and Chandler's was no exception. Eddie enlisted on September 19, 1944, and served in the Pacific with the Army Air Corps for the remainder of the war. About this time Chandler married the former Ferne Streveler, an Iowa native. (It was the second marriage for Eddie.) The newly married Chandlers were living in Los Angeles, where Ferne gave birth to Edward Oliver Chandler Jr. on April 18, 1945. Later the couple had another son and a daughter.

Major League pitchers Red Ruffing and Tex Hughson had given Chandler pitching tips while the three were in the service. Eddie benefited from their advice and pitched so well in service games in Guam, he attracted the attention of big league scouts. Tom Downey of the Dodgers eventually signed Chandler and told him to report to Brooklyn's 1946 spring training camp in Daytona Beach. (Both the Dodgers and the press thought Chandler's age was twenty-four, not twenty-nine.) On April 2 Chandler pitched for the "regulars" against the Dodgers' Class Triple-A affiliate, the Montreal Royals, allowing only one run through seven innings.

Chandler traveled north with the Dodgers in 1946 but was optioned to the Fort Worth Cats of the Class Double-A Texas League, where he had a remarkable season. He won a team-high twenty games, lost only six, posted a 2.00 ERA while striking out a career-high 174 batters, and was selected to the Texas League All-Star team. Led by Chandler's performance, the Cats won the Texas League regular season title, but they lost in the playoffs to the Dallas Rebels.

Eddie's stellar 1946 season attracted the attention of the Dodgers' management, and in 1947 he was again invited to spring training. The team used him as both a starter and a reliever that spring, and he performed admirably in both roles. Roscoe McGowen, sportswriter for the *New York Times*, predicted that Chandler's poise and determination would guarantee him a spot on the roster. He turned out to be right. When the Dodgers broke training camp, Chandler was on the team.

Ed Chandler made his Major League debut on April 18, 1947. The Dodgers were playing the New York Giants, in the Giants' home opener at the Polo Grounds. After the Dodgers' starter, Vic Lombardi, was roughed up, Chandler entered the game in the fourth inning, his team down 4–2.

He held the Giants scoreless for two innings before giving up back-to-back home runs to Bobby Thomson and Willard Marshall. Two weeks later, on May 1, Chandler had a strong relief performance against the Cubs, which the *New York Times* called "a brilliant rescue job."[1]

On May 11 Chandler made his only start for the Dodgers, taking the loss in the second game of a doubleheader against the Philadelphia Phillies. Over the next month Chandler made six appearances in relief, with varying degrees of success. On June 17 the team optioned him back to Fort Worth, subject to a twenty-four-hour recall. Chandler remained with Fort Worth for the rest of the season as a starting pitcher. He compiled a 6-5 record with an impressive 2.78 ERA.

Apparently encouraged by Chandler's late-season success at Fort Worth, the Dodgers brought him back to spring training in 1948. But he failed to make the team, and again found himself headed to Fort Worth. The Cats finished first in the Texas League and won the league championship, although Chandler was just 12-13. Chandler was the Game One starter for Fort Worth in the Dixie Series against the Southern Association champions, the Birmingham Barons. Eddie pitched a five-hitter in winning 5–1 before a raucous crowd at Birmingham's historic Rickwood Field. It was a very satisfying homecoming for a native son.

In February 1949 Chandler was recalled to the Dodgers, but he was returned to Fort Worth at the end of April without appearing in a regular-season game. For the Cats in 1949, Eddie was 13-9, and the team won its third Texas League regular title in four years. In those three seasons, Chandler was 45-31 with a 2.80 ERA and was selected to the Texas League All-Star team twice.

In October 1949 the Dodgers moved Chandler to the St. Paul Saints, their Class Triple-A affiliate in the American Association. Chandler posted a 9-7 record for the 1950 Saints, but his earned run average climbed nearly a full point, which may have been a factor in the organization's decision to leave him unprotected in the off-season Minor League draft. On November 16, 1950, he was selected by the Chicago Cubs.

Eddie went to spring training with the Cubs in 1951 and made the Opening Day roster. He did not get into a game with the Cubs, however, and was released to the Los Angeles Angels, Chicago's affiliate in the Pacific Coast League. Chandler worked mostly in relief during the '51 season, winning five games against seven losses, while pitching only ninety innings, his lowest full-season total since Pocatello in 1941. His ERA ballooned to 5.50. In 1952 Chandler returned to the starting rotation and pitched much more effectively. In thirty-six starts, he was 16-14 with a 3.51 ERA for the sixth-place Angels.

Chandler dropped to 7-12 in 1953, and then, early in the 1954 season, he was dealt to league rival San Francisco. He rebounded nicely and surpassed his '53 win total by mid-July. Overall, Chandler was 12-11 with a 3.34 ERA for the Angels and Seals. After appearing in only seven games in 1955, the Seals released him, ending his professional baseball career.

After baseball, Chandler remained in the Los Angeles area and pursued two passions, the stock market and golf. By 1960 he had created his own investment firm, Chandler and Company. When the Dodgers moved to Los Angeles after the 1957 season, Chandler rekindled many of his old friendships with people he knew throughout their organization. He would often pitch batting practice for the Dodgers at the Coliseum, and when he started his own investment firm, he was quick to sign Dodgers as clients. In 1966 Chandler started his own mutual fund and was also involved in real estate.

Chandler pursued golf with the same vigor that he pursued stocks. The sports pages in Los Angeles in the late 1950s, the 1960s, and even into the 1970s are peppered with references to Eddie Chandler winning or placing in amateur golf tournaments. He played in many pro-am events as well and seems to have been always available to play in golf tournaments involving current and former ball players. As Chandler approached age sixty, the tournament success, quite naturally, dwindled.

Ferne Chandler died in Los Angeles in 1990. At some point, possibly after his wife died, Chandler moved to Las Vegas. He died there on July 6, 2003, at the age of eighty-six. While Eddie Chandler had little success in the Major Leagues—just fifteen games with no victories, one loss, and a 6.37 ERA—he did have a good Minor League career. He played on one championship team and on three others that won regular-season titles. He won 103 games against 86 losses and finished with a lifetime ERA of 3.50.

# Chapter 32. Marv Rackley

*Rob Neyer*

| AGE | G | AB | R | H | 2B | 3B | HR | TB | RBI | BB | SO | BAV | OBP | SLG | SB | GDP | HBP |
|---|---|---|---|---|---|---|---|---|---|---|---|---|---|---|---|---|---|
| 25 | 18 | 9 | 2 | 2 | 0 | 0 | 0 | 2 | 2 | 1 | 0 | .222 | .300 | .222 | 0 | 0 | 0 |

Marvin Eugene Rackley was born on July 25, 1921, in Seneca, South Carolina, a mill town just up the road from Clemson University in the northwestern corner of the state. (Like many professional players of his time, Rackley would later take a "baseball age," claiming to have been born in 1922.) Marv's parents were Thomas (aka Turp) and Blanche Rackley. Turp was a loom fixer in the local cotton mill. As of the 1930 U.S. census, there were six children, four girls, and two boys in the Rackley family. Marv was the fourth child and the second son.

Rackley entered Organized Baseball in 1941 with Valdosta in the Class D Georgia-Florida League, where he batted .322 in 133 games. He opened the 1942 season with Durham (North Carolina) in the Class B Piedmont League, but he struggled, finishing the season with a couple of months as a Dayton Duck in the Class C Mid-Atlantic League.

On October 5, 1942, Rackley entered military service with the Army Air Force at Fort Jackson, South Carolina. He spent the next three years stationed at Craig Field, a fighter pilot training base five miles southeast of Selma, Alabama. Rackley played baseball on a regular basis at Craig Field.[1]

Perhaps as much as any player, Rackley seems to have been *helped* by his years in the service. Despite having shown just modest talent in the Minors, he went to spring training with the Dodgers in 1946. With veteran outfielders Dixie Walker and Pete Reiser both holding out, manager Leo Durocher raved about Marvin Rackley: "Let me tell you about this kid. He's been in the service, and I never heard of him before he reported here. He looks

Marv Rackley's problem was that the Dodgers had too many left-handed-hitting outfielders.

like another Paul Waner—stands at the plate just like Paul—and he's as fast as George Stirnweiss, to give you an idea. If this kid can hit like Waner, he'll be a hell of a ball player."[2]

Not many kids hit like Paul Waner, but Rackley won a spot with the Class Triple-A Montreal Royals, a big jump from his last professional engagement. Despite playing in just 124 games, he still led the International League in both triples (14) and steals (65). One of the league's fastest players,

"Rabbit" Rackley was right at home with the Royals, who led the IL in both categories. Rackley was not the Royals' only speedster, nor was he their most famous; when Rackley patrolled right field, he could look toward the infield and see No. 9 on the back of second baseman Jackie Robinson.

Thanks to (among others) Robinson and Rackley, the Royals went 100-54 for the league's best record, smashed Newark and Syracuse in the IL playoffs, and finally topped Louisville, champions of the American Association, in the six-game Little World Series.

Rackley, however, was not ready to head home to South Carolina. Instead, he and two other white Minor Leaguers—including Al Campanis, Robinson's double play partner in Montreal—joined Jackie on a quick barnstorming tour and battled Honus Wagner's All-Stars in five cities.

Rackley broke camp with Brooklyn in 1947. But on June 15—cut-down day—he was demoted to the St. Paul Saints of the American Association, the Dodgers' other Class Triple-A affiliate. Rackley had played in eighteen games but started just once: on June 10 he played right field and drove in the Dodgers' only run with a ninth-inning single against Reds ace Ewell Blackwell. With the Dodgers in Chicago, it would have been a relatively quick trip to St. Paul. But Rackley, not eager to return to the Minors, had another idea. According to Roscoe McGowen in the *Times*, Rackley stated his plans this way:

> I'm going back to Brooklyn to see my wife and find out what she thinks about it. I didn't get a chance with the Dodgers. I was started in one game against the best pitcher in the league, got one hit and drove in a run. If that was a trial, I didn't do so badly, did I?
>
> I have no envy or criticism of some of the other boys, such as Hermanski and Snider. I'm glad they're getting a chance. I'm merely kicking because I don't feel I got the same chance—and I certainly have it over them in experience.

McGowen reported that Rickey, then with the club in Chicago, would return to New York in his private plane, accompanied by (among others) his wife and Marvin Rackley. "During the ride," McGowen suggested, "it may be that he will convince Rackley it is a good thing to go to St. Paul."

Rackley did go to St. Paul, and he batted .316 in sixty games. The records suggest that he was recalled by the Dodgers almost exactly two months after his demotion, but that might have been a paper move, because he did not play for Brooklyn the rest of the '47 season. After the Dodgers lost the World Series that fall, his occasional teammates—whose full losers' shares came to $4,081—voted Rackley, Eddie Chandler, and four other minor contributors $300 apiece.

Why hadn't Rackley gotten a real chance to play for the Dodgers in 1947? It probably did not help that he was relatively small—five feet ten and 170 pounds—had very little power, and did not throw well. Some years later in Dodgers executive Fresco Thompson's memoir, he recalled this conversation with Branch Rickey about Rackley:

> "What about Marvin Rackley?" Rickey asked me. Rackley was a whiz at Montreal.
>
> I volunteered, "I think Rackley is a pretty good ballplayer for a little fellow."
>
> He gazed at me searchingly. "Do you know of any league that just uses little fellows?"
>
> "No, sir," I answered.
>
> "Alright then, begin again and tell me what kind of a ballplayer is Rackley?"
>
> "Just fair and of doubtful major league ability," I summed him up.[3]

Thompson's introduction to this little story includes some questionable details, which makes the recalled-some-years-later conversation with Rickey questionable, too. And while this might tell us something interesting about Rackley's abbreviated career as a Dodger, the real problem in 1947 was simply that the club had a surfeit of left-handed-hitting outfielders: not only starters Dixie Walker and Pete Reiser but also Gene Hermanski, Arky Vaughan, Al Gionfriddo, and rookie Duke Snider. In 1948, with Walker gone, Gionfriddo gone, and Reiser's role reduced, Rackley would get his shot.

Half a shot, anyway. Hermanski and Snider both deserved (and got) their time, and rookie George "Shotgun" Shuba—yet another lefty-hitting outfielder—won his spurs, too. Aside from a few weeks back in Montreal, Rackley played roughly half the time, sometimes in left field and sometimes in center. Rickey couldn't have been disappointed when Rackley batted .327, though he might have wondered why Rackley hit zero home runs and stole only eight bases.

It might have been in 1948 when Rackley contributed to the development of rookie pitcher Carl Erskine, who later would write, "Marvin Rackley, my former Dodger roommate, conditioned his thinking by reading Scripture. He got me in the habit of packing my own Bible on road trips."[4]

Playing time in 1949 was even more scarce, as Snider took over in center field. For Rackley, there was another complication: the Dodgers traded him to Pittsburgh for Johnny Hopp, *another* lefty-hitting outfielder (who was actually acquired to play first base if anything should happen to Gil Hodges). The transaction was made on May 17; in addition to Hopp, the Pirates also threw in $25,000. Then things started getting weird.

Not long after joining the Pirates, Rackley complained of a sore throwing arm. His new employers suspected that Rickey had obtained Hopp (and $25,000) under false pretenses. Of course, Rickey claimed that he'd known nothing of a sore arm, telling the *New York Herald Tribune*'s Harold Rosenthal, "I then spoke in turn to Burt Shotton, my manager, and Clyde Sukeforth, the coach, about the arm. Neither of them knew of any sore arm the boy had when he was with the club. Our trainer, Doc Wendler, said that Rackley had made a report of a sore arm in spring training, but didn't

think it was anything. Everyone had a sore arm in spring training."[5]

By June 6 Rickey offered to return Hopp and the $25,000 to Pittsburgh, who accepted even though Rackley had gone 11 for 35 as a Pirate and Hopp was hitless in fourteen at bats with Brooklyn. (Rackley wasn't quite finished annoying Rickey. Upon rejoining the Dodgers, he was reported to have said, "My arm's all right, now that I'm back with the Dodgers.")

With the Dodgers returning to the World Series in 1949, after a one-year absence, Rackley started Game Two because of Carl Furillo's groin injury. He went hitless in two at bats before leaving in the fourth inning with a back injury. Rackley also started Game Five and took the collar again before being lifted for a pinch hitter in the seventh. His last official appearance as a Dodger came in the bottom of the sixth; he grounded out to first base. At that point the Dodgers trailed 10–2, and would eventually lose the game and, consequently, the World Series.

Along with occasionally giving Rickey a headache, Rackley had hit just one home run and stolen just one base in sixty-three games as a Dodger that season. Rickey had seen enough. Five days after the World Series, he sold Rackley to Cincinnati for $60,000, conditionally; the next April, the Reds decided to keep Rackley (then, the purchase price was reported as just $30,000).[6]

Rackley played in only five games for the Reds, batting just twice, before they sold him to Seattle in the Pacific Coast League.[7] He would not play in the Majors again but continued in the high Minors through 1955, closing out his career with the Atlanta Crackers of the Southern Association.

In early 2011 the eighty-eight-year-old Rackley and the former Hazel Cleland, whom he married on November 23, 1946, still lived in his native South Carolina, just a few miles from his birthplace.

# Chapter 33. **Gil Hodges**

*John T. Saccoman*

| AGE | G | AB | R | H | 2B | 3B | HR | TB | RBI | BB | SO | BAV | OBP | SLG | SB | GDP | HBP |
|-----|---|----|----|----|----|----|----|----|-----|----|----|------|------|------|----|-----|-----|
| 23 | 28 | 77 | 9 | 12 | 3 | 1 | 1 | 20 | 7 | 14 | 19 | .156 | .286 | .260 | 0 | 3 | 0 |

Gil Hodges was born Gilbert Ray Hodge on April 4, 1924, at Princeton, Indiana, in the state's southwestern corner. The origin of the discrepancy between his birth name of Hodge and the name by which he became well known is unclear; however, the family name was Hodges at least by the time of the 1930 U.S. census. Gil's parents were Irene K. (Horstmeyer) and Charles P. Hodges. When Gil was seven years old, the family, including Gil's older brother, Robert, and younger sister, Marjorie, moved thirty miles north to Petersburg. Big Charlie, as Gil's father was known, did not want his two sons to work in the coal mines as he did. (Big Charlie lost an eye and some toes in various mining accidents and died of a heart embolism in 1957.)

Charles Hodges taught his sons how to play sports, and Gil was a four-sport athlete at Petersburg High School. He ran track and played baseball, basketball, and football, earning a combined seven varsity letters. In 1941, like his brother before him, Gil was offered a Class D contract by the Detroit Tigers, but he declined it and instead enrolled at St. Joseph's College on an athletic scholarship. St. Joseph's, located near Indianapolis, had a well-regarded physical education program, and Gil had designs on a college coaching career. He played baseball and basketball for the Pumas and was a member of the Marines ROTC.

After his sophomore year, he was offered a contract by local sporting-goods store owner and part-time Dodgers scout Stanley Feezle. The lure of playing in the Major Leagues was too much this time, and Hodges left St. Joseph's and signed with Brooklyn, who then sent him to Olean, New York.

Gil Hodges was still a second-string catcher in 1947.

He worked out with the Class D Oilers but did not appear in a game.

Brooklyn called up the nineteen-year-old Hodges late in the 1943 season. He made his debut at Crosley Field on October 3, the Dodgers' last game of the year. Facing Cincinnati's Johnny Vander Meer, Gil went 0 for 2 at the plate and made two costly errors at third base. Eleven days later, he entered the Marine Corps and was sent to Hawaii, first to Pearl Harbor and later Kauai. Hodges served as a gunner for the Sixteenth Anti-Aircraft Battalion. From Hawaii he went to Tinian, the sister island of Saipan in the South Pacific. In April 1945 Sergeant Hodges, now assigned to his battalion's operations and intelligence section, landed on Okinawa with the assault troops and was subsequently awarded the Bronze Star. Don Hoak, a future Dodgers teammate, said, "We kept hearing stories about this big guy from Indiana who killed Japs [Japanese soldiers] with his bare hands."[1] Discharged in February 1946, Hodges went to spring training with Brooklyn.

The solidly built Hodges stood a half inch over six feet one and weighed 200 pounds. He batted and threw right-handed and was considered big for a baseball player of that era. However, Hodges was a gentle giant, often playing the role of peacemaker during on-field brawls. His hands were so large that teammate Pee Wee Reese once remarked that he could have played first base barehanded but wore a mitt because it was fashionable.

Dodgers president Branch Rickey sent the now twenty-two-year-old Hodges to the Newport News (Virginia) Dodgers, the club's entry in the Class B Piedmont League, where he was converted from infielder to catcher. Gil played 129 games, hitting .278 with eight home runs for Newport News. For his efforts Hodges was named to the all-league team. He went to the historic and tumultuous Dodgers 1947 spring training and made the team. He was the second-string catcher but played just twenty-four games behind the plate as the backup to Bruce Edwards.

On May 17 at Forbes Field, Hodges, batting for pitcher Harry Taylor, singled off Pittsburgh's Fritz Ostermueller for his first Major League hit. Gil hit his first Major League home run on June 18, at Chicago's Wrigley Field. His blast came in the seventh inning with one on against Cubs starter Hank Borowy and broke a 3–3 tie.

Hodges appeared in twenty-eight games overall in 1947, hitting an anemic .156. He clearly needed more playing time, but he was not going to get it behind the plate. With Roy Campanella on the way to take over for Edwards, another position change for Hodges was in order. Dodgers manager Leo Durocher "put a first baseman's glove on our other rookie catcher, Gil Hodges. . . . Three days later," Durocher said, "I'm looking at the best first baseman I'd seen since Dolph Camilli."[2]

In 1948 Hodges played ninety-six games at first base, but he was the catcher in thirty-eight games as well. With thirteen errors at first, his fielding percentage was .986, the only year he played regularly that he fielded under .990. In addition, he contributed eleven home runs and seventy runs batted in for the third-place Dodgers. He would not drive in fewer than one hundred runs over the next seven seasons, nor would the Dodgers finish lower than second place over the next eight.

On December 26, 1948, Hodges married the former Joan Lombardi, a Brooklyn girl from the Bay Ridge section. With Joan, Hodges made a permanent home in Brooklyn, one of the few Dodgers to do so, and raised four children: Gil Jr., who would spend some time as a player in the New York Mets' Minor League system, Irene, Cynthia, and Barbara. (At this writing, Joan Hodges still lives in that same house in Brooklyn.) This no doubt made Gil "one of them" in the eyes of the fans. Walter O'Malley, the Dodgers' owner, stated, "If I had sold or traded Hodges, the Brooklyn fans would hang me, burn me, and tear me to pieces." Lastly, the very busy Hodges used the GI Bill to earn his degree at Oakland City College in Indiana during the 1947 and 1948 off-seasons.

By 1949 the Brooklyn Dodgers were poised for the most productive period in the franchise's history. The fabled lineup was in place: Roy Campanella behind the plate, Hodges at first, Jackie Robinson at second, Pee Wee Reese at short, Billy Cox at third, Duke Snider in center, and Carl Furillo in right with a rotating cast in left. The team did not disappoint; Brooklyn won the National League pennant, edging the St. Louis Cardinals by one game. Hodges was now a key contributor. His first career grand slam came on May 14 off the Braves' Bill Voiselle. Hodges hit for the cycle on June 25 in a 17–10 victory at Forbes Field. Gil hit a single, a double, a homer, and then a triple before hitting his second homer of the game in the ninth. He was 5 for 6 with four RBIs for the day.

Hodges appeared in his first All-Star Game and went 1 for 3 with a run scored. For the season, he tied with Snider for the team lead in home runs with 23, and his 115 RBIs were second on the team to Robinson. Brooklyn's pennant euphoria was short-lived, however, as the Dodgers lost the World Series to the New York Yankees in five games. Hodges drove in four of the team's fourteen runs in the Series.

The next two years, 1950 and 1951, brought consecutive second-place finishes. Hodges's power numbers continued to improve, as he averaged 36 home runs and 108 RBIs for the two seasons. He established his career high in runs scored in 1951 with 118, one of three seasons in which he topped 100. He also established a career high in strikeouts, 99, which led the league. (He finished in the top ten in strikeouts eleven times in his career.)

In the 1951 All-Star Game, Hodges went 2 for 5, including a two-run homer. However, his biggest day came on August 31, 1950, when he became the fourth Major Leaguer to hit four home runs in a nine-inning game. He went 5 for 6 and had nine RBIs that night at Ebbets Field, hitting the home runs off four different Boston Braves pitchers. His seventeen total bases also tied a Major League record.

The Dodgers won pennants in 1952 and 1953, only to fall again each time to the Yankees in the Series. In 1952 Hodges hit 32 home runs and drove in 102, while in 1953 he had 31 home runs and 122 RBIs, despite hitting just .181 through May 23.

The slump with which he began the 1953 season actually had carried over from the 1952 World

Series and cemented the legendary bond between Hodges and the Brooklyn fans. In the seven-game Series, he went 0 for 21 with five walks. Instead of booing their first baseman, the Ebbets Field faithful embraced him, cheering him warmly, sometimes with standing ovations, before each at bat.

In his classic *The Boys of Summer*, Roger Kahn writes, "The fans of Brooklyn warmed to the first baseman as he suffered his slump. A movement to save him rose from cement sidewalks and the roots of trampled Flatbush grass. More than thirty people a day wrote to Hodges. Packages arrived with rosary beads, rabbits' feet, mezuzahs, scapulars."

In his book, *The Game of Baseball*, Hodges recalled that slump in his typical humble fashion:

> The thing that most people hear about that one is that a priest [Father Herbert Redmond of St. Francis Roman Catholic Church] stood in a Brooklyn pulpit that Sunday and said, "It's too hot for a sermon. Just go home and say a prayer for Gil Hodges." Well, I know that I'll never forget that, but also I won't forget the hundreds of people who sent me letters, telegrams, and postcards during that World Series. There wasn't a single nasty message. Everybody tried to say something nice. It had a tremendous effect on my morale, if not my batting average. Remember that in 1952, the Dodgers had never won a World Series. A couple of base hits by me in the right spot might have changed all that.[3]

Undoubtedly, his experience of the slump helped him later in his managerial career, when he took over struggling expansion teams.

The 1954 season saw the Dodgers finish in second place and Hodges post career highs in batting average (.304), home runs (42), RBIs (130), and slugging (.579). It was his second consecutive year over the .300 mark. Hodges had 19 sacrifice flies, yet another career high, which also led the Major Leagues by a wide margin. On the last day of the regular season, September 26, Hodges had a solo shot and provided the only run rookie Karl Spooner needed for a 1–0 Dodgers victory. The homer was the twenty-fifth Gil hit at Ebbets Field in 1954, establishing a new club record. His 42 homers and 130 RBIs were both second in the National League in their respective categories. It was the closest he would come to winning a home run or an RBI title.

In 1955 the Brooklyn Dodgers won their first and only World Series. Hodges, now thirty-one years old, contributed 27 homers, 102 RBIs, and a .500 slugging percentage to the Dodgers' first-place finish. Brooklyn clinched the '55 pennant on September 8 with a 10–2 drubbing of Milwaukee, the earliest a team had clinched the pennant in the eighty-year history of the National League. For the fifth time in nine years, they met the Yankees in the World Series. Gil hit .292 (7 for 24) with 1 homer, 3 walks, and 5 RBIs. Hodges drove in the only two runs scored in the seventh and deciding game of the Series, and recorded the final put-out on a throw from Reese.

Hodges would appear in two more World Series, 1956 and 1959. He continued to play as a regular over the span of those years, averaging 26 home runs and 82 runs batted in. Hodges homered once in each Series; in the 1956 seven-game Series loss to the Yankees, he had a hand in twelve of the Dodgers' twenty-five runs, and he batted .391 in the 1959 Los Angeles Dodgers Series win over the Chicago White Sox. In that Series, he won Game Four with a solo homer in the bottom of the eighth that snapped a 4–4 tie. In all, Hodges played in thirty-nine World Series games, compiling a .267 average (35 for 131) with 5 homers, 21 RBIs, and 15 runs scored.

Gil was active for parts of four more seasons, but knee and other injuries limited his playing time. Despite the Dodgers' move to Los Angeles, the Hodges family maintained their home in Brooklyn, and after the 1961 season, the newly formed New York Mets selected Gil in the first

National League expansion draft. He hit the first home run in Mets history, on April 11, 1962. Overall, he appeared in fifty-four games for the woeful '62 Mets, hitting .252.

Hodges began 1963 as an active player but retired when the two-year-old Washington Senators asked him to be their manager. After clearing waivers, Gil was traded to Washington for outfielder Jimmy Piersall on May 23, ending his playing career. Fittingly, Hodges's last Major League hit was an RBI single on May 5, 1963, against the San Francisco Giants. Gil Hodges hit his 370th and final home run on July 6, 1962. Until April 19 of the next season, when Willie Mays hit career home run 371, Hodges had the most home runs by a right-handed batter in National League history.

Each season after Hodges's arrival, the expansion Senators improved on their record from the previous season, peaking with a 76-85 record in 1967. On December 4, 1964, Senators management engineered a seven-player trade with the Dodgers. The Senators received Hodges's former teammate, slugging outfielder Frank Howard, pitchers Phil Ortega and Pete Richert, first baseman Dick Nen, and third baseman Ken McMullen.

These players were the core of the Senators franchise for the next several years and helped Hodges bring the Senators from tenth place to their surprising sixth-place finish in 1967. Although he had one year left on his contract, Hodges would not be around to guide the Senators in 1968. When Wes Westrum resigned as manager of the New York Mets in September 1967, the Mets sought out Hodges as his replacement.

Joan Hodges had never been more than an infrequent commuter to the nation's capital, and Gil still had financial interests in bowling alleys in Brooklyn. Given Gil's popularity in the New York area, he was a natural fit for the Mets. While Senators general manager George Selkirk did not want to lose Hodges, he eventually relented, aided by a Mets payment of $100,000 and a player to be named (pitcher Bill Denehy was sent to the Senators on November 27). Hodges then signed a three-year, $150,000 contract to manage the Mets.

The Mets had never finished above .500, but they were just four games below that mark at the 1968 All-Star break. They could not maintain the pace, however, and lost forty-six of the next eighty-two games. On September 24, 1968, the forty-four-year-old Hodges suffered a "mild" heart attack during a game in Atlanta. In addition to the stress, which he always kept bottled up, and his father's early death from an embolism, he also had developed a smoking habit on Okinawa, contributing factors for an attack so early in life. The '68 Mets did move up one position in the standings, to ninth place, a twelve-game improvement over 1967. There was little in their second-half performance that would predict the much greater improvements still to come.

Gil's first winning season as manager came with the 1969 Mets, a team that went 100-62, twenty-seven wins more than the previous year. They were led by rising star pitchers Tom Seaver, Jerry Koosman, and promising rookie Nolan Ryan, as well as left fielder Cleon Jones and center fielder Tommie Agee. The Mets beat the Atlanta Braves in three straight games in the National League Championship Series, and defeated the heavily favored Baltimore Orioles in five games in the World Series. Hodges was voted Manager of the Year for turning the lovable losers into world champions. The Mets finished with identical 83-79 records in each of the next two seasons. For Hodges, there would be no more championships.

The spring of 1972 saw the first modern players' strike. On April 2, Easter Sunday, Hodges played golf at the Palm Beach Lakes golf course in Florida with coaches Joe Pignatano, Rube Walker, and Eddie Yost. The first two were old Brooklyn Dodgers pals, while Yost had been with Hodges since the Senators days. As they walked off the final hole of their twenty-seven-hole day toward their rooms at the Ramada Inn, Pignatano asked Hodges what time they were to meet for dinner. Hodges answered him, "7:30," and then he fell to the pavement. He was pronounced dead of a coronary at 5:45 p.m. in West Palm Beach.

The Mets were scheduled to open the season in Pittsburgh on April 7, the day of the funeral, but the players agreed to forfeit the game to attend. The Pirates graciously canceled the game, which was not played anyway because of the lingering strike. Coach Yogi Berra took over the stunned Mets as Hodges's replacement and led the Mets back to the World Series in 1973.

Hodges's funeral Mass easily could have been held at St. Patrick's Cathedral in Manhattan, but that would not have been in keeping with his unassuming ways. During his funeral Mass, held at his Flatbush parish church, Our Lady Help of Christians, the Reverend Charles Curley said, "Gil was an ornament to his parish, and we are justly proud that in death he lies here in our little church." Repeating the story of Father Herbert Redmond's concern for Hodges's slump, Father Curley said, "This morning, in a far different setting, I repeat that suggestion of long ago: Let's all say a prayer for Gil Hodges."[4] Gil is buried in Brooklyn's Holy Cross Cemetery.

In the years since Hodges's death, much attention has been given to his absence from the Hall of Fame. Hodges was eligible for the Baseball Writers' Association of America vote from 1969 until 1983. In each year, he received more votes than as many as ten men who were ultimately elected to the Hall.

Hodges led all first basemen of the 1950s in the following categories: home runs (310), games (1,477), at bats (5,313), runs (890), hits (1491), runs batted in (1,001), total bases (2,733), strikeouts (882), and extra-base hits (585). He made the All-Star team eight times, every year from 1949 to 1955 and again in 1957, the most of any first baseman of the time. In addition, Hodges won the first three Gold Gloves awarded at his position and was considered the finest defensive first baseman of the era. Also, he was second among all players in the 1950s in home runs and RBIs, third in total bases, and eighth in runs.

The bridge that spans the East Fork of the White River in northern Pike County, Indiana, is now named the Gil Hodges Memorial Bridge. A space was left at the bottom of the stone monument to someday include the wording of Hodges's Cooperstown plaque.

# Chapter 34. **George Dockins**

*Russell Wolinsky*

| AGE | W | L | PCT. | ERA | G | GS | GF | CG | SHO | SV | IP | H | BB | SO | HBP | WP |
|-----|---|---|------|-----|---|----|----|----|-----|----|----|---|----|----|-----|-----|
| 30 | 0 | 0 | .000 | 11.81 | 4 | 0 | 2 | 0 | 0 | 0 | 5.1 | 10 | 2 | 1 | 0 | 0 |

George Woodrow Dockins was a soft-tossing, perpetually sore-armed left-handed pitcher. He was born in Clyde, Kansas, to Joseph and Ida (Moffatt) Dockins on May 5, 1917. One of four children, he attended Joines School, just north of Clyde, until the eighth grade. As a youth, Dockins loved baseball and played in the Ban Johnson League in nearby Concordia, Kansas.

In 1939 the Cardinals' Branch Rickey signed Dockins to his first professional contract. He began his pro career with the Class D Hamilton (Ontario) Red Wings of the PONY League, where he posted a 15-5 record with a 2.93 ERA. Dockins spent the next two seasons with the Mobile Shippers of the Class B Southeastern League. In 1941 he was the league's top pitcher, winning twenty games with a league-leading 2.05 ERA.

Dockins started the 1942 season with the Rochester Red Wings of the International League. After splitting six decisions, he was optioned to the New Orleans Pelicans of the Southern Association, where he fared much better. George joined the Pelicans on May 27 and showed "poise . . . [,] control, and a world of stuff."[1] Leading the circuit in winning percentage, he posted a 14-5 mark, walking only twenty batters in 160 innings. On August 12, he tossed eight and two-thirds hitless innings against Little Rock, before an infield single spoiled his bid for a no-hitter.

That September, Dockins was one of nine farmhands added to the Cardinals' winter roster.[2] St. Louis pilot Billy Southworth fully expected him to make the big league club in 1943. *New Orleans Statesman* sportswriter Val J. Flanagan predicted Dockins and fellow Pelicans lefty Bill Seinsoth

George Dockins appeared in just four games, making his final big league appearance on August 19.

"are expected to become the next [Howie] Pollet-[Ernie] White combination for the Cardinals."[3] The Associated Press selected Dockins and George Munger of the Columbus Red Birds as the best Cardinals rookie pitching bets for 1943.[4]

But, instead, Dockins was the Opening Day starting pitcher for the Columbus Red Birds. He

had been optioned to the American Association club, subject to twenty-four-hour recall, but spent the entire season with the Red Birds. Dockins won sixteen games and was named to the league's All-Star team. His three-hitter clinched the playoff semifinals over Milwaukee. Columbus then defeated Indianapolis for the league championship. Dockins did not appear in the Junior World Series, in which the Red Birds bested Syracuse of the International League.

A sore left elbow landed Dockins on the voluntarily retired list for the entire 1944 season. His arm was still sore in the spring of 1945, but Southworth took a chance and kept Dockins on the St. Louis roster, bringing him along slowly. In May, after a couple of brief but effective mound stints, Dockins left the club for treatment, but he returned two weeks later.

On June 23 Dockins pitched six and two-thirds innings in relief at Wrigley Field, picking up his second win of the season. On July 22, again in relief, he blanked the Dodgers for six innings in stifling, 100-plus-degree St. Louis heat. Two days later, "Dockins was just as hard to crack," the *Brooklyn Daily Eagle*'s Harold Burr observed.[5] He again halted Brooklyn's offensive attack, this time tossing six and two-thirds shutout innings and earning the win.

Based on these impressive relief outings, Southworth decided to give Dockins a chance as a starter. St. Louis, battling Chicago for the National League pennant, needed help at the back end of the rotation to complement right-handers Red Barrett and Ken Burkhart and left-hander Harry Brecheen. "I like Dockins'[s] spirit," said Southworth, who had been impressed with the southpaw since his fourteen-win season for New Orleans in 1942. "[Earlier in 1945], his arm was sore and he was going to [Dr. Robert Hyland, the Redbirds' physician], for daily treatment. But when I was pretty short on pitchers, he volunteered for re-

lief duty, saying, 'I think I can hold them for a few innings.'"[6]

Dockins responded by winning his first three starts. In his first big league start, on July 29, he bested the Pirates 6–4. Five days later, at Forbes Field, Dockins again topped the Pirates in another complete-game effort. On August 8 he hurled a six-hit shutout against the Giants at the Polo Grounds. On September 1 at Sportsman's Park, with St. Louis trailing Chicago by only three games, Dockins won, 3–2, over Cubs veteran Claude Passeau.

An enthusiastic crowd of more than 34,000, the largest to watch the Cardinals at home in more than six years, turned out the next day for a Sunday doubleheader with the Cubs. In the opener, with the score tied 1–1 in the tenth inning and the bases loaded, Southworth called on Dockins again. He yielded a pinch-hit, three-run double to Frank Secory, good for a 4–1 Chicago victory.

On September 7 he was "in rare form," shutting out the Boston Braves while allowing only three hits and a walk.[7] The victory was his eighth of the season, and his last in a Major League uniform.

Dockins next faced Chicago on September 19 in St. Louis, with the Cardinals now trailing the Cubs by two games. Dockins took a 1–0 lead into the ninth inning, but allowed the tying run. Chicago scored three more in the tenth, and the Cardinals lost, 4–1. Still, the *St. Louis Post-Dispatch*'s J. Roy Stockton wrote that Dockins appeared "as cool as the cucumbers he raises on his Kansas farm."[8] Southworth commented that you could not have asked for a better-pitched game for nine innings than that which George Dockins hurled.[9]

The Cardinals ended the season in second place, three games behind Chicago. Dockins's final ledger for the season showed eight victories and six defeats, with a 3.21 earned-run average in thirty-one games, twelve of them starts.

During the winter of 1945–46, there were rumors that New York Giants skipper Mel Ott, looking for left-handed pitching, would deal for

Dockins. Instead, Brooklyn—now run by Branch Rickey—picked up the twenty-nine-year-old lefty on April 19, 1946, for the $7,500 waiver price. It was Dockins's effective pitching against the Dodgers and the pennant-bound Cubs in 1945 that attracted Brooklyn's interest. Dodgers official Bob Finch, speaking for Rickey, announced, "I [Rickey] signed Dockins to his first pro contract. He has a lovely curve and a fairly good fastball."[10] If nothing else, the signing of Dockins would remove the "thorn in Brooklyn's flesh" that the southpaw inserted "last year with his relief hurling" against the Dodgers.[11]

Saddled with arm problems again, Dockins was optioned to the Fort Worth Cats on May 1 without ever having donned a Brooklyn uniform. In his second start for the Class Double-A Texas League Cats, on May 22 (he won his first), George left the mound after a lone inning pitched. He did not return until mid-July.

As he did in 1945, Dockins returned from arm woes and pitched well. That August he hurled four consecutive complete games and allowed only one run. Dockins finished the season at Fort Worth with a 12-6 record and a 2.17 ERA, while walking only thirteen batters in 158 innings. Brooklyn skipper Leo Durocher was fully expecting Dockins to return to the Dodgers in 1947, but once more the sore left arm interfered. For the second time in his professional career, George went on the voluntarily retired list. This time he returned to his native Clyde, Kansas, to work in the lumber business.

By June, Dockins felt well enough to pitch and applied to the commissioner's office for reinstatement. Rickey flew from Chicago to Fort Worth to arrange the transfer. On June 20, 1947, Dockins pitched five strong innings in an exhibition game against the Danville (Illinois) Dodgers of the Three-I League. Nine days later, on June 29, Dockins made his Dodgers debut.

Called on in the eighth inning of the nightcap at the Polo Grounds, he surrendered consecutive home runs to the first two New York Giants batters he faced, Johnny Mize and Willard Marshall. Mize's blast slammed against the upper-right-field deck. Two seasons earlier, pitching for the Cardinals in the same ballpark, Dockins allowed nineteen-year-old Whitey Lockman a home run in his first big league at bat, the ball landing in the same area as Mize's did.

Discussing his blast for a book published five decades later, Lockman more or less summed up his home run and Dockins's big league career in a somewhat cruel comment: "Hit it off a fellow named George Dockins, a left-handed pitcher for the Cardinals. People still ask me . . . and I tell them, and no one's ever heard of him. And I guess with my home run, no one's heard of him since."[12]

After this performance, Dodgers manager Burt Shotton became reluctant to use his newest pitcher. Dockins saw action about once every two weeks. He quickly became an afterthought on the Dodgers' mound staff, serving as the club's mop-up man. He made his final Major League appearance on August 19, 1947, in an 11–3 drubbing by the Cardinals at Ebbets Field. Less than a week later, Dockins was gone from the club.

Overall, the six-foot, 175-pound southpaw's "contribution" to the 1947 Dodgers amounted to a mere four regular-season appearances, all in relief. The ten hits Dockins allowed in five and one-third innings, along with an ERA of 11.81, earned him a trip back to Fort Worth on August 25.

At Fort Worth in 1948, pitching almost exclusively in relief, he was uncharacteristically injury-free and effective in the season's early weeks. Dockins was named the starting pitcher and hurled four shutout frames when Fort Worth took on the Texas League All-Stars on July 13.

When Cats skipper Lee Burge was fired on June 22, Dockins served as one of three interim managers before Bobby Bragan was hired. During that interim period, Fort Worth went undefeated in ten games. "While the club was at home," wrote sportswriter Blackie Sherrod, "the temporary manager [Dockins] was greeted with wild applause every time he took his walk to the third base coaching box."[13] "I considered staying away, not wanting to jinx the team," Bragan later admitted.[14] Despite his success and popularity as a pilot, Dockins was never again asked to manage a professional baseball club.

That September he suffered a broken nose when he was struck by a line drive during batting practice, missing a week of action. He pitched a final season for Fort Worth in 1949, without distinction. Realizing his chances of again making a Major League roster were slim, Dockins put himself on the voluntarily retired list in March 1950 for the third and final time. He was thirty-two years old.

After retiring from professional baseball, Dockins returned to Clyde, where he tried his hand at several occupations, including carpentry, farming, and dairy production. He retired from the Hutchinson Manufacturing Company in 1980.

George had married Lucy Mae Brichat in Manhattan, Kansas, on July 23, 1937. The couple had one son, Kenneth. On January 22, 1997, George Dockins died in a pasture a quarter mile north of Clyde at the age of seventy-nine. He is buried in Clyde's Mount Hope Cemetery. Dockins left his wife, son Kenneth, two grandchildren, and two great-grandchildren. Lucy Dockins died on January 5, 2007. Dockins had been named to the Kansas Baseball Hall of Fame in 1959. The lone ball field in Clyde, Kansas, is named after him.

# Chapter 35. Eddie Stanky

*Alex Edelman*

| AGE | G | AB | R | H | 2B | 3B | HR | TB | RBI | BB | SO | BAV | OBP | SLG | SB | GDP | HBP |
|---|---|---|---|---|---|---|---|---|---|---|---|---|---|---|---|---|---|
| 31 | 146 | 559 | 97 | 141 | 24 | 5 | 3 | 184 | 53 | 103 | 39 | .252 | .373 | .329 | 3 | 7 | 5 |

One can statistically evaluate with some degree of accuracy the worth of a baseball player to his team. However, sometimes a player stands out because of characteristics that inspire his teammates and draw the admiration and respect of fans. Eddie "The Brat" Stanky was one of those players. Stanky was a gritty, scrappy individual, not gifted with natural talent. He worked long and hard to achieve the success he attained. Just five feet eight and 170 pounds, Stanky seemed so much more imposing as he flew into second base with a feet-first, spikes-raised slide to break up a double play.

He was born Edward Raymond Stankiewicz, on September 3, 1915, to Frank and Anna Stankiewicz.[1] The family shortened the name to Stanky when Eddie was a boy. In his childhood years in the blue-collar Philadelphia neighborhood of Kensington, Eddie developed the belligerent, enthusiastic, win-at-all-costs attitude that would make him so successful—and reviled—in later life.

Stanky batted just .243 in his senior year at Philadelphia's Northeast High School, but his drive was exceptional. His single-mindedness and aggressiveness on the field distinguished him from everyone else, even at an early age. "It was baseball that Eddie came to high school for," said Lester Owen, Stanky's high school coach. "He said he was going to be a pro baseball player. That was that. No one doubted him. He wasn't conceited. He was an ordinary boy with extraordinary ambition."[2]

That ambition helped get Stanky a contract with his hometown Philadelphia Athletics. In 1935 he was sent to play shortstop for the Greenville (Mississippi) Buckshots of the Class C East

Eddie Stanky was Jackie Robinson's earliest important backer.

Dixie League. After a few weeks, a young, homesick, and discouraged Stanky sent his mother a letter asking for money for train fare home. The response was stern. Eddie was not welcome back at home—quitters weren't wanted in Anna Stanky's family. Eddie stayed in Greenville and finished the year with a .301 batting average and eighty runs scored in 104 games.

In 1936 Stanky moved to Portsmouth (Ohio)

of the Class C Middle Atlantic League. He raised his batting average thirty-six points and improved in almost every offensive category. Near the end of the season, he was sent to Williamsport of the Class A New York–Pennsylvania League. He played the last eleven games of 1936 and the first fourteen games of 1937 for Williamsport before returning to Portsmouth (now in the Piedmont League). Eddie had played shortstop, second, third, and even pitched during his first two years in the Minors, but he was now a full-time second baseman.

With Portsmouth in 1938, he hit .283, drew 127 walks, and was hit by a pitch 20 times en route to scoring 110 runs. Early in the 1939 season Stanky was sent to the Macon (Georgia) Peaches of the Class B South Atlantic League. The manager at Macon was Milt Stock, who was also a part-owner of the club. Stock, a fourteen-year Major Leaguer, saw that Stanky, a right-handed batter, had an excellent eye but no power. He put him in the leadoff position and urged him to be patient at the plate. It worked. Stanky had three excellent seasons at Macon and made the All-Star team in 1940.

Years later, when Stanky was managing the St. Louis Cardinals, he credited Stock with "planting the seed" that helped him blossom into a successful player and manager. At the time, though, it was hardly a certainty that Stanky would make the Majors. It was becoming apparent that despite his small size, he had a disproportionately large temper. Stock taught Eddie to control himself and told him that being thrown out of games (as happened fifteen to twenty times a year) hurt his team's chances of winning. But Milt wasn't the only Stock who had a special relationship with Stanky; his daughter, Myrtle "Dickie" Stock, fell in love with her father's little infielder, and they were married on April 11, 1942.

Shortly after the wedding, Stock dealt his new son-in-law to the Milwaukee Brewers of the American Association, where Eddie enjoyed his best— and last—season in the Minors. He finished the year with the league's best batting average (.342) and was named its MVP. Stanky's manager at Milwaukee was Charlie Grimm. In 1943 the Chicago Cubs made Grimm their manager, and Eddie followed his skipper to Chicago.

Stanky's inability to back down from a challenge and his habit of crowding the plate led to several beanings during his career. The first, in the Minors, was so severe that it left him with a fractured skull and a loss of hearing that kept him out of the armed forces. On April 21, 1943, in the first inning of his Major League debut, Stanky stepped to the plate against Pittsburgh's Rip Sewell. He was hit in the head by a pitch.

As the Cubs' second baseman that summer, he hit an uninspiring .245. In 1944 Don "Pep" Johnson arrived to take his place, and Stanky found himself warming the bench while Johnson made the All-Star team. Eddie made a simple demand of Grimm: Play me or trade me.[3] Grimm acquiesced and on June 6 dealt Stanky to the Brooklyn Dodgers for lefty pitcher Bob Chipman.

In Brooklyn, Stanky replaced the navy-bound Billy Herman at second base, and in 1945, his first full season with the Dodgers, he started to make a name for himself. His hard-nosed style of play ingratiated him with the fans, who loved his spirited approach to the game. Stanky drew 148 walks in 1945—a National League record at the time; he also led the league in runs scored with 128.

Brooklyn fans adored him. He was given nickname upon nickname: "Stinky" and "Muggsy" were popular. However, the most famous nickname, the one that stuck with him, was "The Brat," a reference to the snarling, clamorous, hot-headed edge to Stanky that came out in moments of high emotion or tension. The Brat was more of Stanky's on-field alter ego. The off-field Eddie Stanky was less of a dervish, very attentive, and spent much time learning about what it might take to be a Major League manager.

Stanky loved being a Dodger and the fans loved him, honoring him with an Eddie Stanky Day on September 8, 1946. His respect for the Dodgers uniform and the team it represented outstripped everything. In May 1946 he was involved in a fistfight with a former teammate, Cubs shortstop Lennie Merullo, that was so unruly it nearly "inspired a riot."[4]

In 1947 Stanky was elected to his first All-Star squad. He got 141 hits, scored 97 times, and made just 12 errors at second base in helping spark Brooklyn to the pennant. The 1947 season was also the year Jackie Robinson integrated baseball. Peter Golenbock, in his book *Bums*, contends that Stanky told Robinson when he reported to the Dodgers that he didn't like him but that they would "play together and get along" because they were teammates.[5] More recent research has challenged this. Jonathan Eig, in his book *Opening Day: The Story of Jackie Robinson's First Season*, says that "in accounts written shortly after the 1947 season," both Rickey and Robinson "rated Eddie Stanky as Robinson's earliest important backer."[6]

"Dad talked about that first game and Jackie a lot," said Stanky's son Mike. "He was so impressed by Jackie's raw ability and the way he dealt with everything he had to handle, that, despite what's been written over the years, they became really close. I think they both discovered that, despite their obvious differences, they were alike, very much alike."[7]

Brooklyn lost the '47 World Series to the Yankees in seven hard-fought games, during which Stanky hit .240. Days after Stanky signed his 1948 contract, and reported to the Dodgers' training facility in the Dominican Republic, Rickey traded him, on March 6, to the Boston Braves for utility man Carvell "Bama" Rowell, first baseman Ray Sanders, and $40,000.

Stanky received the most votes of any second baseman in the National League All-Star voting for 1948, and he was hitting well over .300 at the break. But while at Ebbets Field for a July 8 battle against the Dodgers, he collided with Dodgers third baseman Bruce Edwards and emerged with a broken ankle and a torn ligament. He was unable to play in the All-Star Game and did not return to action until September 19, when the Braves were close to sewing up their first pennant in thirty-four years. Boston, with Sibby Sisti handling most of the second-base duties in Eddie's absence, made Stanky a pennant winner for the second year in a row. The Dodgers finished in third place.

In the World Series, the Braves lost to Cleveland in six games. Despite Stanky's leg being "a little below par," Boston manager Billy Southworth named him to the starting lineup and played him in each contest.[8] Playing through the pain, Stanky had a .524 on-base percentage, with 7 walks and 4 hits. When doctors operated on him two months later, they removed two bone fragments from his ankle joint.

From the start of spring training in 1949, Southworth began to work his players extra hard, and some of them bridled at this treatment. It was to be the beginning of a long year, filled with controversy, for both Eddie and his teammates.

Stanky batted a solid .285 with ninety runs scored. But he started making enemies in the clubhouse, amid rumors that he would take over the managing job from Southworth. One controversy erupted on July 23 in a game against Pittsburgh. The team's best pitcher, Warren Spahn, was on base in the third inning. Spahn was credited with a stolen base after a hit-and-run called by leadoff man Stanky, who had his manager's blessing to call plays, went awry. Later in the game, Spahn again reached first, and again Eddie sent him to second on a hit-and-run. This time Stanky made contact, grounding the ball to third. Spahn made second on a wild throw and went for third, where he was tagged out. In the ninth inning on this hot

ALEX EDELMAN

day, Spahn blew a three-run lead, and the Braves lost, 12–9.

Reporters immediately assumed that Spahn had run too much on the base paths and had been tired during that last inning on the mound. The blame for "exhausting" Spahn was placed squarely on Stanky for calling the hit-and-runs. Leo Monahan of the *Boston American* said Stanky's teammates were grumbling about The Brat's assumed authority. Another writer said Eddie's mates were outraged at his "takeover attitude."[9] Stanky was livid. His response dripped with frustration, and his anger was palpable in every word. As *The Sporting News* reported him saying, "I'm always playing to get another run for my club and prevent the other team from getting runs . . . so far as taking over, I only do what I can to win the games and leave that 'takeover attitude' to second-guessing bushers. I resent the implication that I exceeded my authority in putting on plays. I have always co-operated with any manager I played for 100 percent. I have always played to win. And that's the way I'll continue until I quit the game."[10]

The incident was the low point of the season. Southworth, reportedly on the verge of a breakdown, left the team on August 16 with the Braves in fourth place at 55-54. Coach Johnny Cooney replaced him as manager, but when Southworth announced that he would be coming back in 1950, Stanky was all but gone from the team. On December 14, 1949, the ax fell, and Stanky and his double-play partner, Al Dark, were traded to the New York Giants—managed now by Leo Durocher—for outfielders Sid Gordon and Willard Marshall, infielder Buddy Kerr, and right-handed pitcher Sam Webb.

The rift between Stanky and Durocher that followed Eddie's trade from Brooklyn was quickly repaired. Durocher let Stanky play the way he wanted, and Stanky thrived. In 152 games during the 1950 season, he hit .300, with a league-high .460 on-base percentage and 115 runs scored, and he also led the league in walks (144) and times being hit by a pitch (12). He was named to the National League All-Star squad, was selected as Player of the Year by the New York Baseball Writers' Association, and finished third in the league MVP voting.

More important, with free rein and total agreement from his manager, the Stanky style of play flourished. The Giants improved from a 73-81, fifth-place finish in 1949 to an 86-68 mark and third place during Stanky's first season with the club.

In an August 12 game, second baseman Stanky started to wave his arms, mimicking the pitcher's windup, while a Phillies hitter stood in the batter's box. After a warning from umpires that Stanky did not heed, he was ejected from the game. Philadelphia catcher Andy Seminick, the victim of Stanky's antics, was not satisfied with the punishment and took out Stanky's replacement, Bill Rigney, in a violent collision at second base. Police were required to quell the ensuing bench-clearing brawl. Durocher protested the contest and said, "What's wrong with trying to fool the batter, anyway? Everyone tries to do that one way or another." Commissioner Ford Frick wasn't buying the excuse: he ordered umpires to eject any player who engaged in similar tactics.[11]

Things got even more exciting in 1951, when Stanky hit a career-high fourteen home runs and scored eighty-eight runs. However, his batting average and on-base percentage each dropped almost sixty points. The Giants, in what became known as the Miracle at Coogan's Bluff, made a late-season sprint to force a three-game playoff with the Brooklyn Dodgers. While Bobby Thomson jogged around the bases after his season-ending home run, Stanky jumped on the back of his manager, standing in the third base coaching box, and the two danced jubilantly together down the baseline.

The Giants lost the World Series to the Yankees in six games, Stanky hitting a lackluster .136, but more memorable than his anemic batting average was a run-in with Yankees shortstop Phil Rizzuto. In Game Three, on a hit-and-run that failed, Stanky was thrown out by at least fifteen feet, but when Rizzuto, covering second, leaned over to tag him out, Stanky kicked the ball out of his glove. The ball dribbled into center field, and Stanky scrambled to third. The play kept a Giants rally going and ignited a five-run outburst that won the game.

In December 1951 the St. Louis Cardinals sent pitcher Max Lanier and outfielder Chuck Diering to the Giants for Stanky, who assumed the position of player-manager for the Cardinals. Just a year removed from one of his best seasons ever, and still in his prime, Stanky began to remove himself from the playing field, appearing in just fifty-three games in 1952 and seventeen in 1953.

Stanky tried to manage the same way he played: uncompromisingly and smartly. He tolerated no laziness and had fines for players not in the dugout for the first and last pitch of the game, not advancing runners, and similar infractions. He feuded with players who resented his strict style of play, with umpires whose calls he disagreed with, and with the media, who, for the first time it seemed, weren't on his side. The Brat was almost dictatorial. "The men will play up to the fullest of their capabilities. . . . I do not plan to let anyone take advantage of me. . . . I am not a martinet and I am not a sucker."[12]

Stanky's method seemed to work. He was *The Sporting News*'s Manager of the Year in 1952, when the Cardinals went 88-66 and contended for much of the season. In 1953 the club finished in third place for the second straight year. Eddie was no longer an active player in 1954, a year in which the Cards faltered and finished in sixth place. Unpopular with his players, Stanky's days in St. Louis were numbered. "He wanted you to play as if today's game was your first or your last," said one of his players, shortstop Dick Schofield.[13] Stanky was unable to realize that the way he had played was not the way that he should manage.

The end came just thirty-six games into 1955, with the Cardinals mired in fifth place. Beer magnate August A. Busch Jr., the Cardinals' new owner, had "decided that Stanky was too much foam and not enough body" and replaced him with Harry Walker on May 28.[14]

The Brat had learned much from his mentors, but what he never seemed to learn was that players of the 1950s would never be unquestioningly obedient and that "discipline should be laced with understanding," as columnist Arthur Daley of the *New York Times* put it. Stanky grimly remarked that he would "stay in baseball . . . even if I have to go to a Class D league."[15]

Stanky took a job managing the Minneapolis Millers of the American Association. The Millers finished in fourth place, and again Eddie was out of a job. He wanted to return to the Giants as a coach and had the blessing of club president Horace Stoneham, but the Giants' pilot, Bill Rigney, said no. Instead, Stanky took a job as a coach for the Cleveland Indians under freshman manager Kerby Farrell. He remained there for two years.

Eddie did well in his role with the Indians. He tried to be a loyal organization man. He taught Indians hitter Bobby Avila the "intentional foul" that had made him such a successful player in his day, and he stayed on when Farrell was replaced by Bobby Bragan, and then again when Bragan was replaced by Joe Gordon. Future Major League manager Joe Altobelli, who was a part-time first baseman on that Cleveland team, called Stanky the best third base coach he ever saw.[16]

Ultimately, Indians ownership cleaned house, and Stanky left the club at the end of 1958. He returned to the Cardinals as a special assistant to general manager Bing Devine, where his role consisted of scouting and evaluating Major and Minor League talent. Devine was fired by the Cardinals in 1964 and moved on to become GM of the

Mets. Stanky joined him in New York but did not stay there long, as he was quickly hired by the Chicago White Sox to be their manager for the 1966 campaign.

Stanky's predecessor in Chicago, Al Lopez, was a gentle, soft-spoken man who had been popular with his players. Lopez treated his players with kid gloves; Stanky rode them and pushed them to be the best they could be. Lopez played percentage-driven, orderly baseball that rarely employed aggressive plays like the hit-and-run and delayed steals; Stanky was the exact opposite, managing the same way he had played. By 1960s standards, his methods were almost incomprehensibly aggressive. Where most teams never used more than 60 pinch runners in a season, Stanky used 144 in 1966 and 127 in 1967.

Unable to adjust to their new run-and-gun style, the White Sox finished the 1966 season in fourth place. But by the start of the 1967 season, Stanky had fired many of the coaches he had inherited in 1966, installing those he thought would help convey his philosophy to the players. Stanky's forceful managing, able pitching staff, and a solid fielding team that made few mistakes helped keep the White Sox competitive deep into one of baseball's most gripping seasons.

Embroiled in a battle with Boston, Minnesota, and Detroit for first place, Stanky's pitching-rich team was going strong in late August, tied with the Red Sox for first despite being one of the league's weakest-hitting clubs. Eddie had his players motivated and playing way over their heads, but barely anyone seemed to notice. Because of their lack of fireworks on offense and inconsistent clutch hitting, the White Sox were called dull. Hometown fans, who should have been coming to the ballpark in droves to see the hustle-filled baseball the South Siders were playing, instead stayed away.

On August 13, after a tough game in Minnesota that Chicago lost, 3–2, on a controversial call in the ninth, Vice President Hubert Humphrey wait-ed outside the clubhouse to meet with the team. He ended up waiting there for a long time while Stanky talked to his players. "Humphrey can't hit," said Stanky. "What do I need with him?"[17]

The Brat later apologized to Humphrey for making him wait, but the incident was indicative of his single-mindedness when it came to his team. Still, despite it all, the White Sox went into the last week of the season seemingly World Series–bound. NBC came to Comiskey Park to set up cameras. To win the pennant, the White Sox would have to beat the lowly Athletics in Kansas City and then the eighth-place Senators. But they lost a doubleheader to Kansas City and then were shut out by the Senators, eliminating them from contention. The White Sox finished in fourth place, three games behind the champion Red Sox.

Notwithstanding the massive letdown that was the end of the 1967 season, Stanky's contract was renewed for four years by White Sox owner Arthur Allyn for the "outstanding managerial job he did in the greatest American League race in history."[18]

But the White Sox lost their first ten games in 1968, and sixty-nine games later, Stanky was asked to resign—replaced, ironically, by former manager Al Lopez. That last partial season was excruciatingly painful. Toward the end of his tenure, Stanky was so frustrated with the inability of the White Sox to produce runs that after a third straight loss by one run, he instituted a $5 fine for players who failed in certain clutch situations. It didn't matter; the White Sox finished the season in eighth place.

Back home in Alabama, Stanky secured the coaching job in 1969 at the University of Southern Alabama. After the relative glamour of the Major Leagues, college ball was different. "I had played in beautiful parks with beautiful locker rooms," he said. "At Southern Alabama, I inherited a rock pile for a ball field, with no dugouts, a four-foot-high fence around it and no grass in the infield."[19]

Stanky transformed that little school into a great college baseball team. For the next fourteen years, beginning in 1969, teams led by Stanky went 488-193. He did not have a single losing season.

Best of all, Eddie finally changed his win-at-all-costs philosophy. He adopted an "everyone plays" style. "I'm a believer in participation," he said. "The one record I care about came in a game against Vanderbilt in 1971. I played thirty-eight men in one nine-inning game. Everyone got in. Some seasons, I've carried as many as forty-five players on a team." Stanky loved coaching students, and he later said the biggest thrill was when his players graduated and "their mothers come up and embrace me for helping along their sons. There is something about a mother's tears at graduation. I can't weigh it."[20]

Stanky sent forty-three of his players to the Major Leagues, as his team became a Sun Belt Conference powerhouse. "He brought the University of South Alabama from just about point-zero to a national power in three years," said a successor as coach, Steve Kittrell, who played under Stanky.[21]

There was a brief moment in the midst of his years at Southern Alabama where it seemed as though Stanky would resume his Major League managerial career. On June 23, 1977, he became manager of the Texas Rangers and piloted them to a 10–8 victory. The next day, he quit. He told team president Eddie Robinson, "I can't take the job . . . I'm homesick for my family." Greeted by reporters back at the University of South Alabama, he was asked if he was back for good. "You're damn right I am," he responded.[22]

Stanky weathered a heart attack and open-heart surgery to coach the school for another six years before retiring in 1983. In one of his last games, Eddie showed a flash of his "Brat" persona, being thrown out of the contest for cursing an umpire. "If there is anything I can't stand," he said after the game, repeating one of his favorite sayings, "it's an umpire who doesn't know the rules."[23]

On June 6, 1999, Eddie Stanky died in a hospital in his hometown in Fairhope, Alabama, after a heart attack. He was eighty-three. Stanky was survived by his wife, son, three daughters, and eight grandchildren.

# Chapter 36. Timeline, June 30–July 14

*Lyle Spatz*

Monday, June 30, at Philadelphia—Brooklyn had fourteen hits to defeat Schoolboy Rowe, 7–4, ending Rowe's thirteen-game winning streak at Shibe Park. Carl Furillo had two doubles and a triple, raising his batting average to .342. Jackie Robinson and Philadelphia's Del Ennis both extended their hitting streaks: Robinson to seventeen games, and Ennis to nineteen. Rex Barney had a shutout until the eighth inning, when the Phillies scored all their runs. Hank Behrman finished up. 38-28, Second, .002 percentage points behind.

Tuesday, July 1, at Philadelphia—Joe Hatten had a 3–0 lead over the Phillies after five innings but failed to survive the sixth. The Phillies rallied against him and Clyde King for five runs and a 5–3 victory. It was the fifth consecutive start in which Hatten had failed to survive the sixth inning. Arky Vaughan had a two-run homer for Brooklyn in the first inning. Jackie Robinson had a single, extending his hitting streak to eighteen games, but Del Ennis, twice walked intentionally, had his streak end at nineteen. 38-29, Second, .002 percentage points behind.

Wednesday, July 2, vs. New York—Brooklyn moved past the Braves into first place behind Ralph Branca's eleventh win, an 11–3 pounding of the Giants. Bruce Edwards had a three-run homer in the Dodgers' nine-run fourth inning, while Arky Vaughan, with a double, and Carl Furillo, with a triple, each drove in two runs in the inning. Jackie Robinson extended his hitting streak to nineteen games. 39-29, First, 1 game ahead.

Thursday, July 3, vs. New York—The Giants used five home runs (two by Bobby Thomson), a nine-run second inning, and a seven-run third to deal the Dodgers their most lopsided defeat of the season. The 19–2 win by New York moved the Giants into second place. Hal Gregg, the first of four Brooklyn pitchers, was the loser. The only bright spot for the Dodgers was Jackie Robinson's bunt single, which raised his hitting streak to twenty games. 39-30, First, ½ game ahead.

Friday, July 4, vs. New York (2)—Brooklyn won both ends of the holiday doubleheader, smashing the Giants 16–7 in the morning game and nipping them 4–3 in the afternoon contest. Each team used five pitchers in the morning game, with the win going to Hugh Casey. Arky Vaughan, Dixie Walker, and Pee Wee Reese each hit solo home runs in the second game, but the game winner came on Gene Hermanski's pinch single in the ninth. Unlike the first game, when managers Burt Shotton and Mel Ott each used five pitchers, Harry Taylor and New York's Mort Cooper pitched complete games. Jackie Robinson's consecutive-game batting streak reached twenty-one in the morning game, but Cooper ended it in the afternoon. The team sent rookie outfielder Duke Snider to St. Paul of the American Association. 41-30, First, 1 game ahead.

Saturday, July 5, vs. Boston—Bill Voiselle pitched Boston back into first place with a 4–1 victory over Vic Lombardi. Voiselle allowed just six hits, including two apiece by Spider Jorgensen and

Jackie Robinson. 41-31, Second, .002 percentage points behind.

Sunday, July 6, vs. Boston—Ralph Branca shut out the first-place Braves on three hits for his twelfth win of the season. Brooklyn's 4-0 triumph allowed the Dodgers to leapfrog Boston back into first place, giving them a one-game lead at the All-Star break. 42-31, First, 1 game ahead.

Monday, July 7—Not scheduled. 42-31, First, 1 game ahead.

Tuesday, July 8—All-Star Game. 42-31, First, 1 game ahead.

Wednesday, July 9—Not scheduled. 42-31, First, 1 game ahead.

Thursday, July 10, vs. Chicago (2)—Ralph Branca pitched eight and one-third innings to win the first game, 5–3. Branca then tossed two and two-thirds innings in relief of Harry Taylor in the nightcap to gain his second win of the day, 4–3. Jackie Robinson's two-run homer off Chicago's Hank Borowy, and three-hit games by Eddie Stanky and Arky Vaughan, led the way in game one. Carl Furillo homered with two on in the first inning of game two, but the Cubs fought back to tie the score in the eighth. The Dodgers won in the tenth on Spider Jorgensen's double and Arky Vaughan's single. 44-31, First, 2 games ahead.

Friday, July 11, vs. Chicago—Vic Lombardi tossed his first complete game of the season, a 5–0 three-hit shutout of the Cubs. Lombardi also had two hits, as did Dixie Walker, while five different Dodgers each drove in a single run. The win, combined with Boston's loss to Cincinnati, raised Brooklyn's lead to a season-high three games. 45-31, First, 3 games ahead.

Saturday, July 12, vs. Chicago (2)—Brooklyn won both ends of a doubleheader to complete a five-game sweep of Chicago, improving its season record against the Cubs to 14–2. A six-run seventh inning helped Joe Hatten win the opener, 7–2. The second game, won by Hugh Casey, was a thriller. Trailing 4–2, the Dodgers tied it in the eighth on Dixie Walker's two-run homer. Then, after the Cubs went ahead again in the ninth, run-scoring singles by Arky Vaughan and Carl Furillo gave the Dodgers a 6–5 win. 47-31, First, 3½ games ahead.

Sunday, July 13, vs. Cincinnati—Clyde King made his first start of the season a winning one. King pitched a complete-game six-hitter as the Dodgers downed the Reds 9–1 for their seventh consecutive win. King also had a double and three runs batted in. Jackie Robinson, Pee Wee Reese, and Bruce Edwards each had three hits for Brooklyn. 48-31, First, 3 games ahead.

Monday, July 14, vs. Cincinnati—The Reds, behind Bud Lively, ended Brooklyn's seven-game win streak, thrashing the Dodgers 9–1. Lively allowed just one hit, a second-inning double by Spider Jorgensen that drove in Pee Wee Reese. Reese, who had walked, was the only other Brooklyn base runner, as their last twenty-two batters went down in order. Ralph Branca had his own personal seven-game winning streak snapped. 48-32, First, 3 games ahead.

# Chapter 37. Arky Vaughan

*Ralph C. Moses*

| AGE | G | AB | R | H | 2B | 3B | HR | TB | RBI | BB | SO | BAV | OBP | SLG | SB | GDP | HBP |
|-----|-----|-----|-----|-----|-----|-----|-----|-----|-----|-----|-----|-----|-----|-----|-----|-----|-----|
| 35 | 64 | 126 | 24 | 41 | 5 | 2 | 2 | 56 | 25 | 27 | 11 | .325 | .444 | .444 | 4 | 2 | 0 |

Hall of Famer Arky Vaughan spent most of his career playing shortstop for the Pittsburgh Pirates, but he was a valuable member of the Brooklyn Dodgers for his last four years in the Major Leagues. He played a key role as a reserve on the pennant-winning 1947 squad. Vaughan's presence on the team in any role was unusual, to say the least. He had nearly fomented a players' strike in 1943, when he became irate over manager Leo Durocher's reprimanding a teammate in the press. He then quit the team at the end of the season and sat out three full years before returning in 1947.

Vaughan's career achievements were remarkable. In 1935 Vaughan led the National League with a .385 batting average, and his .318 lifetime average is second among all shortstops to Honus Wagner's .327. Over his career Vaughan walked 937 times, while striking out just 276 times. He was among the most difficult players to double up, grounding into only 70 double plays in the last thirteen years of his fourteen year career. (GDP was not tracked in 1932.) Vaughan's on-base percentage was an impressive .406, while his slugging percentage was a highly respectable .453. An All-Star selection for nine consecutive years, he compiled a .364 batting average in All-Star Games, and he was the first player to hit two home runs in one.

Joseph Floyd Vaughan was born on March 9, 1912, in Clifty, Arkansas, a farm village about twenty-five miles northeast of Fayetteville. When Arky was seven months old, his parents, Robert and Laura Vaughan, moved the family, including two older sisters, to Mendocino County near San Francisco. They later relocated to Fullerton, Cal-

Arky Vaughan sat out three full seasons before returning in 1947.

ifornia, where Robert found work in the California oil fields. Joseph Floyd Vaughan's childhood friends began calling him Arky as soon as they learned of his birthplace, and he was known as Arky Vaughan for the rest of his life.

At five feet ten inches and 175 pounds, Vaughan was a multisport star at Fullerton High School. In addition, he played on the undefeated Cypress Merchants of the Orange County Winter League in 1930–31. A neighbor of Vaughan's tipped off

Pirates scout Art Griggs about the youngster's abilities, and Griggs signed him in January 1931.

Playing his first season of professional baseball for the 1931 Wichita Aviators of the Class A Western League, the nineteen-year-old Vaughan made an immediate impact. He batted .338 with 21 home runs, 81 runs batted in, and a league-leading 145 runs scored and 43 stolen bases. Vaughan's performance earned him a promotion to the Pirates.

Weak-hitting, good-fielding Tommy Thevenow had been the Pirates' regular shortstop in 1931, and manager George Gibson started him at the position in the 1932 opener. Five days later, on April 17, the twenty-year-old Vaughan made his Major League debut, striking out as a pinch hitter against Cincinnati's Larry Benton. Vaughan got his first start at shortstop on April 28, after Thevenow broke a finger. The left-handed-hitting Californian made an impressive debut with two triples and three runs batted in. The next day, facing future Hall of Fame pitcher Eppa Rixey, Vaughan went 2 for 4. Now firmly established as the Pirates' starting shortstop, Vaughan had a 5-for-5 day on June 7. He hit his first Major League home run on July 26, off Jim Mooney of the New York Giants.

Vaughan's rookie batting average was .318, but he struggled in the field, committing a league-leading forty-six errors. On August 11, Vaughan, the youngest player in the National League, made a crucial error in the tenth inning that allowed the Chicago Cubs to beat Pittsburgh and take over first place in the NL. The Pirates eventually finished second, four games behind the Cubs.

In 1933 Vaughan played shortstop in all but two of the Pirates' games and began to exhibit good power as well as outstanding speed. On May 1 he and catcher Earl Grace both slugged grand slams in a rout of the Philadelphia Phillies. For Vaughan, whose home run was inside-the-park, it was the first of his four Major League grand slams. On June 24 he hit for the cycle, going 5 for 5 with five RBIs against Brooklyn.

Teammate Lloyd Waner recalled Vaughan's speed in an interview with author Donald Honig: "For going from home plate to second base I don't think there was anybody who could match him." Vaughan batted an impressive .314 for the '33 Pirates, as they again were runners-up in the National League.

After Vaughan again made forty-six errors at shortstop, the Pirates hired their legendary shortstop Honus Wagner as a coach. Wagner even roomed with his young protégé on the road. According to a Wagner biographer, Wagner wasn't much of an instructor, but his presence and guidance helped Vaughan settle down. "They said if I couldn't make a shortstop out of Arky Vaughan, nobody could," Wagner recalled almost two decades later. "Of all the players I tried to help, he's the best and the one that went the farthest."

Fifty-one games into the 1934 season, the Pirates replaced manager George Gibson with Pie Traynor. Pittsburgh slumped to fifth place, but the twenty-two-year-old Vaughan sparkled, batting an NL fourth-best .333, with a career-high 42 doubles, 11 triples, 12 home runs, and 94 RBIs. He made his first appearance in the All-Star Game, which was played at the Polo Grounds in New York. Vaughan entered the game in the fifth inning as a pinch hitter and remained in the game, going hitless and compiling two put-outs and an assist in the field.

In 1935 Vaughan had the best season of his career. He was hitting .401 in mid-September, but an eight-game slump lowered his final batting average to .385. Arky led the league in walks (97), on-base percentage (.491), and slugging percentage (.607), and his 19 home runs and 99 runs batted in were career highs. His .491 on-base percentage remains the highest ever for a Pirates player. Vaughan finished third in the baseball writers' vote for the National League's Most Valuable Player; however, *The Sporting News* selected him as their MVP in the National League and as the shortstop on their postseason Major League All-Star team.

Vaughan continued to put up impressive numbers in 1936, batting .335 with 78 runs batted in. His patience and selectivity at the plate produced a career-high 118 walks, the third consecutive year he had led the National League in walks. Vaughan also topped the league in on-base percentage for the third consecutive year, and he scored a league-best 122 runs.

In 1937 Vaughan hit only five home runs, but two came in one game, against Carl Hubbell on May 13. Arky played twelve games in the outfield, but none at third base during the season. Yet he started at third base in the All-Star Game, going 2 for 5 in an NL loss at Washington.

Throughout the summer of 1938, the Pirates battled New York, Chicago, and Cincinnati for the league lead. With a week left in the season, the Pirates led Chicago by two games. Sparked by player-manager Gabby Hartnett's fabled "Homer in the Gloamin," the Cubs swept a three-game series from the Pirates at Wrigley Field and won the pennant by two games over Pittsburgh. Vaughan batted .322 for a second consecutive year and was again third in the league's MVP race. He was selected for his fifth consecutive All-Star Game, but he did not play.

Once considered a liability defensively, Vaughan improved his fielding dramatically from 1938 through 1940. He led the NL three times in assists, twice in put-outs, and once each in total chances per game and double plays. He did, however, commit a league-leading fifty-two errors in 1940.

The Pirates fell to sixth place in 1939, their final season under Pie Traynor. Vaughan batted a solid .306 and again made the All-Star team. He started at shortstop for the National League at Yankee Stadium and scored his team's only run. A few days later, on July 19, Vaughan hit for the cycle for the second time in his career, again going 5 for 5.

In 1940, under new manager Frankie Frisch,

Vaughan batted an even .300, drove in 95 runs, and led the National League in runs scored and triples. The 1941 season was Vaughan's last year in Pittsburgh. Playing in only 106 games, he hit .316 with 6 home runs and just 38 RBIs. Vaughan's playing time was limited by two injuries. In mid-season he suffered a spike wound and was out of the lineup for two weeks. Then, on August 30, he suffered a concussion when he was hit in the head by a pitch during an exhibition game in London, Ontario. Vaughan tried to return to the lineup, but he had severe headaches, and the team doctors ordered him to bed.

Despite his drop in production, Vaughan was again selected as the starting shortstop for the National League All-Star team. In the All-Star Game at Briggs Stadium in Detroit, Vaughan had perhaps his most memorable performance. After getting a single early in the contest, he homered in the seventh with a man on base, putting the NL ahead, 3–2. In the next inning, Vaughan hit his second successive two-run homer, raising the NL's lead to 5–2. Vaughan appeared to be the day's hero until Ted Williams of the Red Sox won the game for the American League, 7–5, with a dramatic ninth-inning three-run homer.

On December 12, 1941, the Pirates traded their popular and perennial All-Star shortstop to the Brooklyn Dodgers for pitcher Luke Hamlin, catcher Babe Phelps, outfielder Jimmy Wasdell, and second baseman Pete Coscarart. "Many of the Pirate faithful shook their heads," wrote Fred Lieb. "They didn't want to see Arky get away."

Playing mostly at third base in 1942 for the Dodgers and their fiery manager, Leo Durocher, Vaughan hit .277 as Brooklyn won 104 games, but they still finished two games behind pennant-winning St. Louis. In his final All-Star Game, at the Polo Grounds, Vaughan played third base and went hitless in two at bats.

Vaughan rebounded in 1943 with a solid performance in what turned out to be his final season as a regular player. He batted .305 and led the NL in stolen bases and runs scored. He played in ninety-nine games at shortstop and fifty-five at third base.

On July 10 of that year, manager Durocher suspended pitcher Bobo Newsom for insubordination. Dodgers second baseman Billy Herman remembered, "I was having breakfast together with Augie Galan and Arky Vaughan at the New Yorker Hotel. Vaughan was a guy who always had everybody's respect, as a ballplayer and as a man. He never said too much, but everybody admired and respected him." Vaughan read a newspaper interview in which Durocher made accusations against Newsom. Herman recalled that Vaughan was quiet but seemed to be upset by what he read. Later, at the ballpark, Vaughan angrily confronted Durocher, who confirmed that he had given the interview. Herman recalled, "Arky didn't say another word. He went back to his locker and took off his uniform—pants, blouse, socks, cap—made a big bundle out of it, and went back to (Durocher's) office.

"'Take this uniform,' he said, 'and shove it right up your ass.' And he threw it in Durocher's face. 'If you would lie about Bobo,' he said, 'you would lie about me and everybody else. I'm not playing for you.'"

Most of his teammates sided with Vaughan and decided not to play that afternoon against Pittsburgh. Durocher, with help from general manager Branch Rickey, eventually persuaded all the Dodgers—except Vaughan—to play. Arky and Newsom watched the start of the game in street clothes from the right-field stands. Rickey asked Vaughan to return to the team, and he did. Arky was back on the bench in uniform before the end of the game.

At season's end, possibly still upset with Durocher, Vaughan decided to put his baseball career behind him. He returned to his Northern California cattle ranch with his wife, Margaret, his former high school sweetheart whom he had married in 1931, and their four children. Vaughan

remained in retirement until 1947, when Rickey coaxed him back to the Dodgers.

At the age of thirty-five, after missing three full seasons, Vaughan managed to hit .325 as a part-time player. The season was marked by the one-year suspension of Durocher and the historic debut of Jackie Robinson. Vaughan served as a respected, calming clubhouse influence for the Dodgers and Robinson that season. After Vaughan's death, Robinson remembered, "He was one of the fellows who went out of his way to be nice to me when I came in here as a rookie. Believe me, I needed it. He was a fine fellow."

The Dodgers won the National League pennant in 1947, and Vaughan had an opportunity to play in his only World Series. Facing the Yankees, Vaughan drew a walk and belted a double in three pinch-hitting appearances. Vaughan returned to the Dodgers in 1948 as a part-time player, but by 1949, wanting to be closer to home, he joined the San Francisco Seals of the Pacific Coast League. In his final season of professional baseball, Arky batted .288 in ninety-seven games.

Following his retirement from baseball, Vaughan devoted all his energies to his family, his ranch, and his hobby of fishing. On August 30, 1952, he and a friend, Bill Wimer, sailed their fishing boat to Lost Lake, east of the Northern California town of Eagleville. The lake, in the crater of an extinct volcano, had reportedly never been sounded. The skiff capsized and, according to a witness, Vaughan and Wimer started swimming for shore. The men swam about sixty-five yards in the chilly water and were only twenty feet from shore when they sank in water that was twenty feet deep. Later reports stated that Vaughan was trying to save Wimer, who, it was reported, could not swim. Their bodies were recovered early the next morning. Vaughan was forty years old.

The baseball world mourned his passing. Pee Wee Reese called Vaughan "a steady, easy-going guy, and (he) had a good long life to look forward to." Cookie Lavagetto said, "I never knew a finer fellow or a better team man." Charlie Dressen said, "I knew him for many, many years. He was a great team man." National League president Warren Giles said, "The whole sporting world lost a gentleman and a fine competitor in the death of Arky Vaughan. He contributed much to National League prestige in the fourteen years he played with the Pirates and Dodgers. I am deeply sorry to hear of his tragic death."

Ignoring his accomplishments, the Baseball Writers' Association of America never gave Vaughan more than 29 percent of their votes for the Baseball Hall of Fame (75 percent is required for election). Vaughan dropped off the BBWAA ballot after 1968, and not until 1985 did he at last gain election, by a vote of the Veterans' Committee.

Yet Arky Vaughan remains relatively unknown in comparison to his fellow Hall of Famers. Overlooked and underappreciated, Vaughan ranks among the top shortstops and offensive stars of his or any era.

# Chapter 38. **Duke Snider**

*Warren Jacobs*

| AGE | G | AB | R | H | 2B | 3B | HR | TB | RBI | BB | SO | BAV | OBP | SLG | SB | GDP | HBP |
|-----|---|----|---|---|----|----|----|----|-----|----|----|-----|-----|-----|----|----|-----|
| 20 | 40 | 83 | 6 | 20 | 3 | 1 | 0 | 25 | 5 | 3 | 24 | .241 | .276 | .301 | 2 | 0 | 1 |

A strong, accurate throwing arm, grace, and athleticism made Duke Snider one of the great center fielders of the 1950s. He played sixteen of his eighteen seasons for Brooklyn and Los Angeles, where his .300 batting average, 389 home runs, and 1,271 RBIs rank him as perhaps the greatest Dodger hitter ever. Blessed with remarkable ability, competitiveness, and a drive to succeed, Snider was also cursed with the tag of unlimited potential.

Edwin Donald Snider was born to Ward and Florence (Johnson) Snider on September 19, 1926. He was their only child. Ward had been a semi-pro baseball player in his native Ohio. Most accounts list Snider's birthplace as Los Angeles, but according to writer Al Stump, he was born in Belvedere and grew up in Compton, a city surrounded by Los Angeles.

Nicknamed "Duke" by his father for his self-assured swagger, Edwin grew rapidly as he entered adolescence, reaching six feet in height and weighing 150 pounds in high school. Duke participated in football, basketball, baseball, and track at Compton High School. He had a powerful arm, once throwing a sixty-three-yard touchdown pass. He was high scorer on the same basketball team as Pete Rozelle, the future commissioner of the National Football League. On the baseball team, he pitched and batted cleanup.

Snider performed well at a Dodgers' tryout camp in Long Beach, California, and was offered a contract calling for a $750 bonus and a salary of $250 a month. The Pittsburgh Pirates subsequently offered him a $15,000 bonus, but Duke honored his Dodgers contract.

Invited to 1944 spring training at Bear Moun-

Duke Snider was a player who needed to be kicked to perform at his best, according to manager Burt Shotton.

tain, New York, Snider quickly demonstrated both his baseball talent and a difficult temperament. Cold and homesick—he failed to bring a coat—the seventeen-year-old moped instead of following directions to run laps. After apologizing for his behavior, Snider was inserted into the lineup against the West Point team and belted a long three-run homer. General manager Branch Rickey profusely praised Snider's power, arm, and the "steel springs in his legs."

At the end of camp, Duke was sent to Newport News, Virginia, in the Class B Piedmont League, where he played 131 games, batting .294 while leading the league with 34 doubles and 9 home runs. In the outfield he compiled 25 assists.

Duke's potential forced the Dodgers' brass to overlook his growing pains. When manager Jake Pitler flashed a take sign, Snider became infuriated. Duke would return to the dugout and kick the water bucket in anger, demanding to be sent immediately to another team in the Dodgers organization. His temper erupted whenever he failed to connect at the plate. After his first season in professional baseball (which also included a brief stay with the Class Triple-A Montreal Royals), Snider enlisted in the navy, serving eighteen months during 1945 and part of 1946.

In 1946 he played sixty-eight games at Fort Worth in the Class Double-A Texas League. Though he batted only .250, Rickey was enthralled by Snider's potential, his explosive swing, his grace in the field, and his blazing speed on the bases. Duke was considered the jewel of the Dodgers organization.

In 1947 Snider performed well enough in spring training to make Brooklyn's Opening Day roster as a backup outfielder. He had his first Major League hit in his big league debut—a single off Boston's Si Johnson on April 17.

Jackie Robinson joined Snider in making the climb from the Minor Leagues to the big club that season. Duke, who admired Jackie for his courage and his athleticism, occasionally ate with him and kidded with him around the batting cage trying to ease the burden Robinson carried. When asked by some of his new teammates to sign a petition against Jackie, Snider refused.

Snider had a limited role with the 1947 Dodgers. In forty games, he hit .241 with twenty-four strikeouts in eighty-three at bats as a pinch hitter and part-time outfielder. While he struggled at the plate, he proved to be a gifted center fielder. But

for all Snider's gifts, he was immature, moody, and temperamental. Manager Burt Shotton pegged Snider as a player who needed to be kicked to perform at his best.

On July 4 the Dodgers sent him to the St. Paul Saints of the American Association. There he hit .316 with twelve home runs in sixty-six games. He returned to the Dodgers at the end of the season and was a spectator at their World Series defeat by the Yankees. Snider received a quarter share of World Series money. After the season, he married Beverly Null, his high school sweetheart. (They raised four children: Pam, Kurt, Kevin, and Dawna.)

Rickey decided to teach the strike zone to Snider as a way to help his most gifted player harness his abundant potential. At spring training in 1948, Rickey and batting coach George Sisler worked intently with Snider to correct his tendency to lunge and overswing at the plate. The work was slow and difficult, but Snider learned the strike zone. Spring training in 1948 was the turning point of Duke's career. He later told Rickey's biographer Murray Polner, "Without [Rickey], I would never have made it."

Snider was assigned to Montreal to start the season in the International League. In seventy-seven games, he hit .327 with 17 home runs and 77 runs batted in. According to writer Ray Robinson, Duke once refused to bunt when ordered to do so by Montreal manager Clay Hopper. Instead, Snider angrily swung away, blasting a home run. Snider apologized to Hopper, who fined Duke for missing a sign and chastised him for his insolent behavior.

On August 6 Snider was recalled to Brooklyn. He played in fifty-three games, batted .244, and hit the first five home runs of his eighteen-year Major League career. Duke soon found Ebbets Field to his liking. It was tailor-made for a left-handed pull hitter. Snider could take aim at a right-field fence just 297 feet from the plate. At the start of the 1949 season, Shotton told him he would be the everyday center fielder and bat third until he demonstrated he was unable to do the job. With growing confidence, Duke proved that he belonged with the Dodgers, hitting a solid .292 with 92 RBIS, while tying Gil Hodges for the club lead with 23 home runs.

The Dodgers and the Cardinals went down to the last day of the season in a fight for the pennant. Duke came to the plate in top of the tenth inning of a 7–7 game with Philadelphia and stroked a single up the middle that scored Pee Wee Reese with the run that clinched the pennant for the Dodgers.

In the World Series, the Dodgers fell to the Yankees in five games. Snider had a terrible Series, striking out eight times in the five games to tie a record held by Rogers Hornsby. Duke was only 3 for 21 at the plate and failed to drive in a single run.

On May 30, 1950, in the second game of a doubleheader at Ebbets Field, Duke had one of the greatest games of his career. Facing Philadelphia's Russ Meyer, Snider hit long home runs over the right-field screen onto Bedford Avenue in the first and third innings. In the fifth he smacked a Blix Donnelly pitch over the center-field wall for his third home run of the game. In his fourth at bat, against Bob Miller, Duke hit a rising line drive that struck one foot below the top of the right-field screen. The ball was hit so hard that he was held to a single.

Snider went on to bat .321 and finish in the National League's top five in eight offensive categories, leading in hits (199) and total bases (343). In 1950 the Dodgers came down to the last day of the season needing a victory to force a playoff for the pennant. Brooklyn was hosting the Phillies, whom they trailed by one game in the standings. With runners on first and second in the ninth inning of a 1–1 game, Duke lined a hit to center field off Robin Roberts. Center fielder Richie Ashburn gathered Snider's hit on one bounce and easily threw out

Cal Abrams, the runner from second, at the plate. In the top of the tenth, Dick Sisler hit a three-run homer to defeat the Dodgers and clinch the pennant for Philadelphia.

Snider's batting average declined to .277 in 1951. He still managed to hit 29 home runs and drive in 101 runs. In fourteen fewer at bats than in 1950, Snider had eighteen more strikeouts and grounded into fourteen more double plays. Duke was disappointed in his failure to produce down the stretch when seemingly one big hit might have helped the Dodgers clinch the pennant. Brooklyn had gotten off to a hot start under manager Charlie Dressen, building a thirteen-game lead over the Giants by August 11. But the Giants won thirty-seven of their final forty-four games to tie for first place and force a best-of-three playoff for the pennant.

The Giants and Dodgers split the first two games. Game Three was played at the Polo Grounds. The Dodgers took a 4–1 lead into the bottom of the ninth. Bobby Thomson's home run capped an amazing rally to lift the Giants into the World Series. As the ball cleared the left-field fence, Snider dropped to a knee and slammed his glove against the ground in frustration.

At the age of twenty-five, Duke's hair was already turning gray. After the 1951 season, he asked to be traded. Duke felt unable to live up to the high expectations associated with playing in New York. The Dodgers had no intention of parting with Snider and attempted to reassure him.

His teammates considered Snider a crybaby, a pouter with a personality problem, and a spoiled mama's boy. Finally, even Reese, the mild-mannered team captain, denounced Snider's behavior, telling him to grow up and stop his moaning.

In 1952 Dressen benched Duke during an August slump. Eventually, Snider returned to the lineup and led the Dodgers to the pennant and another World Series date with the Yankees. Over the last six weeks of the season, he raised his final average to .303, while chipping in 21 homers and 92 runs batted in.

In the sixth inning of Game One, in Brooklyn, Duke hit a two-run homer against Yankees ace Allie Reynolds. He had his best performance in Game Five at Yankee Stadium. He belted a 420-foot two-run homer off Ewell Blackwell in the top of the fifth inning and then made a leaping catch of Yogi Berra's hot liner in the bottom of the inning. After the Yankees took the lead, the Dodgers came back to tie the game in the seventh on Snider's hit. The game went into the eleventh inning, when Snider doubled off the bullpen railing to score Billy Cox with the winning run. After five games, the Dodgers held a 3–2 lead, with the final two games scheduled in Brooklyn.

In Game Six, Snider slugged solo home runs in the sixth and eighth innings. But the Dodgers lost, 3–2. In the final contest, Snider popped out against Yankees reliever Bob Kuzava with the bases loaded in the seventh inning. Kuzava blanked the Dodgers over the final two innings and clinched the championship for the Yankees. Still, Snider had a tremendous Series, going 10 for 29 with four home runs and eight RBIS. He felt he had truly arrived as a Major League player.

The next season, 1953, was the first of Snider's five consecutive forty-plus home run seasons. At twenty-six years old and entering the prime of his career, Duke finished in the top four in ten offensive categories and placed third in the MVP balloting. He hit .336 with 198 hits, 42 home runs, 126 RBIS, and 16 stolen bases. He led the league in runs scored (132) and in slugging (.627). The Dodgers repeated as pennant winners but again were beaten by the Yankees in the World Series. Snider was 8 for 25 with 1 home run and 5 RBIS in six games.

Snider had another outstanding season in 1954. He tied Stan Musial for the league lead with 120 runs scored and finished third in batting average, second in RBIS, and among the top three in six other offensive categories. Duke battled the Giants'

Don Mueller and Willie Mays for the batting title. The three were virtually tied going into the final day of the season, but Duke's 0-for-3 left him third in the race at .341, his career high.

Snider made perhaps his most memorable defensive play in a game at Philadelphia's Connie Mack Stadium on May 31, 1954. With two outs in the bottom of the twelfth inning, the Dodgers clinging to a 5–4 lead, and the potential tying and winning runs on base, Willie "Puddin' Head" Jones hit a scorching shot to left-center field. Snider raced to his right, dug his spikes into the fence, and leaped skyward while extending his glove as high as he could stretch his arm. He made a sensational one-handed catch to preserve the Dodgers' victory before crashing to the turf.

Snider's one defensive shortcoming was with ground balls; he rarely charged them, despite repeated admonitions from Reese. Word quickly spread around the league. Runners would not even hesitate at second on a ground ball to the outfield, consistently taking the extra base when the ball was hit to Snider, despite his strong throwing arm.

In 1955 Duke had his fourth season with a .300 batting average, 30 or more homers, and 100 or more RBIS. He led the National League in runs scored (126) and RBIS (136) while hitting .309 and blasting 42 home runs. Snider was honored as *The Sporting News*'s Player of the Year. His teammate Roy Campanella edged Duke by five points in the balloting for the Most Valuable Player Award. But individual statistics and honors paled in comparison to the team's accomplishment as Brooklyn won its first and only World Series championship.

After a sensational first half, Snider was the starting center fielder for the National League in the All-Star Game. After the All-Star break, he slowed down. One day he was booed vociferously. He erupted in the clubhouse, telling anyone within earshot that the Brooklyn fans were the worst in the league. Reese attempted to intercede with the writers on Duke's behalf, saying that Snider was upset and didn't mean it. Snider insisted that he meant every word and wanted his temperamental outburst printed. When he took the field the next day, the Brooklyn faithful booed Snider as never before. Duke responded with three hits, turning the catcalls into cheers.

The pennant-winning Dodgers again took on the Yankees in the World Series. In the third inning of Game One in Yankee Stadium, Snider belted a solo home run off Whitey Ford that hit the third deck in right field, but the Dodgers lost, 6–5.

Game Four was played in Ebbets Field. Snider connected for a three-run homer off Johnny Kucks that dented an automobile on Bedford Avenue. The 8–5 Dodger victory squared the Series at two games apiece.

The Dodgers won Game Five, 5–3. Yankees starter Bob Grim threw Duke an inside curve ball in the third inning and an outside curve ball in the fifth inning. Each time, Snider pounded the pitch over Ebbets Field's right-field screen for a solo home run, becoming the first player to hit four home runs in two different World Series.

The Dodgers lost Game Six, 5–1, to tie the Series at three victories apiece. Snider was injured in the Yankee Stadium outfield after stepping on a wooden sprinkler cover and twisting his left knee. He was forced to leave the game after three innings. Despite his injured knee, Duke was in the lineup for Game Seven. He went 0 for 3, but Johnny Podres shut down the Yankees, 2–0. Snider was 8 for 25 in the Series with seven RBIS.

The 1956 release of a magazine article written with Roger Kahn, "I Play Baseball for Money, Not Fun," reinforced a perception that Duke was immature, self-absorbed, and whiny. More than fifty newspaper articles castigated Snider, calling him a brat and a problem child for his complaints about the travel, the time away from his growing family, abuse from fans, the weight of unfulfilled expectations, and his desire to leave baseball to grow avocados. Snider had recently purchased sixty acres in Fallbrook, California, north of San Diego, where he had begun to plant avocados with his business partner, former Brooklyn catcher Cliff Dapper.

One criticism that especially bothered Snider was that he benefited from being the only left-handed hitter in a lineup of strong right-handed batters, and that he was ducking left-handed pitchers. Years after his playing career ended, Snider vehemently rejected this charge, pointing to his .308 average against southpaws in 1954.

Brooklyn captured their sixth pennant in ten seasons in 1956. In the decisive final game, Snider hit two home runs, drove in four runs, and made a spectacular catch to stifle a Pittsburgh rally. While his batting average dipped below .300 (.292), he still managed to connect for forty-three home runs, a career best that led the National League. Snider drove in 101 runs, his sixth season topping the century mark.

The Dodgers and the Yankees met again in the World Series. Snider went 7 for 23 with four RBIS, batting over .300 in his fourth consecutive World Series, but the Yankees recaptured the world championship in seven games.

The Dodgers won five National League pennants and placed second three times from 1949 through 1956. But 1957 was the end of an era. The Dodgers fell to third place, eleven games behind Milwaukee. Snider played in 139 games, as his knee continued to bother him. (He had surgery after the season.) He hit forty or more home runs for the fifth consecutive season, tying the National League record held by Ralph Kiner (surpassed by Sammy Sosa, 1998–2003). Snider was the last player to homer at Ebbets Field, slamming two home runs off Philadelphia's Robin Roberts on September 22. He was also the first batter to hit forty home runs while driving in fewer than a hundred runs (he had ninety-two).

After the 1957 season, the Dodgers and the Giants left New York to continue their rivalry in California. Although born and raised in Southern California, Snider hated to leave Brooklyn, where he had many friends and fans. He left behind memories of great performances and a unique ballpark seemingly built for his multitalented game.

Los Angeles welcomed Snider as a native Californian. As the best-known player in Los Angeles, he had a daily radio show and earned the highest salary on the team ($46,000). The Dodgers played in the Los Angeles Coliseum, an aging, oval-shaped, 90,000-seat football stadium built to host the 1932 Olympics. Duke was the only Dodger to hit a home run over the right-center-field fence during the 1958 season. The vast distances to center field, right-center, and right field negated Snider's ability to pull the ball with power.

Duke played 106 games in 1958, as he suffered from a recurrence of knee trouble after a spring training auto accident, a back injury, and an arm strain. He was the only regular to hit over .300 (batting .312) but saw a precipitous decline in home runs (from 40 to 15) and RBIs (from 92 to 58). The aging Dodgers registered their worst record since 1944, finishing seventh, two games ahead of the last-place Phillies. With more than 1.8 million paid admissions, the Dodgers' first season in their new home was a financial success, but a failure on the field.

With twenty cortisone shots for his ailing knee, Snider played in 126 games in 1959. He was still a fine outfielder, but to take some of the stress off his knee, he began playing in right field and left field, where less running was required. Snider topped .300 for the seventh time (.308), tallied 23 homers, and led the team with 88 RBIs, despite striking out in nearly 20 percent of his at bats.

The Dodgers ended the 1959 season in a tie with Milwaukee. They swept the Braves in a two-game playoff and then defeated the Chicago White Sox in six games to win the World Series. Snider hit his final Series home run in Game Six in Chicago, off

Early Wynn. Snider's World Series totals include a .286 batting average with 11 home runs and 26 RBIs in thirty-six games.

Snider's career was now winding down. Slowed by knee trouble, he hit only .243 in 1960 and was sent to the bench to make way for youngsters Tommy Davis and Willie Davis. On April 17, 1961, Snider hit his 370th home run to pass Ralph Kiner on the all-time list. In his next at bat, Duke suffered a broken right elbow when Bob Gibson hit him with a pitch. Playing only eighty-five games that season, Snider platooned in the outfield with his roommate, Ron Fairly, and with Frank Howard.

By 1962 Snider, Jim Gilliam, and John Roseboro were the only position players remaining from Brooklyn. In honor of his sixteen years with the Dodgers, Duke was named captain of the team. Wearing white sideburns and a bit stout at thirty-five, Snider collected the first Los Angeles hit in the new Dodger Stadium on April 10. On May 30 the Dodgers made their first trip to the Polo Grounds to play the newly created New York Mets. Duke received a thunderous ovation when he smashed a batting-practice home run.

Snider came to the plate only 158 times in 1962, batting .278 with just five home runs. At one point in the season, Duke did not leave the bench to play defense for seven consecutive weeks. After the Dodgers lost another three-game playoff to the Giants, rumors began to circulate that Duke had played his final game for Los Angeles. Upon the Dodgers' arrival in Albuquerque for an exhibition game on April 1, 1963, he learned that he had been sold to the Mets.

Snider considered retirement, but general manager Buzzie Bavasi encouraged Duke to continue his career with the Mets. Snider needed five more hits to join the 2,000-hit club, and eleven more home runs to reach 400, a dual feat accomplished by only six other batters in baseball history at that time. Snider was also promised a job with Los

Angeles upon the completion of his playing career, assuaging some of his hurt over the sale.

Snider played in 129 games for the Mets, his highest total since 1957. For sentimental reasons, the New York fans were happy to see Duke back in New York, but his past greatness was a distant memory. Although he was in good condition, his aching legs prevented him from running in the outfield and on the bases with anything approaching his previous panache.

Batting .243 in 354 at bats, Duke did blast 14 home runs to achieve 403 for his career. On April 11 he hit his first home run as a Met, off lefty Warren Spahn. Five days later, Jim Maloney was the victim of Snider's 2,000th base hit. His 400th home run was hit off Bob Purkey on June 14.

Snider decided to play in 1964, but he asked the Mets to trade him to a contender so he might have a chance to participate in one more World Series. The Dodgers expressed some interest in reacquiring him, but before a deal could be struck, the Mets sold Snider to the Giants. It was shocking to conceive of Snider playing for the Dodgers' great rival. With four children to support, Duke took the sale in stride. He was glad for the chance to return to California and be closer to his family.

Beverly and the children remained at home in Fallbrook, California, during the school year, while Duke lived by himself in an apartment. Snider mostly pinch-hit for the fourth-place Giants, batting a career-low .210 in just 167 at bats. He collected the final four home runs of his career.

In addition to his avocado ranch, Snider had invested in a bowling center in Fallbrook. The bowling center was not a success and closed. Snider also had to sell his beloved ranch. He continued to live in Fallbrook, but with the end of his active playing career, he needed to work to support his family.

Duke returned to the Dodgers, scouting and managing in the Minor Leagues through 1968. In 1969 he moved to the San Diego Padres, rejoining Buzzie Bavasi. Snider broadcast Padres games for three years, then served as a batting instructor. In 1973 he became a broadcaster and part-time batting instructor for the Montreal Expos.

Snider first became eligible for election to the Hall of Fame in 1970, but perhaps because of his difficult relationship with the writers, or because there was a sense that Duke failed to reach his potential, he garnered only 17 percent of the votes that year. His percentage gradually rose until 1980, when he received 86 percent of the votes (75 percent was needed) and was elected to the Hall.

During the 1981 Major League Baseball strike that canceled one-third of the season, Terry Cashman wrote a song that paid tribute to the baseball stars of the 1950s. "Talkin' Baseball" became a smash hit and kept Duke Snider in the forefront of public consciousness. Cashman saluted New York's three Hall of Fame center fielders of the 1950s using the choral refrain "Willie, Mickey, and the Duke." Another triumph for Snider during the decade was the publication of his best-selling autobiography, *The Duke of Flatbush*.

Duke retired from the Expos after the 1986 season. He suffered a heart attack in 1987, lost twenty-five pounds, and underwent valve replacement surgery. His legs continued to bother him and he had to give up golf, eventually undergoing additional surgeries.

In the 1980s and 1990s, the growing baseball memorabilia business afforded retired players the chance to earn thousands of dollars for appearing at card shows and signing autographs. As a Hall of Fame member, Snider was in demand. But he took some of his appearance fees in cash and failed to declare those payments on his income-tax returns. In 1995 he and fellow Hall of Famer Willie McCovey were indicted for tax evasion. Both pleaded guilty, and Snider cooperated with the investigation to avoid jail time.

At his sentencing in federal court in Brooklyn, Snider admitted failing to report more than $100,000 in income from promotional appearances and card shows from 1984 to 1993. He was given two years' probation, fined $5,000, and ordered to pay as much as $57,000 in back taxes, interest, and penalties. Snider apologized, accepting responsibility for his actions. His reputation damaged, Snider told reporters that he had made the wrong choice.

Duke Snider died in Escondido, California, on February 27, 2011. He will always be remembered fondly in Brooklyn as the catalyst for the Dodgers' greatest moment, their victory in the 1955 World Series.

# Chapter 39. **Ralph Branca**

*Paul Hirsch*

| AGE | W | L | PCT. | ERA | G | GS | GF | CG | SHO | SV | IP | H | BB | SO | HBP | WP |
|-----|-----|-----|------|------|-----|-----|-----|-----|-----|-----|-------|-----|-----|-----|-----|-----|
| 21 | 21 | 12 | .636 | 2.67 | 43 | 36 | 5 | 15 | 4 | 1 | 280.0 | 251 | 98 | 148 | 6 | 7 |

Ralph Theodore Joseph Branca is a New York guy. He was born on January 6, 1926, in Mount Vernon, just outside New York City, as the fifteenth of seventeen children. His middle name was a celebration of the first President Roosevelt, who also hailed from the Empire State.[1] His elementary and high school years were spent in Mount Vernon. He attended New York University, where he also played basketball, and was signed by the Dodgers after a local tryout camp.[2]

Branca's father, John Branca, came to America from Italy as a child with his family in 1888. Ralph was named after his grandfather, Raffaele, who took the name Ralph in the United States. Ralph's mother was Katherine Berger, who was born in Hungary. Katherine and John married on October 17, 1902. At various times, John was a trolley conductor, a machinist, and a barber.[3]

Ralph married Ann Mulvey in 1951. She was a New York girl from a prominent family. Her parents, James and Dearie Mulvey, owned a share of the Dodgers, and her maternal grandfather, Steve McKeever, had been president of the Brooklyn club.[4] At the end of his playing career, Branca was offered an opportunity to stay in baseball as a pitching coach for Los Angeles in the Pacific Coast League, but "I just didn't want to go to California," he said in a 2008 interview.

Instead, Branca became a financial executive in and around New York City, work he found satisfying. "When you can hand somebody a check for $300,000 in 1961 based on a life insurance policy her husband had purchased from me, you feel good. You feel like you've had a positive effect on that person's life." He later combined his

Ralph Branca was Brooklyn's best pitcher, winning twenty-one games at age twenty-one.

baseball prominence, his financial acumen, and his desire to help others when he ran the Manhattan-based Baseball Assistance Team (BAT) for seventeen years, an organization formed to help those who had had careers in baseball but were facing difficult financial circumstances in their post-baseball lives.[5] His daughter Mary married former New York Mets manager Bobby Valentine in 1977, and his other daughter, Patricia, also made a life in New York.

As a Brooklyn Dodger, the six-foot-three, 220-

pound right-hander was involved in two of the biggest moments in baseball history, which were also prominent moments in the fabric of American culture. One was the integration of baseball by Jackie Robinson in 1947, and the other was as the man who threw the pitch hit for a home run by Bobby Thomson that won the 1951 National League pennant for the New York Giants. In 1947 the twenty-one-year-old Branca became the second-youngest National Leaguer to win twenty games.[6]

The Brooklyn club signed Branca out of New York University in 1943, when he was just seventeen years old. He had played both baseball and basketball for NYU. The Dodgers sent him to Olean (New York), their affiliate in the Class D Pennsylvania-Ontario-New York League, where he split ten decisions. Branca was promoted to the Montreal Royals of the International League, Brooklyn's top farm team, in 1944. He had a 4-5 record for the Royals when the Dodgers called him up on June 7. Five days later, he made his Major League debut, allowing two hits in three and one-third innings of a 15–9 loss to the Giants. Branca split the 1945 season between Brooklyn and St. Paul of the American Association, but he spent all of 1946 with the Dodgers. He won only three games, but he pitched very well in September and was Brooklyn's starter in Game One of the playoffs against St. Louis. His combined record for his first three seasons with the Dodgers was a mediocre 8-9.

By 1947 the Dodgers were one of the most prominent franchises in baseball. Brooklyn had drawn nearly 1.8 million fans to Ebbets Field in 1946 and would inch over that figure in 1947. The Dodgers had lost a playoff to St. Louis for the 1946 pennant and were considered a strong contender for the 1947 flag. Their most visible newcomer was Jackie Robinson, the International League's Most Valuable Player in 1946.

"As I look back, I'm proud that I was tight with Jackie," Branca said. "He was a great competitor and a great teammate. The timing of bringing him to the team was perfect. I've always been proud that baseball integration beat the government's integration by seven years and that I was a part of it. My friendship with Jackie continued after baseball. We played golf together and we both worked in Manhattan and saw each other a lot while he was with Chock full o' Nuts."

As Branca saw it, Robinson's acceptance by the Dodgers was directly related to their recognition of his ability to help the team win. "Some saw it right away, for others, it took until the middle of the year, but by the second half of the season everyone saw it. We all wanted the glory of the World Series, and it was pretty clear we weren't going to get there without Jack."

According to Branca, the southern culture that prevailed in baseball clubhouses at the time was not an issue for the Dodgers. "Once we knew he belonged, it was fine," he said. The opposition was a different story. "Jackie was helping to beat them, and they were mad."

The 1947 season was the high point of Branca's Major League career. His twenty-one wins, second best in the league, were nearly a quarter of his lifetime total of eighty-eight. He also led the National League in starts and was second in strikeouts and third in earned run average.[7] Branca was chosen as an All-Star but did not appear in the game. He was the starter and loser in Game One of the World Series against the Yankees and appeared twice more in relief, picking up a win in Game Six.

In 1948 Branca's win total dropped to fourteen and his ERA went up by nearly a run, to 3.51. "I was 12-5 at the [All-Star] break in 1948. [Actually, he was 10-6.] Then, a couple of my, shall we say, lower IQ teammates, were playing burnout by throwing the ball to each other as hard as they could trying to hurt each other's hands. One of the throws got away and hit me in the shin. The leg swelled and it turned into an infected bone lining. I spent three weeks in the hospital with periosteomyelitis and only got two wins [actually four] in the second half."[8]

According to Branca, the bone infection settled in his shoulder, and as a result he could not throw as hard through 1949 and 1950. Nevertheless, he was 13-5 in '49 and led the league in winning percentage, though his ERA climbed to 4.39.[9] By 1950 manager Burt Shotton used him mostly in relief, and Branca remembers that season, in which he went 7-9, as "a waste." He was little help as the Dodgers lost the pennant to Philadelphia on the last day of the regular season.

As 1951 started, things were looking up for Branca. The Dodgers were in first place for most of the year, and "by throwing in the bullpen every day," he said, "my arm started to get stronger." He made his first start that year on May 28, and after throwing a two-hit shutout against the Pirates on August 27, his record was 12-5.

But September and October were difficult for Branca and the Dodgers. He started six games that the Dodgers lost, as his record for the season dropped to 13-12. The Dodgers had a thirteen-game lead after an August 11 doubleheader and played a little over .500 the rest of the way. The Giants, meanwhile, went 37-7 down the stretch, caught the Dodgers on the last weekend, and beat them in a playoff culminated by the famous "Shot Heard 'Round the World" home run off Branca by Bobby Thomson.[10]

In January 2001, Joshua Prager, a reporter for the *Wall Street Journal*, published the details of a sign-stealing scheme the Giants rigged in the Polo Grounds, their home ballpark. The scheme involved a telescope from windows in the center-field clubhouse, a buzzer rigged under dirt in the bullpen, and a reserve catcher positioning his body and equipment to tip off the batter as to which pitch was coming. Prager's story confirmed for the public what Branca had been told by his Detroit Tigers roommate Ted Gray in 1953. Gray was friends with Giants reserve outfielder Earl Rapp

and was told the story. Branca said Thomson knew what was coming on October 3, 1951, and while he still had to hit it, the information was certainly useful.[11]

"I begrudge the Giants the 1951 pennant," Branca said emphatically in the 2008 interview. "They deprived our owner of money he deserved, they deprived our fans of the joy of a pennant winner, and they deprived my teammates and me of the fame and glory that comes from playing in the World Series. What the Giants did was despicable. It involved an electronic buzzer. No one else used that. Sometimes you could see people in the center-field scoreboard in Chicago or wherever using towels to give signals and you could do something about it. The buzzer was undetectable, and it was wrong."

Branca kept the story essentially to himself until Prager's article appeared. He appeared with Thomson on television and at autograph shows, and generally played the role of good sport for half a century. The two ex-players thrown together by fate became close friends—a friendship that Branca said became strained after Prager's public exposure of the Giants' scheme.[12]

The sign-stealing revelations and the reactions to those revelations have "affected my relationship with Bob. We're not as close. We haven't done a card show in two years, and we don't talk as often," Branca said. "Part of that might be that he moved down South," Branca allowed. "He was one of the soldiers; he wasn't one of the leaders. Still, he okayed it, and he used it."

Branca said he was especially disappointed in Giants captain Alvin Dark and former teammate Eddie Stanky. An observant Catholic, Branca says he takes umbrage because Dark and Stanky claimed to be very religious. Most of his vitriol, though, was aimed at Giants owner Horace Stoneham, manager Leo Durocher, and coach Herman Franks, the man in the clubhouse with the telescope. "They were the generals," Branca said.

Thomson's home run, regardless of the circumstances, was the beginning of a steep downhill slide in Branca's baseball career. In spring training of 1952, he fell off a chair while playing Monopoly in the clubhouse and landed on a Coke bottle.[13] Branca said that threw his back out of alignment, a situation that still plagued him a half century later. "Our trainer was an osteopath, which was basically a chiropractor with two years of medical school, and he didn't think to check my alignment," sighed Branca. "Using a lift might have helped me then." In later years, Branca turned to using lifts in his shoes to cope with the effects of his 1952 accident.

As it was, Branca appeared in only sixteen games for the 1952 Dodgers, and none in a World Series loss to the Yankees. On July 10, 1953, the American League's last-place Detroit Tigers claimed him after he was waived out of the National League.[14] "The Detroit trainer worked hard on me, but he didn't check my alignment either," Branca remembered. "The state of sports medicine was nothing like it is today." Branca went 7-10 in thirty-four games over parts of two seasons with the Tigers before receiving his release in July 1954.[15]

Later in 1954, Branca called the Yankees to pitch batting practice. Manager Casey Stengel and pitching coach Jim Turner were impressed enough to activate him, and he went 1-0 in five games.[16] Branca went to spring training in 1955 with the Minneapolis Millers, the top Minor League affiliate of the Giants. He hurt his arm while pitching nine innings in a spring training game, but he said he didn't tell the trainer. Millers manager Bill Rigney let Branca go when he was ineffective in subsequent outings.

Thinking his career was over, Branca said, he accepted an invitation to Old Timers Day at Yankee Stadium in 1956, but he discovered while preparing for that game that his velocity had returned. He contacted Dodgers general manager Buzzie

Bavasi and spent the last month of the 1956 season with Brooklyn. He made one appearance, on September 7, and in two innings allowed one hit and two walks and struck out two.[17]

Branca accompanied the team on its postseason tour of Japan and hurt his arm again—he said manager Walter Alston did not allow him sufficient time to warm up before a relief appearance. The Dodgers invited him to spring training in 1957, but he failed to make the team. The Los Angeles Angels of the Pacific Coast League offered Branca a coaching job that he turned down, ending his baseball career.

While Branca seemed to harbor some bitterness over how his career ended, Bavasi said in 2006 that he did not intend for Branca to pitch much in his last stint with the team. "I brought him in not to pitch, but in order for him to retire as a Dodger," Buzzie said. It seems either that the team and the player were not on the same page regarding expectations, or that time has clouded memories.

Ralph and his wife, Ann, have lived in the same country club community in Rye, New York, since the middle 1960s. Branca has sung publicly and has earned praise for his strong baritone. He is also a devoted poet and holds the record for seventeen consecutive wins on the television game show *Concentration*.[18] He has been personally and financially successful and is one of the most famous baseball players of his era, even if he feels his pitching potential was largely unrealized due to a series of negative circumstances. He was through as a ballplayer by the time he turned thirty, but in his decade in the big leagues, he bore witness to and directly participated in two of the most famous baseball events of the twentieth century.

## Chapter 40. **Clyde King**

*James L. Ray*

| AGE | W | L | PCT. | ERA | G | GS | GF | CG | SHO | SV | IP | H | BB | SO | HBP | WP |
|-----|---|---|------|-----|---|----|----|----|-----|----|------|----|----|----|-----|-----|
| 23 | 6 | 5 | .545 | 2.77 | 29 | 9 | 12 | 2 | 0 | 0 | 87.2 | 85 | 29 | 31 | 0 | 0 |

Clyde Edward King spent more than sixty years in professional baseball as a player, scout, pitching coach, manager, and general manager with more than a dozen teams. Along the way, he played with Jackie Robinson, coached Bob Gibson, managed Willie Mays, and even fired Yogi Berra.

King was born on May 23, 1924, in Goldsboro, North Carolina. He was one of seven children born into a family headed by his father, Claude, who worked as a foreman at a local lumberyard. Three of the seven children came with his mother, Maggie (McMillan) King, from a previous marriage.

When he was five years old, the country fell into the Great Depression. Although he describes his family and origins as modest rather than poor, Clyde's own stories about his childhood tell a very different story. Perhaps the most telling is how the King brothers made their own baseball equipment. An old abandoned leather sofa provided the leather and the stuffing needed to make a glove. A tree whose trunk was a little thicker than the barrel of a bat was cut down, stripped, whittled, and finally sanded down smoothly into a baseball bat. Baseballs were constructed out of rock, twine, and heavy tape.

King's first real baseball coach was Pat Crawford, a member of the world champion 1934 St. Louis Cardinals, who coached Clyde's school team. King later said Crawford "had a profound influence on my early life because of what he taught me, the most important of which was Crawford's motto that 'perfect practice makes perfect.'"[1] In other words, practice every day like it's

Clyde King had a career-low 2.77 ERA in 1947, but manager Shotton did not use him in the World Series against the Yankees.

a real game, and you'll be ready when it's time to compete.

King was an ace pitcher in high school and also pitched in 1939 for a semiprofessional team, Borden Mills. That squad was made up of young players whose careers were on the rise, former Minor League stars, and even a handful of ex–Major Leaguers. But the fifteen-year old King was undaunted. "They were a bunch of grown men[, but]

176

I could hold my own with them and do fairly well," he said in his autobiography.[2]

After high school, King enrolled at the University of North Carolina at Chapel Hill, where he spent his first year playing baseball and basketball. In April 1944 the Brooklyn Dodgers signed the glasses-wearing, nineteen-year-old right-hander to a contract that featured a $5,000 up-front bonus.

The six-foot-one, 175-pound King immediately joined the Dodgers; there would be no Minor League priming for the youngster. He rode the bullpen bench for a while but finally made his first appearance on June 21, 1944, in relief against the New York Giants at Ebbets Field. King came in with two on and one out in the ninth. Phil Hausmann greeted him with a single to load the bases. Mel Ott then doubled, scoring two runs, and Joe Medwick singled, driving in two more.

When King returned to the locker room, he learned that general manager Branch Rickey wanted to see him as soon as possible. The first thing Rickey asked was "What kind of a pitcher are you? What pitches do you throw?" King responded that he threw a fastball and a curve, but his curve was much better. Rickey asked why King had chosen to throw only fastballs in his disappointing debut. King replied that catcher Mickey Owen had told him to throw all heaters. Rickey then told King, "This is your first lesson, young man. You're in charge. You're the pitcher. Nothing can happen until you throw the ball, so you throw the pitch you want to throw."[3] King took the advice to heart. Throwing a healthy dose of curve balls, King made fourteen appearances that season, throwing forty-three and two-thirds innings, winning two games, and losing one, with a 3.09 ERA.

His stay with the Dodgers was interrupted by a stint of almost two months with the Richmond (Virginia) Pilots of the Class B Piedmont League, the result of a deal in which the Dodgers acquired Pilots pitcher-manager and former Major League star Ben Chapman. King made his debut with

Richmond on August 7, blanking league-leading Portsmouth 1–0 on four singles. Inserted into the Richmond rotation, he won six games and lost three, as well as another win in the league playoffs.

Recalled by the Dodgers after the playoffs ended, King earned his first big league win with a complete-game 3–2 victory over the St. Louis Cardinals on September 27. "That was my first win, and it felt great to be a starter," King wrote in his autobiography. "It felt even better, however, to be a reliever, and I'm so glad that [Dodgers manager] Leo Durocher made me a reliever. I loved coming into games that were on the line. I liked the pressure."[4] King also had his first Major League hit that day, a swinging bunt single off Cardinals pitcher Bud Byerly in the third inning.

Unlike many of his contemporaries, King lived a very clean life; he did not smoke, drink alcohol, or chase women. As he said, "A strong faith in God has been a major force in my life since I became a Christian at age twelve."[5]

After the '44 season, King returned to the University of North Carolina, where he kept in shape by playing on a "B" basketball team. In 1945 he appeared in forty-two games for Brooklyn, forty of them in relief, and posted a 5-5 record with a 4.09 ERA. King was a member of a National League all-star team that toured U.S. bases in Hawaii, Manila, and elsewhere in the Pacific following the 1945 season. Upon his return, he discovered he had been classified 1-A by his local draft board.

King spent spring training with the Dodgers, who then optioned him to Mobile of the Class Double-A Southern Association just before the 1946 season began. He reported to Fort Bragg, North Carolina, for a preinduction physical in June but was rejected for service. He then rejoined Mobile, where he finished the season with thirteen victories, nine defeats, and a 3.57 ERA.

On November 29 King married his college sweetheart, Norma Surles, and the couple settled in King's hometown of Goldsboro. For the next fifty years, King worked in baseball as a player, coach, manager, scout, and general manager for teams all over the country. But every off-season, he returned home to Goldsboro, Norma, and, in time, his three daughters: Normie, Princie, and Janet. Of his beloved North Carolina home, King said, "I was born here and raised here. I know the people here and I love the pace of life. Each year when the baseball season ended, I couldn't wait to get back here."[6]

King was back in Brooklyn in 1947. He pitched in twenty-nine games, won six, lost five, and had a career-low 2.77 ERA. The Dodgers won the pennant, but King did not appear in the World Series against the Yankees.

In 1948 Clyde developed an infection in the index finger of his pitching hand that prevented him from throwing. The team doctor lanced the finger, which may have only worsened the matter, and King spent most of the season with the Dodgers' International League team in Montreal. On June 9 the Phillies claimed him on waivers, but he never pitched for them, and five days later Brooklyn reclaimed him.

King started the 1949 season in Montreal, as part of a pitching rehabilitation plan. His rehabilitation lasted two years in the Minors, although he did find success with a new pitch, a slider, and won 17 games in 1949 and 13 in 1950. He returned to the Dodgers in 1951 and had his best season, with career highs in games (48), wins (14), innings (121⅓), and games finished (31). He also had 6 saves.

By the end of the season, however, King was developing serious arm and shoulder troubles. Because of the injury, King was held out of the three-game playoff series between the Dodgers and the Giants to settle the National League pennant. He was sitting in the dugout when Bobby Thomson hit the pennant-winning home run off Ralph Branca.

King struggled through the pain in 1952, when he pitched in twenty-three games. Although he had a 2-0 record, his ERA ballooned to 5.06. A week after the season ended, the Dodgers traded him to the Cincinnati Reds for catcher Homer "Dixie" Howell and cash. King played the final year of his Major League career for the Reds, appearing in thirty-five games, all in relief. His record was just 3-6 and his ERA was an unimpressive 5.21. King's last Major League appearance came on September 27, 1953, the nine-year anniversary of his first Major League win.

In 1954 King pitched for the Class Triple-A Indianapolis Indians and the Double-A Tulsa Oilers, and in 1955 for the Class Double-A Atlanta Crackers. He then retired from pitching at the age of thirty-one. In his Major League career King appeared in two hundred games, won thirty-two and lost twenty-five, and posted an earned run average of 4.14. He played on two pennant winners, the 1947 and 1952 Dodgers, but never had a chance to pitch in the World Series.

King was named manager of the Atlanta Crackers on July 23, 1955. In 1956 the Crackers won the Southern Association pennant and playoffs, but lost to Houston of the Texas League in the postseason Dixie Series. The next year, he managed the Hollywood Stars to a third-place finish in the Pacific Coast League. For years the Stars had been the biggest attraction in Southern California baseball. However, when the Dodgers announced they were moving from Brooklyn to Los Angeles, the Stars' owners sold the team to a group in Salt Lake City, and King was out of a job. He soon found another one, managing the 1958 Columbus (Ohio) Jets to a fourth-place finish in the International League.

On August 3, 1959, King, who had been working as a coach for the Cincinnati Reds, was hired to manage the Rochester Red Wings of the International League. He led them to a 21-19 record down the stretch, but the team finished a disappointing fifth. The Red Wings went to Cuba for spring training in 1960. This was before the United States embargo on travel to the country, but it was after the revolution, and Fidel Castro was the nation's prime minister. The Red Wings played a game against the University of Havana, just as King's Dodgers had done in spring training of 1947, when a much younger King had pitched and won against the school's star pitcher. Prior to the 1960 game, King and the Havana manager were called to the mound as part of an opening-pitch ceremony, and it was Castro who was to throw out the pitch. Before he did, however, Castro told King that it was he who had pitched and lost for the University of Havana that day thirteen years earlier.

King had success in 1960 and 1961, leading the Red Wings to two straight International League championship games, both of which they lost. In 1962 the team lost in the first round of the playoffs, and King was let go. He spent the 1963 and 1964 seasons as a roving pitching instructor for the St. Louis Cardinals, and in 1965 the Pittsburgh Pirates made him their pitching coach. He spent the next three seasons in Pittsburgh, where he coached such notable hurlers as Vern Law, Roy Face, and Steve Blass.

King left the Pirates after the 1967 season. In 1968 he managed the Phoenix Giants, San Francisco's affiliate in the Pacific Coast League, and the next spring he was named skipper of the big league club. His first season in San Francisco was a moderate success. With an offense that featured Willie McCovey, Willie Mays, and Bobby Bonds, and a pitching staff anchored by Gaylord Perry and Juan Marichal, San Francisco made a run at the National League West Division title. They eventually finished second, three games behind the Atlanta Braves. Clyde was brought back to manage in 1970. But the team got off to a slow start, and on May 23 he was fired.

King then moved on to manage the Atlanta Braves' Class Triple-A team in Richmond of the International League in 1971 and 1972. In 1973 he

moved to Atlanta as assistant general manager. In the middle of 1974, the Braves fired manager Eddie Matthews. They replaced him with King, who led the team to a 38-25 mark over the final sixty-three games of the season. On the Braves team that year was Hank Aaron, making King the only man to have managed both Willie Mays and Hank Aaron. King began the 1975 season at the helm, but he was fired in late August when the team was well out of the race for the division title.

Thinking that his days as a manager might be over, King began looking for a front-office position with another team. That team turned out to be George Steinbrenner's New York Yankees. King's first position with the team was as a scout. Steinbrenner often assigned King to one player for a few days or weeks, usually to help diagnose a problem with a pitcher's motion and then to fix the problem. King called himself a troubleshooter. He served in this capacity until 1982, interrupted by stints as a pitching coach in 1978 and 1982.

King made many decisions and offered input on free agents, young talent, and managerial performance. He helped put together Yankees teams that won five division titles, three American League pennants, and World Series titles in 1977 and 1978. But by 1982 the team's fortunes had begun to change. After one hundred games, the team, under Bob Lemon and then Gene Michael, was just 50-50. Steinbrenner fired Michael and replaced him with King. Clyde managed the Yankees for the last sixty-two games, but Steinbrenner replaced him with Billy Martin for the 1983 season.

King stayed with the Yankees as a scout, and in 1984 he was named general manager, a position he held for three seasons. Perhaps the most difficult thing he had to do as general manager happened on April 28, 1985. Prior to the start of the season, Steinbrenner announced that Yogi Berra, the team's manager during the 1984 season, would remain in place for the entire 1985 campaign. However, the Yankees began the year slowly, and despite his earlier promise, Steinbrenner decided to sack Berra. He did not, however, do it face-to-face. Rather, he dispatched King to deliver the bad news.

King stayed with the Yankees for the next twenty years, serving as a scout, a troubleshooter, a pitching coach, and in various front-office capacities. He called himself a loyal Yankee and remained a close friend and confidant of Steinbrenner until Steinbrenner's death in 2010.

In 1986 King was involved in the creation of the Baseball Assistance Team, a charity that provides help to former Minor League and Major League players who have fallen on tough times. For nearly twenty years, he remained active in BAT, an organization that has helped hundreds of former players.

By his own admission, Clyde King was not a top pitcher, but he certainly had an interesting and varied career: his youth connected him to the Gashouse Gang; his playing career linked him with Jackie Robinson and Roy Campanella; he witnessed close-up Bobby Thomson's and Bucky Dent's pennant-winning home runs; he managed Juan Marichal and Willie Mays and Hank Aaron; and he survived thirty years with George Steinbrenner. That sounds like a pretty rich baseball life.

Clyde King died in Goldsboro at age eight-six on November 2, 2010.

# Chapter 41. **Jake Pitler**

*Stanley H. Bard*

Although he was the first base coach, fans rarely if ever saw Jake Pitler in the coach's box, as he patrolled the baseline urging on his Brooklyn Dodgers. Few of them knew Pitler had once played in the Major Leagues with men like Honus Wagner or that he had been an outstanding Minor League manager.

Jacob Albert Pitler, the son of Russian Jewish immigrants Frederick and Yetta Pitler, was born in New York City on April 22, 1894, the eldest of seven children. Jake was still a child when the family moved to Beaver Falls, Pennsylvania, where Frederick plied his trade as a junk dealer. By 1910 the Pitlers (the original spelling was Peitler) were in Pittsburgh, where Frederick was now selling produce. Jake and his two brothers helped the family finances by selling newspapers on Pittsburgh street corners.

Often he sold papers near Forbes Field, and he became friendly with the Pirates players. Jake's interest in baseball soon resulted in his playing with semipro teams in the Pittsburgh area. (Another newsboy became a lifelong friend—the future owner of the Pittsburgh Steelers, Art Rooney.) Pitler's two newsboy-brothers also found a niche in sports: Harry became a lightweight boxer and later managed heavyweight Billy Conn; Dave played quarterback for the University of Pittsburgh football team.

Jake entered professional baseball in 1912, primarily as a way of earning money, according to his son, Larry. Baseball was a way of making a living without having a formal education. Pitler began his professional baseball career in 1912 with Connellsville (Pennsylvania) in the Class D Ohio-Penn-

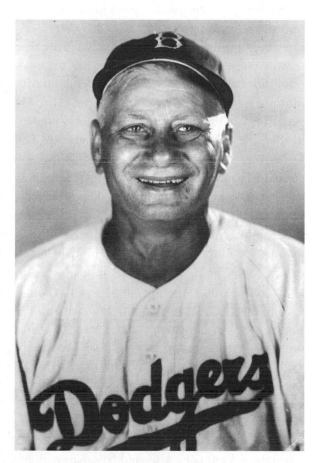

Jake Pitler was very adept at stealing signs from his first base coaching box.

sylvania League, but the team disbanded on June 12. The next year, 1913, found him playing second base for the Jackson Convicts of the Class D Southern Michigan Association (there was a state prison in the city). Jake spent 1914 with the team, now designated Class C and renamed the Chiefs, and batted .301. He started the 1915 season with Jackson, but when the league collapsed in July, the Detroit Tigers signed him and sent him to the Chattanooga (Tennessee) Lookouts of the Class A Southern Association.

Pitler spent all of 1916 with the Lookouts and started the 1917 season there. After forty-two games, he was hitting a league-leading .364, when, on May 22, the Pirates acquired his contract for utility infielder Bill Gleason and cash. The 1916 Pirates had nine different players at second base that season and were looking for stability at the position. Pitler made his Major League debut on Memorial Day at Forbes Field against the Cubs. He was 1 for 4 in the first game of the holiday doubleheader and had another hit in the nightcap. The *Chicago Daily Tribune* said, "Jake Pitler, the new second baseman for the Pirates, displayed a lot of skill, got one hit in each game and handled things like a veteran in the infield." For the rest of the season, the five-foot-eight, 150-pound second baseman played in the same infield as Honus Wagner. At age forty-three, Wagner was in his last campaign and playing part-time, mostly at first base.

William Phelon, writing in the August 1917 issue of *Baseball Magazine*, said, "Jake Pitler has done good work on the sack, and seems to be an aggressive, hustling young fellow." On August 22 Jake and the Pirates played a twenty-two-inning game in Brooklyn, losing 6–5. It was the longest National League game ever played up to that time. Pitler was 3 for 9 in the contest and set a record for put-outs in a game by a second baseman with fifteen. Jake played in 109 games for last-place Pittsburgh and hit just .233. He was much better in the field. His .966 fielding percentage was second to Boston's Johnny Rawlings among the National League regular second basemen.

The Pirates could not have been entirely satisfied with Pitler's play. In January 1918 they traded promising young pitcher and Pittsburgh native Al Mamaux, spitballer Burleigh Grimes, and infielder Chuck Ward to obtain veteran second baseman George Cutshaw and right fielder Casey Sten-

gel from the Brooklyn Robins. In seven seasons with Brooklyn, Cutshaw had averaged .260 and his fielding was solid as well. The twenty-three-year-old Pitler's days as a Major League player were over. Jake got into only two games for the Pirates in 1918, with his last, on May 24, as a pinch runner.

Burton and Benita Boxerman, in volume 1 of their book *Jews and Baseball*, wrote that in 1918 the Pirates assigned Pitler to Jersey City, but instead he jumped to outlaw baseball in Pennsylvania and was banned from Organized Baseball.

Evidently, Pitler was sent to Jersey City, because on June 14 the *Jersey Journal* was positively gushing with enthusiasm over his impending arrival. The *Journal* called Pitler "one of the best players in the Pirate crew." The article continued, "It was only through the strongest personal appeal that [Pirates owner] Barney Dreyfuss consented to Pitler's coming here. He is by far the cleverest infielder that has participated in the games on the new International circuit and will prove a wonderful tonic to the team; also the strongest kind of an attraction while the Jerseys are on tour. Pitler will be the highest salaried man in the league."

The enthusiasm was short-lived, however. It is unclear if Pitler ever reported. On June 22 the *Jersey Journal* was reporting the "desertion" of "Capt. Jake Pitler." By July 7 the *Duluth (Minnesota) News-Tribune* reported that Pitler had left the Pirates to join the war effort. Apparently, Jake, who was single with no dependents, went to work for the Aluminum Corporation of America and played on the company team.

After the war ended, the Pirates sold Pitler's contract to the Vernon (California) Tigers in the Pacific Coast League. Jake did not want to be that far from home and never reported to Vernon. Instead, he stayed home and signed on as the player-manager of the Oil City Independents, a team in the semipro Oil Stove League. He had the same role with the Independents the next season and, according to the 1920 U.S. census, he was employed as a manager in a billiards hall as well.

Pitler returned to Organized Baseball in 1928 with the Binghamton (New York) Triplets of the New York–Pennsylvania League. He played 136 games for the Class B Triplets, hitting .285 with twenty-four doubles. He committed thirty-nine errors at second, a total no doubt inflated by the rough Minor League infields.

Pitler became a player-manager in 1929 for the Elmira Colonels of the New York–Penn League, guiding the Colonels to a fifth-place finish. The Colonels were second in 1930, and then last in 1931. Pitler was fired in midseason, but he soon found employment as a player with the Hazleton (Pennsylvania) Mountaineers in the same league.

Pitler managed the Mountaineers again in 1932, led the Springfield (Ohio) Chicks of the Class C Middle Atlantic League in 1933, and returned to the New York–Penn League with the Scranton Miners in 1934. Pitler managed at Portsmouth (Ohio) of the Middle Atlantic League in 1935, his last year as an active player, and Wilkes-Barre (Pennsylvania) of the New York–Penn League in 1936.

Jake then managed the short-lived Jeannette Bisons in the Class D Pennsylvania State Association in 1937 (his son said Pitler owned the team). The Bisons folded on June 10, after playing twenty-four games. In 1938 Pitler took a job as the director of the Atlantic Baseball Schools in Binghamton, New York, a group of amateur teams sponsored by the Atlantic Refinery.

In 1939 the Brooklyn Dodgers placed a team in Olean, New York, in the newly formed Class D PONY League. The league consisted of teams in Pennsylvania, Ontario, and New York. The Dodgers were looking for a field and business manager at an annual salary of $1,500. The business manager of the Elmira team in the Eastern League knew Jake well and recommended him for the job. Pitler became the manager and led the team to two consecutive league championships, in 1939 and 1940. This began not only his long association with the Brooklyn Dodgers but also his personal friendship with Walter O'Malley, one of the Dodgers' owners.

From 1938 to the end of his career, Pitler's fate was tied to the Brooklyn organization. Upon arriving in Olean, his fiery nature and entertaining antics on the field became a legend in the area and contributed to the building of a fierce rivalry between Olean and the team in Jamestown, New York. An online history of the Olean Oilers recalls Jake as its "likable and crowd[-]pleasing manager from 1939 thru 1943." The history continues, "Jake is the man that most people remember and is still talked about. He was the fiery pepper pot who guided Olean from 1939 to 1943. Jake was the real drawing card at the gate, one of the few managers who could make that claim." Larry Pitler recalled that whenever Olean and Jamestown played each other, Jake and the Jamestown manager, Greg Mulleavy, got together before the game to plan "arguments" to pepper the game and enliven the fans.

Pitler's skill in recognizing and bringing along talent sent to Brooklyn such players as Duke Snider, Clem Labine, and Ralph Branca. Pitler was also credited with pointing out to Branch Rickey Jr., then head of the Dodgers' farm system, a young walk-on at an open tryout in Olean named Gil Hodges. Pitler reportedly told Rickey, "Don't let that kid get away."

After five years at Olean, the longest such tenure of any of the team's managers, Pitler was promoted to manage Newport News (Virginia) of the Piedmont League in 1944 and 1945, and then Danville (Illinois) in the Three-I League in 1946.

For the 1947 season, the Dodgers brought Pitler to Brooklyn to be their first base coach. He soon became recognized by the players as a premier sign stealer, helping batters and runners at first base.

When Pitler came to spring training, he befriended Jackie Robinson, and the two remained close friends to the end of their days. Pitler continued as a coach for the Dodgers until they moved to the West Coast after the 1957 season.

Pitler served under four Brooklyn managers: Leo Durocher, Burt Shotton, Charlie Dressen, and Walter Alston. "He's one of the hardest workers I've ever seen," Shotton once said. "He lives baseball and he was a wonderful influence on young players." Pitler, for his part, never spoke ill of any of the managers for whom he worked, nor was he ever baited into choosing a favorite, no matter how many times the press asked. He also made a statement of principle during his coaching career by never suiting up on the Jewish High Holidays if they fell during the season.

When the Dodgers moved to Los Angeles, Pitler chose to retire rather than move west. In an interesting coincidence, he was replaced as first base coach by the same Greg Mulleavy with whom he had conspired in the PONY League years before. Mulleavey had been the Dodgers' chief scout for the Northeast. When he moved west with the Dodgers, O'Malley asked Pitler to take over Mulleavy's scouting duties. Jake acquiesced and scouted for the team in New York, Pennsylvania, and Canada, while based in Binghamton, New York.

Pitler came to be beloved by Brooklyn fans. They honored him in 1954 and again on August 25, 1956, with Jake Pitler Night. Jake Pitler died on February 3, 1968, in Binghamton. He was seventy-three years old. He left his wife, Henrietta, and his son, Lawrence.

## Chapter 42. Brooklyn Dodgers in the 1947 All-Star Game

*Lyle Spatz*

The American League won the 1947 All-Star Game, 2–1. The game was played at Chicago's Wrigley Field on July 8. Baseball returned All-Star voting to the fans in 1947, but only one Dodger, right-fielder Dixie Walker, was selected to start. Walker grounded out in the first inning against Detroit's Hal Newhouser and flied out in the fourth against the Yankees' Frank Shea.

National League manager Eddie Dyer of the St. Louis Cardinals chose four additional Dodgers for the team, and three participated. When the American League came to bat in the sixth inning, Pee Wee Reese replaced the Cardinals' Marty Marion at shortstop and Eddie Stanky replaced the Phillies' Emil Verban at second base.

The two combined on a 6-4-3 double play in the top of the inning but did little on offense. Reese struck out and walked in his two at bats, while Stanky went 0 for 2. Bruce Edwards replaced Walker Cooper behind the plate in the seventh inning but did not bat. Pitcher Ralph Branca did not appear.

*Lyle Spatz*

Tuesday, July 15, vs. Pittsburgh (2)—Pittsburgh extended Brooklyn's losing streak to three games by pounding the Dodgers 12–4 and 9–3. Preacher Roe, who relieved Roger Wolff in the fourth inning of game one, and Jim Bagby Jr., who went all the way in game two, were the winners. Both Brooklyn starters, Harry Taylor and Joe Hatten, were chased early. Wally Westlake batted in seven runs in the opener, three on a bases-loaded double and four on a grand slam off Hugh Casey. Pee Wee Reese had four hits in the second game, and Jackie Robinson had three, but the Dodgers left a combined twenty-four runners on base in the two games. 48-34, First, 2½ games ahead.

Wednesday, July 16, vs. Pittsburgh—The Dodgers returned to their winning ways with a 10–6 win over the Pirates. Hank Behrman won his first game of the season after three losses, two of which came while he was a member of the Pirates. Jackie Robinson, with a single and two doubles, had three of Brooklyn's fourteen hits, while Dixie Walker had three runs batted in. 49-34, First, 2½ games ahead.

Thursday, July 17, vs. Pittsburgh—The last-place Pirates made it three out of four with a 7–1 rout behind ex-Yankee Mel Queen. Ralph Kiner, Hank Greenberg, and Jimmy Bloodworth each hit solo home runs off Clyde King in the fourth inning to give Pittsburgh a 3–0 lead. The Pirates added four more runs in the seventh against Hal Gregg and Rex Barney. Brooklyn's lone run came in the eighth on a double by Pete Reiser and a single by Dixie Walker. 49-35, First, 2½ games ahead.

Friday, July 18, vs. St. Louis—Ralph Branca had a perfect game for seven innings before yielding a leadoff single to Enos Slaughter in the eighth. That was the Cardinals' only hit as Branca shut them out, 7–0. It was his third shutout of the season and his first win over St. Louis after three straight defeats. The batting stars for Brooklyn were Eddie Stanky, with three hits, including two doubles and a triple, and two runs batted in, and Jackie Robinson, who homered and drove in three runs. 50-35, First, 3 games ahead.

Saturday, July 19, vs. St. Louis—The Cardinals had fourteen hits, twelve off starter Vic Lombardi, in a 7–5 victory that moved them to within four and a half games of the first-place Dodgers. Murry Dickson, in relief of Howie Pollet, was the winner. The highlight for the fans was Jackie Robinson's steal of home, which was part of a double steal, with Dixie Walker swiping second. 50-36, First, 2½ games ahead.

Sunday, July 20, vs. St. Louis—In the top of the ninth with the Cardinals ahead 2–0, Ron Northey hit a high fly to deep right center. Center fielder Pete Reiser jumped for the ball but failed to make the catch, and the ball dropped back on the field. Right fielder Dixie Walker then relayed it to Eddie Stanky, whose throw to catcher Bruce Edwards nailed Northey at the plate. First base umpire Larry Goetz ruled the ball in play, but third base umpire Beans Reardon had signaled to Northey that it was a home run. Northey then slowed down, and he was ruled out at the plate. In the bottom of the ninth, the Dodgers scored three runs to "win" the game, 3–2. The Cardinals protested the game, saying Northey had been deceived by the umpire and would have scored if he had not slowed down. National League president Ford Frick upheld the protest and awarded Northey a home run. However, he did not order the game resumed in the top of the ninth with St. Louis ahead 3–0, which would have been the normal procedure called for by the rules. He allowed the Dodgers' runs to stand and ruled the game a 3–3 tie. All the records counted (Pete Reiser had three hits and Dixie Walker had two) except for the pitchers' win and loss. The game was replayed in its entirety as part of a doubleheader on August 18. 50-36, First, 2½ games ahead.

Monday, July 21, vs. Cincinnati (2)—The largest crowd of the season to date saw the Dodgers come from behind in both games in sweeping a doubleheader from the Reds, 7–4 and 4–3. Trailing in the first game, 4–2, Brooklyn scored two runs in the sixth and three in the seventh to win for reliever Vic Lombardi. In the second game, the Dodgers trailed 3–2 after six, but they tied it in the seventh on a Dixie Walker home run and won it in the ninth. Bruce Edwards, who had three hits in the first game, singled to drive in Carl Furillo with the game winner. Joe Hatten went the distance. After the games, both teams left on the same train for Cincinnati, where they would begin a three-game series. 52-36, First, 3½ games ahead.

Tuesday, July 22, at Cincinnati—The Reds scored a first-inning run off Ralph Branca, but the Dodgers scored the next twelve to win 12–1. Brooklyn had a six-run sixth against Bud Lively, who had one-hit them eight days earlier, and added five more in the eighth against two relievers. Bruce Edwards and Gene Hermanski each had three hits; Hermanski and Eddie Stanky had doubles; Jackie Robinson had a triple; and Dixie Walker hit a home run. 53-36, First, 4½ games ahead.

Wednesday, July 23, at Cincinnati—The Dodgers broke a 2–2 tie with a run in the eighth, then added two in the ninth to win 5–2. Hank Behrman, with relief help from Hugh Casey, was the winner. Ken Raffensberger went the distance for Cincinnati. Pee Wee Reese, celebrating his twenty-eighth birthday, had two hits, as did Jackie Robinson and Carl Furillo. 54-36, First, 4½ games ahead.

Thursday, July 24, at Cincinnati—Vic Lombardi tossed a six-hit 6–1 complete-game victory that gave Brooklyn a sweep of the five games in Cincinnati. The Dodgers scored three unearned runs in the first inning against the Reds' starter, Johnny Vander Meer. Pee Wee Reese had three of Brooklyn's seven hits. 55-36, First, 5½ games ahead.

Friday, July 25, at Pittsburgh—The Dodgers stretched their winning streak to six games, downing the Pirates, 4–1, before the largest crowd of the season at Forbes Field. The streak would have been seven games, but National League president Ford Frick ruled that the July 20 game against St. Louis was a tie and not a Brooklyn win. Harry Taylor allowed just seven hits in winning his eighth game. Meanwhile, the Dodgers were limited to six hits by Mel Queen and two relievers, but they included a home run by Eddie Stanky and two doubles by Carl Furillo. Brooklyn remained five and a half games ahead of the now second-place St. Louis Cardinals. 56-36, First, 5½ games ahead.

Saturday, July 26, at Pittsburgh—After six and one-third innings, Ralph Branca was coasting along with a 4–0 lead and seemed well on his way to his seventeenth victory. But the Pirates erupted for four runs, the last three on a Jimmy Bloodworth home run, to tie the game. The Dodgers bounced back with two in the ninth to win 6–4, the victory going to Hugh Casey, who drove in the winning run on a squeeze play. Carl Furillo had three hits for Brooklyn, and Jackie Robinson had a home run. 57-36, First, 5½ games ahead.

Sunday, July 27, at Pittsburgh (2)—By winning both ends of the doubleheader, the Dodgers extended their winning streak to nine games. Brooklyn won the opener, 8–4, and the nightcap, 11–4. The two wins, combined with the Cardinals' loss to the Braves, extended the Dodgers' lead to seven full games. Brooklyn built an 8–0 lead in game one, before the Pirates rallied late against starter Hank Behrman and scored four runs. Carl Furillo continued his hot hitting with four more hits, including three doubles. Pee Wee Reese and Spider Jorgensen each had three hits. Hal Gregg went all the way in game two, as the Dodgers pinned the loss on former teammate Kirby Higbe. Among Brooklyn's twelve hits were three by Pete Reiser and two each by Jackie Robinson and Dixie Walker. Robinson and Reiser connected for back-to-back home runs. The second game was interrupted twice by showers and then called after seven innings because of the Pennsylvania blue laws. 59-36, First, 7 games ahead.

Monday, July 28, at Chicago—Joe Hatten and the Cubs' Johnny Schmitz each pitched eight scoreless innings before the Dodgers scored four in the ninth for a 4–0 win. Hatten's three-hitter was his eighth consecutive win against Chicago and extended Brooklyn's winning streak to ten games. 60-36, First, 7 games ahead.

Tuesday, July 29, at St. Louis—Playing before the largest crowd of the season in St. Louis, the Dodgers won their eleventh consecutive game, 4–0. They increased their lead over the second-place Cardinals to eight games, as Harry Taylor pitched Brooklyn's second straight three-hitter. Taylor was also the batting star with three runs batted in. 61-36, First, 8 games ahead.

Wednesday, July 30, at St. Louis—Trailing 10–4 in the last of the ninth, the Cardinals scored six runs after two were out to send the game into extra innings. Brooklyn then scored in the tenth on a hit by Pee Wee Reese to win 11–10. The Dodgers' twelfth consecutive win dropped the Cardinals and Giants nine games back. Clyde King, Brooklyn's fourth pitcher, hurled the final inning and a third to earn the win. The Dodgers had fourteen hits, including three by Eddie Stanky and two each by Jackie Robinson, Gene Hermanski, Bruce Edwards, and Carl Furillo. Stan Musial had four hits for St. Louis. 62-36, First, 9 games ahead.

Thursday, July 31, at St. Louis—After sweeping the Cardinals for their thirteenth straight victory, the Dodgers' lead was now ten games. Pee Wee Reese had the winning hit, as he had the day before. His ninth-inning triple drove home Bruce Edwards to give Brooklyn the 2–1 win. Vic Lombardi went all the way for his sixth win. 63-36, First, 10 games ahead.

# Chapter 44. **Pee Wee Reese**

*Rob Edelman*

| AGE | G | AB | R | H | 2B | 3B | HR | TB | RBI | BB | SO | BAV | OBP | SLG | SB | GDP | HBP |
|-----|-----|-----|-----|-----|-----|-----|-----|-----|-----|-----|-----|-----|-----|-----|-----|-----|-----|
| 28 | 142 | 476 | 81 | 135 | 24 | 4 | 12 | 203 | 73 | 104 | 67 | .284 | .414 | .426 | 7 | 7 | 2 |

Outside MCU Park in Coney Island, there stands a statue of two baseball players. Both are famed Brooklyn Dodgers. Both are Hall of Famers whose legends transcend batting averages and fielding percentages. One is a white Kentuckian. The other is an African American from California. They are Pee Wee Reese and Jackie Robinson.

The statue depicts a simple act that was extremely brave for its time: 1947, when America was a separate but unequal society and Robinson became the first of his race to play Major League ball in the twentieth century. That May, according to legend, the Dodgers were battling the Reds at Cincinnati's Crosley Field, located about a ninety-minute drive from Louisville, Reese's hometown. The crowd was mocking Jackie during infield practice. The opposing players were razzing him. The scene was growing uglier by the second. In a display of support for his teammate, Pee Wee calmly strode from his shortstop position toward Jackie on the right side of the infield and placed his left arm around the black man's shoulder: an act that is commemorated by the statue.

This demonstration quieted the fans, and the Reds. It was a crucial moment in Robinson's evolution from outsider to big leaguer. Just as significantly, it defined the character and career of Pee Wee Reese, the quietly forceful captain of the postwar Brooklyn Dodgers.

Harold Henry Reese was born on July 23, 1918, on a farm located between Ekron and Brandenburg in Meade County, Kentucky, about forty-five miles south of Louisville. The Reese family, headed by Harold's father, Carl Marion Reese, and his

Pee Wee Reese said about his acceptance of Jackie Robinson, "I was just trying to make the world a little bit better."

mother, Emma (Allen) Reese, relocated to Louisville when he was seven years old. The youngster earned his nickname not for his diminutive size—he was five feet nine and weighed 140 pounds when he signed his first professional contract at the age of twenty, and added one inch and 20 pounds when fully grown. Instead, he was called Pee Wee because of his predilection for playing marbles. As a preteen, he was runner-up in a *Louisville Courier-Journal* pee-wee marbles competition.

Pee Wee also loved playing baseball, even though his size prevented him from earning a starting job on the Louisville Manual High School team; he admitted he got into only five games during his senior year. In fact, in 1956 *The Sporting News* ran a 1934 photo of "a Louisville amateur team" that featured Pee Wee's older brother, Carl Jr., in uniform. Fifteen-year-old Pee Wee was in the shot but was dressed in street clothes. He was the team's batboy.[1]

As a boy, Reese helped support his family by delivering newspapers and selling box lunches. After graduating from high school in 1936, he held several jobs, the most prominent of which was as an apprentice cable splicer for the telephone company. "I was really tiny in high school," he recalled years later. "Climbing up and down those poles really built me up."[2] In the meantime he kept playing ball, primarily for a team representing the New Covenant Presbyterian Church.

Reese's club won the 1937 Louisville city championship. He was its sparkplug, and at season's end the Louisville Colonels of the American Association signed him to a professional contract. He was given a $200 signing bonus, and his starting salary was $150 a month. In 1938 Reese hit a solid .277 and stole twenty-three of twenty-four bases. His fielding percentage was only .939, but he impressed with his steady play and maturity, and it was while playing in Louisville that Reese earned a second nickname: The Little Colonel.

At the time, the Colonels had no Major League affiliation. But in September, Tom Yawkey, owner of the Boston Red Sox, was part of a group that purchased the team for $195,000. Reportedly, the deal was completed so that the Red Sox would be guaranteed the rights to Reese. According to *The Sporting News*, "The deal was guarded with such secrecy that some officials of the Louisville club

actually did not know that [the Red Sox] were interested in the Colonels."[3]

Pee Wee might have become the Red Sox shortstop if not for the presence of Joe Cronin, the team's player-manager. Cronin, who was to keep playing for another six seasons, showed no interest in relinquishing the shortstop position. So midway through the 1939 campaign, the Red Sox sold Reese to the Brooklyn Dodgers for $35,000 and four players to be named later, each of whom was valued at $10,000. Upon consummating the deal, it was decided that Reese would finish the season in Louisville and come to the Dodgers' training camp the following spring.

A news item published in *The Sporting News* on July 27 dubbed Pee Wee (who was referred to throughout as "Pewee") a "sensational 19-year-old shortstop." At the time he was hitting .278 and leading the American Association with twenty-five stolen bases; he finished the campaign with thirty-five steals in thirty-six attempts. Larry MacPhail, Brooklyn's general manager, called him "the most instinctive base-runner I've ever seen."[4]

Ted McGrew, a Dodgers scout, chimed in, "What amazes me is how much he's learned in so short a time." Donie Bush, the Colonels' manager and one of the team's co-owners, told *The Sporting News* that he "thinks Reese is the best-fielding shortstop he's seen in his thirty-one years in the game." The paper added, "Bill Meyer, manager of the Kansas City Blues, and Babe Ganzel, St. Paul pilot, when informed of Reese's sale . . . called him the best infield prospect in the league. Reese also was described as "probably the most popular player ever to wear a Louisville uniform."[5]

At the time, Pee Wee was anxious to play in Boston and was disconsolate upon learning of the sale, which was consummated while he was in Kansas City, playing for the American Association All-Stars. When a newspaperman told him about the deal, he reportedly responded, "Oh, not Brooklyn!"[6] Reese's reasoning was that the Dodg-

ROB EDELMAN

ers then had a well-earned reputation for on-field ineptitude. Their record the previous season was 69-80, good for seventh place. In 1937 they were a sixth-place club with an even worse record: 62-91. "I was crushed," Reese recalled years later. But he readily admitted that the deal "turned out to be the greatest break of my life."[7]

Before making it into an in-season box score, Reese was hyped for stardom. An ad featured in *The Sporting News* on March 21, 1940, was headlined "On his way to the top! With LOUISVILLE SLUGGERS." It featured an image of Pee Wee, with a "B" on his cap, swinging a bat. The copy read, "Harold 'Pee-Wee' Reese with the Louisville Colonels in 1939, now at the Brooklyn Training Camp, stands a good chance of carving a permanent spot for himself with the Dodgers. Reese is one of the younger users of Louisville Sluggers."[8]

It was in spring training in Clearwater, Florida, that player-manager Leo Durocher, the Dodgers' incumbent shortstop, hit grounder after grounder to the baby-faced rookie. After one such session, an exhausted Durocher quipped, "He'll do. I'll be the bench manager."[9] Leo also mentored the young infielder. "Leo could be tough," Reese recalled. "He fined me $50 one day for being out of position on a relay, but he taught me a lot, including to be myself, not try to be Leo Durocher."[10]

Pee Wee made his Dodgers debut on April 23, 1940. The Boston Bees (as the Braves were then called) were in Brooklyn, and Reese went 1 for 3 with a walk and a run batted in. He also made a throwing error.

On May 26 he hit his first big league home run, a game winner against the Phillies in the tenth inning that broke a 1–1 deadlock. Then on July 3, with the score tied 3–3 against the Giants in the ninth inning, Reese, as reported in *The Sporting News*, "rammed one of Hy Vandenberg's fast ones against the foul pole of the upper left tier [of the Polo Grounds] to clear the sacks and sink the Gi-

ants."[11] On August 4, in the second game of a Sunday doubleheader against the Cubs, Reese drove home two runs with a sixth-inning single. Then in the bottom of the ninth inning, he homered off Claude Passeau to tie the score at 6–6. Dolph Camilli's eleventh-inning four-bagger won the game.

More significant than his hitting, Reese immediately distinguished himself as a slick fielder and first-class base runner. He was particularly adept at turning his back to home plate and scooting into left field to nab a pop-up, and dashing from his shortstop position to second base to scoop up a grounder headed toward center field and fire the ball to first for the out. However, due to injury, his rookie season proved to be tough going. On June 1, in a game against the Cubs at Wrigley Field, hurler Jake Mooty tossed Reese a high inside pitch. Pee Wee was temporarily blinded by the white-shirted fans in the center-field bleachers, and he froze. Mooty's pitch hit Reese in the head. He was carted off to the Illinois Masonic Hospital, where he remained for two and a half weeks. Upon his return to the lineup, on June 21, Reese promptly singled, doubled, and tripled.

Then a broken heel bone, which he sustained while sliding into second base in Brooklyn on August 15, ended his season. These injuries kept Pee Wee out of all but eighty-four games, in which he hit a respectable .272. He began the 1941 campaign with a brace on his ankle, yet he still played in 152 games. His average, however, dropped to .229. Reese felt he contributed little to Brooklyn's first National League pennant winner since 1920.

In 1942 during spring training, Dorothy "Dottie" Walton, Pee Wee's hometown sweetheart, headed south to visit the ballplayer in the company of Patricia Hurst, the girlfriend of fellow Dodger Pete Reiser. On March 29 Dottie and Pee Wee were married in the First Presbyterian Church in Daytona Beach. Later that day, Pat and Pete also wed. The Reeses eventually had two children, Barbara and Mark.

After hitting .255 that season, Reese enlisted in the U.S. Navy and spent most of the next three years in the Pacific Theater with the Seabees, the navy's Construction Battalion. While returning from Guam on board ship, a fellow Seabee informed him he had just heard that the Dodgers had signed a black ballplayer. Plus, he was a shortstop. Would this player upstage Pee Wee, and take his job? At first, Reese was disbelieving. After all, blacks could not play beside whites. They would weaken under the pressure of everyday competition, let alone a pennant race. Pee Wee had been taught that, explicitly and implicitly, his entire life. But, of course, the Dodgers had indeed signed Jackie Robinson.

Reese returned to the Dodgers for the 1946 season, during which he played in 152 games and hit a solid .284. The following year, he also hit .284 and walked 104 times, leading the National League. But his notoriety that season transcended these or any other stats.

At the outset of the 1947 season, the Dodgers promoted Robinson to the Majors. Reese was well aware that some teammates and fans, neighbors and friends, and even family members vehemently opposed his playing with an African American. The shortstop was, after all, a product of a segregated southern culture, and he had never had a catch with an African American, never had a close relationship with an African American, and reportedly never had shaken the hand of one. But he was aware of racism American-style. In his youth, Pee Wee's father reportedly had pointed out to him a tree with a long branch in Brandenburg that had been used for lynching black men, and he implied that such actions were unjust. So a sense of fairness had been instilled in him, and he was determined to accept his new teammate, no matter what. When several Brooklyn players began passing around a petition protesting Robinson's presence on the Dodgers, Pee Wee rebuffed them, declining to sign it.

Decades later, Reese explained his rationale by observing, "If he's man enough to take my job, I'm not gonna like it, but, dammit, black or white, he deserves it."[12] He added that he often would approach Robinson on the field and chat with him for all to see. It was this expression of solidarity on that one May day in Cincinnati that is best remembered today.

Robinson could not recall what Reese said to him—if he said anything. According to Ralph Branca, their teammate, Reese's gesture communicated to the players in the opposing dugout, "Hey, he's my friend. It says *Brooklyn* on my uniform and *Brooklyn* on his and I respect him."[13] Years later, he explained his action by telling Roger Kahn, "I was just trying to make the world a little bit better. That's what you're supposed to do with your life, isn't it?"[14]

On one level, this story is apocryphal. Duke Snider, for one, recalled that the incident took place in Boston. According to an account in *The Sporting News* published in 1956, it first occurred during a 1947 exhibition game in Fort Worth, when "a foghorn-voiced Texas fan 'got on' Jackie with the kind of comments that need not be described," and later on in the season, in Boston, where Reese "made almost an identical gesture—the gesture that told the world that Robinson was his teammate."[15] Then in 1984 the very same paper reported that the incident took place in Cincinnati. In a 1952 magazine article and his book *Wait Till Next Year*, published in 1960, Robinson himself recalled that the incident took place in Boston—in 1948. Carl Erskine claimed to be present when it happened, and he did not become a Dodger until 1948. According to some recollections, Reese made his gesture during infield practice. Others recalled that it occurred during the game, prior to the home team's at bat. The 1984 *Sporting News* account had it taking place in-game, when the Dodgers were in the field, after Jackie had committed an error.

But the essence of the tale is spot-on—for it was during that 1947 campaign that Reese and Robinson became friends. Often, while on the road, the duo competed on the tennis court and golf course. As Reese noted, the comradeship "just happened, and Jackie appreciated it. I told him I wasn't trying to be the great white father. We became very close friends. . . . He was just a fine individual, one of the greatest competitors I've ever seen."[16]

Their relationship was such that Reese could effectively employ humor to ease a tense situation. On one occasion, when the Dodgers were scheduled to play an exhibition game in Atlanta, Robinson received a letter threatening his life. Reese responded by teasing his teammate. "Don't come near me," he kidded Robinson. "I don't want to get shot."[17]

On the field, Robinson spent the 1947 season as the Dodgers' first baseman. He then was switched to second base, where he and Reese developed into an outstanding double play combination. In 1949 Branch Rickey, the Dodgers' president and general manager, named Reese the team's captain, telling Pee Wee, "You're not only the logical choice, you are the only possible choice; the players all respect you."[18] Afterward, Reese's teammates began referring to him by a third nickname: The Captain. One of his duties was to remain atop the Ebbets Field dugout steps prior to the beginning of each game and wave the starters onto the field.

"He took charge out there," noted Robinson, "in a way to help all of us—especially the pitchers. When Pee Wee told us where to play or gave some of us the devil, somehow it was easy to take. He just has a way about him of saying the right thing."[19]

The following season, there even was talk that Rickey would name Reese player-manager, replacing Burt Shotton. At the time the team was in transition, with many of Pee Wee's early teammates having been replaced by those who formed the nucleus of the 1950s Brooklyn clubs. But Rick-

ey felt that Reese, who by then was well-practiced in adjusting the team's defense and strategizing with the pitcher, was no mere relic of the old guard of Dodgers. He was, instead, most valuable to the team as player and field captain. So Shotton remained manager in 1950. He was replaced by Charlie Dressen in 1951; Walter Alston took over for Dressen three years later. Regarding Reese's holdover status, Rickey pronounced, "Reese? Last of the old Dodgers? Wouldn't it be better to say he is the first of the new Dodgers?"[20]

As the 1950s progressed, a debate raged in New York over which of the city's teams had the best players. Just as Brooklyn fans favored Duke Snider in center field, while Giants aficionados chose Willie Mays and Yankees rooters preferred Mickey Mantle, there were also endless debates comparing the prowess of Pee Wee versus the talents of Yankees shortstop Phil Rizzuto. Which one was the slicker fielder? Which one was the superior bunter? Which one was better in the clutch? Which one was the more inspirational team leader? Meanwhile, by 1953 Branch Rickey had left Brooklyn and was running the Pittsburgh Pirates. He attempted to trade for Reese to captain the punchless Pirates. Walter O'Malley, the Dodgers' new owner, flatly refused.

What was inarguable, however, was Dodgers fans' adoration of their shortstop. He was a special favorite in Brooklyn, with Pee Wee Reese fan clubs sprouting up across the borough. The ballplayer was particularly attentive toward youngsters. Unlike so many other Major Leaguers, he won a reputation for never brushing them off and for honestly and thoughtfully answering their questions.

On July 22, 1955, just before his thirty-seventh birthday, Pee Wee Reese Night was held at Ebbets Field. It was quite an event. A pregame ceremony took almost one hour to complete, during which Reese was presented with $20,000 worth of gifts, including a new Chevrolet, $3,000 worth of United States Savings Bonds, two hundred pounds of food in a freezer, and honorary membership in the Teamsters Union. A hoarse-voiced Pee Wee told the crowd, "When I came to Brooklyn in 1940 I was a scared kid. To tell you the truth, I'm twice as scared right now."[21] After the top half of the fifth inning, two vast birthday cakes were wheeled onto the field. The ballyard's lights were lowered, and the 33,000 fans on hand lit matches or turned on cigarette lighters and serenaded their shortstop with a hearty "Happy Birthday."

That season, the Dodgers yet again made it to the World Series. And yet again they faced the New York Yankees, who had defeated them all five previous times they had battled. Pee Wee had a solid Series, scoring five runs and hitting .296. As usual, his contributions transcended what might be culled from a box score. In the bottom of the sixth inning of Game Seven, Billy Martin walked, Gil McDougald bunted safely, and Yogi Berra bashed the ball into the left-field corner. Surely, this would be an extra-base hit and would net the Yankees a pair of runs. But left fielder Sandy Amoros snared the ball before it hit the ground. Reese, meanwhile, ran out to short left field to take Amoros's cutoff throw. He quickly spun around and fired a strike to Gil Hodges to double McDougald off first—and preserve the Dodgers' shutout.

Appropriately, it was Reese who fielded the final ball hit by a Yankee in Game Seven. The date was October 4, 1955. The time was 3:43 p.m., and the Dodgers were beating the Bronx Bombers, 2–0. Pee Wee's toss of Elston Howard's ninth-inning, two-out grounder to Hodges closed out the Series, and the season. Finally, the Brooklyn Dodgers were the world champions.

Reese now was a veteran Major Leaguer, but he still was a first-rate player. In its 1956 season preview, *Sports Illustrated* listed Reese as the team's number one "mainstay."[22] Regrettably, he twisted his back early in spring training, and there was some concern as to how this would impact his sea-

son. He ended up playing in 147 games, 136 at shortstop and 12 at third base. While his statistics remained respectable, collectively they were down from previous seasons. But he remained a powerful presence in the Ebbets Field locker room, ensconced in an armchair and smoking a pipe, and he readily mentored his younger teammates, dispensing sage, hard-nosed advice. At one point, Johnny Podres, then in his early twenties, complained that he was losing too many low-scoring games. When, he wondered, will the Dodgers run up the score for him? Reese's counsel was brief, and pointed: Perhaps, the veteran suggested, the young hurler needed to win some 1–0 games himself. This quieted Podres down. Years later he admitted it was a lesson well learned.

During each season a number of Dodgers, including Reese and Duke Snider, lived in the Bay Ridge section of Brooklyn and drove to and from Ebbets Field during home stands. After a game, Snider often wanted to hastily depart the ballyard and head home. "Duke, Duke," Reese once told him, "if you're hurryin' out of the clubhouse, you're hurryin' out of baseball."[23]

The 1956 season, however, was Reese's last as a regular. In 1957 he got into only 103 games, with his batting average shrinking to .224. He played shortstop in just twenty-three contests; most of the time, he patrolled third base. Twenty-five-year-old Charlie Neal, then being groomed as Pee Wee's replacement at short, played the position in one hundred games.

In 1958 the Dodgers abandoned Brooklyn for Los Angeles. That season Reese got into only fifty-nine games. His .224 batting average was identical to his 1957 mark. His poor showing paralleled the fortunes of the Dodgers, who finished the year entrenched in seventh place.

Given his team's new West Coast address, Pee Wee also went Hollywood, becoming one of the first of the Dodgers to accept a movie or television acting role. He appeared as himself in "A Question of Romance," a TV drama about a young woman torn between her expertise on baseball and her insecure, baseball-hating boyfriend. When it was learned that Reese would be on the show, he was kidded by his teammates, who compared him to everyone from Gregory Peck and Tyrone Power to Frankenstein. "A Question of Romance" aired on November 9, 1958, on CBS-TV's *General Electric Theater.*

But clearly, Reese's career as an active player was winding down. At season's end, the Dodgers' hierarchy allowed him the option of becoming a coach. *The Sporting News* reported that the Cleveland Indians were interested in him as a player, but he explained, "And as long as I'm in baseball I would like to stay with the Dodgers. I realize there's no place for me in their youth movement, but maybe I'll stay on as a coach."[24] On December 18, 1958, Buzzy Bavasi, the Dodgers' general manager, announced that Reese had retired as a player and accepted a position on manager Walter Alston's coaching staff. "He could have remained on the active roster of another major-league club[,] but the Dodgers, in rebuilding their team, must make room for another youngster," Bavasi declared. "That's baseball."[25]

From 1946 through 1956, the final year he was the team's regular shortstop, Reese's batting average was generally in the .270s or .280s. His highest home run total was 16, in 1949. That season, he led all National League shortstops with a .977 fielding percentage and topped the NL with 132 runs scored. His highest RBI total was 84 and his highest hit total was 176, both in 1951. In 1952 he topped the senior circuit with 30 stolen bases.

Reese's lifetime batting average was .269. All told, he appeared in 2,166 games, had 2,170 hits, and is the Dodgers' all-time leader with 1,338 runs scored and 1,210 walks. He hit .272 in forty-four World Series games. In the 1955 Fall Classic, he established a mark for shortstops by taking part in seven double plays in a seven-game series, a record he equaled the following season.

These generally unspectacular statistics obscure Reese's value to the Dodgers. Even though he hit .300 just once—in 1954 when, at age thirty-six, his average was .309, with a career-best slugging percentage of .455 and second-best on-base percentage of .404—he finished in the top ten in the National League MVP voting on eight occasions. He was a top-notch bunter and hit-and-run man. He made the NL All-Star Team in 1942 and each season from 1946 to 1954. In 1948, 1949, and 1953 he was an All-Star Game starter. In all the years in which Reese was the team's full-time shortstop, the Dodgers never finished lower than third place.

After spending the 1959 season as a Dodgers coach, Reese segued into a new career as a color man on televised baseball broadcasts. First he replaced Buddy Blattner as Dizzy Dean's partner on CBS-TV's *Game of the Week*. He worked at CBS from 1960 to 1965; during his final season there, he and Dean broadcast twenty-one New York Yankees home games on *Yankee Baseball Game of the Week*, and the two were partnered on *Sports with Dizzy Dean and Pee Wee Reese*, a chat show. Then in 1966 he moved over to NBC-TV, where he was paired with Curt Gowdy. In March 1969 NBC abruptly announced that Reese had been fired. It was a mystery to him as to why his contract was not renewed. "Did I talk too much?" he wondered. "Didn't I talk enough?"[26]

He added, "I spent three great years with NBC and six with CBS. But it's going to feel strange to be out of baseball this year. I've been in the sport for thirty years."[27] He needn't have worried. Scant weeks after leaving NBC, Pee Wee was hired to join Ed Kennedy in the Cincinnati Reds broadcast booth, replacing Frank McCormick. He remained with the Reds for two seasons, and then finished his career with a lengthy stint in the employ of the Louisville-based Hillerich & Bradsby Company, the maker of Louisville Slugger bats. He served as director of the organization's college and professional baseball workforce and as sales representative with Major League ball clubs. He also represented Hillerich & Bradsby at public functions.

In 1984 Reese's uniform number—which, appropriately, was "1"—was retired by the Dodgers. That same year, the veterans' committee elected him to the Baseball Hall of Fame. His Hall of Fame plaque reads as follows: "Shortstop and captain of great Dodger teams of 1940s and '50s. Intangible qualities of subtle leadership on and off field. Competitive fire and professional pride complemented dependable glove, reliable base-running and clutch-hitting as significant factors in 7 Dodger pennants. Instrumental in easing acceptance of Jackie Robinson as baseball's first black performer."

As he aged, Reese suffered a variety of illnesses. He was afflicted with prostate cancer, which he overcame. Then in March 1997 doctors removed a malignant tumor from his lung, and he underwent radiation treatment. Adding to his woes was a broken hip. By this time he was making few public appearances.

Pee Wee Reese died at his Louisville home two years later, on August 14, 1999. He was eighty-one years old, and he had been married to his beloved Dottie for fifty-seven years. He was survived by her, his son and daughter, three grandchildren, and two great-grandchildren. The first Saturday after Reese's death, flags at Dodger Stadium were flown at half-staff. His funeral was held at Louisville's Southeast Christian Church. There were 2,000 attendees, among them practically all of Reese's surviving teammates, from Joe Black to Don Zimmer. He was buried in Rest Haven Memorial Cemetery in Louisville.

Speaking at Reese's funeral, Joe Black, the African American Dodgers hurler, declared, "Pee Wee helped make my boyhood dream come true to play in the majors, the World Series. When Pee Wee reached out to Jackie, all of us in the Negro League smiled and said it was the first time that a white guy had accepted us. When I finally got up to Brooklyn, I went to Pee Wee and said, 'Black people love you. When you touched Jackie, you touched all of us.' With Pee Wee, it was No. 1 on his uniform and No. 1 in our hearts."[28]

ROB EDELMAN

# Chapter 45. **Bruce Edwards**

*Ralph Berger*

| AGE | G | AB | R | H | 2B | 3B | HR | TB | RBI | BB | SO | BAV | OBP | SLG | SB | GDP | HBP |
|-----|-----|-----|-----|-----|-----|-----|-----|-----|-----|-----|-----|------|------|------|-----|-----|-----|
| 23 | 130 | 471 | 53 | 139 | 15 | 8 | 9 | 197 | 80 | 49 | 55 | .295 | .364 | .418 | 2 | 10 | 2 |

The Brooklyn Dodgers had great teams in the immediate postwar years, teams that would win pennants or fight for them until the last day of the season (and sometimes beyond). No team can be successful, though, without a significant presence behind the plate. In the early part of the 1946 season, the Dodgers were struggling to find that presence. Manager Leo Durocher knew the men he had—Ferrell Anderson and Don Padgett—were not the answer. Durocher was desperate to trade for a catcher, even approaching the Cardinals' manager, Eddie Dyer. Dyer demurred, telling Leo he was not going to help his closest rival.

Sometimes the trade not made is the best move, and such was the case for Durocher and the Dodgers in 1946. Forced to go to their farm system, Brooklyn called up young Bruce Edwards from their Mobile (Alabama) team in the Class Double-A Southern Association. Edwards, fresh from Military service and mature beyond his years, would be just what Leo needed, solidifying the defense and contributing greatly to the Dodgers' successes of 1946 and 1947.

Charles Bruce Edwards was born in Quincy, Illinois, on July 15, 1923, to Wade and Elsie Edwards. Wade was a truck driver and Elsie a housewife. The family moved to Sacramento, California, in time for Bruce to attend Sacramento High School.

Dodgers scouts Tom Downey and Bill Svilich signed the seventeen-year-old Edwards in 1941 at a tryout camp in San Mateo, California. The Dodgers sent him to the Santa Barbara Saints of the Class C California League. Edwards, a right-

Bruce Edwards finished fourth in the voting for the National League's Most Valuable Player Award, the highest-rated Dodger.

handed hitter, batted .259 with 10 doubles, 1 triple, and 1 home run in fifty-three games. After a brief stay with Santa Barbara in 1942, where he was converted from an outfielder to a catcher, he moved up to the Durham (North Carolina) Bulls of the Class B Piedmont League. It was the last professional baseball for Bruce Edwards for three years. Bruce enlisted in the army in January 1943 and served in a tank destroyer unit in Holland, France, and Germany.

Back from the service in 1946, Edwards began the season with Mobile, where he was batting .332 in sixty-two games for the Bears. Looking for help behind the plate, the Dodgers called him up, and on June 23 he played his first big league game. Edwards had an RBI double in his first Major League at bat. The hit came in the second inning off Cardinals left-hander Harry Brecheen and helped the first-place Dodgers defeat the second-place Cardinals, 4–2.

The twenty-three-year-old Edwards caught in ninety-one games in 1946, including one stretch of thirty-four games in which no opposing runner stole a base. On August 15 he had three assists in one inning. Edwards had his first Major League home run on September 8, off Mike Budnick of the Giants at Ebbets Field. Three days later he caught all nineteen innings of a 0–0 suspended game against Cincinnati at Ebbets Field, the Major Leagues' longest scoreless game ever.

The Dodgers ended the season tied for first place with St. Louis but lost the first two games of the three-game playoff. After joining the team, Edwards batted .267 with 13 doubles and 25 runs batted in. Arthur Daley of the *New York Times* thought that during the second half of the season, Edwards might have been the best catcher in either league. Eddie Dyer, perhaps regretting a trade not made, believed the youngster almost won the pennant for Durocher.

Nicknamed "Bull," Edwards stood five feet seven and weighed 175 to 185 pounds at various stages of his career. His first full season with the Dodgers, 1947, showcased his talent behind the plate and at bat. Rookie Dixie Howell was supposed to challenge Edwards for playing time, but the challenge never materialized. By April 2 Durocher said only three men were certain starters for the upcoming season: Eddie Stanky, Pee Wee Reese, and Bruce Edwards. A week later, Bruce was sidelined with a sore right shoulder, an unfortunate harbinger of his baseball future.

Edwards was well enough to play in Brooklyn's historic season opener on April 15. He was the Dodgers' starting catcher in Jackie Robinson's first Major League game. Bruce was 0 for 2 at the plate, but he did have an RBI in Brooklyn's 5–3 victory. He had a much better game on May 21 against the Cardinals. Edwards had a single, a double, and a home run against Brecheen in a game at St. Louis that the Dodgers would eventually win in ten innings.

The next day, when the Dodgers returned from their western swing, Edwards went to Johns Hopkins Hospital in Baltimore to have his sore shoulder evaluated. Roscoe McGowen of the *New York Times* said the team would miss Edwards if he were sidelined for any length of time. As it turned out, Edwards missed no time. He started the next game, in which he had two hits and threw out two would-be base stealers.

Another of Edwards's offensive highlights of the 1947 season came on July 2, at home against the Giants. His three-run home run sparked a nine-run fourth inning and led to a Brooklyn victory. On July 31 the sore-shouldered Edwards threw out Stan Musial in a key situation. The Dodgers had blown a ten-run lead but managed to prevail in the tenth inning, 11–10. His first career grand slam home run came on August 15, against the Phillies' Schoolboy Rowe at Shibe Park.

Edwards played in 130 games in 1947, hitting .295. His eighty RBIs were third best on the Dodgers, exceeded only by Dixie Walker and Carl Furillo. He established career highs in most offensive categories, including hits, home runs, triples, walks, and runs scored. Defensively, Bruce led all National League catchers in chances, putouts, and double plays for the pennant-winning Dodgers. He was selected to the National League's

All-Star team, and he played two innings in the All-Star Game as a replacement for starter Walker Cooper.

Edwards played in all seven games of the World Series, as the Dodgers fell to the New York Yankees. He batted just .222, had only two RBIS, and hit into a double play that ended the Series. Edwards figured to remain as the Dodgers' first-string catcher in 1948, but another injury and the emergence of rookie Roy Campanella diminished his playing time in Brooklyn. He appeared in ninety-six games, batting .276 with eight home runs.

Durocher and Burt Shotton, who replaced Leo as manager in midseason, played Edwards at several different positions in 1948. In addition to his catching forty-eight games, he played twenty-one games in the outfield and fourteen at third base, but he struggled at both new positions. The forty-eight games behind the plate were the most Edwards would have in a Major League season from that point on. He remained a backup for the rest of his Major League career.

Edwards batted .209 in sixty-four games in 1949, and just .183 in fifty games in 1950, as the experiment to make him an outfielder or third baseman was canceled. He played just five games at those positions in 1949 and none in 1950. Bruce made his last World Series appearance in 1949, getting a single in two pinch-hitting opportunities in Brooklyn's five-game loss to the Yankees.

On June 15, 1951, the Dodgers traded Edwards, along with pitcher Joe Hatten, outfielder Gene Hermanski, and infielder Eddie Miksis, to the Chicago Cubs for pitcher Johnny Schmitz, catcher Rube Walker, outfielder Andy Pafko, and infielder Wayne Terwilliger. The Dodgers were in Chicago at the time of the trade. The next day Carl Erskine was on the mound for Brooklyn and Edwards, in his new Cubs uniform, got a small taste of revenge. He slammed Erskine for a three-run homer, snapping a 3–3 tie, and batted in four runs to lead the Cubs to a 6–4 victory. Overall, Edwards hit a combined .237 in sixty-eight games in 1951, including .363 as a pinch hitter.

Edwards, playing in just fifty games in 1952, batted .245, but he continued to be a reliable pinch hitter, going 7 for 24 (.291). Even with his limited playing time, Edwards was valuable to the Cubs, serving as a pitching coach without portfolio. Bob Rush credited Bruce with helping him develop his hard curve ball. Armed with the new pitch, Rush won seventeen games for the fifth-place Cubs and shaved more than a run off his 1951 ERA.

In 1953 Edwards, now thirty years old, was named the player-manager of the Springfield (Massachusetts) Cubs of the Class Triple-A International League. He played only first base for the last-place team, hitting .286. Relieved of his duties during the season, he became the player-manager of the Des Moines Bruins of the Class A Western League.

In 1954 the Cubs brought him back as a player, but after appearing in only four games, they sent him back to the Minors, where he batted a healthy .298 in 106 games for the Los Angeles Angels of the Pacific Coast League. Edwards also played sixteen games with the Des Moines Bruins in '54, batting .353.

On December 11, 1954, the Washington Senators purchased Edwards from the Cubs for $15,000. Washington manager Charlie Dressen, who had coached and managed Bruce in Brooklyn, hoped Edwards could light a fire under the team because of his credibility in the clubhouse as well as on the field. Bruce spent the entire 1955 season with the Senators but appeared in only thirty games and batted an anemic .175. There was, however, one positive development for him that season: on September 20, Edwards married the former Geraldine Peterson.

After Washington released him in February 1956, Edwards started the new season with the Vancouver Mounties of the Pacific Coast League. He was hitting .295 when the Cincinnati Redlegs signed him as a free agent on July 18. Bruce appeared in only seven games for Cincinnati, including his last Major League game on September 13, 1956. He also played in ten games for the Southern Association's Memphis Chicks that year.

Cincinnati released Edwards on January 18, 1957, ending his Major League career. Though Bruce had mostly been a backup, he did have his moments of glory. In 1946, while appearing in fewer than one hundred games, he finished fourteenth in the voting for the National League's Most Valuable Player. The next year, 1947, his best season ever, Edwards was fourth in the MVP voting. In 1947 and 1951, he was named to the National League All-Star squad.

After releasing him, the Redlegs hired Edwards to manage their Visalia team in the California League. As their player-manager, Edwards led the team to the pennant in 1957. He hit .309 in eighty-seven games for the Class C club. In 1958 he was relieved in midseason as the team finished in fourth place.

In his ten Major League seasons, Edwards appeared in 591 games, with a .256 batting average. In addition to his contributions on the field, he was valued for his savvy handling of pitchers and his general knowledge of the game. New York sportswriter Dan Daniel offered this praise: "For catching skills, handling hurlers, general mobility, and general value to his club, give me Bruce Edwards of the Brooklyn Dodgers."

After retiring from baseball, Edwards was an inventory control analyst for thirteen years at an aerospace firm in Sacramento and then a movie projectionist at several movie houses in the area.

Bruce Edwards died of a heart attack on April 25, 1975, in Sacramento at the age of fifty-one. He was survived by his wife, Geraldine, daughters Muriel and Cindy, and sons Kim and Michael. He is buried in the Memorial Lawn Cemetery in Sacramento.

# Chapter 46. The Protested Game of July 20, 1947

*David W. Smith*

It is well known that a manager may formally protest a game only if he claims an umpire has made a decision contrary to the rules. Dissatisfaction with a specific call (safe/out, ball/strike, fair/foul) is not grounds for a protest.

However, sometimes things get a little murky. Take, for example, the game of July 20, 1947, played by the Dodgers against the St. Louis Cardinals in Ebbets Field. A protest by the Cardinals that day was upheld, although the specific rule that was violated is hard to pin down. Also, the remedy decreed by National League president Ford Frick went beyond the protest rules.

Let's address these two points separately, beginning with a short summary of what happened on the field that day. Jim Hearn pitched a great game for St. Louis, allowing no runs, two walks, only four singles, and holding a 2–0 lead through eight innings. In the top of the ninth with two outs and the bases empty, Cardinals right fielder Ron Northey hit a "towering drive" to the wall in center off Hugh Casey.[1] Dodgers center fielder Pete Reiser leaped but couldn't get it.

Umpire Larry Goetz, working at first base in the three-man crew, ran into the outfield and immediately called "No," ruling that the ball hit the top of the wall. Beans Reardon was the other base umpire, and as Northey approached third base, Reardon signaled that it was a home run. Northey naturally slowed his pace as he continued to the plate, where umpire Jocko Conlan called him out, ending the inning.

Roscoe McGowen described it in the *New York Times*: "There was a lapse of a couple of seconds before the ball dropped back on the field, where [right fielder Dixie] Walker picked it up and fired it to [second baseman Eddie] Stanky, who relayed it to [catcher] Bruce Edwards." The picture accompanying the story shows a sliding Northey was tagged out on a close play.[2] *The Sporting News* has a picture of the play at the plate from a different angle.[3]

The Cardinals immediately and vehemently protested, saying that Northey had been deceived by Reardon. The consensus in the press box and from the umpires (in later testimony) was that the slow-footed Northey would almost certainly have been safe had he not slowed down.

Manager Eddie Dyer formally protested the game, and the Dodgers came to bat, still trailing by two runs. The Cardinals used three pitchers to face seven batters but obtained only one out as Brooklyn collected three hits, a walk, and a stolen base (coupled with a throwing error by catcher Joe Garagiola) and used three pinch hitters to score three times, apparently winning the game, 3–2.

President Frick's ruling was released on July 25, and he tried to be Solomon-like as he reached an unorthodox decision. The starting point was to accept the widespread view that Northey would have scored except for Reardon's action. Therefore, Frick ruled that Northey was to be credited with a home run. However, he also let stand the three Dodgers runs in the bottom of the ninth, and the game went in the books as a 3–3 tie, with all individual records counting in the official totals. Only Casey's win and Murry Dickson's loss were expunged. A replay of the entire game was scheduled as part of a doubleheader on August 18, when the Cardinals were next scheduled to be in Brooklyn.

What rule was violated? The rule book does not specifically address confusing or deceptive actions by umpires, so Frick made a common-sense determination that the events on the field (a) were caused by the umpire and (b) were unfair to the Cardinals. The stated procedure in the rule book for an allowed protest is to resume the game at the point of the protest. In this case that would mean the Cardinals should still be batting with two outs in the top of the ninth and a 3–0 lead. The three Dodgers runs in the bottom of the ninth would be wiped out. Frick explained his action by stating that "fairness, common sense and sportsmanship must govern any decision not explicitly covered by the rules."[4]

There are two questions that remain unanswered: (1) Where was Reardon standing when the play began? (2) Why did Northey slide? It is interesting to note how umpires choreograph their movements when there are only two men working the bases. Even though Northey was a left-handed batter, it seems likely that with the bases empty, Reardon was on or near the left-field foul line. Such a position would be consistent with the facts that Goetz ran into the outfield to view the play and that Reardon was near third to make an indication to Northey.

The sliding question is more vexing. If Northey believed that Reardon gave him the homer sign, then why would he slide? The story in *The Sporting News* says he "jogged" to the plate. Perhaps he noticed the ball coming in and decided that Reardon was wrong, causing him to speed up and then slide in an attempt to evade the tag.

Final note: The tie game was played off as the second half of a day-night doubleheader on August 18, meaning that the Dodgers charged separate admission for the two games. The attendance at the first game was 32,781 and at the second was 33,723. The Dodgers donated "all receipts of the night game, amounting to $46,000, plus a probable $4,000 from the Frank Stevens concession stands, to the Brooklyn War Memorial Fund, Inc." The Dodgers won both games that day, by scores of 7–5 and 12–3.[5]

# Chapter 47. Joe Hatten

*Joseph Wancho*

| AGE | W | L | PCT. | ERA | G | GS | GF | CG | SHO | SV | IP | H | BB | SO | HBP | WP |
|-----|---|---|------|-----|---|----|----|----|-----|----|----|----|----|----|-----|----|
| 30 | 17 | 8 | .680 | 3.63 | 42 | 32 | 2 | 11 | 3 | 0 | 225.1 | 211 | 105 | 76 | 5 | 6 |

After four seasons of double-digit victories as a starter for the Dodgers (1946–49), left-handed pitcher Joe Hatten started only twenty-eight games over the next three seasons. He then departed the Major Leagues for a long career in the Minors.

When Hatten was asked what single thrill he remembered from his days as a Major Leaguer, he replied, "I remember Brooklyn and liked it very much. I can't just pick out any one thrill. Every day was a thrill while playing in Brooklyn. I thought they were a great bunch of fans."[1]

Joseph Hilarian Hatten was born on November 7, 1916, in Bancroft, Iowa. He was the fourth of eleven children (six girls and five boys) born to Frank and Gertrude Hatten. Frank owned a harness-making shop, a lively trade in a period when horses were still important to American commerce.

Joe's first experience at playing baseball was at the Junior American Legion level as a teenager. When he grew too old for Legion ball, he played semipro baseball around Bancroft for four years. In 1938 Hatten signed a Minor League contract with Sioux City of the Nebraska State League. However, the Cowboys released him a month into the season, and there is no evidence that he got into any games.

Hatten signed the next year, 1939, with Crookston (Minnesota) of the Class D Northern League. In his first full professional season, he led the team in victories, posting a 14-14 win-loss record for the last-place club. He had an earned run average of 3.02 and led the league with 299 strikeouts, including 21 in one game. In 1940 Hatten played for the Dodgers' Class B Anniston (Alabama) farm club of the Southeastern League. The

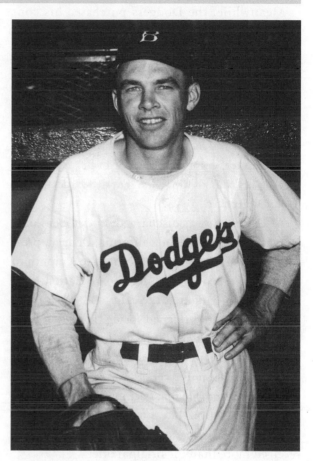

Joe Hatten won seventeen games in 1947, sixteen against second-division teams.

competition was tougher and Joe slipped to 7-18 with a 5.31 ERA. Yet in 1941 Hatten found himself pitching at the top Minor League level, with the unaffiliated Minneapolis Millers of the American Association. He won five and lost six, pitching both in a starting role and in relief.

Andy Cohen of the Dodgers had been scouting Hatten as a Minor Leaguer. Based on Cohen's report, Brooklyn acquired the six-foot, 175-pound southpaw from the Millers in December 1941. Hatten started the 1942 campaign with the International League's Montreal Royals, the Dodgers' top farm team. He won four games and lost two before being called up for navy service on May 25.

Meanwhile, the Dodgers purchased his contract. "But it was going to be a long time before I could pitch for them," he recalled.[2] Hatten served in the navy for forty-one months, ten of which were overseas in the Pacific, Australia, and India. Back in the United States, he was stationed at the Naval Air Station in Livermore, California. Hatten pitched on service teams both overseas and at Livermore, compiling a record of 85-25. While serving his tour of duty, Joe married Zanette Easley on March 20, 1944.

After Hatten was discharged, in October 1945, he played winter ball in California. Dodgers president Branch Rickey offered him $450 a month to pitch for the Brooklyn club in 1946. Hatten, now twenty-nine, balked at the offer and was a holdout as the Dodgers opened spring training in Daytona Beach, Florida. "I'll be glad to pay him what he will be worth if he proves himself," said Rickey. "But I think he should report and start for what he has been offered. He must demonstrate that he can pitch in the National League and win."[3] Eventually the two men came to an agreement, and Hatten received more than the original offer.

Brooklyn manager Leo Durocher was impressed the first time he saw Hatten pitch that spring. "No doubt about it, this Hatten looks like a real pitcher," the Dodgers' skipper said. "He pours that thing by you, and he isn't half trying yet. He ought to be something when he's ready to cut loose. All you have to do is look at him and you know that if he can control it, he can be the best southpaw the Dodgers have ever had."[4]

Hatten won his Major League debut on April 21, 1946, at Ebbets Field. He outdueled New York

Giants pitcher Bill Voiselle to earn the 2–1 decision. The 1946 race was a nip-and-tuck battle between the Dodgers and the St. Louis Cardinals. On the next-to-last day of the season, Hatten pitched Brooklyn to a win over the Boston Braves. The victory extended his winning streak to six and gave him fourteen wins for the season.

Both the Dodgers and the Cardinals lost on the final day of the season, forcing a best-of-three playoff, the first playoff in Major League history. Howie Pollet defeated the Dodgers, 4–2, in the first game. Hatten started the second game and was knocked out in the fifth inning. The Cardinals won the game, giving them the pennant.

Hatten had posted a fine 14-11 record in 1946 while leading the Dodgers with thirteen complete games and a 2.84 ERA. However, he was second in the league in walks (110) and first in the league in hit batters (7). Control problems plagued Hatten throughout his Major League career. Except for 1950, his walks exceeded his strikeouts every season.

Before the start of the 1947 season, baseball commissioner Happy Chandler suspended Durocher for one season for "an accumulation of unpleasant incidents" and "publicity-producing affairs." Rickey tapped an old friend, Burt Shotton, to come out of retirement and lead the Dodgers. Rickey believed that Shotton would be able to handle the issues that would occur during Jackie Robinson's first year in the big leagues. Hatten started the Dodgers' opener, on April 15, 1947, and worked six innings. He left for a pinch hitter trailing 3–1, but the Dodgers rallied to win, 5–3.

Hatten finished the season with a 17-8 record and a 3.63 ERA. Perhaps his most impressive day came in a September 14 doubleheader in Cincinnati. Joe pitched a complete game to win the opener and then held the Reds to one hit over the final five and two-thirds innings to win the nightcap. The two victories that day were numbers fifteen

JOSEPH WANCHO

and sixteen for the year. (Sixteen of Hatten's seventeen wins in 1947 came against the second-division Reds, Cubs, and Phillies.)

Brooklyn managed to hold off the Cardinals this time and won their first pennant since 1941. After Brooklyn lost the first two games of the Series at Yankee Stadium, they returned home for Game Three. Hatten started for the Dodgers, but it was not one of his better performances. He gave up six runs in four and one-third innings, including a two-run home run to Joe DiMaggio. But the Dodgers bounced back to win, 9–8, with Hugh Casey getting the victory in relief. Hatten pitched out of the bullpen for the remainder of the Series, making brief appearances in the final three games.

Durocher returned from his suspension to manage the Dodgers in 1948. He said of Hatten, "I've been hammering away at Joe to keep his curve ball low. When he gets it across the letters, they murder him. He came to see me the other day. 'I've got it now, Leo,' was all he said, but that was all I wanted to hear."[5]

In July, Durocher resigned and was named manager of the New York Giants. Shotton was recalled from his retirement in Florida to again take over as Brooklyn's manager. Hatten completed his third straight season with over two hundred innings pitched. His record for the third-place Dodgers was 13-10 with a 3.58 ERA.

The Dodgers returned to the top of the National League in 1949, edging the Cardinals by one game. Hatten was 12-8 that season, but his earned run average ballooned to 4.18. In the 1949 World Series against the Yankees, Hatten pitched in Game Four, giving up three earned runs in an inning and one-third of relief. He pitched a third of an inning in Game Five, as the Yankees made quick work of Brooklyn, winning the Series four games to one.

The addition of Preacher Roe in 1948, the promotion of Don Newcombe in 1949, and the maturation of Carl Erksine spelled the end for Hatten as a full-time starter for the Dodgers. He started a

combined fourteen games for Brooklyn in the 1950 and 1951 seasons, with most of his appearances coming in relief.

Shotton vehemently denied placing Hatten in his doghouse for ineffectiveness, yet he hardly gave him a vote of confidence: "All the time I have been at Brooklyn Joe has been a very brilliant pitcher some times and a very mediocre pitcher other times. I think he is a pretty good spring pitcher. Last summer, I believed I had others who were going better, that's all. That's Hatten's history. He's either very good or very bad. One thing about him, it doesn't take long to find out whether he got it or not."[6]

Following the 1950 season, in which the Dodgers finished second to the Phillies, Branch Rickey was forced out at Brooklyn by co-owner Walter O'Malley. Manager Shotton was fired and replaced by Charlie Dressen. Soon Hatten left Brooklyn as well, being dealt to the Chicago Cubs as part of an eight-player deal on June 15, 1951. Hatten, outfielder Gene Hermanski, infielder Eddie Miksis, and catcher Bruce Edwards went to the Cubs, in exchange for pitcher Johnny Schmitz, catcher Rube Walker, infielder Wayne Terwilliger, and outfielder Andy Pafko.

Chicago finished the 1951 season in last place, thirty-four and a half games behind the pennant-winning Giants. Hatten was 2-6 for the Cubs, but at spring training in 1952 he earned the praise of manager Phil Cavarretta and pitching coach Charlie Root. "The way Hatten's going this spring," said Cavarretta, "I think he's going to be very valuable to us. It's nice to have those 200-inning pitchers, especially those like Hatten who know how to win."

Root said, "Hatten's in such great physical condition that he can go for quite a few years yet, and the wonderful thing is that he's got all the savvy and doesn't have to learn the hard way anymore. Lots of fellows don't really get good until they pass 31 or 32. Joe's had a few lean years now, and has had enough rough moments to know what it's all about."[7]

However, Joe failed to live up to those expectations. In thirteen games, including eight starts, he went 4-4 with a 6.08 ERA. He pitched in his last Major League game, as a reliever, on July 4, 1952, in St. Louis, and then he was optioned to the Los Angeles Angels of the Pacific Coast League. "I guess I was just rockin' along up there," he said. "It was an awful shock to discover that all the clubs would waive on me."[8] For his Major League career, Hatten won sixty-five games and lost forty-nine with an ERA of 3.87.

During the rest of 1952, he was 8-8 for the Angels as a starter. In 1953 he posted a 17-11 record for the Angels with a 3.34 ERA. His 152 strike-outs led the league. His victories included a seven-inning no-hit, no-run game against San Diego on June 7. Altogether, he pitched nine Minor League seasons, almost all at the Class Triple-A level, after leaving the big leagues and won ninety-three games while losing eighty-seven.

In 1960, at the age of forty-three, Hatten retired to Redding, California, where he began a new career as a mailman for the Unites States Postal Service. He returned to his hometown of Bancroft, Iowa, every year until 1981 for the annual old-timers' game or Joe Hatten Day. The street leading to the sandlot ball diamonds was renamed Joe Hatten Drive.

Joe Hatten died in Redding on December 16, 1988, after a struggle with cancer. He was survived by his wife and their five children, sons Donald and William and daughters Donna, Judy, and Barbara. Hatten is buried at the Inwood/Ogburn Cemetery in Shingletown, California.

## Chapter 48. Timeline, August 1–August 17

*Lyle Spatz*

Friday, August 1, at Chicago—Catcher Clyde Mc-Cullough hit a ninth-inning two-out, two-run homer off Hugh Casey to give the Cubs a 10–8 victory and end Brooklyn's winning streak at thirteen. Joe Hatten, Hank Behrman, and Clyde King preceded Casey on the mound. Dixie Walker had three hits for Brooklyn, including a pair of doubles. 63-37, First, 9 games ahead.

Saturday, August 2, at Chicago—Chicago racked up seventeen hits against Harry Taylor and six successors on the way to a 12–7 victory. Peanuts Lowrey and Eddie Waitkus each had five hits for the winners. 63-38, First, 8 games ahead.

Sunday, August 3, at Chicago—Johnny Schmitz, who had pitched eight scoreless innings against the Dodgers in his previous start, pitched nine today. Schmitz's 6–0 win gave Chicago a sweep of the series, while cutting Brooklyn's lead over the Cardinals to seven games. Umpire Bill Stewart issued a warning to Brooklyn starter Ralph Branca about throwing high and tight to several Chicago batters. 63-39, First, 7 games ahead.

Monday, August 4, at Boston—Dixie Walker hit the one hundredth home run of his career, a two-run blast off Bill Voiselle in the tenth inning, to defeat the Braves 4–2. Hugh Casey pitched four and two-thirds innings in relief to earn his eighth win. Arky Vaughan had three hits for Brooklyn, while Pete Reiser and Jackie Robinson helped Casey with sparkling defensive plays. 64-39, First, 7 games ahead.

Tuesday, August 5, at Boston—Brooklyn's lead over St. Louis dropped to six games after the Dodgers lost 4–2 to the Braves' Johnny Sain. Boston catcher Hank Camelli had a two-run double off Hal Gregg in the sixth inning to break what had been a 2–2 tie. 64-40, First, 6 games ahead.

Wednesday, August 6, at Boston—Warren Spahn's fourteenth win and a three-run homer by Bob Elliott off loser Joe Hatten powered the Braves to a 7–3 win. Spahn held the Dodgers to six singles and a Jackie Robinson double, as Brooklyn lost another game off its first-place lead. 64-41, First, 5 games ahead.

Thursday, August 7, at Boston—Red Barrett's three-hitter gave Boston its third straight victory over the Dodgers. Harry Taylor went the distance and allowed only five hits in taking the 3–1 loss. Johnny Hopp had three hits and two runs batted in for the Braves. For the third consecutive day, a Brooklyn loss and a Cardinals win combined to shave a full game off the Dodgers' lead, which was now down to four games. 64-42, First, 4 games ahead.

Friday, August 8, vs. Philadelphia—Ralph Branca threw his fourth shutout of the season as the Dodgers, playing their first game at Ebbets Field in eighteen days, defeated the Phillies 5–0. Bruce Edwards had three hits, while Eddie Stanky, Pete Reiser, Carl Furillo, and Dixie Walker each had two in leading Brooklyn's thirteen-hit attack. 65-42, First, 4 games ahead.

Saturday, August 9, vs. Philadelphia—First base-man Howie Schultz, whom the Dodgers had sold to Philadelphia in May to make room for Jackie Robinson, hit a sixth-inning grand slam off Vic Lombardi to lead the Phillies to a 5–3 win. The Dodgers loaded the bases with one out in the ninth, but Carl Furillo hit into a game-ending double play. 65-43, First, 4 games ahead.

Sunday, August 10, vs. Philadelphia—Joe Hatten shut out the Phillies, 2–0, limiting them to five hits. Brooklyn scored individual runs in the first and eighth innings, each the result of a Dixie Walker single that scored Eddie Stanky. Despite the win, the Dodgers lost a half game off their lead after St. Louis won a doubleheader from Pittsburgh. The Cardinals had now won ten of their last eleven games. 66-43, First, 3½ games ahead.

Monday, August 11—Not scheduled. With the Cardinals' win over the Cubs, the Dodgers' lead, which had been ten games eleven days earlier, was now down to three games. 66-43, First, 3 games ahead.

Tuesday, August 12, vs. Boston—The Braves battered Ralph Branca, Hank Behrman, and Rex Barney for fifteen hits in thumping the Dodgers 9–2. Boston's Bill Voiselle and Clyde Shoun limited Brooklyn to seven hits. By winning for the seventh time in the last eight games, the Braves moved to within six and a half games of the lead. The third-place Giants were six back, and the second-place Cardinals were still three behind. 66-44, First, 3 games ahead.

Wednesday, August 13, vs. Boston—A four-run first inning and a five-run fifth inning led the Dodgers to a 10–5 win. Jackie Robinson started both rallies with bunt singles. Clyde King, in relief of Harry Taylor, was the winner. 67-44, First, 3½ games ahead.

Thursday, August 14, vs. Boston—Carl Furillo celebrated Carl Furillo Day at Ebbets Field with an eighth-inning single that drove in Eddie Stanky with the game's only run. Vic Lombardi allowed four singles in besting Warren Spahn, 1–0. 68-44, First, 4½ games ahead.

Friday, August 15, at Philadelphia—Bruce Edwards's ninth-inning grand slam off Schoolboy Rowe was the big blow in Brooklyn's 8–1 win at Philadelphia. Joe Hatten raised his record to 5-0 against the Phillies this season. Jackie Robinson had four hits for Brooklyn while Pete Reiser and Edwards each had three. 69-44, First, 4½ games ahead.

Saturday, August 16, at Philadelphia—Pinch-hitter Bobby Bragan hit a ninth-inning, run-scoring double off Oscar Judd to give Brooklyn a 5–4 victory. Bragan was batting for winner Hugh Casey, who took over for starter Ralph Branca to start the seventh inning. Hank Behrman retired the Phillies in order in the home ninth to preserve the victory. Jackie Robinson had two doubles, and Carl Furillo had his one hundredth hit of the season and two runs batted in. The Cardinals' loss to Pittsburgh extended the Dodgers' lead to five and a half games. 70-44, First, 5½ games ahead.

Sunday, August 17, at Philadelphia (2)—Knuckle-baller Dutch Leonard shut out the Dodgers, 4–0, in the first game of the doubleheader. Clyde King was the loser. Brooklyn was ahead 5–4 in the bottom of the seventh inning of game two, but because of the Pennsylvania blue laws forbidding play after 6:59 p.m., the score reverted to the 4–4 tie it had been at the end of six innings. The game would be completed on September 25. Pete Reiser had three hits and three runs batted in for Brooklyn, but starter Hal Gregg failed to hold a 4–0 lead. (The next day, Commissioner Frick ruled that the Phillies had used stalling tactics to make sure the blue law restriction would kick in. He ruled the game should resume from the point where it had been suspended—in the bottom of the seventh inning with Harry Walker facing Hugh Casey, a 2-0 count, nobody on, and nobody out.) 70-45, First, 4½ games ahead.

# Chapter 49. **Howie Schultz**

*Stew Thornley*

| AGE | G | AB | R | H | 2B | 3B | HR | TB | RBI | BB | SO | BAV | OBP | SLG | SB | GDP | HBP |
|-----|---|----|----|----|----|----|----|----|-----|----|----|------|------|------|----|-----|-----|
| 24 | 2 | 1 | 0 | 0 | 0 | 0 | 0 | 0 | 0 | 0 | 0 | .000 | .000 | .000 | 0 | 1 | 0 |

Howie Schultz combined Major League careers in baseball and basketball during the 1940s. Nicknamed "Stretch," the six-foot-six Schultz had already started his professional baseball career while still a student and one of the stars of the basketball team at Hamline University in St. Paul, Minnesota.

Howard Henry Schultz was born July 3, 1922, and grew up in St. Paul. His parents, Leo and Minnie, were also St. Paul natives. Leo Schultz worked for the Montgomery Ward company for thirty-five years, running the shipping-and-receiving dock through the Great Depression. "We had food on the table and clothes on our back," Schultz said of the Depression years. "We never suffered."

Schultz was the second of three children. His brother, Louis, was born two years before him, and his sister, Lorraine, two years after him. In 1926 the family moved to a house three blocks north of Lexington Park, home of the St. Paul Saints of the American Association.

Leo Schultz was an avid baseball fan. A member of the St. Paul Municipal Baseball Board and the board for amateur baseball in the state, he spent a great deal of time with friends at Lexington Park, watching the Saints. Howie caught the baseball bug from his dad and attended his first Saints game by the time he was six.

Schultz began playing basketball when he was in the eighth grade in a Saturday morning program at Concordia College in St. Paul. The man who oversaw the program, Dick Siebert, played professional baseball while coaching the Concordia Academy (high school) basketball team in the off-season. Schultz first played on organized baseball and basketball teams as a ninth grader. From there

Howie Schultz was sold to Philadelphia in early May when the Dodgers realized Jackie Robinson could handle the first base position by himself.

he went to Central High School, playing both sports in his junior and senior seasons.

After graduating from Central in 1940, Schultz enrolled in Hamline University, which was only about a mile from his home. Despite being a small college, Hamline was establishing a national reputation for its basketball team under coach Joe Hutton. Schultz played basketball but not baseball for Hamline.

In the summer of 1940, Lou McKenna, who was the general manager of the Saints, asked Schultz if he would be interested in playing in the Class C Northern League following his first year at Hamline. Schultz said yes and played for the Grand Forks (North Dakota) Chiefs in 1941.

In Howie's sophomore season at Hamline, the Pipers won the National Association of Intercollegiate Basketball (NAIB) title. The United States had entered World War II by that time. Schultz had a late draft number and did not get his call until the summer of 1942. However, he was deferred from military service because of his height. He played again for Grand Forks, but the St. Paul Saints purchased his contract in August, and he finished the 1942 season in the American Association.

Schultz played his junior season of basketball during the winter of 1942–43 and then left school to go to spring training with the Saints. "My dad said, 'I hate to see you leave school, but if you're going to have an opportunity, you might really have it now because of the elimination of so many guys going into the service.' Obviously, he was right."

Schultz did well with the Saints in 1943 and was seen by Brooklyn Dodgers president Branch Rickey during an August game in Louisville. A few days later, the Dodgers acquired Schultz from St. Paul for $40,000 and four players—pitchers Rube Melton and Ed Spaulding and infielders Joe Orengo and Jack Bolling. (The following season, the Dodgers developed a working agreement with St. Paul and eventually purchased the team, but the Schultz deal occurred when the Saints were still an independent team.)

Schultz made his Major League debut at Ebbets Field in an August 16 twilight game against the St. Louis Cardinals. Facing Mort Cooper, he lined out to third baseman Whitey Kurowski his first time up. In the fifth, he singled. The next inning, he capped a two-run rally with a run-scoring double off the left-field fence.

"First Sacker Wins Fans" was one of the sub-headlines in the *New York Times* the next morning. Rickey was pleased at Schultz's great start. He had recently traded fan-favorite Dolph Camilli to the Giants and thought it crucial for Schultz, Camilli's replacement at first base, to win over the Brooklyn fans immediately.

In forty-five games with Brooklyn in 1943, Schultz had a .269 batting average with thirty-four runs batted in. His only home run during the season came on August 22, at Ebbets Field, off Xavier Rescigno of Pittsburgh.

Schultz returned to Hamline in the fall of 1943 to continue his studies. Originally a business and economics major, he switched to social studies when he decided to go into teaching. He did not play basketball for Hamline that winter.

After playing in 138 games for Brooklyn and hitting eleven home runs with eighty-three RBIs in 1944, Schultz was back at Hamline for his fifth year of college and his fourth and final season of basketball. His amateur eligibility became an issue as the Pipers prepared to play City College of New York (CCNY) at New York's Madison Square Garden as part of a college doubleheader.

On Thursday, December 21, 1944, a week before the CCNY game, the Pipers had defeated the professional Harlem Globetrotters in a game in Rochester, Minnesota. The Amateur Athletic Union eventually sanctioned the CCNY-Hamline game, and Schultz scored eleven points as the Pipers beat CCNY 47–42. A few weeks later, Hamline twice played DePaul, which had George Mikan as its center. The first game was played before a crowd of 15,752 at Chicago Stadium on January 20. Schultz had thirteen points for Hamline, but DePaul won, 45–41. Mikan had twenty-six points. In a rematch four days later at the St. Paul Auditorium, DePaul won again, 49–40. Schultz was the game's high scorer with twenty-one points. Mikan had seventeen.

During his final year at Hamline, Schultz's draft

status changed. He recalls the mood of the country during the Battle of the Bulge in December of 1944 and resentment toward professional athletes for not being in the service. "Virtually all of us were reclassified 1-A," he said. "I got my notice of reclassification right at the end of my first semester [late January of 1945]. I went to the draft board and asked when I would be called."

Schultz was informed that he probably would not be called until at least April but that he was not to leave town. Schultz called Rickey and explained his situation. Rickey optioned him to St. Paul, and Schultz played home games with the Saints (as well as games the team played at Minneapolis). He graduated from Hamline and, following his commencement went back to the draft board to inquire about his status. He was told that his papers had been recalled and that he was free to do whatever he wanted.

Schultz was called back up by the Dodgers, but after two weeks with Brooklyn, he got a telegram to report to Fort Snelling in Minneapolis for a preinduction physical. When his height was measured at more than seventy-eight inches, he was classified as 4-F again. "I went back to Brooklyn, didn't do very much, and around the middle of August, Rickey optioned me to Montreal."

With the war over, Schultz was able to spend the entire 1946 season with Brooklyn. A right-handed hitter, he played primarily against left-handed pitching, with Ed Stevens playing against right-handers. The Dodgers and St. Louis Cardinals finished the regular season in a first-place tie, necessitating the first tiebreaker playoff series in Major League history. The first game was in St. Louis, and the Cardinals had left-hander Howie Pollet on the mound. Schultz came up in the third inning with the Dodgers trailing 1–0 and hit a home run to tie the game. St. Louis retook the lead, but Schultz cut the gap to one run with a run-scoring single in the seventh. The Cardinals held on, however, for a 4–2 win.

The series shifted to Brooklyn, and Schultz was on the bench as right-hander Murry Dickson pitched for St. Louis. The Cardinals took an 8–1 lead into the last of the ninth. The Dodgers scored three runs, but left-hander Harry Brecheen, in relief of Dickson, fanned Schultz, pinch-hitting for Dick Whitman, to end the game and Brooklyn's season.

The 1946 season also marked the end of the color barrier that had long been in effect in Organized Baseball. Schultz recalls playing in a couple of exhibition games against Jackie Robinson of the International League's Montreal Royals in Daytona Beach that spring. He got to know Robinson better in 1947 as the Dodgers moved their training camp to Havana, Cuba. Robinson was still on the Montreal roster, but it was clear what the Dodgers had in mind for him. Schultz arrived late for spring training because he was playing professional basketball in the off-season for the Anderson (Indiana) Packers of the National Basketball League. On the plane from Miami to Havana with Schultz was Brooklyn scout Clyde Sukeforth, who had scouted Robinson with the Kansas City Monarchs of the Negro American League. Sukeforth told Schultz that Robinson would be brought up by the Dodgers, and because the team had Eddie Stanky at second base, Robinson would be playing first base.

In the Dodgers' regular-season opener, Robinson was in the starting lineup as Brooklyn's first baseman. Schultz entered the game as a defensive replacement and did not play again for nearly a month. He pinch-hit in a May 9 game in Philadelphia and after the game was sold to the Phillies for a reported $50,000.

The team Schultz joined is remembered for its abusiveness toward Robinson. "It was embarrassing," said Schultz. Of Philadelphia Phillies manager Ben Chapman, possibly the worst of the bunch, Schultz shook his head and said sadly, "He was still fighting the Civil War. He was just very unhappy with the situation. He just didn't feel that blacks should be there. There were enough guys on that team from the south who jumped on the bandwagon.

"I was playing first [for the Phillies in a game against the Dodgers] and Jack got on. The abuse was almost continuous. And I said, 'Jack, how can you handle this crap?' And he said, 'Oh, I'll have my day.' That's all he said. And, of course, he did."

Schultz played in 114 games for the Phillies in 1947, hitting just .223, and decided not to play in 1948. However, the Phillies lured him back. Because he was playing basketball again, Schultz missed spring training. "I couldn't hit a balloon." Philadelphia put him on waivers, and the Cincinnati Reds claimed him. Ted Kluszewski, a left-handed-hitting first baseman, was in his first full year with the Reds, and initially Schultz and Kluszewski were platooned. After Schultz got hurt, having had his wrist sliced open when he was spiked at first base, Kluszewski began playing regularly.

Schultz played his final Major League game on September 8, 1948, and then refused an assignment to the Minor Leagues, ending his professional baseball career. He continued to play pro basketball in the winter, and he earned more money in that sport than in baseball. However, the wear of two sports took its toll on him. "I was not built to sustain a long [baseball] season," Schultz said. "I got weak. I always felt that if I hadn't played basketball the year before and just stuck to baseball, I could have hit my .250, .260. I had too big a strike zone, and I didn't have the quick wrists.

"I was probably at the top level a better basketball player than I was a baseball player. I could compete with anybody at that time, including Mikan, Arnie Risen [center for the Rochester Royals, now in the Basketball Hall of Fame], any of the top centers that were playing in the league at that time."

The Anderson Packers, sponsored by the Duffey Packing Company, were members of the National Basketball League until the league merged with the Basketball Association of American to create the National Basketball Association (NBA) in 1949. The 1949–50 season was Schultz's fourth with the Packers, and his first as a coach. He found the dual roles of player and coach to be difficult, and at midseason was traded to Fort Wayne, where he went back to only playing. (His NBA coaching record was 21-14 for a winning percentage of .600.)

Schultz married Gloria Tellejohn, whom he met at Hamline University, on March 9, 1945, in Hamline United Methodist Church in St. Paul. They had two children: Howard Jr., known as Skip, born January 10, 1949, and Becky, born January 12, 1950. When Becky was born, the couple decided to settle in St Paul. Howie chose not to return to Fort Wayne in the fall of 1950. Instead, he got a chance to play and coach closer to home. A new league, the National Professional Basketball League, was formed and included four teams that had been dropped by the NBA. Another team in the league was the St. Paul Lights, and Schultz was chosen to coach and play for the team. However, the Lights folded on December 20, less than two months into the season.

The next year Schultz found another local team to play for, the NBA Minneapolis Lakers. Schultz spent the entire season with the Lakers in 1951–52 and played during the 1952–53 season before they released him in February 1953. This ended his career in professional sports, but he was still playing semiprofessional baseball in Minnesota. Schultz played for several town teams during the 1950s.

Schultz had begun teaching at Mechanic Arts High School in the fall of 1954, while also serving as the school's baseball and basketball coach. In 1965 he succeeded Joe Hutton as Hamline's basketball coach. He also coached baseball and taught physical education and coaching theory. In 1972 Schultz went back to the St. Paul school system, coaching basketball. He retired from the school system in 1986.

In 1988, he and Gloria moved to a townhome overlooking a golf course in Stillwater, Minnesota, a river town about twenty miles from St. Paul, and for many years they spent their winters on a golf course in Naples, Florida.

Howie Schultz was eighty-seven when he died in Stillwater on October 30, 2009, following a four-month battle with cancer. He was survived by Gloria and their two children.

# Chapter 50. **Pete Reiser**

*Mark Stewart*

| AGE | G | AB | R | H | 2B | 3B | HR | TB | RBI | BB | SO | BAV | OBP | SLG | SB | GDP | HBP |
|-----|-----|-----|-----|-----|-----|-----|-----|-----|-----|-----|-----|-----|-----|-----|-----|-----|-----|
| 28 | 110 | 388 | 68 | 120 | 23 | 2 | 5 | 162 | 46 | 68 | 41 | .309 | .415 | .418 | 14 | 3 | 2 |

Only a handful of people who saw Pete Reiser in his prime are still around today. Those who did have two things in common: they remember when the Dodgers belonged to Brooklyn . . . and they cannot watch an athlete streak toward an outfield fence without feeling just a little sick to their stomachs. Pete was a 5-foot-10½, sinewy-strong 185-pounder who generated more speed, power, and pure energy than seemed physically possible from that modest frame. The only thing that could stop Pete was an unpadded stadium wall.

Harold Patrick Reiser was born on March 17— St. Patrick's Day (hence his middle name)—1919, in St. Louis, Missouri. He was the sixth of nine living children born to George and Stella (Boody) Reiser. As a boy, his friends and family called him Pete, after the cowboy movie hero Two-Gun Pete. He loved westerns, and as a child he often walked around the neighborhood with a pair of toy six-shooters holstered to his belt. Eventually his nickname became "Pistol Pete."

Reiser's father, a good semipro pitcher, began flinging pitches to his son at an early age; and at an early age, Pete could hit them. Pete's older brother Mike often brought him along to play in his sandlot games. Thus, at least in modern parlance, Pete spent much of his youth "playing up." Mike was later signed out of high school by the New York Yankees, but he contracted scarlet fever shortly thereafter and died.

Reiser was good at every sport he tried. As a fourteen-year-old at Holy Ghost Parochial School, he impressed a local soccer scout enough to earn $50 a game—more than his dad was making in a week. He was a terrific football player, bowl-

Leo Durocher said Pete Reiser "might have been the best ballplayer I ever saw."

er, and ice skater, too; and he was ambidextrous. Pete threw and batted right-handed as a boy, but he could swing around and do almost as well left-handed. His sports fantasy, however, did not take place on the diamond. Raised in a devout Catholic family, he dreamed of becoming a football star for Notre Dame.

At William Beaumont High School, Reiser was the team's shortstop. He was not big, but he was fast. He also had a powerful arm and a live bat, and he was unrelenting on defense. He believed

215

there was no ball he could not get to. This was not a major issue in the infield, where players are encouraged to leap and dive and spin. In the outfield, where Reiser would ultimately play, his imprudence would lead to his downfall.

At fifteen, Reiser sneaked into a St. Louis Cardinals tryout, where he out-threw and outran more than eight hundred other boys. He was disappointed when he returned home without a contract, but later a Cardinals scout, Charlie Barrett, visited the Reiser home and explained why they hadn't made a big deal about Pete at Sportsman's Park. The Cardinals didn't want word leaking out to the Browns, with whom they shared the ballpark, or anyone else. The scout also admitted they'd had their eye on him since grade school. The Cardinals knew Pete wasn't old enough to sign to a contract, so they got permission from George Reiser to hire the boy as a "chauffeur."

That summer Reiser drove around the South with Barrett as he visited the Cardinals' farm teams. At each stop the teenager would take the field and test himself against the bush leaguers. It was on these trips that Reiser got his first glimpse of life on the road. He had never eaten in a restaurant in his life. He liked it.

Just as planned, Reiser was signed by the Cardinals in 1937, after high school. He played shortstop for two Class D teams—New Iberia (Louisiana) of the Evangeline League and Newport of the Northeast Arkansas League. In 1938 Commissioner Kenesaw Mountain Landis ruled that the Cardinals' system tied up so many young players that it went against the interest of baseball. Landis broke up their Minor League monopoly by cutting loose dozens of players, who were then dispersed to other teams through a kind of Depression-era free agency. Of these players, Pete Reiser was arguably the best. More to the point, he was the one Rickey most wanted to keep.

Rickey contacted his one-time associate Larry MacPhail, who was now running the Brooklyn Dodgers. They worked out a gentlemen's agreement. The Dodgers would sign Reiser, hide him in the low Minors for a couple of years, and then trade him back to the Cardinals. Rickey called Pete and told him to sign with Brooklyn no matter what they offered. This kind of chicanery was contradictory to baseball rules, and had Landis learned of the arrangement, he would have stopped it.

Pete followed orders, signed with the Dodgers for $100, and was sent to Superior (Wisconsin) of the Class D Northern League, where he hit .302 with fifty-five extra-base hits. He was still hitting right-handed at the time, but once he revealed that he was ambidextrous, coaches encouraged him to swing around to the left side, to take better advantage of his speed. He would hit almost exclusively left-handed for the better part of the next ten years.

Reiser first caught the eye of the Dodgers' new player-manager, Leo Durocher, when he arrived at spring training in 1939. It was a hot day and Durocher did not feel like playing shortstop. He asked Pete to play the position. What happened next is part of baseball lore. Pitchers literally could not get Reiser out. In eleven trips to the plate over three games, he collected three walks, four singles, and four home runs. Durocher, who had been pining for a left-handed power threat, had one dropped right in his lap—from Class D ball, no less!

Durocher started telling the beat writers that Reiser would be his Opening Day shortstop. He was ready to take the rookie under his wing, as he would do twelve years later with Willie Mays. When glowing articles started showing up in the New York papers, MacPhail received a phone call from an enraged Rickey accusing him of a double-cross. MacPhail sent Durocher a telegram instructing him to stop playing Reiser—phenom or not. He needed more instruction and was to be sent to the Minor League camp.

Durocher, who hated to be second-guessed when it came to players, ignored these orders.

MacPhail then boarded a flight south so he could deal with Leo face-to-face. Durocher was just as conniving as Rickey and MacPhail, but he also had a big mouth, so MacPhail was not about to tell him the real story behind Pistol Pete. An argument ensued during which MacPhail fired Durocher. The next day they settled their differences; nevertheless, Durocher could see MacPhail was serious about Reiser. He optioned Pete to the Minors as ordered.

That year Reiser suffered the first of many serious injuries he would endure during his professional career. Playing the outfield with Class A Elmira (New York), he felt a sharp pain while throwing a ball to the infield. He continued to play for two weeks until the pain became unbearable. X-rays showed that he had fractured his arm. He underwent an operation to remove bone chips from his right elbow, and he played in only thirty-eight games in 1939. Toward the end of the season, he returned for a few games, throwing left-handed.

Reiser was back in Elmira to start the 1940 season, but the Dodgers realized he had nothing left to prove there. He was batting .378 when they promoted him to their top farm team, in Montreal, and from there he arrived in Brooklyn and appeared in his first game on July 23. After a 0-for-9 start, he batted .293 in fifty-eight games and was one of Durocher's most-used bench players.

Reiser worked his way into the starting lineup early in 1941, playing center field between veterans Joe Medwick and Dixie Walker. Pistol Pete started hot and stayed hot, torturing enemy pitchers at the plate and on the base paths, while making remarkable catches and throws in the outfield. His teammates and the Brooklyn fans knew they were seeing something rare and special.

Reiser finished the year with a .343 average to win the batting crown by a wide margin. He led the National League with 39 doubles, 17 triples, 117 runs scored, and a .558 slugging percentage, and finished second to teammate Dolph Camilli in voting for the Most Valuable Player Award.

The Dodgers and the Cardinals battled through a grueling summer atop the standings. The lead changed hands often, and neither team could open up more than a three-game bulge. In mid-September the Dodgers arrived in St. Louis for a three-game series nursing a one-game lead. Freddie Fitzsimmons won the opener in extra innings, the Cardinals won the second game, and then Brooklyn broke a scoreless tie in the eighth inning of the third game to win 1–0. The Dodgers maintained their advantage the rest of the way to win the pennant by two and a half games.

In the World Series, the Dodgers lost two of the first three games to the Yankees. In Game Four, Reiser's fifth-inning two-run homer over the Ebbets Field scoreboard off Atley Donald gave Brooklyn a 4–3 lead. But Mickey Owen's infamous "dropped third strike" with two out in the ninth allowed the Yankees to rally for a 7–4 win. A day later, the Yanks clinched the Series with a 3–1 victory.

On March 29, 1942, during spring training, Pete married his fiancée, Patricia Hurst, near Daytona Beach, Florida. That same day, Pete and Pat served as best man and maid of honor at the wedding of his roommate, Pee Wee Reese. The Reisers' first daughter, Sally, was born in St. Louis on March 20, 1943.

As good as Pete Reiser had been in 1941, he was even better in 1942. Few who saw him in the season's first half questioned whether he would repeat as batting champ. Some—including Reiser himself—thought he could follow up Ted Williams's .406 campaign in 1941 with a .400 season of his own. Reese was having a fine year, too. Sportswriters were calling Pete and Pee Wee the Gold Dust Twins.

On July 18, 1942, the Dodgers had an eight-game lead over the Cardinals when they went to

St. Louis for a four-game series. Reiser, batting .356, was riding an eleven-game hitting streak. In the eleventh inning of a 6–6 tie on July 19, Enos Slaughter belted a long drive off Johnny Allen. Reiser raced toward the center-field wall, narrowly avoiding the flagpole that rose from the playing field, and caught Slaughter's hit in full stride—and then hit the concrete wall an instant later. The ball fell from his glove, and although dazed, he threw the ball to the cutoff man, Reese. By the time Reese fired the ball home, Slaughter had circled the bases to win the game.

All attention turned to No. 27, who lay on the field motionless, facing the sky, his shoulder separated and blood trickling from his ears. When Durocher reached him, the manager started to cry. Pete was carried off on a stretcher and woke up the next morning in the hospital with a fractured skull and a brain injury. The Cardinals' team doctor examined him and recommended that he not return to the field that season. In the era before the effects of a concussion were fully understood, Reiser did what gamers do—he returned to the diamond as soon as he could walk. He was dizzy, had a hard time focusing, and felt weak, but there was no keeping him out of the lineup.

He would never be the same player again.

Reiser hit .244 from July 25, the day he returned, to the end of the season, even trying to switch-hit to minimize the pain in his shoulder. The Dodgers' lead evaporated down the stretch as St. Louis edged Brooklyn by two games. From the heights of July, Reiser ended up batting .310, but still led the league with twenty steals. Before the injury, teammate Billy Herman—who had played with Hall of Famers Chuck Klein and Hack Wilson—said Pete Reiser was the greatest player he had ever seen on a baseball field.

After the season, Reiser attempted to enlist in the navy, but he flunked his physical and was classified 4-F. In January 1943 he tried again, this time at an army recruiting office. He was about to be re-

jected when an officer recognized him and waved him through. Soon he was on his way to Fort Riley in Kansas.

If baseball was tough on Pete Reiser's body, military life was even tougher. One day, after a long march in below-zero weather, he started feeling woozy and was diagnosed with pneumonia. Doctors were ready to issue a medical discharge when the base commander realized he had the great Pete Reiser in the infirmary. He decided to keep him at Fort Riley so he could play for the camp team after he recuperated. The deal he made with Pete was that he could be excused from all duties, leave the base virtually whenever he liked, and have his own private room.

Over the next two years, Fort Riley put together quite a team. It included Joe Garagiola, Lonny Frey, Harry Walker, Al Brazle, Murry Dickson, Rex Barney, Ken Heintzelman, and Frank "Creepy" Crespi. One player who didn't make the club was an African American lieutenant who was told he had to play with the base's colored team. Of course, there was no colored team at Fort Riley, so he watched the players practice awhile and then turned and walked away. It was Reiser's first encounter with his future Brooklyn teammate, Jackie Robinson.

Even on an army team, Reiser was incapable of letting up. Once, he was chasing a fly ball and burrowed right through the thick hedge that formed the outfield wall—and down a ten-foot drainage ditch on the opposite side. He separated his shoulder and couldn't throw. So he simply switched to a right-handed glove and threw with his left arm, as he had in Elmira in 1939.

In 1945 Reiser was transferred to Camp Lee, in Virginia. When the war ended, he was almost sent to Japan as part of a team that would play exhibitions to entertain the troops. Luckily for him, a base doctor looked at his medical records and was appalled. Clearly, he never should have been allowed into the army in the first place. Pete was discharged early in 1946, in time to catch up with the Dodgers in spring training.

The Brooklyn brass noticed right away that their former star no longer had a Major League arm. Previously, there had been discussions within the organization that he might be better off in the infield, if only from a self-preservation standpoint. But now that was out of the question. Of course, in his first exhibition start Pete drilled three hits and drew three walks, so he wasn't about to lose his starting job in the outfield.

Pete's season ended early with a fractured fibula, suffered during a stolen base attempt against the Cubs. Prior to that he had reinjured his shoulder and limped through a series of minor pulls, sprains, and strains. The shoulder got so bad that he was moved to left field, and he often threw the ball underhand. In an August game with the Cardinals, he ran into the left-field wall chasing a Whitey Kurowski hit. While convalescing at home, he burned his hands lighting the oven for his wife. It just wasn't Pete's year. (It wasn't the Dodgers' year either—they wound up the season tied with the Cardinals, then lost two straight in a playoff for the pennant.)

Even so, Reiser could still run. He led the league in 1946 with thirty-four stolen bases—including seven steals of home. He batted .277 in 122 games and led the team with eleven home runs, three of which were inside-the-park. By the time he hurt his ankle, however, his swing had become hitched and choppy because of the aching shoulder. He was basically a slap hitter in the second half. He simply wasn't driving the ball with the same authority anymore.

The 1947 Dodgers had an entirely new look. Robinson was now the man who made the Dodgers go. This stroke of historic good fortune helped to counter a second straight injury-plagued campaign for Reiser, whose grim encounter with the center-field wall at Ebbets Field provided the lowlight for an otherwise brilliant Dodgers season.

Chasing a ball hit by Culley Rikard of the Pirates, Pete snagged it on the dead run an instant before slamming into the fence. He held onto the ball for the out, but he fractured his skull. The injury was so bad that he was given the last rites, and he lay in a hospital bed for five days hovering between life and death.

When Pete Reiser *was* in the lineup in 1947, he was a solid contributor. In 110 games, he batted .309 with some power and plenty of speed. He finished a distant second to Robinson in the National League stolen-base race, with fourteen. The Dodgers won with Pete and without him. At season's end their record was 94-60, five games better than the second-place Cardinals.

The ill effects of the head injury—plus a sore leg—were evident in the World Series against the Yankees. Reiser misplayed a couple of balls in the first two games—both losses at Yankee Stadium. He started Game Three but injured his ankle on a steal attempt. Manager Burt Shotton replaced him with Carl Furillo in the second inning, and Pete spent the remainder of the Series as a bench player.

Reiser saw action as a pinch hitter in the pivotal ninth inning of Game Four, when Bill Bevens tried to complete the first World Series no-hitter. With the Yankees leading 2–1, manager Bucky Harris had Bevens intentionally walk Pete with two outs and Al Gionfriddo on second. A free pass to put the winning run on base was hardly sound baseball strategy, but it had been a wacky game up to that point, with Bevens already having walked nine hitters.

Sensing an opportunity, Shotton sent Eddie Miksis in to run for Pete and sent Cookie Lavagetto in to hit for Eddie Stanky. Lavagetto took Bevens's second offering the other way and hit it against the screen in right field. By the time Tommy Henrich retrieved the ball and got it back to the infield, Miksis was on his way home with the winning run.

The Yankees and Dodgers split the next two

games. Reiser saw his last bit of playing time by drawing a walk in Game Five and then heading to the bench with Miksis running for him again. Furillo was now the team's center fielder. The Dodgers led Game Seven in Yankee Stadium, but Joe Page shut them down in a five-inning relief stint and the Yankees came back to win, 5–2.

Pete Reiser was never a regular player again. In 1948 Durocher returned to the Brooklyn dugout from his one-year suspension and saw that Pete was no longer capable of playing the outfield. Still recalling the young superstar from 1941 and 1942, Durocher believed that he could at least keep the potent Reiser bat in the lineup, so he played him at first base in spring training. Stanky was a holdout and Rickey planned to trade him, which would create an opening at second for Robinson. Pete was a candidate for the first-base job—until Leo saw him in action and realized that he needed to look elsewhere. Pistol Pete had gained a few pounds and was sluggish around the bag.

Reiser saw sporadic playing time in the outfield and spelled newcomer Billy Cox at third base for a few games. Mostly he was used as a pinch hitter and fill-in outfielder. He spent much of the 1948 season on the injured list and finished with a .236 average in sixty-four games. After the season, Pete asked Rickey to trade him. Rickey obliged, engineering a minor swap with the Boston Braves in December for journeyman outfielder Mike Mc-Cormick and infielder Nanny Fernandez.

Though still no more than a bench player, Reiser, now thirty, enjoyed a minor renaissance in Boston in 1949. He saw action in the outfield and at third and collected nineteen extra-base hits among his total of sixty. He batted .271 and stole three bases. Additionally, his second daughter, Shirley, was born in Boston on July 11 of that year.

Pete's 1950 campaign was a different story. His average sank to .205. The Braves released him after the season. Less than a week after leaving the Braves, Branch Rickey—now running the Pitts-

burgh Pirates—acquired Reiser for the third time. He proved to be a handy bench player for manager Billy Meyer, hitting .271 in seventy-four games. Rickey released him after the season but offered him a chance to manage the Pirates' farm club in New Orleans. Pete turned down the opportunity. He felt he had some more good baseball in him. He was signed by the Cleveland Indians in February 1952. Cleveland's manager, Al Lopez, had been a catcher with Pittsburgh when Reiser broke in.

Reiser functioned primarily as a pinch hitter in 1952, playing just ten games in the outfield. He batted a paltry .136 with three homers in the first half and played his final game as a Major Leaguer on July 5. The injury that ended his career was a separated shoulder, suffered while sliding in a game against the Yankees. Pete might have stayed with the Indians, but he was needed at home by his wife, Pat. Sally, the younger of their two daughters, had severe developmental problems, and he wanted to be closer to home while they decided their next move. When he told Lopez why he was saying good-bye to baseball, Lopez cried. Like everyone who had seen Pete Reiser in his prime, he was saddened that a good guy and great player had suffered such relentlessly horrible luck.

After baseball, Reiser owned a car dealership and worked as a carpenter. In 1955 Dodgers general manager Buzzy Bavasi offered him the manager's job at the Dodgers' Class D affiliate in Thomasville, Georgia. Pete enjoyed managing and coaching, and he did a good job with the youngsters that season. When the Dodgers finally won the World Series in the fall, he felt great pride. If he couldn't get a ring, he was delighted that Pee Wee could.

Over the next few years, Reiser was assigned to manage the Dodgers' top Minor League hitting prospects, including Tommy Davis and Frank Howard. In 1960 he accepted an invitation to join manager Walter Alston's staff in Los Angeles. When the team moved to Chavez Ravine in 1962

MARK STEWART

and adopted a small-ball strategy, Pete's coaching insights became invaluable to the team's success. He had already been working with shortstop Maury Wills on the finer points of base stealing, helping to transform Wills into the league leader in 1960 and 1961. With the stolen base now one of the team's primary weapons, Pete and Maury set out to make a little history.

They developed a set of unwritten rules—when to go, when not to go, and how to distinguish a legitimate stolen base from what Reiser called a "honeymoon steal." He also urged Wills to level with Alston when he felt that a pitcher's pickoff move was too hard to read. Alston would not bunt Wills to second unless he knew that he couldn't steal, so honesty was an important policy. The result was a 104-steal season, breaking Ty Cobb's record and earning Wills the Most Valuable Player Award. Wills later called Reiser his "mentor."

Reiser continued coaching for the Dodgers through the 1964 season. He got his long-awaited World Series ring in 1963, when Los Angeles swept the Yankees. In 1965 the Dodgers assigned him to manage the Spokane (Washington) Indians, their affiliate in the Pacific Coast League. Pete's stay in Spokane was cut short when he suffered a heart attack while hitting fungos that spring. He was forty-six at the time.

Reiser returned to the game in 1966 at the behest of Durocher, who was now managing the Chicago Cubs. As a fellow coach for Los Angeles in the early 1960s, Durocher had come to admire Reiser's rapport with young players. Pete especially liked working with Latino players. He felt they brought the same aggressiveness and joy to the game that he had so many years earlier. Pete even served as an interim manager for the Cubs' Texas League team in Dallas–Fort Worth that season.

Reiser stayed with the Cubs through 1969 before accepting an offer from another Dodgers coaching compatriot, Lefty Phillips, who was now managing the California Angels. In 1970 Pete worked with Sandy Alomar on his base stealing and Alex Johnson on his batting. Alomar topped thirty steals for the first time (and would do so again in 1971). Johnson won the batting title. How much credit Reiser could take for this transformation is pure conjecture. The taciturn Johnson must have driven Pete crazy, particularly with his attitude on defense, which was the polar opposite of Pete's. To Johnson, walls weren't for crashing into. They provided shade on hot days.

Reiser spent two years on Phillips's staff and left when the team fired the manager and hired Del Rice for the 1972 season. The welcome mat was out for Pete in Chicago as long as Durocher was there, and in 1972 Pete returned to coach for the Cubs. He stayed with them through the wild 1973 NL East race, when Chicago was part of a five-way logjam. During a brawl with the Giants that season, someone slugged Pete and he disappeared under the pile, unconscious.

Reiser did some scouting for the Cubs in the late 1970s, until he couldn't hold up to the travel anymore. After the 1981 season, he announced to Pat that he was retiring for good. Two days later, on October 25, the newswires carried the story of his death in Palm Springs, California, at sixty-two. The cause was listed as a respiratory illness (emphysema). Pete had been a heavy smoker since his teen years. Pat Reiser died in 2001.

There is no official count of Reiser's baseball injuries, but the best guess reads something like a dozen collisions with unpadded fences, five skull fractures (though he claimed only four), a chronically dislocated shoulder, two broken ankles, damaged knee cartilage, torn muscles in his left leg, and two beanings in the days before batting helmets. As a player he was carried off the field on a stretcher eleven times—six times conscious, five times not.

Most players must wait for decades to appreciate their legacy. In the case of Pete Reiser, he could look at two things he had helped to create—one

with pride and the other with irony. The Dodgers, a hapless collection of clowns and losers in the
years before he arrived in Brooklyn, now believed
they could win every year. Pete had helped to make
them believers with his phenomenal 1941 season.

Also, by the early 1950s most teams had either
installed warning tracks or at least planned to,
and some stadiums were also starting to pad their
walls. The first padded wall at Ebbets Field was
made of cork. Given how hard Reiser hit that wall,
it is doubtful anything other than modern foam
cushioning would have saved him.

Alas, in the heat of the moment, Pete Reiser just
never could pull up and play it off the wall. Every fly ball was his to catch, and catch them all he
would—or kill himself trying.

# Chapter 51. **Tommy Tatum**

*Dan Mullen*

| AGE | G | AB | R | H | 2B | 3B | HR | TB | RBI | BB | SO | BAV | OBP | SLG | SB | GDP | HBP |
|---|---|---|---|---|---|---|---|---|---|---|---|---|---|---|---|---|---|
| 27 | 4 | 6 | 0 | 0 | 0 | 0 | 0 | 0 | 0 | 0 | 1 | .000 | .000 | .000 | 0 | 0 | 0 |

Tommy Tatum played parts of fourteen seasons in professional baseball, but it was for a single moment—a product of timing more than anything else—that made Tommy Tatum part of American baseball history. On April 18, 1947, Tatum batted third for the Brooklyn Dodgers in an early season visit to the Polo Grounds for a meeting with the Giants. The third of just four games he would appear in during his final stint with the Dodgers, Tatum found himself batting between fellow rookie Jackie Robinson and star right fielder Dixie Walker. With the score tied at 1–1 in the third inning, Robinson belted a Dave Koslo pitch for his first Major League home run.

As Robinson crossed the plate, Tatum greeted him with outstretched arms. A photographer captured a moment representing racial integration in baseball that made its way to doorsteps throughout the city on the back page of the next day's *Daily News*. An encouraging welcome to modern baseball's first African American was about the biggest contribution Tatum gave Brooklyn in the 1947 season. He would have only one more at bat with the team—an unsuccessful trip as a pinch hitter on May 8 against the Cardinals—before he became the casualty of an unusually deep Brooklyn outfield.

Tommy was born V T Tatum to Emmit and Lessie Tatum in the north Texas town of Decatur on July 16, 1919. He picked up the name Tommy in his youth, since the "V T" did not stand for anything. Tatum honed his game on the sandlots of Oklahoma City under the tutelage of Oklahoma coaching legend Roy Deal. A talented and polished all-around player by his late teens, Tatum starred

Tommy Tatum played four games for the Dodgers before they sold him to Cincinnati on May 13.

on Deal's Gassers, a sandlot team sponsored by the Oklahoma Natural Gas Company. Known locally as the "Red Fox" for the color of his hair, Tatum caught the eye of Detroit scouts who offered him a contract with the Tigers in 1939, upon his graduation from Capitol Hill High School.

The right-handed-hitting Tatum, who was six feet tall and weighed 185 pounds, spent one season in the Detroit organization, batting .254 for the Class C Henderson (Texas) Tigers as a nineteen-year-old. Despite leading the team with nine triples, and being one of the team's youngest players, he failed to impress the parent club. After he was granted free agency, along with twenty other Detroit Minor Leaguers, on January 14, 1940, the Dodgers signed Tatum and assigned him to Nashville of the Southern Association.

Again one of his league's youngest players, Tatum was up for the challenge in 1940. Used mostly as a utility player, he batted .307 with 7 triples in 264 at bats for a Nashville team that finished the season with 101 wins and just 47 losses. During Minor League Baseball's centennial celebration in 2001, the 1940 Nashville Volunteers were recognized as the forty-seventh-best Minor League team ever.

In 1941 Tatum returned to Nashville, where he had an even better year in a full-time role, primarily as a center fielder. He batted .347 with forty extra-base hits in 105 games before being brought to Brooklyn. Tommy made his Major League debut on August 1 in Chicago, playing center field and batting sixth. In the first inning, he faced left-hander Vern Olsen, with Joe Medwick on third and Dolph Camilli on first. The Nashville recruit gave a good account of himself with an RBI double. It would be the high point of his Major League career. Tatum appeared in seven more games, batting .167 (2 for 12) with just the one run batted in overall.

On Christmas Eve 1941, Tatum married Alberta Marie Moody in Nashville. The couple would have two sons: Terry, born in 1944, and Dennis, born in 1947. Tatum went to training camp with the Dodgers in 1942 and had a good spring. However, the club thought he needed more seasoning and sent the twenty-two-year-old Tatum to the Montreal Royals of the International League.

Tommy spent the entire 1942 season with Montreal, teaming with Carl Furillo, Stan Rojek, and other top prospects on the fast track to Brooklyn. Tatum, who played almost exclusively at third base for the '42 Royals, struggled to a .226 average in 156 games.

By January 1943 Tatum was in the U.S. Army Signal Corps, eventually serving in the Pacific Theater of Operations. Like many professionals, Tatum played baseball during his time in the armed forces. While in Hawaii he played for the Wanderers, an entrant in the Hawaii Baseball League. Reportedly, Tatum had twenty-two hits in his first forty-three at bats, but he also suffered an injury to his throwing arm from which he would never fully recover.

After returning to baseball in 1946, Tatum would again be a part of one of baseball's all-time most successful Minor League teams, the one-hundred-win Montreal Royals. Tatum batted .319 and stole twenty-eight bases in 129 games that season, teaming with Marv Rackley and Jackie Robinson on a team loaded with speed. Tatum played first and second base for the first time in his professional career, doubtless a sign his arm was giving him trouble. The Royals won the International League pennant and then defeated the Louisville Colonels in the Junior World Series, in which Tatum contributed several key hits. After the season he was named to the International League All-Star team and came in third in the league's MVP voting.

While Robinson immediately offered a spark as Brooklyn's everyday first baseman, Rackley and Tatum struggled to find playing time in an overcrowded Dodgers outfield. Stuck behind imbedded stars Pete Reiser and Dixie Walker, along with second-year man Carl Furillo and a plethora of other options, including veteran Arky Vaughan, Tatum found his way into only four games in the first month of the season.

On May 13 Brooklyn sold the now twenty-seven-year-old Tatum to the Cincinnati Reds for

DAN MULLEN

an estimated $15,000. In Cincinnati, Tommy saw regular action for the only time in his big league career. With the Dodgers in town at the time of the transaction, Tatum wasted no time gaining revenge on his former employer.

In his first game in a Reds uniform, he drove in more runs than he had in his entire time with the Dodgers, courtesy of a two-run single in Cincinnati's 7–5 victory. The next day, Tatum had one of the best games of his career. He belted his only Major League home run, a first-inning solo shot off former teammate Joe Hatten, and stole a base in the Reds' 2–0 victory.

Tatum went on to establish himself as a capable member of the Reds' lineup, batting .273 with 5 doubles, 2 triples, and 16 RBIs in sixty-nine games. He stole 7 bases without being caught and put together a seven-game hitting streak in mid-August that included four multi-hit games. Tommy played his last Major League game on September 24, 1947. Over eighty-one games in the big leagues, he compiled a .258 batting average.

In 1948 Tatum was with the Reds' Class Double-A affiliate Tulsa Oilers, where he enjoyed one of the most productive campaigns of his professional career. When he was named to the Texas League All-Star squad in early July, he was leading the circuit in runs scored, hits, RBIs, batting average, and stolen bases. He paced the Oilers to a second-place finish and led the Texas League with a .333 average.

Tatum spent the 1949 season bouncing from system to system; he played briefly with the Reds' Class Triple-A squad in Syracuse before being shipped to the Red Sox organization, where he suited up for Class Double-A Birmingham and Class Triple-A Louisville. Tommy hit .285 overall, with 24 doubles, 1 triple, and 4 home runs.

In 1950 Tatum found a home back in the Dodgers' farm system at Fort Worth of the Texas League, serving as a player-coach with former teammate and player-manager Bobby Bragan. At age thirty, the "Red Fox" had become known as the "Old Red Fox," but his base-running ability still drew praise. *Baseball Digest* printed a *Fort Worth Star-Telegraph* feature on Tatum's "come-up slide" and delayed steal in an article pronouncing him the Texas League's best base runner. "If the center fielder has to come in to field the ball and makes a little lob throw to shortstop or second baseman thinking that the play is all over," Tatum said of his cunning maneuver, "you've got a real chance of going on in and scoring ahead of the relay. As you're nearing the bag, keep your eye on the coverer . . . [, and] when he gives the clue, you make the 'come-up slide' which will get you off running, in case the ball gets away." Playing some third base in addition to the outfield, Tatum's offensive production dropped off, as he batted just .223 in 115 games.

The next year, Tatum remained in the Texas League as the player-manager of the Oklahoma City Indians, where he remained for the better part of five years before being replaced midway through the 1955 season. He hit .297 in his first season at the helm, but his average dwindled in each succeeding year. The Indians' best regular-season finish during the Tatum era was 1954, when they finished third. In 1952, however, the Indians parlayed their fourth-place finish into a berth in the league finals before succumbing.

Tatum briefly considered joining old teammate and then Pirates manager Bobby Bragan for the 1956 season to help Pittsburgh's woeful running game, but he ultimately passed on the offer, deciding to remain in Oklahoma. After baseball, he worked as an insurance broker and was active as a Mason, achieving thirty-second-degree status.

Tatum remained in Oklahoma City until his death, at age seventy, on November 7, 1989. He is buried in the Resurrection Memorial Cemetery in Oklahoma City. He was survived by his wife, Marie; his sons, Terry and Dennis; and numerous grandchildren.

# Chapter 52. **Timeline, August 18–August 31**

*Lyle Spatz*

Monday, August 18, vs. St. Louis (2)—The Dodgers won both ends of a day-night doubleheader over the visiting Cardinals, defeating St. Louis's two left-handed aces, Howie Pollet and Harry Brecheen. The second game was a replay of the protested July 20 game that had been declared a tie. Brooklyn's 7–5 and 12–3 wins raised their first-place lead over the second-place Cardinals to six and a half games. Vic Lombardi went eight innings to win the first game, though he needed Hugh Casey to bail him out of a ninth-inning jam. Lombardi then pitched three scoreless innings in relief of Harry Taylor in the night game. Brooklyn had twenty-two hits in the two games, including two triples by their hottest hitter, Bruce Edwards, and a home run by Jackie Robinson. 72-45, First, 6½ games ahead.

Tuesday, August 19, vs. St. Louis—Catcher Del Rice drove in four runs with two doubles and a home run to lead the Cardinals to an 11–3 win. Al Brazle was the winner; Hank Behrman, the second of four Dodger pitchers, was the loser. Jackie Robinson had three hits, while Pete Reiser, Pee Wee Reese, and Dixie Walker each had two. 72-46, First, 5½ games ahead.

Wednesday, August 20, vs. St. Louis—The Cardinals' twelve-inning 3–2 win gave them a split in the four-game series. Ralph Branca had a one-hitter going into the ninth inning, but the Cards rallied for two runs to tie the score and then won it in the twelfth against Hugh Casey. 72-47, First, 4½ games ahead.

Thursday, August 21, vs. Cincinnati—Brooklyn bounced back from its disappointing loss to the Cardinals a day earlier with an 8–1 thrashing of the Reds. Clyde King went the distance, defeating Ewell Blackwell, the league's best pitcher. Arky Vaughan had three hits for the Dodgers, while the Reds helped Brooklyn's cause by committing four errors. 73-47, First, 5 games ahead.

Friday, August 22, vs. Cincinnati—Dixie Walker had four hits and scored the winning run as Brooklyn defeated the Reds, 6–5, in twelve innings. After the Reds tied the game in the ninth with two runs against Hugh Casey, Hank Behrman came on and retired eleven batters in a row. The Dodgers had fifteen hits, including six doubles and a Walker triple. 74-47, First, 6 games ahead.

Saturday, August 23, vs. Cincinnati—The Dodgers scored five first-inning runs against Johnny Vander Meer on their way to an 8–5 win. Vic Lombardi, Brooklyn's best pitcher for the past month, went the distance. Jackie Robinson had three singles and stole his twenty-third base of the season. Both Eddie Stanky and Pee Wee Reese had to leave the game with spike wounds. Reese's was the more serious, and the Dodgers accused Cincinnati's Bert Haas of spiking Reese deliberately. The Reds remained upset at an incident two days earlier when Pete Reiser barreled into Ewell Blackwell in a play at the plate. 75-47, First, 6 games ahead.

Sunday, August 24, vs. Pittsburgh—Ralph Branca, with relief help from Hugh Casey, downed the

Pirates, 3–1. Eddie Miksis and Stan Rojek filled in for Brooklyn's injured double-play combination of Eddie Stanky and Pee Wee Reese. Each had a run batted in, with Miksis's coming on a home run. 76-47, First, 6 games ahead.

Monday, August 25, vs. Pittsburgh—Brooklyn scored seven runs in the second inning, routing former teammate Kirby Higbe. Stan Rojek had the big blow of the inning, a bases-loaded triple. The Dodgers then withstood a late rally against Clyde King and Hugh Casey to win, 11–10. Pete Reiser homered for Brooklyn, as did Eddie Miksis, for the second straight day. 77-47, First, 6 games ahead.

Tuesday, August 26, vs. Pittsburgh—The Pirates pounded Hal Gregg, Rex Barney, and Dan Bankhead for twenty hits in a 16–3 drubbing of the Dodgers. Bankhead, whom the Dodgers had purchased from the Negro American League's Memphis Red Sox a few days earlier, became the first African American to pitch in the Major Leagues. Although he didn't pitch very well, Bankhead had the further distinction of hitting a home run in his first big league at bat. Eddie Miksis had his third home run in three days. 77-48, First, 6 games ahead.

Wednesday, August 27, vs. Chicago—Joe Hatten yielded a three-run homer to Bob Scheffing in the first inning and the Cubs added three more in the sixth to win 6–3. Johnny Schmitz went the route for Chicago. Cookie Lavagetto had a home run, and Eddie Miksis continued his hot hitting with three more hits. 77-49, First, 6 games ahead.

Thursday, August 28, vs. Chicago—Spider Jorgensen drove in four runs, three of them on a first-inning bases-loaded double, to lead Brooklyn to a 6–2 win. Vic Lombardi allowed two solo home runs to Bill Nicholson, but that's all the Cubs

could get off him and reliever Hank Behrman. Eddie Stanky returned to action, putting Eddie Miksis back on the bench. The Cardinals' loss to the Giants increased Brooklyn's first-place lead over St. Louis to seven games. 78-49, First, 7 games ahead.

Friday, August 29, vs. New York—Ralph Branca pitched a four-hitter to defeat the Giants 6–3. The Dodgers broke a 1–1 tie with five runs against Dave Koslo and reliever Joe Beggs in the sixth, the final run coming on Jackie Robinson's steal of home. 79-49, First, 7½ games ahead.

Saturday, August 30, vs. New York—A two-run pinch single by Cookie Lavagetto capped a three-run eighth-inning rally as the Dodgers downed the Giants, 3–1. Clyde King went eight innings to get the win. Hugh Casey pitched the ninth. Andy Hansen had held Brooklyn to two hits through seven innings but had to leave with an injured finger. Ken Trinkle took the loss. 80-49, First, 7½ games ahead.

Sunday, August 31, vs. New York—A home run by Willard Marshall gave the Giants 182 home runs for the season, tying the mark set by the 1936 Yankees. But Bruce Edwards was the hitting star with two singles, a home run, and five runs batted in. In all, the Dodgers had twelve hits to win, 10–4, behind Hank Behrman and Vic Lombardi. 81-49, First, 7½ games ahead.

# Chapter 53. **Eddie Miksis**

*Peter M. Gordon*

| AGE | G | AB | R | H | 2B | 3B | HR | TB | RBI | BB | SO | BAV | OBP | SLG | SB | GDP | HBP |
|-----|---|----|---|---|----|----|----|----|----|----|----|-----|-----|-----|----|-----|-----|
| 20 | 45 | 86 | 18 | 23 | 1 | 0 | 4 | 36 | 10 | 9 | 8 | .267 | .337 | .419 | 0 | 2 | 0 |

"Miksis will fix us," Branch Rickey promised Dodgers fans in 1948. Brooklyn management loved Eddie's slick fielding, speed, and attitude. The Dodgers thought so highly of the six-foot, 180-pound shortstop, they bought a controlling interest in his Minor League club in 1944 just to get him. Miksis became a valuable Major Leaguer, but it seemed that every time he was about to get a starting job, a future Hall of Famer beat him out of it.

Edward Thomas Miksis was born on September 11, 1926, in Burlington, New Jersey, a suburb of Philadelphia and Trenton. He was the third son of John C. and Pauline T. Miksis. Both had immigrated to the United States in 1909, John from Lithuania and Pauline from Poland. Eddie would eventually have five siblings—three brothers and two sisters.

Miksis starred in baseball and other sports at Trenton High School, and he signed with the Dodgers in 1944 at the age of seventeen. With the United States in the midst of World War II, and so many big leaguers in the armed forces, it was common for raw players to be rushed to the Majors. After seventy-two games with the hometown Trenton Packers of the Class B Interstate League, Miksis was called up by the Dodgers. Manager Leo Durocher was so enamored of Eddie's skills that he made him his starting shortstop.

Miksis made his Major League debut on June 17, 1944, against the Phillies at Shibe Park. Eddie came in as a pinch runner for Paul Waner and scored the first of four runs in a ninth-inning rally. He then played shortstop in the bottom of the

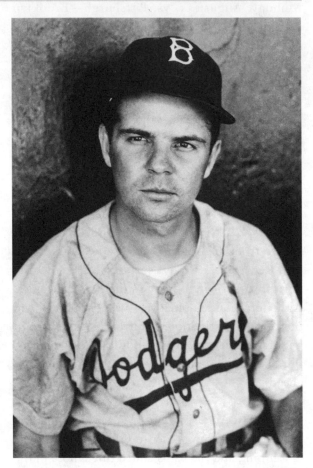

Eddie Miksis hit four home runs in 1947, with three coming on successive days.

ninth. Eddie had his first Major League hit in the July 4 doubleheader in Cincinnati. It came off veteran Harry Gumbert in the seventh inning of the second game. Miksis bunted down the first base line and collided with the Reds' six-foot-four first baseman Frank McCormick. Eddie was badly shaken, but he was safe. Miksis played in only ten games at shortstop during the rest of the season, and fifteen games at third base. He hit .220 in ninety-one at bats.

It was clear Miksis needed seasoning, but Uncle Sam had first call on his services. He spent 1945 and much of 1946 in the navy. Eddie managed to play some baseball while stationed at the Naval Training Center in Bainbridge, Maryland, where he was part of the center's team.

After his discharge Miksis joined the Dodgers on July 2, 1946, hitting .146 in twenty-three games over the remainder of the season. Despite his lack of experience, Miksis was in the Major Leagues to stay. During his fourteen years as a big leaguer, mostly with the Dodgers and the Chicago Cubs, Eddie served mainly in a utility role. In only four of those years did he appear in more than one hundred games.

Miksis spent the 1947 season as a pinch runner and occasional backup to second baseman Eddie Stanky. He hit a career-high .267, with four home runs in eighty-six at bats, and had just one error in eighty-four chances in the field. Eddie's first home run, a solo shot, came on May 28, 1947, at the Polo Grounds. The right-handed-hitting Miksis connected off Giants right-hander Hub Andrews. Eddie hit his other three home runs on successive days, August 24, 25, and 26, at Forbes Field while filling in for Stanky, who was out with an injury. Miksis played thirteen games at second and said, "I probably helped Stanky get cured much quicker by the way I was playing." The Dodgers' brass figured that Miksis's four home runs in eighty-six at bats projected to twenty or more over a full season. They were convinced he was their second baseman of the future.

In the 1947 World Series, Miksis figured in one of the most celebrated rallies in baseball history. In Game Four, with the Yankees leading the Series two games to one, and the game 2–1, Bill Bevens took a no-hitter into the bottom of the ninth inning at Ebbets Field. Bevens walked two but got two outs, and was one out away from the first World Series no-hitter. Pinch runner Al Gionfriddo was on second and Miksis, also pinch-running, was on first as Cookie Lavagetto came up to pinch-hit for Stanky.

Years later, Miksis said that with two outs, the Yankees' first baseman, George McQuinn, was playing off the bag. "That let me take a very big lead. I took off as soon as Lavagetto made contact and was past second before the ball came down." Lavagetto's fly hit the right-field wall, and by the time the Yankees got the ball to the plate, Miksis was sliding home with the winning run to "the biggest explosion of noise in the history of Brooklyn." The Series was tied, two games apiece. But the Yankees won in seven games. Miksis, playing mostly in a substitute role, had one hit in four at bats. Eddie received a full share, $4,081, of the World Series money allocated to the losing team.

Despite winning the 1947 pennant, the 1948 Dodgers were a team in transition. Leo Durocher, suspended for the '47 season, returned, even though Burt Shotton had led Brooklyn to a first-place finish. Some older stars were slowing down because of age or injuries, and Branch Rickey had promoted more young players from his farm system.

When Stanky was traded to the Boston Braves during the off-season, Miksis may have expected to start at second base in 1948. His expectations were likely fueled by the press. In February 1948, Roscoe McGowen of the *New York Times* positively gushed, reporting, "Miksis, a tall strong youngster with home run power, has played every infield position as well as the outfield and has shown aptitude, if not perfection, in all positions." Rickey often crowed about his "baby." Eddie was not destined to be a regular, however. Jackie Robinson, who had played first base in 1947, moved to second base, again relegating Miksis to a backup role.

Miksis played in more games in 1948 (86), and had more at bats (221) than in any other year with the Dodgers, but he hit just .213 with only two home runs. He had only about half as many at bats during the pennant-winning 1949 season, batting .221 and playing mostly third base. He batted .286 in seven at bats during the World Series, which ended in another Dodgers loss to the Yankees.

As the 1950s dawned, the Dodgers were content with having Miksis fill in whenever Jackie Robinson or Pee Wee Reese needed a day off. Eddie was still in his twenties, so he asked for a trade to a team that would play him regularly. On June 15, 1951, the Dodgers sent Miksis, outfielder Gene Hermanski, catcher Bruce Edwards, and pitcher Joe Hatten to the Chicago Cubs for outfielder Andy Pafko, catcher Rube Walker, pitcher Johnny Schmitz, and infielder Wayne Terwilliger. The Dodgers wanted to get the slugging Pafko to play left field as they sought to extend their six-game lead over the second-place Giants.

Though he had lobbied for a trade, Miksis could not understand the deal that was made. "I thought it was probably the dumbest trade that was ever made," he said years later. "They had a fourteen and a half [sic] game lead and traded half their ballclub and went out and lost it in the last game of the season."

While the Dodgers and Giants battled for the pennant, Miksis became Chicago's regular second baseman, replacing Terwilliger. He batted a career-high .265 for the last-place Cubs, and his eleven stolen bases were the tenth most in the league.

In 1952 Miksis injured his right knee on Opening Day. As he tried to play through it, his average fell to .232 in ninety-three games. Even though he was not as sharp physically, Miksis still showed plenty of baseball brains. On June 11 he saved a game for the Cubs just by noticing the way a player ran the bases. The Phillies had the bases loaded in the fourth inning of a 1–1 game. Richie Ashburn lined an apparent single to center, scoring Jack Mayo and Connie Ryan and sending Tommy Brown to third. After the play was over, Miksis called for the ball and stepped on second. The umpire ruled Brown out for not touching the base, making the apparent hit a force play and nullifying the two runs.

Miksis said, "I didn't see Brown miss second. But when he rounded the bag he glanced back with a guilty look. I was playing a hunch. Psychology, you know." While the Dodgers were winning the pennant, the Cubs finished the season in fifth place. It was a measure of Miksis's importance to the club that general manager Wid Mathews said, "Where would we be without Miksis?"

Eddie rested his knee over the winter and got the second-base job back in 1953. A Cubs press release touted him as "one of the keys in the Cubs' plan to rise to the first division this season." Miksis set career highs in games played (142), plate appearances (624), at bats (577), hits (145), stolen bases (13), and strikeouts (59). Overall, he hit .251 with 8 home runs (all solo shots) and 39 runs batted in.

Miksis split his time in the field between second base and shortstop. He managed a mediocre .954 fielding percentage at each position. Among the eight regular second basemen in the National League, Miksis played in the second fewest games but had the most errors and, by far, the worst fielding percentage. The Cubs finished the season in seventh place.

In 1954 the Cubs gave the keystone jobs to a pair of rookies, Gene Baker at second and future Hall of Famer Ernie Banks at short. Always the gentleman, Eddie lent Banks a glove for the first week of spring training even though it was clear that Banks and Baker would put Eddie back on the bench. Although he played in only thirty-eight games and hit .202, the 1954 season was not a complete loss for Miksis. On February 6, in Philadelphia, he married the former Rosemarie Valovage, whom he'd met at a Polish social function.

In 1955 the twenty-seven-year-old Miksis became the Cubs' regular center fielder. He hit .235,

PETER M. GORDON

but with career highs of 9 home runs and 41 RBIS. He led National League center fielders in fielding percentage (.989, tied with Duke Snider)—the only time he would lead the league in any category.

Manager Stan Hack wanted more offense from his outfield, so Miksis was relegated to a utility role in 1956. He played 114 games at second base, shortstop, third base, and the outfield. The Cubs traded him to the St. Louis Cardinals before the 1957 season. He played sporadically and was batting .211 when the Cardinals sold him to the Baltimore Orioles on September 19. Baltimore released him on May 15, 1958, after he had appeared in just three games. Two days later the Cincinnati Redlegs signed Miksis as a free agent. He got into sixty-nine games for the Reds and hit a mere .140.

Eddie retired after the 1958 season. He moved to Huntingdon Valley, Pennsylvania, and became a salesman for a trucking company. He had a brief resurgence of fame in 1964 when he received one vote for the Hall of Fame. That vote prompted one newspaper to call for a congressional investigation into Hall of Fame voting. Sportswriter Phil Pepe contacted Eddie after the vote to ask him his opinion. Eddie had no illusions about the quality of his baseball career, saying of the unknown voter, "I think the person who voted for me was a true baseball expert. He wasn't interested in statistics. . . . He must have had a few beers before he made out his ballot."

Miksis lived the rest of his life in Huntingdon Valley. He died on April 8, 2005, at the age of seventy-eight. He was survived by his wife, Rosemarie, daughters Jeanine, Rose Marie, and Christina, and sons Edward Jr. and Joseph. Eddie Miksis never was a star, but he always appreciated that he could play baseball for a living. When asked what his greatest thrill was as a ballplayer, he answered, "Getting paid every two weeks."

# Chapter 54. **Stan Rojek**

*Edward W. Veit*

| AGE | G | AB | R | H | 2B | 3B | HR | TB | RBI | BB | SO | BAV | OBP | SLG | SB | GDP | HBP |
|-----|---|----|---|---|----|----|----|----|----|----|----|-----|-----|-----|----|----|----|
| 28 | 32 | 80 | 7 | 21 | 0 | 1 | 0 | 23 | 7 | 7 | 3 | .263 | .322 | .288 | 1 | 3 | 0 |

Late in the afternoon of September 22, 1942, propelled by a Lew Riggs single, pinch runner Stan Rojek rounded third base and scored a ninth-inning run that sent the Brooklyn Dodgers and the New York Giants into extra innings. A five-foot-ten, 170-pound shortstop, appearing in his first Major League game, Rojek found himself in the midst of one of the all-time great pennant races. Three seasons would pass before Rojek got another taste of Major League baseball.

Stanley Andrew Rojek was born on April 21, 1919, in North Tonawanda, New York, located on the Niagara River between Buffalo and Niagara Falls. His parents were Andrzej (later anglicized to Andrew) and Apolonia Rojek. Andrew, a house carpenter, a building contractor, and lastly a dairy farmer, was born in Wylawa, Galicia (now part of Poland), and had immigrated in 1905. Stan was the second of three boys and had an older sister, Julia.

After graduating from North Tonawanda High School—where he also played basketball—Rojek played semipro baseball in western New York. He attracted the attention of Brooklyn scout Dick Fischer and subsequently signed with the Dodgers in 1939. Stan was assigned to the Class D PONY League in Olean, New York, just eighty-four miles south of his home. Rojek hit .320 in Olean, then worked his way through the Brooklyn farm system. He was with the Class C Dayton (Ohio) Wings in 1940 and the Class B Durham (North Carolina) Bulls in 1941. Promoted to Montreal, the Dodgers' top farm team, in 1942, he hit .283 and was named to the International League All-Star team. He was a late September call-up to Brooklyn, but he got into just the one contest.

Stan Rojek was a valuable fill-in for Pee Wee Reese and Eddie Stanky.

The next baseball game Stan Rojek played was a pick-up game in 1943 at the U.S. Army's Keesler Field in Mississippi. Rojek, like many Major and Minor Leaguers, had been called to serve in World War II. Stan was prime material for the war effort, twenty-four-years-old, single, and in great physical condition.

By July 1945 Rojek was in the Pacific, at Isley

Field on Saipan, and playing for the Seventy-Third Bomb Wing Bombers, whose roster included Major Leaguers Sid Hudson, Tex Hughson, and Mike McCormick. Rojek led the players on the Twentieth Air Force tour of the Pacific Islands with a .363 batting average and had three home runs. "The wars years may have retarded the chances of some young players, but I am one of the fortunate," he told *The Sporting News*. "I am leaving the Army a better player because I had the experience of playing with and against seasoned major league stars. I played more than 200 games in the Army, and I didn't do badly."[1]

Discharged in December 1945, Rojek looked forward to returning to Brooklyn and earning the starting assignment at shortstop. Unfortunately for him, he was a member of one of the few teams where he could not compete for that role. The Dodgers had future Hall of Famer Pee Wee Reese firmly entrenched at short. Rojek served as his backup, getting into just forty-five games, hitting .277 (13 for 47).

The right-handed-hitting Rojek made his first Major League hit an important one. On May 8, 1946, pinch-hitting for pitcher Les Webber, Rojek singled off Reds southpaw Clyde Shoun to drive in the first run of an eventual ninth-inning, four-run rally. He stayed in the game to play second base in the bottom of the ninth and had another single in the tenth. Brooklyn and St. Louis famously posted identical records in the '46 campaign, and Rojek appeared in the first Major League playoff game. Stan pinch-hit for Kirby Higbe in the top of the fifth inning and drew a free pass. It was his last contribution of the season.

Rojek played in only thirty-two games in 1947, but he started more games than the previous year, filling in for the injured Reese at short and for Eddie Stanky at second. He also played nine games at third. From August 24 through September 1, Rojek was the starting shortstop for all ten games. The Dodgers were 7-3 in that span and Stan bat-ted .314 with six RBIS and made no errors in the field. Overall, he committed only 2 errors in 116 chances (.983) and hit .263 (21 for 80). He showed very little power, though, managing only one extra-base hit.

Stan did not appear in the 1947 World Series but did receive a full share, $4,081, of Brooklyn's allotment. In November, with the winter meetings and the Minor League draft looming, Branch Rickey was looking for roster flexibility. One of his first moves was to shed Rojek and first baseman Ed Stevens. The pair were sold to the Pittsburgh Pirates for a reported $50,000.

Initially, Rojek's Pirates teammates called him "Reject" because he had been dumped by the Dodgers. He also was called "The Happy Rabbit" because of his projecting front teeth, his attitude, and his quickness in scurrying around shortstop.

The way was cleared for Rojek to secure the everyday shortstop role, when three weeks after his transfer to Pittsburgh, the Pirates' shortstop, Billy Cox, was traded to Brooklyn. With regular work, Rojek flourished. He played shortstop in all of the Pirates' 156 games as Pittsburgh rose from last place in 1947 to fourth place in 1948. He had 29 errors in 766 chances for a .962 fielding average, slightly better than the league average. He led all shortstops with 475 assists, and his 91 double plays were second only to Reese's 93.

New Pittsburgh manager Billy Meyer called Rojek "a pennant-winning shortstop."[2] The lead-off hitter for 153 games, Rojek, who hit .290 with 27 doubles, 5 triples, 4 homers, and 51 RBIS, led the league in plate appearances (713) and at bats (641). He finished third in the National League in hits (186) and stolen bases (24). Impressively, he finished tenth in the vote for the National League Most Valuable Player. It was by far his best season as a Major Leaguer.

Rojek probably got much satisfaction in 1948 from the Pirates' defeating the Dodgers thirteen times in twenty-two games. On July 25 he had eight hits in nine at bats as Pittsburgh and Brooklyn split a doubleheader; overall, he hit .323 against his old mates and slugged .444, each well above his season average. Yet in 1949 his offensive statistics declined sharply. On April 27, against the Cardinals, Rojek, who had two hits and scored two runs in the game, was twice hit by a pitch. The second one, in the ninth inning, was a beaning by pitcher Ken Johnson that sent Rojek to the hospital.

Rojek said after the beaning he was never the same. He said his teammates "noted that I was just a fraction of a second hesitant in my swing. It wasn't that I was afraid. It was just my reaction wasn't there anymore. And you need every fraction of a second you can get in trying to hit a round ball with a round bat, especially if that ball is thrown some ninety-plus miles per hour."[3] His batting average fell to .244 for the year, and in 1950 he batted .257 in seventy-six games while being platooned with twenty-three-year-old Danny O'Connell.

Branch Rickey, who had moved from the Dodgers to the Pirates and had cut Rojek's salary, had promised to give the fun-loving infielder a raise if he married. Stan wed Audrey Moeller, but Rickey failed to pay up, and in May 1951 he traded Stan to the Cardinals for outfielder Erv "Four Sack" Dusak and first baseman Rocky Nelson.

Rojek batted .274 in fifty-one games for the Cardinals, backing up Solly Hemus. In January 1952 the Cardinals sent him on waivers to the St. Louis Browns. With the Browns he played in only nine games, the last one on May 13—his last game in the Major Leagues—before being sent to Toledo of the American Association. After the season, the Browns sent Rojek to the Dodgers in a deal that brought Billy Hunter to St. Louis. It was not quite full circle for Rojek—he never played for the Dodgers, and he spent 1953 through 1955 as a part-time infielder for Dodgers' farm clubs in Mobile, Montreal, and St. Paul.

After the 1955 season, the thirty-six-year-old Rojek retired from baseball and joined his brothers, Anthony and Theodore, in the family's dairy business in North Tonawanda. In 1961 the three brothers opened Rojek's Park Manor Bowling Lanes. Hall of Fame manager Joe McCarthy, a resident of the area, rolled the first ball. Family members said the bowling alley idea more than likely came from Stan Musial, who visited Rojek often. "They were two Polish guys talking and laughing," commented Rojek's nephew, Jim Rojek. The brothers operated the bowling alley for twenty-five years.

In June 1977 North Tonawanda renamed Payne Field, a city ballpark, Stan Rojek Field. Rojek is also enshrined in the Brooklyn Dodgers Hall of Fame. Stan and his wife were divorced during the 1980s, according to nephew Jim, and she moved to Florida.

Rojek suffered a stroke in 1995. He died on July 9, 1997, in North Tonawanda. He was survived by a son, Bart, a daughter, Betty Valek of Southington, Connecticut, and five grandchildren. Rojek is buried in Mount Olivet Cemetery in Tonawanda.

# Chapter 55. **Dan Bankhead**

*Rory Costello*

| AGE | W | L | PCT. | ERA | G | GS | GF | CG | SHO | SV | IP | H | BB | SO | HBP | WP |
|-----|---|---|------|-----|---|----|----|----|-----|----|----|---|----|----|-----|-----|
| 27 | 0 | 0 | .000 | 7.20 | 4 | 0 | 1 | 0 | 0 | 1 | 10.0 | 15 | 8 | 6 | 1 | 1 |

Dan Bankhead was the first African American pitcher in the Major Leagues. However, Bankhead's big league career was brief and unsatisfying, and so even the black newspapers never covered him in depth. He also passed away before historians could record his personal memories. As with many black ballplayers of his day, Bankhead's career was multinational. He started in Puerto Rico, made detours to the Dominican Republic and Canada, and then knocked around Mexico well into his forties. A respectable hitter, Dan often played the field, while coaching and managing as well.

Bankhead's talent drew comparisons to Bob Feller, but control problems and an old injury hindered him. Coping with racial obstacles was another big issue—even fellow Negro Leaguers such as Buck O'Neil thought so.[1]

This "quiet, pleasant man" had other sides to his personality.[2] Sometimes he simply did not act in his own best interest—he lost two jobs under a cloud. His brothers Sam (age seventy) and Garnett (age sixty-three) both died by gunshot following quarrels. Dan also had a temper, which a weakness for women allegedly provoked. His family life was at times tumultuous. Yet as he battled illness and lived hand to mouth in his final years, he finally attained peace.

Daniel Robert Bankhead was born on May 3, 1920, in Empire, Alabama. His parents, Garnett Bankhead Sr. and Arie (Armstrong) Bankhead, had five boys and two girls who lived to adulthood. Four of Dan's brothers played in the Negro Leagues. (Another brother, James, born roughly two years before Dan, apparently died young.) Bankhead's given name appears simply as "Dan"

Dan Bankhead was the Major Leagues' first African American pitcher.

in his military records, in the Social Security system, and on his gravestone. Dan's son William F. Bankhead believes that his father shortened it at some point.

Empire is about thirty miles northwest of Alabama's largest city, Birmingham. It is in the coal country that fueled Birmingham's steel industry. Garnett (who played baseball himself) worked for a lumber company, on a loading facility, and as a coal miner. These were hard and dangerous jobs—

but in the Jim Crow South, they were a step up from sharecropping.

Dan attended public schools in Birmingham. In 1940 he joined the local Negro League team, the Black Barons. He tried out as a shortstop, but he threw so hard that the Barons made him a pitcher.[3] Negro League statistics are patchy, but records show that Dan pitched two scoreless innings in the East-West All-Star Game in 1941.

In the winter of 1941–42, Bankhead played ball overseas for the first time. The Puerto Rican Winter League was in its fourth season, and many great Negro Leaguers were there: Josh Gibson, Willard Brown, Willie Wells, and Dan's eldest brother, Sam.

Dan pitched again for Birmingham in 1942, but in April 1943 he enlisted in the Marine Corps. The Montford Point Marines of Camp Lejeune, North Carolina, were not trained as combat units.[4] Even so, the all-black troops became historically significant as an important step toward the integration of American military forces. Dan was part of the Montford Point baseball team, which remained in the States for the duration of the war and toured as a "morale raiser." In addition to pitching, he played shortstop and the outfield.[5]

At least once, Bankhead got leave to pitch for the Black Barons. On June 5, 1944, Dan struck out seventeen New York Black Yankees as he fired a three-hit shutout in the nightcap of a doubleheader. The game was played at Yankee Stadium before an estimated crowd of 12,000.[6]

Sergeant Bankhead left the service in June 1946 and joined the Memphis Red Sox of the Negro American League. Dan was again selected for the East-West All-Star Game—two were held that year—and he got the win for the West in the second.

Sometime in the mid-1940s, Bankhead married Linda Marquette, who was not African American. The slender, graceful woman had gone to school in Kansas City and also attended the Chicago Conservatory of Music. According to Dan's son William, they met while she was performing as a jazz singer. The couple had a daughter named Waillulliah, whose name was patterned after the famous actress Tallulah Bankhead, a member of a prominent Alabama family.

William Bankhead believed (with reason) that "Lulu" was actually a foster child. A 1947 article noted that she was nine years old and that her parents had been married for ten years.[7] If that were the case, Dan and Linda would have been about seventeen and fifteen, respectively, upon their wedding.

With Linda and Lulu in tow, Bankhead returned to Puerto Rico in the winter of 1946–47.[8] Pitching for the Caguas Criollos, he went 12-8 and led the league in strikeouts. He also stole twelve bases.

Back with Memphis in 1947, Dan played with his brother Fred. That year was the first time that any of the Bankhead men were teammates; Garnett Jr. also appeared briefly with the Red Sox in '47, possibly after Dan left. In July, Dan again got the win in the East-West All-Star Game.

Scouts George Sisler and Wid Matthews alerted Brooklyn's Branch Rickey. The Dodgers were short on pitching, so Rickey purchased Bankhead's rights from Memphis for a reported $15,000.[9]

Rickey biographer Lee Lowenfish said, "Rickey was happy that Dan Bankhead's color did not attract overwhelming press attention when the pitcher arrived in Brooklyn."[10] However, author Jules Tygiel differed, writing that "[Bankhead] received a terrific workout from photographers and newshounds."[11]

Rickey wanted to test his new pitcher in the Minors first, but the Dodgers needed him more. The twenty-seven-year-old rookie's debut came in relief against Pittsburgh on August 26. Black fans made up roughly a third of that day's Ebbets Field crowd of 24,069. A very nervous Bankhead drilled Wally Westlake with his first pitch and was hit hard. However, he also homered in his first Major League at bat.

Bankhead pitched just ten more innings in three more games over the rest of the season. He remained on the Dodgers' roster for the World Series, appearing as a pinch runner in Game Six.

In spring 1948 the Dodgers trained in the Dominican Republic. News stories from what was then Ciudad Trujillo stated that Dan "was converted into a gardener [outfielder] because of his batting power and speed afoot."[12] The experiment was abandoned, though. Returning to the mound, Bankhead went 20-6 with a 2.35 ERA for the Nashua Dodgers of the Class B New England League. In August he was promoted to the Class Triple-A St. Paul Saints of the American Association, where he won all four of his decisions.

After another winter in Caguas, Bankhead was assigned to Brooklyn's other Class Triple-A team, the International League's Montreal Royals, in 1949. He again went 20-6, but he also issued 170 walks.

In the winter of 1949–50, after barnstorming in the Southwest with a group of black players led by Luke Easter, Bankhead was back in Puerto Rico. He led the league in strikeouts again and also hit seven home runs. Before the 1950 season, Bankhead had been mentioned in several trade rumors, but he stayed with Brooklyn and got all nine of his Major League wins. His first came in relief of Don Newcombe at the Polo Grounds on April 28.

Dan took his first four decisions, and just when he looked to be settling in as an important member of the rotation, his recurring shoulder problems returned. The root cause was apparently a dislocation suffered at the age of seventeen.[13] Dan's last start that year came on July 31, but he continued to work frequently out of the bullpen. He finished the year with a record of 9-4, starting twelve times in forty-one appearances. Control was a problem, as he walked eighty-eight in 129⅓ innings.

The Bankheads were in the Dominican Republic in the winter of 1950–51, where in March they welcomed son William. Dan's shoulder problems worsened in 1951. He pitched just fourteen innings in seven games for the Dodgers and was mostly ineffective. In late July, Brooklyn sold Bankhead's contract to Montreal; he never made it back to the Majors.

Perhaps his most lasting big league moment came during a clubhouse debate, when he told Jackie Robinson, "Not only are you wrong, Robinson—you are loud wrong."[14]

It took Dan more than a month to pick up his first win in the International League, and he finished with a 2-6 record with a 3.91 ERA. Arm trouble limited him to only thirteen innings in five games for Montreal in 1952, and he was released in July.[15] Bankhead went back to the Dominican Republic as a player-manager, but he did not last long. After a wild on-field brawl, Dan was fined and jailed. In late August he was fired after quarrels with the club president, Dominican dictator Rafael Trujillo's brother-in-law.[16]

In 1953 Bankhead played for Drummondville in the Canadian Provincial League, mainly in the field. Quite a few black ballplayers were in this league, plus some former big leaguers. Late that July, Bankhead went to Mexico, where he would spend nearly all of his remaining fourteen years in the game. Dan batted and pitched year-round, though there was a gap in the summer of 1958. William Bankhead remembers seeing his father arrested in Brooklyn after a stormy domestic dispute. To the best of his knowledge, though, Dan and Linda (who died in 2007) never got divorced. Throughout the years in Mexico, William said, "he used to come home and make pit stops."[17]

Dan played and managed in some obscure Mexican circuits in 1961–62. He must have inspired a following—one hundred fans traveled five hundred miles in August 1962 to cheer for him on Dan Bankhead Day in Puebla. The veteran pitched a complete game and won, 13–1.[18]

Bankhead was the manager of Martínez de la Torre in the Veracruz League at the start of the 1962 winter season, but he was fired in November with only a cryptic report that it was done "for the good of the club."[19] After ten seasons away, he resurfaced in Puerto Rico as a player-coach with Caguas, also briefly serving as interim manager. William Bankhead recalled that Dan left the club after another domestic dispute with Linda, but he soon joined Ponce.

Bankhead managed extensively in Mexico in the mid-1960s. In 1966, at age forty-six, he enjoyed his last hurrah as a player with Reynosa. But after managing Aguascalientes in 1967, his time in baseball ended. Like many men in this position, he did not have another good career option—the game was his life. Cornelius "Doc" Settles, whose mother and two aunts grew up with Dan in Alabama, described what happened.

"From what I understand," said Settles in 2008, "everything started to implode for Dan in Mexico." William Bankhead said, "He was pitching more than balls, you know what I mean? Too many kids, too many intimacies. There are several kids down in Mexico that I know of. And you can't live in a foreign country without money."

"The nearest oasis was Houston," Settles continued. "Dan was facing inner turmoil when he first came to Houston. He was trying to get back on his feet. But he stepped in right when I needed somebody in my life. He was so humble, and he had a down-home sensibility that grounded him. I was just a teenager, and he was always willing to share a few moments with me and my brothers tossing baseballs and playing games. I will never forget Dan Bankhead burning up my hand while trying to catch one of his pitches. Even in his final days Dan could still toss a mean fastball."

Bankhead spent his final years working for a small service company delivering food goods and supplies to small businesses and restaurants across Houston. At some point in the 1970s, he was di-

agnosed with lung cancer and was in and out of the Veterans Administration hospital in Houston. "You could see him erode," Settles said. "He'd have his ups and downs, but he knew. He just got more and more humble. He was resolved to make peace. Dan's final days living in Houston were filled with reflection, days of happiness." Eventually, he succumbed on May 2, 1976, a day short of his fifty-sixth birthday.[20]

Thanks to the VA, the old Marine was buried under a modest bronze marker in Houston National Cemetery. "I don't remember if any of his old teammates came to the funeral," Settles said. "It was a small and quiet event. I don't think he was in touch with them. It was in the past and he didn't dwell on it."

Settles has fond memories of Bankhead. "He had a personality you wanted to be around. He left you with positive things. I was able to enjoy his laughter and his jokes and his smiles. I just wish we knew more about what he went through as an African American baseball trailblazer."

# Chapter 56. Timeline, September 1–September 19

*Lyle Spatz*

Monday, September 1, vs. Philadelphia (2)—As was the case on July 4, the Labor Day "holiday doubleheader" was a morning-afternoon affair with separate admissions. In the morning game, Joe Hatten shut out the Phillies, 5–0, and in the afternoon contest, Oscar Judd shut out the Dodgers by the same score. Ralph Branca started the afternoon game on just two days' rest and suffered his tenth loss. Hatten, the complete-game winner in the morning, pitched two-thirds of an inning in relief and Phil Haugstad made his Major League debut. 82-50, First, 6½ games ahead.

Tuesday, September 2—Not scheduled. 82-50, First, 6½ games ahead.

Wednesday, September 3—Not scheduled. 82-50, First, 6 games ahead.

Thursday, September 4, at New York—A crowd of just under 50,000 saw Vic Lombardi shut out the Giants, 2–0. Lombardi raised his career record against New York to 10-1. Pete Reiser had three hits, and Pee Wee Reese celebrated his return to the lineup with a seventh-inning home run. 83-50, First, 6½ games ahead.

Friday, September 5, at New York—The Dodgers' magic number was reduced to sixteen following their 7–6 win. Brooklyn scored two runs in both the eighth and ninth innings to take a 7–4 lead and then held on as the Giants scored two in the home ninth. Phil Haugstad, the third of four Brooklyn pitchers, got his first Major League win. The loss went to the Giants' sensational rookie Larry Jan-sen, ending his ten-game winning streak. Dixie Walker and Bruce Edwards each had three hits, with Walker garnering two runs batted in and Edwards three. 84-50, First, 7 games ahead.

Saturday, September 6, at New York—Ralph Branca went all the way, but failed in his second attempt to win his twentieth game, as the Dodgers lost to Ray Poat, 3–2. Spider Jorgensen accounted for three of Brooklyn's six hits. 84-51, First, 6 games ahead.

Sunday, September 7, at New York—The Dodgers got home runs from Dixie Walker, Cookie Lavagetto, and Gene Hermanski but lost to the Giants, 7–6. The Giants, now the all-time team home run champions, also had three, including Johnny Mize's forty-sixth. Lavagetto played first base in place of Jackie Robinson, whose sore back kept him out of the lineup for the first time this season. The Dodgers used nineteen players, including five pitchers. Clyde King took the loss. 84-52, First, 5½ games ahead.

Monday, September 8—Not scheduled. 84-52, First, 5½ games ahead.

Tuesday, September 9, at Chicago—Rookie Cliff Aberson's eighth-inning grand slam off starter and loser Vic Lombardi led the Cubs to a 4–3 victory as the Dodgers opened their final western swing. Aberson was pinch-hitting for Johnny Schmitz, who earned the win. Pee Wee Reese had three hits for Brooklyn, but his error on a potential double play in the eighth inning allowed the Cubs to stay alive. 84-53, First, 4½ games ahead.

Wednesday, September 10, at Chicago—Joe Hatten, with late-inning help from Hugh Casey, downed the Cubs 5–1. The game was tied 1–1 after six innings, but doubles by Dixie Walker and Spider Jorgensen and a home run by Eddie Stanky won it for the Dodgers. Jackie Robinson batted cleanup for the first time this season and had two hits. 85-53, First, 4½ games ahead.

Thursday, September 11, at St. Louis—The Dodgers defeated the Cardinals 4–3 in the opener of the final series between the two teams. The win raised Brooklyn's lead to five and a half games. The game was packed with tension, and at one point in the third inning, home-plate umpire Beans Reardon had to step between St. Louis catcher Joe Garagiola and Brooklyn batter Jackie Robinson. Robinson had harsh words for Garagiola, who he thought had deliberately stepped on his foot in a play at first base the previous inning. Robinson later had a two-run homer, but it was pinch hitter Cookie Lavagetto's single in the eighth inning that drove in the game-winning run. Ralph Branca, aided by a solid relief effort by Hank Behrman, won his twentieth game of the season. Branca became Brooklyn's first twenty-game winner since Whit Wyatt and Kirby Higbe in 1941. 86-53, First, 5½ games ahead.

Friday, September 12, at St. Louis—The Cardinals closed to within four and a half games again with an exciting, seesaw 8–7 victory. A pinch-hit two-run homer off Howie Pollet by recently recalled rookie Don Lund sparked a four-run rally in the ninth that put the Dodgers ahead 7–6. But St. Louis came right back in its half of the inning when Enos Slaughter slugged a two-run double off Ralph Branca to drive in the tying and winning runs. Branca, who had notched his twentieth

win the day before, was brought in by Burt Shotton expressly to pitch to Slaughter. Hank Behrman, who allowed the two runners to reach, was the loser. Jackie Robinson, back batting second, had two hits; Dixie Walker, batting cleanup, had three. Stan Musial had a bases-loaded triple for the Cardinals. *The Sporting News* named Jackie Robinson the Rookie of the Year for 1947. 86-54, First, 4½ games ahead.

Saturday, September 13, at St. Louis—The Cardinals rallied for three runs in the last of the ninth inning, but came up a run short. Brooklyn's 8–7 win allowed the Dodgers to leave St. Louis with a 5½-game lead. Three hits each by Pee Wee Reese, Jackie Robinson, Gene Hermanski, and Dixie Walker led the Dodgers' nineteen-hit attack. Vic Lombardi allowed twelve hits but was the winner. Hal Gregg and Hank Behrman also pitched for Brooklyn. 87-54, First, 5½ games ahead.

Sunday, September 14, at Cincinnati (2)—The Dodgers defeated the Reds, 13–2 and 6–3, to move seven games ahead of St. Louis and reduce their magic number to seven. Joe Hatten was the winner in both games, going all the way in the opener and pitching the final five and two-thirds innings in the nightcap. Brooklyn had twenty-nine hits in the two games, including five by Jackie Robinson and four by Dixie Walker. Pee Wee Reese led the attack in the first game with four runs batted in. 89-54, First, 7 games ahead.

Monday, September 15—Not scheduled. 89-54, First, 7½ games ahead.

Tuesday, September 16, at Cincinnati—Twenty-one-year-old Ralph Branca won his twenty-first game of the season, topping the Reds 7–3. Pete Reiser and Gene Hermanski homered for the Dodgers and Bruce Edwards had three runs batted in. Brooklyn's eleventh consecutive win against

Cincinnati, combined with the Cardinals' loss to the Giants, raised the Dodgers' lead to eight and a half games and reduced their magic number to four. 90-54, First, 8½ games ahead.

Wednesday, September 17, at Pittsburgh—Brooklyn's magic number was reduced to two after Hal Gregg defeated the Pirates, 4–2, while the Cardinals were losing to Boston. Jackie Robinson and Don Lund each had two hits and a home run. 91-54, First, 9½ games ahead.

Thursday, September 18, at Pittsburgh—Home runs by Carl Furillo, Bruce Edwards, and Jackie Robinson helped stake the Dodgers to a 7–4 lead. But the Pirates rallied for three in the eighth and got a home run from Wally Westlake off Clyde King in the ninth to win, 8–7. Ralph Kiner also homered for Pittsburgh, his fiftieth of the season. It came off starter Jack Banta, who was making his Major League debut. Johnny Van Cuyk also made his Major League debut, pitching an inning and one-third of scoreless relief. Despite the loss, the Dodgers were assured of at least a tie for the pennant after the Cardinals lost to the Braves. 91-55, First, 9½ games ahead.

Friday, September 19—Not scheduled. 91-55, First, 9 games ahead.

# Chapter 57. **Phil Haugstad**

*Bob Buege*

| AGE | W | L | PCT. | ERA | G | GS | GF | CG | SHO | SV | IP | H | BB | SO | HBP | WP |
|-----|---|---|------|-----|---|----|----|----|-----|----|-----|----|----|----|-----|----|
| 23 | 1 | 0 | 1.000 | 2.84 | 6 | 1 | 1 | 0 | 0 | 0 | 12.2 | 14 | 4 | 4 | 0 | 0 |

Every red-blooded American boy growing up during the Great Depression dreamed of playing in the World Series, preferably in Yankee Stadium. Philip Donald Haugstad came close twice, missing by one day in 1947 and by one pitch to Bobby Thomson in 1951.

Phil entered the world on February 23, 1924, in Black River Falls, Wisconsin. He was the second of four sons of Paul and Jennie Haugstad, who operated a modest dairy farm in rural Jackson County, in the west-central part of the state.

The Haugstads were churchgoing Lutherans. Jennie, whose maiden name was Peasley, was English on her father's side, German on her mother's. Paul's parents had emigrated, separately, from Norway in 1882. Phil was five years old when the stock market crashed in October 1929. The crash hit small farmers extremely hard. The four sons—in descending order, Robert, Philip, Harold, and Arthur—pitched in with the farm chores. Their mother taught in one-room schoolhouses in the area. Phil's father hired out as a carpenter and joined the Civilian Conservation Corps. Phil picked beans and cucumbers for the Humbird Canning Factory.

The Haugstad brothers attended Pleasant View School, a one-room frame structure with a big wood stove in the basement and two outdoor toilets in back. The brothers walked to school, three miles each way, sometimes in temperatures as cold as forty degrees below zero.

Phil attended Alma Center High School, where he was elected president of the Future Farmers of America and appeared in a couple of one-act plays. His main interest, however, was sports. He

Phil Haugstad's victory against the Giants on September 5 was his only big league win.

excelled in basketball and baseball, winning nearly every game he pitched and hurling three no-hitters.

In his prime, Phil carried 165 pounds on a wiry six-foot-three frame, but brother Bob said, "My God, he could pick up one side of the back end of a pickup truck. He was mighty strong, all muscle." Art said, "Some pitchers have a soft ball when it hits your mitt. Phil's was like a bowling ball hitting your mitt, just drove you back. They compared him with Bob Feller at times."

On May 12, 1942, Haugstad graduated from Alma Center High School. In early 1943, with war raging in Europe and in the Pacific, he drove to the recruiting office in Eau Claire and enlisted in the Army Air Corps.

Phil was assigned to the aircraft mechanics school at Keesler Army Airfield in Biloxi, Mississippi. The facility provided four weeks of basic training for new recruits and focused on special training in maintenance of the B-24 bomber. After basic, Phil was sent to Peterson Field in Colorado Springs, Colorado.

Although not fond of the regimentation of military life, Phil enjoyed skiing in the mountains of Colorado. He also found access to his other favorite sport. "The military had all these baseball teams," brother Bob noted. "They had a couple of B-17s that would fly these guys to different tournaments, other service teams and what-not. A lot of them were big-league players or very famous people playing."[1]

On Valentine's Day 1946, Sergeant Phil Haugstad was honorably discharged at Camp McCoy, about twenty-five miles south of his home. He promptly signed a Minor League contract with the Brooklyn Dodgers organization. The scout who signed him was Ernie Rudolph, a native of Black River Falls.

A month after returning to civilian life, Haugstad was at the Dodgers' spring training camp in Daytona Beach, Florida. He had begun camp with the St. Paul Saints, Brooklyn's Class Triple-A team in the American Association, but later was assigned to the Class C Grand Forks (North Dakota) Chiefs of the Northern League.

During the 1946 season Phil was the workhorse of the Grand Forks pitching staff, leading his club in nearly every category. He won fifteen games for a sixth-place team and created a good-enough impression that in 1947 he made the big jump back to St. Paul.

By the end of June, Haugstad had recorded nine victories with only one loss. He was selected to the league's All-Star team, an honor somewhat diminished by the fact that no All-Star game was played. The scheduled three-day break was used instead to make up postponed games, and each All-Star was simply given a wristwatch.

In late August, Phil was 15-6 when Brooklyn general manager Branch Rickey decided to add him to the Dodgers' roster for the September pennant run. Rickey let him pitch one more game, on August 29. Phil hurled a complete game and beat the Kansas City Blues, but as a result he did not report to the Dodgers until September 1. He was one day too late for World Series eligibility.

On September 1, Phil rode the train from the Twin Cities to New York City, and then caught a taxi to Ebbets Field. The Dodgers were playing a morning-afternoon Labor Day doubleheader against the last-place Phillies.

Haugstad arrived at the park just twenty minutes before the afternoon game and fought his way through the mob outside, only to be refused entrance by the gate attendant. Two hours later, having gained admittance, he was pitching the final two innings of the first Major League ballgame he had ever seen. "He always remembered walking in there and seeing all the people and how big the park was," his son, Hal, said. "He was just amazed."

That day was Phil's biggest thrill in baseball. "I was too tired to be scared," he told a reporter. "I just threw what Bruce Edwards called for. But in between, I sorta pinched myself to make sure I was in the big time."[2]

Four days later, Phil worked two scoreless innings in relief against the Giants in the Polo Grounds and earned his first victory—destined to be his only victory—in the Major Leagues.

The Dodgers won the pennant, but they lost the World Series to the Yankees in seven games. Haugstad was permitted only to sit and watch. His teammates did vote him a partial share of the Series money, though.

Phil started the 1948 season with the Dodgers, but on May 1, having pitched just one inning, he was optioned back to St. Paul. He brought with him his fiancée, Esther Laffe from Humbird, Wisconsin. On Tuesday, May 11, Phil and Esther were married in a candlelit ceremony in Bethlehem Lutheran Church in St. Paul. Five hours after the wedding, Phil pitched a four-hitter to beat the Kansas City Blues, 5–1. Phil and Esther would have three children: Judy, the eldest, and Hal, the youngest, were born in Black River Falls; Nancy, the middle child, was born in Brooklyn.

After the season Phil and his bride traveled to Havana, Cuba, for a belated four-month honeymoon, albeit a working honeymoon. Phil pitched in the Cuban Winter League for the Marianao Tigers.

At spring training in 1949, Phil learned to change his pitching motion and said confidently, "I think I've got the control problem about licked."[3] He smoothed out his violent delivery and maintained better balance. Assigned again to St. Paul, he enjoyed his best season, winning twenty-two games and leading the Saints to their first regular-season title in eleven years. However, he still averaged more than five and a half walks per nine innings.

St. Paul won sixteen of its first seventeen games in 1949, and then struggled to hold on. In the final game of the regular season, in Milwaukee, the Saints faced a do-or-die situation—win and they capture the pennant, lose and they finish second. The Saints won, as Haugstad allowed just one run before tiring and needing relief in the final inning. His tiring was hardly surprising. He had pitched seven tough innings the night before in a tense one-run Saints victory.

The American Association playoffs were not a success for the Saints. Despite leading three games to one, they lost the series to the Milwaukee Brew-

ers. For this Phil received nine days' additional pay, at $29.94 per diem, a total of $269.46.

Immediately after the final game, Phil traveled to St. Louis to join the Dodgers, who were fighting the Cardinals for the National League flag. Phil watched the last nine games of the season in a Dodgers uniform but never got into a game. The Dodgers overtook the Cards and won the pennant, but as in 1947, Phil was not eligible for the World Series roster.

In 1950 Phil was again pitching in St. Paul, not Brooklyn, who still considered him too wild for the big leagues. He won sixteen games and lost eleven, with a 3.89 ERA, but walked 125 batters in 229 innings.

Haugstad was back with the Dodgers in 1951 for his only full season in the Majors. That season ended when Thomson homered off Ralph Branca to win the pennant for the Giants. The Dodgers had several other pitchers whom manager Charlie Dressen could have called upon, all better rested than Branca. One of them was Phil Haugstad, whom they had used in short relief all year.

According to Phil's daughter Judy, whenever that game was discussed in her father's presence, "Dad said with a smile, 'I'm glad I was not the pitcher of that home-run ball.'"

At the start of September of 1951, the Dodgers visited the Polo Grounds sporting a comfortable seven-game lead over the Giants. They left two days later having been crushed twice, 8–1 and 11–2. Slap-hitter Don Mueller blasted a record-tying five home runs in the two games, one off Haugstad in each game. Haugstad responded a few moments later by hitting Bobby Thomson with a fastball and then brushing back Willie Mays.

The following February the *New York Times* reported that Haugstad had told Dressen, "I can win here. I've been seeing other pitchers come up that I used to beat in the minors." Roy Campanella agreed with him, saying, "I can't understand why Haugstad isn't a winning pitcher because there's hardly anybody in the league with a more wicked fastball."[4]

Phil could no longer be optioned to the Minors. The Dodgers had to keep him on their roster, trade him, or put him on waivers. They chose the latter course, and on May 25, 1952, without having appeared in a game for the Dodgers, Phil was sold to the Cincinnati Reds. He appeared in nine games with Cincinnati, the final one on July 1. The last pitch he threw in the big leagues was slammed for a three-run homer by Enos Slaughter. The next day Haugstad was placed on waivers, claimed by the St. Louis Browns, and assigned to the Toronto Maple Leafs, the Browns' International League farm club.

The final three seasons of Phil's sojourn in Organized Baseball were characterized by arm troubles and address changes—Toronto, San Antonio, and Charleston, West Virginia.

At Charleston, Phil suffered with arm trouble and was twice removed from the roster. In June the team released him for good. He was thirty-one years old. Despite an ailing right arm, he was not ready to accept his severance from baseball. He signed with the Huron Elks of the Basin League, a South Dakota semipro circuit. He won his first start but was cut loose after two weeks.

The final stop was the Williston Oilers in the ManDak (Manitoba-Dakota) League. It was an independent league in North Dakota and Canada, with a reputation as a last refuge for former Negro Leaguers and ex–big league and Minor League ballplayers. But Haugstad's arm was dead, and Williston released him, ending his baseball career.

"He was offered a job with the Brooklyn Dodgers after he quit," Phil's daughter Judy related, "but he wanted to do his own thing." He started a logging business. At first he employed two or three other men. Later the number rose to ten or twelve. Along the way Phil built his own tree harvester. Brother Bob said, "He was very talented in so many things. Welding and everything else.

He could have made lots of money, but he was too busy inventing stuff."

Phil's family said they believe that fixing and inventing cost him his health. "Dad didn't smoke," Judy explained, "but he was always out there in the garage without any ventilation when he was welding on his trucks and trailers. He ended up with emphysema and bad lungs. He was on oxygen his last few years of life. That welding did him in."

Before losing his health, Phil liked hunting and fishing and camping with his family. He also liked bowling and golfing with friends. What Phil especially enjoyed, though, was water-skiing, which he continued to do well into his fifties.

Haugstad had always been a quiet person, but as his health deteriorated, he became increasingly so. He spent more time in bed as his legs began to retain fluid. In 1994 Phil received an invitation to attend a Brooklyn Dodgers reunion in New York City. He had not seen most of his old teammates for four decades or more. His health made the journey problematic, but in the end his family decided he should go.

When he returned home, Phil said with eloquent simplicity, "Just seeing them again made it all worthwhile for me." On October 21, 1998, Phil Haugstad died in Black River Memorial Hospital. He is buried in Riverside Cemetery in Black River Falls.

# Chapter 58. **Don Lund**

*Jerry Nechal*

| AGE | G | AB | R | H | 2B | 3B | HR | TB | RBI | BB | SO | BAV | OBP | SLG | SB | GDP | HBP |
|-----|---|----|----|----|----|----|----|----|-----|----|----|-----|-----|-----|----|-----|-----|
| 24 | 11 | 20 | 5 | 6 | 2 | 0 | 2 | 14 | 5 | 3 | 7 | .300 | .391 | .700 | 0 | 0 | 0 |

For most former big leaguers, their time as an active player is the zenith of their athletic careers. This was not the case for Don Lund, who as a career .240-hitter appeared in only 241 games with the Brooklyn Dodgers, St. Louis Browns, and Detroit Tigers over parts of seven seasons. His ten-year stint as a professional baseball player was simply one part of a captivating fifty-year journey through the worlds of intercollegiate athletics and professional baseball. This journey included being present, as a rookie player, at one of baseball's historic moments and later, as an executive, helping to build a World Series championship team. Lund also spent several years as a scout and a Major League coach. At the collegiate level he was a nine-letter athlete, coached an NCAA championship baseball team, and served as an administrator in one of the country's premier athletic departments.

Donald Andrew Lund was born to Andrew and Marguerite Lund on May 18, 1923, in Detroit, Michigan. Don had one sibling, an older sister, Virginia. His father, an automobile worker, took his son to his first Major League game in 1929 to see Don's favorite player, Charlie Gehringer, play against Babe Ruth and the Yankees.

Lund began his baseball career on the Detroit sandlots and rose to prominence while playing for Southeastern High School. He was a three-sport star there from 1939 to 1941. Don was named to the All-Metropolitan basketball team for three years and in his senior year was named both All-City and All-State. In football, he captained the team in his senior year while being named All-City. He was also president of his graduating class.

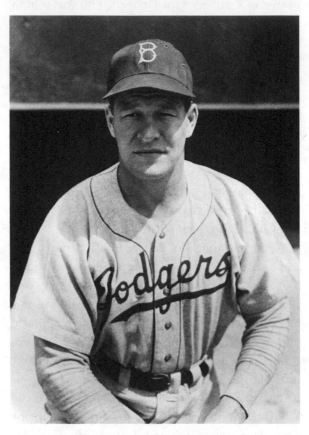

Don Lund's first big league home run came on September 12 as a pinch hitter against Cardinals ace Howie Pollet.

Lund was recruited by several Midwest colleges, but he chose to attend the University of Michigan in nearby Ann Arbor. At a time when freshmen were not eligible for varsity teams, Don became a nine-letter athlete. Playing during the World War II era, he was rejected for military service due to a "trick knee." While in college, he married Betty Huff, his high school sweetheart. They would remain married for more than fifty years before Betty died in 1998.

Lund was a fullback on the 1943 Michigan team that shared the Western Athletic Conference championship with a 6-0 record. In 1944 he became the starting fullback and regular punter, while also serving as co-captain. The Wolverines lost to Ohio State, 18–14, in the final game for the Big Nine championship.

Don was named MVP of the team; nevertheless, he considered baseball his favorite sport in college. "The most fun of all was baseball. It was just great." The baseball team, under coach Ray Fisher, a former big league pitcher, won conference championships in 1944 and 1945. For his college career, Lund had a .307 batting average and was team captain in his senior year.

After graduation, Don had to choose between baseball and football. He was the first-round pick of the National Football League's Chicago Bears in 1945, but at that time professional football lacked the prestige of Major League Baseball. Meanwhile, the legendary baseball star George Sisler, a Michigan alumnus, had been scouting Lund. The day after Don graduated, Sisler accompanied him to New York to meet with Branch Rickey, another Michigan graduate. When Rickey asked what it would take to sign him, Lund replied, "$7,500 and a major league contract." They agreed quickly. "I should have asked for $25,000," Lund recalled.

After signing in June of 1945, Lund went directly to the big leagues. He appeared in four games with no hits in three at bats before being optioned to St. Paul of the American Association, where he hit .263 in seventy-eight games. In 1946 Don experienced what was likely his worst season in professional baseball. He missed part of spring training due to the birth of his daughter Susan in Detroit. After batting only .200 in fourteen games with St. Paul, Lund was assigned to San Diego in the Pacific Coast League. There he again struggled, hitting only .152 in thirty-three at bats. Don was then

told to report to the Fort Worth Cats of the Texas League. The morning he reported to the Fort Worth team he was informed that Branch Rickey wanted him in Mobile instead. He batted a meager .240 in seventy-four games for the Southern Association Bears.

The 1947 season was a different story. At training camp Don was assigned to the Montreal Royals, Brooklyn's Class Triple-A team in the International League. The Royals played most of their spring training games against the Dodgers. Lund's hitting prowess returned. He hit several home runs, including one against Ralph Branca in the final game of the exhibition season at Ebbets Field. Three Montreal players were selected to start the season with the Dodgers: Lund, Jackie Robinson, and Spider Jorgensen. All three were signed to big league contracts on the same day. After signing, Don and Jorgensen left via a back entrance while the press flooded the room to cover the Robinson story. Don played sparingly in the early season, and in May he was sent back to St. Paul, where he hit .280 in ninety games with sixteen home runs.

After finishing the season in St. Paul, Lund joined the first-place Dodgers in St. Louis. On September 12, Don was sent up as a pinch hitter in the ninth inning with a man on base and the Dodgers trailing by three runs. Facing Cardinals ace Howie Pollet, he came through with his first big league home run. Two days later Lund started the second game of a twin bill against Cincinnati and delivered two doubles in a 6–3 victory. On September 17 in Pittsburgh, he had two hits, including his second home run. A few days later the Dodgers clinched the pennant. Lund finished the season with six hits in twenty at bats for an even .300 batting average. Don was ineligible for the World Series but watched from the stands as the Dodgers lost in seven games to the Yankees.

On June 28, 1948, with Lund batting a lowly .188, the Dodgers sold him on waivers to the St. Louis Browns. Don learned about the sale while reading the newspaper at dinner. In 2004 Lund remembered St. Louis as being very hot, "but it was the big leagues and I was playing." Used primarily against left-handers, he had a .248 average with three home runs in sixty-three games for the sixth-place Browns.

Before the start of the 1949 season, Lund was traded to his hometown Detroit Tigers, which was a dream come true. That winter, "I was working out at my local high school and someone came up to me and said, 'Hey Don, you just got traded to the Tigers.'" Don made the Opening Day roster; however, he was sold to Toledo of the American Association on May 19 after only two plate appearances. He spent the entire season with the Mud Hens, finishing with a .298 average, 17 home runs, and 81 RBIS.

At the start of the 1950 season, the Tigers informed Don they had sold him outright to Toledo and he could not be reacquired without going through the unrestricted draft. Lund traveled to Cincinnati to protest his status to Commissioner "Happy" Chandler. The protest was unsuccessful. Chandler told Lund, "It's a rule and there is nothing I can do about it."

Much to his dismay, Don spent the next three years playing in the Tigers' Minor League system. Nevertheless, he used this period to build relationships that would pay future dividends. Lund befriended Jim Campbell, who later became the Tigers' general manager, and Jack Tighe, who went on to manage the team. In 1950 Don spent another season in Toledo, where his average dropped to .245, but he had a career high twenty-three home runs. Back in Toledo in 1951, he hit .259 playing for manager Tighe.

In 1952 both Lund and Tighe moved to Buffalo of the International League, where Don hit .302 with sixteen home runs. That September the last-place Tigers, under GM Charlie Gehringer, brought Lund back to Detroit. Don had two hits in his first game back and finished with a .304 average while playing in eight games. Early in 1953 a spot opened in the Tigers' outfield, and Lund was inserted into the lineup. He finished the season with a .257 average and had career highs in games played (131) and plate appearances (470).

After finishing the previous season thirty-four games under .500, the 1954 Tigers went with youth in the outfield, including rookie Al Kaline. Lund struggled in his reduced role. Through late July he had appeared in only thirty-five games with sixty at bats while hitting a paltry .130. On July 29 the Tigers sent him to the Minneapolis Millers, the New York Giants' American Association farm team, in exchange for Hoot Evers. Don finished the season with the Millers hitting .287 with six homers in forty-two games.

During the off-season Lund, at age thirty-one, evaluated his options. The Tigers offered him a position as a Michigan-area scout. Rather than return to Minneapolis, "I figured I had better take advantage of that," he recalled in 2009. Don worked as a scout for the next two seasons. In October 1956 Jack Tighe was named to manage the Tigers and selected Lund to be his first base coach. Tighe was replaced in mid-1958 by Bill Norman, who retained Lund as a coach.

The 1958 season was also the last of Ray Fisher's thirty-eight years as baseball coach at Michigan. Offered the job as his replacement, Lund resigned from the Tigers to accept the position. The Wolverines had a losing record in 1959, Don's first season. The 1960 team included Lund's first recruits and improved its record to 19-12-1. Among those recruits was future Major League catcher Bill Freehan.

Lund's 1962 Wolverines finished second in the Big Ten but qualified for the NCAA tournament, where they surprised everyone. The Wolverines advanced to the College World Series and claimed the championship in a fifteen-inning 5–4 victory over Santa Clara. Lund was named Coach of the

Year by the American Association of College Baseball Coaches.

In September 1962 Don's old Minor League acquaintance Jim Campbell was named general manager of the Tigers. Campbell recruited Lund to become his replacement as director of Minor League operations. Don accepted the position, and it was on to a new challenge, building the Tigers' farm system. The culmination of that work came in 1968. Seven of eight position players for the world champion Tigers that year were products of Lund's farm system.

Lund remained with the Tigers until 1970, when he accepted Michigan's offer to serve as assistant athletic director. Eventually he was promoted to associate athletic director, where he served until his retirement in 1992. For many years Don was also the commentator on Michigan football radio broadcasts with play-by-play announcer Bob Ufer.

In his later years Lund had numerous honors bestowed upon him. In 1984 Don was inducted into the Michigan Hall of Honor. In 1987 he was elected to the Michigan Sports Hall of Fame. In 1999 his No. 33 University of Michigan baseball jersey was retired. As of 2011, Don Lund still lives near the university, just outside of Ann Arbor.

# Chapter 59. **Vic Lombardi**

*Lawrence Baldassaro*

| AGE | W | L | PCT. | ERA | G | GS | GF | CG | SHO | SV | IP | H | BB | SO | HBP | WP |
|-----|---|---|------|-----|---|----|----|----|-----|----|-----|-----|----|----|-----|-----|
| 24 | 12 | 11 | .522 | 2.99 | 33 | 20 | 9 | 7 | 3 | 3 | 174.2 | 156 | 65 | 72 | 2 | 4 |

At five feet seven and 158 pounds, Vic Lombardi was hardly an imposing figure on the mound. But the left-hander had enough talent and guile to pitch in 538 games over a seventeen-year professional career, including six seasons in the Majors with two starts in the legendary 1947 World Series. He was also a good-enough athlete to win a National Left-Handed Open Golf title and to work as a teaching professional until his death at the age of seventy-five.

Victor Alvin Lombardi was born on September 20, 1922, in Reedley, California, twenty-two miles southeast of Fresno. He was the son of Biagio Vito Lombardi, a farm worker who had emigrated from Italy, and Lena (Freitas) Lombardi, the daughter of Portuguese immigrants and the mother of five children from a previous marriage. When Vic was young, the family moved thirty-eight miles south to Tulare. As a pitcher at Tulare High School, he played for Pete Beiden, who would later become a legendary coach at Fresno State University.

Lombardi was signed as an amateur free agent in 1941 by Brooklyn Dodgers scout Tom Downey. That year, at age eighteen, he began his professional career with the Johnstown Johnnies of the Class D Pennsylvania State Association. Twice striking out 19, as well as 18 and 17, he finished with 204 strikeouts and posted a 12-3 record, with a league-leading 1.85 ERA. He ended the season by going 1-1 for the Santa Barbara Saints, Brooklyn's Class C affiliate in the California League.

In 1942 Lombardi had a 9-4 record and a 3.08 ERA with Santa Barbara before being promoted to the Durham (North Carolina) Bulls in the Class B Piedmont League, where he was 4-1 with a 2.06

Vic Lombardi started the season poorly, but he was Brooklyn's most effective pitcher in the month of August.

ERA. After marrying Adrienne Grimaud on December 18, 1942, he did not play professional baseball again until 1945. (Lombardi and his wife had two daughters, Victoria and Christine. The couple divorced in 1951.) For reasons that are lost to history, Lombardi chose to sit out the entire 1943 season. Nor did he play pro ball the following season when he served in the navy from May 13 to June 6, 1944. (According to a 1945 article in the *Fresno*

*Bee*, Lombardi was released from the service because of faulty vision.)

In 1945 the twenty-two-year-old Lombardi pitched well enough in spring training to make the Dodgers' depleted wartime pitching staff. "He reminds me of Bill Sherdel when Wee Willie pitched for the Cardinals," said Dodgers president Branch Rickey. "If Lombardi does not make it, I will be the most surprised man in baseball."[1]

Wearing No. 18, he made his Major League debut on April 18, 1945, pitching two hitless innings in relief against Philadelphia. Ten days later he notched his first victory, giving up one hit in two innings of relief in a 4–3 win over the New York Giants. On May 2, at Ebbets Field, Lombardi made his first start, pitching eight innings in a 3–1 loss to the Boston Braves. He went on to pitch 203⅔ innings, posting a 10-11 record with a 3.31 ERA in thirty-eight appearances.

Lombardi was slight in stature even by the standards of his era. Inevitably, writers mined the thesaurus to come up with appropriately descriptive adjectives. In addition to the more mundane "little" and "diminutive," Lombardi was also called "the mite southpaw," the pint-sized southpaw," "pint-sized portsider," "pony pitcher," "the welterweight pitcher," and "the midget southpaw." And, because he wore glasses at times during his career, he was also the "bespectacled little left-hander."

But when Lombardi came up big against the Dodgers' hated crosstown rivals, "little Vic" became known by a new moniker: "Giant Killer." In his rookie season Lombardi beat the Giants four times, twice in relief, without a loss.

In 1946, his second year with the Dodgers, Lombardi had one of his two most productive seasons. Pitching against restored postwar lineups, he had a career-high thirteen wins (against ten losses) and a career-best ERA of 2.89. That year the Dodgers moved from a third-place finish in 1945 to a final-day tie for first with the St. Louis Cardinals. St. Louis won the pennant with a two-game sweep in a best-of-three playoff. Lombardi pitched in relief in both games.

Moreover, Lombardi was even more dominant against the Giants in 1946 than he had been as a rookie. Each of his first four starts against New York resulted in complete-game wins. Then, after a 3–2 victory in which he got a no-decision, he beat the Giants for a ninth straight time on August 12. In fact, the Dodgers won all seven games that Lombardi started against their interborough rivals in 1946. In six of those games, he gave up a total of nine runs; the other start was an 8–5 complete-game win on July 4.

Lombardi's streak of nine straight career wins against the Giants came to an abrupt end in the third game of the 1947 season when he was routed after three innings. Facing the Giants eight days later, Lombardi came on in relief in the third, gave up only three hits in seven innings, and got the win. He started only one more game against New York that year, but it was a masterpiece. On September 4 he threw a five-hit 2–0 shutout, allowing only one Giants runner to reach second base.

Lombardi pitched well in 1947, going 12-11 with a 2.99 ERA. Only Ralph Branca, with twenty-one, and Joe Hatten, with seventeen, had more victories for the pennant-winning Dodgers. While Lombardi's personal statistics were not quite as impressive as those of the previous season, relative to his peers he had a better year than in 1946. Among National League pitchers, he was fourth in fewest hits allowed per nine innings, fifth in lowest opponents' batting average, and tied for sixth in shutouts.

A *Chicago Tribune* story of March 31, 1997, on the occasion of the fiftieth anniversary of Jackie Robinson's Major League debut, noted that Lombardi welcomed his new teammate in 1947. "I had a lot of black kids who were my friends here [Fresno], growing up," he said. "I wasn't prejudiced. The only thing I was prejudiced about was [jerks]. And they come in all colors. If you're a good guy, you're my friend. If you're [a jerk], see ya later. It's that simple."

The 1947 World Series was the first of six postwar meetings between Brooklyn and the Yankees. After the Yanks won the opener, Brooklyn manager Burt Shotton chose Lombardi to start Game Two, in Yankee Stadium. In four-plus innings, he allowed five runs on nine hits, including a home run, three triples, and two doubles.

The Dodgers bounced back to win the next two games at Ebbets Field before losing the fifth game. With Brooklyn on the brink of elimination, Lombardi was tapped to start Game Six, again at Yankee Stadium. It proved to be, in the words of John Drebinger of the *New York Times*, "one of the most extraordinary games ever played." Before a then-record Series crowd of 74,065, the Dodgers jumped out to a 4–0 lead, but after holding the Yanks to one single in the first two innings, Lombardi gave up two runs in the third before being relieved by Branca. Two more singles brought in two more runs to tie the score at 4–4, with all four runs charged to Lombardi. Brooklyn eventually won to tie the Series, but the Yankees won the deciding game the next day.

Game Six of the 1947 World Series proved to be Lombardi's last with the Dodgers. On December 8 he and pitcher Hal Gregg were traded to the Pittsburgh Pirates for pitcher Preacher Roe, third baseman Billy Cox, and infielder Gene Mauch. In a separate deal, the Dodgers sold Dixie Walker to the Pirates for the $10,000 waiver price.

At the time, *The Sporting News* reported that the "midget southpaw" was the "surprise name in the trade," adding "his departure weakens an already shabby hurling corps."[2] In his three seasons with Brooklyn, Lombardi won thirty-five and lost thirty-two with a 3.07 ERA in 112 games.

In 1948, his first year with the Pirates, Lombardi appeared in thirty-eight games and compiled a 10-9 record. On September 24, local Italian Americans organized Vic Lombardi Night at Forbes Field, presenting the honoree with luggage and a silver set.

The Pirates, who had finished seventh in 1947, jumped to fourth in 1948, then fell to sixth and eighth in Lombardi's remaining two seasons. He appeared in thirty-four games in 1949 but made only twelve starts, compiling a 5-5 record with a 4.37 ERA. In 1950, his final year in the Majors, he started only two games for the last-place Pirates, going 0-5 with a 6.60 ERA. By then he was hampered by a rotator cuff injury.

In his six-year Major League career, Lombardi compiled a 50-51 record with a 3.68 ERA in 223 games. Of his 100 starts, 42 were complete games. In 1993 Lombardi was inducted into the Brooklyn Dodgers Hall of Fame along with Al Gionfriddo. At the time, Lombardi was quoted in the *Fresno Bee* as saying, "Brooklyn fans were a different breed. It was a family thing. You walked down the street, and everyone knew you. The team was different too, even for then. We went to the ballpark together, we left together, we ate together; it was just one big family. No one got out of line. There were no bad actors. It wasn't the same when I went to Pittsburgh. There were some good players but more individuals.

"I was a pretty good pitcher. I wasn't great, that's for sure. I was a middle pitcher. I could win ten or twelve games a year, pitch 200 innings and complete quite a few games. I could throw 85 to 88 mph. The ball moved pretty good, and I had pretty good control."[3]

Only twenty-eight when his big league career ended, Lombardi returned to the Minors. He spent the next nine years in the Pacific Coast and International Leagues, primarily as a starter. After one year with Hollywood in the PCL, he played for Toronto in the IL from 1952 to 1954 before returning to the PCL, where he pitched for Seattle (1955–56), San Diego (1956–58), and Portland (1958–59). Joe Astroth, the catcher for San Diego in 1956, Lombardi's first year with the team, recalled that

Lombardi "needs another pitch to get back. We'd work out on the sidelines, working on the spitter."[4] When Lombardi retired at the age of thirty-six, his eleven-year Minor League record—both before and after his stay in the Majors—was 140-80 with a 3.42 ERA.

In the 1947–49 editions of the *Baseball Register*, Lombardi's hobby was listed as hunting. But in the 1950 edition, hunting was replaced by golf. Whenever he took up the game, he played it well enough to become a teaching professional by 1958. And in January 1967 he won the seventh annual National Left-Handed Open Golf Championship in Hollywood, Florida. As a teaching pro, he worked at the Sierra View Golf Course in Visalia and the Airways, Palm Lakes, and Riverside courses in Fresno. Then, from the late 1980s until he died in 1997, he was at the Fig Garden Golf Club in Fresno.

In November 1963 Lombardi married one of his golf students, twenty-year-old Bonnie Bryant, a native of Tulare who joined the LPGA tour in 1971. According to Lombardi's daughter Victoria, the marriage lasted less than a year. Another of Lombardi's pupils was Patti Liscio, a ten-year LPGA tour player who met him in 1993 and worked with him until his death in 1997. She said they became very good friends, adding, "If there wasn't a forty-year difference in age, we'd have been married. He was a gift."

The former Major League pitcher retained his competitive drive as a golfer. To supplement the modest income he made as a teaching pro, he would team up with a partner against another twosome in money matches. One of his regular partners was Jerry Hagopian, who met Lombardi in the 1960s. Hagopian said he once asked Lombardi who was the toughest hitter he faced. "Stan Musial," replied Lombardi. "I never could get him out. I hated the son of a bitch. Every Christmas he'd send me a card and write: 'Merry Christmas, Vic. Hope to see you next year.'"

Just as he had on the mound, Lombardi looked for any competitive edge he could get on the links. "He liked to rib people and try to aggravate you before, during and after a match," said Liscio. "One of his favorite sayings was, 'You lose your head, you lose your ass.'"

Another golfing buddy was Gus Zernial, who led the American League in home runs and RBIs in 1951 while playing with the Philadelphia Athletics. Zernial met Lombardi when both lived in condos on the Palm Lakes golf course. "He taught me how to hit the golf ball," said Zernial. "He helped [PGA tour player] Jerry Heard and a lot of state golfers. He had a tremendous local following. He wouldn't play unless he played for money. He was a better golfer on the tee. He always talked people out of strokes. Everyone wanted to beat Vic."

Lombardi, who was inducted into the Fresno Athletic Hall of Fame in 1978, was proud of his Major League background and enjoyed its benefits. "He was a proud man," said his daughter Christine. "He had great pride in presenting himself as an athlete."

Lombardi was a private man; even those who spent a lot of time with him confessed to not knowing him well. "He was a good friend," said famed golfer Gary Bauer, "but he never let anyone get very close to him. He was an enigma. He was very closed-mouthed about his family." Victoria Lombardi said of her father, "He had a good life, but he was a lonely man. His professional life filled him up."

In December 1997, Lombardi, who had undergone quadruple heart bypass surgery previously, drove himself to Community Hospital in Fresno when he felt some pain in his chest. When informed that he needed a second bypass surgery, he told friends he wasn't concerned and that he would soon be playing golf again. The surgery went well, but when he was taken off the heart machine the doctors were unable to restart his heart. Lombardi died on December 3, 1997, at the age of seventy-five and is buried in Tulare Public Cemetery.

# Chapter 60. Jack Banta

*Jimmy Keenan*

| AGE | W | L | PCT | ERA | G | GS | GF | CG | SHO | SV | IP | H | BB | SO | HBP | WP |
|-----|---|---|------|------|---|----|----|----|-----|----|-----|---|----|----|-----|-----|
| 22 | 0 | 1 | .000 | 7.04 | 3 | 1 | 1 | 0 | 0 | 0 | 7.2 | 7 | 4 | 3 | 1 | 1 |

Jack Banta was a hard-throwing right-handed pitcher who threw with a deceptive sidearm delivery. He played in parts of four seasons in the Majors with the Brooklyn Dodgers, but it was his performance on the final day of the 1949 season, in Philadelphia, that gained Banta his everlasting place in Brooklyn Dodgers history. Because St. Louis was in the process of winning their game in Chicago, a Dodgers loss would necessitate a three-game playoff with the Cardinals for the National League pennant.

Brooklyn took an early 5–0 lead, but the Phillies rallied to tie the score at 7–7 after six innings. Banta, who had entered the game with two outs in the bottom of the sixth, shut down the Phillies the rest of the way, giving up only two hits and a walk. After the Dodgers took a 9–7 lead in the top of the tenth, Banta retired the Phillies in the bottom of the inning to seal the victory and give Brooklyn the NL flag.

Jackie Kay Banta was born in Hutchinson, Kansas, on June 24, 1925. He was the only son of Glen and Blanche (Hutsell) Banta. Glen, a barber by trade, later opened a popular billiards parlor in Hutchinson. Jack's parents were dedicated baseball fans, and early on they instilled in him an appreciation and passion for the game.

Jack pitched on the local Optimist baseball team on the sandlots of Hutchinson until he was seventeen. He graduated from Hutchinson High School (which had no baseball team) in 1943 and took a full-time warehouse job. The teenager tried to enlist in the military in World War II, but a bad knee kept him out of the service.

Dodgers scout Burt Wells, who had seen Banta

Jack Banta made his Major League debut on September 18, 1947.

play in 1942, was driven by the war-induced player shortages to sign young talent. In 1944 Wells invited Banta to a tryout in Springfield, Missouri, where the Dodgers' American Association affiliate, the St. Paul Saints, were practicing.

It did not take long for the 6-foot-2½, 175-pound Banta to impress everyone at the Saints camp with his blazing fastball, and he was quickly signed. Brooklyn general manager Branch Rickey first assigned Banta to the Newport News (Virginia) team in the Class B Piedmont League. After he pitched in three games at Newport News, the Dodgers sent him to their Class D affiliate in Olean, New York.

Banta was Olean's best pitcher (12-5, 3.10 ERA) and primary pinch hitter (21 hits and an overall .304 batting average). Late in the '44 season he was promoted to the Montreal Royals of the International League. In fourteen games with the Royals, Banta went 1-4, giving him a 14-9 record with a 3.42 ERA with the three teams.

Banta spent the entire 1945 season with the Royals, winning twelve games and losing nine, as Montreal finished first in the regular season but lost out in the finals of the Governors' Cup playoffs. He also experienced shoulder trouble for the first time, but after a few weeks of rest was able to resume his place in the rotation.

In August 1946, after winning nine games and losing six with Montreal, Banta was transferred to St. Paul. Montreal was cruising to the International League crown, while St. Paul was in the midst of a tight American Association pennant race. Jack won three games and lost two for the Saints, who also used him as a left-handed pinch hitter.

Banta returned to Montreal in 1947, and from the outset of spring training he was "locked in" on the mound. "This should be the year for that boy to arrive," Royals manager Clay Hopper told the press.[1] In June, Banta, who pitched with a sidearm crossfire motion, hurled twenty-nine consecutive scoreless innings. Four days after the streak ended, he pitched a 4–0 shutout against Baltimore. During the streak, he allowed twenty hits, walked fourteen, and struck out forty-seven. After witnessing Banta's whitewash of Baltimore, International League president Frank J. Shaughnessy estimated the hard-throwing twenty-two-year-old would easily bring $100,000 on the open market.

On June 11, 1947, in the midst of Banta's scoreless streak, Dodgers pitcher Rube Melton was demoted to Montreal. Branch Rickey intended to call up Banta to replace Melton. However, manager Hopper balked at the exchange, telling Rickey that numerous doubleheaders loomed and he needed all of his pitchers. Rickey could certainly have pressed the issue, but he decided that Banta needed a bit more Minor League experience and let Hopper keep him.

Banta finished the season at 15-5 for the Royals, striking out 199 in 199 innings and leading the league with seven shutouts. His accomplishments earned him a September call-up to the Dodgers. Banta made his Major League debut on September 18, 1947, in an 8–7 loss to the Pittsburgh Pirates. He pitched in two more games with Brooklyn before the season ended but was ineligible to play in the World Series against the Yankees that year.

In 1948 Banta went to spring training with the Dodgers in the Dominican Republic. Once again he showed his dominant form, tossing a seven-inning no-hitter against Montreal and allowing just one run in twenty-seven innings of work in the Grapefruit League. Dodgers manager Leo Durocher said, "Banta can really fire that ball. If he continues to give us pitching like this I may not have any mound problems."[2]

Banta earned a spot on the Dodgers' roster, but after a relief appearance against the Giants and a losing start against the Braves, he was optioned to Montreal. Banta spent the rest of the 1948 season with the Royals, tying Rochester's Bill Reeder for the most wins in the league with nineteen. His 193 strikeouts also led the league. Banta continued to pitch well in the postseason, helping Montreal win the International League playoffs and the Junior World Series.

Back with the Dodgers in 1949, Banta had his best year in the Majors. Pitching mostly in relief, he won ten games—including the pennant-clincher—with a 3.37 ERA. Brooklyn again lost the World Series to the Yankees, this time in five games. Banta pitched in relief in three of the games, and his 3.18

ERA was the lowest among Dodgers relief pitchers. He earned $6,000 in salary that season, plus $4,081 in World Series money.

Banta reported to the Dodgers for spring training in Vero Beach in 1950 ready to pick up where he left off. But he injured his shoulder a few days after he arrived in camp. The injury was diagnosed as floating cartilage, the same problem he had encountered in 1945. He continued to pitch through the pain, but his control suffered. After posting a 4-4 record with the Dodgers, he was sent to Montreal, remaining there for the rest of the season. He was 4-7 with a 4.92 ERA in nineteen games, seventeen of them starts. He walked eighty-seven batters in ninety-seven innings.

By the spring of 1951, Banta was still in considerable pain and began getting injections of novocaine in his shoulder. The novocaine eased the pain while he pitched, he told reporters, but after it wore off, "I can't lift my arm."

Speaking about his career-ending injury years later, Banta said, "In those days anything that was wrong with you was tendinitis. They never heard of a rotator cuff. They'd take an x-ray and if they didn't find any bone chips they didn't know what was wrong with you."[3]

The Dodgers, puzzled by Banta's injury, sent him to a dentist to have impacted wisdom teeth removed, hoping that would relieve the pain in his shoulder. After a few weeks in camp with the 1951 Dodgers, Banta was sent home to rest for a month. After that he joined the Fort Worth Cats, the Dodgers' affiliate in the Class Double-A Texas League. Jack pitched only fourteen innings over seven games for the Cats without a decision.

In 1952, with his shoulder still ailing, Banta joined the Dodgers' Lancaster (Pennsylvania) club in the Class B Interstate League as a player-coach. He made a few appearances at first base but did his best work on the mound as a relief pitcher. The former strikeout artist went 5-2 with a 3.98 ERA in twenty-eight appearances.

Banta retired as a player after that season. He had a brief stint as a scout for the Dodgers before taking a job as a manager in the Brooklyn farm system. He managed from 1953 through 1957 at the Class C and Class D levels, leading the Shawnee (Oklahoma) Hawks to a first-place finish in the Sooner State League in 1954.

With his involvement in Organized Baseball over, Banta, who was one season shy of qualifying for a Major League pension, settled down to family life in Hutchinson with his wife, the former Jackie Gaylor, and their three children, Michael, Kristie, and Lee Ann. Jack and Jackie had married in Hutchinson on February 1, 1949.

During his playing days, Banta had worked in the off-season as an accountant. In 1956 the Kansas native took a job with the Dillon Corporation, a supermarket chain based in Hutchinson. He spent thirty-four years with the company. Jack was an avid golfer, who consistently shot par or under, and a great pool player. He also enjoyed hunting and fishing.

In 2004 Banta was inducted into the Kansas Baseball Hall of Fame. This accolade had been offered to him earlier, but he had always declined the honor. Finally, he relented and accepted; but his health was failing at the time, and he was unable to attend the installation ceremony.

In his later years, Banta suffered from cardiovascular problems. He died on September 17, 2006, at the age of eighty-one. He was survived by his wife and their three children, four grandchildren and four great-grandchildren. Jack Banta is buried in Hutchinson's Penwell-Gabel Cemetery.

# Chapter 61. **Johnny Van Cuyk**

*David Greisen*

| AGE | W | L | PCT. | ERA | G | GS | GF | CG | SHO | SV | IP | H | BB | SO | HBP | WP |
|-----|---|---|------|------|---|----|----|----|-----|----|-----|---|----|----|-----|-----|
| 25 | 0 | 0 | .000 | 5.40 | 2 | 0 | 1 | 0 | 0 | 0 | 3.1 | 5 | 1 | 2 | 0 | 0 |

The number of professional baseball players active in the area known as the Fox River Valley of Wisconsin reached its pinnacle during the 1940s and 1950s, after the formation of the Class D Wisconsin State League in 1940. Left-handed pitcher John Henry Van Cuyk, who began his professional career in that league, eventually had a brief Major League career with the Brooklyn Dodgers.

Van Cuyk was born to Henry and Anna Van Cuyk in Little Chute, Wisconsin, on July 7, 1921. Little Chute, directly east of Appleton and the Fox River, has been known for its Dutch inhabitants since the 1800s. Henry was born in the Netherlands in 1896 and came to the United States with his parents, Johannes and Gertrude. They settled in Kimberly, Wisconsin, near Little Chute.

John was one of five children, four boys and a girl. His youngest brother, Chris, was a left-handed starting pitcher for parts of three seasons (1950–52) with the Dodgers. "He had much better baseball ability than I had," John said. "He was six feet seven and weighed 260 pounds and by God, could he throw that ball. But it went to hell because if a lady winked at him, boy, be careful."

As a child, John was known as "the kid that plays ball." "I'd walk up and down the street early in the morning with a bat, glove, and ball and get a bunch of kids together and walk across the river to Little Chute and play all day. All summer long, that's all we did. From seven in the morning until it was dark at night." When Van Cuyk told others he was going to be a professional baseball player when he grew up, they laughed. "Nobody thought it was possible for someone from Kimberly to make it to the Major Leagues," he said.

Johnny Van Cuyk was thought by *Baseball Digest* to be a Rookie of the Year candidate in 1947.

Van Cuyk became a five-sport varsity letter winner at Kimberly High School. He was a standout for the Papermakers in football, basketball, and baseball and also ran track and boxed. "In football I was an end and could run like a damn deer. My dad used to say, 'If you get in trouble, throw the ball to John. He can run like hell when somebody's chasing him.'" The six-foot-one, 190-pound Van

Cuyk tried fighting as an amateur boxer, but it didn't go as well. "I got the [bleep] kicked out of me in boxing." Van Cuyk is enshrined in the Kimberly High School athletic hall of fame and is one of a very few athletes in the school's history to earn five varsity letters in a single year.

Van Cuyk's professional baseball career began in 1940 with the Appleton Papermakers, an unaffiliated team in the Wisconsin State League. Van Cuyk personified the typical Wisconsin State League player: he was young, inexpensive, and a long shot to make the Majors. His salary with Appleton was $65 a month, but he earned additional cash—"50 bucks a start"—throughout the season by pitching for the village team in Kimberly.

Van Cuyk was back with Appleton in 1941, by which time the Papermakers had become a Cleveland Indians affiliate. He had a combined 10-16 record for the two seasons before putting his baseball career on hold because of World War II. He was drafted by the army, served as a military policeman, and advanced to the rank of sergeant. "I had it pretty good in the service, but it was all because I could play ball," Van Cuyk said.

He pitched mostly for the battalion team at Camp Grant, Illinois, but after being transferred to an army facility in Los Angeles, he heard about a semipro team sponsored by Paramount Studios in Hollywood. He asked for a tryout, made the team, and pitched in thirty-five games, winning thirty-one of them. Van Cuyk struck out 530 batters in 302 innings. And the competition wasn't easy—many of the teams he pitched against were loaded with professional stars. Best of all for Van Cuyk, he was paid $100 for each game he pitched.

Tom Downey, a scout for the Brooklyn Dodgers, signed Van Cuyk immediately after he finished his military obligation. "When I signed with the Dodgers I got a $20,000 bonus, which at that time was like getting millions nowadays." When he told his dad about the money, his dad replied, "Nobody's worth that kind of money!"

In the spring of 1946, Van Cuyk trained with the Dodgers before they assigned him to the Fort Worth Cats of the Texas League. His pitching was strong and steady throughout the year. He finished with eighteen victories and eight defeats for the regular-season champions and led the league in ERA (1.42), strikeouts (207), and shutouts (6). Van Cuyk was the Game One starter in the opening round of the Texas League playoffs, shutting out Tulsa on two hits. After the season, he returned to Kimberly to work at a local coal yard and live with his wife, the former Josephine Fiers, and her parents.

As the result of his impressive season in Fort Worth, Van Cuyk appeared on the front cover of the April 1947 edition of *Baseball Digest* as a rookie-of-the-year candidate. He made the Dodgers' Opening Day roster, but within weeks he was pitching for the International League's Montreal Royals, Brooklyn's top Minor League team.

Van Cuyk was 12-9 when Brooklyn recalled him in September. He made his Major League debut on September 18 against the Pittsburgh Pirates at Forbes Field. Van Cuyk had entered the game in the fifth inning with two outs, the bases loaded, and the score tied, 3–3. He allowed a run to score and then pitched a scoreless sixth inning before Eddie Miksis pinch-hit for him in the top of the seventh.

Miksis walked and scored on a home run by Jackie Robinson, putting Van Cuyk in line for the win in what would have been the pennant-clinching victory. But Wally Westlake's home run in the bottom of the ninth gave Pittsburgh an 8–7 win. Van Cuyk made his second, and final, appearance of the season in Brooklyn's next game, on September 20 at Ebbets Field, throwing the final two innings of an 8–1 loss to the Boston Braves.

While Van Cuyk was eligible to pitch in the 1947 World Series against the New York Yankees, he never saw action. Nevertheless, he cited the seven-game Series as one of his fondest memories in baseball. "Yankee Stadium was altogether different from any ballpark I ever played in," he said. "To walk in there and see 60,000 people up in those seats was a thrill."

Van Cuyk was fond of playing for Leo Durocher, the club's manager in 1948. He called Leo "the greatest manager in baseball," adding, "I never saw Durocher chew anybody out in front of anybody. If you had an ass-chewing coming for something—you made a mistake on the mound or something like that—he'd call you into his office and tell you, and it was done. No other manager did that."

Van Cuyk's next two seasons were much like his rookie year. He spent the majority of the season pitching for Montreal and made a combined five relief appearances for the Dodgers. His last trip to the mound in a Dodgers uniform came on May 9, 1949, in a 14–5 loss to the St. Louis Cardinals. He finished the season in Montreal, compiling a 10-10 record, the third straight year he had won ten or more games for the club. The Royals won the 1949 Governors' Cup by defeating the Buffalo Bisons four games to one for the International League championship. After the season, Van Cuyk appeared in two games for Cienfuegos in the Cuban Winter League.

In 1950 Van Cuyk began the season with the American Association's St. Paul Saints, the Dodgers' other Class Triple-A affiliate. He made thirty-eight appearances for the Saints, primarily as a reliever. Back in St. Paul the next year, Van Cuyk appeared in thirty-six games, including ten starts. It was the sixth consecutive year he saw action in at least thirty Minor League games.

Van Cuyk's tenure with the Saints came to an end when he was purchased by the Oakland Oaks of the Pacific Coast League before the 1952 season. He appeared in sixty-one games for manager Mel Ott, all but one in relief, and had a 9-3 won-lost record and a 2.67 ERA. On May 6, 1953, the Oaks sold Van Cuyk to the San Diego Padres of the PCL. He appeared in seventeen games for Oakland in 1953, but a dispute with the ball club over money eventually led to his retirement. "I retired and was offered a job to manage in Albuquerque for the Dodgers. I turned it down (for family reasons) and Tommy Lasorda took the job."

Van Cuyk returned to Kimberly with his family, which included his wife and two sons, John Jr. and Lonny, both of whom were adopted in Montreal while he was playing for the Royals. He resumed working at the coal yard that regularly employed him during the off-seasons. In 1954 he received an offer that would prompt yet another change of address for the family. "Ben Sternberg, from Rochester, Minnesota, called and wanted me to come there and play semipro baseball in the Southern Minny League with the Rochester Royals," he said. That wasn't all: Sternberg, a real estate businessman, also had an opening in his company, and so Van Cuyk became a real-estate agent. He continued to play for the Royals until the league disbanded for financial reasons in March of 1960.

Van Cuyk and his wife moved back to Kimberly in the early 1970s, and he started a second long-term, post-baseball career in automobile sales. In the mid-1970s the couple moved to Las Vegas, Nevada, and Van Cuyk worked at a Ford dealership as a sales manager. They spent roughly five years out West before he took a similar position at a Ford dealership in Appleton. Altogether, Van Cuyk put in thirteen years in the real-estate industry, and eighteen in the automotive field. In his later years he worked part-time at a golf course in Rochester and commented, "I like it there because all we talk about is baseball."

In January 1988 Van Cuyk's high school sweetheart and wife of forty-six years, Josephine, died of bone cancer. She was sixty-two years old. The two were married on January 3, 1942, shortly before he entered the army.

After Josephine's death, Van Cuyk moved to

Cleveland, Ohio, to live with John Jr. and his family. While he was there, he began dating Kay Canfield, a friend from Rochester, Minnesota, whose husband had just died. According to John Jr., "The next thing you know, they got married."

The couple made a permanent home in Rochester, with the exception of a one-year stay in Las Vegas. John said they were deeply attached to baseball and watched as many Minnesota Twins games as possible. The former Major Leaguer's heart remained with the Dodgers, however. "They're still my team, and they always will be," he said.

Throughout his life Van Cuyk served as a role model for others, most notably his two sons. "He was very competitive, but he never pushed us into baseball," they said. "While he always worked hard, he and Mom took the time and came to our events and were always very complimentary."

While his days with the Brooklyn Dodgers were limited and he never had a pitching decision in the Majors, Van Cuyk collected an ample store of Major League memories. He appeared on a World Series roster, played for Hall of Fame managers Leo Durocher and Mel Ott, and witnessed the successful integration of baseball by teammate Jackie Robinson. The franchise rewarded him for his "outstanding consistent relief pitching" from 1947 to 1949 by inducting him into the Brooklyn Dodger Hall of Fame in 1999.

Van Cuyk died in Rochester on July 10, 2010, three days short of his eighty-ninth birthday. He is buried at St. Agnes Cemetery in Kellogg, Minnesota. Van Cuyk was survived by his wife, Kay; his sons, Lonny and John Jr.; six grandchildren; and eight great-grandchildren.

# Chapter 62. Timeline, September 20–September 28

*Lyle Spatz*

Saturday, September 20, vs. Boston—Johnny Sain's twentieth victory prevented the Dodgers from clinching the pennant. Brooklyn's five errors, including two each by Pee Wee Reese and Bruce Edwards, contributed to its 8–1 loss. Eddie Stanky's first-inning error was the key to Boston scoring four unearned runs. Dick Whitman, who had spent the season at Montreal, celebrated his recall with a pinch-hit single. Vic Lombardi was the victim of the nonsupport. A St. Louis victory kept the Cardinals alive for another day. 91-56, First, 8 games ahead.

Sunday, September 21, vs. Boston—The Dodgers lost their third consecutive game, and their third consecutive opportunity to clinch the pennant. Warren Spahn matched Johnny Sain's feat of the day before by winning his twentieth game. Spahn tossed a 4–0 shutout. He allowed just six hits, half of them to Pee Wee Reese. Ralph Branca, trying for his twenty-second win, was the loser. The Cardinals were rained out. 91-57, First, 7½ games ahead.

Monday, September 22—Not scheduled. After beating the Cubs in an afternoon game, the Cardinals lost the night game, clinching the pennant for Brooklyn. 91-57, First, 7½ games ahead.

Tuesday, September 23, vs. New York—The new National League champions celebrated Jackie Robinson Day with a 6–1 win over the Giants. New York's only run came on a home run by Bobby Thomson off Joe Hatten, who pitched the first five innings. Dan Bankhead blanked the Giants over the final four. 92-57, First, 7½ games ahead.

| Final 1947 National League Standings | | | | | | |
|---|---|---|---|---|---|---|
| Team | G | W | L | T | PCT | GB |
| Brooklyn Dodgers | 155 | 94 | 60 | 1 | .610 | — |
| St. Louis Cardinals | 156 | 89 | 65 | 2 | .578 | 5.0 |
| Boston Braves | 154 | 86 | 68 | 0 | .558 | 8.0 |
| New York Giants | 155 | 81 | 73 | 1 | .526 | 13.0 |
| Cincinnati Reds | 154 | 73 | 81 | 0 | .474 | 21.0 |
| Chicago Cubs | 155 | 69 | 85 | 1 | .448 | 25.0 |
| Philadelphia Phillies | 155 | 62 | 92 | 1 | .403 | 32.0 |
| Pittsburgh Pirates | 156 | 62 | 92 | 2 | .403 | 32.0 |

Wednesday, September 24, vs. New York—After pitching five innings of one-hit ball, Hal Gregg turned over a 4–0 lead to Willie Ramsdell, who was making his Major League debut. The Giants jumped on Ramsdell for six runs (only two earned) in the sixth inning and won the game, 6–5. 92-58, First, 6½ games ahead.

Thursday, September 25, at Philadelphia (2)—The Dodgers won two games from the Phillies, 7–5 and 5–2. The first was the completion of the August 17 game that had been halted in the bottom of the seventh inning with Brooklyn ahead 5–4. The Dodgers scored single runs in the eighth and ninth innings to make a winner of Hugh Casey. In the regularly scheduled game, the Dodgers broke a 2–2 tie with three runs in the tenth. Willie Ramsdell was credited with his first Major League win. 94-58, First, 6½ games ahead.

Friday, September 26—Not scheduled. 94-58, First, 6 games ahead.

Saturday, September 27, at Boston—Tommy Holmes hit a two-out single in the ninth inning to score Connie Ryan and give the Braves the 2–1 win. Erv Palica, Brooklyn's fifth pitcher, was the loser. 94-59, First, 5 games ahead.

Sunday, September 28, at Boston—The Dodgers closed out the season with a 3–2 loss at Braves Field. A ninth-inning error by first baseman Ed Stevens let in the winning run. Johnny Sain won his twenty-first game while rookie Jack Banta suffered his first Major League loss. 94-60, First, 5 games ahead.

# Chapter 63. **Willie Ramsdell**

*John Harry Stahl*

| AGE | W | L | PCT. | ERA | G | GS | GF | CG | SHO | SV | IP | H | BB | SO | HBP | WP |
|-----|---|---|------|-----|---|----|----|----|-----|----|-----|---|----|----|-----|----|
| 31 | 1 | 1 | .500 | 6.75 | 2 | 0 | 1 | 0 | 0 | 0 | 2.2 | 4 | 3 | 3 | 1 | 0 |

Willie Ramsdell, nicknamed "Willie the Knuck," mixed a colorful personality with the unpredictable knuckle ball to produce a thirteen-year professional baseball career. Ramsdell made two brief pitching appearances for the 1947 Brooklyn Dodgers but was ineligible for the World Series. He subsequently pitched in thirty-two games for the Dodgers over the next two seasons, and then played for both the Cincinnati Reds and the Chicago Cubs before his Major League career ended in 1952.

James Willard Ramsdell was born in the small town of Williamsburg, Kansas, on April 4, 1916, to James E. and Hazel Ramsdell. James was a railroad worker.[1] According to Willie, his parents named him after Jess Willard, a native Kansan and the heavyweight boxing champion of the time.[2]

Ramsdell's father was a former semipro pitcher and initially taught him the game. Willie graduated from Chanute High School, about eighty miles south of Williamsburg, which is midway between Wichita and Kansas City. In 1935 he pitched in four of the seven games that led the Prince Howard team of Kansas City, Missouri, to the Ban Johnson championship.[3] In 1938 a friend of his father's got him a successful tryout with his first professional team in Big Spring, Texas.[4]

With the Big Spring Barons in the Class D West Texas–New Mexico League, Ramsdell began using the knuckle ball out of desperation. Initially, Willie relied on mixing his good curve ball with a very ordinary fastball. But he quickly discovered that the region's thin air flattened out his curve, making him ineffective. His manager, Charles Barnabee, suggested that he try the knuckle ball or

Willie Ramsdell was called up in September and split two decisions in the season's final week.

quit the game. With little to lose, Ramsdell took his skipper's advice and discovered that he could throw the flutter ball with success.

Adapting quickly, James Willard Ramsdell morphed into Willie the Knuck.[5] At five feet eleven and 165 pounds, yet oozing self-confidence, Ramsdell realized he was able to get batters out in critical situations. Years later he often joked that he gave up his fastball to throw the knuckler.

From 1938 to 1941 at Big Spring (the club played

out of Odessa, Texas, for part of 1940), Ramsdell won 60 games and pitched 840 innings. He did this even though opposing batters averaged more than a hit or a walk per inning against him. He would bend but seldom break. Assessing his pitching skills, the *Big Spring Daily Herald* wrote, "[He] never looked like he could throw hard enough to break an egg shell." The newspaper concluded, however, that he had the "think tank" to succeed as a pitcher.[6]

Ramsdell's best year with the Class D club was in 1941, when he posted a 25-9 record in 282 innings with a 2.94 ERA.[7] He clinched the first regular-season pennant for Big Spring by starting both games of a doubleheader and pitching two complete-game shutouts.[8]

Willie's likeable, happy-go-lucky personality also made him an off-the-field favorite. Repeatedly characterized as "loquacious" by the *Herald*, Ramsdell liked talking (occasionally using a profanity to emphasize his point) and having fun. In the off-season, he stayed in Big Spring, working and pitching semipro baseball for the town's biggest employer.

Promoted to Class C in 1942, he spent a chaotic season with two teams: Santa Barbara in the California League (which folded in midseason) and Muskogee, Oklahoma, in the Western Association. Even amid the distractions associated with a midseason franchise shift, Ramsdell won twenty games and lost only eleven.

The Western Association was one of the many Minor Leagues that suspended operations during World War II. From 1943 through 1945, Ramsdell was back in Wichita, working and playing for semipro teams sponsored by two defense-related companies: Coleman Lamp and Cessna Aircraft. After divorcing his first wife, with whom he had two children, Willie married his second wife, Opal Schupbach, in 1943 in Wichita.[9]

When the Texas League resumed operations in 1946, Ramsdell joined the Fort Worth Cats, recently purchased by the Dodgers. He posted a respectable 17-7 record in 206 innings. Unfortunately, his off-the-field fun-loving ways continued. In mid-July the *San Antonio Light* reported that Willie had been suspended indefinitely by his manager, Ray Hayworth, for "continued violation of training rules." After apologizing, he resumed pitching a few days later.

In 1947 Ramsdell went to spring training with the Dodgers, and again he reportedly had a very good time off the field. He got a lukewarm vote of confidence from his manager, Leo Durocher, before Commissioner Happy Chandler suspended Durocher for the season for associating with gamblers. Assessing Ramsdell, Durocher called him a one-pitch (the knuckle ball) pitcher. "There is nothing in his repertoire to mix it with," Durocher said. "Every time he winds up, he practically advertises 'here comes my knuckler but I defy you to hit it.'" Durocher admiringly described Willie's knuckle ball movement: "The thing dances up and down and sideways as if it were hung on a rubber band."

Nevertheless, the Dodgers sent Ramsdell to Fort Worth, where he posted a 21-5 record with a 2.25 ERA, his third twenty-win season in the Minor Leagues. Thirteen of the victories came in succession. Ramsdell led the Texas League in winning percentage (.808) and was selected as a league All-Star.

In late September 1947, after the Dodgers had clinched the National League pennant, the club brought up Willie and a few other Minor Leaguers to finish out the season and rest the regulars for the World Series. Willie appeared twice in relief, registering a 1-1 record with a 6.75 ERA.[10]

Ramsdell's first Major League appearance was a disaster. Relieving in the sixth inning against the New York Giants at Ebbets Field on September 24, he hit the first batter he faced with his first pitch and then walked the next hitter. After two outs, Buddy Kerr doubled home the two runners.

Brooklyn catcher Gil Hodges then dropped a third strike (which would have been the third out) with the batter reaching first base. Ramsdell walked the next two hitters, forcing in a run. Walker Cooper drove in all three runners with a double. In all, six runners scored, and Ramsdell was tagged with the loss.[11]

He fared better the next day, picking up the victory in relief at Philadelphia. Ineligible for the 1947 World Series, Willie spent the Series watching from the dugout.[12] After the season, the National Baseball Congress, the umbrella organization for semipro baseball, named Ramsdell 1947's "most valuable" graduate of its ranks. Willie was the first player to receive the award for his Minor League achievements.[13]

In 1948 Ramsdell began the season with the Dodgers. He made several relief appearances through April, with mixed results; in his worst effort, he walked three batters and made two wild pitches in two-thirds of an inning.[14]

In May, when the Dodgers reduced their roster to twenty-five players, Ramsdell was sent to Class Double-A Mobile (Alabama) in the Southern Association. He pitched only six innings there before the Dodgers brought him back to replace injured pitcher Hugh Casey. In July, with Casey recovered and Carl Erskine doing well in the Minors, the Dodgers called up Erskine. They sent Ramsdell to Fort Worth, where he stayed for the rest of the season.

Willie quickly overcame the disappointment of his demotion and helped the Cats win the Texas League pennant. He finished with a 7-2 record and a 3.00 ERA in seventy-eight innings, and he won several key games late in the season.[15]

In 1949 Ramsdell pitched the entire season for Hollywood in the Pacific Coast League. Used primarily as a starter, he finished with an 18-12 record with an ERA of 2.60. His manager, Fred Haney, said poor run support prevented Ramsdell from winning twenty games.[16]

"When Ramsdell pitches," said Al Unser, who caught him at Hollywood, "it's a three-way guessing game among the batter, the umpire, and me."[17] After nearly ten years of experience with the knuckler, Willie opted for a meteorological explanation to describe his flutter ball's unpredictability. "I got a suspicion," said the Knuck, "that it has something to do with the dew point."[18]

According to his wife, Opal, Willie's Hollywood time also included a brief appearance on the silver screen. He appeared as a pitcher in the 1950 movie *Kill the Umpire*, starring William Bendix.[19]

Ramsdell began the 1950 season with the Dodgers. Although his knuckle ball remained effective, he continued to have control problems. Ramsdell pitched only six innings in five games for Brooklyn, all in relief. He was sold to Cincinnati on May 10, reportedly for around $20,000.[20] At Cincinnati Ramsdell began as a reliever but ended up as a starting pitcher. His best 1950 performance was his 9–0 shutout of the Cubs on August 8. But scoring runs was a problem for the 1950 Cincinnati club; Ramsdell was one of the primary victims, as the sixth-place Reds were shut out in five of his twelve defeats.[21] He finished with a combined Brooklyn-Cincinnati record of 8-14 with a 3.68 ERA.

Ramsdell remained a starter for the Reds in 1951, and poor run support continued to dog him. Spanning the end of 1950 through the early games of 1951, Ramsdell pitched thirty-three consecutive innings without the Reds scoring a run for him.[22] He wound up the '51 season with a 9-17 mark for the sixth-place team. His thirty-one appearances included ten complete games and one shutout. He pitched 196 innings with a 4.04 ERA, while tying for the National League lead in wild pitches with nine.[23]

In January 1952 the Reds traded Ramsdell to the Chicago Cubs for pitcher Frank Hiller. When injuries struck several Cubs starting pitchers, Chicago used Ramsdell as a starter. Two of his starts against the Dodgers were memorable. His start at Ebbets Field, on May 18, enabled a classic action photo of Jackie Robinson stealing home with a brilliant hook slide. "Goddamn," screamed Willie to catcher Johnny Pramesa. "You shoulda got him."[24]

Starting against the Dodgers again on June 19, Willie found himself being Chicago's "star of the game" as Carl Erskine pitched a no-hitter. Erskine walked Ramsdell before a rain delay stopped the game. When play resumed, Erskine went on to pitch a no-hit, one-walk game. Being Chicago's guest star on Happy Felton's postgame show paid $50. According to Willie, he found himself pulling for Erskine to get the last batter he needed for the no-hitter so he could collect the cash.

Willie's last Major League appearance came in relief on July 15. Nine days later the Cubs released him to Los Angeles in the Pacific Coast League. He finished his Major League career with a 24-39 record and a 3.83 ERA.

Ramsdell finished 1952 with Los Angeles, going 5-6 while being used exclusively as a starter. He followed with brief stints in winter ball in Venezuela (Caracas Leones) and Cuba (Almendares Alacranes). In 1953 he was again pitching in the PCL. Willie began with Los Angeles, but after the Angels released him in early August, he ended with the Portland Beavers.[25]

Ramsdell's last professional season was 1954. After the Beavers released him in early January, he started the season near home as player-manager for Iola, Kansas, in the Class C Western Association. On May 19, however, he quit the hapless club after a 2-17 start. His blunt assessment: "I honestly feel we don't have the material to win in Class C."[26]

Willie then pitched at Beaumont in the Class Double-A Texas League and Colorado Springs in the Class A Western League. After the 1954 season, Ramsdell retired to Wichita. He continued to play semipro ball occasionally for local teams, including the Wichita Boeing Bombers. He reportedly raised cattle on a small farm and enjoyed singing in a local barbershop quartet.

In 1964 Ramsdell was among the twenty-five initial nominees to the Sandlot Hall of Fame, sponsored by the National Baseball Congress. The NBC chose one player from each of their national tournaments from 1935 to 1959.

After a long illness, Ramsdell died in Wichita on October 8, 1969, at age fifty-three. Perhaps reflecting the results of his earlier, happy-go-lucky days, his death certificate cites a wide array of liver-related problems as the principal causes of his death. In his obituary, *The Sporting News* noted that Willie was long on humor but short on luck during his Major League career.

JOHN HARRY STAHL

# Chapter 64. **Dick Whitman**

*Ted D. Smith*

| AGE | G | AB | R | H | 2B | 3B | HR | TB | RBI | BB | SO | BAV | OBP | SLG | SB | GDP | HBP |
|-----|---|----|----|----|----|----|----|----|-----|----|----|------|------|------|----|-----|-----|
| 26 | 4 | 10 | 1 | 4 | 0 | 0 | 0 | 4 | 2 | 1 | 0 | .400 | .455 | .400 | 0 | 0 | 0 |

Dick Whitman's life was described by his brother-in-law Bob Read as "the kind of story that maybe America was built on." A member of "The Greatest Generation" that survived the Great Depression and fought totalitarianism in World War II, he forged a professional baseball career that began in 1942 and ended in 1957. While the war delayed Whitman's big league debut, he eventually played as an outfielder for three pennant-winning teams in his six years as a Major Leaguer. His most notable contribution came as a member of the 1950 Philadelphia Phillies, for whom he served as a pinch hitter and substitute outfielder during the team's pennant drive.

Dick Corwin Whitman was born on November 9, 1920, in Woodburn, Oregon, thirty miles south of Portland. His parents were Clyde Eli Whitman and the former Nancy Margaret Hicks. The couple also had a daughter, Virginia, born in 1928. Clyde was in the Oregon National Guard and saw action at the Mexican border in 1916, and he served in France in World War I.

Dick's baseball abilities were apparent early. After starring for his local high school team, he played alongside fellow future Major Leaguers Johnny Pesky and Joe Erautt in 1938 and 1939 for the Silverton Red Sox, a local semipro team. The Silverton team was highly successful, winning the Northwest regional tournament and competing in the National Baseball Congress semipro championship tournament in Wichita in both those years. The 1939 team went 34-2, finishing third nationally. Pesky, Erautt, and Whitman all made the 1939 national semipro All-Star team.

Upon graduation from high school in 1938,

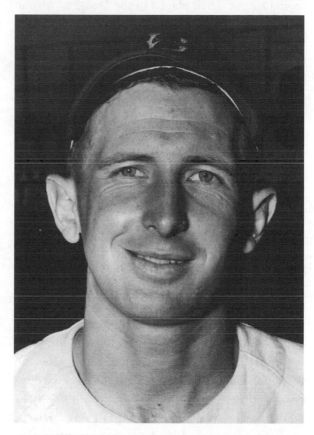

Dick Whitman was a semi-regular in 1946, but he appeared in only four games in 1947.

Whitman enrolled at the University of Oregon, where he was an active member of the Sigma Nu fraternity and played on fraternity teams in a number of intramural sports. On the baseball field, he was a standout center fielder for the Ducks' varsity team from 1940 through 1942, batting .397 for his college career, a mark that still stands as the school record. The team won the Northern Division of the Pacific-8 conference in his junior and senior seasons (1941 and 1942). As a senior, Whitman was captain of the team, leading the way offensively with a .412 average, 3 home runs, and 16 runs batted in, all team highs.

Scout Tom Downey of the Brooklyn Dodgers signed Whitman after his 1942 graduation from Oregon. Dick played in the Dodgers' Minor League system that summer, first for Santa Barbara in the Class C California League, then for the Durham (North Carolina) Bulls of the Class B Piedmont League. But the United States had entered the Second World War the previous winter, and like many able-bodied men of his generation, Whitman entered the military. He had enlisted in the Oregon National Guard in September 1940, with active duty deferred until after his graduation.

Called to active duty in November 1942, he served in the army in Europe from December 1944 until January 1946 as a member of the Eighty-Third Infantry Division, rising to the rank of master sergeant. He suffered shrapnel wounds and frostbite in the Battle of the Bulge and was awarded the Purple Heart and a Bronze Star for bravery in battle, along with three battle stars. He carried a scar on his right cheek as a result of the shrapnel.

Whitman resumed his baseball career after the war and immediately earned a spot on the Dodgers' 1946 roster, hitting .260 with 2 home runs while playing in a career-high 104 games. His 31 RBIS, 39 runs scored, and 69 base hits were also career highs. He made his Major League debut on April 16 in Boston, going 0 for 3 with a run batted in against Johnny Sain. Whitman had his first Major League hit on April 18 in the Dodgers' home opener. With the bases filled, the five-foot-eleven, 170-pound Whitman lined a two-strike pitch from Giants pitcher Harry Feldman to left-center field for a double, driving in two runs.

The 1946 Dodgers were a very good team that fought the Cardinals for first place all season. After action on June 29, the Dodgers opened a four-game lead thanks in part to Whitman's first Major League home run, a two-run blow off Boston's Ed Wright. Roscoe McGowen of the *New York Times* called it a "Ruthian wallop into Bedford Avenue." Whitman would hit only one more Major League home run. The Dodgers and Cardinals had identical records after the 154-game season. A best-of-three playoff series was scheduled to determine the winner of the pennant.

The Cardinals won both games to move on to the World Series. Whitman was a defensive replacement in the first playoff game; he started the second game, going 0 for 4. Later that fall Whitman married Joan Beck, whom he had grown up with in Woodburn and to whom he would remain married until his death.

The Dodgers had a crowded outfield situation in 1947, with Dixie Walker, Carl Furillo, and Pete Reiser as the established starters. While Whitman was considered a good prospect, the Dodgers had other prospects that looked even more promising. Whitman thus spent most of 1947 with the Dodgers' Class Triple-A team, the Montreal Royals. He did well at Montreal, batting .327, slugging ten home runs, and at one point putting together a twenty-three-game hitting streak, the longest in the International League that season.

Whitman appeared in four games for the Dodgers after getting a late-season call-up, but he did not play in the 1947 World Series. He spent more time with the big league club in 1948 and 1949, playing in sixty and twenty-three games, respectively. He batted .291 in 165 at bats in '48, getting most of his playing time as a pinch hitter or spelling Gene Hermanski in right field. He made one appearance in the 1949 World Series, as a pinch hitter in Game Four, striking out against Allie Reynolds to end the game.

After Whitman's disappointing 1949 campaign, in which he batted .184, the Dodgers sold him to the Philadelphia Phillies on October 14. This was part of a general clearing-out of the overstocked Dodger farm system by Branch Rickey, who sold

TED D. SMITH

ten players to various clubs in a matter of days. It was a fortunate move for Whitman, though, since it was with the 1950 Phillies that he had his greatest impact as a Major Leaguer.

The starting outfield for the Phillies that season featured Del Ennis in right, Richie Ashburn in center, and Dick Sisler in left. That trio missed few games during the pennant-winning campaign, but Whitman was the primary outfield sub, playing thirty-two games in the field spread among all three positions. He was also the team's best pinch hitter, going 12 for 39 (.308) in that role and appearing in seventy-five games overall. His twelve pinch hits led the National League.

Whitman appeared in three of the four games against the Yankees in the 1950 World Series, all as a pinch hitter, going 0 for 2 with a walk. He started the 1951 season with Philadelphia but got off to a slow start, appearing in only nineteen games, mostly as a pinch hitter, with only two hits. On June 8 the Phillies sold Whitman to the St. Paul Saints, Brooklyn's Class Triple-A affiliate in the American Association. They made the move to make room for Tommy Brown, who had been purchased from Brooklyn the previous day. Whitman never again appeared in a Major League game.

Whitman continued in the Dodgers' Minor League system through 1954. He was with St. Paul from 1951 through part of 1953. During the 1953 season, he was transferred to Montreal, where he played through 1954. In Montreal in 1954, he was a teammate of future Hall of Famer Roberto Clemente; Royals manager Max Macon sometimes gave playing time to the veteran Whitman over the young Clemente, which severely frustrated the future star. There has been speculation that the Dodgers were attempting to "hide" Clemente from other teams by limiting his playing time. Evidence suggests, however, that Macon's use of the left-handed-hitting Whitman over the right-handed-hitting Clemente in certain situations had

more to do with his affinity for platooning than with a conscious attempt to cover up Clemente's talent.

For the 1955 season, Whitman returned to his native Oregon to play for the Portland Beavers of the Pacific Coast League. Dick had always maintained ties to his home state during his playing career, making his off-season home in Eugene, where he had gone to college. He performed ably for the Beavers, batting .304 and driving in fifty runs while playing regularly in the field.

In 1956 Whitman, by then a thirty-five-year-old veteran of eleven seasons in professional baseball, was hired as a player-manager for the San Jose Jo-Sox in the Class C California League. That year he led the league in batting with a .391 average, playing in 129 of the team's 140 games, mostly in center field. He was named the league's MVP, while leading his team to a third-place finish. Whitman returned for a second season as player-manager in 1957, with his team finishing fifth. It was his final season of professional baseball.

Dick Whitman's baseball career was probably typical of most professional ballplayers', in that it was composed more of laboring in relative obscurity in the Minors than in achieving stardom in the big leagues. Of his thirteen seasons playing professionally, only six included stints in the Major Leagues. Only three of those seasons (1946, 1949, and 1950) did not include at least some time in the Minors. He was never a regular starter in any Major League season, his main contributions coming as a pinch hitter and in giving the regular outfield starters an occasional day off.

Whitman's career batting average as a pinch hitter was .286 (26 for 91), thirty-two points higher than his batting average in other roles; all of his World Series appearances were as a pinch hitter. Yet he always kept his love and passion for the game and enjoyed telling stories of his professional baseball career.

After retiring from baseball, Whitman settled

in San Jose. He worked for the local water company until his retirement in the mid-1980s. He and Joan moved to Peoria, Arizona, in 1991, where he enjoyed golfing and became an avid fan of the Arizona Diamondbacks. Whitman died of a heart attack on February 12, 2003, in Peoria. He was survived by Joan; a daughter, Alison Mettler; and sons Richard and Joseph, along with five grandchildren and two great-grandchildren. Whitman was inducted posthumously into the University of Oregon Hall of Fame in 2004.

Upon his death, Joan said, "He loved baseball, loved playing the game. . . . It was his life and he made it a great life."

# Chapter 65. **Erv Palica**

*Mark Stewart*

| AGE | W | L | PCT. | ERA | G | GS | GF | CG | SHO | SV | IP | H | BB | SO | HBP | WP |
|-----|---|---|------|-----|---|----|----|----|-----|----|----|----|----|----|-----|-----|
| 19 | 0 | 1 | .000 | 3.00 | 3 | 0 | 1 | 0 | 0 | 0 | 3.0 | 2 | 2 | 1 | 1 | 0 |

Erv Palica, a laconic Californian, was little more than a bit player during the 1947 season, but four years later he was at the epicenter of a midseason controversy that may have cost the Dodgers the 1951 pennant.

Palica was born on February 9, 1928, in Lomita, California, a small town west of Long Beach. His parents, Ambrose and Phyllis (Marzurana) Pavliccivich, were German-speaking native Austrians who immigrated to the United States before the beginning of World War I. As the family moved to California from Michigan, around 1920, the surname was shortened to Palica. The youngest of six athletic brothers, Erv honed his skills on the diamond by competing with his siblings. Four of the Palica boys found their way into pro ball during the 1940s. The fifth (and eldest), Christy, was killed in the Philippines during World War II.

There was little mistaking who the real talent in the family was. Even as a skinny adolescent (he ultimately filled out to 6 feet 1½ and 180 pounds), Erv Palica displayed a quick bat, live right arm, strong legs, quick feet, and a seemingly unquenchable thirst for baseball knowledge. He was introspective and polite, rarely speaking unless spoken to; over the years, his demeanor remained essentially unchanged.

After his sophomore season at Narbonne High School in Harbor City, he was chosen to the all–Los Angeles schoolboy team. Palica was among those honored as high school All-Americans in 1944 by *Esquire* magazine, and he was invited to play in the magazine's East-West All-Star Game at the Polo Grounds.

Brooklyn Dodgers scout Tom Downey signed

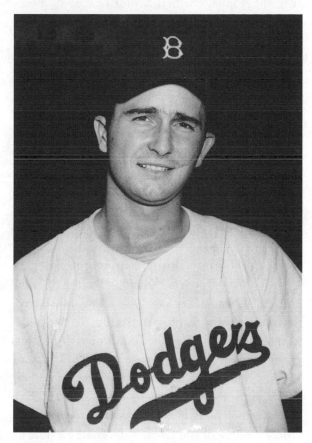

Erv Palica's pitching debut came on September 18 when he threw four balls to the only batter he faced.

Palica on January 25, 1945. The sixteen-year-old high school junior reported to spring training at the team's wartime camp in Bear Mountain, New York. Palica considered himself a pitcher, but general manager Branch Rickey had other plans. Rickey took a liking to Palica's skills and, with Pee Wee Reese still in the service, thought he might have discovered a short-term answer to the team's shortstop needs.

Palica broke camp with the club and saw action in two games as a pinch runner before being farmed out. His first Major League appearance came against the New York Giants at the Polo Grounds on April 21, making Palica (seventeen years, two months, twelve days) the youngest player in the league. His first Minor League stop was with the Mobile (Alabama) Bears of the Class A Southern Association. He was the youngest player on the Mobile club by a good three years. Manager Clay Hopper pointed Palica toward third base, where he toiled for several weeks before getting a chance to pitch in a mop-up role.

This one outing convinced Brooklyn's Minor League brass that Palica had a future on the mound. They sent him to Newport News (Virginia) of the Class B Piedmont League to hone his craft under manager Jake Pitler. In twenty-three mound appearances, Palica went 11-8. He also made twenty nonpitching appearances, filling a utility role for the team and batting .308.

In 1946 the Dodgers trained in Daytona Beach, Florida. When Rickey saw Palica, he recalled having wanted him to play shortstop. To the eighteen-year-old's dismay, he found himself fielding grounders off the bat of coach Charlie Dressen. Dressen informed Rickey that the teenager had no future in the infield.

Nevertheless, Palica was assigned to the Asheville Travelers of the Class B Tri-State League to relearn the shortstop position. The experiment officially ended on May 8, when he threw away eight balls in a game against the Anderson (South Carolina) Athletics. Erv returned to the mound, where he won fifteen games, lost only six, and turned in a nifty 2.51 earned run average.

Palica was optioned to the Class Triple-A Montreal Royals in 1947, reuniting him with manager Clay Hopper. In twenty-five starts, Palica went 12-10 with a 4.18 ERA. He was recalled to Brooklyn on September 14 and had one loss in three games in the waning days of the season. His late call-up made him ineligible for the World Series, which Brooklyn lost to the Yankees in seven games.

Palica's debut as a Major League pitcher came on September 18 in Pittsburgh's Forbes Field. Though he had appeared in the Majors as a base runner in 1945, standing on the mound was a very different and terrifying new experience—and he got a case of the shakes. After throwing four straight balls to the only batter he faced, forcing home a run, manager Burt Shotton replaced him.

Palica made the Dodgers out of spring training in 1948, earning a spot in Leo Durocher's bullpen. Durocher had been the manager when the youngster played for Brooklyn in 1945, but Leo was in the midst of serving a one-year suspension in 1947 during Palica's return to the club. The fiery manager was impressed by Palica's poise in tight spots. There was none of the shakiness from the previous September. He went right after hitters, using his darting fastball to set up the curve when it was working, and occasionally employing a knuckleball. Durocher appreciated a hard-throwing kid who dared to fool hitters with soft stuff. Palica would not be as lucky with the skippers who followed Durocher.

Palica was among Brooklyn's most dependable relievers in 1948. On April 24 he sparkled in a six-inning relief effort against the Phillies, claiming his first Major League win. This earned him a spot in the starting rotation when Harry Taylor was felled by appendicitis. Palica went 6-6 in ten starts and thirty-one relief appearances in 1948.

The 1949 season was something of a breakthrough for Palica. He claimed the top spot in the Brooklyn bullpen, leading the club with forty-nine appearances (forty-eight in relief). Still the youngest player on the club, he notched eight wins and six saves in 1949, while lowering his ERA to 3.62. He was so good that throughout the season, fans and beat writers continually questioned why Shotton kept him in the bullpen. (Shotton was again the manager, having replaced Durocher midway through the 1948 season.) Palica had the poise and arm of a first-rate starter, but the manager did not seem to trust him in that role. During the September stretch, as the Dodgers nailed down their second pennant in three seasons, Erv saw little in the way of meaningful action.

The Dodgers moved on to face the Yankees in the World Series. Palica, still out of favor with Shotton, did not make his first postseason appearance until Game Five after New York had already scored ten runs.

The Dodgers entered 1950 favored to repeat as National League champions. They had a splendid everyday lineup and two superb starters in Don Newcombe and Preacher Roe. Their only weakness was the back end of the starting staff, and Shotton spent much of the year shuttling pitchers in and out of the bullpen. Among them was Palica, who responded the best, making nineteen starts, completing ten, throwing two shutouts, making two dozen relief appearances while winning thirteen games, and keeping his ERA under 4.00. He fanned 131 batters to edge Newcombe for the team high, despite the fact that Newcombe logged sixty-six additional innings.

In retrospect, it is inexplicable that Shotton kept Palica in the bullpen for the better part of three months. Erv didn't win his first game until July; all of his production came in the second half. The lack of confidence in him that Shotton displayed at the end of 1949 had clearly carried over to 1950.

After the Dodgers dropped briefly into fourth place in July, Palica joined the rotation, and the team surged in the second half, closing in on the front-running Phillies. They never caught the Whiz Kids, but they came tantalizingly close in the final week. Palica was one of the stars during this run. From September 19 to 24, he won three games, including an 11–0 two-hitter against the Phillies. During that contest Palica hammered a ball over the fence in Shibe Park with the bases loaded. The

grand slam off rookie Bubba Church was his only Major League home run.

On the next-to-last day of the season, Palica pitched a marvelous 7–3 victory against Philadelphia, extending the Phillies' free-fall to five straight games and pulling the Dodgers within one game of the lead with one to play. The season finale, however, went to the Phillies on Dick Sisler's tenth-inning three-run homer.

In November 1950 Palica flunked his army physical because of high blood pressure. The army kept him at Fort Jay in Brooklyn and reexamined him two weeks later, only to find that the condition persisted. During spring training the following March, Palica was summoned to California by his local draft board. This time he was deemed fit to serve, but soon after he was given a deferment because of his wife Florence's difficult pregnancy. (Palica had married Florence Biondi, a Brooklyn native, on August 6, 1950.) Their baby was due late in the summer, so he would be able to remain a Dodger at least until then.

The 1951 season was also a bitter disappointment for the Dodgers and especially for Palica. Some were predicting a twenty-win campaign, but new manager Charlie Dressen—who had once been assigned to transform him into a shortstop—was not an Erv Palica fan. Dressen had come to view the young hurler as a hypochondriac. He also thought of him as a player who was always ready with a quick excuse. But what irritated Dressen most was Palica's refusal to make greater use of his fastball. Catcher Roy Campanella said Palica's heater had more life than that of any other Dodgers pitcher. So why, Dressen wondered, did he prefer to trick hitters instead of overwhelming them? In the manager's mind, it was a question of courage.

The situation came to a head during a July game against the Pirates at Ebbets Field. Palica had been complaining about a stiff arm and a sore right hip—a painful condition that seemed to afflict his push-off leg for a week or two almost every season. This time it had "popped" while he was on the mound in the tenth inning of a July 8 game against the Phillies. He was pitching to Tommy Brown when it happened, and Clyde King had to hustle in from the bullpen to preserve a 6–4 victory. The other Dodgers recognized that their teammate never quite felt 100 percent and ribbed him about it from time to time; still, they admired his talent and valued his self-effacing humor.

On July 18 Palica was tabbed for mop-up duty after the Pirates took a 10–2 lead. But the Dodgers came back to go ahead 12–11, at which point Palica yielded an eighth-inning home run to Ralph Kiner and a run-scoring single to Pete Reiser. The Pirates won, 13–12. Dressen was livid in the clubhouse. When asked to comment on Palica, he grabbed his throat in a choking gesture and ordered reporters to put it in print. He then launched into a tirade: "He's got more alibis than Carter's has liver pills! If it isn't his fanny it's his arm! If it's not that, it's his groin! If it's not that, he's worried about his wife! If it's not that, he can't run with his high blood pressure! If it's not that, the Army is going to get him!

"The guy is a joke around the team," Dressen continued. "The players laugh at him. One day when he said he was ready, they gave him a big hand of applause in the clubhouse."

When asked about Palica's stuff, Dressen claimed he had yet to see Palica throw a real fastball all season. Finally, he called Palica "a gutless kid who doesn't belong in the majors." Brooklyn general manager Buzzy Bavasi backed up his manager, announcing that he would cut Palica's salary the following season—quite a proclamation considering there was still a half season left to play.

Dressen was criticized by players and fans for his outburst. Billy Meyer, the Pirates' manager, added he had felt the same way as Dressen about many players, but on principle alone had kept those thoughts out of reporters' notebooks. "You don't go and put it in the papers that you think a man is gutless," he admonished. "It isn't ethical."

Bavasi was also openly questioned by his peers. Palica would have fetched six figures in a straight sale to almost any team in baseball. Now that the Dodgers had tipped their hand, they would receive little more than his waiver price if they put him on the market. Branch Rickey Jr., an executive with Pittsburgh, estimated that Dressen and Bavasi had cost Brooklyn $150,000.

Two days later, Bavasi engaged in some ham-handed damage control. He told columnist Dan Daniel that Dressen meant no harm—"he merely wanted to light a fire under Palica"—but that the manager probably should have asked the writers to keep his outburst out of the papers. Bavasi then offered that Shotton had voiced the same frustration about Palica but had "always enjoined the reporters to secrecy."

Erv Palica was never the same after the Pittsburgh incident. The team left him behind on the next road trip, partly as punishment but also to deal with his physical problems. When he rejoined the club, he was banished to the back of the bullpen during a critical time in the pennant race. Palica's record stood at 2-6 and his ERA had ballooned to 4.75 when his season ended prematurely in mid-September, five weeks after the birth of his first child, Joanne. With mother and baby doing well, the army told him it was time to report.

Palica spent all of 1952 and most of the 1953 season in the service, staying in shape by pitching for the base team at Fort Dix, New Jersey. Although his discharge wasn't scheduled until the end of the '53 season, Palica received approval from Commissioner Ford Frick to pitch for the Dodgers on days when he wasn't otherwise engaged. He was in uniform for an early August series with the Braves, and Dressen, perhaps hoping to prove there were no hard feelings, inserted him into a tight game. Palica faced six batters and five of them reached base.

Dressen used Palica just four times that year, as the Dodgers cruised to the pennant. Erv watched as a noncombatant while his teammates dropped another Fall Classic to the Yankees.

Palica was back in shape for spring training in 1954. He was delighted to return to a clubhouse devoid of Dressen, who had been replaced by Walter Alston. Palica made twenty-two relief appearances and three starts in '54 but failed to show his old form.

After the season the Dodgers traded Preacher Roe and Billy Cox to the Baltimore Orioles. When Roe chose to retire, the Dodgers sent Palica to the Orioles instead. Erv was handed a starting role by Baltimore manager Paul Richards. He went 5-11 with a 4.13 ERA for the seventh-place Orioles.

Palica returned to Baltimore for the 1956 season, serving as a spot starter and reliever during another losing year. From 1957 through 1959, he pitched for the Orioles' Pacific Coast League team, the Vancouver Mounties, posting records of 15-12, 15-13, and 13-10.

In 1960 Palica was offered a job in the Boston Red Sox organization, but he did not make the big club. He pitched in one game for the Minneapolis Millers before returning to the West Coast, this time with the Seattle Rainiers, a Cincinnati farm team.

After several more seasons in the Minors, Palica called it a career at the age of thirty-five. He finished with a Minor League record of 115-83. As a Major Leaguer, his record was 41-55 in 246 appearances.

Palica then returned to Southern California and found work as a longshoreman. In 1971 the Mets flew him in for an old-timers' game at Shea Stadium. The Dodgers, just a stone's throw away from his Huntington Beach home, never asked him back.

Palica stayed in touch with Duke Snider and a handful of other former Brooklyn teammates, including Wayne Belardi, a fellow Californian. His home was uncluttered by baseball keepsakes. He had a Schaefer beer mug from some long-forgotten postgame TV guest appearance. And there was the 1949 team ring, according to Florence his only prize possession.

Palica was toiling on the docks near his home in Huntington Beach when he suffered a heart attack. He died on May 29, 1982, at age fifty-four. He was survived by his wife, Florence, and all five of his children—daughters Joanne, Dianne, and Suzanne, and sons Daniel and Wayne.

# Chapter 66. **Ed Stevens**

*Jim Kreuz*

| AGE | G | AB | R | H | 2B | 3B | HR | TB | RBI | BB | SO | BAV | OBP | SLG | SB | GDP | HBP |
|---|---|---|---|---|---|---|---|---|---|---|---|---|---|---|---|---|---|
| 22 | 5 | 13 | 0 | 2 | 1 | 0 | 0 | 3 | 0 | 1 | 5 | .154 | .214 | .231 | 0 | 0 | 0 |

Ed Stevens was born in Texas on January 12, 1925, in the town that twenty-five years earlier had witnessed the worst natural disaster in the United States, the 1900 Galveston Hurricane. Stevens grew up in Galveston playing baseball with his brother and his friends. He was a left-handed-hitting, left-handed-fielding first baseman who was big by 1940s standards—six feet one and 190 pounds.

In 1941, at the age of sixteen, he was signed to a contract by the Brooklyn Dodgers. He spent his first professional season with the Big Spring (Texas) Bombers of the Class D West Texas–New Mexico League. Stevens did well, finishing with a .271 batting average and thirteen home runs in 117 games.

Ed started the following year, 1942, with the Lamesa (Texas) Dodgers in the same league, Big Spring having dropped out of the league. His .367 average and .633 slugging percentage resulted in a midseason move to the Johnstown Johnnies of the Class D Pennsylvania State Association, where he hit .273 over the final forty-six games of the season.

The Dodgers liked what they saw, and after Ed was forced to sit out the 1943 season with an injury, they assigned him in 1944 to their top farm club, the Montreal Royals of the International League.

Stevens batted .271 with 16 home runs and 102 runs batted in at Montreal in 1944. The following season he did even better, batting .309 with 19 home runs and 95 RBIs in 110 games. The 1945 Royals finished in first place, but minus Stevens, they lost to the Newark Bears in the playoffs.

Ed Stevens was sent to the Minors in 1947 to make way for Jackie Robinson to play first base.

Called up by the Dodgers in August, Ed made his Major League debut in the first game of a doubleheader against Cincinnati on August 9. Inserted in the sixth inning, he went 0 for 1, but he started the second game and went 3 for 5 with an RBI and a run scored.

His first Major League hit came off Reds pitcher Howie Fox; his first home run was on August 19, off Pittsburgh's Fritz Ostermueller. In all, the twenty-year-old Stevens played in fifty-five games for the 1945 Dodgers, finishing with a respectable .274 average and twenty-nine RBIS.

Asked about his memories of playing during World War II, Stevens recalled walking along the Galveston seawall, wearing his blue and white Brooklyn warm-up jacket, holding future wife Margie's hand, when a car drove by and a young man inside hollered out, "You lousy bum!" Stevens assumed the heckler thought the Dodgers jacket was an advertisement that he was a draft-dodger, and not that he was a "lousy bum from Brooklyn."

The 1946 season was full of promise, not only for Stevens but also for the Dodgers. They had a good mix of ballplayers—Eddie Stanky, Dixie Walker, Pee Wee Reese, Pete Reiser, and Carl Furillo—plus the best general manager in the game, Branch Rickey, and a competent manager in Leo Durocher.

Stevens platooned at first base with right-handed hitter Howie Schultz in '46. Playing in 103 games, he had a .242 batting average, 10 home runs, and 60 runs batted in. When the regular season ended, the Dodgers were tied for first place with the St. Louis Cardinals, and a best-of-three playoff series was needed to decide the pennant winner.

The Cardinals took the first game in St. Louis, 4–2, behind left-hander Howie Pollet with Schultz at first base and Stevens on the bench. Schultz got two hits, including a home run and batted in both Brooklyn runs.

The second game, played in Brooklyn, was Stevens's opportunity to match Schultz's performance, and he did it with two hits—a single and a triple—while driving in two runs. He drove in Augie Galan in the bottom of the first inning with a two-out single to put the Dodgers up 1–0. Then, with the Dodgers facing an 8–1 deficit and down to their final at bat, Stevens again drove in Galan, this time with a triple. Stevens later scored on Carl Furillo's single, but it was not enough: the Cards took the second game 8–4 and the series, 2–0. Stevens's two hits were among only five the Dodgers could muster against Cardinals right-hander Murry Dickson.

Ed Stevens was always sure of himself at the plate with a bat in his hands, but he did not carry that same level of confidence early on with his glove. While fielding hard-thrown balls from his infielders that either were in the dirt or took a short hop in front of him, he would make a quick stab down at the ground with his mitt. Occasionally he would come up empty, resulting in an error on either him or the other infielder.

It was not until 1946 that Dodgers shortstop Pee Wee Reese, just back from World War II, pulled Stevens aside one day and tutored him on the art of fielding. Pee Wee told Ed he should get in a crouched position, with his glove touching the ground, and field the ball while bringing his glove up vertically, exactly the opposite of how Stevens had been practicing. The tip greatly improved his fielding and allowed him to be more comfortable at the plate as a result. Back then, it was not normal for a veteran to help a rookie, so it really made an impression on this young ballplayer, and he became a lifelong Reese friend and fan as a result.

In 1947 the Dodgers moved their spring training to Havana, Cuba, in part to help Jackie Robinson avoid the racism of the American South. Robinson had played second base at Montreal in 1946, but the Dodgers had veteran Ed Stanky at second and decided to use Jackie at first base.

Stevens's recollection of Jackie Robinson was that he was the consummate teammate, got along with everyone, and was the most focused individual he had ever met. When Robinson stepped onto the playing field, he was there to win, and nothing was going to get in his way, Stevens said. He had the utmost respect for Jackie. On a wall in his Houston home he hung a photo of the two young men side by side, smiling, while leaning over the dugout steps at Ebbets Field.

Shortly after the season began, Branch Rickey told Stevens that if he would agree to go down to

Montreal to make room for Robinson, and that if he had a good year, Rickey would try to trade Stanky to another team. This would enable Robinson to move to his natural position at second base in 1948, and allow Stevens to play first base. Stevens said Rickey promised him he would be Brooklyn's first baseman for ten to fifteen years, as long as his abilities held up. Ed replied that he did not see any reason why he had to leave the Brooklyn club, and that he had made the team and deserved to play.

According to Stevens, Rickey supposedly replied, "Well, I'm going to reward you if you'll do this for me, if you'll go down there and get in shape." Ed said he knew Rickey had already made up his mind, so he agreed. Stevens hit .290 with 27 home runs and 108 RBIs for the Royals. Late in the season, Rickey brought him back to the big club, but three days too late to qualify for the 1947 World Series roster. Then, on November 13, 1947, Rickey sold both Stevens and infielder Stan Rojek to the Pittsburgh Pirates.

Stevens spent three seasons, 1948–50, playing for the Pirates, taking over first base from the departing Hank Greenberg. In his first season, he batted behind Ralph Kiner, who led the National League with forty home runs. Every time Kiner hit a home run, Stevens said, the opposing pitcher threw at the next batter (Stevens). Ed reminded Kiner of this when they met for breakfast in Houston in 1991 while Kiner was in town for an autograph session. Kiner's reply was a soft chuckle and a big grin.

Stevens played in 128 games for the Pirates in 1948 and 67 in 1949. He had his best Major League season in '48, with 10 home runs, 19 doubles, and career highs in RBIs (69) and hits (109). He also had a great year in the field, committing just 4 errors for a .996 fielding percentage. In 1950 Stevens appeared in just seventeen games, and in midseason the Pirates sent him to their Class Triple-A affiliate at Indianapolis. He finished the 1950 season

and played the entire 1951 season with Indianapolis. In 1952 Ed signed with the Toronto Maple Leafs of the International League, where he was the regular first baseman through 1956. During that span, he hit 100 home runs and had 524 RBIs. He led the league in RBIs twice and was named to two postseason All-Star teams. In 2009 he was inducted into the International League Hall of Fame.

Now well into his thirties, Stevens moved frequently in the '57, '58, and '59 seasons, playing for five teams in the International League, American Association, and Southern Association. He sat out the 1960 season and retired after seventeen games with Mobile (Alabama) of the Southern Association in 1961.

With his playing days over, Stevens became a full-time scout for the Minnesota Twins. Over the years, Ed scouted for several clubs, including the Seattle Mariners and Oakland A's.

Asked about the one player he misjudged while scouting, he didn't hesitate—Nolan Ryan. He explained that he missed on Ryan by coming to the same conclusion that all the other scouts and Houston Colt .45s general manager Paul Richards had—that Ryan was too skinny and would blow out his arm quickly. The lone exception was Red Murff, the scout who signed Ryan for the New York Mets. Ed always regretted "the one that got away."

When Stevens retired from baseball, he was forty-two days short of the number required for earning pension benefits. He was able to make up that difference in 1981, when San Diego Padres manager Jack McKeon allowed coach Eddie Brinkman to step aside for forty-four days while Stevens filled his position.

Ed Stevens and his wife, Margie, now live in a quiet neighborhood in southwest Houston. Ed had married Margie Lee Saxon on April 16, 1943, in Meadsville, Mississippi. The couple had three daughters: Janice, born in 1946; Barbara, born in 1950; and Vikki, born in 1953.

JIM KREUZ

# Chapter 67. **Walter O'Malley**

*Andy McCue*

Walter Francis O'Malley, the owner who dragged baseball franchises across the country and baseball management into the twentieth century, was born in New York City on October 9, 1903.

A boy who barely played the game, O'Malley wound up drawing comparisons to Adolf Hitler, Joseph Stalin, and Mephistopheles after moving his successful Brooklyn Dodgers franchise to Los Angeles for the 1958 season. He was called the most powerful man in baseball and the real commissioner during the 1960s, but his team wound up producing the free agent identified most closely with breaking the reserve clause and revolutionizing the economics of Major League Baseball.

Walter was the only child of Edwin and Alma (Feltner) O'Malley. Edwin was a clerk in the dry-goods business who subsequently moved to the distant reaches of Queens and migrated to real estate and Democratic politics. He spent a stormy seven years as city commissioner of public markets. The increasingly affluent Edwin shipped Walter off to Culver Academy, an exclusive and expensive prep school in northern Indiana.

From Culver, Walter moved to the University of Pennsylvania, graduating in 1926. His main claim to fame at Penn was as a student organizer and politician. He was the first Penn man ever elected class president in both his junior and senior years, and he was selected as "Spoon Man" by his classmates, one of Penn's high honors each year.

Walter moved to another Ivy League school, Columbia University, for law school. However, after one year, he dropped out of Columbia and moved his law studies to night school at Fordham University. He was out of the Ivy League and back

Walter O'Malley was already moving to take control of the club during the 1947 season.

with the Catholic strivers. O'Malley later said his father had lost all his money.

Edwin apparently hadn't lost all his influence in the city, however, for Walter immediately landed a job that paid the night-school bills. It was in the city's engineering department, and O'Malley would subsequently claim he had studied engineering at Penn. His transcript, however, reveals no engineering courses and some early difficulties with mathematics. Nevertheless, he subsequently moved to an engineering firm that did business with the city, and then he opened Walter F.

O'Malley Engineering Co. while completing Fordham Law in 1930.

The Depression was not a good time to enter the legal field, but O'Malley's opportunistic eye soon found a niche to suit the times. It started, he said, when a priest who needed a will picked him out of the phone directory because O'Malley was a good County Mayo name. Among the dying man's assets were mortgage bonds on properties that were going bankrupt because tenants didn't have the money to pay the rent.

O'Malley conceived of a scheme that reorganized these real estate investments to allow the debts to be paid off. He brought his idea to George V. McLaughlin, head of the Brooklyn Trust Co., which had made the loans that funded many of these real estate ventures. McLaughlin bought the idea and, more importantly, he took on O'Malley as a protégé.

One of McLaughlin's biggest headaches was the Brooklyn Dodgers, a small business in financial terms, but one with a high profile that could bring the bank much adverse publicity. The death of Charles Ebbets and Edward McKeever in 1925 had left the team's board split evenly between Ebbets's heirs and those of the McKeever family.

In 1938 McLaughlin pushed the heirs into providing better management. On a recommendation from St. Louis Cardinals general manager Branch Rickey, their first choice, the board hired Larry MacPhail to run the team. MacPhail made a great deal of progress both on and off the field before resigning to serve in World War II. Late in 1942 the board turned again to Rickey, and this time he accepted. Rickey wanted a new lawyer for the team, as the team's current firm also handled matters for the National League and Rickey thought conflicts might arise. McLaughlin recommended O'Malley, who joined the team in the winter of 1942–43.

In late 1944 he, Rickey, John L. Smith of Pfizer Chemical, and Andrew Schmitz, a Brooklyn insurance man with ties to McLaughlin, were announced as buyers of the 25 percent of the team owned by the heirs of Edward McKeever. Schmitz soon dropped out. In mid-1945 the Rickey-O'Malley-Smith triumvirate bought the 50 percent of the team that had been owned by the Ebbets estate. At McLaughlin's insistence, the 75 percent owned by the triumvirate had to be voted as a block, to prevent the kind of 50–50 splits that had plagued the team during the 1930s.

O'Malley's role on the team was to deal with legal and business affairs, leaving Rickey to concentrate on identifying and nurturing on-field talent. O'Malley worked with the radio and television contracts and sponsorships. He dealt with the maintenance of Ebbets Field. He served as liaison to the Catholic hierarchy when Leo Durocher's marriage to Laraine Day led to a threatened withdrawal of Catholic youth groups from the Knothole Gang program.

Within a couple of years, the internal politics of the team had settled down to a duel between Rickey and O'Malley, two strong-willed, highly intelligent men with a desire to run the team. The prize was the vote of John Smith, an experienced and thoughtful business executive who approached his ownership with the eyes of a prudent fan. Within the partnership agreement, whoever got Smith's vote controlled the 75 percent of the stock.

In 1950, soon after Smith died, O'Malley bought out Rickey's 25 percent. Because the partnership agreement was still in place, this effectively gave him control of the team. Smith's widow was content to be a silent partner and eventually sold out to O'Malley when the Dodgers moved to Los Angeles.

O'Malley moved to make changes. He put his baseball people, notably Emil J. "Buzzie" Bavasi, in charge of the farm system and the Major League team while he concentrated on business operations and a new stadium.

He began an extensive promotion of group sales and city promotions. Group sales extended the team's contacts with youth, religious, corporate, and service groups. City promotions brought fans to the ballpark from the suburbs that were springing up on Long Island, draining people from Brooklyn. O'Malley negotiated the broadcasting contracts and worked on the development of the Dodgers' Vero Beach property, a former navy base in Florida that Rickey had acquired after World War II for use as a spring training complex.

O'Malley turned marketing into a year-round function for the front office at a time when some teams still closed their offices for several months during the winter. He began to expand the number of promotions and jumped on opportunities for publicity. But all of O'Malley's promotions weren't enough to stem the steady attendance decline that affected all of baseball in the decade after World War II. Television and suburbanization were the big trends, and O'Malley came to regret his earlier decision to maximize television revenue by putting as many games on television as possible.

Strong performance on the field helped keep the team performing well and drawing better than others. But that couldn't slow an overall attendance decline. When the Dodgers won their first World Series, in 1955, attendance that year was less than 60 percent of what it had been eight years earlier.

By 1955 Ebbets Field was forty-three years old and showing its age. In addition, O'Malley's customers now came from their suburban homes in cars rather than on foot, subway, or bus. And there were barely five hundred parking spaces to accommodate them.

O'Malley floated plans for a modern stadium in *Collier's* magazine. He began talking up the team's need, and possible locations. He was willing to pay for the stadium; he sought the city's assistance in putting together the acreage he would need for both the structure and adequate parking. The city was not responsive.

The key figure in city government was Robert Moses, and O'Malley's relationship with Moses was complex. Moses was willing to bargain only if O'Malley would fit into Moses's plans, one of which was the redevelopment of some swampy land near LaGuardia Airport in the borough of Queens into a World's Fair site and large park. He was willing to build the Dodgers a stadium there. O'Malley pointed out that the site wasn't in Brooklyn and he wouldn't be able to own it. Moses said too bad.

O'Malley tried to raise the pressure on the city in a number of ways. In 1955 he announced that the team would play seven 1956 home games at Roosevelt Field in Jersey City. In late 1956 he sold Ebbets Field and its land to a housing developer. In 1957 he ostentatiously entertained Los Angeles officials at spring training in Vero Beach. Los Angeles badly wanted a Major League team, and its mayor was only too happy to crow that talks had been very positive.

At some point during this period, as Moses's intransigence persisted, Los Angeles's offer shifted from bargaining chip to real possibility in O'Malley's eyes. Some thought O'Malley had made his decision to move early on. Los Angeles officials were sure he didn't make it final until after the 1957 season, when the National League finally gave O'Malley and New York Giants owner Horace Stoneham permission to move.

Led by newspaper reporters and columnists who were losing two-thirds of the biggest sports franchises in town, New York reacted with vitriol. O'Malley had always suffered a tenuous relationship with the press. When he took over from Rickey, the initial reaction was positive, since Rickey had a reputation as sanctimonious and cheap. But that soon soured. O'Malley was, said Red Barber after leaving the team's radio booth, "a devious man, about the most devious man I know."

It would take decades for all the factors in O'Malley's decision to become both clear and accepted. Faced with declining sales, flat costs, and no hope of the stadium he felt would revive his position, O'Malley had done what many other businessmen were doing in the 1950s. He left New York.

Los Angeles was so hungry for Major League baseball that people flocked to the Los Angeles Coliseum. They set records for an Opening Day crowd and a day-game crowd. They doubled the Brooklyn single-game record. A million people had come out by early July, when they also passed the 1957 attendance in Brooklyn. Despite a putrid team on the field and steadily declining crowds through the season, they broke the Dodgers' annual attendance record by September.

The 1959 team drew over 2 million people, plus over 90,000 for each of three World Series games, each day setting a fresh record. The Dodgers won the Series in six games over the Chicago White Sox.

After a series of court battles, Dodger Stadium opened in April 1962, two years after O'Malley's planned debut. Both the stadium and the team that played there were an immediate success. From dugout seats to in-stadium restaurants, from a message board to terraced parking lots removing the need for people to climb stairs or ramps to their seats, Dodger Stadium was full of new ideas. It was the first large baseball stadium built without pillars that blocked the view from some seats.

The team lost a heartbreaking playoff series in 1962 (attendance 2.75 million) but won the World Series in 1963 (attendance 2.5 million) and 1965 (2.5 million again). Walter O'Malley paid off the $18 million it had taken to build the stadium. Now in his sixties, O'Malley was being hailed or condemned as "the real commissioner of baseball." In 1962 Bill Veeck tabbed O'Malley "Boss of Baseball." He probably was the most powerful figure in the game, but that didn't mean O'Malley always got what he wanted.

In late 1960, while he was still worried about building and financing his stadium, an American League expansion team was thrust into his territory as a tradeoff for the National League's return to New York City. O'Malley made lemonade, requiring that the new team, to be owned by Gene Autry and called the Angels, be a tenant in his new stadium. Their rent would give O'Malley more cash to pay off the stadium's building costs.

O'Malley unsuccessfully opposed such measures as the amateur draft, which began in 1965, and further expansion in 1969. Still, when owners stalled over selecting a new commissioner in 1969, it was O'Malley's proposal of Bowie Kuhn that carried the day.

The Dodgers, meanwhile, had been creating the business model other franchises were following. There was a beautiful stadium and a successful baseball operation, but there was also a strong front office emphasizing marketing and promotion. Significantly, O'Malley was also the first owner to pay extensive attention to the Hispanic market, broadcasting Dodgers games in Spanish from the team's first year in Los Angeles.

By 1970 Walter O'Malley was sixty-seven and ready to hand over the reins to his son Peter. Peter had been groomed by running Minor League operations and then Dodger Stadium. In early 1970 he became president of the team, running it on a day-to-day basis and putting an even stronger emphasis on marketing.

Walter became chairman of the board and continued to represent the team in baseball-wide discussions. As the 1970s progressed, it became clear that baseball's biggest issue was its relationship with the Major League Baseball Players' Association, surging under the leadership of Marvin Miller.

With O'Malley's perceived role as both *éminence grise* and labor moderate, it was ironic that the case that broke the back of the owners' economic position arose from the Dodgers. In 1975 Andy Messersmith, a pitcher who had won twenty games for the Dodgers the year before, asked the

Dodgers to give him a no-trade clause. The Dodgers, citing long-standing policy, refused. After acrimonious exchanges with general manager Al Campanis, the issue was bucked up to Peter O'Malley. By the time Peter passed the negotiations on to Walter, Messersmith already was strongly committed to testing free agency. Miller also had persuaded Dave McNally, a longtime Baltimore Orioles and Montreal Expos pitcher, to join the fight. Messersmith and McNally eventually took the case to arbitration, and the arbitrator ruled as everyone expected, opening the free agency era.

By the end of the Messersmith crisis in early 1976, O'Malley was in declining health. He retired even further from management of the team, although he still attended spring training. Kay (Hanson) O'Malley, whom Walter married in 1931, died on July 12, 1979. Walter died the next month, on August 9. They had two children, Teresa, born in 1933, and Peter, born in 1937.

The O'Malley image over the years has focused on the morality of his moving the Dodgers from Brooklyn to Los Angeles. What has been lost in the focus on greed and morality is a recognition of the other effects, good and bad, that O'Malley had on the game. His management practices turned the Dodgers into the unchallenged model other sports franchises would follow. His emphasis on customer service, promotions, and relentless marketing radically changed the way not just baseball teams, but all sports franchises, did business.

Author Roger Kahn, who probably observed O'Malley more than any other writer had, summed him up as "an earth force lightly filtered through a personality."

# Chapter 68. John L. Smith

*Andy McCue*

The headline on John Lawrence Smith's *New York Times* obituary called him a "noted chemist," a label the unassuming executive would have appreciated. It wasn't until later that the story mentioned he was a part-owner of the Brooklyn Dodgers. To the non–baseball world, Smith had made his name as an executive of Charles Pfizer & Company, and especially for his role in leading the Brooklyn company's successful effort in pioneering the mass production of penicillin. His leadership was critical in moving Pfizer from a chemical supplier into an international pharmaceuticals giant. But to the baseball world of the late 1940s, he was the pivot on which the ownership of the Dodgers balanced.

Smith was born in Krefeld, Germany, on February 10, 1889, as Johann Schmitz, the son of Gottfried and Johanna (Dollbaum) Schmitz. Krefeld was the center of the German velvet industry, and Gottfried moved his family to Stonington, Connecticut, in 1892 to pursue opportunities in Stonington's velvet mills. While they spoke German at home, the family formally changed its name to Smith in 1918, presumably as the result of anti-German agitation during World War I. John, who was naturalized in 1908, used the Anglicized version from the time he entered the working world at age seventeen.

Gottfried and his four other children remained in Stonington, mostly working in the mills, but John had larger ambitions. In 1906 he moved to New York City, looking for work as a chemist. He found a job as a laboratory assistant with Pfizer in Brooklyn and began to take classes at Cooper Union. While working and studying, Smith found time for baseball (which he said he played poorly) and track (where he did better). It was the beginning of a lifelong interest in sports.

In 1914 Smith got his degree in chemistry, married Mary Louise Becker, and moved to E. R. Squibb, where he oversaw the development of a large-scale ether-making facility at their plant in New Brunswick, New Jersey. In 1919 he returned to Pfizer, becoming plant superintendent. He would remain at Pfizer the rest of his life.

The Pfizer company Smith rejoined specialized in producing chemicals used by food and beverage manufacturers as well as druggists, as it had since its founding in 1849. Smith would push Pfizer to a much stronger emphasis on research into both chemistry and production methods. In the 1920s, John McKeen, who would succeed Smith as Pfizer's president, described the man who had recently hired him:

> [Smith was] neat, orderly, and impeccably dressed. Seated at his desk, his daily attire was an immaculate high-starched collar and a four-in-hand necktie in the fashion of the day. In his daily visits through the plant, Mr. Smith appeared with sleeves rolled up, no collar or tie, and delved into the operations, moving into all areas, including those that were hot and humid as well. He was personally on hand for the start-up of any operation and kept an eye on any new construction in progress. He worked long hours, nights and Saturdays, was acquainted with all details of the operations, and was a thoroughly competent scientist.

By 1929 Smith was a vice president of the firm and living the upper-middle-class life. As his responsibilities grew, Smith showed an eye for people as well as research and management. Smith's benevolence with the employees was balanced by a driving desire for results. By the 1940s Pfizer employees were working on a revolutionary product and process, one that would cement Smith's place in the world of pharmaceuticals.

In 1928 Scottish physician Alexander Fleming noticed a mold in his laboratory that destroyed bacteria. He sought funding from the British government for further research but was denied. After World War II began in late 1939, the government began to reexamine research proposals to identify those that might help win the war. Suddenly, there was money to continue Fleming's research, which soon confirmed the antibiotic properties of penicillin.

With many pressures on its own economy, the British turned the possibilities of penicillin over to the United States in early 1941, and Washington sought the help of American chemical companies. Pfizer wanted to explore adapting the deep-tank fermentation process. There was intense pressure not just to produce it, but to produce it in useful quantities. Eventually, after much trial and error, the deep-tank fermentation process began to produce in quantity. By D-Day, it was just under forty thousand cases worth of production per month. Half of the world's penicillin was coming from Pfizer's Brooklyn plants, and the price per dose had dropped from $20 in early 1943 to $1. The company's first public stock offering was oversubscribed and the shares' value soared on Wall Street. Smith's reward was Pfizer's presidency in 1945.

By then Smith had embarked on his baseball career. He was fifty-six by the time of this promotion and his days of baseball playing and track were behind him. But his interest in sports had never left him.

One of his favorite ways to relax was to spend an afternoon at Ebbets Field watching the Dodgers. He was encouraged in this relaxation by George V. McLaughlin, president of the Brooklyn Trust Company, which served as the bank for Pfizer and most of Brooklyn's largest companies.

McLaughlin was deeply entangled with the Dodgers and must have seen Smith as a possible solution to one of the team's problems. The problems had started with the death of Charles Ebbets in 1925, which left ownership evenly split between Ebbets's heirs and the McKeever family. For over a decade after Ebbets's death, the two camps squabbled, and moves to repair the team's deteriorating financial condition died in 50–50 votes.

In 1938, with the death of the last McKeever brother, McLaughlin persuaded the heirs to bring in Larry MacPhail to run the team. MacPhail put together the pennant-winning 1941 team and substantially reduced the team's debt, then left in late 1942 to join the army.

McLaughlin got the board to hire Branch Rickey and suggested Rickey hire a young lawyer named Walter O'Malley, a McLaughlin protégé who was very good at managing troubled properties. These moves solved the Dodgers' financial problems, but that was only the beginning for McLaughlin. The Dodgers had paid back the bank's loans, but Brooklyn Trust also operated as trustee for both the Ebbets heirs and those of Edward McKeever. He had a fiduciary duty to protect their interests, and a duty to the bank to get back the money he had lent the heirs against the value of their shares. They wanted to cash out, and he had to find buyers who would satisfy the heirs, get the bank repaid, and not do anything that would tarnish the bank's reputation for protecting one of Brooklyn's most popular institutions.

Smith, McLaughlin decided, was a key piece of the puzzle. The afternoons at Ebbets Field introduced Smith to Rickey, who had the brains and experience to run the baseball operation, and to O'Malley, who had the business acumen. The problem was that Rickey had no capital, and

O'Malley only a modest amount. With the explosive growth of Pfizer, Smith had plenty.

McLaughlin also knew the sale had to be structured properly. The deadlocks between the Ebbets and McKeever groups had hamstrung Dodgers management for over a decade. He had to find a mechanism that would avoid deadlocks within the board and ensure that somebody truly controlled management.

In those conversations at the ballpark, McLaughlin broached the idea that Smith and O'Malley buy Edward McKeever's shares. Smith says he insisted Rickey be added to the group. Brooklyn insurance man Andrew Schmitz, another Brooklyn Trust client, was added as a fourth partner. In November 1944 the group made the purchase. That led to part two of McLaughlin's plan—that the group should buy out the Ebbets heirs as well, giving them not just an investment, but control. When Andrew Schmitz decided he wanted out, the Smith-Rickey-O'Malley triumvirate bought his shares and the Ebbets shares as well in August 1945.

For Smith, the Dodgers were a hobby, a chance to relax. He thoroughly enjoyed his spring training trips, going swimming or piloting a wheeled buggy powered by a sail around the nearby beaches. He accompanied the team to Havana, Venezuela, and Panama. At times he sailed a boat from New York to Vero Beach for spring training.

Smith would invite colleagues, customers, and others to his Ebbets Field box for a little relaxation. One frequent guest was Alexander Fleming himself. After World War II, Pfizer brought Fleming to their Brooklyn plant at least once a year. Smith, ever the good host, took him to Ebbets Field. Fleming was intrigued by the game and wound up with quite a collection of Dodgers-autographed paraphernalia. Smith was also active in charitable activities, such as the Brooklyn Industrial Home for the Blind, the Brooklyn Public Library, the Brooklyn Eye and Ear Hospital, and the Brooklyn YMCA.

At Pfizer, Smith was fending off an attempt at unionization and presiding over the transition of a chemical company selling to other firms into a pharmaceuticals manufacturer selling consumer products. The basis for the transition was the development of a research capability under Smith's leadership and the profits generated from penicillin. The research already was bearing fruit. In 1948 a Pfizer chemist invented tetracycline, the first of the broad-spectrum antibiotics. As Terramycin, it became the first drug to be marketed to the public under the Pfizer name. In later decades Pfizer would turn out such breakthrough drugs as Lipitor, Zoloft, and Viagra. Smith would move from Pfizer's president to chairmanship of the board in 1949.

While Pfizer dominated his time, he also made room for weekly meetings of the Dodgers' ownership, and it soon became clear that he was the balance wheel between the poles of Rickey and O'Malley, two talented, ambitious men who each wanted control of the team.

Over time, Smith would come to side most often with O'Malley. But he'd also contracted lung cancer, and a February 1950 operation took him out of circulation for a couple of months. When he returned, he was weak. He died July 10 of that year. His shares passed to Mary Louise, whom Smith had clearly placed in O'Malley's camp.

Mrs. Smith's position was complicated by the size of her husband's estate, probated at $4,116,241, half of which, including the Dodgers stock, was willed to her. With O'Malley's ability to use the Smiths' vote to control the team, Rickey knew his days were numbered and began the process that led to O'Malley's buying him out.

Mrs. Smith eventually sold out to O'Malley as the team was leaving Brooklyn for Los Angeles. She remained a Vero Beach spring visitor until her death in 1961. John and Mary Louise Smith are buried in Stonington.

# Chapter 69. **Red Barber**

*Warren Corbett*

The man who broadcast Jackie Robinson's first season with the Dodgers recalled that, as a boy in Sanford, Florida, "I saw black men tarred and feathered by the Ku Klux Klan and forced to walk the streets. I had grown up in a completely segregated world." Red Barber confessed that when he learned the Dodgers would field a black player, his first reaction was to quit his job.

Walter Lanier "Red" Barber—"Red" for the color of his hair—was born in Columbus, Mississippi, on February 17, 1908. Seventy years later he was one of the first two broadcasters honored by the National Baseball Hall of Fame, along with his rival and sometime partner Mel Allen. Curt Smith, who chronicled the history of baseball broadcasting in two books, wrote in *The Storytellers*, "The Ol' Redhead was white wine, crepes Suzette and bluegrass music; Mel, beer, hot dogs and the United States Marine Band."

Red's father, William Lanier Barber, was a locomotive engineer from Brown's Creek, North Carolina. His mother, Selena Martin, was an English teacher and school principal from an old Mississippi family. She insisted that her children practice what she taught. "My mother gave me an ear for language. . . . She gave me my interest in religion, too," he wrote. "My father didn't have the education my mother did, but he was a wonderful raconteur, a natural storyteller. He'd sit out on the front porch and tell stories by the hour." The Barbers later had a second son, William Martin, and a daughter, Effie Virginia.

The Barbers moved to Sanford, Florida, near Orlando, when Walter was ten years old. He was a high school football halfback and kicker at five

Red Barber called 1947 "the year all hell broke loose."

feet eight and 165 pounds. He graduated first in his class and was rewarded with a twenty-dollar gold piece. His first ambition was to be an end man (the lead comedian) in a minstrel show, and he performed in blackface during high school and college. While he was working his way through the University of Florida as a waiter and boardinghouse manager, one of his housemates, Ralph Fulghum, asked him to read a research paper on the university radio station. As Red put it, "Then came the great turning point of my life. I know that Satan took Christ up on a mountain and showed him the world and said, 'If you bow down to me I'll give it all to you.' Christ wasn't tempted, but I was. Fulghum tempted me out of all proportion. He said, 'If you come out and read this paper I'll buy you dinner tonight.'" Barber made his radio debut reading a paper titled "Certain Aspects of Bovine Obstetrics."

That led to a job with the station, WRUF, and to his first sports assignment: Florida's opening football game in 1930. He called his debut "undoubtedly the worst broadcast ever perpetrated on an innocent and unsuspecting radio audience." He was so bad that he was pulled off the air and other announcers tried their hands at the next two games. During those weeks, Barber began attending football practice and picking the brains of an assistant coach. He learned how to prepare for a broadcast. He talked his boss into giving him another chance, and the sportscaster's career began.

Barber encountered the other passion of his life in Gainesville: Lylah Murray Scarborough, a nurse who treated him when he was taken into the infirmary one night after an accident. They were married in 1931. On September 17, 1937, Red and Lylah's daughter, Sarah, was born. Sarah, their only child, later became a professor of English.

Ambitious for a better job, Red took time off from WRUF and rode buses to Atlanta, Louisville, Cincinnati, and Chicago for auditions, but stations were not hiring during the Depression. In 1934 the Cincinnati Reds' new general manager, Larry MacPhail, persuaded owner Powel Crosley Jr. to put the team's games on the air. An executive at WLW, a station owned by Crosley, remembered the young man from Florida and hired him as the club's first play-by-play announcer at $25 a week, less than he was paid in Gainesville. On Opening Day he broadcast the first Major League game he had ever seen. "That was the most joyous day of my life, next to my wedding day," he remembered.

In 1935 Red called the first of thirteen World Series, over the Mutual network. What he remembered most vividly was the pregame briefing by Commissioner Kenesaw Mountain Landis. Judge Landis summoned the announcers from all the networks (there were no exclusive rights deals then) and in his customary Sermon-on-the-Mount style, lectured them, "Don't editorialize. Report." Landis's admonition was prompted by Ted Husing's 1934 Series broadcasts, when Husing criticized the umpires. Husing was banned from the Series forever after.

Many of Barber's successors in the booth have called him the first reporter to broadcast baseball. "I've heard tapes of Red Barber in the 1930s and '40s," Bob Costas told the *Los Angeles Times*, "where he tells you there's a line single to left-center and he tells you how many times it bounced before the center fielder picked it up. You needed that then. Today, even the very good announcers will very rarely describe a guy's stance or the peculiarities of a guy's windup, because they've been subconsciously influenced by television even though they're on the radio."

Allan Barra, in the online magazine *Salon*, described listening to tapes of Barber's broadcasts: "There were no complex statistics, no hype, and, of course, no visuals. Just poetry. When the wind was blowing the flag. A description of how the fielders were set. An anecdote or two about each player. With nothing to work with but words, Barber painted a picture of the game that kick-started my own imagination in a way that technology never could."

Barber's best-known innovation for broadcasters was a simple device to remind him to repeat the score frequently for listeners who had just tuned in: He kept a three-minute egg timer, an hourglass, on his desk in the booth. Every time the sand ran down, he repeated the score and flipped his timer over. Dozens if not hundreds of later announcers would adopt this prop.

An important part of the early play-by-play

man's job was the re-creation of out-of-town games. Broadcasters didn't begin traveling with teams until after World War II. The announcer in a studio hundreds of miles from the ballpark used Western Union's telegraphic pitch-by-pitch accounts to simulate a live broadcast. Most broadcasters tried to make the re-creation seem as realistic as possible—using sound effects of recorded crowd noise, cranking up the volume for an exciting play; two pieces of wood banged together to simulate the crack of the bat; recorded organ music. "My reaction was just the opposite. I wanted the audience to know at all times that I was doing a re-creation," Barber said in a 1985 appearance on KCMO radio in Kansas City, Missouri. He used no sound effects and placed his microphone close to the telegraph key, so listeners heard the beeps of Morse code.

"You did that broadcast from a series of mental pictures," Barber said. "I made it my business to mentally photograph every player—how he looked, how big he was. . . . I memorized the idiosyncrasies, the habits. . . . I memorized how each pitcher pitched. So as I stood in the studio I saw the game."

When Larry MacPhail left Cincinnati for Brooklyn in 1939, he took Barber with him to the nation's media capital. Red brought the down-home idiom of his southern roots to the borough whose residents were ridiculed for speaking of "dem" and "dose." Many people who lived in Brooklyn in the 1940s have insisted that they could walk down any street in the borough and never miss a pitch, because Barber's voice was wafting out of every window and every passing car. During World War II he became a civic institution as chairman of Brooklyn's Red Cross blood drive and host of radio War Bonds sales.

New York offered Barber unmatched opportunities. According to the Pro Football Hall of Fame, he called the first National Football League championship game to be broadcast nationwide,

in 1940, when the Chicago Bears buried the Washington Redskins, 73–0. He regularly broadcast football games of the professional Brooklyn Dodgers and New York Giants, as well as Princeton University. He also hosted entertainment programs with bandleaders Sammy Kaye and Woody Herman and singers Lena Horne and Mario Lanza. For nine years after World War II, he was the director of sports for CBS, where he first heard Fordham University student Vince Scully.

During the war, Dodgers general manager Branch Rickey was signing as many promising young players as his scouts could find, laying the groundwork for a decade of success. He was also laying the groundwork for an even more important move. Months before he signed Jackie Robinson, Rickey confided his plan to Barber. Red said he was the first one outside Rickey's family to hear that Rickey intended to break Organized Baseball's sixty-year-old color line: "I believe he told me about it so far in advance so that I could have time to wrestle with the problem, live with it, solve it."

Barber never admitted any racist feelings. In his history of Robinson's rookie year, *1947: When All Hell Broke Loose in Baseball*, he declared, "I was not a racist." He wrote in his autobiography, "The Negroes who came and went through our lives were always treated with the utmost respect and with a great deal of warmth and a great deal of affection." At the same time, he acknowledged, "There was a line drawn, and that was that." Southerners of Barber's generation never encountered a black person in a situation of social or economic equality until they reached middle age. That was that.

After Rickey's revelation, Barber told Lylah, "I'm going to quit." She suggested they have a martini and sleep on it. His wife's cooler head prevailed, but Barber said, "It really tortured me." Eventually he concluded, "All I had to do when he came was treat him as a fellow man, treat him as a ballplayer, broadcast the ball." In his 1991 interview with Bob Costas, Barber recalled, "I don't think I ever said he was a Negro. I didn't have to. Everybody knew who he was." He also owned up to his self-interest: "Economics has a way of being the hidden persuader. I valued the job at Brooklyn."

The rookie Robinson led the Dodgers to the 1947 World Series. That classic included two of Barber's most famous games. In Game Four, Yankees right-hander Bill Bevens took a no-hitter into the ninth inning, while walking ten. Brooklyn pinch hitter Cookie Lavagetto came to bat with the Dodgers trailing by one run and two runners on base: "Two men out, last of the ninth. The pitch. Swung on. There's a drive hit out toward the right-field corner. Henrich going back. He can't get it. It's off the wall for a base hit. Here comes the tying run—and—here's—the winning run."

On National Public Radio's *Morning Edition* on April 23, 1982, Barber told host Bob Edwards, "When all of the excitement was over for a little bit, I just sort of caught my breath and without thinking about it, Bob, I said, 'Well, I'll be a suck-egg mule.'"

Edwards asked why he said that. Barber replied, "When you're doing something such as you and I are doing, live radio without any preparation, no script, you are just concentrating on your work and something just comes out. . . . When you realize that things suddenly come out of your subconscious or your unconscious when you're talking to an open microphone, sometimes it frightens you."

In the sixth game, Brooklyn had a three-run lead when Joe DiMaggio came to bat. In Barber's words: "Here's the pitch. Swung on, belted. It's a long one deep to left center. Back goes Gionfriddo. Back, back, back, back, back, back. He makes a one-handed catch against the bullpen. Oh, doctor. [Pause for crowd noise.] He went exactly against the railing in front of the bullpen and reached up with one hand and took a home run away from DiMaggio." Barber said those calls demonstrated

an important rule for a play-by-play broadcaster: on a long drive, watch the outfielder; he'll be the first to know whether it's catchable. Thus, "Back goes Gionfriddo." "Henrich going back. He can't get it."

More than thirty years later, a young broadcaster named Chris Berman on the upstart cable network ESPN adopted "back, back, back," he said, as a tribute to Barber.

Barber was celebrated for his vivid imagery, all the more memorable because he brought the country sayings of his southern upbringing to urban Brooklyn. Cincinnati public radio station WVXU assembled this Red Barber sampler:

The game "is just as tight as a brand-new pair of shoes on a rainy day."

"They'll tear up the pea patch before the day is over."

"The bases are FOB—they're full of Brooklyns." (He acknowledged he made this up after seeing the term, which meant "free on board" in the shipping industry, and turning it over in his mind.)

His most enduring coinage was "sitting in the catbird seat." In Barber's lexicon that meant a batter with a three-ball, no-strike count or a team with a comfortable lead.

Ernie Harwell, who broke into big league broadcasting under Barber in 1948 and lasted for fifty-five seasons, told WVXU, "The ironic thing was, he was a very cultured man, and on the air he sounded like some guy from the backwoods, you know. . . . And he really wasn't. He loved the opera and he loved the classics and all that kind of stuff. He lived on Park Avenue in New York."

Vin Scully, who inherited Red's mantle as "Voice of the Dodgers," joined the broadcasts in 1950 as a twenty-two-year-old. "His work ethics were so strong that he imbued me with that spirit," Scully told WVXU. "Get to the ballpark early. Check, check, recheck. Talk to players, managers constantly. And that rubbed off on me."

In 1950 attorney Walter O'Malley bought Rickey's 25 percent interest in the Dodgers and took control of the franchise. Red's relationship with the new owner was touchy. "O'Malley wanted to cut me down to size," he wrote in his autobiography. "He is a devious man, about the most devious man I ever met." Barber broadcast his thirteenth World Series in 1952, again sharing the NBC radio and television microphones with Mel Allen. It would be his last.

Ever since the Gillette Company bought exclusive rights to the Series in 1939, Barber had chafed at the company's cavalier treatment of announcers. By 1953 Gillette paid the broadcasters just $200 a game "for the biggest sports event on coast-to-coast television," he fumed. Barber declined to broadcast the '53 Series when the company refused to negotiate his fee. When Red told O'Malley what had happened, O'Malley's reply— "That's your problem"—ended Barber's relationship with the Dodgers. His contract for the Brooklyn broadcasts had expired, and the sponsors had made no move to renew it.

A few days after he left the Dodgers, Red was hired by the Yankees. The new job was quite a comedown. For twenty years in Cincinnati and Brooklyn, he had been the principal broadcaster, handing out assignments to his assistants. He decided how many innings they would call, who would do which commercials, who would handle pregame and postgame shows.

The Yankees' principal broadcaster, Mel Allen, was the most famous sports announcer in the country. Red was hired to handle pregame and postgame shows on televised home games and to work a few innings of play-by-play. He traveled with the team only occasionally. "Mel accepted me as an equal," he insisted. "He could not have been nicer to me either then or all through the years we worked together."

Red was forced to adjust, grudgingly, to fundamental changes in the broadcasting industry. In 1939 he had broadcast the first Major League game on television over NBC's experimental station W2XBS, when only a few dozen homes had TV sets. In the 1950s television became the dominant medium. Like many other radio veterans, Barber never accepted television. He endured it. He explained why in *Rhubarb in the Catbird Seat*: "On TV it's the director's show, and the broadcaster is an instrument of his, like a camera. On radio, it's my show, where my knowledge and experience and taste and judgment decide what goes and what doesn't. On radio, you're an artist. On TV, you're a servant."

Barber deplored the invasion of the broadcast booth by retired ballplayers—he dismissed them as "former-great-star-expert[s]." By 1965, after the Yankees fired Allen for "popping off," Barber was sharing the booth with three of those "experts": ex-shortstop Phil Rizzuto, ex–second baseman Jerry Coleman, and Joe Garagiola, a onetime backup catcher who had parlayed a quick wit and a trove of real and invented anecdotes about his boyhood pal Yogi Berra into a broadcasting career. Garagiola committed what Barber considered the unforgivable sin: "He cut in on me in the middle of sentences. . . . He ran over fellows."

CBS had bought the Yankees, and network executive Michael Burke took over as the team's president in September 1966. He curtly informed Barber, "We have decided not to seek to renew your contract." Barber thought he knew why. On a chilly, rainy day near the end of the 1966 season when baseball's marquee franchise fell to last place, the Yankees played a home game before 413 fans. Barber wrote in *The Broadcasters*, "This was the smallest crowd, by far, in the history of the massive ballpark built by Babe Ruth, Ed Barrow, and Colonel Jake Ruppert." He asked the television director for a shot of the empty seats. The director refused, and Barber was told that the order came from the CBS executive who supervised Yankee broadcasts. But Barber was still a reporter. As he recalled it, he said, "I don't know what the paid attendance is today—but whatever it is, it is the smallest crowd in the history of Yankee Stadium . . . and this smallest crowd is the story, not the ballgame."

According to the University of Florida's Smathers Library, where Red's papers are housed, he broadcast play-by-play on thirteen World Series, four baseball All-Star Games, five Army-Navy games, one Sugar Bowl, two Rose Bowls, eight Orange Bowls, and four NFL championship games. That career was over.

At age fifty-eight Barber began what he called his retirement at his home in Key Biscayne, Florida, near Miami. But it was an active retirement. He wrote a syndicated newspaper column and four books, and he did sportscasts for Miami radio and TV stations. Cable television impresario Ted Turner hired Barber and Mel Allen to call the 1978 Little League World Series, one of the most bizarre anachronisms in broadcasting history.

That same year, he and Allen—forever linked—became the first broadcasters honored by the National Baseball Hall of Fame. They received the Ford C. Frick Award for "major contributions to baseball," an award named for the commissioner Barber despised.

Red would take one more star turn on a national stage, introducing himself to a generation of listeners who knew only the Los Angeles Dodgers and who, if they followed baseball at all, followed it primarily on television. In 1981 he joined NPR's *Morning Edition* as a regular commentator, appearing for four minutes every Friday at 7:35 a.m. Eastern time.

The host of *Morning Edition*, Bob Edwards, lovingly captured those years in *Fridays with Red*, published after Barber's death. The Barbers had left the fast-growing Miami area for the smaller city of Tallahassee, where Lylah had attended Florida State College for Women, the predecessor of Florida State University. Tallahassee station WFSU-FM ran an audio line to their home, and Red

broadcast from a desk in his office. Nominally, the spot was a sports commentary. In reality, it was a free-form conversation about just about anything, often including his flower garden and the adventures of his cats. He talked about opera, quoted Victor Hugo and Kahlil Gibran, and delivered condensed versions of some of the sermons he had preached as a lay reader in the Episcopal Church.

To the buttoned-down Edwards—who had every word of his broadcasts scripted, even "I'm Bob Edwards"—it was both a nightmare and a delight. Red insisted that his segment be live. He made it unpredictable. A producer would call him on Thursday to discuss topics for the next morning's broadcast. By Friday, Red had often changed his mind and took off in a totally unexpected direction. Edwards described himself as Barber's straight man. Because Red talked about his camellias so often, Edwards's wife planted one in their backyard. Red wanted to know what variety it was. Edwards replied, "Pink."

"Red's spot on 'Morning Edition' was the most popular feature of any program on public radio," Edwards wrote. "And for many listeners, Red was a reminder of a father, a grandfather, or a favorite uncle they had—or wished they had." Barber was as much a perfectionist as ever: Edwards said he could hear the click of Red's stopwatch at the beginning and end of his allotted four minutes. His career had come full circle: from noncommercial station WRUF in 1930 to noncommercial NPR more than fifty years later. In his first NPR broadcast, he said, "I'm a child of radio."

In the 1980s Lylah developed Alzheimer's disease, and much of the rest of Red's life was devoted to caring for her. "By the time I met him in the early '80s, he was so frail it seemed a gust of wind might take him away," Edwards wrote. Barber had suffered various physical ailments since the 1940s, going deaf in his left ear and surviving a heart attack and surgery for ulcers that removed much of his stomach. On October 8, 1992, he begged off the next day's broadcast, blaming a sore throat. On that Friday he drove himself and Lylah to a hospital. He underwent emergency surgery for an intestinal blockage and fell into a coma.

Red Barber died at eighty-four on October 22, 1992, at the Tallahassee Memorial Regional Medical Center. The *New York Times* reported that the cause of death was pneumonia and other complications from surgery. His ashes were buried in his yard, beneath five camellias. In his *Morning Edition* tribute, Bob Edwards said, "One of the great voices of America will speak to us no more, and the camellias will never smell as sweet." Red would not have liked that; camellias have no scent.

In Sanford, Florida, where Red grew up, a municipal park bears his name. In Tallahassee, where he lived his last years, Florida State University's Center for Public Broadcasting sits at 1600 Red Barber Plaza. His alma mater, the University of Florida, annually awards the Red Barber Radio Scholarship—$700 to a junior or senior majoring in telecommunications, with a preference to students planning to pursue careers in sports broadcasting. In Los Angeles, Red's heir, Vin Scully, continued into the twenty-first century as the voice of the Dodgers.

# Chapter 70. Connie Desmond

*Rob Edelman*

In the 1940s Red Barber was solidly entrenched as the Brooklyn Dodgers' lead broadcaster. But he was not the team's lone play-by-play man. The "Old Redhead" was ably assisted by Connie Desmond, whose delivery befitted the era in that it was unhurried, calming, and wholly agreeable.

Decades after Desmond last described a game in Brooklyn, those in the know acknowledged his flair for painting verbal portraits of ballgames. Jack Craig, writing in the *Boston Globe*, referred to Desmond as "late and legendary."[1] The *New York Times*'s George Vecsey called him "vastly underrated."[2] Fellow *Times* sportswriter Gerald Eskenazi wrote, "He had a classic radio voice, with no regional accent, and a smooth if nondramatic delivery."[3] Barber himself noted, "He had a warm personality, a warm, pleasant voice. He knew his business impeccably."[4]

Given his abilities, Desmond might have emerged as a broadcaster of the stature of a Barber, a Mel Allen, or a Vin Scully. What held him back was an inability to control his intake of alcohol.

Cornelius "Connie" Desmond Jr. was born in Toledo, Ohio, on January 31, 1908, the youngest of four children born to Cornelius and Ruth Desmond. He graduated from the University of Notre Dame in 1931 and began his career the following January in his hometown, where his pleasant voice won him a spot crooning and introducing dance bands on WSPD radio. But Connie yearned to broadcast baseball and emulate his idol, the velvety-voiced Ty Tyson, the announcer of University of Michigan football games and Detroit Tigers baseball games.

He got his opportunity a couple of years lat-

er when General Mills began sponsoring baseball broadcasts, including approximately twenty-five Toledo Mud Hens games. A play-by-play man was needed, and Desmond won the job. He labored to perfect his low-key style, and in 1940 General Mills promoted him to the Columbus (Ohio) Red Birds, the St. Louis Cardinals' top farm club. For the following two seasons, he called Red Birds games on WCOL radio.

In 1942, while in spring training with Columbus, Desmond was offered what a young play-by-play man then would have considered an ideal job: coming to New York and working with Mel Allen as a New York Yankees and New York Giants home-game broadcaster. Desmond readily accepted, but his tenure with Allen was brief. After the season, he was hired by the Brooklyn Dodgers as a replacement for Al Helfer, who had joined the navy. The April 15, 1943, *Sporting News* announced that Desmond "has been selected by the J. Walter Thompson Agency as Red Barber's new assistant in the Old Gold broadcasts of the Brooklyn Dodgers' games."[5]

The key word here is "assistant." With Barber established as the Dodgers' celebrity broadcaster, chances for career enhancement within the Brooklyn organization were limited. Desmond instead remained the supporting player, a mop-up man rather than a full-fledged broadcast partner. His duties included preparing and updating the statistics that would be at Barber's fingertips as he called the game, broadcasting the fifth inning, reporting the out-of-town scores, and reading most of the commercials.

At this time, recalled soon-to-be Dodgers play-by-play man Vin Scully, "There was never any interplay on the air. I know Red always felt one man, one voice."[6] And so it could only be Barber, and not Desmond, who broadcast the breakup of Bill Bevens's no-hitter by Cookie Lavagetto in the ninth inning of Game Four of the 1947 World Series. It could only be Barber, and not Desmond, who made the call on Al Gionfriddo's catch of a ball hit by Joe DiMaggio in Game Six.

It was for good reason, then, that a 1948 newspaper ad hyping Dodgers radio and television broadcasts featured Barber's name before Desmond's—and in a larger type size.[7] (CBS-TV began airing Brooklyn's home games in 1947. The team switched its affiliation to WOR-TV three years later.) Also in 1948, the *New York Times* reported that Barber and Desmond gave blood in response to a newly instituted Red Cross blood donor program. Yet the emphasis on Barber's participation further reflected on his massive popularity and Desmond's second-string status. The piece was headlined "Red Barber Gives Blood." The "Old Redhead" was cited at the top of the account, with the third and final paragraph beginning, "Mr. Barber was accompanied by his broadcasting associate, Connie Desmond, who also donated blood."[8]

What's more, during the 1948 campaign, Barber temporarily left his position to recover from a bleeding ulcer. Instead of elevating Desmond, Dodgers president Branch Rickey summoned Ernie Harwell, then broadcasting Atlanta Crackers games on WSB radio, as Barber's substitute. In securing Harwell's services, Rickey even agreed to send the Crackers one of his players, catcher Cliff Dapper.

What, then, prevented Desmond from emerging out of Barber's shadow? "Many thought [Desmond] rivaled Barber in ability," wrote Ted Patterson in *The Golden Voices of Baseball*.[9] One only can assume that his fondness for the bottle was damaging him professionally. Knowledge of his penchant for drinking at the time can only be

speculated upon. However, Patterson observed that "alcoholism plagued him throughout his career, limiting his great potential."[10]

So Desmond's status in the broadcast booth remained unchanged. By 1950 it was Barber who had his own television program, *Red Barber's Club House*, broadcast on CBS-TV. It was announced in February that Barber would be heading south to cover spring training. His show would be temporarily replaced by *Saturday Sports Review*, with Desmond filling in and reporting the sports news. During the off-season, Desmond also assisted Barber on WHN's New York Giants football broadcasts and worked on the Barber-hosted CBS *Football Roundup*. He accepted other on-air assignments, including broadcasting National Invitation Tournament college basketball games and offering play-by-play of college football, including Bowl games.

By the late 1940s Barber had become the director of sports at CBS. In November 1949 he assigned Scully, a freshly minted Fordham University graduate, to work the CBS Radio booth at the Boston University–University of Maryland football game at Fenway Park. It was Scully's first post-college play-by-play work, and he accomplished the equivalent of tossing a game-winning touchdown. Barber asked Scully to broadcast the Harvard-Yale contest in New Haven the following weekend. That winter, at Barber's urging, Scully was hired to join him and Desmond in the Dodgers' broadcast booth to replace the departing Ernie Harwell.

Clearly, Scully was on the rise with the Dodgers. In 2003 he recalled his connection with his two older colleagues when he noted, "That relationship boiled down to, and came out over the air[,] as the father, Red Barber; the older brother, Connie Desmond[;] and the kid. Whatever that relationship brought to the booth, it apparently came out over the air. Those people in Brooklyn who were exposed to it have told me that they don't expect to ever hear anything like it again."[11]

"That relationship" was fated to last just four seasons. During the 1953 campaign, Walter O'Malley, now in control of the Dodgers, began pressuring Barber to become more of an on-air team rooter, a tactic that was not to Barber's taste. When O'Malley failed to back Barber's request for extra payment by the Gillette Company for broadcasting the 1953 World Series, Barber resigned.

The 1954 baseball season began with Scully and Desmond as the primary Dodgers broadcasters, with André Baruch hired to do some reporting and play-by-play and read most of the commercials.

Given his proven abilities and his seniority with the Dodgers, and with the formidable presence of Barber no longer a factor, Desmond—who was just in his mid-forties—finally was positioned for major stardom in the New York broadcast market. During the season, he was the focus of a print ad for Schaefer beer. The ad copy read, "Folks who drink for enjoyment prefer Schaefer—it's *real* beer," and the visual featured a smiling Desmond, with Barber nowhere in sight.[12]

A WOR-TV camera sat behind Desmond as he hoisted a glass of brew. The only problem was, he did not just "drink for enjoyment"—and his predilection for alcohol was about to demolish his career in Brooklyn. According to Barber, Desmond simply could not hold his liquor, and he occasionally even failed to appear for Dodgers broadcasts.

So almost immediately, Scully was anointed the team's prime broadcaster. Fittingly, it was Scully rather than Desmond who pronounced over the air, on October 4, 1955, after Elston Howard grounded out to Pee Wee Reese to give Brooklyn its first World Series title, "Ladies and gentlemen, the Brooklyn Dodgers are the champions of the world."[13]

Midway through that campaign, Desmond's drinking had resulted in his sudden disappearance from the Dodgers' broadcast booth. *The Sporting News* noted that he was "on sick leave," and he apparently was fired at season's end.[14] He begged to

be reinstated, and Walter O'Malley agreed to afford him one final opportunity. In February 1956 the media reported that Desmond was slated to remain a member of the Dodgers' play-by-play team, which now consisted of Scully and Al Helfer.

Then on August 10, 1956, the *New York Times* tersely announced that Desmond had "resigned as a baseball announcer for the Brooklyn Dodgers."[15] No explanation was given for his departure. But according to *Boston Globe* columnist Jack Craig, Desmond clearly "lost his job because of alcoholism."[16] Observed baseball broadcasting historian Curt Smith, "Connie took a knockout future—and flushed it down the flask."[17]

While Desmond did not completely disappear from the world of sports and media, never again did he enjoy the stature of working beside someone of the caliber of a Red Barber or Vin Scully. His plight, in fact, was quite the opposite. In the early 1960s, future *New York Times* sportswriter Gerald Eskenazi was working at the paper as a copyboy. One day, a secretary informed him that a Mr. Desmond wished to speak with someone in the sports department. "I came to the reception area and was greeted by a quick-smiling Connie Desmond, who stood up, shakily," Eskenazi recalled. "Clearly, he was drunk."[18] Desmond first asked for Arthur Daley, the paper's sports columnist, who was out of the office. Then, he attempted to borrow $5 from young Eskenazi.

In 1964 Desmond's name surfaced in a report about the Red Carpet Network, a new FM radio station that would provide music, news reports, and stock quotations for taxi drivers and their passengers. Desmond was listed as executive vice president and general manager of the company. Suffice it to say that the Red Carpet Network did not revolutionize FM radio.

Desmond eventually resettled in Toledo, where he returned to his professional roots as a Mud Hens broadcaster. He died on March 10, 1983.

In his time Desmond may have been a top-

ROB EDELMAN

quality play-by-play man. "If you never heard the late Connie Desmond, you missed a great baseball broadcaster," wrote Joe Falls in *The Sporting News*.[19] But in relation to his legacy, perhaps most telling was his obituary, published with no byline in the *New York Times*. It consisted of one sparse paragraph:

> Connie Desmond, who broadcast Brooklyn Dodger baseball games in the 1940's and 1950's with Red Barber, died last Thursday in Toledo, Ohio. He was seventy-five years old. Mr. Desmond is survived by his wife, Virginia; a sister, Bette; a son, Jim; a daughter, Cathy, and three grandchildren.[20]

# Chapter 71. Advertising and the Dodgers in 1947

*Roberta J. Newman*

The year 1947 was a banner year for the Brooklyn Dodgers. At the same time as the newly desegregated Dodgers seized the National League pennant, the team expanded its appeal to a demographic not traditionally served by Organized Baseball. It was also a banner year for the advertising industry. With the abatement of wartime shortages, 1947 marked the beginning of a period of unparalleled consumption, fueled by a newly invigorated Madison Avenue. And just as the 1947 Dodgers, both as a real team and as an emblem of a community, would come to serve the advertising industry, so too would the advertising industry serve the Dodgers.

In order to assess the relationship between the 1947 Dodgers and the advertising industry, it may be instructive to look, however briefly, at the state of American consumer culture, and by extension the state of advertising, at this pivotal time in history. The period immediately following World War II was one of rapid economic expansion. "Economic growth," writes James T. Patterson, "was indeed the decisive force in the shifting attitudes and expectations in the post-War era."[1] "These were above all years of nearly unimaginable consumption of goods," he notes. "Between 1939 and 1948, clothing sales jumped three-fold, furniture, four-fold, liquor five-fold and household appliances, including TVs, five-fold."[2] Given the fact that consumer goods were in short supply during the war, it is not surprising that most of this growth occurred between 1946 and 1948.

But what was behind this postwar consumer frenzy? What induced Americans to spend with abandon? Clearly, a reaction against the deprivations of the Depression and wartime was behind a good part of postwar consumerism. But Americans, accustomed by necessity to frugality, were not in the habit of consuming. They had to be directed to do so. This was the job of advertising, which James B. Twitchell describes as "the culture developed to expedite the central problem of capitalism: the distribution of surplus goods."[3] And surplus goods there were aplenty, as is generally the case after a major war.

In addition to the postwar surplus that needed to be sold, factories geared up for wartime production had to be put to new use. So, too, was there a need to employ new technologies developed during the war. Taken together, these factors fed what was to become one of the largest producers of culture in America, the advertising industry. In many ways 1947 was a transitional year for advertising. The "creative revolution" in advertising was still nearly a decade away. But while ads in the print media still resembled those of wartime, they were far more plentiful, as were the goods they sold. At the same time, a new media, soon to become the nation's primary vehicle for advertising as well as a major durable good, was emerging. Indeed, 1947 may be seen as the beginning of the age of television.

So how did the postwar advertising boom play out in Brooklyn, and more importantly, how did it relate to the Dodgers? Although Brooklynites, like all Americans, had just emerged from a global war, their home, formerly the fourth-largest city in America but always the poor stepsister to "the city," was essentially provincial, isolated from Greater New York as a whole. A seemingly diverse area, early postwar Brooklyn was really a patchwork of distinct neighborhoods, which Carl Prince describes as a "borough of marbleized ghettoes," with little in common with one another. Writes Prince: "A corollary to this was the frequently confrontational nature of ethnic relationships in the borough, a hostility that matched the sense of isolation without. The Dodgers formed an ameliorating force for unity in Brooklyn, but the team's local mystique did not miraculously bring all the people to love each other. Still, the Dodger presence helped."[4] Perhaps the best way to advertise to such a fragmented demographic was to invoke the one element that served to unify it, the Dodgers. As such, the team was featured prominently in local advertising in 1947.

A natural place for the advertising industry to place ads in order to appeal to Dodgers fans was in the borough's major news organ, the *Brooklyn Daily Eagle*. In addition to the ubiquitous advertising for Dodgers games, both at home at Ebbets Field and against the archrival Giants at the Polo Grounds, the Dodgers were invoked in non-game-related print ads throughout the *Eagle*. Naturally, most of Dodgers-related advertising was concentrated in issues from April through mid-October, baseball season, though even in the off-season the Dodgers were never entirely absent from the paper's advertising pages.

Businesses linking themselves to the Dodgers in the Brooklyn paper were, by and large, local. Lindsay Laboratories and Pharmacy, close by the Brooklyn Academy of Music, for example, welcomed the Dodgers at the outset of the season, urging *Eagle* readers to drop in to request a schedule of the team's home games, and presumably to spend some money on health and beauty items, many newly available following the war, and perhaps have a soda at the fountain. And because watching baseball and otherwise consuming was apt to make a person hungry, Lee's Chinese restau-

rant, just a stone's throw from Ebbets Field, trumpeted its proximity to the Dodgers, urging readers to convene there before and after games.

Regional and national advertisers also understood that the way to appeal to *Eagle* readers, presumably Dodgers fans all, was to allude to the team in their advertising. The Baltimore and Ohio Railroad, freed from wartime travel restrictions, appealed to Dodgers fans who might be planning a foray out of Brooklyn, however briefly, in an ad featuring a cartoon representation of an angry player informing a stone-faced umpire that "we wuz robbed," followed by rather twisted copy reading, "But Brooklynites say that with pleasure when they discover that B&O rids them of inconvenience, traffic problems and baggage worries."[5] The makers of Durex double-edge razor blades regularly ran contests in the *Eagle*, offering free tickets to fans who could describe in twenty-seven words or fewer who was the best player at a given position. While fans of all three teams were invited to enter, Dodgers fans were privileged, Brooklyn's team always receiving top billing in the *Eagle* ads.

Naturally, winning the 1947 pennant brought joy to fans across Brooklyn. It also brought visions of dollar signs to *Eagle* advertisers. Page after page of ads placed by local businesses filled the *Eagle* between September 23 and October 2 congratulating the team for clinching a trip to the World Series. Some offered fans souvenirs, others claimed to be the ideal location to celebrate after a Dodgers win, and still others simply linked their names to that of the team, as if to become winners by association. But they all trumpeted their connection to the Dodgers. As might be expected in a booming consumer economy, banks competed fiercely for the accounts of Brooklyn's residents. South Brooklyn Savings and Loan, one of at least a dozen banks to place a congratulatory ad in the *Eagle*, offered fans a "FREE World Series souvenir baseball bank," invoking Brooklyn pride with the copy "It's a homer! It's just the thing for your desk in the office and the bureau at home." Not explicitly mentioned, but suggested by the ad copy, is the assumption that once those "base hit nickels, dimes and quarters grow to home run dollars," the best place for them would naturally be the South Brooklyn Savings and Loan.[6] Not to be outdone, the Williamsburgh Savings Bank, the Brooklyn Trust Company, and the Lafayette National Bank of Brooklyn, as well as the Dime, Fulton, and Roosevelt Savings banks, all offered their congratulations to the team in the pages of the *Eagle*.

The Marine Roof of the upscale Hotel Bossert, a few blocks down Montague Street from the Dodgers' offices, offered itself as a place to "Celebrate our Victory" by "Dancing to the music of Hugo."[7] The equally elegant St. George Hotel, home to several of the team's players during the season, attempted to appeal to Dodgers fans with poetry, of sorts. "Congratulations, Brooklyn team / For every hit and run / You're in the groove, you're on the beam / you've triumphed, conquered, won," read its print spot.[8] Local saloons and eateries from Bay Ridge to Flatbush, from Fort Greene to Midwood, from Flatlands to Bushwick, places with names like Gallagher's Subway Inns and the Hole in the Wall, Hoes and the White Shutter, Flynn's Cabaret, and Hammy's Pantry urged fans to "Dodge in and Celebrate," or something of the sort.[9]

Purveyors of consumer goods produced by the repurposed war machine also jumped on the Dodgers bandwagon. Like the Dodgers, Abraham & Straus, Brooklyn's iconic department store, had a great year in 1947, expanding and adding, among other things, a new furniture department christened Contemporama.[10] A&S, as it was commonly known, frequently implemented Dodger tie-ins in its advertising, not only at the season's successful conclusion but also throughout the year. Indeed, earlier in the season the retailer emphasized its Brooklyn roots by connecting itself to an amateur baseball series, also sponsored by the *Eagle* and the team, appropriately titled Brooklyn

Against the World.[11] The store's ad copy reads, "When Brooklyn boys set out to lick the World— look out world," declaring Brooklyn to be "Dodger Town."[12] Moreover, A&S would claim agency in the team's success. "Whee! We're in! Bring on those Yankees," screams a half-page A&S ad, as if the retailer naturally was at least partly responsible for winning the pennant.[13]

Another downtown Brooklyn department store, Loeser's, also got in on the act. Taking a page from a discount clothing purveyor and local politician, Abe Stark of Ebbets Field's "Hit Sign, Win Suit" fame, Loeser's promised a free nine-by-twelve-foot Karastan rug to the Dodger who hit the first home run of the Series at Ebbets Field.[14] Of course, Abe Stark placed a congratulatory ad, as well. These major retailers were joined by Bohack Food Stores, a Brooklyn and Long Island grocery chain, which ran a quarter-page ad depicting a gigantic cartoon ballplayer in a Dodgers uniform waving a banner reading "NL Champs," sitting upon a pile of presumably vanquished National Leaguers, each wearing a cap identifying him as a representative of the other clubs, in front of a brightly shining sun illuminating the Brooklyn Bridge. The ad asks *Eagle* readers, "Who's a Bum?"[15]

The *Eagle* was not the only news outlet to benefit from dollars generated by Dodgers-related advertising, especially at World Series time. Ads invoking Brooklyn's team also appeared in the *New York Times* and the city's other media outlets. For the most part these ads did not appeal strictly to Dodgers fans, but invoked the team and its fans in relationship to New York's other teams. For example, George-Wally Haberdashers and Hatters, located in Manhattan, notes that a featured hat might be "seen at the stadium," without specifying which of the city's three Major League ballparks it meant. The ad claimed, "Whether you're a Yankee or a Dodger fan, you're always a winner in this ever popular off-the-face style by Dobbs."[16] This ad, which appeared in the *Times* on October 1, was clearly intended to draw consumers from fans of not one, but two, of the city's teams, capitalizing on the fortuitous occurrence of an all–New York Subway Series. And if a Giants fan just happened in, he too could be the proud owner of a fashionable Dobbs. Unlike the ads in the fundamentally local *Eagle*, targeted directly at Brooklynites, George-Wally Haberdashers covered all its bases.

Given the combined popularity and success of the Dodgers, it is no surprise to find product endorsements and testimonial ads by individual Dodgers players in the pages of the print media, especially in New York. Testimonials were, after all, the meat-and-potatoes of the advertising industry, coming to prominence in the 1920s. Dixie Walker, perhaps the team's most popular player, endorsed one of the borough's own home brews, Schaefer Beer, in the *New York Times*. The testimonial seems to be aimed at New York baseball fans in general, referring to Walker as "baseball's hardest hitting outfielder," who calls the Brooklyn brew the "finest beer I ever tasted."[17] Implicit in the ad is the notion that by consuming Walker's favorite beer, Walker's fans and other connoisseurs might indirectly share in the player's talent. Schaefer drinkers needed only to open a cold one to "be like Dixie," becoming hard-hitters themselves, both literally and figuratively.

Eventually, Schaefer, soon to become known as "the one beer to have, if you're having more than one," would cement a major sponsorship deal with the Dodgers organization, but not in 1947. Indeed, it took until 1951 for the brewery to grab a long-desired piece of the Dodgers' sponsorship pie, the result of Branch Rickey's reluctance to take money from the beer industry.[18] The Schaefer sign, with its light-up "H" for a hit and "E" for an error, was added to the Ebbets Field scoreboard, right above Abe Stark's sign, in 1951. Eventually, Connie Desmond, one of the team's broadcasters, would pitch

the brew to the team's fans. But in 1947 Walker was the sole Dodger to tout the pleasure of quaffing a cold Schaefer.

Although the majority of Dodgers-related advertising appeared in the local print media in 1947, occasionally national ads also invoked the team and its players. Once again, Dixie Walker was one of the primary vehicles by which baseball fans and newspaper readers in other cities would consume the Dodgers. In fact, for many Americans outside New York, Walker, through his endorsement advertising, was the face of the Dodgers of 1947. Walker sold Wheaties and Wonder Bread to readers of the *Chicago Tribune* and the *Washington Post*. He also pitched Raleigh cigarettes, an endorsement that appears to be counterintuitive on more than one level. That Walker, an athlete and a "role model" to American boyhood, would be paid to claim "New Raleigh 903 is Smoother, Milder, Better Tasting" seems well-nigh incredible by early twenty-first-century standards.[19] But it was not at all unusual for Walker and celebrity athletes like him to be paid to lend their names and images to cigarette advertising. Neither was it unusual for Walker, a nonsmoker, to endorse a product he did not use. It was not until 1961 that the Federal Trade Commission enforced "Truth in Advertising" laws, mandating that celebrities endorse only products they actually use.[20] The fact that Walker endorsed Raleigh, rather than Old Golds, also appears odd by contemporary standards. Old Golds were, after all, the Dodgers' radio sponsors. In a clear example of a product tie-in, during Dodgers broadcasts, a home-team home run was an "Old Goldie." Yet despite the fact that Walker's Raleigh testimonial might read as a conflict of interest, neither was it uncommon in 1947 for a ballplayer to endorse a brand produced by his team's sponsor's competitor.

Dixie Walker was not the only member of the 1947 Dodgers to endorse products, both locally and nationally. Shortstop Pee Wee Reese, for example, pitched for Rheingold Beer, one of Schaefer's primary competitors in the New York market. But perhaps no single player had a bigger impact on Dodgers-related advertising than the 1947 Rookie of the Year, Jack Roosevelt Robinson. As has been well documented, on April 15 Robinson stepped onto Brooklyn's playing field, beginning the slow, inexorable process of desegregating Major League Baseball. And Robinson's impact on Dodgers-related advertising was nearly as large as his impact on baseball, as a whole.

Naturally, Robinson's debut had an immediate effect on advertising in the black press. Neighborhoods served by the *Amsterdam News*, the *Chicago Defender*, the *Pittsburgh Courier*, and the *Baltimore Afro-American*, among other traditionally black publications, grew substantially during the 1940s, the result of a second "great migration" of laborers from the South seeking economic opportunities and improved living conditions not available in rural regions firmly under the thumb of Jim Crow. Writes James T. Patterson, "This was a massive migration in so short a time—one of the most significant demographic shifts in American history—and it was often agonizingly stressful."[21] Instantly, a significant new group of consumers might be reached through Dodgers-related advertising. This demographic differed from the team's traditional fan base in more ways than one, which is made apparent by the ads intended to appeal to the new target market.

Over the course of the 1947 season, any number of New York businesses targeting African American consumers linked themselves to Robinson in the pages of the *Amsterdam News* and the *New York Age*. Local businesses in Brooklyn's own rapidly expanding predominantly black neighborhood, Bedford-Stuyvesant, were no exception. The Silver Rail Bar and Grill on Fulton Street, for example, advertised a "Jackie Robinson Gift Party," noting in parenthetical small print, "Jackie will

not appear in person."[22] Harlem's baseball fans were also targeted by local businesses advertising in New York's black press. Following a Dodgers-Giants match at the Polo Grounds, Bowman's Henry Armstrong Melody Room at St. Nicholas Avenue and 125th Street invited Robinson's fans to celebrate with friends at their establishment, though no gift appears to have been involved.

Of course, Robinson's appeal extended well beyond New York City. Resembling the congratulatory ads for the pennant-winning Dodgers that appeared in the *Eagle* at the end of the season, page after page of advertising linking local black businesses in other cities with substantial African American communities across the country also appeared in black newspapers outside New York. A page of ads that ran in the *Courier* during the Dodgers' first visit to Pittsburgh is representative of congratulatory advertisements placed in the black press. Ads for Vet Sales Company Army-Navy Surplus, Evans Tailors, and Anderson's Service Stations all invoke Robinson. United Clothing and Furniture Company, offering easy weekly payments, lauds the African American infielder. More importantly, Virgil H. Lucas and A. A. Lenior, attorneys, tell Robinson, "We're rooting for you," in their ad.[23] Each of these ads has something else in common. In every case, the team name is nowhere to be seen. Herein lies a clear distinction between congratulatory ads in the *Courier* and the other black newspapers and those placed in the *Eagle*. Like Lucas and Lenior, small local businesses in African American neighborhoods outside of New York make it clear that it is Robinson, not the Dodgers as a team, with whom they wish to be associated.

Jackie Robinson, like Dixie Walker, also endorsed national products, not only in the black press but in mainstream print media as well. While Walker sold Wonder bread to white readers of the nation's papers, Robinson sold Bond bread in the black press, primarily in New York. Not only does

Robinson's Bond endorsement ad, which ran repeatedly throughout the season, include a personal testimonial, it also offers consumers a trade card with an image of the Dodger. "Your grocer will give you a pocket-size reproduction of this Jackie Robinson photograph, free for the asking," reads the advertisement.[24] Presumably, while in the market, shoppers would also fill their carts with groceries, including Bond bread.

And like Walker, Robinson, also a nonsmoker, endorsed cigarettes, in this case the Dodgers' sponsor, Old Golds, in ads featuring action photographs of Robinson with facsimile autographs bearing the legend "For a treat instead of a treatment."[25] Robinson's Old Gold ads differ from the local ads in the black press. Not only was Old Gold a national brand, but Robinson's endorsement appeared in mainstream papers as well as in the black press. Indeed, it might be said that Robinson's national product endorsements, whose number grew throughout his career, may have led to changes in the way in which African Americans were perceived by the majority of American consumers. It is, moreover, a little ironic that Robinson and Walker served, individually, as the advertising faces of the 1947 Dodgers. Walker, who initially had opposed Robinson's joining the Dodgers, was traded after the 1947 season, while Robinson continued to be the advertising face of the team throughout his career.

Throughout the 1947 season, one theme surfaced in print advertising, whether the outlet was black or mainstream, national or local. Wherever the Dodgers had fans, print ads sold televisions. Commercial television, which was introduced during a Dodgers game on July 1, 1941, with a short spot for Bulova clocks, had been halted due to the war but resumed after hostilities ceased.[26] On March 1, 1947, the Dodgers announced the first agreement by a Major League team to televise all seventy-seven home games, co-sponsored by Ford Motor Company and General Mills.[27] Ford, along

with Gillette, would also go on to sponsor the 1947 World Series.[28] In reality, the impact of television advertising in 1947 was small, as was ad revenue. After all, fewer than 1 percent of all American households owned sets.[29] A new twelve-inch receiver cost approximately $300.[30] That sum represented 10 percent of the median family income in 1947.[31] Therefore, very few viewers were aware of the poor quality of the commercials shown during Dodgers broadcasts, regular season and World Series alike.[32] Most who saw the games did so in taverns and saloons. But television in 1947 relied on baseball for content. As James Walker and Robert Bellamy write, "The RCA chairman, David Sarnoff[,] observed . . . [,] 'We [television makers] had to have baseball games and if they demanded millions for the rights, we would have to give it to them.'"[33] "Television did not create baseball," Walker and Bellamy note, "but baseball helped to create television. Newly minted television stations were not the only ones that need baseball to fill their broadcast hours. Television manufacturers need appealing programs to push consumers to buy their first sets."[34]

And sell sets they did. Ads for televisions appeared all over the print media in 1947, especially in New York. Bressner Radio, Inc., offered *Eagle* readers "a season's pass to Ebbets Field" with the new DuMont 1947 Teleset. The model, illustrated in the ad, depicts a huge console with a tiny screen. What is on that screen? Of course, it is a crude drawing of the action on the field.[35] Ads for televisions evoking the Dodgers, placed by Davega, a New York–area appliance chain, were almost ubiquitous in virtually every regional print outlet during the 1947 season. One Davega ad, published in both the *Times* and the *Amsterdam News*, predicted a Yankees-Dodgers World Series as early as August, in an attempt to sell Philco televisions, offering easy installment payments as well as free delivery.

RCA, not to be outdone, placed a full-page ad in

the *New York Times*, making sure consumers were aware of the fact that not only the Dodgers but also the Giants and the Yankees broadcast their home games. RCA's ad included the promise that "several television cameras strategically located cover the baseball diamond to bring you a close-up of the action wherever it occurs. The engineer can switch from one camera to the other for the best view."[36] Why buy any other brand?

In many ways 1947 was the heyday for Brooklyn as well as the Dodgers, but changes were afoot. Following the lead of his father, a real-estate developer who fled his Bedford-Stuyvesant neighborhood when an African American family moved in, Bill Levitt broke ground on Long Island for what would become the largest private housing project in American history. The lily-white subdivision was to be called Island Trees, but the name Levittown stuck.[37] "Suburbs had long surrounded major cities, but there had been relatively little residential building in the 1930s and early 1940s, and the fantastic sprawl of suburbia was only beginning in the mid-1940s," writes Patterson.[38] And what did Bill Levitt offer free to new homebuyers in his development? A television set. Why make the trip to Ebbets Field, when the Dodgers could come to you in the comfort of your brand-new, two-bedroom Cape or Colonial? Indeed, with the breaking of ground in Levittown, white flight from New York had begun. Many of the *Eagle*'s readers, avid Robinson fans all, would soon begin the exodus out of Brooklyn, headed for Long Island, New Jersey, and points west. Ten years later, the Dodgers would follow.

In many ways, Dodgers-related advertising, a sign of postwar prosperity and consumerism, may be seen as a bellwether for what was to come. The team's fans would retreat into their new homes, complete with their Contemporama furniture and labor-saving appliances purchased at A&S, not the one in Brooklyn, but in the store's branches in New Jersey and on Long Island. They would watch Jackie Robinson steal home in Game One of the 1955 World Series on RCA televisions, perhaps purchased at Davega's. Still, the mark of these wholesale changes, which may be traced to the early postwar years, would not be truly felt for nearly a decade. Unlike the 1955 Dodgers, the 1947 Dodgers did not win the World Series; nevertheless, it most certainly was a great year for Brooklyn, its team, and Dodgers-related advertising.

# Chapter 72. **The 1947 World Series**

*Tom Hawthorn*

Before the first pitch, two simple facts made the 1947 confrontation between the Brooklyn Dodgers and the New York Yankees one for the history books. The feisty, daring, brilliant Jackie Robinson patrolled first base for the Brooklyn Dodgers, becoming the first African American to appear in the World Series. He played in games seen not only by those fortunate enough to hold tickets but also, in this first televised Series, by an unseen audience who caught the games at taverns, facing store display windows, and in private homes.

On the field, several matchups held promise. How would Brooklyn's young Ralph Branca, who had gone 21-12 in the season, handle Yankees slugger Joe DiMaggio, whose career-low (thus far) twenty home runs still led the club? How would the Yankees' pitchers hold Robinson on base after he led the National League with twenty-nine stolen bases?

As it turned out, the Series would be remembered for cameos by bit players—an unheralded right-hander who, despite issuing ten walks, had recorded twenty-six outs without giving up a base hit; a pinch hitter who delivered a Hollywood ending; and a miraculous catch by a onetime coal miner who was stepping onto the outfield grass at Yankee Stadium for the first time.

## Game One: Yankees 5, Dodgers 3

The opening game attracted stars of the stage and screen to Yankee Stadium. The Hollywood contingent included comedian Danny Kaye and actress Laraine Day, who earlier in the year had married Dodgers manager Leo Durocher, who was under suspension for consorting with gamblers. News-

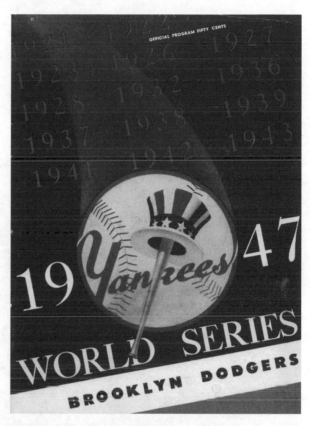

A 1947 World Series program.

paper photographers snapped Durocher shaking hands with Happy Chandler, the baseball commissioner who had issued the punishment.

Political dignitaries included former president Herbert Hoover; New York City mayor William O'Dwyer, who tossed out the first ball; and New York governor Thomas E. Dewey, who would be selected the Republican nominee for president the following June.

Al Schacht, the "Clown Prince of Baseball," performed impersonations for the amusement of

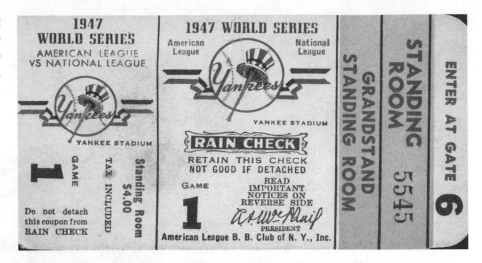

A four-dollar standing room ticket in the Grandstand for Game One.

Pee Wee Reese scores in Game One as Joe Page covers the plate. The umpire is Bill McGowan.

the crowd, among them Joe DiMaggio's mother, who sat with her son Dominic, an outfielder with the Boston Red Sox.

Batting second, Robinson coaxed a walk from Yankees starter Frank Shea, a twenty-six-year-old rookie who had gone 14-5 during the season. Robinson stole second, only to get caught in a rundown between second and third after Shea snagged a comebacker to the mound. Robinson managed to stay alive long enough for the batter, Pete Reiser, to get as far as second. Reiser scored on Dixie Walker's single.

For the first four innings, Branca, the Brooklyn right-hander, mastered the Yankees, who failed to get a single runner on base. Joe DiMaggio opened the home half of the fifth by legging out an in-

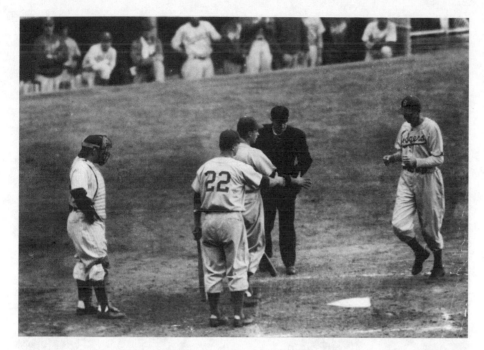

Gene Hermanski (22) and batboy Stan Strull greet Dixie Walker after his home run in Game Two. Yogi Berra is the catcher and Babe Pinelli is the home plate umpire.

field single to shortstop. A base on balls and a hit batsman loaded the bases for Johnny Lindell, who drove in a pair with a double to left. Another walk reloaded the bases. Yankees manager Bucky Harris sent Bobby Brown up as a pinch hitter for Shea. With the count 2-0, Dodgers manager Burt Shotton replaced Branca with Hank Behrman, who walked Brown, forcing in a run. Two more runs scored on Tommy Henrich's single. The five runs stood up for the Yankees, as the Dodgers managed only single runs against lefty Joe Page in the sixth and seventh innings.

### Game Two: Yankees 10, Dodgers 3

Allie Reynolds went the distance to put the Yankees up two games to none. The Yanks got on the scoreboard against Vic Lombardi with two singles to open the first, with George Stirnweiss scoring as Lindell grounded into a double play.

The Yanks led, 3–2, after the fourth, thanks to some poor fielding. Brooklyn's Reiser had a miserable game in center field. A hit that should have been a single slipped past him for a triple; he stumbled while pursuing a fly ball, which also resulted in a triple; a third fly landed for yet another three-bagger as he fell down. The three Yankee triples tied a World Series record.

Nor was Reiser alone in his misery. A ball landed for a double as three Dodgers stood around waiting for someone to take charge. A possible double play was lost when Eddie Stanky dropped a toss from Behrman, once again on in relief, Robinson muffed a bunt. The official scorer charged the sloppy Dodgers with only two errors—to Reiser and Stanky—but the Brooklyn fielding was awful. "It just wasn't the Dodgers' day," *The Sporting News* reported.

The Yankees scored runs in six of eight innings, erasing all doubt as to the outcome when four runners crossed the plate in the seventh.

### Game Three: Dodgers 9, Yankees 8

The Series moved to Ebbets Field, where the Dodgers chased starter Bobo Newsom with six runs in the second inning. The score was 7–2 by the end of the third, 9–4 after four.

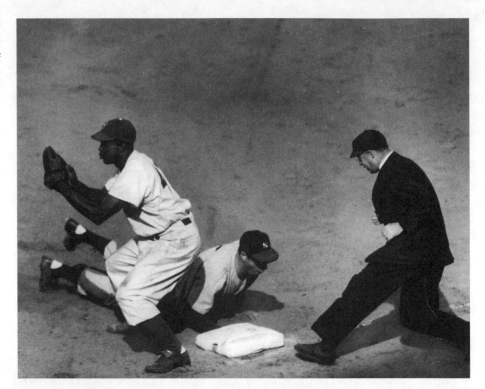

Joe DiMaggio dives back to first base safely after a pickoff attempt.

Hugh Casey, Pee Wee Reese, Joe Hatten, and Eddie Stanky (*left to right*) exchange congratulations with a seated Dixie Walker following Brooklyn's 9–8 victory in Game Three of the 1947 World Series.

Phil Rizzuto steals second base in Game Four. Eddie Stanky covers the bag while Pee Wee Reese backs up the play. The umpire is Babe Pinelli.

The Yankees kept nibbling away against starter Joe Hatten and reliever Branca. DiMaggio smacked a two-run homer into the left-field stands in the fifth for his first RBI in the Series. They added another in the sixth on doubles by Brown and Henrich. Yogi Berra's smash over the scoreboard in right—the first pinch-hit home run in World Series history—narrowed the score to 9–8.

The first two runners in the Yankees eighth got on base on a walk and a single, but the threat diminished when DiMaggio hit into a double play. The next four Yankees batters went quietly, with

Hugh Casey, who pitched the final two and two-thirds innings, getting credit for the win.

## Game Four: Dodgers 3, Yankees 2

The Yankees chased Harry Taylor before the Brooklyn starter recorded an out. They scored a run in the top of the first when DiMaggio walked with the bases loaded following two singles and an error by Pee Wee Reese. A double play prevented more damage.

For the Yankees, Floyd "Bill" Bevens gave up two walks in the bottom of the first, though he managed to get out of trouble without surrendering a hit. The six-foot-three, 210-pound right-hander issued another walk in the second, a walk and a wild pitch in the third, and another two walks in the fifth, with Spider Jorgensen eventually scoring on a fielder's choice. Bevens gave up more bases on balls in the sixth and seventh, but through eight innings, he had yet to be touched for a hit.

Going into the ninth, the Yankees nursed a 2–1 lead. (Back in the fourth, a Billy Johnson triple off Hal Gregg had been followed by a Lindell double.) The Yankees loaded the bases with Henrich coming to the plate. Casey came on in relief to replace Behrman. On the first pitch, Henrich grounded a one-hopper back to Casey, who started an inning-ending pitcher-to-catcher-to-first double play.

The drama of that confrontation had barely abated when attention returned to Bevens's bid for the first no-hitter in World Series history. Bruce Edwards flied out to left. One down. Carl Furillo walked. Jorgensen fouled out on a pop to first. Two down. Reiser came on to hit for the pitcher, while Al Gionfriddo ran for Furillo. After Gionfriddo stole second, Reiser was walked intentionally. Eddie Miksis took his place as the runner.

Now, Harry "Cookie" Lavagetto stepped to the plate as a pinch hitter for Stanky. Cookie swung and missed on Bevens's first pitch. But he sent the next offering clattering off the right-field fence for a double as both runners raced home. In that instant Bevens lost his no-hitter and the game, as Brooklyn tied the Series.

Delirious fans poured onto the field. Jubilant teammates pounded Lavagetto on the back, while supporters surrounded the celebrating players. One fan snatched Cookie's cap. Police escorted him to the dugout. In the bedlam Bevens walked in glum silence to the Yankees' dressing room. On the radio Red Barber said, "Well, I'll be a suck-egg mule!"

*Life* magazine called the ninth-inning confrontation the "most exciting two minutes in history of World Series" (an odd headline for a sport played without a clock). "It was an inning that will never be forgotten," *The Sporting News* judged correctly.

Casey got the win, his second, though he made just a single pitch.

## Game Five: Yankees 2, Dodgers 1

Frank Shea returned to the mound for the Yankees, retiring the first ten batters he faced. Meanwhile, his own single in the fourth drove in Aaron Robinson from second base with the game's first run. In the fifth, DiMaggio homered off starter Rex Barney, who was soon replaced. The two runs would be all the Yankees needed.

Shea frustrated the Dodgers, who managed only to scratch out a run in the sixth after Gionfriddo and Reese walked and Robinson singled. With two outs in the ninth and a runner on first, Lavagetto came to the plate again as a pinch hitter. Here again was a chance for Lavagetto to snatch victory from defeat. This time, however, he struck out as Shea gained his second Series victory.

"A hero one day—a bum the next," Lavagetto said afterward in the clubhouse.

## Game Six: Dodgers 8, Yankees 6

After two games of pitching dominance, the batters came to the fore on a return to Yankee Stadium. Neither starter—Vic Lombardi for the Dodgers, Allie Reynolds for the Yankees—lasted through the third inning.

The first three Dodgers batters hit singles, though Brooklyn managed just two runs—one scoring on a double play and the other on a passed ball by Sherm Lollar.

The Dodgers jumped to a 4–0 lead before the Yankees got on the board, but a lead-off double by Lollar in the third followed by a Spider Jorgensen error and five singles tied the game. The home side went ahead by a run in the fourth when Yogi Berra's single scored Aaron Robinson.

The Dodgers responded with four runs of their own in the sixth with a pair of doubles and a trio of singles for an 8–5 lead. In the home half of the inning, Gionfriddo came in as a replacement in left field, the first time he had ever played the field at Yankee Stadium. With two outs and George Stirnweiss on second and Berra on first, DiMaggio stepped to the plate. He took a mighty swing at a Joe Hatten offering.

The left-fielder raced back "like a miscreant into the deepening shadows," according to one account, before snagging the potential home run at the 415-foot marker.

"I put my head down and ran," Gionfriddo recalled later. "I looked over my shoulder once and knew I was going in the right direction. When I got close to the fence, I looked over my left shoulder and then jumped practically at the same time and caught the ball over my shoulder. I turned in the air coming down and hit the fence with my butt. I caught it in the webbing."

DiMaggio, not known for showing emotion on the field of play, kicked at the base path dirt in frustration. The catch preserved a three-run lead that lasted until the bottom of the ninth.

The Yanks loaded the bases on a walk and two singles. With one out and Hugh Casey on the mound, the Yankees scored a run on a fielder's choice. With the tying run on first and himself representing the Series-winning run, Stirnweiss grounded to the pitcher for an easy out at first. The Yanks had left thirteen men on base.

## Game Seven: Yankees 5, Dodgers 2

Burt Shotton sent Hal Gregg to the mound at Yankee Stadium for the deciding game. Days earlier, the right-hander had kept the Dodgers close in a long relief stint opposite Bevens's no-hit bid. The Yankees' Bucky Harris countered with Shea, who had won Games One and Five.

Eddie Stanky singled and Reese walked in the first, but both men were thrown out on steal attempts by Yankees catcher Aaron Robinson.

The Dodgers got on the scoreboard in the second, when Gene Hermanski's triple to right was followed by a single by Edwards. When the next batter, Furillo, also singled, Shea was yanked in favor of Bevens, the near-hero of Game Four. The first batter he faced, Jorgensen, rapped a double, scoring Edwards. More damage was limited when Phil Rizzuto fielded a grounder by Gregg and gunned down Furillo at the plate.

The Yankees got a run back in the bottom of the inning when a pair of walks was followed by a single by Rizzuto, bringing home George McQuinn.

In the fourth, the home side chased Gregg, scoring two runs to take a 3–2 lead.

In the sixth, Rizzuto got on with a bunt single, stole second, and scored on pinch hitter Allie Clark's single.

The Yankees made it 5–2 in the seventh when Billy Johnson, who had tripled, scored on Aaron Robinson's sacrifice fly.

Joe Page, who had come on in relief in the fifth, kept the Dodgers scoreless the rest of the way. In the ninth, Eddie Miksis singled with one out, but Edwards hit a grounder to Rizzuto, whose toss to Stirnweiss started a game-ending, Series-ending, double play. The Yankees had their eleventh World Series title, while the Dodgers would continue to pursue their first.

# Chapter 73. Al Gionfriddo

*Rory Costello*

| AGE | G | AB | R | H | 2B | 3B | HR | TB | RBI | BB | SO | BAV | OBP | SLG | SB | GDP | HBP |
|-----|---|----|----|----|----|----|----|----|----|----|----|------|------|------|----|----|----|
| 25 | 37 | 62 | 10 | 11 | 2 | 1 | 0 | 15 | 6 | 16 | 11 | .177 | .346 | .242 | 2 | 1 | 0 |

"Running! turning! leaping! like little Al Gionfriddo—a baseball player, Doctor, who once did a very great thing."

The great thing novelist Philip Roth described in *Portnoy's Complaint* was Gionfriddo's racing, twisting catch to rob Joe DiMaggio of extra bases or a three-run homer and save Game Six of the 1947 World Series for Brooklyn. Alas, the twenty-five-year-old Gionfriddo never played in the Major Leagues again. Yet more than sixty years later, his spectacular grab remains a potent memory. Red Barber's exciting radio call, a classic action photo, dozens of writers, and thousands of fans all helped the play live on. At root, though, is the appeal of a hard-working little guy's moment in the sun.

Albert Francis Gionfriddo (pronounced Gee-on-FREE-doe) was born March 8, 1922, in Dysart, Pennsylvania. Dysart is northwest of Altoona, about ninety miles east of Pittsburgh. Al's father, Paul Gionfriddo, was a coal miner. The family's roots are Sicilian. Paul (originally Paolo) was born in the town of Solarino in Siracusa province and learned the trade of stone mason. He immigrated to the United States in the early 1900s.

Paul and his wife, the former Rose Rametta, daughter of a fellow coal miner from Calabria, had thirteen children, of whom Al was the seventh. Only ten reached adulthood. The Gionfriddo parents conversed in Italian, but they wanted their children to speak English. "Al could speak some broken Italian," his second wife, Susan Jacobsen Gionfriddo, recalled in 2008. "He could understand it better." The youngsters also grew up American thanks to sports. Sue notes that the Dysart baseball team "was half Gionfriddos, be-

Al Gionfriddo came to the Dodgers from Pittsburgh as part of the May 3 trade that sent Kirby Higbe to the Pirates.

tween his brothers and cousins." Al played center field for the nearby American Legion team, the Cresson Juniors, and Jim played left field.

Al also attended high school in Cresson, roughly twelve miles south of Dysart. As a running back in football, he won a scholarship to nearby St. Francis University, but his calling was on the diamond. At age nineteen, in 1941, before graduating from Cresson High, Al signed with the Pittsburgh Pirates. He had been discovered in August 1940 in the Legion's Pennsylvania state tournament. The scout was quite likely Patsy O'Rourke, a Philadelphian.

"His father felt he should have been working, but it was a dream come true for Al," said Sue Gionfriddo. "It was also a ticket out of the mines. He spent some time there, maybe a summer." Gionfriddo said in 1972, "I worked in the coal mines, and I didn't like that. I signed for $65 a month and the love of baseball. I just wanted to get into baseball."[1]

Al joined the Oil City Oilers in the Class D Pennsylvania State Association. He followed a strong first season by making the circuit's all-star team in 1942. Gionfriddo was just five feet six and roughly 160 pounds—but he could run. "The Dysart Deer," who also had been a sprinter in high school, was already making a name for sensational catches.[2]

With World War II in full swing, Al was ordered to report to his draft board that August. He joined the army in February 1943 but received a medical discharge the following January. "He was running the obstacle course, which he did very well," Sue said. "His commanding officer had some kind of bet and wanted him to do it again, but Al ruptured his stomach. After he was discharged, he went back to school and finished up."

Gionfriddo then resumed his baseball career with the Albany (New York) Senators in the Class A Eastern League. Noted for his hustle and "one of the most aggressive spirits in baseball," Al was the consummate lead-off man. His twenty-eight triples are still the Eastern League's single-season record.

On May 22, 1944, Al and Arlene Lentz—his childhood sweetheart—got married in Albany.[3] After the Eastern League season ended, the Pirates called up Gionfriddo, and he made his Major League debut at the Polo Grounds on September 23. He went 1 for 6 in four games. His first hit, a single, came on September 27 off Al Javery of Boston at Braves Field.

Gionfriddo's only season as a big league regular was 1945. He hit .284 with 2 home runs and 42 RBIs in 122 games. That July, the Cresson draft board recalled the "pride of the Pittsburgh bobbysoxers"; however, he got an extension, since Arlene was expecting their first child. Meanwhile, the war ended.[4]

Gionfriddo made *The Sporting News*'s all-rookie team in 1945, but after Ralph Kiner joined the Pirates, he played in just sixty-four games in 1946. In late August, Al underwent an appendectomy, which ended his season.[5] He returned in October to play with a group of touring Major Leaguers skippered by Pirates coach Honus Wagner. The opponents were an African American squad headed by Jackie Robinson.[6]

Gionfriddo's most intriguing baseball activity in '46 came off the field. He was involved in the Pirates' strike vote that June, the key to a failed bid to organize baseball's labor movement two decades before Marvin Miller's arrival.[7] Al wondered whether his activism might have been held against him when he was later buried in the Minors.[8]

After working in the off-season as a fireman on the Pennsylvania Railroad, Gionfriddo came to the plate just once for the Pirates in early 1947. Then on May 3 he went to Brooklyn in the trade for pitcher Kirby Higbe. Legend has it that Gionfriddo carried the deal's large cash component in a satchel.

Al was upset when he heard of the trade, as he was just building up a tire business in Pittsburgh. He remained unhappy even after he was assured that he would stay with the Dodgers as a backup outfielder.[9] He appeared in thirty-seven games for Brooklyn and batted a meager .177. Yet despite his small role on the field, he had a subtle influence in the clubhouse, as shown by his locker-room support for Jackie Robinson.[10]

"Al was disappointed by the trade at first," Sue Gionfriddo confirmed. "But a bad thing turned into a good thing. He got the opportunity to be part of history, and he cherished it." After the World Series ended, Dysart declared October 12 "Al Gionfriddo Day." A crowd of 5,000 people gathered to greet the local hero, who played center field as Dysart defeated Coalport in an exhibition game.[11]

Gionfriddo went to spring training in the Dominican Republic with the Dodgers in 1948. In April, though, Brooklyn sent him outright to their top farm club, the Montreal Royals of the International League. Despite playing well in Cuban winter ball, he was never able to return to the crowded and competitive Brooklyn outfield.

Al's obituary in the *New York Times* says, "He remained bitter toward Branch Rickey. . . . Gionfriddo maintained that Rickey reneged on a promise to bring him back to the majors, leaving him sixty days short of qualifying for a pension."[12]

Al remained in Montreal through 1951. Between the 1951 and 1952 seasons, he was transferred to Brooklyn's other top farm club, St. Paul of the American Association. After he refused the St. Paul assignment, the Dodgers sent him to the Fort Worth Cats, their Class Double-A affiliate in the Texas League, to serve as a player, coach, and road secretary. From there Gionfriddo journeyed through the Minors at successively lower levels, including a stretch in 1953 as player-manager of Drummondville in Canada's Provincial League.

The Dodgers organization released him at the end of that season. An article in the *Hayward (California) Daily Review* stated that "Al moved with the wife and three children from Altoona to Van Nuys, California, with the intention of giving up baseball. But former teammate Chuck Connors talked him into staying in the game."[13] Gionfriddo played from 1954 through 1956 in the Class C California League and then retired at age thirty-five.

After his playing days ended, Al remained in California. With a wife and a houseful of kids to support, he worked double shifts at the Tulare County Juvenile Hall in Visalia and the Tulare County Boy's Camp.[14] Later he became an insurance salesman in Visalia. He was closely involved with youth baseball and encouraged the kids to get a college education.[15]

During the 1961 season, Al scouted central California for the San Francisco Giants. From 1962 through 1964, he was general manager of the Minor League team in Santa Barbara, a farm club of the Mets and then the Dodgers. Sue Gionfriddo remembered, "The Dodgers wanted him to move, and he didn't want to go. Tommy Lasorda went instead."

After that, Gionfriddo went into the restaurant business. He worked at an oyster bar in the Santa Barbara suburb of Goleta; then he bought it and renamed it Al's Dugout. Al and Arlene divorced in March 1971. On July 22, 1973, he married Sue, whom he had met five years earlier—she played first base for a women's team he'd organized.

In 1974 Gionfriddo sold the restaurant. He then became an athletic equipment manager and trainer at San Marcos High in Santa Barbara. There he remained for fifteen years before retiring in 1988. During this time, he also served as a part-time scout for Cincinnati.[16]

Al kept active tying handmade fishing lures and serving as a marshal two days a week at the Sandpiper Golf Course in Goleta.[17] He also played golf several times a week. He had a single-digit handicap when he was younger, and it hovered between ten and twelve in later years.

Al long believed that ballplayers of his generation had been denied justice.[18] In July 1996 he joined four other former Major Leaguers—Cy Block, Pete Coscarart, Dolph Camilli, and Frank Crosetti—in filing a class action suit concerning Major League Baseball's commercial use of "their names, voices, signatures, photographs and/or likenesses." Al also brought his own separate action, but over the next five years their legal battles all proved fruitless.

"Al was very disappointed," said Sue. "He was

RORY COSTELLO

passionate about his beliefs. The old guys were cut out, he said—they were part of the history, but not part of the solution. I remember Pete Coscarart telling Al, 'You know, they're just going to wait for us to die. Then it'll go away.'"

In 1995 the Gionfriddos moved to Solvang, a quaint Danish-style village thirty miles northwest of Santa Barbara. Six days after his eighty-first birthday, on March 14, 2003, Al was enjoying a round of golf on one of the two courses at Alisal Guest Ranch in Solvang. On the fifth green, he was stricken by a fatal heart attack. "There were no pre-existing health issues," Sue noted. The attack "was massive and sudden. His friends tried to revive him, but they couldn't."

Former Dodgers manager Tom Lasorda, who had been Al's roommate in Montreal, commented, "He was an outstanding ballplayer and friend. He wore the Dodger uniform proudly, and we're losing a great Dodger."[19]

Gionfriddo was survived by four of his six children with Arlene: Susan, Gary, Alene, and Ray. Two other children, son Robert and daughter Kris, predeceased him. Al also had fourteen grandchildren and seven great-grandchildren.

Gionfriddo is buried in Santa Barbara Cemetery. His headstone bears an inscription of a crossed baseball bat and golf club. Yet he will always be associated with his "thrill of a lifetime" feat from October 1947.

# Chapter 74. **Cookie Lavagetto**

*Mathew Sisson*

| AGE | G | AB | R | H | 2B | 3B | HR | TB | RBI | BB | SO | BAV | OBP | SLG | SB | GDP | HBP |
|-----|---|----|----|----|----|----|----|----|----|----|----|------|------|------|----|----|----|
| 34 | 41 | 69 | 6 | 18 | 1 | 0 | 3 | 28 | 11 | 12 | 5 | .261 | .370 | .406 | 0 | 1 | 0 |

Harry Arthur "Cookie" Lavagetto is best known for one swing of the bat against Bill Bevens of the New York Yankees on an October day in 1947. But his baseball career, as a player and manager, was much more than that. The six-foot, 170-pound Lavagetto played professional baseball for ten seasons over a fourteen-year span, losing four seasons to service in the navy during World War II. Lavagetto, a four-time All-Star at third base, had a career batting average of .269 and played in two World Series as a member of the Brooklyn Dodgers, in 1941 and 1947. He was the last manager of the American League Washington Senators, from 1957 through 1960, and the first manager of the Minnesota Twins when the Senators relocated there for the 1961 season.

Lavagetto's parents were Luigi S. and Adelaide (Lavagett) Lavagetto, both born in Italy in the mid-1870s. Luigi arrived in the United States in 1901; Adelaide arrived in 1906. Harry, the youngest of four boys, was born on December 1, 1912, in Oakland, California, and christened Enrico Atillio Lavagetto.[1] His name was "changed" twice. After his Catholic Church confirmation, the middle name "Attilio" became "Arturo." And on his first day of school, he was told by his teacher that in English "Enrico" was either "Henry" or "Harry." He decided on Harry, and from that day forward he was known as Harry Arturo Lavagetto. It was during these early days at school in Oakland that Harry met Mary Poggi. It was a long courtship; they didn't marry until 1945. "Our families used to go mushroom-hunting together in the hills above Oakland," Lavagetto recalled.[2]

Playing Major League baseball had always

Cookie Lavagetto was a part-time player in 1947, his final big league season.

been young Harry's dream. Shortly after graduating from Oakland Technical High School, he had a tryout with San Francisco of the Pacific Coast League.[3] Living just across the bay, Lavagetto was eager for the chance to play professional baseball so close to home. But he flopped during the tryout and assumed his goal of playing in the big leagues was over. Moreover, his father had been pressuring him to start earning a living.

A week after the tryout, Lavagetto heard of a game that was being put together between some big leaguers on the West Coast who were about to leave for spring training and an All-Star semipro team. Proceeds of the game were to go toward an insurance fund to pay for hospital bills for semipro players who got injured.

Lavagetto was picked to play for the semipro team, and was slated to come into the game after the fifth inning with other substitutes. When he came to bat, his team was down two runs and the bases were loaded with two outs. On the mound was Al "Pudgy" Gould, who had played two seasons (1916–17) with the Cleveland Indians and had a long career in the Pacific Coast League. Harry hit a Gould pitch high off the right-field wall for a bases-clearing double, securing the lead and eventually the win for the semipros. After the game, he received nine offers to play professionally.

Lavagetto called that hit his greatest moment in baseball. "Everything stemmed from that one shot I hit," he told Washington sportswriter Bob Addie. "There would have been no big-league career, no chance to spoil Bevens's no-hitter. One swing changed the whole course of my life because I was almost to the point, after being released by San Francisco, where I was going to give up the idea of ever playing big-league ball."[4] Lavagetto signed with Cookie DeVincenzi, owner of the Pacific Coast League's Oakland Oaks. Harry became known as "Cookie's boy" and, eventually, just plain Cookie.[5]

Lavagetto began his professional career as a second baseman with the Oaks in 1933, batting .312 in 152 games.[6] Pittsburgh Pirates scout Bill Hinchman signed him, and he spent three seasons (1934–36) with Pittsburgh, moving between second base and third. In 1934, his rookie season, Lavagetto played in eighty-seven games, all at second base, but his playing time decreased sharply in each of the next two years. Lavagetto's combined batting average for his three seasons in Pittsburgh was .249.[7]

On December 4, 1936, the Pirates traded Lavagetto and pitcher Ralph Birkofer to the Brooklyn Dodgers for pitcher Ed Brandt.[8] Lavagetto played in one hundred games at second base in his first year with the Dodgers, but for the rest of his Major League career, he was primarily a third baseman. In Cookie's first season with Brooklyn, he batted .282 with seventy runs batted in. The next season, 1938, Lavagetto became an All-Star for the first time, and in 1939 he had the best season of his career, batting .300 with eighty-seven RBIS.

Lavagetto had the reputation of being somewhat of an oddball during his playing days. "Cookie was a character," said a sportswriter who covered the Dodgers then. "He walked funny and always needed a shave," the writer told *Sports Illustrated*. "His shirt would be hanging out of his pants, and he wore his hat at a weird angle. Cookie would just sit there, not realizing he looked any different than the next guy." Lavagetto was well liked in the clubhouse and often enjoyed making his teammates laugh. "Oh, I used to know it," Lavagetto told *Sports Illustrated*. "I used to enjoy wearing one sock up, the other down. I don't know why exactly. I just enjoyed it."[9]

Lavagetto was chosen for the All-Star Game in every season from 1938 through 1941. After not playing in the '38 and '39 games, he was the National League's starting third baseman in 1940 and a pinch hitter in 1941. The Dodgers won the NL pennant in 1941 but lost to the New York Yankees in the World Series. In January 1942, with the United States at war, Cookie applied for enlistment in the navy. On February 17 in San Francisco, he was sworn in as an aviation machinist's mate first class, and shortly afterward reported for duty at the Alameda (California) Naval Air Station.

"We don't think enough credit has been given to Cookie Lavagetto for his enlistment in naval aviation," wrote Bob Considine on February 3,

1942, in his weekly column "On the Line." "After all, most of the athletes who have gotten wild applause of late for their patriotism were drafted into the services. Lavagetto, several times chosen as the best third baseman in the National League, and with five or six prosperous years of baseball before him, was in Class 3-A and might have remained there even if we were invaded as deep as Akron. He enlisted the moment his brother, whom he had been supporting (along with a number of others), got a defense job. He felt morally called upon to give to the government his ability to fly a plane. Anyway, my lid's off to a good, game guy who, with a minimum of fanfare and under no compulsion, is doing his bit."

Considine's mention of flying was a reference to the fact that in 1938 Harry and teammate Dolph Camilli decided to take flying lessons. After they got their pilot's licenses, Dodgers chief executive Larry MacPhail heard about it and, irate, fined the pair $500 apiece for activities detrimental to the ball club.

While with the navy in California, Cookie played baseball whenever he could. He competed against the same Oakland Oaks team for whom he had once played. Lavagetto played for the navy team in an Army-Navy All-Star game on July 5, 1943, at Seals Stadium in San Francisco. While stationed at the Livermore (California) Naval Air Station in '43, he played for a navy team that won sixty of its seventy games.[10]

Soon after he married Mary Poggi, on April 10, 1945, Cookie was reassigned to Hawaii, where he managed a navy team that included Stan Musial. In 1946, with World War II over, Lavagetto returned to the Dodgers at the age of thirty-three. He had missed four seasons, and his skills had eroded. "I was washed up," he told *Sports Illustrated*. He played in only eighty-eight games in 1946 and forty-one in 1947.[11] His last big league season was 1947, and Cookie went out with a flourish.

The Dodgers won the pennant in '47 and faced the New York Yankees in the World Series. It was during that Series that Lavagetto solidified himself in baseball history and lore. On October 3, with the Yankees leading the Series two games to one, Bill Bevens was on the mound for the Yankees at Ebbets Field. In the bottom of the ninth inning, the Yankees led, 2–1. Although he had walked eight Dodgers, Bevens was just three outs away from throwing the first World Series no-hitter. Bruce Edwards, the Dodgers' first batter, flied out. Carl Furillo worked Bevens for the pitcher's ninth walk. Spider Jorgensen fouled out. There was one more out to go.

Dodgers manager Burt Shotton sent Al Gionfriddo in to run for Furillo. Gionfriddo stole second, while Bevens was pitching carefully to Pete Reiser. With a 3-1 count on him, Reiser was given an intentional walk, Bevens's tenth walk of the game. Eddie Miksis pinch-ran for Reiser, and Shotton sent the right-handed-hitting Lavagetto up to pinch-hit for the right-handed hitting Eddie Stanky.

Lavagetto had always been a good clutch hitter, and there was no better situation than this. Bevens's second pitch to Cookie was high and outside. Lavagetto smashed the ball over right fielder Tommy Henrich's head and off the wall. Gionfriddo scored from second. Henrich threw the ball home, but the relay arrived at the plate just as the speedy Eddie Miksis slid in with the winning run. Lavagetto's smash robbed Bevens of a no-hitter and a victory, and the Series was tied. Lavagetto was mobbed in the center of the field by his teammates and needed a police escort to get to the dugout. Bevens later told Lavagetto, "We were told to throw you high and outside." Harry replied, "That's just where I like them."

The hit was Lavagetto's last in the Major Leagues. He was released by the Dodgers on May 3, 1948. After his release, Lavagetto returned to the Oakland Oaks, where he played through 1950 under managers Casey Stengel and Charlie

Dressen. Dressen was hired as the Dodgers' manager in 1951, whereupon Lavagetto quit playing and signed on with Brooklyn as a coach. When Dressen was refused a two-year contract after the 1953 season, Cookie sent owner Walter O'Malley a telegram that read, "Please accept resignation." The loyalty Lavagetto had toward Dressen was strong, and he followed Dressen back to Oakland as a coach.

In 1955 Dressen was named manager of the Washington Senators and brought Lavagetto with him. After two disappointing seasons, Dressen was fired early in the 1957 season. The managing job was offered to Cookie but, ever loyal to Dressen, he refused it. Only after Dressen begged him to accept did he take the job, his first as a manager. Lavagetto never thought of himself as anything but a coach, and he had a tough time at first adjusting to the position. Cookie was used to being out of the spotlight and had always deflected sportswriters' questions to Dressen. He liked playing cards with the players and enjoyed his anonymity.

That all changed for Lavagetto when he became a manager. The life free of mental strain was gone and he was thrust into the limelight. People now wanted to hear what he had to say. On the road he was given a suite in the team's hotel. He did not like being alone and missed having a roommate. He also did not like deciding the batting order and the pitching rotation, and making decisions during games. What bothered him most was dealing with the losses of a last-place team. Eventually the constant worrying took a toll on Cookie, and he began to have trouble sleeping and eating and even broke out in hives.

After a while, Lavagetto became confident enough to run the team and realize that he could handle the job. It took time for the Senators to improve, but eventually they did. After finishing in eighth place during the first three seasons under Lavagetto, the team improved to fifth in 1960.[12]

Following the 1960 season, owner Calvin Griffith moved the team to Minnesota, where Lavagetto became the first manager of the new Minnesota Twins. Cookie and the team were welcomed to Minnesota with open arms, and Cookie was an instant celebrity. He was treated like royalty in the Twin Cities; he was given cars from local dealerships, and he had his own radio show before each home game. Cookie's reaction was "I prefer to remain in obscurity."[13]

Despite the warm welcome, Lavagetto's time as manager of the Twins lasted just fifty-nine games. With the team's record at 23-36, he was replaced by one of his coaches, Sam Mele. Griffith cited the team's sluggish start and differences in opinion on player talent as his reasons for firing Lavagetto. "He wanted to get rid of just about everybody I wanted to keep," Griffith said.[14]

Lavagetto took the rest of the season off and then returned to coaching with the newborn New York Mets in 1962. He remained with the Mets through 1963. In 1964 he moved closer to home after a false diagnosis of lung cancer and a related operation. He hired on that season as a coach with the San Francisco Giants and stayed with the Giants until he retired after the 1967 season.

Lavagetto died on August 10, 1990, at his home in Orinda, California. He and his wife had two sons: Michael, who became a Catholic priest, and Ernest.

# Chapter 75. Al Gionfriddo's Memorable Game Six Catch

*Rory Costello*

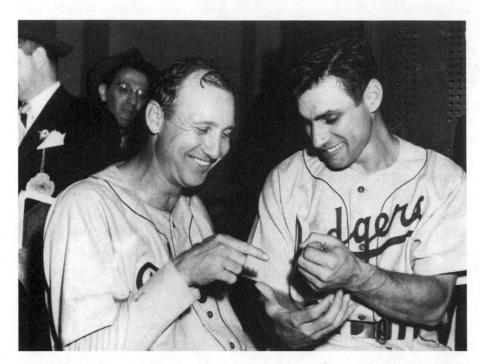

Dixie Walker and Al Gionfriddo celebrate in the clubhouse after Gionfriddo's memorable catch in Game Six of the 1947 World Series. (Courtesy of the Los Angeles Dodgers)

In the bottom of the sixth inning of Game Six of the 1947 World Series, Al Gionfriddo replaced Eddie Miksis in left field. Normally an infielder, Miksis had gone in as a replacement for Gene Hermanski. As Dodgers broadcaster Red Barber later wrote, Brooklyn pitcher Joe Hatten was "wobbly."[1] After a sharp line-out, George Stirnweiss walked, Tommy Henrich barely missed a homer before fouling out, and Yogi Berra singled. Then Barber, on the Mutual radio network, called the moment that defined Gionfriddo for the rest of his life and beyond:

> Joe DiMaggio up, holding that club down at the end. Big fellow sets, Hatten pitches—a curveball, high outside for ball one. Sooo, the Dodgers are ahead, 8–5. And the crowd well knows that with one swing of his bat this fellow's capable of making it a brand-new game again. Outfield deep, around toward left, the infield over-shifted. Here's the pitch, swung on—belted! It's a long one deep into left center—back goes Gionfriddo! Back-back-back-back-back-back . . . he makes a one-handed catch against the bullpen! Ohhh-hooo, Doctor!

Television, a World Series first that year, caught the iconic Yankee Clipper's rare flicker of emotion as he kicked the dirt near second base. Joe D. was still miffed after the game. "'Don't write this in the paper,' [DiMaggio] told a group of reporters, 'but the truth is that if he had been playing me right, he would have made it look easy.'"[2] Gionfriddo himself later admitted that he was playing shallow, and a couple of steps overshifted to the left, at the direction of coach Clyde Sukeforth.[3] This heightened the drama of his sprint.

Al recounted the play many times over the years, most vividly in Roger Kahn's book *The Era, 1947–1957.* He described "Death Valley" in old Yankee Stadium, making the catch as a lefty, and getting a good jump. "'I picked up DiMaggio's ball good. . . . I didn't think I had a chance. . . . I put my head down and I ran, my back was toward home plate and you know I had it right. I had the ball sighted just right.' After all these years, Gionfriddo laughs in gorgeous triumph."[4]

DiMaggio became more gracious about the play in later years. Talking with Al to a group of children, Joe said, "Some big guy wouldn't have ever made the Catch. A big guy woulda backed off and left it to go over the fence. But this little guy. He always had to work harder than anybody else . . . he never gave up."[5] DiMaggio and Gionfriddo also got together in 1974 to offer their recollections for the television program *The Way It Was.*[6]

Though most stories at the time said the ball would have been a home run, debate remains. Even then, it was not unanimous. Associated Press writer Frank Eck noted that "many in the [Yankees] dressing room believed the ball would have hit the iron fence for at least a triple."[7] DiMaggio biographer David Jones quoted historian Eric Enders: "This was merely an example of the halo granted DiMaggio by the New York media. Film of the play clearly shows that it would not have left the park. Indeed, Gionfriddo caught the ball two full steps in front of the fence."[8]

Al himself always thought he stopped it from going out. At the time, he told *The Sporting News,* "Bobby Bragan was in the bullpen, and he said it would have cleared the fence by from one to two feet."[9] On the radio Red Barber (who was not giv-

en to hyperbole) said, "He took a home run away from DiMaggio."

Visual evidence is questionable. Newsreel footage does not show the play from start to finish; there are even allegations it may be a staged re-enactment. However, an expert in the field, Doak Ewing, proprietor of Rare Sportsfilms, Inc., says, "Anybody who thinks that doesn't know film. There are a couple of different views out there, with different angles, but how could you stage that crowd?" Sue Gionfriddo added, "Al had been asked, and he felt that the newsreel footage was accurate. It was always his understanding that it was live."

Along with the fans' reaction, reality shows in the way Gionfriddo loses his cap on the run and then gets it back from the center fielder (though one cannot make out Carl Furillo's distinctive profile). The left-field umpire—the use of six umpires was another first from the '47 Series—also enters the frame to give the "out" sign. Alas, umpire Jim Boyer passed away in 1959; his view is unknown.

Decades later, other authors have drawn and fostered (mis)impressions from this clip. For example, another DiMaggio biographer, Richard Ben Cramer, describes Al as "dancing a spirited tarantella, unsure where to run, which way to turn, how to get under the ball."[10] Jonathan Eig called it a "stumbling, bumbling play."[11] These descriptions belie Gionfriddo's skill as an outfielder—and many other contemporary accounts. For one, Hall of Famer Bill Terry called it "the greatest catch I've ever seen."[12]

Photographers got Pee Wee Reese to pose kissing Al on the cheek, though "finally Reese, grinning as happily as all the other Dodgers, pretended annoyance and called out: 'Let somebody else kiss this little guy. I'm tired of it.'"[13]

"I've signed thousands of that picture," Gionfriddo remarked in 2000.[14] In 1991 he said, "You think, 'Geez, how in the world do these people remember?' They were there when they were teenagers, I guess, and they tell their sons, their grandkids."[15] Hollywood portrayed this very thing in a tender deathbed scene from the 1989 film *Dad* with Jack Lemmon and Ted Danson.

Sue Gionfriddo recalled, "He used to say, 'If all the people that said they were there that day actually were there, Yankee Stadium must have held a million.'"

# Chapter 76. **Lavagetto Ends Bill Bevens's No-Hit Attempt**

*Joe Dittmar*

Pete Reiser, Hugh Casey, Pee Wee Reese, and Dixie Walker surround Cookie Lavagetto after his game-winning hit in Game Four.

Before the 1947 season began, the Yankees hired Dodgers coach Charlie Dressen away from Brooklyn. The incident precipitated such public animosity between the two clubs that Commissioner Happy Chandler was forced to intervene. Among the accusations were several that smacked of gambling. In the end Chandler suspended Dressen for thirty days and Brooklyn manager Leo Durocher for the season for "consorting" with gamblers. Each team was fined $2,000. Fittingly, the two teams were to meet seven months later for a drama-filled seven-game World Series. With the favored Yankees leading two games to one, the clubs met for Game Four at Brooklyn's Ebbets Field. The thriller provided a storybook finish with tragic overtones.

New York started Bill Bevens, a mediocre 7-13 right-hander who was a few weeks shy of his thirty-first birthday. Bevens experienced a lot of bad luck throughout the regular season, in part the residue of his seventy-seven walks in only 165 innings. Rookie Harry Taylor, who had a promising season aborted due to an elbow injury in August, got the call for the Dodgers.

The Yankees wasted no time jumping on Taylor. The first two batters, George Stirnweiss and Tommy Henrich, both singled, and Yogi Berra reached first on an error. Another walk, to Joe DiMaggio, forced in a New York run and sent Taylor to an early shower. Hal Gregg assumed the pitching duties for Brooklyn and got a pop-up and a double

play grounder to extinguish a potentially big inning for the Yankees. In the home half of the first, the Dodgers worked Bevens for two walks, but both runners were left stranded.

In the third, DiMaggio walked with two outs. George McQuinn then tapped a ball near the plate, and Brooklyn catcher Bruce Edwards threw wildly to first. DiMaggio, on a sign from third base coach Dressen, tried to score on the errant throw but was cut down easily at the plate on a throw by right-fielder Dixie Walker. The play provided the second-guessers with ample grist during the following few days. In the bottom of the inning the Dodgers' Eddie Stanky led off with a walk and advanced to second on a Bevens wild pitch. But Johnny Lindell helped the Yanks escape damage with a tumbling catch of Jackie Robinson's foul fly.

New York added a second run in the fourth when Billy Johnson tripled, and Lindell doubled him home.

The Dodgers finally took advantage of Bevens's wildness in the fifth. The first two batters, Spider Jorgensen and Gregg, walked. Although Brooklyn had yet to hit safely, they now had six free passes from the big right-hander. Stanky sacrificed both runners into scoring position. Pee Wee Reese then sent a ground ball to shortstop Phil Rizzuto who tossed out Gregg running to third. Jorgensen scored on the play, making it 2–1.

To start the eighth, Hank Behrman replaced Gregg on the mound for the home club. Behrman withstood an error by Jorgensen but ran into serious trouble in the ninth. Lindell singled sharply past third before Rizzuto forced him at second. Bevens then sacrificed and was safe on a fielder's choice when Edwards threw late to second. When Stirnweiss singled to center, the Yankees had the bases loaded and a golden opportunity to put the game out of reach.

Brooklyn called in their ace reliever, Hugh Casey, to face the dangerous Henrich. Casey had won the previous day's 9–8 contest, and now, on his first offering, Henrich grounded sharply back to the mound, which led to a snappy 1-2-3 double play, pulling the Dodgers out of potential disaster. They still had no hits but were only one run down.

Thanks to a great catch by Henrich with his back to the wall in the bottom of the eighth, Bevens recorded his only perfect inning of the contest and carried his 2–1 lead into the final frame.

Bevens's high-wire act finally caught up with him in the strategy-filled, fatal ninth. After Edwards flied out to the wall in left, Carl Furillo collected the Dodgers' ninth walk. That pass tied the 1910 mark for one World Series game set by Jack Coombs, but when Jorgensen fouled out, Bevens was one out away from the first World Series no-hitter. Al Gionfriddo, running for Furillo while Pete Reiser batted for Casey, stole second. This changed Yankees manager Bucky Harris's thinking about pitching to Reiser. Although the talented outfielder was injured and couldn't run well, New York decided to walk him. It was the tenth walk for Brooklyn and a disaster-inviting strategy, putting the winning run on base. Brooklyn skipper Burt Shotton sent in reserve infielder Eddie Miksis to run for Reiser.

The cat-and-mouse game reached another level when, for only the second time during the 1947 season, Eddie Stanky, a right-handed batter, was lifted for a pinch hitter. Cookie Lavagetto, another right-handed batter, was an aging veteran who had seen limited action during the season but was always a dangerous hitter. Cookie swung and missed, leaving Bevens only two strikes away from victory and fame. But fate had its day as Lavagetto drilled the next offering high off the right-field wall. The ball bounced around long enough for Gionfriddo to score the tying run and Miksis to tally the game winner. Bevens's almost no-hitter had turned into an unforgettable loss.

# Chapter 77. **Most Valuable Player Award**

*Lyle Spatz*

The Baseball Writers' Association of America put seven Dodgers on their National League Most Valuable Player Award ballots, including six of the top thirteen. Boston Braves third baseman Bob Elliott was the top vote-getter, followed by Cincinnati Reds pitcher Ewell Blackwell and New York Giants first baseman Johnny Mize.

The most valuable Dodger, according to the writers, was Bruce Edwards, the second-year catcher, who finished in fourth place. Four voters placed Edwards at the top of their ballots, giving him more first-place votes than anyone except Elliott, who had nine. Edwards batted a solid .295 in 130 games, and did an outstanding job of handling the often-erratic Brooklyn pitching staff.

Brooklyn's rookie first baseman Jackie Robinson, with a .297 average, 125 runs scored, and a league-high 29 stolen bases, was fifth. Other Dodgers receiving votes were shortstop Pee Wee Reese (eighth place), pitchers Ralph Branca and Hugh Casey (eleventh and twelfth, respectively), second baseman Eddie Stanky (tied for thirteenth), and right fielder Dixie Walker (nineteenth).

The Walker vote is one of the more intriguing in the history of postseason awards. He received one first-place vote, but the other twenty-three writers omitted him from their ballots. Walker had been heavily involved in the preseason resistance to Robinson; nevertheless, he had a fine year, batting .306 and leading the team in runs batted in with ninety-four. His one first-place vote seems misplaced, but even more so does his being completely overlooked by the other writers.

# Chapter 78. **Rookie of the Year Award**

*Lyle Spatz*

In a vote that included first-year players from both leagues, the Baseball Writers' Association of America's Rookie of the Year Award in 1947 went to Jackie Robinson. The Brooklyn first baseman batted .297, scored 125 runs, and had a league-leading 29 stolen bases. His numbers, impressive as they were, did not tell the whole story of Robinson's accomplishments. Despite the added pressure of being Major League Baseball's first African American player in the twentieth century, he was the team's sparkplug, and his daring on the bases was responsible for many forced errors by the opposition.

Four other rookies, two from the National League and two from the American League, received votes. Larry Jansen of the New York Giants, who won twenty-one games and had a league-leading .808 winning percentage, was second. New York Yankees pitcher Frank Shea was third. Shea, 14-5, had a .737 winning percentage to lead the American League.

Philadelphia Athletics first baseman Ferris Fain, who batted .291 and finished second in the American League in on-base percentage, was fourth. Cincinnati Reds outfielder Frank Baumholtz, a .283 hitter, finished just behind Fain.

# Chapter 79. Cy Young Award

*Lyle Spatz*

Official recognition of baseball's best pitcher did not begin until 1956, when Brooklyn's Don Newcombe won the first Cy Young Award. Starting in 1967, two awards were given, one to the best pitcher in each league. While there was no official vote in 1947, two retrospective attempts have been made to determine the likely pre-1956 Cy Young winners for each league. The two, one by the Society for American Baseball Research and one by awards historian Bill Deane, agree that the 1947 winner in the National League clearly would have been Cincinnati's Ewell Blackwell.

Blackwell led the league in wins (22), complete games (23), and strikeouts (193), while finishing second in earned run average (2.47) and hits allowed per nine innings (7.48). He threw a no-hitter against the Boston Braves and just missed another in his next start, which Brooklyn's Eddie Stanky broke up with a ninth-inning single. Blackwell, who finished second to Bob Elliott in the voting for Most Valuable Player, was also the National League's starting pitcher in the All-Star Game.

Because there was no separate award for them, pitchers were always well represented in the MVP voting, especially in the World War II era. The National League winner in 1942 had been Mort Cooper of the Cardinals, while American League pitchers had captured three consecutive MVP awards in the era: Spud Chandler of the New York Yankees in 1943, and Hal Newhouser of the Detroit Tigers in both 1944 and 1945.

In the majority of cases, the pitcher with the highest MVP vote total was the winner of the Retroactive Cy Young Award. Therefore, it's not too large a leap of faith to assume that the order in which pitchers finished in the MVP voting in 1947 would have been the same had there been a Cy Young vote. Giants rookie Larry Jansen (21-5) would have finished second, with two Brooklyn right-handers—Ralph Branca and Hugh Casey—taking the next two slots.

The twenty-one-year-old Branca was the ace of the staff for the pennant-winning Dodgers. In addition to winning twenty-one games, he finished second in the league in strikeouts and innings pitched and third in earned run average. Casey (10-4) finished thirty-seven games for the Dodgers and led the NL with a retroactively determined eighteen saves. Philadelphia's Dutch Leonard would have finished fifth, with Boston's Warren Spahn and Johnny Sain gaining the final two spots.

# Chapter 80. Dodgers Attendance in 1947

*John Pastier*

The years immediately following World War II were a golden age for baseball attendance. In 1945 the Major Leagues drew more than 10.8 million, breaking a fifteen-year-old record. The next year, they eclipsed that total by more than 70 percent, attracting more than 18.5 million paying fans. The 1947 season was even better, producing nearly 19.9 million paid-for and filled seats.

That year was especially productive for the National League. It outdrew the American League for the only time between 1944 and 1952, overcoming the junior circuit's formidable 27 percent advantage in seating capacity to lead it by nearly 10 percent. Brooklyn topped the league with more than 1.8 million at home and nearly 1.9 million on the road—both were league records. If one includes the World Series, those numbers rise to more than 1.9 million and nearly 2.2 million. The home figures are particularly impressive considering that the Dodgers were limited by playing in a park with 34,000 seats, the league's second smallest. By filling nearly 79 percent of Ebbets Field's available seats, they set a Major League record that stood for thirty-five years, until the Los Angeles incarnation of the team filled Dodger Stadium to 79.6 percent of capacity while drawing 3.6 million.

Counting their World Series home games, the Dodgers attracted more than 38 percent of the total NL gate as hosts or as visitors. Their games, home and away, drew 87 percent better on average than NL games not involving the team. Including the World Series, more than 4.1 million paying fans saw the Dodgers play in 1947.

Along the way to setting these full-season records, the Dodgers notched several notable daily figures. Facing the Giants at Ebbets Field on August 30, they set a Brooklyn single game record of 37,512. On August 18, playing the Cardinals in a day/night, separate-admissions doubleheader, they drew 66,504—a one-day Ebbets Field record. On Labor Day, 63,621 turned out for separate-admission morning and afternoon games against the Phillies. These records stood unbroken through the Brooklyn years.

There were also some impressive road crowds. On May 11, 40,720 fans packed Shibe Park for a Dodgers-Phillies doubleheader, the largest crowd ever to see a Phillies or A's contest in that park's history. Exactly a week later, the Cubs and Dodgers drew 46,572, a single-game Wrigley Field record that still stands, even though seating has been expanded. This turnout easily topped the All-Star Game (41,123), which was held at Wrigley that year.

In six of their seven NL road parks, the Dodgers attracted the largest crowd of the season. (In the seventh, Crosley Field in Cincinnati, they drew the second largest.) At Shibe Park, they drew two of the three highest turnouts. At Forbes Field in Pittsburgh, they produced the season's two largest crowds, at Sportsman's Park in St. Louis the top four, and at the Polo Grounds, by far the league's biggest venue, they attracted the top six. In the World Series, the Dodgers helped draw Yankee Stadium's four biggest daytime crowds of the season. Three of those games took place during the work week, and three topped 70,000, a figure that had never been reached in a Series game before. The overall World Series gate of 389,763 was a record at the time, and the October 5 crowd of

74,065 set a New York City postseason record that has stood sixty-two years.

At the time, this unprecedented fan interest in the Dodgers was largely attributed to Jackie Robinson's remarkable drawing power in his rookie year. Informed contemporary observers repeatedly affirmed Robinson's ability to turn out crowds and attract a new audience. At the Ebbets Field season opener, it was estimated that 14,000 fans—more than half the attendance that day—were black. Assessing Robinson's career, Dodgers publicist Arthur Mann declared that his "status is beyond evaluation as [the] greatest box-office draw since Babe Ruth." Even before Jackie's first season was over, *Time* magazine said that he "has pulled about $150,000 in extra admissions this season." This was big money at the time, representing well over 100,000 added tickets, and was thirty times Robinson's salary.

Broadcaster Red Barber wrote that "wherever Jackie played, he drew large crowds. He became the biggest attraction in baseball since Babe Ruth. Robinson put serious money into the pockets of every NL owner." Dodgers traveling secretary Harold Parrott, previously a sportswriter, observed that "Robinson drew the fans to pack the ballparks wherever we went in 1947." Sportswriter Jimmy Cannon declared him to be "the most lucrative draw since Babe Ruth. Later writers also echoed these sentiments. In 1984, Peter Golenbock wrote that Robinson "had become an attraction of Ruthian dimensions." Roger Kahn was a bit more cautious, calling him "the game's greatest box-office attraction in 1947."

At first the novelty of a black Major Leaguer attracted the big crowds that were bolstered by unprecedented numbers of African Americans in the stands, as well as whites who were rooting both for and against Robinson and baseball integration. But soon, novelty was supplanted by a desire to see the fresh and exciting brand of aggressive base running that Robinson brought from the Negro Leagues. What Babe Ruth did with his big bat in the twenties, Robinson did with his feet in 1947. That year, black journalist Wendell Smith summed up the phenomenon in a snappy piece of doggerel: "Jackie's nimble / Jackie's quick / Jackie's making the turnstiles click."

At a three-day conference held in 1997 at Long Island University commemorating the fiftieth anniversary of Robinson's debut, one presenter expressed great skepticism about such "starry-eyed myths" of Robinson's 1947 box-office prowess. Henry D. Fetter, a Los Angeles entertainment and litigation attorney and enthusiastic admirer of "the well financed and brilliantly managed Yankees," charged many of the observers cited above with collectively "overstating Robinson's impact on attendance," and he objected to, but never fully defined, "the Robinson-Rickey myth." His presentation later appeared in *Jackie Robinson: Race, Sports, and the American Dream*, a selection of the conference presentations edited by Joseph Dorinson and Joram Warmund published in 1998.

In contrast to contemporary observers who actually witnessed the Dodgers' attendance phenomenon day after day, Fetter used numerical analysis to create what he felt to be "a more accurate perspective on attendance and fan reaction to Robinson in 1947." But he also went well beyond that pivotal year, tracking absolute and relative declines in Dodger attendance through 1956, and ending his argument by saying, "In the end, stemming the declining fortunes of major league baseball in Brooklyn as a business in Brooklyn was one burden that was too great even for Robinson to bear." Not only is that chronologically far afield for an analysis titled "Robinson in 1947: Measuring an Uncertain Impact," but it also seems to be rebutting a claim about Robinson's role in saving the Brooklyn franchise that no one, other than Fetter, had actually made.

Fetter's argument is often detailed, but not necessarily comprehensive or well-balanced. He offers certain facts and interpretations that bolster his case, but he ignores others that weaken it. For example, he notes that the Dodgers had more road dates in 1947 than the year before, which accounted for part of their road attendance gain. But he doesn't mention that their Ebbets Field gains occurred despite having fewer home dates. He correctly notes that Dodger home attendance, while topping its record-setting 1946 season, did not rise to a great degree. But he doesn't mention that in the same year, Yankees' attendance actually fell, as did American League attendance as a whole. Significantly, as previously mentioned, 1947 was the only year between 1944 and 1952 in which the National League was able to overcome a steep seating capacity disadvantage and outdraw the Junior Circuit. Is it unreasonable to think that Robinson's debut season played a significant role in this once-in-nine-years event?

Individual games are also cited selectively, and not always informatively. Rather than trying to rebut all of Fetter's inaccurate or debatable claims, I'll focus on events of Robinson's first week or so in Brooklyn: "Robinson's arrival in Brooklyn was conspicuous for the absence of hometown reaction it generated. . . . Rather than dominating the news (even the baseball news), Robinson's call-up yielded top billing on the city's sports pages to the continuing furor [over the] stunning suspension . . . of Leo Durocher as Dodger manager for the season." Durocher's arbitrary suspension by Commissioner Happy Chandler was indeed a bombshell, but it did not get top billing over Robinson that day, at least not in the city's leading newspaper. The *New York Times* gave Robinson's signing a full-page-width, eight-column headline on its first sports page (page 20), while Durocher earned a seven-column headline on the second sports page (page 21).

Fetter continued (nonchronologically), "Ebbets Field had been barely one-third full on April 10 when Robinson made his first Brooklyn appear-

ance, in a Montreal uniform in a Royals-Dodgers exhibition game." The attendance was 14,282, which the *Times* called "the biggest crowd to watch the Dodgers this spring."

Fetter wrote that "Robinson's local debut, the year before in a Montreal-Jersey City game, by contrast, had drawn over 25,000 to Roosevelt Stadium." The Jersey City contest was the first twentieth-century appearance by a black player in an official league game in organized baseball. The Brooklyn game was an exhibition between the Dodgers and their top Minor League club, with Robinson still a Dodgers farmhand, as he had been for the entire previous season.

Jersey City openers were only incidentally about baseball. They were primarily demonstrations of civic and political fealty to Mayor Frank "Boss" Hague and his legendary political machine, and they invariably drew full houses or better. Immediately following the Montreal exhibition game, Robinson debuted as a Dodger in a set of Ebbets Field exhibition games against the Yankees that drew more than 79,441, a three-game record for this traditional spring series. Fetter did not mention this example of Robinson's drawing power.

"The season opener crowd at Ebbets Field was the smallest at any National League ballpark that day. . . . The 26,000 [actually, closer to 27,000] fans at Ebbets Field that day fell far short of the 39,000 who turned out that same afternoon to see the Yankees open the season in the Bronx. (Not to mention the 27,306 fans attending the races at Jamaica Race Track that afternoon.)" Confining this Opening Day comparison to a single date and league creates the impression that this was the smallest first-game crowd of 1947, but it wasn't even close. Four big league teams failed to reach 10,000, and two of those fell short of 5,000. The defending world-champion Cardinals failed to draw even half the Dodgers' figure, falling short of 12,000. The Yankee comparison is misleading, since their home park held more than twice that of the Dodgers. One could accurately say that on that day, there were about 5,300 empty seats in Brooklyn, compared to about 30,000 in the Bronx. The racetrack comparison is simply a red herring.

"In their second home game . . . Dodger attendance fell to 10,252." Second games usually dipped below Opening Day levels in that era, as they still often do. In 1947 half the Major League teams drew less than the Dodgers for their second home games, averaging fewer than 6,000 fans. Fetter does not mention that, or that the Yankees' second-game attendance plunged to 8,350.

Fetter also presented two graphs attempting to show a negative correlation between 1947 NL attendance gains and black population in the league's various cities. These diagrams each showed a scatter-plot of eight data points but included no trend line. Much of the input data was inaccurate or conceptually questionable, but the fundamental flaw was that three-quarters of the games represented in the data did not involve the Dodgers at all, and therefore had little or no relevance to the issue of Robinson's drawing power.

The question of Jackie Robinson's effect on attendance is a complex one and cannot be definitively answered by looking at numbers alone, even if the analyis is done even-handedly. Red Barber noted that "the Dodgers often played before turnaway crowds" and "there has not been another season like it"; and, of course, official attendance figures take no note of fans who came to the ballpark but couldn't get in. About 37 percent of the Dodgers' home crowds exceeded park capacity, as was the case with about 16 percent of their road dates. It seems safe to say that at those games, even more fans were on hand but were denied admission after standing room was filled.

Taking a few steps back from the thicket of possible analytical details of the Dodgers' 1947 games, the most useful picture that emerges is that a team with the league's second-smallest ballpark capacity managed to set attendance records for two years in succession, and to fill a greater proportion of its seats than any club did either before, or for another third of a century after.

This is not simply a matter of cold, abstract numbers, but an indication of unprecedented passion and energy in the stands. The fans of 1947 were witnessing not only a fresh new approach to Major League Baseball but also a watershed event in the nation's social and ethical evolution. Barber's words bear repeating: "There has not been another season like it."

# Chapter 81. Ownership Issues in Brooklyn

*Andy McCue*

Red Barber called 1947 the year "When All Hell Broke Loose in Baseball." The team Barber broadcast for, the Brooklyn Dodgers, was at the center of that year's headlines. Jackie Robinson broke the color barrier. Leo Durocher was banned from the game.

Behind the headlines, in the quiet of the boardroom at the team's 215 Montague Street headquarters, issues that would profoundly affect the Dodgers, and indeed all of baseball, were being shaped by three men. Two of the triumvirate would leave large marks on the history of baseball, and the third would choose which of those two would finally control the team.

The issues on the table often seemed routine. Should they add additional seats in center field? Should they agree to pay their accountants more? Who should sponsor radio broadcasts? But each of these issues wound itself around larger ones. How much should it spend on its scouting and farm systems? What should be done about Ebbets Field?

To understand the arguments playing out in the minutes of these board meetings, it is necessary to understand how the ownership of the Dodgers was structured—and how that structure set the pattern for how the partnership would come apart.

The story begins in 1912, as Charles Ebbets struggled to finish the stadium that would bear his name. He ran short of cash and sold half his franchise to Stephen and Edward McKeever, brothers who brought both money and construction experience to the project. Things ran smoothly through pennants in 1916 and 1920. By 1925 the *New York Times* would describe the Dodgers as "one of the soundest organizations financially in professional baseball."

That began to change with the death of Charles Ebbets in April of that year, followed by that of Ed McKeever eleven days later. Both men had multiple heirs with multiple interests. The board soon settled into a thirteen-year stalemate, with the feuding McKeever and Ebbets interests each holding exactly 50 percent. The team descended into serious debt, a situation exacerbated by the Great Depression. Even when the National League stepped in to name a president to act as arbitrator, matters did not improve. By the end of the 1937 season, phone service had been cut off to the team's offices because the bills had not been paid.

Effectively, the team was controlled by the Brooklyn Trust Company and its chairman, George V. McLaughlin. The team owed the bank over $700,000, and it had also loaned money to both the Ebbets and McKeever heirs, with their shares in the team as collateral. McLaughlin and the league pressured the two factions to find an executive they both could accept, and who could bring the team out of its financial troubles. James Mulvey, husband of Stephen McKeever's daughter Dearie, went to St. Louis to lure Branch Rickey. Rickey demurred, but he recommended that the team hire Larry MacPhail, who most recently had run the Cincinnati Reds.

MacPhail arrived for the 1938 season and turned the franchise around. By the end of 1942, the Dodgers had won a pennant and barely missed another. Despite borrowing another $200,000, MacPhail had reduced the franchise's debt to

Brooklyn Trust to $350,000 and had $150,000 in the bank. Then, with World War II raging, Larry MacPhail went off to the army.

Again the board went to Branch Rickey, and this time he accepted. Rickey soon perceived the economic opportunity presented by the recovering franchise. His perception was reinforced by the purchase offers that began to come in from outsiders.

McLaughlin was the arbiter of any sale, for he had multiple responsibilities. As chairman of Brooklyn Trust, he had to make sure that his bank was repaid. As the trustee for the Ebbets and McKeever heirs, he had to ensure that they got a fair price for their holdings. As a leading citizen of Brooklyn, conscious of the public-relations nightmare Dodger problems could bring his bank, he had to make sure one of the borough's gems was well-managed and stable.

Part of the equation was bringing in the right people. Rickey offered decades of baseball experience, and he had hired a McLaughlin protégé named Walter O'Malley to act as the team's lawyer and to keep an eye on the business side. But Rickey had no capital to invest and O'Malley didn't have enough. From the ranks of the bank's clients, McLaughlin recruited two wealthy men, Andrew Schmitz, an insurance broker, and John Smith, a top executive with the chemical manufacturer Pfizer Inc. In November 1944 McLaughlin sold the group the Edward McKeever heirs' 25 percent. In August 1945 the group added the Ebbets heirs' 50 percent, with Schmitz dropping out.

The other part of the equation was the ownership structure. McLaughlin vividly recalled the paralysis occasioned by the 50–50 votes between the Ebbets and McKeever factions, so he pushed the new owners to create a structure that could avoid such deadlocks. Rickey, O'Malley, and Smith each owned 25 percent.

The three partners agreed that they would vote their shares as a bloc. Within the bloc, whatever side of an argument two could agree on would become the position of the controlling 75 percent of the stock. Given personalities as strong as Rickey's and O'Malley's, it was inevitable that John Smith would be the swing vote.

The routine issues were just that—routine. Hire Charles Vacchris and Co. to add the center-field seats. Pay the accountants more. Let cigarette maker P. Lorillard sponsor the radio broadcasts.

The political issues were tougher and began to reveal a fundamental split between Rickey and O'Malley. At first, it looked as if the unhappiness of Dearie (McKeever) and Jim Mulvey would push the partners closer together. The Mulveys were upset that they hadn't been offered a chance to buy more of the team when McLaughlin put together the triumvirate.

In June 1946 Mulvey had been pushed off the board of directors. He said it was because he was raising objections to Rickey's policies. "They did not like hearing those exceptions," he told *The Sporting News*. Rickey's response, while not public, was more detailed. He told Commissioner Happy Chandler that Mulvey voted negatively on even the most routine matters; that he constantly asserted in board meetings that his family hadn't gotten the team because McLaughlin wanted the stock for himself, and that O'Malley was just a front for McLaughlin; and that Mulvey argued constantly for more dividends to shareholders rather than investing money in the team. He also made vague allegations to the press that hurt the Dodgers' image, Rickey said.

In 1947 Mulvey was still refusing to play ball. He asserted his rights to attend the September stockholders' meeting and paid a stenographer to create a verbatim transcript, which he refused to share with his co-owners, who were worried about legal action. He asked to audit the company's books and was refused. The triumvirs remained united, despite pressure from Chandler to reach an accommodation and, preferably, put Mulvey back on the board. They did agree to Mulvey's claim of back pay for service as a corporate officer, but they wouldn't go any further.

But the exchanges with Mulvey were revealing cracks among the triumvirate. The importance of some would not be clear until later. Mulvey was constantly calling for dividends. Rickey, O'Malley, and Smith were against that, but Rickey and O'Malley had different reasons. Rickey wanted to pour money into developing the farm system. O'Malley wanted to put money aside for a new ballpark to replace the aging Ebbets Field. This wasn't a crack that would split Rickey and O'Malley then, but it revealed a major O'Malley concern that would flower after he gained full control of the team.

The Mulvey campaign that would contribute greatly to Rickey's departure was Mulvey's quest to create dividends by cutting expenses. He questioned everything, from large expenses to purchase Minor League clubs or players, to the number of free passes that were being issued. He wanted lots of detail, and the club wasn't willing to give it to him.

These questions, however, resonated with John Smith, whose close control of spending was a hallmark of his management at Pfizer Inc. Because of the triangular structure of the partnership agreement, Smith's vote would be the one to decide between Rickey and O'Malley.

The issues were diverse, and Smith did not always side with O'Malley. Rickey wanted to set up a massive spring training camp at a former navy pilot–training facility outside Vero Beach, Florida. The land was free, but O'Malley expressed concern at the cost of converting the base to a baseball camp and worried that Vero Beach's relative isolation would limit the ability to draw the exhibition game crowds that helped finance spring training. Rickey persuaded Smith.

O'Malley wanted to take the money offered for television rights to Dodgers home games. Rickey worried that it would cut down attendance. O'Malley persuaded Smith.

Rickey wanted a corporate plane to take him around to Minor League cities and Dodgers tryout camps. He wanted more scouts. He wanted to buy the St. Paul franchise of the American Association for $175,000, a move Smith agreed to only with the promise of economies elsewhere.

Rickey moved into football, taking a franchise in the All-America Football Conference. From that conference, the San Francisco 49ers and Cleveland Browns would enter the National Football League. The Brooklyn (football) Dodgers would be merged with the New York (football) Yankees and leave a puddle of red ink, $300,000 in 1947 alone. That loss was covered by the sale of prospects. Irv Noren, Sam Jethroe, and Chico Carrasquel all went on to decent Major League careers, but the revenue from their sales was eaten by the football venture rather than falling to the bottom line.

The pattern was becoming clear. John Smith was happy operating in the background, but when he did give his first major interview, he expressed some surprise that sportswriters criticized Branch Rickey for parsimony. "I have read that Rickey is cheap. As treasurer of the Brooklyn club, I think that he is extravagant," Smith told Michael Gaven of the *New York Journal-American* early in 1948. By the middle of that year, John Drebinger of the *New York Times* was reporting that "the majority of stockholders, represented by Walter O'Malley and John L. Smith, were not seeing eye-to-eye with Brother Rickey on a number of things."

With that word "extravagant" hanging in the air, Rickey turned once again to his main concern, his own future as a team executive. In late 1942, when Rickey joined the Dodgers, he had received a five-year contract. In 1946 that contract was extended to October 1950. But from 1947 to 1950, Rickey fought a losing battle to persuade O'Malley and Smith to extend it further. The problem was the amount of Rickey's compensation. He received a $50,000 annual salary, plus 10 percent of the team's pretax profits. To put this in perspective, the Major League minimum salary was $5,000, and the salaries of the Dodgers' players of the late 1940s topped out at $23,500. The bonus provision also was troublesome, for as chief executive, Rickey could make decisions that affected how big those profits were. He could sell players, for example, if he needed cash. In fact, the pretax profits were substantial. From 1947 through 1949, the team's net income before taxes fell just short of $2.7 million, or not quite $90,000 a year for Rickey over three years.

By 1950 it was obvious to Rickey that his contract would not be renewed. The issue became even more obvious when John Smith died in July of that year. His widow, Mary Louise Smith, was clearly taking her cues from O'Malley. If Rickey were to take employment elsewhere in baseball, he'd have to sell his Dodgers stock. The inexorable provisions of the partnership agreement came into play.

Rickey decided to force the issue, using another clause in the agreement between the three partners. He offered to sell his stock to the others. Smith, who was terminally ill, wasn't interested. O'Malley, outsmarting himself, offered Rickey the amount Rickey had paid for the stock five and six years before. That had been when World War II and its uncertainties still hung over the team, and when people hadn't begun to perceive its financial potential. Infuriated, Rickey turned to a friend, John Galbreath, owner of the Pittsburgh Pirates, who wanted Rickey to be his general manager. Galbreath led Rickey to William Zeckendorf, a New York real estate man who was willing to pay $1 million for Rickey's 25 percent. The partnership agreement allowed O'Malley to match that price. So he swallowed hard and paid.

The triumvirate had become one man.

# Epilogue

*Lyle Spatz*

## Pitchers

KIRBY HIGBE, May 3, 1947: Traded to the Pittsburgh Pirates with pitcher Hank Behrman, pitcher Cal McLish, catcher Dixie Howell, and infielder Gene Mauch, for outfielder Al Gionfriddo and $100,000.

RUBE MELTON, June 3, 1947: Pitched for Brooklyn in his final Major League game.

ED CHANDLER, June 14, 1947: Pitched for Brooklyn in his final Major League game.

GEORGE DOCKINS, August 19, 1947: Pitched for Brooklyn in his final Major League game.

HAL GREGG, December 8, 1947: Traded to the Pittsburgh Pirates with pitcher Vic Lombardi for third baseman Billy Cox, utility infielder Gene Mauch, and pitcher Preacher Roe.

VIC LOMBARDI, December 8, 1947: Traded to the Pittsburgh Pirates with pitcher Hal Gregg for third baseman Billy Cox, utility infielder Gene Mauch, and pitcher Preacher Roe.

HUGH CASEY, September 30, 1948: Released.

HANK BEHRMAN, March 26, 1949: Sold to the New York Giants.

JOHNNY VAN CUYK, May 9, 1949: Pitched for Brooklyn in his final Major League game.

WILLIE RAMSDELL, May 10, 1950: Sold to the Cincinnati Reds.

JACK BANTA, June 21, 1950: Pitched for Brooklyn in his final Major League game.

REX BARNEY, September 4, 1950: Pitched for Brooklyn in his final Major League game.

HARRY TAYLOR, September 10, 1950: Sold to the Boston Red Sox.

JOE HATTEN, June 15, 1951: Traded to the Chicago Cubs with outfielder Gene Hermanski, infielder Eddie Miksis, and catcher Bruce Edwards, for pitcher Johnny Schmitz, catcher Rube Walker, infielder Wayne Terwilliger, and outfielder Andy Pafko.

DAN BANKHEAD, July 18, 1951: Pitched for Brooklyn in his final Major League game.

PHIL HAUGSTAD, May 25, 1952: Sold on waivers to the Cincinnati Reds.

CLYDE KING, October 10, 1952: Traded to the Cincinnati Reds for catcher Dixie Howell and cash.

RALPH BRANCA, July 10, 1953: Sold on waivers to the Detroit Tigers.

ERV PALICA, March 17, 1955: Traded to the Baltimore Orioles for first baseman Frank Kellert and cash.

## Catchers

BOBBY BRAGAN, June 27, 1948: Played for Brooklyn in his final Major League game.

BRUCE EDWARDS, June 15, 1951: Traded to the Chicago Cubs with pitcher Joe Hatten, outfielder Gene Hermanski, and infielder Eddie Miksis, for pitcher Johnny Schmitz, catcher Rube Walker, infielder Wayne Terwilliger, and outfielder Andy Pafko.

GIL HODGES, October 10, 1961: Drafted by the New York Mets in the 1961 expansion draft.

## Infielders

HOWIE SCHULTZ, May 10, 1947: Sold to the Philadelphia Phillies.

COOKIE LAVAGETTO, September 28, 1947: Played for Brooklyn in his final Major League game.

STAN ROJEK, November 14, 1947: Sold to the Pittsburgh Pirates.

ED STEVENS, November 14, 1947: Sold to the Pittsburgh Pirates.

EDDIE STANKY, March 6, 1948: Traded to the Boston Braves for outfielder Bama Rowell and first baseman Ray Sanders.

SPIDER JORGENSEN, May 17, 1950: Sold to the New York Giants.

TOMMY BROWN, June 8, 1951: Traded to the Philadelphia Phillies for outfielder Dick Whitman and cash.

EDDIE MIKSIS, June 15, 1951: Traded to the Chicago Cubs with pitcher Joe Hatten, outfielder Gene Hermanski, and catcher Bruce Edwards, for pitcher Johnny Schmitz, catcher Rube Walker, infielder Wayne Terwilliger, and outfielder Andy Pafko.

JACKIE ROBINSON, September 30, 1956: Played for Brooklyn in his final Major League game.

PEE WEE REESE, September 26, 1958: Played for Brooklyn in his final Major League game.

## Outfielders

TOMMY TATUM, May 1, 1947: Sold to the Cincinnati Reds.

AL GIONFRIDDO, September 28, 1947: Played for Brooklyn in his final Major League game.

DIXIE WALKER, December 8, 1947: Sold to the Pittsburgh Pirates.

DON LUND, June 28, 1948: Sold on waivers to the St. Louis Browns.

ARKY VAUGHAN, September 22, 1948: Played for Brooklyn in his final Major League game.

PETE REISER, December 15, 1948: Traded to the Boston Braves for outfielder Mike McCormick and third baseman Nanny Fernandez.

MARV RACKLEY, October 14, 1949: Sold to the Cincinnati Reds.

DICK WHITMAN, November 14, 1949: Sold to the Philadelphia Phillies.

GENE HERMANSKI, June 15, 1951: Traded to the Chicago Cubs with pitcher Joe Hatten, infielder Eddie Miksis, and catcher Bruce Edwards, for pitcher Johnny Schmitz, catcher Rube Walker, infielder Wayne Terwilliger, and outfielder Andy Pafko.

CARL FURILLO, May 7, 1960: Played for the Los Angeles Dodgers in his final Major League game.

DUKE SNIDER, April 1, 1963: Sold to the New York Mets.

# Notes and References

## General References

Eig, Jonathan. *Opening Day: The Story of Jackie Robinson's First Season*. New York: Simon & Schuster, 2007.

Golenbock, Peter. *Bums: An Oral History of the Brooklyn Dodgers*. New York: G. P. Putnam's Sons, 1984.

Kahn, Roger. *The Boys of Summer*. New York: Harper & Row, 1972.

———. *The Era, 1947–1957*. Boston: Houghton Mifflin, 1993.

Lowenfish, Lee. *Branch Rickey: Baseball's Ferocious Gentleman*. Lincoln: University of Nebraska Press, 2007.

Silverman, Matthew, Michael Gershman, and David Pietrusza, eds. *Baseball: The Biographical Encyclopedia*. Kingston NY: Total/Sports Illustrated, 2000.

*The Sporting News Baseball Guide*.

*The Sporting News Baseball Register*.

*New York Times*.

*Sporting News*.

U.S. Census Bureau. 1910 census (*Thirteenth Census of the United States*).

U.S. Census Bureau. 1920 census (*Fourteenth Census of the United States*).

U.S. Census Bureau. 1930 census (*Fifteenth Census of the United States*).

Ancestry.com.

Baseball-Almanac.com.

BaseballInWartime.com.

BaseballLibrary.com.

Baseball-Reference.com.

DeadballEra.com.

FindaGrave.com.

GenealogyBank.com.

ProQuest.com.

Retrosheet.org.

SABR.org.

National Baseball Hall of Fame and Library, Cooperstown, New York.

ProQuest Historical Newspapers archive.

## 2. Spring Training in Havana

1. Daniel, "Training Horizons Widen," 11.

2. Koppett, *Concise History*, 225. Koppet writes, "Durocher told the sportswriters, or something like that."

3. Brown, "Cuban Baseball."

4. Diamond, *Importance of Jackie Robinson*, 43.

5. Allen, *Dixie Walker*, 158.

Allen, Maury. *Dixie Walker of the Dodgers: The People's Choice*. With Susan Walker. Tuscaloosa: University of Alabama Press, 2010.

———. *Jackie Robinson: A Life Remembered*. London: Franklin Watts, 1987.

Diamond, Arthur. *The Importance of Jackie Robinson*. San Diego: Lucent Books, 1992.

Frommer, Harvey. *Rickey and Robinson: The Men Who Broke Baseball's Color Barrier*. New York: Macmillan, 1982.

Koppett, Leonard. *Koppett's Concise History of Major League Baseball*. New York: Carroll & Graf, 2004.

Polner, Murray. *Branch Rickey*. New York: Atheneum, 1982.

Robinson, Jackie, and Alfred Duckett. *I Never Had It Made*. New York: G. P. Putnam's Sons, 1972.

Brown, Bruce. "Cuban Baseball." *Atlantic Monthly* online, July 1984.

Echevarria, Roberto Gonzalez. "The '47 Dodgers on Havana: Baseball at a Crossroads." *Spring Training*, 1996. http://www.springtrainingmagazine.com/history3.html#havana.

Daniel, Dan. "Training Horizons Widen for Majors." *Sporting News*, February 26, 1947.

Kimball, Bob. "Out-of-the-Ordinary Spring Training Sites." *USA Today*, February 13, 2009.

"Is They . . . or Is They Ain't His Guests?" *Sporting News*, March 26, 1947 (photo caption).

Branch Rickey biography. Baseball Biography Project. http://bioproj.sabr.org.

"High Jinxes and High Hopes in Havana." MovieTone News, 1947.

### 3. Jackie Robinson

1. Kahn, *Boys of Summer*, 358.

2. Vincent X Flaherty—Jackie Robinson Scrapbooks per Tygiel, *Baseball's Great Experiment*, 60.

3. Flaherty—Robinson Scrapbooks, Tygiel, *Baseball's Great Experiment*, 60.

4. Unattributed—Jackie Robinson Scrapbooks, Tygiel, *Baseball's Great Experiment*, 60.

5. *Sporting News*, November 1, 1945.

6. *Pittsburgh Courier*, November 3, 1945.

7. John Crosby, *Syracuse Herald*, November 12, 1972.

8. *Pittsburgh Courier*, April 27, 1946.

9. Joe Bostic, *Amsterdam News*, April 27, 1946.

10. Sam Maltin, *Pittsburgh Courier*, October 12, 1946.

11. *Brooklyn Eagle*, October 24, 1945.

12. Robinson, *I Never Had It Made*, 64.

13. Golenbock, *Bums*.

14. Arnold Schechter, *Sports Illustrated*, April 22, 1985.

15. *Sporting News*, November 1, 1945.

16. *New York Daily News*, July 20, 1972.

Frommer, Harvey. *Rickey and Robinson: The Men Who Broke Baseball's Color Barrier*. New York: Macmillan, 1982.

Jacobs, Bruce. *Baseball Stars of 1953*. New York: Timely Comics, 1953.

Marshall, William. *Baseball's Pivotal Era, 1945–51*. Lexington: University Press of Kentucky, 1999.

Moffi, Larry, and Jonathan Kronstadt. *Crossing the Line: Black Major Leaguers, 1947–1959*. Jefferson NC: McFarland, 1994.

Polner, Murray. *Branch Rickey: A Biography*. New York: Atheneum, 1982.

Robinson, Jackie, and Alfred Duckett. *I Never Had It Made*. New York: G. P. Putnam's Sons, 1972.

Rosenthal, Harold. *The 10 Best Years of Baseball: An Informal History of the Fifties*. Chicago: Contemporary Books, 1979.

Shatzkin, Mike, and Jim Charlton. *The Ballplayers: Baseball's Ultimate Biographical Reference*. New York: Arbor House, William Morrow, 1990.

Tygiel, Jules. *Baseball's Great Experiment: Jackie Robinson and His Legacy*. New York: Oxford University Press, 1997.

———. *Extra Bases: Reflections on Jackie Robinson, Race, and Baseball History*. Lincoln: University of Nebraska Press, 2002.

———. *The Jackie Robinson Reader: Perspectives of an American Hero*. New York: Penguin Books, 1997.

Wilber, Cynthia J. *For the Love of the Game: Baseball Memories from the Men Who Were There*. New York: William Morrow, 1992.

Ardolino, Frank. "Jackie Robinson and the 1941 Honolulu Bears." *National Pastime: A Review of Baseball History* 15 (1995): 68–70.

Kirk, Al, and Robert Bradley. "Jackie Robinson and the L.A. Red Devils." http://www.apbr.org/reddevils.html.

### 4. Branch Rickey

*Current Biography Yearbook 1945*. Bronx NY: H. W. Wilson, 1945.

Polner, Murray. *Branch Rickey: A Biography*. New York: Atheneum, 1982.

Chamberlain, John. "Brains, Baseball, and Branch Rickey." *Harper's*, April 1948, 346–55.

Dexter, Charles. "Brooklyn's Sturdy Branch." *Collier's*, September 15, 1945, 116.

Fitzgerald, Ed. "Sport's Hall of Fame: Branch Rickey, Baseball Innovator." *Sport*, May 1962, 62–63, 88–90.

Holland, Gerald. "Mr. Rickey and the Game." *Sports Illustrated*, March 7, 1955, 38.

Rice, Robert. "Profiles: Thoughts on Baseball." Pts. 1 and 2. *New Yorker*, May 27, 1950, 32–42; June 30, 1950, 30–45.

Farrington, Dick. "Branch Rickey, Defending Farms, Says Stark Necessity Forced System." *Sporting News*, December 1, 1932, 3.

Branch Rickey papers. Library of Congress.

## 5. Leo Durocher

1. Durocher, *Nice Guys*, 34.
2. Durocher, *Nice Guys*, 46.
3. Eskenazai, *Lip*, 248.

Claerbaut, David. *Durocher's Cubs: The Greatest Team That Didn't Win*. Dallas: Taylor Publishing, 2000.

Day, Laraine. *Day with the Giants*. Edited by Kyle Crichton. Garden City NY: Doubleday, 1952.

Durocher, Leo. *The Dodgers and Me: The Inside Story*. Chicago: Ziff-Davis, 1948.

———. *Nice Guys Finish Last*. With Ed Linn. New York: Simon & Schuster, 1975.

Eskenazi, Gerald. *The Lip: A Biography of Leo Durocher*. New York: Quill, William Morrow, 1993.

Feldmann, Doug. *Miracle Collapse: The 1969 Cubs*. Lincoln: University of Nebraska Press, 2006.

Heidenry, John. *The Gashouse Gang: How Dizzy Dean, Leo Durocher, Branch Rickey, Pepper Martin, and Their Colorful, Come-from-Behind Ball Club Won the World Series and America's Heart during the Great Depression*. New York: Public Affairs, 2007.

Mann, Arthur. *Baseball Confidential: Secret History of the War among Chandler, Durocher, MacPhail, and Rickey*. New York: David McKay, 1951.

Marlett, Jeffrey. "Durocher as Machiavelli: Bad Catholic, Good American." In *The Cooperstown Symposium on Baseball and American Culture, 2007–2008*, edited by Bill Simons, 38–50. Jefferson NC: McFarland, 2009.

Prager, Joshua. *The Echoing Green: The Untold Story of Bobby Thomson, Ralph Branca, and the Shot Heard Round the World*. New York: Pantheon, 2006.

Tygiel, Jules. *Baseball's Great Experiment: Jackie Robinson and His Legacy*. 25th anniversary edition. New York: Oxford University Press, 2008.

Williams, Peter. "You *Can* Blame the Media: The Role of the Press in Creating Baseball Villains." In *Cooperstown Symposium on Baseball and American Culture (1989)*, edited by Alvin L. Hall, 343–60. Westport CT: Meckler Publishing and SUNY College at Oneonta, 1991.

Hazucha, Andrew. "Leo Durocher's Last Stand: Anti-Semitism, Racism, and the Cubs Player Rebellion of 1971." *NINE: A Journal of Baseball History and Culture* 15, no. 1 (Fall 2006): 1–12.

Mandell, David. "The Suspension of Leo Durocher." *National Pastime: A Review of Baseball History* 27 (2007): 101–4.

Shaplen, Robert. "The Nine Lives of Leo Durocher." *Sports Illustrated*, June 6, 1955.

Treder, Steve. "A Legacy of What-Ifs: Horace Stoneham and the Integration of the Giants." *NINE: A Journal of Baseball History and Culture* 10, no. 2 (2002): 71–101.

Woodward, Stanley. "That Guy Durocher!" *Saturday Evening Post*, June 3, 1950, 25–27.

## 6. Kirby Higbe

Higbe, Kirby. *The High Hard One*. With Martin Quigley. New York: Viking Press, 1967.

Honig, Donald. *Baseball When the Grass Was Real*. New York: Coward, McCann & Geoghegan, 1975.

James, Bill. *The New Bill James Historical Baseball Abstract*. New York: Free Press, 2001.

———, and Rob Neyer. *The Neyer/James Guide to Pitchers*. New York: Fireside, 2004.

Light, Jonathan Fraser. *The Cultural Encyclopedia of Baseball*. Jefferson NC: McFarland, 1997.

"Ex-Dodger, Cub Pitcher Kirby Higbe." *Chicago Tribune*, May 8, 1985.

"Feller, Higbe Hurled for Legion Also-Rans." *Sporting News*, June 8, 1960.

Kirby Higby obituary. *New York Times*, May 7, 1985.

"Phils Sell Higbe to Dodgers for $100,000." *Chicago Daily Tribune*, November 12, 1940.

"USO All-Stars Top Manila, 5–4." *New York Times*, January 4, 1946.

Bedingfield, Gary. "Kirby Higbe." Baseball in Wartime. http://www.baseballinwartime.com/player_biographies/higbe_kirby.htm.

Kemp, Bill. *Illinois-Indiana-Iowa League: Minor League Baseball in the Middlewest, 1901–1961.* Three-eye .com. http://www.three-eye.com/playersH.html.

Kirby Higby file. Baseball Hall of Fame.

## 7. Bobby Bragan

1. Research into the Bragan and Downs families was conducted by Maurice Bouchard, using the 1910 and 1920 U.S. censuses; the information was confirmed in a telephone interview with Bobby Bragan on January 14, 2010.
2. Bragan and Guinn, *You Can't Hit the Ball,* 55.
3. Bragan and Guinn, *You Can't Hit the Ball,* 112.
4. Bragan and Guinn, *You Can't Hit the Ball,* 3–4.
5. Statistics found at Baseball-Reference.com.
6. *Sporting News,* December 30, 1953.
7. Bragan and Guinn, *You Can't Hit the Ball,* 229.

Bragan, Bobby, and Jeff Guinn. *You Can't Hit the Ball with the Bat on Your Shoulder: The Baseball Life and Times of Bobby Bragan.* Fort Worth: Summit Group, 1992.

Duvall, Bob. "Whatever Became Of—." *Baseball Digest,* February 1971, 73.

Brands, Edgar G. "Perini, Stengel Majors' Top Men." *Sporting News,* December 30, 1953.

Effrat, Louis. "Giants Bow to Phils, 11–2, 6–5; Losing Streak Now Six Straight." *New York Times,* September 3, 1940.

"Bragan Hits 2 Homers; Phils Beat Reds, 3–1." *Chicago Daily Tribune,* June 19, 1940.

"Jimmy Bragan Dies." *Birmingham (Alabama) News,* June 3, 2001.

"Phils Top Reds, 4–2, as Bragan Stars." *New York Times,* July 31, 1942.

Alabama. Jefferson County. 1910 U.S. census, Population Schedule.

Alabama. Jefferson County. 1920 U.S. census, Population Schedule.

Alabama. Jefferson County. 1930 U.S. census, Population Schedule.

"About Bobby Bragan." Bobby Bragan Youth Foundation. http://www.bobbybragan.org.

"Ancestry World Tree Project." http://www.ancestry.com.

Bedingfield, Gary. "Bobby Bragan." Baseball in Wartime. http://www.baseballinwartime.com/player_biogra phies/bragan_bobby.htm.

"Bobby Bragan." Texas Baseball Hall of Fame. http://www.tbhof.org.

Claire, Fred. "Bragan an Ageless Wonder." http://mlb.mlb .com/news.

"World War I Draft Registration Cards, 1917–1918." Database and images. http://www.ancestry.com.

Bragan, Bobby. Telephone interview by Maurice Bouchard, January 15, 2010.

## 8. Dixie Walker

Barber, Red. *1947: When All Hell Broke Loose in Baseball.* Garden City NY: Doubleday, 1982.

———, and Robert Creamer. *Rhubarb in the Catbird Seat.* Garden City NY: Doubleday, 1968.

Campbell, Gordon. *Famous American Athletes of Today* (9th ser.). Boston: L. C. Page, 1945.

Creamer, Robert W. *Baseball in '41.* New York: Penguin Group, 1991.

Durocher, Leo. *Nice Guys Finish Last.* With Ed Linn. New York: Simon & Schuster, 1975.

Goldstein, Richard. *Spartan Seasons: How Baseball Survived the Second World War.* New York: Macmillan, 1980.

Marzano, Rudy. *The Brooklyn Dodgers in the 1940s: How Robinson, MacPhail, Reiser and Rickey Changed Baseball.* Jefferson NC: McFarland, 2005.

McGee, Robert. *The Greatest Ballpark Ever: Ebbets Field and the Story of the Brooklyn Dodgers.* New Brunswick NJ: Rivergate Books, 2005.

Robinson, Jackie, and Alfred Duckett. *I Never Had It Made.* New York: G. P. Putnam's Sons, 1972.

Simon, Scott. *Jackie Robinson and the Integration of Baseball.* Hoboken NJ: John Wiley & Sons, 2002.

Ahrens, Art. "The Old Brawl Game." *National Pastime: A Review of Baseball History* 23 (2003): 3–6.

Barber, Red. "Leadoff Man." *New Republic,* July 4, 1983, 28–31.

Boren, Stephen D., and Thomas Boren. "The 1942 Pennant Race." *National Pastime: A Review of Baseball History* 15 (1995): 133–35.

Broeg, Bob. "The '42 Cardinals." *Sport*, July 1963, 40 (7).

Gaven, Michael. "What a Load of Rhubarb." *Baseball Digest*, February 1958, 51 (12).

Graham, Frank, Jr. "Greatest Fight on a Ballfield." *Baseball Digest*, June 1953, 45 (2).

Kavanagh, Jack. "Dixie Walker." *Baseball Research Journal* 22 (1993): 80–83.

MacPhail, Lee. "Year to Remember Especially in Brooklyn." *National Pastime: A Review of Baseball History* 11 (1991): 41–43.

McGowen, Roscoe. "Boss of Bums but Not Bum Boss." *Baseball Magazine*, August 1947, 307 (4).

Panaccio, Tim. "How It Was during the War Years." *Baseball Digest*, January 1977, 68 (3).

Powell, Larry. "Jackie Robinson and Dixie Walker: Myths of the Southern Baseball Player." *Southern Cultures* (Summer 2002): 56–70.

Tiller, Guy. "Prospect for Majors: Dixie Walker." *Baseball Digest*, October 1950, 85 (2).

Wise, Bill. "Dixie Does All Right." *Sport Pix*, June 1949, 8 (5).

Bailey, Judson. "New Players Put Brooklyn There—MacPhail." *Atlanta Constitution*, August 22, 1941.

Berkow, Ira. "Dixie Walker Remembers." *New York Times*, December 10, 1981.

———. "Dixie Walker: You Associate with Blacks till You Know Them." *Burlington North Carolina Times-News*, March 29, 1972.

———. "Ice Water in the Veins." *New York Times*, April 10, 1987.

Broeg, Bob. "Backward, Turn Backward Oh Time . . ." *St. Louis Post-Dispatch*, September 23, 1972.

———. "Fine Alabama Contribution to Baseball." *St. Louis Post-Dispatch*, June 21, 1949.

Bromberg, Lester. "Dodger Fans: Dixie's on Job and Will Be Set for Opener." *New York World Telegram*, February 22, 1947.

Burr, Harold C. "Dixie Walker's More than Man-of-Week to Brooklyn." *Brooklyn Eagle*, July 7, 1946.

Daniel, Dan. "Dixie Bids for Yank Job." *New York World Telegram*, April 5, 1935.

———. "Dixie Walker Ascribes Added Power to Change in Bats." *New York World-Telegram*, July 8, 1946.

Dunnell, Milt. "Dixie Lived Down the Racist Image of Robinson Case." *Toronto Star*, May 19, 1982.

Goldpaper, Sam. "Dixie Walker, Dodger Star of the 1940's, Dead at 71." *New York Times*, May 18, 1982.

Good, Charlie. "League Batting Leader Joins the Toronto Club." *Toronto Daily Star*, August 28, 1931.

Greene, Sam. "Detroit Fans Deride Cochrane for Swapping Walker to Dykes." *Sporting News*, December 9, 1937.

Kirksey, George. "MacPhail's Spending Due to Net Dodger Flag." *Atlanta Constitution*, December 22, 1940.

McGowen, Roscoe. "Dodgers Revolt against Durocher, then Play and Win Game, 23–6." *New York Times*, July 11, 1943.

Rice, Robert. "The Artful Dodger." *PM*, August 8, 1943.

Roeder, Bill. "Walker-Merullo Bout Seen Top Diamond Brawl." *New York World-Telegram and Sun*, July 26, 1954.

Vaughan, Irving. "Baseball Got Dixie Walker in Steel Mill, Also Got Him Out." *Chicago Daily Tribune*, May 14, 1937.

Wolf, Bob. "Dixie Adds Dynamite to Braves' Bats." *Sporting News*, December 26, 1964.

Young, Fay. "End of Baseball's Jim Crow Seen with Signing of Jackie Robinson." *Chicago Defender*, November 3, 1945.

Walker, Stephen. E-mail conversations with the author.

## 9. Carl Furillo

1. Golenbock, *Bums*, 357.
2. Kahn, *Boys of Summer*, 311.
3. Golenbock, *Bums*, 96.
4. Golenbock, *Bums*, 97.
5. *New York Times*, April 5, 1946.
6. Eig, *Opening Day*, 44.
7. Golenbock, *Bums*, 152.
8. *New York Times*, April 16, 1947.
9. *New York Times*, August 15, 1947.
10. Kahn, *Boys of Summer*, 311.
11. Kahn, *Boys of Summer*, 312.
12. Kahn, *Era*, 314.
13. Eskenazi, *Lip*, 268.

14. *New York Times*, September 7, 1953.

15. Golenbock, *Bums*, 405.

16. *Boys of Summer* (documentary film).

17. *Boys of Summer* (documentary film).

Eskenazi, Gerald. *The Lip: A Biography of Leo Durocher*. New York: Quill, William Morrow, 1993.

Lowry, Philip J. *Green Cathedrals*. New York: Walker, 2006.

Lee, Anthony. Personal communication.

*Boys of Summer*. Video Corporation of America, 1983.

## 10. The Suspension of Leo Durocher

1. Quoted in Lowenfish, *Branch Rickey*, 348.

2. See David Mandell, "The Suspension of Leo Durocher," *National Pastime: A Review of Baseball History* 27 (2007): 101–4.

3. Leo Durocher, *Nice Guys Finish Last*, with Ed Linn (New York: Simon & Schuster, 1975), 46–47 (Huggins), 65 (Immerman), 48–55 (Ruth); Gerald Eskenazi, *The Lip: A Biography of Leo Durocher* (New York: William Morrow, 1993), 47–48.

4. Red Barber, *1947: When All Hell Broke Loose in Baseball* (New York: Da Capo, 1982), 19; Eskenazi, *Lip*, 199–200.

5. http://www.baseball-reference.com/managers/durocle01.shtml.

6. Lowenfish, *Branch Rickey*, 407.

7. Lowenfish, *Branch Rickey*, 408.

8. Lowenfish, *Branch Rickey*, 408. See "$750,000 Swindle: Brooklyn Clerk Gravely Steals a Fortune to Buy Some of the Good Things of Life for His Family," *Life*, November 18, 1946.

9. Arthur Mann, *Baseball Confidential: Secret History of the War among Chandler, Durocher, MacPhail, and Rickey* (New York: David McKay, 1951), 38.

10. Lowenfish, *Branch Rickey*, 409.

11. Mann, *Baseball Confidential*, 44.

12. Mann, *Baseball Confidential*, 43–44.

13. Mann, *Baseball Confidential*, 46.

14. Mann, *Baseball Confidential*, 46–47; Eskenazi, *Lip*, 174, 202–3; Happy Chandler, *Heroes, Plain Folks, and Skunks: The Life and Times of Happy Chandler*, with Vance Trimble (Chicago: Bonus Books, 1989), 206–7.

15. Mann, *Baseball Confidential*, 29.

16. Kahn, *Era*, 27 (first quote), 28 (second).

17. Durocher, *Nice Guys*, 235.

18. "Catholics Quit Dodgers Knothole Club in Protest over the Conduct of Durocher," *New York Times*, March 1, 1947, 17; "Manners & Morals: Don't You Want Me to Be Happy?" *Time*, February 3, 1947; Kahn, *Era*, 29 (Brooklyn CYO), 36–37 (Murphy and Chandler); Chandler, *Heroes*, 213; Barber, *1947*, 103.

19. Durocher, *Nice Guys*, 245; Mann, *Baseball Confidential*, 71–72.

20. Barber, *1947*, 125–26 (quoted).

21. Jules Tygiel, *Baseball's Great Experiment: Jackie Robinson and His Legacy*, 25th anniversary edition (New York: Oxford University Press, 2008), 177; Jules Tygiel, *Past Time: Baseball as History* (New York: Oxford University Press, 2000), 113.

22. Durocher, *Nice Guys*, 205; Kahn, *Era*, 36.

23. Kahn, *Era*, 35.

24. Lowenfish, *Branch Rickey*, 421–22.

25. Quoted in Golenbock, *Bums*, 101 (Durocher and MacPhail quotes); see also Mann, *Baseball Confidential*, 102–4.

26. Lowenfish, *Branch Rickey*, 424; Mann, *Baseball Confidential*, 102–15.

27. Louis Effrat, "Chandler Bans Durocher for the 1947 Baseball Season," *New York Times*, April 10, 1947.

28. Lowenfish, *Branch Rickey*, 425; Durocher, *Nice Guys*, 257, 235 (emphasis in original).

29. Arthur Daley, "Sports of the Times: Chandler Flexes His Muscles," *New York Times*, April 10, 1947.

30. "Durocher versus the CYO," *Catholic Digest* 11 (June 1947): 96; reprint from *Catholic Mirror*, April 1947.

31. Leo Durocher, *The Dodgers and Me: The Inside Story* (Chicago: Ziff-Davis, 1948), 273.

32. Chandler, *Heroes*, 221.

33. Kahn, *Era*, 30, 265 (finances); Golenbock, *Bums*, 105.

34. Durocher, *Nice Guys*, 270–71.

35. "Leo Durocher, Laraine Day and a Turbulent Time," http://www.baseball-fever.com/showthread.php?t=70561.

36. Kahn, *Era*, 140–42.

37. Mann, *Baseball Confidential*, 114.

38. For the contrast between "surface" and "deep" crimes, see Carlo Rotella, *Good with Their Hands: Boxers, Bluesmen, and Other Characters from the Rust Belt* (Berkeley: University of California Press, 2004), 119.

## 11. Branch Rickey and the Mainstream Press

1. Chandler, *Heroes*, 219.

2. Marzano, *Dodgers in the 1940s*, 134.

3. Pratkanis and Turner, "Nine Principles," 152; Lowenfish, *Branch Rickey*, 425.

4. Marzano, *Dodgers in the 1940s*, 135.

5. The quote is from a biography of Lester Rodney: Silber, *Press Box Red*.

6. Smith, "Man of Many Faucets."

7. Chandler, *Heroes*, 229.

8. Silber, *Press Box Red*, 102.

9. Lowenfish, *Branch Rickey*, 438.

Chandler, Happy. *Heroes, Plain Folks, and Skunks: The Life and Times of Happy Chandler.* With Vance H. Trimble. Chicago: Bonus Books, 1989.

Golenbock, Peter. "Men of Conscience." In *Jackie Robinson: Race, Sports and the American Dream*, edited by Joseph Dorinson and Joram Warmund, 13–21. Armonk NY: M. E. Sharpe, 1998.

Mardo, Bill. "Robinson—Robeson." In *Jackie Robinson: Race, Sports and the American Dream*, edited by Joseph Dorinson and Joram Warmund, 98–106. Armonk NY: M. E. Sharpe, 1998.

Marzano, Rudy. *The Brooklyn Dodgers in the 1940s: How Robinson, MacPhail, Reiser and Rickey Changed Baseball.* Jefferson NC: McFarland, 2005.

Pratkanis, Anthony R., and Marlene E. Turner. "Nine Principles of Successful Affirmative Action: Branch Rickey, Jackie Robinson, and the Integration of Baseball." In *The Cooperstown Symposium on Baseball and the American Culture, 1997 (Jackie Robinson)*, edited by Peter M. Rutkoff. Jefferson NC: McFarland, 2000. (Also found in *Out of the Shadows: African American Baseball from the Cuban Giants to Jackie Robinson*, edited by Bill Kirwin. Lincoln: University of Nebraska Press, 2005.)

Silber, Irwin. *Press Box Red: The Story of Lester Rodney, the Communist Who Helped Break the Color Line in American Sports.* Philadelphia: Temple University Press, 2003.

Cohane, Tim. "A Branch Grows in Brooklyn." *Look*, March 19, 1946, 69.

Fitzgerald, Ed. "Branch Rickey, Dodger Deacon." *Sport*, November 1947, 58–68.

Lardner, John. "Reese and Robinson: Team within a Team." *New York Times Magazine*, September 18, 1949.

Lowenfish, Lee. "The Gentlemen's Agreement and the Ferocious Gentleman Who Broke It." *Baseball Research Journal* 38, no. 1 (2009): 33–34.

Mann, Arthur W. "Say Jack Robinson: Meet the Dodgers' Newest Recruit." *Colliers*, March 2, 1946, 67–68.

Meany, Tom. "What Chance." *Sport*, January 1947, 12–13, 96–97.

Rice, Grantland. "The Emancipation of Jackie Robinson." *Sport*, October 1951, 12–15.

Sheed, Wilfrid. "Branch Rickey: He Revolutionized Baseball. Twice. And He Was a Penny-Pinching, Scheming Hustler of a Saint, Too." *Sport*, December 1986, 29, 137.

Smith, Leverett T., Jr. "A Man of Many Faucets, All Running at Once: Books by and about Branch Rickey." *National Pastime: A Review of Baseball History* 28 (2008): 53–63.

Washburn, Pat. "New York Newspapers and Jackie Robinson's First Season." *Journalism Quarterly* (Winter 1981): 640–44.

Young, Dick. "Being a Baseball Writer." *Baseball Digest*, January 1953, 83–94.

"Rickey and Robinson." *Crisis*, May 1947, 137.

"Rookie of the Year." *Time*, September 22, 1947, 70.

## 14. Jackie Robinson's First Game

This chapter evolved from the author's presentation at the "Jackie Robinson: Race, Sports, and the American Dream" conference held at the Brooklyn campus of Long Island University on April 3–5, 1997.

## 15. Clyde Sukeforth

1. "Shatzkin's Conversation with Sukeforth."

2. Schultz, "Clyde Sukeforth."

3. Schultz, "Clyde Sukeforth."

4. Anderson, "Clyde Sukeforth."

5. Schultz, "Clyde Sukeforth."

6. "Interview with Clyde Sukeforth," 8.

7. Anderson, "Days That Brought the Barrier Down."

8. Schultz, "Clyde Sukeforth."

Schultz, Randy. "Clyde Sukeforth: Former Player, Coach and Scout Played Roles in Jackie Robinson's Signing and the 1951 N.L. Pennant." *Baseball Digest*, July 2005.

Anderson, Dave. "Clyde Sukeforth, 98, Is Dead; Steered Robinson to Majors." *New York Times*, September 6, 2000.

———. "The Days That Brought the Barrier Down." *New York Times*, March 30, 1997.

Lindholm, Karl. "The Dodgers Yankee, a Maine Man." *Anderson County Independent*, January 15, 2009.

Madden, Bill. "Scout's Honor." *New York Daily News*, July 28, 1996.

Zeigel, Vic. "The SHOT Hits 50, Giants Still Win." *New York Daily News*, October 3, 2001.

"Billy Meyer Quits as Pirates Manager." *New York Times*, September 28, 1952.

"Georgetown Beats Yale Nine." *New York Times*, April 20, 1924.

"Georgetown Nine Win." *New York Times*, April 28, 1925.

"Georgetown Wins, 9–4." *New York Times*, April 19, 1925.

"Sukeforth's Eye Improves." *New York Times*, December 3, 1931.

Clyde Sukeforth's obituary. DeadballEra.com.

"Mike Shatzkin's Conversation with Clyde Sukeforth." 1993 interview. BaseballLibrary.com.

"Interview with Clyde Sukeforth." Maine Memory Network of Southern Maine Center for the Story of Lives, 1998.

## 16. Burt Shotton

1. Kieran, "Sports of the Times: The Boom in Amateur Boxing."

2. Daley, "Sports of the Times: Of Historical Importance."

3. Harrison, "Baseball Season Begins This Week."

4. Drebinger, "Phillies Will Not Be Follies Again."

5. "Chandler Rejects Plea on Durocher."

6. Polner, *Branch Rickey: A Biography*.

7. Sheehan, "Shotton, 62-Year-Old Veteran."

8. Drebinger, "Ottmen Win, 10-4."

9. Sheehan, "Shotton, 62-Year-Old Veteran."

10. Sheehan, "Shotton, 62-Year-Old Veteran."

11. Sheehan, "Shotton, 62-Year-Old Veteran."

12. Sheehan, "Shotton, 62-Year-Old Veteran."

13. "Idle Dodgers Take Flag."

14. McGowen, "Pilot of Brooks Unbowed in Defeat."

15. "Rickey Delighted but Not Surprised."

16. McGowen, "Dodgers Reinstate Durocher as Manager."

17. McGowen, "Dodgers Reinstate Durocher as Manager."

18. Daley, "Sports of the Times: Prophets in Distress."

19. "Fans Here Are Stunned by Sudden Shift."

20. Reichler, "Major Loop Pilots Blow Off Steam."

21. Drebinger, "Dodger Boss Promises Improved Club for 1950."

22. Drebinger, "Shotton Is Engaged to Manage for Another Year."

23. "Through, Says Shotton."

24. "Burt Shotton Would Like to Get Back in Baseball."

25. "The Lip Comes Back."

26. "Shotton Promises Action on Players."

27. "Shotton Promises Action on Players."

28. Golenbock, *Bums*.

29. Golenbock, *Bums*.

30. Golenbock, *Bums*.

31. Golenbock, *Bums*.

32. Golenbock, *Bums*.

33. Nack, "The Breakthrough."

34. Dorinson and Warmund, *Jackie Robinson*.

35. "Letters."

36. Lowenfish, *Branch Rickey*.

37. "Burt Shotton, Who Led Dodgers To '47 and '49 Pennants, Dies."

38. "Burt Shotton, Who Led Dodgers To '47 and '49 Pennants, Dies."

Dorinson, Joseph, and Joram Warmund, eds. *Jackie Robinson: Race, Sports, and the American Dream.* Armonk NY: M. E. Sharp, 1998.

Gough, David. *Burt Shotton, Dodgers Manager: A Baseball Biography.* Jefferson NC: McFarland, 1994.

Polner, Murray. *Branch Rickey: A Biography.* New York: Atheneum, 1982.

Sullivan, Neil J. *The Minors: The Struggles and Triumphs of Baseball's Poor Relation from 1876 to the Present.* New York: St. Martin's Press, 1990.

Thomas, Joan M. "Burt E. Shotton." In *Deadball Stars of the American League*, edited by David Jones, 788–89. Dulles VA: Potomac Books, 2006.

Nack, William. "The Breakthrough." *Sports Illustrated*, May 5, 1997.

"Flatbush Cincinnatus." *Time*, August 11, 1947.

"Letters." *Time*, November 24, 1947.

"The Lip Comes Back." *Time*, December 15, 1947.

Barber, Red. "How to Win a Pennant—by Two Who Did." *New York Times*, September 28, 1947.

Daley, Arthur. "Sports of the Times: Of Historical Importance." *New York Times*, August 21, 1962.

———. "Sports of the Times: Overheard at Ebbets Field." *New York Times*, September 1, 1947.

———. "Sports of the Times: Prophets in Distress." *New York Times*, December 30, 1948.

———. "Sports of the Times: The Passing Baseball Scene." *New York Times*, April 29, 1947.

Dawson, James P. "Durocher Pilot in All-Star Game." *New York Times*, December 30, 1947.

Drebinger, John. "Dodger Boss Promises Improved Club for 1950." *New York Times*, October 11, 1949.

———. "Durocher Elated After 'Social Call.'" *New York Times*, October 9, 1947.

———. "Ottmen Win, 10–4, with 6 Home Runs." *New York Times*, April 19, 1947.

———. "Phillies Will Not Be Follies Again If Shotton Has His Way." *New York Times*, March 20, 1928.

———. "Shotton Is Engaged to Manage for Another Year." *New York Times*, November 9, 1949.

———. "Sports of the Times: It Looks Like the Dodgers, They Say." *New York Times*, July 31, 1947.

———. "Sports of the Times: Managing with a Soft Pedal." *New York Times*, August 10, 1947.

Feeney, Charley. "Playing Games." *Pittsburgh Post-Gazette*, July 25, 1972.

Harrison, James R. "Baseball Season Begins This Week." *New York Times*, April 8, 1928.

Heller, Dick. "Dodgers Handled Unrest to Start '47." *Washington Times*, April 10, 2006.

Kieran, John. "Sports of the Times: Mr. Shotton Spills a Word." *New York Times*, April 14, 1932.

———. "Sports of the Times: The Boom in Amateur Boxing." *New York Times*, April 27, 1931.

———. "Sports of the Times: The Man of Few Words." *New York Times*, March 19, 1933.

McGowen, Roscoe. "Dodgers Reinstate Durocher as Manager for 1948 Season." *New York Times*, December 7, 1947.

———. "Phillies' Hopes Centre on Hitters." *New York Times*, March 22, 1930.

———. "Pilot of Brooks Unbowed in Defeat." *New York Times*, October 7, 1947.

Reichler, Joe. "Major Loop Pilots Blow Off Steam: Burt Shotton, Joe McCarthy On Rampages." *Evening Independent*, May 17, 1949.

Rendel, John. "Burt Shotton Is Retained by Rickey as Dodgers' Manager for 1949 Season." *New York Times*, October 9, 1948.

Sheehan, Joseph M. "Shotton, 62-Year-Old Veteran, Takes Over as Brooklyn Pilot." *New York Times*, April 19, 1947.

Ziegel, Vic. "N.Y. Jaws Dropped When Lip Switched." *New York Daily News*, September 24, 1995.

"Baseball Owners Gather in Chicago." *New York Times*, December 11, 1933.

"Burt Shotton, Who Led Dodgers To '47 and '49 Pennants, Dies." *New York Times*, July 31, 1962.

"Burt Shotton Pays Tribute to Leo Durocher." *Los Angeles Times*, January 20, 1948.

"Burt Shotton Will Manage Columbus in '36." *Chicago Tribune*, November 12, 1935.

"Burt Shotton Would Like to Get Back in Baseball." *St. Petersburg Times*, October 19, 1951.

"Chandler Rejects Plea on Durocher." *New York Times*, April 22, 1947.

"Dodgers Name Grimes Pilot for One Year." *Chicago Tribune*, November 6, 1936.

"Durocher Hopeful of Retaining Post." *New York Times*, November 13, 1942.

"Durocher Says Job Still His." *St. Petersburg Times,* November 3, 1947.

"Fans Here Are Stunned by Sudden Shift; Reactions on Durocher Varied and Violent." *New York Times,* July 17, 1948.

"Idle Dodgers Take Flag as Cards Lose." New York Times, September 23, 1947.

"Rickey Delighted but Not Surprised." *New York Times,* September 23, 1947.

"Rickey Heads Dodgers; Hints of Changes." *Chicago Tribune,* October 30, 1942.

"Shotton Hopes to Stay." *New York Times,* October 27, 1950.

"Shotton Is Named as Coach of Reds." *New York Times,* January 23, 1934.

"Shotton Misses Opener." *New York Times,* April 21, 1948.

"Shotton Promises Action on Players." New York Times, July 17, 1948.

"Through, Says Shotton." *New York Times,* December 2, 1950.

### 17. Ray Blades

1. *New York Post,* April 9, 1947.
2. *Baseball Digest,* December 1966, 74.
3. *Washington Post,* June 12, 1962.
4. *Sporting News,* November 18, 1953, 23.
5. *Los Angeles Times,* May 15, 1927.
6. *St. Louis Post-Dispatch,* April 2, 1939.
7. *St. Louis Post-Dispatch,* September 29, 1939.
8. *St. Louis Post-Dispatch,* June 3, 1940.
9. *Sporting News,* October 22, 1947, 15.
10. *New York Times,* October 7, 1947.
11. *Sporting News,* November 5, 1952, 15.

### 18. Spider Jorgensen

Williams, Pat, and Mike Sielski. *How to Be Like Jackie Robinson: Life Lessons from Baseball's Greatest Hero.* Deerfield Beach FL: Heath Communications, 2004.

Elderkin, Phil. "Spider Jorgensen Recalls Jackie and the '47 Dodgers." *Baseball Digest,* June 1998.

Holland, Gerald. "How Come, Spider?" *Sports Illustrated,* August 28, 1961.

Redmon, Michael. "Pro Baseball in S.B." *Santa Barbara Independent,* June 2, 2010.

The Baseball Cube. http://www.thebaseballcube.com/players/J/Spider-Jorgensen.shtml.

Gazzolo, James. "Spider Jorgensen (obituary)." http://www.thedeadballera.com/Obits/Obits_J/Jorgenson.Spider.Obit.html.

http://www.californiahistorian.com/articles/baseball-spider.html.

http://www.independent.com/news/2010/jun/02/pro-baseball-sb/.

E-mail conversation between Tom Bourke and Jorgensen's daughter Jonel, August 2010.

Kipp, Jack. "Baseball Forced Change in Social Mores." Folsom Historical Society.

### 19. Hal Gregg

Burr, Harold C. "Gregg's Back Okay, Ready to Load Cart." *Brooklyn Eagle,* March 13, 1945.

———. "Introducing Hal Gregg." *New York World Telegram,* March 30, 1944.

Cohane, Tim. "New Serious Attitude Aids Gregg." *New York World Telegram,* September 14, 1945.

Daley, Arthur M. "Sports of the Times, Story of Frustration." *New York Times,* June 20, 1952.

Daniel (Margowitz). "Gregg Most Impressive Pitcher in the National League." *New York World Telegram,* August 9, 1945.

Drebinger, John. "Brooklyn Obtains Three in Exchange." *New York Times,* December 9, 1947.

———. "Yanks Win Series, Page Taking Final from Dodgers 5–2." *New York Times,* October 7, 1947.

Effrat, Louis. "Gregg's Two-Hitter Defeats Phils." *New York Times,* April 20, 1945.

———. "Rookie Pitchers Fail in Brooklyn." *New York Times,* August 19, 1943.

Goren, Herb. "Gregg Becomes Big Factor in Dodgers World Series Plans." *New York Sun,* September 18, 1947.

McGowen, Roscoe. "Cubs' 13 Safeties Rout Dodgers." *New York Times,* August 22, 1943.

———. "Dodgers Blank Pirates: Gregg Gives 3 Hits in 7–0 Conquest." *New York Times,* September 20, 1946.

———. "Double by Reiser Beats Boston, 5–3." *New York Times*, April 16, 1947.

———. "Gregg Halts Phils for Brooklyn, 10–1." *New York Times*, May 7, 1944.

Murphy, Edward T. "Kid Pitcher Amazes Dodgers." *New York Times*, April 2, 1943.

Sheehan, Joseph M. "Dodgers Bow 8–4, after 5–4 Triumph." *New York Times*, August 14, 1952.

———. "Giants Get Gregg, Oakland Star, in Move to Bolster Staff." *New York Times*, June 14, 1952.

"Gregg Can Prove Ott a Prophet." *New York World Telegram and Sun*, June 14, 1952.

"Gregg to Return Home for Spinal Treatment." *New York World Telegram*, July 5, 1944.

"Hal Gregg Gets License to Wed." *New York World Telegram*, May 1, 1946.

"Major Leaguer Lived Out His Life in the Bishop Area." *Inyo Register* (Bishop CA), May 17, 1991.

Obituary, Harold D. Gregg. *Inyo Register* (Bishop CA), May 16, 1991.

"Pirates Tout A New Terry." *New York World Telegram and Sun*, March 23, 1950.

## 21. Hank Behrman

I would like to acknowledge: Bill Carle, Bill Deane, Craig Lukshin, Steven McPherson, Stephen Milman, Rod Nelson, and Roland Sullivan.

1. Murphy, "Behrman Is a Dodger Sleeper."
2. Murphy, "Behrman Is a Dodger Sleeper."
3. McGowen, "33,045 See Dodgers Defeat Braves."
4. Goren, "Behrman Shows Winning Form."
5. Murray, "Behrman Gets Last Laugh."
6. Richman, "Year for Throwing Spat Balls."
7. Richman, "Year for Throwing Spat Balls."
8. McGowen, "Dodgers Defeat Pirates."
9. Burr, "Winter Job for Behrman."
10. Burr, "Winter Job for Behrman."
11. "Behrman Keeps in Shape."
12. Burr, "Winter Job for Behrman."
13. Young, "No Fatted Calf."
14. Holmes, "King Recrowned."
15. McMullen, "It's Happy-Go-Behrman."

Holmes, Tommy. "King Recrowned by New Pitch." *Baseball Digest*, July 1951.

McMullen, Loren. "It's Happy-Go-Behrman." *Baseball Digest*, October 1951.

Richman, Milton. "It Was a Year for Throwing Spat Balls." *Baseball Digest*, January 1949.

Allen, Maury. "Former Dodger Behrman Dies." *New York Post*, January 28, 1987.

Burr, Harold C. "Rickey Picks Winter Job for Behrman as Pick-Shovel Artist." *Brooklyn Eagle*, February 9, 1949.

Daley, Arthur. "Sports of the Times: The Voice of the Turtle." *New York Times*, February 28, 1961.

———. "Sports of the Times: Touching All Bases." *New York Times*, March 29, 1949.

Drebinger, John. "Baseball Season Begins Tomorrow." *New York Times*, April 17, 1949.

———. "Dodgers to Play Pirates Today; Giants Engage Reds Tomorrow." *New York Times*, May 5, 1947.

———. "Giants Are Back at Phoenix Base." *New York Times*, March 29, 1949.

———. "Hatten Wins, 10–3, Aided by 3 Homers." *New York Times*, April 20, 1949.

Effrat, Louis. "Behrman Returns from Montreal to Bolster Dodger Mound Staff." *New York Times*, June 24, 1948.

———. "Dodgers Acquire Negro Shortstop." *New York Times*, February 24, 1949.

———. "Dodgers Top Reds in 13th Inning, 6–5." *New York Times*, June 25, 1946.

Goren, Herbert. "Behrman Shows Winning Form." *New York Sun*, June 29, 1947.

McGowen, Roscoe. "Arrival of Casey Cheers Durocher." *New York Times*, March 4, 1948.

———. "Behrman of Dodgers Halts Braves in His First Big League Start, 4–2." *New York Times*, April 18, 1946.

———. "Braves Set Back Dodgers by 5–4 on Torgeson's Hit in 9th Inning." *New York Times*, July 29, 1947.

———. "Brooks Bow to Blackwell, 4–0, Then Top Reds in 9–8 Slugfest." *New York Times*, June 23, 1947.

———. "Dodgers Seeking Home-Run Hitter." *New York Times*, March 28, 1947.

———. "Gregg Wins in Box for Brooks, 4 to 2." *New York Times*, September 18, 1947.

———. "Montreal Defeats Dodgers by 6 to 1, Homer in

9th Preventing Shut-Out." *New York Times*, April 3, 1946.

———. "Restriction Irks Pilot of Dodgers." *New York Times*, March 7, 1946.

———. "33,045 See Dodgers Defeat Braves, 3–1." *New York Times*, June 28, 1946.

Murphy, Edward T. "Behrman Is a Dodger Sleeper." *New York Sun*, February 19, 1946.

Murray, Arch. "Behrman Gets Last Laugh—He's Back!" *New York Post*, June 10, 1948.

Roeder, Bill. "Unworried by World Conditions, Behrman May Be Big Help to Bums." *New York World-Telegram*, June 24, 1948.

Steiger, Gus. "Flock Glad Behrman Heart Was in Flatbush." *New York Daily Mirror*, October 14, 1947.

Young, Dick. "Giants Buy Behrman For 25 Gs." *New York Daily News*, March 27, 1949.

———. "No Fatted Calf, Flock's Behrman Sulks in Vero." *New York Daily News*, February 26, 1949.

"Behrman Keeps in Shape as Ebbets Field Laborer." *New York Times*, February 9, 1949.

"Behrman to Come Back." *New York Times*, June 11, 1948.

"Dodgers Reclaim King." *New York Times*, June 15, 1948.

"Giants Release Pitcher Behrman to Oakland Team; Six Rookies Are Dropped." *New York Times*, April 2, 1950.

"Henry (Hank) Behrman." *Sporting News*, February 23, 1987.

"Obituary: Ellen Behrman." *Tampa Tribune*, June 14, 2004.

"Other 28—No Title." *New York Times*, September 19, 1948.

"Porterfield Top Pitcher." *New York Times*, December 6, 1948.

"Royals Win No-Hitter." *New York Times*, April 18, 1948.

## 22. Rube Melton

1. *Brooklyn Eagle*, undated article, Melton's Hall of Fame file.

2. *Winona (Minnesota) Republican-Herald*, January 25, 1943.

3. Bill James, *The New Bill James Historical Baseball Abstract* (New York: Free Press, 2001), 206.

4. *Gastonia (North Carolina) Gazette*, April 5, 1964.

5. *Gastonia (North Carolina) Gazette*, June 23, 1934.

6. *Gastonia (North Carolina) Gazette*, March 8, 1935.

7. *Gastonia (North Carolina) Gazette*, September 3, 1935.

8. *Sporting News*, June 18, 1936.

9. *Monessen (Pennsylvania) Daily Independent*, September 4, 1936.

10. *Sporting News*, March 11, 1937.

11. *Sporting News*, June 9, 1941.

12. R. G. Utley and Scott Verner, *The Independent Carolina Baseball League, 1936–1938: Baseball Outlaws* (Jefferson NC: McFarland, 2005), 202.

13. *Sporting News*, June 9, 1941.

14. *Gastonia (North Carolina) Gazette*, February 16, 1940.

15. *Gastonia (North Carolina) Gazette*, April 13, 1940.

16. *Gastonia (North Carolina) Gazette*, July 11, 1940.

17. *Sporting News*, December 19, 1940.

18. *Sporting News*, December 19, 1940.

19. *Sporting News*, January 9, 1941.

20. *New York Times*, July 25, 1941

21. *New York Journal American*, undated article, Melton's Hall of Fame file.

22. *New York Times*, July 25, 1941.

23. *New York Journal American*, undated article, Melton's Hall of Fame file.

24. D. M. Jordan, *Occasional Glory: The History of the Philadelphia Phillies* (Jefferson NC: McFarland, 2002), 179.

25. *New York World Telegram*, December 14, 1942.

26. *Sporting News*, December 17, 1942.

27. *New York World Telegram*, March 12, 1943.

28. *New York World Telegram*, March 19, 1943.

29. *New York Times*, August 16, 1943.

30. *New York World Telegram*, March 23, 1944.

31. *New York World Telegram*, March 27, 1944.

32. *Sporting News*, May 11, 1944.

33. *New York World Telegram*, June 1944.

34. Unknown newspaper article, February 22, 1945, Melton's Hall of Fame file.

35. *Utica (New York) Observer-Dispatch*, March 14, 1947.

36. *United Press International*, March 21, 1947.

37. *New York World Telegram*, June 12, 1947.

## 23. Jackie Robinson and the Jews

1. William M. Simons, "The Athlete as Jewish Standard Bearer: Media Images of Hank Greenberg," *Jewish Social Studies* 44 (Spring 1982): 95–112.

2. See Aviva Kempner's *The Life and Times of Hank Greenberg*, a film that tells the story quite movingly.

3. Hank Greenberg, *Hank Greenberg: The Story of My Life*, edited by Ira Berkow (New York: Times Books, 1989), 191.

4. Pete Hamill, *Snow in August* (New York: Warner Books, 1997).

5. Ken Burns, *Baseball* (TV miniseries, 1994). Burns was not concerned with the fact that the Passover seder did not correspond with Opening Day that year, but that young Henry Foner, from whom he heard this story, was watching Robinson play on April 9 for the Montreal Royals in an exhibition game with the Dodgers the day before Rickey made the announcement that Robinson would be joining the Brooklyn team. Henry Foner, "Mah Nishtanah," in *Jackie Robinson: Race, Sports, and the American Dream*, ed. Joseph Dorinson and Joram Warmund (Armonk NY: M. E. Sharpe, 1998), 71.

6. See Howard Bryant, *Shut Out: A Story of Race and Baseball* (New York: Routledge, 2002).

7. Jackie Robinson, *Jackie Robinson: My Own Story* (New York: Greenberg, 1948), 146–47. Robinson maintained strong connections with Jews throughout his adult life, supported Jewish causes, and subscribed to the theory that there was indeed a special connection between Jews and blacks that united them. In "The Jackie Robinson I Remember," Roger Kahn related telling Robinson the story of being called "Izzy" (a "not terribly subtle code word for Jew") at a prep school he attended. He describes Robinson's response: "When I told Jackie Robinson that story on a slow train through Alabama 44 springs ago, his eyes moistened with pain for that touchdown-scoring, wounded little kid. We barely knew each other, but to use George Washington's noble phrase, Jackie Robinson gave 'bigotry no sanction.' He hated anti-Semitism just as he hated prejudice against blacks—without qualification and from the gut" (*Journal of Blacks in Higher Education* 14 [Winter 1996/1997]: 89). According to Kahn, Robinson would tolerate no slurs against anyone; he would even express his contempt if someone so much as told a "Polish joke." He truly empathized with those who experienced prejudice of any kind (Roger Kahn, interview by the author, December 10, 2005). Robinson saw Jews both as supporters of civil rights and as good role models for blacks to emulate in their struggle for full equality in the United States. He defended Jews against charges of racism, even in the 1960s when it became extremely unpopular in the black community to do so. Arnold Rampersad makes this clear in his definitive biography, *Jackie Robinson: A Biography* (New York: Alfred A. Knopf, 1997).

## 25. Gene Hermanski

1. 1930 U.S. census, Essex County, New Jersey, Population Schedule, Newark (Ward 10), Enumeration District 163, p. 9A, dwelling 55, family 168, Stephen Horomenski; digital images, http://www.ancestry.com; from National Archives microfilm publication T626, roll 1338.

2. "More Than a Game," *New York Times*, June 5, 1973.

3. "Hermanski Leads PONY League in Home Runs," *Olean (New York) Times Herald*, June 21, 1941.

4. "Newman's .354 Bat Gives Pony Crown by Scant Four Points," *Salamanca (New York) Republican-Press*, September 6, 1941.

5. "Oilers Purchase Six New Players; Release Houser," *Olean (New York) Times Herald*, September 11, 1941.

6. "Gene Hermanski," Wikipedia, http://en.wikipedia.org/wiki/Gene_Hermanski, revision dated July 6, 2009. The anonymous author cites as his or her source the *Salem (Massachusetts) Evening News*, August 8, 1943, 8.

7. Roscoe McGowen, "Dodgers Checked by Reds, 9–2 and 4–3," *New York Times*, August 15, 1943.

8. Roscoe McGowen, "Run-Scoring Pass Wins for Higbe, 4–3," *New York Times*, August 16, 1943.

9. "A Mittfull of Nothing," AP Wirephoto caption, *Lowell (Massachusetts) Sun*, August 21, 1943.

10. Gary Bedingfield, "Gene Hermanski," Baseball in Wartime, http://www.baseballinwartime.com/player_biographies/hermanski_gene.htm.

11. Roscoe McGowen, "Double by Reiser Beats Boston, 5–3," *New York Times*, April 16, 1947.

12. Roscoe McGowen, "Dodgers Triumph over Giants, 7–3, and Lead League," *New York Times*, April 27, 1947.

13. Roscoe McGowen, "Brooks Take 2d Place by Point, Erskine Turning Back Cubs, 6–4," *New York Times*, August 6, 1948.

14. "Hermanski and Dodgers Whip Braves, 5 to 2," *Chicago Daily Tribune*, April 27, 1949.

15. "Hermanski in Dodgers Fold for $12,000," *Lowell (Massachusetts) Sun*, February 23, 1950.

16. Al Wolf, "First-Place Acorns Open Angels Series," *Los Angeles Times*, April 27, 1954.

17. "Coast League Club Sells Hermanski to Beaumont," *Chicago Daily Tribune*, January 25, 1955.

18. Edward Prell, "Cubs Break Camp; Start Jaunt Home," *Chicago Daily Tribune*, April 1, 1955.

19. "Hermanski Selling," *Kerrville (Texas) Times*, June 29, 1955.

20. "Sports in the News," *Newport (Rhode Island) Daily News*, October 6, 1955.

21. "A Dodger's Memories," *New York Times*, October 27, 1973.

NewEnglandAncestors.com.

Hermanski, Gene. Series of interviews by Robert H. Schaefer, 2009.

## 26. Hugh Casey

1. *Brooklyn Eagle*, September 20, 1947.
2. *New York Post*, September 23, 1947.
3. *Sporting News*, March 28, 1940.
4. *Los Angeles Times*, October 7, 1938.
5. *Baseball Magazine*, February 1940.
6. *Sporting News*, March 28, 1940.
7. *Baseball Digest*, April 1948.
8. *Baseball Digest*, April 1948.
9. *New York Times*, September 27, 1941.
10. *Los Angeles Times*, April 21, 1936.
11. *Los Angeles Times*, October 6, 1941.
12. *Los Angeles Times*, October 6, 1941.

13. Red Barber, *The Rhubarb Patch: The Story of the Modern Brooklyn Dodgers* (New York: Simon & Schuster, 1954), 59.

14. Casey started two games in 1942 and one in 1946.

15. Reportedly, he realized his arm was sound enough to pitch in the Series only after throwing a baseball at teammate Vic Lombardi. The little left-handed pitcher had accused Casey of babying his arm by spending all his time in the clubhouse's diathermy machine.

16. *Chicago Tribune*, March 26, 1948.

17. *Brooklyn Eagle*, May 21, 1948.

18. Barber, *Rhubarb Patch*, 59.

19. *New York Mirror*, April 22, 1950.

20. *New York World-Telegram and Sun*, July 3, 1951.

21. *Sporting News*, July 11, 1951.

## 27. Rex Barney

Barney, Rex. *Rex Barney's* THANK *Youuuu for 50 Years in Baseball from Brooklyn to Baltimore*. With Norman L. Macht. Centreville MD: Tidewater Publishers, 1993.

*Baseball Guide and Record Book*. St. Louis: Charles C. Spink & Son, 1944, 1948, 1949, 1950.

Barney, Rex. "Can't Anybody Help Me?" *Collier's*, April 16, 1954.

Corio, Ray. "Rex Barney, 72, Dodger Pitcher; Threw a No-Hitter for Brooklyn." *New York Times*, August 13, 1997.

King, Larry. "Rex Barney: Alive, Well and Talkative." *Sporting News*, May 28, 1984.

Madden, Bill. "A Baseball Voice Is Silenced: Rex Barney Dead at 72; Ex-Dodger, Announcer." *New York Daily News*, August 13, 1997.

Young, Dick. *New York Daily News*, September 10, 1948.

Rex Barney player file. Baseball Hall of Fame.

## 28. Tommy Brown

Roberts, Robin, and C. Paul Rogers III. *The Whiz Kids and the 1950 Pennant*. Philadelphia: Temple University Press, 1996.

Traughber, Bill. "Tommy Brown Recalls His Career." SABRgraphs.

Tommy Brown clippings file. Baseball Hall of Fame.

### 29. Harry Taylor

Barber, Red. *1947: When All Hell Broke Loose in Baseball*. Garden City NY: Doubleday, 1982.

*New York Daily News*, 1947.
*Terre Haute Tribune-Star*, 1999.

http://www.sonsofsamhorn.net.

Harry Taylor's player file. Baseball Hall of Fame.

### 31. Ed Chandler

1. "10 Cubs Passes Help Brooks Win by 5–2," *New York Times*, May 2, 1947.

"Angels Grab Pair to Win Oak Series." *Los Angeles Times*, June 16, 1952.
"Brooks Defeated by Cincinnati, 9–6." *New York Times*, June 10, 1947.
"Cards Turn Back Brooks in 10th, 5–4." *New York Times*, June 3, 1947.
"Dodgers Acquire 8 Farm Club Aces." *New York Times*, October 16, 1949.
"Dodgers Lose Pair to Cards, 5–3 and 12–2." *New York Times*, June 15, 1947.
"Durocher off List as 32 Dodgers Draw Full World Series Shares." *New York Times*, October 16, 1947.
"9,000 See Bombers Beat Brooklyn, 4–0." *New York Times*, March 7, 1947.
"Phils Set Back Brooks, 7–3 and 5–4, before 40,952 Fans at Shibe Park." *New York Times*, May 12, 1947.
"Rackley Protests Brooklyn Release." *New York Times*, June 18, 1947.
"Reese Homer Wins for Brooklyn, 7–6." *New York Times*, May 7, 1947.
"3 Rookie Pitchers Sign with Dodgers." *New York Times*, February 16, 1948.
"Yanks Bow in Exhibition in Caracas, 4–3; 2 Rivals Jailed When They Refuse to Pitch." *New York Times*, March 2, 1947.
*Chicago Daily Tribune*, November 17, 1950.

*Dallas Morning News*, May 26, 1946.
*Dallas Morning News*, April 29, 1949.
*Los Angeles Times*, April 27, 1956.
*Los Angeles Times*, October 18, 1956.
*Los Angeles Times*, May 7, 1958.
*Los Angeles Times*, June 20, 1961.
*New York Times*, March 8, 1946.
*Pittsburgh Courier*, April 6, 1946.
*Washington Post*, March 5, 1946.
*Washington Post*, April 3, 1946.

Chandler, Johnny. Telephone interview by the author, August 31, 2009.

Edward Chandler's clipping file. A. Bartlett Giamatti Research Center, Baseball Hall of Fame.

### 32. Marv Rackley

1. Gary Bedingfield, "Marv Rackley Could Fly," Baseball in Wartime, http://baseballinwartime.blogspot.com/2010/03/marv-rackley-could-fly.htmlu (March 26, 2010).
2. Gayle Talbot, "Dodger Pilot Says Walker Is Out, Reiser May Go," *Dothan (Alabama) Eagle*, March 7, 1946.
3. Fresco Thompson and Cy Rice, *Every Diamond Doesn't Sparkle* (New York: David McKay, 1964).
4. Carl Erskine, "The Inside Pitch," *Wisconsin State Journal*, March 3, 1954.
5. Harold Rosenthal, "Pirates Complain of Sore Arm, So Dodgers Take Rackley Back," *New York Herald Tribune*, June 9, 1949.
6. "Reds to Keep Rackley," *New York Times*, April 18, 1950.
7. "Rackley Sold to Seattle," *New York Times*, May 12, 1950.

### 33. Gil Hodges

1. *New York Times*, April 3, 1972.
2. Durocher, *Nice Guys*, 228.
3. Hodges, *Game of Baseball*, 16–17.
4. *New York Times*, April 8, 1972.

Amoruso, Marino. *Gil Hodges: The Quiet Man*. Middlebury VT: Paul S. Eriksson, 1991.
Durocher, Leo. *Nice Guys Finish Last*. New York: Pocket Books, 1975.

Hodges, Gil. *The Game of Baseball*. New York: Crown, 1970.

Zimmerman, Paul, and Dick Schapp. *The Year the Mets Lost Last Place*. New York: World Publishing, 1969.

*New York Times*, April 3–8, 1972.

D'Agostin, Joe. Personal communication.
Edelman, Rob. Personal communication.

### 34. George Dockins

1. *Sporting News*, September 3, 1942.
2. *New York Times*, September 27, 1945.
3. *Sporting News*, September 3, 1942.
4. *New York Times*, March 21, 1943.
5. *Brooklyn Eagle*, July 25, 1945.
6. *Sporting News*, June 7, 1945.
7. *St. Louis Post-Dispatch*, September 8, 1945.
8. *St. Louis Post-Dispatch*, September 20, 1945.
9. *St. Louis Post-Dispatch*, September 20, 1945.
10. *Brooklyn Eagle*, April 20, 1946.
11. *Sporting News*, April 25, 1946.
12. Steve Bitker, *The Original San Francisco Giants* (Champaign IL: Sports Publishing), 1998.
13. *Sporting News*, September 29, 1948.
14. Mark Presswood and Chris Holaday, *Baseball in Fort Worth* (Mount Pleasant SC: Arcadia Publishing, 2004), 57.

### 35. Eddie Stanky

1. 1920 U.S. census, Philadelphia County, Pennsylvania, Ward 33, Philadelphia, Enumeration District 1104, p. 17B, dwelling 353, family 356, Frank Stankiewicz; digital images, http://www.ancestry.com; from National Archives microfilm publication T625, roll 1625.
2. "The Brat," *Time*, April 28, 1952, http://www.time.com/time/magazine/article/0,9171,816375,00.html.
3. Arthur Daley, "Sports of the Times: A Day for Eddie Stanky," *New York Times*, September 8, 1946.
4. Daley, "Day for Eddie Stanky."
5. Golenbock, *Bums*, 160.
6. Eig, *Opening Day*, as quoted by Luther Spoehr in his May 7, 2007, review written for the History News Network, http://hnn.us/roundup/entries/38544.html.
7. Frank Fitzpatrick, "The Ground Ball That Changed America," *Philadelphia Inquirer*, April 8,

2007; William Nack, "The Breakthrough," *Sports Illustrated*, May 5, 1997.

8. Roscoe McGowen, "Southworth Picks Stanky to Play at Second Base for Braves Today," *New York Times*, October 6, 1948.
9. As quoted in Kaese, *Boston Braves, 1871–1953*, 278.
10. John Drohan, "Stanky Says He Had Billy's Approval for Hit-and-Run," *Sporting News*, August 3, 1949.
11. "The Brat."
12. "The Brat."
13. Skipper, *A Biographical Dictionary*.
14. "Relaxed Redbird," *Time*, June 13, 1955.
15. Arthur Daley, "Sports of the Times: Quick Harvest," *New York Times*, June 6, 1955.
16. Dave Anderson, "Sports of the Times: Hot Seat at the Hot Corner," *New York Times*, December 4, 1980.
17. "No Need for Mombo, or Hubert Humphrey," *Ocala (Florida) Star-Banner*, August 25, 1967.
18. "Stanky Is Given 4-Year Contract," *New York Times*, October 1, 1967.
19. "Eddie Stanky, Ex-Player and Manager, Dies," *Wilmington (North Carolina) Morning Star*, June 7, 1999.
20. Colman McCarthy, "Infielder Eddie Stanky, 82, Dies—Called the Brat for Canniness," *Washington Post*, June 8, 1999.
21. "Tradition," University of South Alabama.
22. "'Homesick' Stanky Resigns," *New York Times*, June 24, 1977.
23. "Stanky to Retire," *New York Times*, May 8, 1983.

Kaese, Harold. *The Boston Braves, 1871–1953*. Boston: Northeastern University Press, 2004.

Rains, Rob. *Cardinals: Where Have You Gone?* Champaign IL: Sports Publishing, 2005.

Skipper, John C. *A Biographical Dictionary of Major League Baseball Managers*. Jefferson NC: McFarland, 2003.

Hirshberg, Al. "What Really Happened to the Braves?" *Sport*, January 1950.

"The Incompatibles." *Time*, December 26, 1949.

Berkow, Ira. "Slick, Slicker, Slickest: Reese, Rizzuto, Dark." *New York Times*, January 22, 1996.

"Cards Name Stanky as Personnel Chief." *New York Times*, September 26, 1958.

"Ex-Big Leaguer Eddie Stanky Dies." Associated Press, June 6, 1999.

*New York Times*, October 6, 1948.

*New York Times*, August 18, 1949.

*New York Times*, June 8, 1999.

*Sporting News*, August 24, 1949.

## 37. Arky Vaughan

*The Baseball Dope Book*. St. Louis: Sporting News, 1981.

Fleitz, David. *More Ghosts in the Gallery*. Jefferson NC: McFarland, 2007.

Hageman, William. *Honus: The Life and Times of a Baseball Hero*. Champaign IL: Sagamore, 1996.

Honig, Donald. *Baseball When the Grass Was Real*. New York: Coward, McCann & Geoghegan, 1975.

————. *The October Heroes*. New York: Simon & Shuster, 1979.

McConnell, Bob, and David Vincent, eds. SABR *Presents the Home Run Encyclopedia*. New York: Macmillan, 1996.

Reichler, Joseph L. *The Great All-Time Baseball Record Book*. 1981. Revised by Ken Samelson. New York: Macmillan, 1993.

Tourangeau, Richard "Dixie." "Play Ball 1995" (calendar). Tide-Mark Press.

## 38. Duke Snider

Allen, Lee. *The Giants and the Dodgers: The Fabulous Story of Baseball's Fiercest Feud*. New York: G. P. Putnam's Sons, 1964.

Anderson, Dave. *Pennant Races: Baseball at Its Best*. New York: Doubleday, 1994.

Angell, Roger. *The Summer Game*. New York: Popular Library, 1972.

Barber, Red. *1947: When All Hell Broke Loose in Baseball*. New York: Da Capo Press, 1982.

*A Baseball Century: The First 100 Years of the National League*. New York: Macmillan, 1976.

Chalberg, John C. *Rickey and Robinson: The Preacher, the Player, and America's Game*. Wheeling IL: Harlan Davidson, 2000.

Cohen, Stanley. *Dodgers! The First 100 Years*. New York: Carol, 1990.

Daley, Arthur. *Sports of the Times: The Arthur Daley Years*. New York: Quadrangle/New York Times Book Company, 1975.

Drees, Jack, and James C. Mullen. *Where Is He Now? Sports Heroes of Yesterday Revisited*. Middle Village NY: Jonathan David, 1973.

Drysdale, Don. *Once a Bum, Always a Dodger*. With Bob Verdi. New York: St. Martin's Press, 1990.

Durslag, Melvin. "Manager with a Hair Shirt." In *I Managed Good but Boy, Did They Play Bad*, by Jim Bouton, with Neil Offen, 148–60. Chicago: Playboy Press, 1973.

Enders, Eric. *1903–2003: 100 Years of the World Series*. New York: Barnes & Noble, 2004.

Falkner, David. *Great Time Coming: The Life of Jackie Robinson from Baseball to Birmingham*. New York: Simon & Schuster, 1995.

Fischler, Stan. *Showdown: Baseball's Ultimate Confrontations*. New York: Grosset & Dunlap, 1978.

Forker, Dom. *The Men of Autumn: An Oral History of the 1949–1953 World Champion New York Yankees*. New York: New American Library, 1989.

Frommer, Harvey. *New York City Baseball: The Last Golden Age 1947–1957*. New York: Macmillan, 1980.

————. *Rickey and Robinson: The Men Who Broke Baseball's Color Barrier*. New York: Macmillan, 1982.

Gergen, Joe. *Greatest Sports Dynasties*. St. Louis: Sporting News, 1989.

Goldblatt, Andrew. *The Giants and the Dodgers: Four Cities, Two Teams, One Rivalry*. Jefferson NC: McFarland, 2003.

Goldstein, Richard. *Spartan Seasons: How Baseball Survived the Second World War*. New York: Macmillan, 1980.

————. *Superstars and Screwballs: 100 Years of Brooklyn Baseball*. New York: Dutton, 1991.

Golenbock, Peter. *Dynasty: The New York Yankees, 1949–1964*. New York: Berkeley Books, 1985.

Honig, Donald. *Mays, Mantle, Snider: A Celebration.* New York: Macmillan, 1987.

———. *The October Heroes: Great World Series Games Remembered by the Men Who Played in Them.* New York: Simon & Schuster, 1979.

Hoppel, Joe, and Craig Carter. *The Sporting News Baseball Trivia Book.* St. Louis: Sporting News, 1983.

———. *The Sporting News Baseball Trivia Book 2.* St. Louis: Sporting News, 1987.

Huhn, Rick. *The Sizzler: George Sisler, Baseball's Forgotten Great.* Columbia: University of Missouri Press, 2004.

James, Bill. *The New Bill James Historical Baseball Abstract.* New York: Free Press, 2001.

Kahn, Roger. *Memories of Summer: When Baseball Was an Art and Writing about It a Game.* New York: Hyperion, 1997.

Leonard, John. "Franchise: Dodgerisms, Brooklyn and L.A." In *The Ultimate Baseball Book,* by Daniel Okrent and Harris Levine, 265–84. Boston: Houghton Mifflin, 1981.

Light, Jonathan Fraser. *The Cultural Encyclopedia of Baseball.* Jefferson NC: McFarland, 2005.

Mantle, Mickey. *All My Octobers: My Memories of 12 World Series When the Yankees Ruled the World.* With Mickey Herskowitz. New York: Harper Collins, 1994.

Mays, Willie. *Say Hey: The Autobiography of Willie Mays.* With Lou Sahadi. New York: Simon & Schuster, 1988.

McNeil, William F. *The Dodgers Encyclopedia.* Champaign IL: Sports Publishing, 1997.

Nathan, David H. *Baseball Quotations.* New York: Ballantine Books, 1991.

Nelson, Kevin. *The Golden Game: The Story of California Baseball.* San Francisco: California Historical Society Press; Berkeley CA: Heyday Books, 2004.

Nemec, David. *Players of Cooperstown: Baseball's Hall of Fame.* Lincolnwood IL: Publications International, 1994.

———. "Seventh Inning: 1950–1959." In *The Ultimate Baseball Book,* by Daniel Okrent and Harris Levine, 247–64. Boston: Houghton Mifflin, 1981.

———. *20th Century Baseball Chronicle: Year-by-Year History of Major League Baseball.* Lincolnwood IL: Publications International, 1993.

O'Connor, Anthony. *Baseball for the Love of It: Hall of Famers Tell It Like It Was.* New York: Macmillan, 1982.

Peary, Danny. *Cult Baseball Players: The Greats, the Flakes, the Weird, and the Wonderful.* New York: Simon & Schuster, 1990.

Pepe, Phil, and Zander Hollander. *The Baseball Book of Lists.* New York: Pinnacle Books, 1983.

Phillips, Louis, and Burnham Holmes. *Yogi, Babe, and Magic: The Complete Book of Sports Nicknames.* New York: Prentice Hall, 1994.

Polner, Murray. *Branch Rickey: A Biography.* New York: New American Library, 1982.

Prince, Carl E. *Brooklyn's Dodgers: The Bums, the Borough, and the Best of Baseball 1947–1957.* New York: Oxford University Press, 1996.

Reidenbaugh, Lowell. *Cooperstown: Where Baseball's Legends Live Forever.* St. Louis: The Sporting News, 1983.

———. *Take Me Out to the Ballpark.* St. Louis: Sporting News, 1983.

Ritter, Lawrence. *Lost Ballparks: A Celebration of Baseball's Legendary Fields.* New York: Penguin Studio Books, 1994.

———, and Donald Honig. *The Image of Their Greatness: An Illustrated History of Baseball from 1900 to the Present.* New York: Crown, 1984.

———. *The 100 Greatest Baseball Players of All Time.* New York: Crown, 1981.

Robinson, Ray. *The Home Run Heard Round the World: The Dramatic Story of the 1951 Giants-Dodgers Pennant Race.* New York: Harper Collins, 1991.

Rosenthal, Harold. *The 10 Best Years of Baseball: An Informal History of the Fifties.* Chicago: Contemporary Books, 1979.

Shatzkin, Mike. *The Ballplayers: Baseball's Ultimate Biographical Reference.* New York: Arbor House, 1990.

Snider, Duke. *The Duke of Flatbush.* With Bill Gilbert. New York: Zebra Books, 1989.

Stout, Glenn, and Richard A. Johnson. *The Dodgers: 120 Years of Dodgers Baseball.* Boston: Houghton Mifflin, 2004.

Sullivan, Neil. *The Dodgers Move West*. New York: Oxford University Press, 1987.

Vass, George. *The Game I'll Never Forget*. Chicago: Bonus Books, 1999.

Whittingham, Richard. *The Los Angeles Dodgers: An Illustrated History*. New York: Harper & Row, 1982.

Williams, Dick. *No More Mr. Nice Guy: A Life of Hard Ball*. With Bill Plaschke. San Diego: Harcourt Brace Jovanovich, 1990.

Durslag, Melvin. "The Duke and His Miseries." *Sport*, June 1959, 70–73.

Mann, Arthur. "The Dodgers' Problem Child." *Saturday Evening Post*, February 20, 1954, 27, 111–13.

Snider, Duke. "I Play Baseball for Money, Not Fun." With Roger Kahn. *Collier's*, May 23, 1956, 42–45.

Stump, Al. "Duke Snider's Story." *Sport*, September 1955.

"Sport Visits the Duke Sniders' Ranch." *Sport*, May 1958, 46–49.

Fried, Joseph P. "Snider Gets Probation and a Fine in Tax Scheme." *New York Times*, December 2, 1995.

———. "Snider Was Sentenced First. Who's Next?" *New York Times*, December 5, 1995.

Hunter, Bob. "Dodgers' Snider Battles Tears in Saying 'So Long.'" *Sporting News*, April 13, 1963.

———. "L.A. Fans Stage Dazzling Salute for Snider Night." *Sporting News*, September 7, 1960.

———. "Snider Ties DiMaggio, Hits 361st Home Run of Career." *Sporting News*, June 15, 1960.

Kaegel, Dick. "Baseball Inducts Four in Shrine." *Sporting News*, August 16, 1980.

Kahn, Roger. "The Boys Turn 26." *Los Angeles Times*, February, 22, 1998.

Kremenko, Barney. "Duke of Dodgerdom Still King in Gotham." *Sporting News*, April 20, 1963.

Lang, Lang. "Shrine Doors Open for Kaline, Snider." *Sporting News*, January 26, 1980.

McDonald, Jack. "Giants Obtain Duke to Strengthen Their Bid for King's Row." *Sporting News*, April 25, 1964.

Reidenbaugh, Lowell. "Duke in His Finest Hour Remembers Rickey, Sisler." *Sporting News*, January 26, 1980.

Scholfied, Steve. "Fallbrook's Duke Snider 80 and Going Strong." *North County Times*, September 19, 2006.

Sexton, Joe. "Tax Fraud: Two Baseball Legends Say It's So." *New York Times*, July 21, 1995.

"Duke Sale Bugs Buzzie; 'We'd Have Bought Him!'" *Sporting News*, April 25, 1964.

"Duke Seventh on Homer List." *Sporting News*, April 26, 1961.

"Duke Ties Mize in HR Log." *Sporting News*, June 8, 1960.

## 39. Ralph Branca

1. Joshua Prager, *The Echoing Green* (New York: Pantheon Books, 2006), 118.

2. Prager, *Echoing Green*, 127.

3. Ancestry.com, 1910, 1920, and 1930 U.S. census data.

4. Bob McGee, *The Greatest Ballpark Ever* (Piscataway NJ: Rivergate Books, 2005), 120.

5. Jon Heyman, *Sports Illustrated*, October 3, 2006.

6. Christy Mathewson was several months younger than Branca when he won twenty games for the 1901 New York Giants. Since then, Dwight Gooden, with the 1985 Mets, became the youngest ever to win twenty games.

7. Baseball-Reference.com.

8. The *Journal of Bone and Joint Surgery* does not list periosteomyelitis. Branca's disorder may have been osteomyelitis.

9. Retrosheet.org.

10. Retrosheet.org.

11. Jon Heyman, *Sports Illustrated*, October 3, 2006.

12. Heyman, *Sports Illustrated*.

13. Heyman, *Sports Illustrated*.

14. Baseball-Reference.com.

15. Baseball-Reference.com.

16. Baseball-Reference.com.

17. Baseball-Reference.com.

18. Heyman, *Sports Illustrated*.

All quotes by Ralph Branca are from an interview by the author on September 29, 2008; quotes from Buzzie Bavasi are from an e-mail exchange with the author on October 26, 2006.

**40. Clyde King**

1. King, *King's Legacy*, 6–7.
2. King, *King's Legacy*, 8.
3. King, *King's Legacy*, 38.
4. King, *King's Legacy*, 153.
5. King, *King's Legacy*, 145.
6. King, *King's Legacy*, 173.

King, Clyde. *A King's Legacy*. With Burton Rocks. Lincolnwood IL: Masters Press, 1999.

Chass, Murray. "King Promoted in Yanks Shift." *New York Times*, April 10, 1984.

Fletcher, Walter. "Braves Grant King Two Year Contract." *New York Times*, October 1, 1974.

Martinez, Michael. "Berra Fired by Steinbrenner." *New York Times*, April 29, 1985.

Rogers, Thomas. "Sports World Special, King of the Gumball." *New York Times*, September 6, 1982.

"King Let Go as Manager after 17–16 Loss." *New York Times*, May 23, 1970.

"King Ousted as Pilot of Braves." *New York Times*, August 31, 1975.

"Martin Named Twins Manager, King Takes Over as Giants' Pilot." *New York Times*, October 12, 1968.

"Reese, Branca, King Accept Terms as Dodgers Finish Signing Players." *New York Times*, February 14, 1952.

"Stanky and Head Signed by Dodgers." *New York Times*, January 31, 1946.

"Woodward Said to Replace King." Associated Press, in *New York Times*, October 9, 1986.

**41. Jake Pitler**

"Jake Pitler Dies Upstate at 73; Ex-Coach of Brooklyn Dodgers." *New York Times*, February 4, 1968.

Much of the information for this biography came from the author's interviews with Jake Pitler's son, Larry.

**44. Pee Wee Reese**

1. "At 15, Batboy for Brother's Team."
2. McGowen, "PEE WEE," December 19.
3. Dudley, "Louisville Hails Bush-Red Sox Purchase."
4. Fitzgerald, "$75,000 Deal for Reese."
5. Fitzgerald, "$75,000 Deal for Reese."
6. McGowen, "PEE WEE," December 19.
7. "Five for the Hall."
8. Display ad, *Sporting News*, March 21, 1940.
9. McGowen, "PEE WEE," December 19.
10. Broeg, "Pee Wee Was No Dodger Midget."
11. McGowen, "PEE WEE," December 26.
12. Kahn, "He Didn't Speculate in Color."
13. Bodley, "Robinson Drew Praise."
14. Kahn, *Into My Own*.
15. McGowen, "PEE WEE," December 19.
16. Bodley, "Robinson Drew Praise."
17. "Five for the Hall."
18. McGowen, "PEE WEE," December 19.
19. McGowen, "PEE WEE," December 19.
20. McGowen, "PEE WEE," December 19.
21. Goodwin, *Wait till Next Year*.
22. "Brooklyn Dodgers," April 9.
23. Vecsey, "Reese Has His Heirs."
24. "Game Still Tops to Reese."
25. Finch, "Reese, All-Time Dodger."
26. "NBC Fires Reese."
27. "NBC Fires Reese."
28. "Rachel Robinson Recalls."

Goodwin, Doris Kearns. *Wait till Next Year: A Memoir*. New York: Simon & Schuster, 1997.

James, Bill. *The New Bill James Historical Baseball Abstract*. New York: Free Press, 2001.

Kahn, Roger. *Into My Own: The Remarkable People and Events That Shaped a Life*. New York: Thomas Dunne Books, 2006.

Polner, Murray. *Branch Rickey*. New York: New American Library, 1982.

Bingham, Walter. "Underlying Pessimism: The Los Angeles Dodgers' Great Stars are Aging or Absent, and This Team Will Win No Pennant." *Sports Illustrated*, March 24, 1958.

Creamer, Robert. "The Curtain Rises." *Sports Illustrated*, October 15, 1956.

———. "How to Do It Again." *Sports Illustrated*, March 19, 1956.

———. "Twilight of the Bums." *Sports Illustrated*, April 1, 1957.

"Brooklyn Dodgers." *Sports Illustrated*, September 26, 1955.

"Brooklyn Dodgers." *Sports Illustrated*, April 9, 1956.

"Los Angeles Dodgers." *Sports Illustrated*, April 14, 1958.

"Rachel Robinson Recalls How the Late Pee Wee Reese Helped Jackie Robinson Integrate Baseball." *Jet*, September 13, 1999.

Berkow, Ira. "Reese Helped Change Baseball." *New York Times*, March 31, 1997.

———. "Two Men Who Did the Right Thing." *New York Times*, November 2, 2005.

Bodley, Hal. "Robinson Drew Praise from Many Corners." *USA Today*, April 13, 2007.

Broeg, Bob. "Pee Wee Was No Dodger Midget." *Sporting News*, April 23, 1977.

Dudley, Bruce. "Louisville Hails Bush-Red Sox Purchase; Price under $200,000." *Sporting News*, September 15, 1938.

Finch, Frank. "Reese, All-Time Dodger at Short, Hangs Up Glove to Become Coach." *Sporting News*, December 24, 1958.

Fitzgerald, Tommy. "Brooklyn in $75,000 Deal for Reese, Who 'Didn't Want to Be a Dodger.'" *Sporting News*, July 27, 1939.

Goldstein, Richard. "Pee Wee Reese, 81, Captain of the 'Boys of Summer,' Is Dead." *New York Times*, August 15, 1999.

Kahn, Roger. "He Didn't Speculate in Color." *Los Angeles Times*, August 19, 1999.

Kindred, Dave. "An Artist at Life." *Sporting News*, August 30, 1999.

McGowen, Roscoe, "PEE WEE . . . Pride of Flatbush." *Sporting News*, December 19, 1956.

———. "PEE WEE . . . Pride of Flatbush." *Sporting News*, December 26, 1956.

———. "Robinson's Gone, but Randy Faces New Brooks Battle." *Sporting News*, December 26, 1956.

Miller, Stuart. "Breaking the Truth Barrier." *New York Times*, April 14, 2007.

Plaschke, Bill. "No. 1 on Your Scorecard . . ." *Sporting News*, August 23, 1999.

Samuelsen, Rube. "Dodgers Leave It Up to Reese! Utility Role or a Coaching Post." *Sporting News*, October 29, 1958.

Vecsey, George. "Sports of the Times: Reese Has His Heirs, Even Today." *New York Times*, August 17, 1999.

"At 15, Batboy for Brother's Team." *Sporting News*, December 19, 1956.

"The Day Jackie Robinson Was Embraced." *New York Times*, April 21, 2007.

"Ex-Shortstops to Throw Words on NBC Telecasts." *Sporting News*, April 23, 1966.

"Five for the Hall: Pee Wee Reese." *Sporting News*, August 6, 1984.

"Game Still Tops to Reese after Debut on Video." *Sporting News*, November 19, 1958.

"NBC Fires Reese; Koufax Sent to Bullpen." *Sporting News*, March 22, 1969.

"On the RADIO AIRLINES." *Sporting News*, March 16, 1939.

"Paid Notice: Deaths REESE, PEE WEE." *New York Times*, August 18, 1999.

"Pee Wee Dodger Coach? 'All They Have to Do Is Ask Me.'" *Sporting News*, November 26, 1958.

"Pee Wee Reese Accepts Job with Bat Company." *Sporting News*, July 31, 1971.

"Reese Replaces McCormick on Red Telecasting Team." *Sporting News*, April 5, 1969.

"Reese's Gesture." *New York Times*, August 6, 2000.

"Web Videocasts of Major Games to Open April 16." *Sporting News*, March 23, 1960.

## 45. Bruce Edwards

Caren, Eric C. *Baseball Extra*. Edison NJ: Castle Books, 2003.

Lee, Bill. *The Baseball Necrology*. Jefferson NC: McFarland, 2003.

Prince, Carl. *The Brooklyn Dodgers: The Bums, the Borough and the Best of Baseball*. New York: Oxford Press, 1996.

History News Network. http://hnn.us.

## 46. The Protested Game of July 20, 1947

1. Roscoe McGowen, "Brooks Win by 3–2 with 3-Run Rally," *New York Times*, July 21, 1947.

2. McGowen, "Brooks Win."

3. Dan Daniel, "Replay Ordered on Card Protest of Dodger Win," *Sporting News*, July 30, 1947.

4. Daniel, "Replay Ordered."

5. Roscoe McGowen, "Brooklyn Chases Pollet, Brecheen," *New York Times*, August 19, 1947.

## 47. Joe Hatten

1. Bob Du Vall, *Baseball Digest*, June 1971, 64.

2. McGowen, "Young Man Hatten."

3. McGowen, "Young Man Hatten."

4. Bill Roeder, "No Rest for the Dodgers," Baseball Hall of Fame.

5. Harold C. Burr, "Snider Punches Dodger Ticket and Robot Pitcher Takes a Bow," *Sporting News*, April 14, 1948.

6. Bill Roeder, "Newcombe's Key to Flock Crisis," Baseball Hall of Fame.

7. Chicago Cubs press release, March 26, 1952, Baseball Hall of Fame.

8. Howard Roberts, "Count on Joe," November 25, 1952, Hatten file, Baseball Hall of Fame.

Roberts, Robin, and C. Paul Rogers III. *The Whiz Kids and the 1950 Pennant.* Philadelphia: Temple University Press, 1996.

McGowen, Roscoe. "Young Man Hatten of Brooklyn." *Baseball Magazine* 83, no. 2 (July 1949): 273 (3).

DesMoinesRegister.com.

## 49. Howie Schultz

Thornley, Stew. *Basketball's Original Dynasty: The History of the Lakers.* Minneapolis: Nodin Press, 1989.

Daley, Arthur. "Dodgers Buy Schultz for $40,000, 4 Players: Saints Get Rube Melton, Orengo and First Baseman." *St. Paul Pioneer Press*, August 16, 1943.

Effrat, Louis. "Dodgers Purchase Robinson, First Negro in Modern Major League Baseball." *New York Times*, April 11, 1947.

McGowen, Roscoe. "Schultz in Debut Helps Dodgers." *New York Times*, August 17, 1943.

"Baseball Man in a Basketball Suit." *New York Times*, December 28, 1944.

"City College Five Gets A. A. U. Permission to Play Against 'Ineligible' Howie Schultz." *New York Times*, December 29, 1944.

"Schultz Rejected Again: Dodger First Baseman Exceeds Maximum Service Height." *New York Times*, March 1, 1944.

Schultz, Howard, Jr. Telephone interview by Thomas Bourke, January 31, 2010.

Schultz, Howie. Interview by Stew Thornley, May 25, 2004.

Old-Time Data, Inc. *Professional Baseball Player Database.* Playing record for Howie Schultz.

Year-by-year Hamline University basketball results. Provided by Hamline media relations department.

## 50. Pete Reiser

Durant, John. *The Dodgers.* New York: Hastings House, 1948.

Durocher, Leo. *Nice Guys Finish Last.* With Ed Linn. New York: Simon & Schuster, 1975.

Goldstein, Richard. *Superstars and Screwballs: 100 Years of Brooklyn Baseball.* New York: Dutton, 1991.

Heinz, W. C. *Once They Heard the Cheers.* New York: Doubleday Books, 1979.

Honig, Donald. *Baseball When the Grass Was Real.* New York: Coward, McCann & Geoghegan, 1975.

Jacobson, Sidney. *Pete Reiser: The Rough-and-Tumble Career of the Perfect Ballplayer.* Jefferson NC: McFarland, 2004.

Mann, Arthur. *Branch Rickey: American in Action.* Cambridge MA: Riverside Press, 1957.

McNeil, William. *The Dodgers Encyclopedia.* 2nd ed. Champaign IL: Sports Publishing, 2003.

Shatzkin, Mike, and Jim Charlton. *The Ballplayers: Baseball's Ultimate Biographical Reference.* New York: Arbor House, William Morrow, 1990.

Tiemann, Robert L. *Dodger Classics.* St. Louis: Baseball Histories, 1983.

*Baseball Digest.*

MACO *Baseball Guidebook.*

*Popular Sports.*

*Sport.*

*Sportfolio.*

*Sports Pix.*

*True Baseball Yearbook.*

*New York World-Telegram.*

JockBio.com.

## 51. Tommy Tatum

*Afro-American* (Baltimore).
*Chicago Daily Tribune.*
*Christian Science Monitor.*
*Daily Oklahoman* (Oklahoma City).
*Hartford Courant.*
*Le Petit Journal* (Montreal).
*Louisiana Times-Picayune.*
*Montreal Gazette.*

Tatum, Terry. Telephone interview by Thomas Bourke, Oklahoma City, May 22, 2010.

## 53. Eddie Miksis

Golenbock, Peter. *Wrigleyville.* New York: St. Martin's Griffin, 1999.

"Eddie Miksis: Utility Man Deluxe." *Sports Collectors Digest*, July 31, 1992.

*Brooklyn Eagle.*
*Cincinnati Enquirer.*
*New York Daily News.*

Winslow, Jeanine. Telephone conversation with Tom Bourke, September 7, 2010.

Eddie Miksis player file. Baseball Hall of Fame.

## 54. Stan Rojek

1. Kritzer, "Rojek, Pacific Vet."
2. Johnson, "Rojek Delivers the Year Round," 13.
3. Wiater, "Rojek Was Too Talented to Trade."

Roberts, Robin, and C. Paul Rogers III. *The Whiz Kids and the 1950 Pennant.* Philadelphia: Temple University Press, 1996.

Hart, Karla. "Mighty Mouse That's a Bird." *Baseball Digest*, March 1953.

Johnson, Vince. "Rojek Delivers the Year Round." *Baseball Digest*, October 1948.

Nason, Jerry. "Plate Crowders Ask for It." *Baseball Digest*, August 1955.

———. "Stick It in His Ear." *Baseball Digest*, August 1950.

Billoni, Mike. "Stan Rojek Field Dedicated Today." *Tonawanda (New York) News*, June 13, 1977.

Cardinale, Anthony. "Stanley A. Rojek Dies; Played Shortstop for 3 Major League Teams." *Buffalo News*, July 10, 1997.

Kritzer, Cy. "Rojek, Pacific Vet, Well-Armed for Dodger Infield Fight." *Sporting News*, December 6, 1945.

Rojek, Jim. "Dodger Black." Unpublished article.

Wiater, Ed. "Rojek a Part of Baseball History." *Tonawanda (New York) News*, July 10, 1997.

———. "Rojek Was Too Talented to Trade." *Tonawanda (New York) News*, May 1997.

"Anthony Rojek Dies; Started Dairy." Newspaper article, source unknown.

*Brooklyn Eagle*, September 23, 1942.

Rojek, James. Telephone interview by the author, August 20, 2010.

Articles from the North Tonawanda History Museum Stan Rojek collection. http://www.nthistorymuseum.org/Collections/stanleyrojek.html.

## 55. Dan Bankhead

1. See Moffi and Kronstadt, *Crossing the Line*, 13; Rampersad, *Jackie Robinson*, 184; and Posnanski, *The Soul of Baseball*, 144.
2. Barber, *1947*, 280.
3. Barber, *1947*, 118.
4. As coastal artillery and ammunition supply units, though, they often had to fight off Japanese attacks on supply lines.
5. From the online history of the Montford Point Marines, http://www.mpma28.com/newsletters/newsletter/2854121/44177.htm.
6. "Barons Win by 9–0, 13–0; Triumph over the Philadelphia Stars and Black Yankees," *New York Times*, June 5, 1944.
7. "Wife, Daughter, Dog, Chicken Root for Dan," *Richmond Afro-American*, September 6, 1947.
8. Heaphy, *The Negro Leagues, 1869–1960*, 173.
9. Lowenfish, *Branch Rickey*, 433. Two notes: The won-lost record cited here and also in *The Sporting News* conflicts with the 4-4 mark shown in Holway, *The Complete Book of Baseball's Negro Leagues*. Also, Dan's wife is referred to as "Charlotte."
10. Lowenfish, *Branch Rickey*, 433.

11. Miller and Wiggins, *Sport and the Color Line*, 184.

12. Leo H. Petersen, "Youth, Speed and Fight to Mark 1948 Dodger Team," *Lima (Ohio) News*, March 29, 1948.

13. Moffi and Kronstadt, *Crossing the Line*, 12.

14. Dave Anderson, "Nice Wrong Isn't Really So Terrible," *New York Times*, February 27, 1998.

15. *Charleston (South Carolina) Gazette*, July 20, 1952.

16. Alejandro Martínez, "Dan Bankhead Fined, Jailed in Dominican Republic Riot," *Sporting News*, August 13, 1952; "Bankhead Fired as Manager in Dominican Loop," *Sporting News*, September 3, 1952.

17. Thanks to Doc Settles and William F. Bankhead for sharing their memories.

18. "Bankhead Stars on Big Day," *Sporting News*, August 18, 1962.

19. Roberto Hernández, "Bankhead Fired as Manager; Pinkston Fractures Arm," *Sporting News*, December 1, 1962.

20. "Bankhead Dies," *Charleston (South Carolina) Daily Mail*, May 7, 1976. Of interest in this story is a reference to a wife coming up from Mexico.

Barber, Red. *1947: When All Hell Broke Loose in Baseball*. Garden City NY: Doubleday, 1982.

Crescioni Benítez, José A. *El Béisbol Profesional Boricua*. San Juan, Puerto Rico: Aurora Comunicación Integral, 1997.

Heaphy, Leslie. *The Negro Leagues, 1869–1960*. Jefferson NC: McFarland, 2002.

Holway, John. *The Complete Book of Baseball's Negro Leagues*. Fern Park FL: Hastings House, 2001.

Johnson, Lloyd, and Miles Wolff. *The Encyclopedia of Minor League Baseball*. Durham NC: Baseball America, 1997.

Lester, Larry. *Black Baseball's National Showcase: The East-West All-Star Game, 1933–1953*. Lincoln: University of Nebraska Press, 2001.

Miller, Patrick, and David Wiggins, eds. *Sport and the Color Line: Black Athletes and Race Relations in Twentieth Century America*. New York: Routledge, 2004.

Moffi, Larry, and Jonathan Kronstadt. *Crossing the Line: Black Major Leaguers 1947–1959*. Iowa City: University of Iowa Press, 1994.

Posnanski, Joe. *The Soul of Baseball: A Road Trip through Buck O'Neil's America*. New York: HarperCollins, 2007.

Rampersad, Arnold. *Jackie Robinson: A Biography*. New York: Ballantine Publishing Group, 1997.

Riley, James A. *The Biographical Encyclopedia of the Negro Baseball Leagues*. New York: Carroll & Graf, 1994.

Treto Cisneros, Pedro, ed. *Enciclopedia del Béisbol Mexicano*. Mexico City, Mexico: Revistas Deportivas, S.A. de C.V., 1998.

"Dan Bankhead, 54, Ex-Dodger, Is Dead." *New York Times*, May 7, 1976. *The Sporting News* sometimes presented Bankhead's year of birth as 1921.

Social Security Death Index.

## 57. Phil Haugstad

1. Robert Haugstad, telephone interview, April 22, 2009.

2. Robert Fleming, "How It Feels When a Dream Comes True," *Milwaukee Journal*, September 7, 1947.

3. "Northern League Players Who Made the Majors," http://usfamily.net/web/trombleyd/Northern%20PlayersGL.htm.

4. Roscoe McGowen, "Dressen to Use 5 or 6 Starters on Mound for Dodgers This Year," *New York Times*, February 21, 1952.

Figueredo, Jorge S. *Cuban Baseball: A Statistical History, 1878–1961*. Jefferson NC: McFarland, 2003.

Johnson, Rody L. *Rise and Fall of Dodgertown*. Gainesville: University Press of Florida, 2008.

*Black River Falls (Wisconsin) Banner-Journal*.
*Humbird (Wisconsin) Enterprise*.
*Milwaukee Journal*.
*St. Paul Pioneer Press*.

Personal telephone interviews with Harold Haugstad, Judy Haugstad Tulgren, Robert Haugstad, and Arthur Haugstad.

## 58. Don Lund

Adler, Rich. *Baseball at the University of Michigan*. Chicago: Arcadia Publishing, 2004.

Brandstatter, Jim. *Tales from Michigan Stadium.* Champaign IL: Sports Publishing, 2005.

Harrigan, Patrick. *The Detroit Tigers Club and Community, 1945–1995.* Toronto: University of Toronto Press, 1997.

Husman, John. *Baseball in Toledo.* Chicago: Arcadia Publishing, 2003.

Irwin, James Robert. *Playing Ball with Legends.* Ann Arbor: Edwards Brothers, 2009.

Kelley, Brent. *The Pastime in Turbulence.* Jefferson NC: McFarland, 2001.

Angelo, Frank. "Detroit's Ace Prep Athlete." *Detroit News Pictorial*, April 6, 1941.

Greene, Sam. "Reason for Lund Deal." *Detroit News*, January 26, 1949.

Holmes, Tommy. "Dodgers Collar Michigan's Lund, 200-Pound Outfielder." *Brooklyn Eagle*, June 28, 1945.

McGowen, Roscoe. "Gregg Wind in Box for Brooks, 4 to 2." *New York Times*, September 18, 1947.

———. "Hatten Twice Tops Reds, 13–2 and 6–3." *New York Times*, September 15, 1947.

———. "Redbirds Capture Seesaw Game 8–7." *New York Times*, September 13, 1947.

Roeder, Bill. "Mahatma Cometh Small Fry Goeth." *World-Telegram*, May 8, 1948.

Sylvester, Curt. "Lund Returns to U-M." *Detroit Free Press*, July 18, 1970.

"Coach of Year Award to Don Lund." *New York Times*, January 7, 1963.

"Doby Homer in 9th Downs Tigers 9–8." *New York Times*, May 27, 1953.

"Lund Named Scout." *Benton Harbor News-Palladium*, November 18, 1954.

"132 Pitches Are Tossed." *New York Times*, July 21, 1958.

"Rookies and Groth Enable Tigers to Batter Bosox 6–2." *Syracuse Post-Standard*, September 11, 1952.

"Southeastern Ace All-City Bound Again." *Detroit Free Press*, February 9, 1941.

"Tigers Name Campbell New General Manager." *New York Times*, September 28, 1962.

"Tigers Rehire Coaches." *Washington Post and Times Herald*, October 12, 1958.

"Tighe Signs for Year as Tiger Pilot." *Chicago Tribune*, October 18, 1956.

Dickson, James. "Well-Played: The Story of University of Michigan Three-Sport Legend Don Lund." Ann-Arbor.com, November 23, 2009.

http://bentley.umich.edu/athdept/baseball/baseball.htm.

http://web.baseballhalloffame.org/visit/hof_game/1940s.jsp.

http://www.baseball-reference.com.

http://www.e-yearbook.com/yearbooks/University_Michigan_Michiganensian_Yearbook/1999/Page_188.html.

http://www.mhsaa.com/games/sports/bbb/psl.pdf.

Lund, Don. Interview by Jim Lannen and Art Neff, 2004.

———. Interview by the author, 2009.

*The Michiganensian Yearbook—Class of 1999.* University of Michigan.

## 59. Vic Lombardi

Thanks to Bill Swank and SABR members Lyle Spatz, Maury Bouchard, Tom Larwin, Bill Millhollen, and Mike Wilhelm for their helpful suggestions.

1. "Vic Lombardi Reminds Branch Rickey of Wee Willie Sherdel," *Fresno Bee*, March 28, 1945.

2. *Sporting News*, December 3, 1947.

3. *Fresno Bee*, July 18, 1993.

4. Swank, *Echoes from Lane Field*, 142.

Lieb, Fred. *The Pittsburgh Pirates.* New York: G. P. Putnam's Sons, 1948.

Marazzi, Richard, and Len Fiorito. *Baseball Players of the 1950s.* Jefferson NC: McFarland, 2004.

Mele, Andrew Paul. *A Brooklyn Dodgers Reader.* Jefferson NC: McFarland, 2005.

Swank, Bill. *Echoes from Lane Field: A History of the San Diego Padres, 1936–1957.* Paducah KY: Turner Publishing, 1997.

Winerip, Harold. "Fans Bearing Gifts." *Baseball Magazine*, June 1949.

Baumgartner, Stan. "Don't Sell Those Little Fellows Short." *Sporting News*, January 8, 1947.

*Chicago Tribune.*
*European Stars and Stripes.*
*Fresno Bee.*

Erskine, Carl. E-mail to the author.
Telephone interviews with Victoria Lombardi, Christine Lombardi Ketchum, Navo Arax, Gary Bauer, Jerry Hagopian, Patti Liscio, and Gus Zernial.

Fresno County Hall of Records.
National Military Personnel Records Center, St. Louis.

### 60. Jack Banta

A special thank-you from the author to Jack Banta's daughter Kristie Banta Empey, who generously assisted me with family information, research, and overall support during the writing of this biography. In addition, she put me in touch with her mother, brother, cousin, and Mr. Jolly. I sincerely appreciate all of her help and kindness.

    1. *Sporting News*, July 2, 1947.
    2. *Sporting News*, April 14, 1948.
    3. *Hutchinson (Kansas) News*, August 14, 1994.

*Hutchinson (Kansas) News*, July 11, 2003, and August 14, 1994.
*Reno County (Kansas) New Times*, October 15, 1997.

Banta, Jackie. Telephone interview, July 22, 2010.
Banta, Mike. Telephone interview, July 28, 2010.
Dunsworth, Harold. Telephone interview, July 25, 2010.
Empey, Kristie Banta. Telephone conversation with Tom Bourke, September 17, 2010.
———. Telephone interview. July 22, 2010.
Jolly, Jim. Telephone interview, July 28, 2010.

### 61. Johnny Van Cuyk

Hall, Flem. "Dodgers' Van Cuyk: Rookie of the Year?" *Baseball Digest*, April 1947.
Lev, Norman. "Brooklyn Dodgers Fiftieth." *One More Inning: A Baseball Time Machine for the Future* 10 (January 2006): 101.

Carlson, Heather J. "Fifteen Minutes with John Van Cuyk." *Rochester (Minnesota) Post-Bulletin*, June 13, 2005.
Christopherson, Brett. "Remembering the Titan: Van Cuyk Recalls His Days with Jackie Robinson." *Appleton (Wisconsin) Post-Crescent*, May 20, 2007.
"Cardinals Rout Brooks by 14–5 in Ragged Game at Ebbets Field." *New York Times*, May 10, 1949.
"Cubs and Schmitz Halt Dodgers, 6–0." *New York Times*, May 9, 1948.
"Dodgers' Diamond Is Forever." *Rochester (Minnesota) Post-Bulletin*, October 14, 1999.
"Jerseys Beaten, 8–1, 3–2." *New York Times*, August 9, 1948.
"Newark Stops Royals, 5–1." *New York Times*, May 15, 1947.
"Royals Top Jerseys, 6–3." *New York Times*, May 10, 1947.
"Sain Stops Brooks." *New York Times*, September 21, 1947.
"This Real Estate Agent Had Some Fast Pitches—Van Cuyk Recounts His Days in the Majors." *Rochester (Minnesota) Post-Bulletin*, August 13, 1997.
"Van Cuyk Leading Texas League with 75 Strikeouts." Unidentified newspaper clipping, 1946.
"Westlake Homer Stops Brooks, 8–7." *New York Times*, September 19, 1947.

http://www.littlechutewi.org.
http://www.tripleabaseball.com.
"John Van Cuyk." In "The Oakland Oaks of the 1950s." http://oaklandoaks.tripod.com.
"The 1946 Fort Worth Cats." http://www.fwcats.com.
Thornley, Stew. "Nicollet Park (Minneapolis)." Baseball Biography Project. http://bioproj.sabr.org.

Van Cuyk, John and Kaye. Interview, February 5, 2009.
———. Telephone interview, March 26, 2009.
Van Cuyk, Johnny, Jr. Telephone interview, March 17, 2009.
Van Cuyk, Lonny. Telephone interview, March 17, 2009.
Van Cuyk, Mark. Telephone interview, February 9, 2009.

Harrison, Katerina. "The Fond du Lac Panthers: Fond du Lac's Professional Baseball Team." Fond du Lac Public Library, Fond du Lac, Wisconsin.

### 63. Willie Ramsdell

    1. 1920 U.S. census, Population Schedule, vol. 42,

Enumeration District 211, sheet 6, line 44, James E. Ramsdell.

2. Obituaries, James Willard (Willie) Ramsdell, *Sporting News*, October 25, 1969.

3. Hank Hart, "The Sports Parade," *Big Spring (Texas) Daily Herald*, June 27, 1938.

4. Zeke Handler, "Knuckler Ramsdell Knocks 'Em Over for Cats, Hurling 13 Victories in Row," *Sporting News*, August 17, 1947.

5. George White, "The Sports Broadcast," *Dallas Morning News*, September 9, 1947.

6. Tommy Hart, "Lookin' 'Em Over," *Big Spring (Texas) Daily Herald*, April 14, 1946.

7. SABR Minor League Database, Willie Ramsdell, 1938–54.

8. "Record as Lemesa Is Shutout, 4–0 and 6–0," *Big Spring (Texas) Daily Herald*, September 2, 1941.

9. Opal Smith, telephone interview, June 12, 2009.

10. John Thorn, Pete Palmer, and Michael Gershman, *Total Baseball*, 7th ed. (Kingston NY: Total Sports Publishing, 2001), 1705.

11. James F. Dawson, "Giants' 6-Run Sixth Halts Dodgers, 6–5," *New York Times*, September 25, 1947.

12. Opal Smith, interview.

13. "Baseball Group Tabs Tex Hurler Top '47 Semi-Pro," *Brownsville (Texas) Herald*, December 26, 1947.

14. Harold C. Burr, "Everything in Brooklyn and Rickey Calls It Quite Normal," *Brooklyn Eagle*, April 30, 1948.

15. Blackie Sherrod, "Cats Wind Up in Clover after Grass-Green Start," *Sporting News*, September 29, 1948.

16. Frank Finch, "Stars' Goose-Egg Diet behind Ramsdell Slenderizes Hill Ace's Winning Record," *Sporting News*, August 17, 1949.

17. Finch, "Stars' Goose-Egg Diet."

18. "Ramsdell Knuckler Baffles," *Long Beach (California) Independent*, June 17, 1949.

19. Opal Smith, interview.

20. *People Today*, quoted in Hart, "Looking 'Em Over."

21. Tom Swope, "Reds Can See One Ace, Hunt Second," *Sporting News*, February 21, 1951.

22. "Reds' Attack Again Flops for Hard-Luck Ramsdell," *Sporting News*, May 2, 1951.

23. Pat McDonough, "Furillo Hits Most Times, Zernial Champion Whiffer," *Sporting News*, January 9, 1952.

24. Kahn, *Boys of Summer*, 124.

25. "Ramsdell Picked Up by Portland Nine," *Long Beach (California) Independent*, August 4, 1953.

26. "Ramsdell Quits, Iola Still Loses," *Salina (Kansas) Journal*, May 20, 1954.

*Big Spring (Texas) Daily Herald.*
*Brooklyn Eagle.*
*Chicago Tribune.*
*Cincinnati Enquirer.*
*Dallas Morning News.*
*Kiowa (Kansas) News.*
*Los Angeles Times.*
*San Antonio Light.*

Willie Ramsdell player file. Baseball Hall of Fame.

### 64. Dick Whitman

Bedingfield, Gary. *Baseball in World War II Europe.* Arcadia SC: Arcadia Publishing, 1999.

Johnson, Lloyd, and Myles Wolff, eds. *The Encyclopedia of Minor League Baseball.* 2nd ed. Durham NC: Baseball America, 1997.

Markusen, Bruce. *Roberto Clemente: The Great One.* Sports Publishing, 2000.

Nowlin, Bill. *Mr. Red Sox: The Johnny Pesky Story.* Cambridge MA: Rounder Records, 2004.

Roberts, Robin, and C. Paul Rogers III. *The Whiz Kids and the 1950 Pennant.* Philadelphia: Temple University Press, 1996.

University of Oregon. *Oregana.* Eugene, 1942.

———. *Oregon Hall of Fame.* Eugene, 2004.

Votano, Paul. *Stand and Deliver: A History of Pinch Hitting.* Jefferson NC: McFarland, 2003.

Dexter, Charles. "When It's Time to Call the Other Fellow's Bet, Collins Is the—Ace in the Hole." *Baseball Digest*, July 1956, 71–75.

Thornley, Stew. "Clemente's Entry into Organized Baseball: Hidden in Montreal?" *National Pastime: A Review of Baseball History* 20 (2006).

Bellamy, Ron. "Former UO Star Whitman Dies." *Eugene (Oregon) Register-Guard*, February 18, 2003.

Sexton, Connie Cone. "Major Leaguer Batted in Two World Series." *Arizona Republic*, March 9, 2003.

Old-Time Data, Inc. *Professional Baseball Player Database*. Version 6.0. CD-ROM, 2008.

**65. Erv Palica**

Special thanks to Bruce W. Belcher, Edison High School, Huntington Beach, California; Bill Nowlin, SABR; Robert Plapinger Baseball Books; and the Atlanta Braves. All quotes are from various editions of the *New York World Telegram*.

James, Bill, and Rob Neyer. *Guide to Pitchers*. New York: Fireside, 2004.
Kelley, Brent P. *The Pastime in Turbulence: Interviews with Baseball Players of the 1940s*. Jefferson NC: McFarland, 2001.
McNeil, William. *The Dodgers Encyclopedia*. 2nd ed. Champaign IL: Sports Publishing, 2003.
Shatzkin, Mike, and Jim Charlton. *The Ballplayers: Baseball's Ultimate Biographical Reference*. New York: Arbor House, William Morrow, 1990.
Snider, Duke. *The Duke of Flatbush*. With Bill Gilbert. New York: Zebra Books, 1989.

*Baseball Digest*.
*Sport*.
*Sport Life*.
*Sports Illustrated*.

*Brooklyn Eagle*.
*Milwaukee Journal-Sentinel*.
*Newsday*.
*New York Daily News*.
*New York Herald Tribune*.
*New York Sun*.
*New York World-Telegram*.

CPCbaseballtrivia.blogspot.com.
Findagrave.com.
TheBaseballCube.com.
TV.com.

**66. Ed Stevens**

Heyde, Jack. *Pop Flies and Line Drives: Visits with Players from Baseball's Golden Era*. Victoria BC: Trafford Publishing, 2004.

Stevens, Ed. *The Other Side of the Jackie Robinson Story*. Mustang OK: Tate Publishing, 2009.

*Hartford Courant*.

Stevens, Ed. Interviews by the author.
——. Telephone interview by Thomas Bourke, January 24, 2010.

**67. Walter O'Malley**

Caro, Robert A. *The Power Broker: Robert Moses and the Fall of New York*. New York: Knopf, 1974.
D'Antonio, Michael. *Forever Blue: The True Story of Walter O'Malley, Baseball's Most Controversial Owner, and the Dodgers of Brooklyn and Los Angeles*. New York: Riverhead Books, 2009.
Drysdale, Don. *Once a Bum, Always a Dodger*. New York: St. Martin's Press, 1990.
McGee, Robert. *The Greatest Ballpark Ever: Ebbets Field and the Story of the Brooklyn Dodgers*. New Brunswick NJ: Rivergate Books, 2005.
Miller, Marvin. *A Whole Different Ball Game: The Sport and Business of Baseball*. Secaucus NJ: Carol Publishing Group, 1991.
Moses, Robert. *Current Biography*. New York: H. W. Wilson, 1954, 479–81.
O'Malley, Walter F. *Current Biography*. New York: H. W. Wilson, 1954, 494–95.
Rader, Benjamin G. "O'Malley, Walter Francis." In *American National Biography*. Vol. 16. 716–17. New York: Oxford University Press, 1999.
Sullivan, Neil J. *The Dodgers Move West*. New York: Oxford University Press, 1987.

Allan Roth papers. Baseball Hall of Fame.
Allan Roth papers. Case Western Reserve University.
Branch Rickey and Arthur Mann papers. Library of Congress.

**68. John L. Smith**

Mines, Samuel. *Pfizer: An Informal History*. New York: Pfizer, 1979.
Rodengen, Jeffrey L. *The Legend of Pfizer*. Ft. Lauderdale: Write Stuff Syndicate, 1999.

*The Pfizer Scene* (company magazine).

Obituaries in *New York Times*, July 11, 1950, and *Sporting News*, July 19, 1950.

## 69. Red Barber

Barber, Lylah. *Lylah*. Chapel Hill NC: Algonquin Books of Chapel Hill, 1985.

Barber, Red. *The Broadcasters*. New York: Dial Press, 1970.

———. *1947: When All Hell Broke Loose in Baseball*. Garden City NY: Doubleday, 1982.

———. *Rhubarb in the Catbird Seat*. With Robert Creamer. Garden City NY: Doubleday, 1968.

———. *Show Me the Way to Go Home*. Philadelphia: Westminster Press, 1971.

———. *Walk in the Spirit*. New York: Dial Press, 1969.

Edwards, Bob. *Fridays with Red*. New York: Simon & Schuster, 1993.

Smith, Curt. *The Storytellers*. New York: Macmillan, 1995.

———. *Voices of the Game*. South Bend IN: Diamond Communications, 1987.

Thurber, James. "The Catbird Seat." *New Yorker*, November 14, 1942, 17–20.

*Salon*, November 7, 2000. http://www.salon.com.
*Los Angeles Times*, August 6, 2002.

From the Catbird Seat: Red Barber, a 1993 radio documentary written and produced by Greg Rhodes for public station WVXU in Cincinnati. It included excerpts from Barber's play-by-play broadcasts and his later interviews.

## 70. Connie Desmond

1. Craig, "Schembechler about to Silence Voice of Tigers."

2. Vecsey, "Don't Support Local Cable Shell Game."

3. Eskenazi, *I Hid It under the Sheets*.

4. McNeil, *Dodgers Encyclopedia*.

5. "On the Radio Airlines."

6. Best, "Vin Scully."

7. Display ad, *New York Times*, April 16, 1948.

8. "Red Barber Gives Blood."

9. Patterson, *Golden Voices*.

10. Patterson, *Golden Voices*.

11. Rodenbush, "Q&A with Vin Scully."

12. Display ad, *New York Times*, August 25, 1954.

13. Kepner, "Sixty Years in Dodgers' Booth."

14. Roeder, "Make-Believe Microphone."

15. Adams, "Marisa Pavan."

16. Craig, "Scully Completes Cycle."

17. Smith, *Voices of Summer*.

18. Eskenazi, *I Hid It under the Sheets*.

19. Falls, "Oh, to See Gehrig Play!"

20. "Connie Desmond."

Eskenazi, Gerald. *I Hid It under the Sheets: Growing Up With Radio*. Columbia: University of Missouri Press, 2005.

McNeil, William. *The Dodgers Encyclopedia*. 2nd ed. Champaign IL: Sports Publishing, 2003.

Patterson, Ted. *The Golden Voices of Baseball*. Champaign IL: Sports Publishing, 2002.

Smith, Curt. *Voices of Summer: Ranking Baseball's 101 All-Time Best Announcers*. New York: Carroll & Graf, 2005.

Adams, Val. "NBC Gives Role to Marisa Pavan." *New York Times*, August 10, 1956.

———. "TV Series Slated for Perry Mason." *New York Times*, February 7, 1956.

Best, Neil. "Vin Scully Grew Up as a . . . New York Giants fan!" *Newsday*, May 3, 2008.

Craig, Jack. "Schembechler about to Silence Voice of Tigers; Sportview." *Boston Globe*, December 21, 1990.

———. "Scully Completes Cycle at Fenway; Sportview." *Boston Globe*, July 9, 1989.

Falls, Joe. "Oh, to See Gehrig Play!" *Sporting News*, May 16, 1983.

Hutchens, John K. "Brooklyn's Red Barber." *New York Times*, May 2, 1943.

Lohman, Sidney. "News and Notes from the Studios." *New York Times*, December 31, 1950.

Rodenbush, Jim. "Q&A with Vin Scully." *Pittsburgh Tribune-Review*, April 27, 2003.

Roeder, Bill. "Make-Believe Microphone Vin's Step to Broadcasting." *Sporting News*, August 3, 1955.

Rosenthal, Harold. "Scully Earns TV Plum Four Years Out of Fordham." *Sporting News*, October 14, 1953.

Vecsey, George. "Sports of the Times: Don't Support

Local Cable Shell Game." *New York Times*, March 29, 2002.

Young, Dick. "Clubhouse Confidential." *Sporting News*, February 22, 1956.

———. "Young Ideas: Sleeper: Jays Ahead of Yanks." *Sporting News*, April 18, 1983.

"Barber on Air Again." *Sporting News*, March 22, 1945.

"Connie Desmond." *New York Times*, March 13, 1983.

"On the Radio Airlines." *Sporting News*, April 23, 1942.

"On the Radio Airlines." *Sporting News*, April 15, 1943.

"Radio and Television." *New York Times*, February 25, 1950.

"Radio Network for Taxis Proposed." *New York Times*, December 10, 1964.

"Radio-Video." *New York Times*, January 10, 1950.

"Red Barber Gives Blood." *New York Times*, May 12, 1948.

"Tuning In." *Sporting News*, February 15, 1956.

"Tuning In." *Sporting News*, August 29, 1956.

Derkeiler.com. http://newsgroups.derkeiler.com/Archive/Alt/alt.sports.baseball.ny-mets/2006-09/msg00661.html.

Social Security Death Index. http://ssdi.rootsweb.ancestry.com/cgi-bin/ssdi.cgi.

Wikipedia.com. http://en.wikipedia.org/wiki/Red_Barber#Brooklyn_Dodgers.

## 71. Advertising and the Dodgers in 1947

1. James T. Patterson, *Grand Expectations: The United States, 1945–1947* (New York: Oxford University Press, 1996), 61.

2. Patterson, *Grand Expectations*, 70.

3. James B. Twitchell, *AdCult: USA* (New York: Columbia University Press, 1996), 41.

4. Carl E. Prince, *Brooklyn's Dodgers: The Bums, the Borough, and the Best of Baseball* (New York: Oxford University Press, 1996), 102.

5. Display ad, Baltimore and Ohio Railroad, *Brooklyn Daily Eagle*, August 11, 1947.

6. Display ad, South Brooklyn Savings and Loan, *Brooklyn Daily Eagle*, September 25, 1947.

7. The Bossert, once Brooklyn's most luxurious hotel, is now owned and operated by the Watchtower as a dormitory for Jehovah's Witnesses.

8. Display ads, Marine Roof of the Hotel Bossert, and Hotel St. George, *Brooklyn Daily Eagle*, October 2, 1947.

9. Display ads, *Brooklyn Daily Eagle*, October 2, 1947.

10. Jan Whitaker, *Service and Style: How the American Department Store Fashioned the Middle Class* (New York: St. Martin's, 2006), 315.

11. Federated Department Stores, http://www.ohiohistorycentral.org/entry.php?rec=888, July 8, 2009.

12. Display ad, Abraham & Straus, *Brooklyn Daily Eagle*, September 14, 1947.

13. Display ad, Abraham & Straus, *Brooklyn Daily Eagle*, September 23, 1947.

14. Display ad, Loeser's, *Brooklyn Daily Eagle*, October 1, 1947.

15. Display ad, Bohack Food Stores, *Brooklyn Daily Eagle*, September 23, 1947.

16. Display ad, George-Wally Haberdashers and Hatters, *New York Times*, October 1, 1947.

17. Display ad, Schaefer Beer, *New York Times*, May 29, 1947.

18. Roberta Newman, "Now Pitching for the Dodgers: The Local Character of Baseball and Advertising in Brooklyn, 1890–1957," in *Cooperstown Symposium on Baseball and American Culture 2005–2006*, ed. William M. Simons (Jefferson NC: McFarland, 2007), 81.

19. Display ad, Raleigh Cigarettes, *Washington Post*, July 2, 1947.

20. Roberta Newman, "It Pays to be Personal: Baseball and Product Endorsements," NINE: *A Journal of Baseball History and Culture* 12, no. 1 (2003): 35.

21. Patterson, *Grand Expectations*, 19.

22. Display ad, Silver Rail Bar and Grill, *New York Amsterdam News*, August 30, 1947.

23. Display ads, *Pittsburgh Courier*, May 17, 1947.

24. "Congratulations Jackie Robinson," *New York Amsterdam News*, August 23, 1947.

25. Robinson's Old Gold ads appeared in a variety of news outlets throughout 1947 and for years after.

26. James R. Walker and Robert V. Bellamy, *Center Field Shot: A History of Baseball on Television* (Lincoln: University of Nebraska Press, 2008), 16.

27. "Advertising News and Notes," *New York Times*, March 1, 1947.

28. Walker and Bellamy, *Center Field Shot*, 70.

29. Walker and Bellamy, *Center Field Shot*, 24.

30. Walker and Bellamy, *Center Field Shot*, 26.

31. Patterson, *Grand Expectations*, 63.

32. Walker and Bellamy, *Center Field Shot*, 25.

33. Walker and Bellamy, *Center Field Shot*, 26.

34. Walker and Bellamy, *Center Field Shot*, 26.

35. Display ad, Bressner Radio, Inc., *Brooklyn Daily Eagle*, May 4, 1947.

36. Display ad, RCA, *New York Times*, June 1, 1947.

37. David Halberstam, *The Fifties* (New York: Villard Books, 1993), 131.

38. Patterson, *Grand Expectations*, 11.

## 72. The 1947 World Series

Distel, Dave. "Gionfriddo Recalls His Famous Catch." *Baseball Digest*, February 1973, 70–73.

"Most Exciting Two Minutes in History of World Series." *Life*, October 13, 1947, 44–45.

## 73. Al Gionfriddo

Grateful acknowledgment to Sue Gionfriddo and the Gionfriddo family for their memories. Thanks also to John Petrini and John Zant.

1. Dave Distel, "Moment of Glory," *Los Angeles Times*, November 2, 1972.

2. Joe Szafran, "Scanning the Field," *Oil City (Pennsylvania) Blizzard*, May 26, 1942.

3. *Sporting News*, June 1, 1944.

4. Frederick G. Lieb, "Strongest All-Freshman Team since '41 Named," *Sporting News*, November 1, 1945.

5. Charles J. Doyle, "Crippled Bucs Hear the Door Slam on Cellar," *Sporting News*, September 4, 1946.

6. "Robinson's Stars Split in Opener," *Sporting News*, October 16, 1946.

7. For general discussion of this strike vote, see Rossi, *A Whole New Game*, 10–11.

8. Earl Gustkey, "1947: A Series of Surprising Stars—Lavagetto, Bevens and Gionfriddo Had Their Moments," *Los Angeles Times*, October 17, 1987.

9. Oscar Ruhl, "From the Ruhl Book," *Sporting News*, October 15, 1947.

10. John Zant, "The Catch Heard 'Round the World: Remembering the Day Al Gionfriddo Made Joe DiMaggio Angry, 60 Years Later," *Santa Barbara Independent*, October 4, 2007; Mike Downey, "A Fall Classic," *Los Angeles Times*, August 27, 1997.

11. "Gionfriddo Is Honored; Brooklyn Hero Feted in Home Town—Stars in Ball Game," *New York Times*, October 13, 1947.

12. Richard Goldstein, "Al Gionfriddo, 81; Remembered for '47 Catch," *New York Times*, March 16, 2003.

13. Scott Baillie, "Happy Once Again: Al Gionfriddo Now Playing for Ventura," *Hayward (California) Daily Review*, May 20, 1954.

14. Jack Wood, "Al Gionfriddo and Joe DiMaggio," http://nyenevada.blogspot.com/2008/04/al-gionfriddo-and-joe-dimaggio.html, April 26, 2008.

15. Steve Ledbetter, "Brief Series Hero Gionfriddo Sells Insurance and Baseball," *Titusville (Pennsylvania) Herald*, November 11, 1960.

16. Norm Clarke, "Gionfriddo's Impossible Catch Ranks among Series Legends," *Oxnard (California) Press-Courier*, October 16, 1977.

17. Downey, "Fall Classic."

18. Earl Gustkey, "1947: A Series of Surprising Stars—Lavagetto, Bevens and Gionfriddo Had Their Moments," *Los Angeles Times*, October 17, 1987.

19. "Al Gionfriddo, 81; Dodger Made Game-Saving Catch in '47 Series," *Los Angeles Times*, March 16, 2003.

Barber, Red. *1947: When All Hell Broke Loose in Baseball*. New York: Da Capo Press, 1984.

Frommer, Harvey. *New York City Baseball: The Last Golden Age*. Madison: University of Wisconsin Press, 2004.

Johnson, Lloyd, and Miles Wolff, eds. *The Encyclopedia of Minor League Baseball*. 2nd ed. Durham NC: Baseball America, Inc., 1997.

Rossi, John. *A Whole New Game: Off the Field Changes in Baseball, 1946–1960*. Jefferson NC: McFarland, 1999.

Burr, Harold C. "Rickey Solves Squad-Cutting Worry by Jackpot Deal That Nets $200,000." *Sporting News*, May 14, 1947.

Daley, Arthur. "The Impossible Is Still Happening." *New York Times*, October 6, 1947.

"Gionfriddo Got Thrill of Lifetime Making Catch." *Brooklyn Eagle*, October 6, 1947.

*Gionfriddo v. Major League Baseball*, 94 Cal.App.4th 400, 114 Cal.Rptr.2d 307 (2001).

Ancestry.com. 1910, 1920, and 1930 U.S. census data. Note that the name of Gionfriddo was misspelled each time—as Geofrrido, Goifriddo, and Gomfredo. This source also provided Al's wedding dates and Paul Gionfriddo's place of birth (from military records).

Charney, Frank. "Sunday Postcard." http://www.nantyglo.com/postcards03/may1803.htm, May 18, 2003.

http://bob.sabrwebs.com/content/docs/court_cases/Gionfriddo.pdf.

http://caselaw.lp.findlaw.com/data2/californiastatecases/a078967.doc.

http://www.law.com/regionals/ca/opinions/dec/a091113.shtml.

Links to audiovisual records of the Catch: Red Barber's radio call—http://www.thedeadballera.com/Gionfriddo.mp3; Pathé News newsreel clip—http://www.spokane7.com/blogs/moviesandmore/archive.asp?postID=6961.

Old-Time Data, Inc. *Professional Baseball Player Database*. Version 6.0. http://www.baseball-almanac.com/minor-league.

## 74. Cookie Lavagetto

1. The state of California and the 1920 U.S. census list him as Attilio H. Lavagetto.

2. http://sportsillustrated.cnn.com/vault/article/magazine/MAG1072554/index.htm.

3. http://oaklandoaks.tripod.com/lavagetto.html.

4. Bob Addie, "Destiny Goes to Bat," *Baseball Digest*, August 1956, 43–44.

5. http://sportsillustrated.cnn.com/vault/article/magazine/MAG1072554/index.htm.

6. http://www.baseball-reference.com/minors/player.cgi?id=lavage001har.

7. http://www.baseball-reference.com/players/l/lavagco01.shtm.

8. http://www.baseball-reference.com/players/l/lavagco01.shtml.

9. http://sportsillustrated.cnn.com/vault/article/magazine/MAG1072554/2/index.htm.

10. http://www.baseballinwartime.com/player_biographies/lavagetto_cookie.htm.

11. http://sportsillustrated.cnn.com/vault/article/magazine/MAG1072554/3/index.htm.

12. http://sportsillustrated.cnn.com/vault/article/magazine/MAG1072554/4/index.htm.

13. http://sportsillustrated.cnn.com/vault/article/magazine/MAG1072554/1/index.htm.

14. "Ermer Tabbed as Twins' Pilot 13 Years Ago!" *Baseball Digest*, March 1968, 56.

Some of the biographical information came from an April 11, 2010, telephone interview Thomas Bourke did with Cookie Lavagetto's son Ernest in Walnut Creeek, California.

## 75. Al Gionfriddo's Memorable Game Six Catch

1. Red Barber, *1947: When All Hell Broke Loose in Baseball* (New York: Da Capo Press, 1984), 347.

2. David Halberstam, *Summer of '49* (New York: Harper Perennial Modern Classics, 2002), 49. Halberstam, age thirteen, was in the stands at Yankee Stadium that day. See John Zant, "Gionfriddo's Catch Receives the Stamp of Authority," *Santa Barbara Newsroom*, May 11, 2007.

3. Dave Anderson, "Subway Series Reflections: A Ride on the Carousel of Time," *New York Times*, October 20, 2000.

4. Kahn, *Era*, 127.

5. Kahn, *Era*, 128.

6. Penny Weichel, "Gionfriddo Revisited," *Oil City (Pennsylvania) Derrick*, November 16, 1974.

7. Frank Eck, "DiMag's Blow Called Longest He Ever Hit," *Titusville (Pennsylvania) Herald*, October 6, 1947.

8. David Jones, *Joe DiMaggio* (Westport CT: Greenwood Publishing Group, 2004), 97–98; Eric Enders, *100 Years of the World Series* (New York: Barnes and Noble Books, 2003), 118.

9. Birtwell, Roger. "Little Al Didn't Expect to Stay with Dodgers," *Sporting News*, October 15, 1947.

10. Richard Ben Cramer, *Joe DiMaggio: The Hero's Life* (New York: Simon & Schuster, 2000), 235.

11. Eig, *Opening Day*, 257.

12. "'Greatest Catch I've Ever Seen'—Terry," *Winnipeg Free Press*, October 6, 1947.

13. Roscoe McGowen, "Outfielder Feted for Mighty Catch," *New York Times*, October 6, 1947.

14. Anderson, "Subway Series Reflections."

15. Steve Campbell, "Gionfriddo's Name Still Catchy over 40 Years Later," *Fort Worth Star-Telegram*, August 11, 1991.

## 80. Dodgers Attendance in 1947

Attendance patterns and magnitudes between the end of World War II and the flurry of franchise relocations a few years later were dramatically different than they are today and, without some sense of context, might seem unremarkable by present standards. In those days, a million in a season was a badge of economic health, while now twice that number is regarded as substandard. Today, day-to-day attendance variation is not as dramatic as it was then. In our era, season ticket sales (whether full or partial plans) provide a large and stable base of patronage, while then they were far less common. Now, most games are at night, and thus don't conflict with work schedules; then, night games accounted for less than a fifth of the schedule, meaning that about half the games were unlikely to generate a large turnout. Teams then were heavily dependent on weekend and holiday dates to bolster their bottom lines. Single-admission doubleheaders are now virtually nonexistent but were common then: in 1947 the Dodgers played seven of them at home, usually ensuring a healthy turnout, but also in effect giving seven games away free. They also played five doubleheaders on the road. And today's longer schedules provide roughly 5 percent more home games per team.

Reduced-price or free tickets for knothole gangs and ladies' days helped fill the seats on slow dates, but didn't show up in the official attendance figures. Also, official tallies in the earlier period included only those fans who both bought tickets and attended the game, while today all sold tickets count, whether or not their holders actually show up. Around 1947, seating capacities varied widely between a minimum of below 30,000 and a maximum of nearly 79,000, with a standard deviation of about 15,200. Current ballparks range much more narrowly between about 35,000 and 56,000, with a standard deviation of only about 5,066. Many published seating capacities of the time were approximate (often ending in three or even four zeroes), and frequently contradictory, which is why this article often refers to numerical data in an approximate way. (Fortunately, the most critical capacity figure, that of Ebbets Field, seems reliably defined by a detailed World Series accounting as 31,944 seats.) Even with two parks shared by the leagues, the National League teams had much smaller aggregate and average capacities than the American League, averaging about 37,300 compared to the AL's 47,500. On average, the other thirteen Major League ballparks had about 13,200 more seats than Ebbets Field.

A similar uncertainty applies to cumulative attendance figures: my methodology has been to use Retrosheet numbers as a basis and frequently cross-check them against *New York Times* boxscores or Red Barber citations based on the same source, correcting the former when there is a discrepancy. The result is a set of totals similar to commonly published season totals, but not identical to them.

Ticket prices back then were low; according to one source, AL tickets averaged about $1.25 in 1946. Today, an average MLB ticket runs nearly $27.00—a more than 21-fold hike, compared to an 11.6 times rise in the consumer price index. As a rough estimate, the Major Leagues grossed about $25 million in ticket sales in 1947, compared to about $2 billion in 2009.

## 81. Ownership Issues in Brooklyn

Branch Rickey papers. Library of Congress.

# Contributors

RABBI REBECCA T. ALPERT is an associate professor of religion and women's studies at Temple University. She attended Barnard College before receiving her PhD in religion at Temple University and her rabbinical training at the Reconstructionist Rabbinical College in Wyncote, Pennsylvania. She is the coauthor of *Exploring Judaism: A Reconstructionist Approach* and the author of *Like Bread on the Seder Plate: Jewish Lesbians and the Transformation of Tradition* and *Whose Torah? A Concise Guide to Progressive Judaism*, as well as several edited volumes and numerous articles. Her specialization is religion in America, and she focuses on issues related to gender, sexuality, and race. She has recently taught courses on religion in American public life; Jews, America, and sports; and sexuality in world religions. Her most recent book, *Out of Left Field: Jews and Black Baseball*, was published by Oxford Press in 2011.

LAWRENCE BALDASSARO is a professor emeritus of Italian and a former director of the Honors College at the University of Wisconsin–Milwaukee. He has written for several baseball journals and is a regular contributor to *GameDay*, the Milwaukee Brewers magazine. He is the editor of *Ted Williams: Reflections on a Splendid Life* and a coeditor, with Richard Johnson, of *The American Game: Baseball and Ethnicity*. His latest book is *Beyond DiMaggio: Italian Americans in Baseball* (University of Nebraska Press, 2011).

STANLEY H. BARD is a native of Brooklyn who grew up in the fifties rooting for his beloved Brooklyn Dodgers before they left for the West Coast. His love of the game stems from those early years. As a fan sitting in the right-field stands, Stan saw a lot of Jake Pitler as he grew up in Ebbets Field. Stan attended the State University of New York at Buffalo, giving him his first exposure to the Minor League game. He saw quite a few Buffalo Bisons games at the old War Memorial Stadium. Stan spent most of his professional life in management of nonprofit organizations. Before retiring to western Pennsylvania, Stan and his wife lived and worked in Cincinnati, where he became a loyal Reds fan.

While this is his first attempt at writing a baseball biography, he has published an article, "Return to Ebbets," which appeared in the now defunct *Elysian Fields*.

RALPH BERGER earned a bachelor's degree in social science from the University of Pennsylvania, a master's of public administration from Temple University, and a certificate from the University of Michigan for completion of a human resources program. He has written many biographical sketches for the SABR Biographical Committee. Ralph currently lives with his wife, Reina, in Huntingdon Valley, Pennsylvania. He hopes to continue to write many more articles for SABR.

MAURICE BOUCHARD, who lives in Shrewsbury, Massachusetts, with his wife, Kim, has been a baseball fan since Sandy Koufax struck out Bob Allison for the final out of the 1965 World Series. A SABR member since 1999, Maurice has contributed to several baseball books, including *Lefty, Double-X and the Kid*, and *The 1967 Impossible Dream Red Sox*. He has a BS from SUNY-Albany, an MS from UMASS-Lowell, and an MLIS from Simmons College, just across the Muddy River from Fenway Park.

BOB BUEGE, a Milwaukee native, attended (with his dad) a doubleheader between the Milwaukee Braves and the St. Louis Cardinals at County Stadium on July 5, 1953. Eddie Mathews hit a home run, Warren Spahn pitched a shutout, some of the ballplayers left their gloves on the field between innings, and Bob was hooked for life. He is now retired after forty years as an educator, thirty-four in a Milwaukee public high school and six at the University of Wisconsin–Milwaukee. He is the author of four books, including *The Milwaukee Braves: A Baseball Eulogy* and *Eddie Mathews and the National Pastime*. He has been a SABR member since 1988 and a member of the Ken Keltner Badger State Chapter of SABR since 2001.

WARREN CORBETT, a former Minor League Baseball broadcaster, is the author of *The Wizard of Waxahachie: Paul Richards and the End of Baseball As We Knew It*. He is editor of a trade publication in Washington DC.

RORY COSTELLO is the author of "Twilight at Ebbets Field" (*National Pastime* 26 [2006]), an essay of stadium lore revealing what happened after the Dodgers left Brooklyn. He is a longtime Brooklyn resident but was years too late to have the pleasure of seeing a game at the lovable old ballpark in Crown Heights.

JOE DITTMAR, a corporate trainer in the pharmaceutical industry, has been a leader in the SABR Connie Mack Chapter and was vice chairman of the Records Committee for eighteen years. In addition to numerous articles published in SABR's *National Pastime* and *Baseball Research Journal*, he has authored *Baseball's Benchmark Boxscores*, *The 100 Greatest Baseball Games of the 20th Century Ranked*, and the Sporting News–SABR Research Award–winning *Baseball Records*

*Registry: The Best and Worst Single-Day Performances and the Stories Behind Them*. Joe also teaches a baseball history class at his local community college.

ALEX EDELMAN is an undergraduate at New York University, where he is an English major and a creative writing minor in the College of Arts and Sciences. This is the fifth BioProject collection he has appeared in. His second effort, on 1967 Red Sox pitcher Billy Rohr, received a Jack R. Kavanagh Award. At NYU he has studied under noted authors Darin Strauss, Jonathan Lethem, Nathan Englander, Thomas Bender, and Rachel DeWoskin. A native of Boston, Edelman is also an acclaimed stand-up comic and tours nationally. His 2010 essay on historian Allan Nevins's conception of "Nation" was nominated for the Columbia University Journal of History. He is fond of hockey, his brothers, and anything well-written.

ROB EDELMAN is the author of *Great Baseball Films* and *Baseball on the Web*. His film/television-related books include *Meet the Mertzes*, a double-biography of *I Love Lucy*'s Vivian Vance and fabled baseball fan William Frawley, and *Matthau: A Life*—both coauthored with his wife, Audrey Kupferberg. He is a film commentator on WAMC (Northeast) Public Radio and a contributing editor of *Leonard Maltin's Movie Guide*. His byline has appeared in *Base Ball: A Journal of the Early Game*, *Baseball and American Culture: Across the Diamond*, *Total Baseball*, *The Total Baseball Catalog*, *Baseball in the Classroom: Teaching America's National Pastime*, *The Political Companion to American Film*, and dozens of other books. He authored an essay on early baseball films for the DVD *Reel Baseball: Baseball Films from the Silent Era, 1899–1926*, and he has been a juror at the National Baseball Hall of Fame and Museum's annual film festival. He is a lecturer at the University at Albany, where he teaches courses in film history.

DAVID L. FLEITZ, a computer systems analyst from Pleasant Ridge, Michigan, has written six books on baseball history, including biographies of Joe Jackson, Louis Sockalexis, and Cap Anson, as well as two volumes of biographies of little-known members of the Baseball Hall of Fame. David's latest work, *The Irish in Baseball: An Early History*, was published by McFarland in 2009. A regular contributor to SABR publications, David's work has appeared in SABR's *National Pastime, Baseball Research Journal*, and both of the *Deadball Stars* compilations. He is also a trivia expert, having won the individual trivia competition at three consecutive SABR conventions beginning in 2006.

IRV GOLDFARB saw his first baseball game at Yankee Stadium in 1962, but his first game at the Polo Grounds a year later made him a Mets fan for life. Irv was a disc jockey for twenty-two years in Buffalo, Hartford, and New Haven, Connecticut, and now works at ABC Television in New York. He lives in Union City, New Jersey, with his future wife, Mercedes, a more insane Mets fan than he is. Irv has had chapters published in both *Deadball Stars of the National League* and *Deadball Stars of the American League*; *The Fenway Project*; and *The Miracle Has Landed*. He has been a SABR member since 1999.

PETER M. GORDON wrote his first article for the *Baseball Research Journal* in 1988. He has written for the *National Pastime*, the BioProject, and other SABR publications. He lives in Orlando, Florida, and is a member of the Auker-Seminick Chapter. After a career as a theater director, Peter worked in television programming for NBC, HBO, and PBS, and he moved to Orlando to lead the team that created and developed the programming that enabled the Golf Channel to achieve worldwide success. Peter is now a media consultant, writer, speaker, and published poet. He blogs about content development at www.myprogramidea.blogspot.com.

He has been married for over twenty-five years and has three sons.

DAVID GREISEN has been a high school special education teacher and coach in south-central Minnesota since 2002. He was born and raised in Wisconsin, where he quickly became a lifelong fan of bratwurst, Bob Uecker, and Milwaukee Brewers baseball. He presently resides in Saint Peter with his wife, Marci, and two small children, Owen Gehrig and Callie Anne. Together, they enjoy traveling, staying active, and cheering for the Minnesota Twins.

DON HARRISON is the author of *Connecticut Baseball: The Best of the Nutmeg State* (The History Press, 2008) and a SABR member. A two-time selection as Connecticut Sportswriter of the Year, he covered nine World Series for the *Waterbury Republican-American* and the *New Haven Journal-Courier*. It was his good fortune to chronicle two of the preeminent events in Series history—the Mets' improbable triumph over Baltimore in 1969 and Reggie Jackson's three home runs in the finale of the 1977 Fall Classic. Don's career in public relations embraces work with a corporation in Connecticut's Fairfield County and Sacred Heart University, where he was the founding editor of the college's quarterly magazine. In 2002, as editor, he spearheaded the launch of the *Greenwich (Connecticut) Citizen*, a weekly newspaper. His freelance work has appeared in *The Sporting News*, the *New York Times*, *Connecticut* magazine, and dozens of other publications.

TOM HAWTHORN is a columnist for the *Globe and Mail*, Canada's national newspaper. He joined SABR in 1995. His baseball nickname is E5.

PAUL HIRSCH is the owner of Paul Hirsch Professional Communications, a marketing and public relations firm in Danville, California, and a freelance magazine writer. A SABR member since 1983, he has served on the SABR board of directors, has been chapter leader of the Lefty O'Doul Chapter in San Francisco, was a member of the 1998 SABR Convention Committee, and helped originate the SABR Donor Program. Paul has been married to Debbie Rodd since 1988 and has two children, Rebecca and Mark. His other SABR BioProject subjects include Joe Pignatano, Ed Roebuck, John Kennedy, and Al Ferrara.

WARREN JACOBS is a reference/instruction librarian at California State University, Stanislaus. The campus is located in Turlock in California's Central Valley, east of San Francisco. In addition to providing course-integrated information literacy instruction, Warren also teaches an information literacy credit course online and works as an embedded librarian in the College of Education. Warren regularly reviews new books on education and information science for the journal *Education Libraries*. He is the author of several articles on librarianship. Warren enjoys reading baseball history and biography. Duke Snider is the subject of Warren's first published work on baseball.

WILLIAM H. JOHNSON is a military analyst for the Navy Warfare Development Command. He is a retired naval flight officer and lives in Chesapeake, Virginia. Since joining SABR in 1994, he has contributed biographies to *The Miracle Has Landed* (1969 Mets) and *Go-Go to Glory* (1959 White Sox), as well as the SABR BioProject. In 2010 he was awarded a Yoseloff-SABR grant to continue his research into the history of baseball in eastern Iowa.

JIMMY KEENAN has been a SABR member since 2001. His grandfather Jimmy Lyston, along with his great-grandfather John M. Lyston and John's two brothers Marty and Bill, were all professional baseball players. He is the author of the book *The Lystons: A Story of One Baltimore Family and Our National Pastime*. His biography of Cupid Childs was published in SABR's *National Pas-*

*time* in 2009. In addition, he was the writer and historian for the *Forgotten Birds* documentary, which chronicles the fifty-year history of the Minor League Baltimore Orioles. His prerecorded interview about the 1921 Baltimore Orioles can be heard at the "Second Inning" display at the Sports Legends Museum in Baltimore, Maryland. He has also written biographies for SABR's BioProject. Jimmy is a 2010 inductee into the Oldtimers Baseball Association of Maryland's Hall of Fame and is currently a member of the organization's board of governors.

JIM KREUZ was introduced to SABR by former Major League pitcher Tim McNamara, whose high school catcher was a kid named Gabby Hartnett, whose teammate at Fordham was shortstop Frankie Frisch, and whose best friend on the Boston Braves was an outfielder named Casey Stengel.

MARK LANGILL is the publications editor and team historian of the Los Angeles Dodgers. A member of the front office since 1994, Langill previously covered the team for five seasons for the San Gabriel Valley Newspapers Group. He has written four books, *Dodger Stadium, Los Angeles Dodgers, Dodgertown*, and *Game of My Life: Dodgers*. He has appeared on both television and radio to discuss Dodgers history, including the MLB Network production *Cathedrals of the Game: Dodger Stadium* and ESPN's *30 for 30* documentary *Fernando Nation*.

LEONARD LEVIN saw one game at Ebbets Field and wishes he could have seen more. It was that much fun. A retired newspaper editor who lives in Providence, Rhode Island, he spends much of his time doing baseball research and editing biographies written by SABR members.

JEFFREY MARLETT teaches religious studies at The College of Saint Rose in Albany, New York. He is the author of *Saving the Heartland: Catholic Missionaries in Rural America, 1920–1960*

(Northern Illinois University Press, 2002). He became interested in Leo Durocher while preparing undergraduate ethics courses.

JOE MARREN is an associate professor in the communication department at Buffalo State College. He was a summa cum laude graduate of Buffalo State in 1986, and he received his master's degree in history from St. Bonaventure University in 1996. Marren worked as a newspaper reporter and then editor at a variety of community newspapers in estern New York for eighteen years.

ANDY MCCUE is a retired newspaper reporter, editor, and columnist. He is an active member of SABR, where he has served as president. He is the author of *Baseball by the Books: A History and Bibliography of Baseball Fiction* and is working on a full-length biography of Walter O'Malley.

BOB MCGEE is author of *The Greatest Ballpark Ever: Ebbets Field and the Story of the Brooklyn Dodgers* (Rivergate, 2005), which won the 2005 Dave Moore Award. His sports articles have appeared in the *New York Times* and the *Oakland Tribune*; numerous other contributions have appeared elsewhere. He currently lives in Westchester County, north of New York City, but he's always had a home in Brooklyn.

JACK V. MORRIS is a corporate librarian for an environmental engineering company. He lives in East Coventry, Pennsylvania, with his wife and two daughters. He is not the Jack Morris of World Series fame, though he sometimes wishes he was.

RALPH C. MOSES is a retired clincial social worker, teacher, and long-suffering Cubs fan. He lives in Chicago, where he is raising two young sons. Ralph has previously written articles on Bid McPhee and Vada Pinson for the SABR BioProject.

DAN MULLEN is a managing editor and writer at ESPN Mobile. A second-generation SABR member, Mullen was raised in Greeley, Colorado, and now resides in Wethersfield, Connecticut. Mullen's writing has appeared in several sports publications, including *The Sporting News*, the *New Britain Herald*, *Greeley Tribune*, Rivals.com, and TopProspectAlert.com.

JERRY NECHAL currently works as an administrator at Wayne State University in Detroit. He resides in Sylvan Lake, Michigan. He has previously written about "The Worst Team Ever" in *The Baseball Research Journal* and completed the biography of Mickey Stanley for the book *Sock It to 'Em Tigers: The Incredible Story of the 1968 Detroit Tigers*. Other interests include hiking, architecture, bocce ball, and mountain biking. He still longs for a bleacher seat in old Tiger Stadium.

ROBERTA J. NEWMAN is a cultural historian who has written extensively on sport and the media. She is currently working on a coauthored book-length project dealing with the last days of segregated black baseball. A lifelong Brooklynite, she is a member of the faculty of New York University's liberal studies program.

ROB NEYER is the author or coauthor of six books about baseball, has written more words for ESPN. com than anyone, and is currently SB Nation's national baseball editor.

JOHN PASTIER has been an architect, city planner, design critic, and university teacher. He was awarded a USA Fellowship from the National Endowment for the Arts to research ballpark history and design, and he has written about those topics for SABR publications, other sports periodicals, and professional and general-interest periodicals in print and online. He was the lead author of *Historic Ballparks* (Chartwell Books, 2006) and *Ballparks Yesterday and Today* (Chartwell Books, 2007) and is an editor of a Tiger Stadium book to be published by McFarland. He was a consultant on Camden Yards, Safeco Field, Petco Park, and two Minor League ballparks and an expert witness for the City of Chicago regarding historic landmark status for Wrigley Field. A SABR member since 1988, he was an officer in the society's Alan Roth and Northwest chapters, and he received the USA Today/Baseball Weekly Award for the 1996 SABR national convention's best research presentation.

JAMES L. RAY is an attorney who practices in Philadelphia, Pennsylvania. He has been the feature baseball writer for Suite101 since March 2007, where he has written more than 460 articles on the national pastime. His articles cover a wide breadth of topics, including the origins of the game, the deadball era, the best hitters and pitchers by decade, the Negro Leagues, statistical analysis, and player comparisons. Jim is an active member of SABR who recently published biographies of Roy White, Don Mattingly, and Lou Gehrig for SABR's BioProject.

C. PAUL ROGERS III is president of the Hall-Ruggles (Dallas–Ft. Worth) SABR Chapter and is the coauthor of four baseball books, including *The Whiz Kids and the 1950 Pennant*, written with boyhood hero Robin Roberts, and *Memories of a Ballplayer: Bill Werber and Baseball in the 1930s*, with Bill Werber. His most recent project was with Eddie Robinson, whose memoir *Lucky Me: My Sixty-Five Years in Baseball* was published by the SMU Press in the fall of 2010. His real job is as a law professor at Southern Methodist University in Dallas, Texas, where he served as dean of the law school for nine years.

JOHN T. SACCOMAN is a professor and chair of mathematics and computer science at Seton Hall University in New Jersey. There he team-teaches one of the earliest-known Sabermetrics courses with its founder, Rev. Gabe Costa. They, along with Mike Huber, have coauthored two books published by McFarland—*Understanding Sabermetrics* and *Practicing Sabermetrics*. A char-

ter member of the Elysian Fields Chapter of SABR, John resides in northern New Jersey with his son and fellow Mets fan, Ryan, and his Red Sox–loving wife, Mary. He learned about the Brooklyn Dodgers from his mother, Paula, and hopes to meet Mrs. Joan Hodges in Cooperstown some day.

ROBERT H. SCHAEFER has been a SABR member since 1995 when he retired from the aerospace industry. He has performed investigations in several areas of baseball history and has presented some of his findings at a number of SABR national conventions. He is a three-time recipient of the annual McFarland-SABR Award for the best baseball research, being honored for his work in 2000, 2001, and 2003. His essays have appeared in SABR's *National Pastime* and *Baseball Research Journal*, NINE: *A Journal of Baseball History and Culture*, and *Base Ball: The Early Game*.

MATHEW SISSON, a SABR member from Dartmouth, Massachusetts, is a lifelong Red Sox fan. He currently lives in Watertown, Massachusetts, and works as an internal management consultant for one of Massachusetts's major health insurance providers. Matt is a graduate of the University of New Hampshire, where he majored in health management and policy, and holds an MBA from Clark University. Matt has written for *Baseball Digest Daily* and *Seamheads* and has had his work featured on ESPN.com, Fangraphs, and Beyond the Boxscore. In addition to his online work, Matt has also contributed articles in the Maple Street Press's 2009 and 2010 *Yankees Annual*.

DAVID W. SMITH has been a biology professor at the University of Delaware since 1975. He is a lifelong baseball researcher, joining SABR in 1977 and making many research presentations at national and regional SABR meetings. He also has several publications in SABR research journals and in 2005 was the recipient of SABR's Bob Davids Award. He is the founder and president of Retrosheet, a nonprofit organization dedicated to the collection and public distribution of play-by-play data from Major League games free of charge. Almost all of his research has relied on the use of this detailed play-by-play information to examine subtle aspects of the playing of the game that can only be addressed with this type of data. He is a frequent consultant for many Major League teams, sportswriters, television shows, and the Hall of Fame on historical baseball records.

TED D. SMITH grew up loving baseball, and he never lost that love. He incorporated that passion into every part of his life. He grew up in Alabama and moved to California during his college years. He received a master's in information and library science from UCLA in 1992, where he became an avid fan of the Dodgers. His work as a University of Oregon librarian from 1994 to 2009 included developing and teaching a popular freshman seminar, "How to do Baseball Research." Ted passed away in 2009 and is survived by his wife, Kathy, and two sons, Collin and Trevor.

LYLE SPATZ has been a SABR member since 1973 and chairman of the Baseball Records Committee since 1991. He is the author of five books on baseball history and the editor of two baseball record books. His latest book is *Dixie Walker: A Life in Baseball* (McFarland, 2011). Lyle, who lives in Florida with his wife, Marilyn, saw his first game on July 5, 1947—at Ebbets Field.

JOHN HARRY STAHL is a retired CPA with a lifelong interest in baseball. He and his wife, Pamela, celebrated their fortieth wedding anniversary in late 2011. They are blessed with two grown children, Rebecca and Jared, and one grandson, Noll. This is John's seventh SABR player biography.

MARK STEWART has spent twenty-five years as a sportswriter. He has profiled more than five hundred athletes in print and online and has written more than fifty nonfiction baseball books for chil-

dren and adults. He has had the pleasure of meeting several of the players profiled in this book, including Duke Snider, Gil Hodges, and Jackie Robinson, who often played tennis with his father when Mark was a little boy. Mark is a founding partner of the sports information website JockBio.com.

RICK SWAINE is a baseball historian and longtime SABR member. Born and raised in Miami and a graduate of Florida State University, he is a semi-retired CPA who resides in the Tallahassee area and is involved in financial consulting and vintage baseball collectibles. He also coaches and plays in adult baseball leagues and tournaments throughout the Southeast. Rick specializes in writing about baseball's unsung heroes. He has authored three full-length books: *Beating The Breaks: Major League Ballplayers Who Overcame Disabilities*, *The Black Stars Who Made Baseball Whole: The Jackie Robinson Generation in the Major Leagues*, and *The Integration of Major League Baseball: A Team by Team History*. He is also a contributor to SABR's *National Pastime* and *Baseball Research Journal*, *Black Ball: A Negro Leagues Journal*, and the SABR BioProject.

STEW THORNLEY, a SABR member since 1979, received the SABR-Macmillan Award in 1988 for his first book, *On to Nicollet*, a history of the Minneapolis Millers. He enjoys visiting graves of notable people and has been to every known grave of baseball Hall of Famers. He is an official scorer for Major League Baseball for Minnesota Twins home games. He and his wife and fellow SABR member, Brenda Himrich, live in Roseville, Minnesota, with their two cats.

ADAM J. ULREY is a lifelong Los Angeles Dodgers and Cleveland Indians fan who lives in Dexter, Oregon, with his wife, Jhody, their son, Camran, and their three dogs, Behr, Susie, and Montana. He works at Sacred Heart Hospital in Eugene,

Oregon. Adam was a contributing writer to the 2006 book *Deadball Stars of the American League* and many of the team BioProject books. He enjoys spending as much time as possible fly fishing on his creek and in the lakes and rivers of Oregon.

EDWARD W. VEIT, an eleven-year member of SABR, presently operates the press box elevator for the Baltimore Orioles at Camden Yards. Born in Philadelphia, he is a lifelong fan of the Phillies and particularly expert about the 1950 Whiz Kids ("I grew up with them"). Ed holds degrees from West Chester University, Johns Hopkins University, and Loyola University of Maryland and is retired from teaching English in Baltimore County Schools. Along with a teaching career, Veit spent five years as a Washington DC policeman and still follows the Washington Senators in Minnesota.

JOSEPH WANCHO lives in Westlake, Ohio, and has worked at AT&T since 1994 as a process/development manager. Joe is a lifelong Cleveland Indians fan and a SABR member since 2005. He has contributed to several other SABR bio book projects and has written more than a dozen biographies on the SABR BioProject website.

RUSSELL WOLINSKY is a Bronx native and a lifelong National League/New York Mets fan with a particular fascination with the baseball history of New York City. Working in the library of the National Baseball Hall of Fame and Museum in Cooperstown for several years, Russell contributed regularly to the museum's publications as well as writing a column, "Can of Corn," a collection of biographies of lesser-known Major Leaguers, for the Hall's website. He is currently working on a pair of full-length baseball books: an overview of the 1969 season and a history of the 1903 New York Highlanders. Russell currently resides in Rye, New York.